STATES *of* MIND

STATES *of* MIND

American and Post-Soviet

Perspectives on

Contemporary Issues

in Psychology

Edited by

Diane F. Halpern *&*

Alexander E. Voiskounsky

New York   Oxford   ■   Oxford University Press   1997

Oxford University Press

Oxford   New York

Athens   Auckland   Bangkok   Bogota   Bombay   Buenos Aires
Calcutta   Cape Town   Dar es Salaam   Delhi   Florence   Hong Kong
Istanbul   Karachi   Kuala Lumpur   Madras   Madrid   Melbourne
Mexico City   Nairobi   Paris   Singapore   Taipei   Tokyo   Toronto

and associated companies in
Berlin   Ibadan

Copyright © 1997 by Oxford University Press, Inc.

Published by Oxford University Press, Inc.
198 Madison Avenue, New York, New York 10016

Oxford is a registered trademark of Oxford University Press

Library of Congress Cataloging-in-Publication Data
States of mind : American and post-Soviet perspectives on contemporary
issues in psychology / edited by Diane F. Halpern and Alexander E.
Voiskounsky.
   p.   cm.
Includes bibliographical references and index.
ISBN 0-19-510350-5 (cloth)
ISBN 0-19-510351-3 (paper)
1. Psychology—United States.   2. Psychology—Former Soviet
republics.   I. Halpern, Diane F.   II. Voiskounsky, Alexander E.
BF121.S826   1997
150'.947—dc20   96-28089

1 3 5 7 9 8 6 4 2

Printed in the United States of America
on acid-free paper

Preface

The idea for this book grew from several months of discussions between the editors when Halpern, the American editor, was teaching psychology classes at Moscow State University where Voiskounsky, the Russian editor, had worked as a student and then as a professor for most of his adult life. It seemed obvious to us that we could learn a great deal about psychology if we could trade places and view contemporary issues with each other's eyes and against a backdrop of political thought that was diametrically opposed to the one we had each known. We were immediately struck by the differences in how we thought about contemporary issues in psychology and the way we made sense of thoughts, actions, and feelings. Unwittingly, we became participants in the process we wanted to observe.

Even as we planned this book, the differences in how we thought about topics in psychology and in the world came into focus. These differences became apparent as we selected topics that we believed to be important at the present time and into the future and the way we decided to organize the topics. For example, it was obvious to Halpern, the American, that politics, persuasion, and lying belonged together as a conceptual unit. For Voiskounsky, the Russian, it was equally obvious that politics, prejudice, and ethnic psychology were the most logically connected topics. As we discussed the differences in our thinking, we became aware of the way sociopolitical experiences had differentially shaped the organization and boundaries of these concepts for each of us. In the Soviet Union, the major political issues were the repeated attempts of ethnically distinct republics (e.g., Armenia, Lithuania, Estonia, Azerbijan, and others) to become independent. Thus, in the Russian mind, the primary concerns of politics were prejudice and ethnicity.

In the United States, politics is often an exercise in persuasion because of the choices that need to be made by ordinary citizens in a multiparty political system. But it was only after extended discussion of these deep-rooted differences in how we think about politics that we could understand why the other editor had such "strange" thoughts. Given that this is the English-language version of this book, we decided to use an organization of topics that is more meaningful to Western readers. We plan to reorganize topics for the Russian-language version so that it will be more compatible with the way former Soviets, other former communists, and current communists think about these concepts. We offer this explanation to readers who may be wondering how we negotiated the countless issues that arose from this international enterprise. We hope that this background information will provide readers with some insight into our own states of mind as we planned and wrote this book.

In many instances, we had to depart from standard practices in editing an academic book so that readers would understand and appreciate the important differences and similarities in American and post-Soviet psychologies. This is why we cannot honestly call this an edited book, but neither of us has an appropriate word in our native language for what it is. The plan was to get outstanding psychologists from the countries that once constituted the Soviet Union and from the United States to write companion chapters on particular topics. This way, we would have an excellent summary of selected fields in psychology from each tradition, with the rare chance to compare them and to speculate about future directions. As we conferred on this book, we found that we had to modify our original plan.

Perhaps we need a new word to describe the role of the editors in producing this book. The term "assisted authors" comes to mind, but it reminds the American editor of "assisted suicide," not exactly the connotation she wants to give to this collective effort. For various reasons, we have assumed a much more intrusive role in the production of many of the chapters than is normally assumed by editors. We sincerely thank all of the authors for their cooperation and understanding.

First, there was the problem of translations. Any translation needs to go beyond a simple correspondence of words to capture the meaning and flavor of a piece. Often, there is a choice of several words that might fit a translation, and each offers a different connotative meaning. In other instances, there seemed to be no good way to translate a word or phrase, and a short description had to be substituted. But we even went beyond that. There are major style differences between former Soviets and native English writers. In order to keep the style consistent throughout the book, we had to adopt a single style and then edit all of the chapters to keep them stylistically harmonious.

Most important, some of the information that was presented in the original Russian, and even some that was written in English, would not have been understandable to a majority of English-language readers. Background information often had to be provided. For example, there is a reference to the administrative status of cities in the chapter on environmental/ecological psychology, contributed by two respected Latvian psychologists. This passage could not be understood without an explanation of how cities in the Soviet Union were assigned an administrative status and how consumer goods were distributed according to the status of a city. In instances like this one, we took the liberty of explaining what would be needed to make the chapter understandable to readers who did not grow up in the Soviet Union.

Another example is a reference to the Old Testament as a basis for creating an ethic of honesty and truth in the Russian chapter on the psychology of truth and lies. To English-speaking readers, the reference would be to the Judeo-Christian ethic, but to Russians the term "Judeo" would not be included in the label for this reference. This created the problem of referring to the Ten Commandments as though they were not part of Judaism (a strange thought to Westerners) or of changing the way the terms are used in Russian. In this example, we included the term "Judeo" in parentheses so that Western readers would understand the reference but so that it would also stand apart from the way former Soviets would refer to it. There is no definitive way of knowing if the omission of the word "Judeo" from this ethic reflects random processes in the way terms evolve or if the omission is a deliberate reflection of anti-Semitism.

We also tried to add a genuine feel for the lives of the people whom the authors wrote about. Communal living spaces in the former Soviet Union, for example, had many features in addition to crowded kitchens and long lines to use the bathroom. These arrangements also meant a loss of privacy and easy access to information about anyone's activities. It made spying easy during the Stalin years and created the need to dissemble even among those with whom people shared living space. The secondary problems created by shared living spaces need not be explained for those who lived in these housing arrangements, but an explanation was needed for most English-language readers.

In all cases, drafts of the chapters were shown to the authors to ascertain that we did not alter the essential meaning they wished to convey, even if we altered almost everything else. We are very lucky to have had such a fine group of understanding authors who allowed us this freedom.

Finally, the reader will see that some of the citations to foreign language publications are not in the standard format of the American Psychological Association. In addition, some names may be spelled inconsistently because of the difficulties of translating various alphabet systems into English. Problems such as these are inherent in international projects that involve numerous languages and widely different conventions for scholarly work.

We have many people to thank for their assistance with this book. First, we thank Natella Voiskounsky for her patient translations, editing skill, and good nature. We can't image how we could have completed this project without her. We also thank the Rockefeller Foundation for providing us with a month in which to work together in beautiful Bellagio, Italy. This allowed us the opportunity to work together closely in a continuous interchange of ideas and explanations. We thank the Fulbright Foundation for awarding the American editor (Halpern) a fellowship so that she could teach at Moscow State University in Russia and work with the Russian editor (Voiskounsky). We also thank Kevin Kopelson, at the University of Iowa, for his suggestions for the title. Finally, we thank the authors who so graciously shared their expertise with us. We hope that you, the reader, will come away with a better idea of psychology and the way people are understood in these opposite sides of the world.

San Bernardino, California   D. F. H.
Moscow, Russia   A. E. V.
December 1996

Contents

Contributors

Diane F. Halpern, Ph.D., is Professor and Chair of Psychology at California State University, San Bernardino. She has won many awards for her teaching and research, including the Distinguished Life-Time Contribution to Education Award given by the American Psychological Association, the California State University's State-Wide Outstanding Professor Award, the Outstanding Alumna Award from the University of Cincinnati, the Silver Medal Award from the Council for the Advancement and Support of Education, and the G. Stanley Hall Lecture Award from the American Psychological Association. She is the author or editor of several books: *Thought and Knowledge: An Introduction to Critical Thinking* (3d ed., 1996), *Thinking Critically about Critical Thinking Instruction* (1996), *Sex Differences in Cognitive Abilities* (2d ed., 1992), *Enhancing Thinking Skills in the Sciences and Mathematics* (1992), *Changing College Classrooms* (1994), and *Student Outcomes Assessment* (1987). Halpern was the guest co-editor, with Susan G. Nummedal, of a special issue of the journal *Teaching of Psychology* titled "Psychologists Teach Critical Thinking" and guest editor of a special double issue of the journal *Learning and Individual Differences* titled "Psychological and Psychobiological Perspectives on Sex Differences in Cognition: I. Theory and Research" (1995) and "II. Commentaries and Controversies" (1996).

Alexander E. Voiskounsky, Ph.D., is Professor of Psychology at Moscow University after M. V. Lomonosov and is a member of the Russian Psychological Union and MosCHI. He considers himself a follower of Lev Vygotsky, the founder of the cultural-historical psychological theory. His research concerns mediation of human behavior, with an emphasis on the effects of changes in technology on behavior, an interest that reflects his belief that information-related media are creating major advances in human psychological development. His most recent research is a psycholinguistic analysis of language usage in international network communication. Voiskounsky is the author of the popular science monograph *Ja Govorju, My Govorim* (I speak, we speak) (1982, 1990), which sold over 300,000 copies (including Bulgarian translations). Topics covered in this monograph include communication between mother and child, writer and reader, and advertiser and consumer and other forms of communication such as gaze contact, groupthink, kipu (knotted ropes used by South American Indians), sign language, voice mail, videoconferences, inner speech, and computer-mediated communication.

Paul A. Bell, Ph.D., is Professor of Psychology at Colorado State University. He is a Fellow of the American Psychological Association and the American Psychological Society. He is a past President of APA Division 34 (Population and Environmental Psychology) and President-Elect of the Rocky Mountain Psychological Association. His publications include the textbook *Environmental Psychology* (with Greene, Fisher, and Baum), now in its fourth edition. His research interests include environmental stress, management of scarce resources, and designing environments for the cognitively impaired elderly.

Boris S. Bratus, Ph.D. and Dr. Sci., is a Full Professor of Psychology at Moscow University after M. V. Lomonosov and the head of a laboratory at the Psychological Institute after L. G. Schukina, Russian Academy of Education. His earlier books and papers are dedicated to personality abnormalities. His current work is on the psychology of culture, morals, religion, and personality theory. He is the originator of the psychology of religion. He is on the Editorial Boards of the *Voprosy Psikhologii* (Questions of psychology) and the *Moskovsky Psikhoterapevtichesky Zhurnal* (Moscow psychotherapeutic journal). Bratus is a member of the Russian Academy of Natural Sciences and a corresponding member of the Russian Academy of Education. He has edited (and contributed to) the forthcoming first Russian textbook on the psychology of religion. Bratus is the author of 12 monographs in Russian, one of which is translated into English (*Anomalies of Personality: From the Deviant to the Norm* [1990]).

Sergei Deryabo, Ph.D., is a senior researcher at the Daugavpils Pedagogical University (Latvia). He received his doctorate from the Psychological Institute after L. G. Schukina, Russian Academy of Education (Moscow). His research field concerns the connections between people and other living things (plants, animals, etc.). A pioneer in ecological/environmental psychology in Eastern Europe, he is the author or co-author of three monographs on this topic.

Paul Ekman, Ph.D., is Professor of Psychology at the University of California, San Francisco. He is the author or editor of 11 books. His next book, *What the*

Face Reveals, will be published by Oxford University Press in 1997. He received the American Psychological Association's Distinguished Scientific Contribution Award in 1991 and an honorary doctor of humane letters from the University of Chicago in 1994. His two main areas of research and writing concern emotion and expression and lying.

Evgueny I. Golovakha, Ph.D. and Dr. Sci., is Deputy Director of the Institute of Sociology, National Academy of Sciences of the Ukraine (Kiev). His research field includes personality theory, psychology and sociology of politics, life-span perspective, and social psychiatry. His applied work is in the analysis of social problems that emerged after the Chernobyl disaster and the sociological and social psychological variables involved in the transition from a totalitarian to a democratic society, with special emphasis on the dynamics of ethnic tolerance and intolerance in the Ukraine. He is the author or co-author of eight books in Russian and Ukrainian.

Bonnie L. Green, Ph.D., is Professor of Psychiatry and Director of Psychosocial Research at Georgetown University. She is the editor of the *Journal of Traumatic Stress* and served on the post-traumatic stress disorder (PTSD) advisory committees for the *DSM-IIIR* and *DSM-IV*. She received the Laufer Award for Outstanding Contributions in Research from the National Organization for Victim Assistance. She has been conducting National Institute of Mental Health–funded research on the long-term psychological sequelae of a variety of traumatic events for two decades. Recent studies have addressed PTSD in women with breast cancer and the contribution of unique aspects and dimensions of trauma history to various psychosocial and physical health outcomes.

Nicole E. Holland is a doctoral student in social-personality psychology at the Graduate School and University Center of the City University of New York. She is the recipient of a dissertation award from the Graduate School. Her current research involves assessing factors of academic success among African American college students. She has co-authored publications and presented several conference papers that address issues related to racial identity.

Jonathan S. Kaplan, M.A., is a graduate student in the doctoral program in clinical psychology at the University of California, Los Angeles. In 1991, he received a B.A. in Asian studies from Tufts University. During 1993 and 1994, he assisted with research on ethnicity and emotion at the University of California, Berkeley. Recently, he completed his master's thesis on the relationship among ethnicity, treatment outcome, and the source of a client's referral to mental health treatment. His research interests include cross-cultural and cross-ethnic issues related to the field of mental health.

Aksel Kirch, Ph.D., is the head of the Ethnopolicy Working Group at the Institute of International and Social Studies, Estonian Academy of Sciences (Tallinn). He graduated from the University of Tartu (Estonia) and received his Ph.D. in sociology at Moscow University. His research interests include social and educational mobility of young people. He is currently investigating ethnic processes and ethnic policy in the post-Soviet Baltic republics. Kirch is a research consultant of the Round Table of Ethnic Minorities for the President of Estonia. He has contributed to many monographs and journals. His most recent monograph, which he co-edited with Michael Geistlinger, is *Estonia: A New Framework for the Estonian Majority and Russian Minority* (1995).

Marika Kirch, Ph.D., is a senior research fellow at the Institute of International and Social Studies, Estonian Academy of Sciences (Tallinn). She graduated from the University of Tartu (Estonia) as a social psychologist and received her Ph.D. in sociology at Moscow University. Her earlier research was concerned with the value orientations and social psychology of youth. Her most recent research is in ethnic studies of Estonia residents. She is an adviser for the Division of Higher Education and Research, Ministry of Culture and Education of Estonia. Among her most recent publications is the monograph *Changing Identities in Estonia: Sociological Facts and Commentaries* (1994), which she co-edited with David Laitin.

Vera A. Kol'tsova, Ph.D., is the head of the History of Psychology and Historical Psychology Laboratory at the Institute of Psychology, Russian Academy of Sciences (Moscow). She is among the leading experts in the history of Russian psychology and is also interested in epistemology and historical psychology, the psychology of communication, and the history of psychology in general. She has thoroughly analyzed the psychological views of M. V. Lomonosov, V. M. Bekhterev, A. S. Makarenko, and many other prominent Russian researchers. Kol'tsova is on the Editorial Boards of the *Psikhologicheskii Zhurnal* (Psychological journal) and the publications series (Nauka Publishers) of the works of most prominent late psychologists.

Teresa L. Kramer, Ph.D., is a clinical psychologist and Assistant Professor of Clinical Psychiatry at the University of Cincinnati College of Medicine. She is also Assistant Director of the Traumatic Stress Studies Center and has published articles on exposure to sexual assault, combat, and natural disasters. She is also Director of Child and Adolescent Services at University Psychiatry Services, an outpatient practice of the Department of Psychiatry. Her clinical specialty is in the area of child, adolescent, and family trauma. She is also a reviewer for the *Journal of Traumatic Stress.*

Dmitry A. Leontiev, Ph.D., is Associate Professor of Psychology at Moscow University after M. V. Lomonosov. He is interested in theories of personality, motivation research, media and advertising theories and practice, empirical aesthetics, and the psychology of art. He is Vice-President of the Moscow Psychological Society and a member of the International Society for Theoretical Psychology, the International Society for the History of Behavioral and Social

Sciences (Cheiron), the International Society for Cultural Research in Activity Theory, and the International Association of Empirical Aesthetics. Leontiev is on the Editorial Boards of *Psikhologicheskii Zhurnal* (Psychological journal), *Journal of Viktor-Frankl-Institute* (Wienna), and *Alter Ego* (Riga). He has participated in the construction and adaptation of various psychological tests.

Madrudin S. Magomed-Eminov, Ph.D., is the head of the Laboratory of Personality and Stress Studies at the Psychology Department, Moscow University after M. V. Lomonosov. His interests include motivation research, personality theory, stress studies, and psychoanalytic theories. He has originated applied work dealing with the post-trauma stress disorders characteristic of victims and veterans of war—principally in Afghanistan and Chechnya. He is Director of the Psychological Services Bureau at the Russian Union of Afghani War Veterans and President of the Psychoanalytical Association. Magomed-Eminov is a member of Psychology International. He is the author of a monograph and of numerous research and popular science publications.

Natasha B. Meshalkina is a postgraduate student at the Institute of Psychology, Russian Academy of Sciences (Moscow). She received a B.A. from the Psychology Department, Moscow University after M. V. Lomonosov. Her research area is the origin and development of the psychological health field and conceptions of psychohygiene in Russia at the turn of the century. Her papers and conference presentations (Moscow, 1993; Nizhny Novgorod, 1994) are on the history of psychological studies of alcoholism and psychohygiene in Russia.

Olga V. Mitina, Ph.D., is a research fellow at the Psychology Department, Moscow University after M. V. Lomonosov. She has degrees in both mathematics and psychology from Moscow University. Her research work is in political and ethnic psychology, and she lectures in mathematical psychology. Her applied work is in developing methods of personal constructs theory and semantic differential to investigate the constructs underlying the structure of the mind (consciousness). She is also conducting cross-cultural research on the psychology of feminism.

Peter E. Nathan, Ph.D., began his work in alcoholism while on the faculty at Harvard Medical School, where he launched a program of research on basic psychosocial variables associated with alcoholism. He then moved to Rutgers University, where he served as Professor and Director of Clinical Psychology Training. While at Rutgers, he established the Alcohol Behavior Research Laboratory and assumed the directorship of Rutgers' Center of Alcoholic Studies. He then served as Vice-President for Academic Affairs at the University of Iowa, and, most recently, has returned to the Psychology Department as the University of Iowa Foundation Distinguished Professor. In 1988, he became a member of the work group to consider changes in the diagnostic criteria for Substance Abuse Disorders for the *DSM-IV*, as well as the *DSM-IV* Task Force, and in 1990, he was appointed to the National Advisory Council on Alcohol Abuse and Alcoholism of the National Institutes of Health. He has written or edited 18 books and 200 journal articles, most of them dealing with alcohol abuse or dependency.

Yury N. Olegnik, Ph.D., is Dean of the Psychology Department and Chair of General Psychology and History of Psychology, Institute of Youth (Moscow). He is also a senior research fellow at the Institute of Psychology, Russian Academy of Sciences. He is interested in the history of Russian psychology, mostly in the 20th century. He has investigated the genesis of differential psychology conceptions and studies in Russia. He is an expert in biographical studies of prominent researchers and in searching through archives. He is the Secretary of the Editorial Board of the publications series (Nauka Publishers) of the works of most prominent late psychologists. He is editor or co-editor of (or contributor to) numerous publications and collective volumes on the history of psychology.

Natalya V. Panina, Ph.D. and Dr. Sci., is the head of the Department of Sociology at the Institute of Sociology, National Academy of Sciences of the Ukraine (Kiev). Her research interests include the social psychology of comprehension, political and ethnic psychology, and sociology. Her applied work is in measuring the dynamics of life satisfaction, monitoring psychiatric changes as a function of ethnicity, studying social problems resulting from the Chernobyl disaster, the measurement of ethnic attitudes, and research on the peculiarities of the transition from a totalitarian to a democratic society. She is co-author of four books (in Russian and Ukrainian).

Victor F. Petrenko, Ph.D. and Dr. Sci., is the head of a research laboratory on the psychology of communication and psychosemantics at the Psychology Department, Moscow University after M. V. Lomonosov. He is a Full Professor of Psychology. He is interested in various fields in psychology and related sciences: personality theories, psychology of consciousness and the unconscious, personal constructs theory, political psychology, psycholinguistics, ethnic studies, artificial intelligence, semantic theories, and empirical art studies. Petrenko is an originator of a new branch of psychology of human consciousness research. He is on the Editorial Boards of *Psikhologicheskii Zhurnal* (Psychology journal) and *Social Sciences Today*. He is a member of the European Association of Personality Psychology and the European Association of Psychology of Personal Constructs. He is the author of three monographs and numerous publications in journals and edited volumes.

Vello Pettai received a B.A. degree from Middlebury College and a Ph.D. in political science from Columbia University. His research interests are in ethnic studies and democracy development in the Baltic republics (mostly Estonia and Latvia). His research results are published in the *Journal of Democracy, Nationalities Papers,* and the *Journal of Baltic Studies and Post-Soviet Studies*. He is a visiting lecturer in political science at the University of Tartu (Estonia), 1995–1996.

Anthony R. Pratkanis, Ph.D., is Professor of Psychology and Director of the Graduate Program in Social Psychology at the University of California, Santa Cruz. A Fellow of the American Psychological Association, he is the co-author of *Age of Propaganda* and co-editor of *Attitude Structure and Function* and of *Social Psychology* (volumes 1–3). Just after the turn of the century, his grandfather immigrated from Lithuania to Vandergrift, Pennsylvania, where he worked in the steel mills.

Pamela Trotman Reid, Ph.D., is Professor of Psychology at the Graduate School and University Center of the City University of New York. She also serves as the Associate Provost and Dean for Academic Affairs. She is a Fellow of the American Psychological Association and has held many national offices, including serving as President of the Division of Psychology of Women and a member of the Executive Council of the Division for the Psychological Study of Ethnic Minorities. Her publications have focused on the intersection of racism and sexism, as well as on gender development, particularly among African American children and families.

Timothy A. Salthouse, Ph.D., is Professor of Psychology at the Georgia Institute of Technology. His research has been supported by the National Institute on Aging since 1978, including Research Career Development Awards and MERIT Awards. He is the author of four books and over 100 articles and is the current editor of the journal *Psychology and Aging*.

Galina U. Soldatova, Ph.D., is a senior research fellow at the Institute of Ethnology and Anthropology, Russian Academy of Sciences (Moscow). She received her doctorate in social psychology from the Institute of Psychology, Russian Academy of Sciences. Her research field is ethnic psychology, and she is interested in theory, research methods, and fieldwork. Having spent her childhood in the Caucasus region of the Soviet Union, she is particularly well qualified to investigate the complex ethnic problems of that region. Soldatova is conducting joint work with colleagues from abroad, mostly from the United States. She is the author of numerous publications (a dozen of them in English). Forthcoming are a monograph and a collective monograph that she co-authored with two other authors.

Stanley Sue, Ph.D., is Professor of Psychology at the University of California, Los Angeles. He is Director of the National Research Center on Asian American Mental Health, a National Institute of Mental Health–funded research center. Sue has received a number of awards, including the American Psychological Association Distinguished Contributions to Psychology in the Public Interest Award, the Distinguished Contribution Award for the Study of Diversity from the American Association of Applied and Preventive Psychology, and the Distinguished Contributions Award from the Asian American Psychological Association. His research work examines ethnicity and mental health.

Eric D. Sundstrom, Ph.D., is Professor of Psychology at the University of Tennessee and a Fellow of the American Psychological Association and the American Psychological Society. His publications include *Work Places: Psychology of the Physical Environment in Offices and Factories* (1986) and a chapter in *Handbook on Environmental Psychology* (1987). His research focuses on the ecology of work-group effectiveness. He maintains an active practice as an organizational consultant.

Philip E. Tetlock, Ph.D., is Distinguished Professor of Psychology at the University of California, Berkeley, and Visiting Burtt Professor at Ohio State University. He is co-winner of the Woodrow Wilson Book Award from the American Political Science Association, as well as the recipient of the Behavioral Science Research Prize from the American Association for the Advancement of Science and the Distinguished Scientific Contribution Award for Early Career Achievement from the American Psychological Association. His most recent book (with Aaron Belkin) is *Counterfactual Thought Experiments in World Politics* (1996).

Tarmo Tuisk is a research fellow at the Institute of International and Social Studies, Estonian Academy of Sciences (Tallinn). He received his B.A. from the Tallinn Technical University (Estonia). He is affiliated with the Ethnopolicy Working Group. Tuisk is conducting fieldwork on the sociology of ethnic tolerance and intolerance in Estonia and is a contributor to a number of research journals and edited volumes.

Vitold Yasvin, Ph.D., is a lecturer and senior research fellow at the Daugavpils Pedagogical University (Latvia). He received his doctorate at the Psychological Institute after L. G. Schukina, Russian Academy of Education (Moscow). He is the author or co-author of two monographs on environmental and ecological psychology, the field in which he has conducted highly significant and pioneering work.

Victor V. Znakov, Ph.D. and Dr. Sci., is a senior research fellow at the Institute of Psychology, Russian Academy of Sciences (Moscow). He graduated from the Psychology Department, Leningrad (now St. Petersburg) University. His research field is the psychology of comprehension and the psychology of moral choice. Znakov is on the Editorial Board of the *Psikhologicheskii Zhurnal* (Psychology journal). He is the author of two monographs and numerous publications in journals and edited volumes (mostly in Russian). Znakov is a member of the New York Academy of Sciences.

STATES *of* MIND

Introduction

Psychology in a Sociopolitical Context

Diane F. Halpern *&* Alexander E. Voiskounsky

It was an unprecedented event in contemporary history. In an (almost) blood-less coup, a major world power and the largest country on earth made a 180-degree turn in its political orientation. In 1991, the Soviet Union began its tor-tuous march toward capitalism. The official belief system of approximately 200 million Soviet citizens for most of the 20th century was abandoned as the prin-ciples of free enterprise replaced those of a planned economy. The collapse of communism created aftershocks that have been felt throughout the world. The demise of the largest communist power in the world has profoundly altered the way Westerners and former Soviets view each other and themselves.

Political belief systems are, at their heart, psychological theories. They are implicit theories of motivation, personality, mental health, human development, education, and social interaction—topics that are the very lifeblood of psychol-ogy. We cannot separate the way in which people think and act from the soci-ety in which they live, nor can we view human thought and behavior without the lens of one's own culture. What is normal? When will people help others? How can violence be reduced? Why do we hate? What is the best way to raise children? How do we love, develop, or learn? These are among the many ques-tions of psychology, and although there are universal principles and standards, there are also variations that depend on the time, place, and tradition in which people live and the vantage point from which we view their lives.

The rapid change in the Russian political system created a unique opportu-nity to study the way in which topics of psychological inquiry are framed and develop. Both prior to 1991 and for many years following the "capitalist revolution," there has been very little exchange of information between psychologists in the West and in the former Soviet countries. Psychology, as a discipline, is usually traced to the 1879 German laboratories of Wilhelm Wundt, the father of scientific psychology, who used the methods of introspectionism to examine the structure of the mind. Wundt's disciples defined psychology during its neonatal period in both Russia and the West, but other models of human thought and behavior soon became the dominant paradigm. The seminal work of the great Russian physiologist Ivan Pavlov is well known in the West, but fewer than a handful of Soviet psychologists have been influential in the development of Western psychological thought. Knowledge of Western developments in psychology has also been extremely limited in the former republics of the Soviet Union. Recent political events have permitted a unique opportunity to see how two major world powers have defined contemporary psychological issues and the way in which they collect and interpret data that bear on these issues.

The change has been profound. It seems that almost every former Soviet or frequent visitor to the former Soviet countries has his or her personal vignette about a moment or incident when the magnitude of the change from communism to capitalism "hit home." For the first author (Halpern), it occurred during a visit to the prestigious Academy of Sciences Institute for Psychology in Moscow. During an earlier visit in 1990, when the Soviet Union still existed as a communist country, she sat stiffly at a long, formal table with stone-faced officials under the watchful eyes of large portraits of Lenin and Gorbachev (who was the Soviet leader at that time). At a return visit in 1994, in the new capitalist Russia, she sat at the same long, formal table with the same stone-faced officials, but this time only two bright rectangles of wallpaper marked the places where the portraits of Lenin and Gorbachev had been hanging. This may seem like an insignificant indicator of the magnitude of the change, but the two blank rectangles spoke as loudly as the men whose portraits had previously occupied that space. The psychologists who met at this formal table in the Institute of Psychology were no longer under the watchful gaze of communism.

Access to Western Information in the Soviet Union

Access to the Western literature in psychology was strictly controlled in the Soviet Union. Only those areas of study that were relevant to and supportive of the communist ethic were freely available. This meant that there were many Western journals and books available in fields like human factors and ergonomics, which concern the compatibility of machine design for efficient and comfortable use by humans—an important topic in a country where the production of military machinery and the exploration of space were paramount. By contrast, there was no need for Soviet psychologists to read the research literature on topics like prejudice or ethnic psychology because the ideal Soviet society was allegedly unmarred with pejorative emotions like prejudice and ethnicity, even in a multiethnic state, was irrelevant as long as one was a good communist. Just as there was no need for research in these areas, there was also no need for theoretical treatises on topics like these because the "answers" were provided by the communist political belief system. Prejudice, like alcoholism, prostitution, criminality, and virtually all other negative aspects of other societies, was caused by capitalism. Anyone who questioned the roots of these societal ills was in need of intensive "reeducation."

There was also no reason for Soviet psychologists to research areas like political psychology or methods of persuasion because there was only one political system and advertisements were of the most primitive kind, as is often the case when there is no competition. Although not labeled as such, the propaganda was unbearable as the media told only of the great successes of communism and portrayed Western countries as crime-ridden slums filled with the homeless poor juxtaposed with images of the opulent living conditions of the super-rich and exploitive capitalists. Because of uncompromising restrictions on what could be studied and what could be read, much of Soviet psychology developed independently from that in the West.

When there are no political choices, there is no need to persuade citizens how to vote—only that they *are* to vote. The physical act of voting was a simple matter: the ballot was to be deposited in the official receptacle without making any marks on it. Voting was compulsory in the 1950s and 1960s, despite the fact that there was only one political party and one candidate for each office. In these strictly pro-communist decades, a carrot-and-stick approach was used to ensure that citizens voted. For example, during times of food shortages, desirable produce, often oranges, appeared in the markets on election days so that those who arrived at the voting places early would be able to purchase them. The consequence for the failure to vote was an undesirable activity, such as a visit with a party official to explain why a vote was not cast.

Of course, over the 100 years constituting the last century, there were periods in which there was relatively more academic freedom than in other periods. The means with which the dominant political views were expressed and freedom of inquiry was permitted did not remain static over this long period of time. There were tremendous differences between the czarist years and the Stalinist years and during the periods of the interregnum and post-Stalinism. For example, the influential developmental psychologist Lev Vygotsky conducted his groundbreaking studies before the most repressive period of Stalin's era, and the highly regarded physiologist Alexander Luria made his most influential contributions soon after Stalin's death, a time when pressures to conform to the Marxist ideology were temporarily eased. Differences in openness to new ideas, however, were more of degree than of kind. Secrecy, control, and censorship were the overriding principles between 1917 and 1991, which left researchers in psychology in the Soviet Union with limited autonomy concerning what they could investigate, read, write, or say.

In the immediate years following the Revolution of 1917, the Marxist-minded Soviet psychologists were strongly behavioristic, and the study of the mind that had been favored by Wundt and his students was deemed unacceptable. Marxist-based conceptions of psychology were quick to emerge. Sergei Rubinstein and Lev Vygotsky were devoted Marxist psychologists with great common appeal. They initially espoused the belief that Marxism was an evolving theory of human behavior and that as psychologists they had much to contribute to its development. The newly formed governmental regime made them realize that they were quite mistaken in their view of Marxism as an ideology capable of changing. Marxism became a psychopolitical doctrine that was immutable and highly dogmatic.

Marxism was ideologically compatible with the Kantian notion that people are born with a mind that is a blank slate, a *tabula rasa*, on which experience makes indelible marks. If society could provide the "right" experiences, then its citizens could avoid the angst caused by the capitalist mentality. At the same time in the West, behaviorism was also flourishing, although it was not grounded in a communist belief system.

The pioneering work of Pavlov fit well into the behaviorist Zeitgeist that immediately followed the revolution because he was able to demonstrate the power of learning about contingencies. Pavlov arranged the learning environment so that even a dog could learn to react to a bell as though it were food. If learning could exert such powerful influences on dogs, imagine what would be possible if contingencies were arranged correctly for human society. Although Pavlov's work was a source of great pride to the Soviets, Pavlov, the person, was somewhat of an embarrassment. He managed to secure research funding from the government at a time when none was available by threatening to relocate his laboratory in the West. He also made an open and defiant display of his religious beliefs. Much to the chagrin of officials, Pavlov would make the sign of the cross every time he passed a church. Perhaps even more embarrassing was his obstinate insistence on wearing the medals he had been given by the then-defunct czarist regime, an action that showed complete disregard for the new government that had recently killed the same czar!

Lev Vygotsky and Anton Makarenko were Soviet developmental psychologists who worked with homeless children in the years following the Revolution of 1917. During the repressive periods from the mid-1930s to mid-1950s, Soviets were forbidden to read Vygotsky's work. Thanks to the efforts of Alexei Leontiev, a prominent disciple of these psychologists, the work of Vygotsky was triumphantly republished in 1956 in the Soviet Union and was later exported to the West where it has achieved great prominence. The second author (Voiskounsky) was struck with the incredible international influence of Vygotsky when, during a discussion with Andy Lock, a New Zealand psychologist, Lock confessed that the first book in psychology that he had ever purchased was written by Vygotsky. There is still much interest in New Zealand and in the West in the Vygotskian creative heritage, and Vygotsky's conceptual work regarding learning and human development seems to be increasing in popularity throughout the world. Other Soviet psychologists who have attained popularity in Western Europe, but who are still relatively unknown in the United States, include Bluma

Zeigarnick, Alexei Leontiev, Sergei Rubinstein, Pietr Gal'perin, Daniel Elkonin, and Boris Ananiev.

The official Soviet response to the highly influential work of the psychologist Sigmund Freud was complicated by the fact that it was not immediately apparent how to interpret Freud's work using a Marxist philosophy. Freud's early work was conducted in Vienna, and thus was not far from the Soviet border. Russian translations of the works of Freud were available in the 1920s, and they were initially interpreted as being compatible with Marxism. It was "clear" that Freud was studying the ways in which a bourgeois capitalist society oppressed its citizens. It was similarly clear that a society based on the superior principles of communism would result in much less unhappiness. Later, Freud's writings disappeared from public libraries because the Freudian idea of a powerful unconscious was interpreted as being incompatible with communism.

The works of Freud, along with those of other "forbidden" authors, were maintained in a restricted area of the Lenin Library in Moscow and a few other libraries in the Soviet Union. The location of the mammoth Lenin Library, and the fact that it housed much of the restricted literature, is an important reason why serious researchers from every part of the vast Soviet Union relocated to Moscow. Only those with "appropriate" clearance and academic credentials were permitted access to the restricted books and journals stored in the Lenin Library. Ordinary citizens could not read these works, but academics could be labeled "appropriate" after meeting with a librarian (who surely was a KGB confidant) and attesting to facts that might include having no acquaintances who were dissidents, the absence of undesirable affiliations (such as a Jewish grandmother or the like), and having no criminal record that would show disrespect for the communist beliefs. Of course, access would be denied to anyone who espoused an interest in original ideologically minded research. The banning of Freud's books probably had the unintended effect of making them even more desirable, and typewritten copies would sometimes circulate secretly among those who were eager to learn about what they were not supposed to be reading.

In the last 25 years, Western psychology has become increasingly cognitive in its orientation, with a virtual explosion in papers being written in this field. Much of the most recent work was also not widely available in the Soviet Union, but probably not for ideological reasons. A highly effective way to control access to what is read is simply to use a nonconvertible currency. The ruble could not leave the country, and because the ruble was the currency of Russia, ordinary citizens could not purchase Western books or journals that were not available in the state-run Russian stores. A second reason for the scarcity of contemporary literature in cognitive psychology is the deterioration of the Soviet economy. As the Soviet economy plummeted, the cost of journals and texts skyrocketed. The coincident of ideological secrecy and a poor economy meant that recent journals would be available on an irregular basis and only at those libraries with the largest budgets. Thus, it was mostly large-city libraries in Moscow and, to a lesser extent, St. Petersburg that carried more recent subscriptions. This resulted in the continued dominance of Muscovites as the academic leaders in psychology and most other academic fields. Today, subscriptions to scientific journals are mostly available through donations provided by international societies to large libraries.

Even when controversial material was theoretically available, it was missing from the shelves. Sometimes, articles with titles that suggested they might contain dissident content were cut out of journals that were otherwise intact. Of course, no Soviet official would admit this degree of censorship, but it was commonly acknowledged by researchers who spent many frustrating hours attempting to track down a desired reference. Among the many Russian expressions that were coined to capture the frustration of everyday experiences, it was frequently said that "We have everything available, and we have nothing available." This short phrase indicates that, while a wide range of reading material was supposedly available for public access, actually finding the material was a far more difficult task than official public policy would admit.

Psychology in the Soviet Union also suffered because it was considered to be a low-status field of study. For decades, it was widely considered to be a fascinating, but somewhat peripheral field. There were few jobs available for psychologists with advanced training because the number of academic institutions was small and hospitals preferred to use their allocated positions for medical personnel. Most of the colleges scattered throughout the vast regions in the Soviet Union were the so-called pedagogical institutions, where psychology was taught to prospective teachers with the goal of equipping them with the fundamentals of learning theory in preparation for their future jobs. For the most part, education in psychology at these institutions was, at best, cursory and often of poor quality, as well. It was extremely difficult to obtain an advanced education in psychology. For decades, the greatest competition for entry into Moscow State University was among students who wanted to enter the psychology department, a fact that remains true today. Thus, while psychology attracted the very best students, it was not accorded the status or job security associated with other fields of study. With relatively few advanced students, there was little need for access to contemporary literature in the field.

Access to Soviet Information in the West

The science and practice of psychology in the 15 republics that constituted the Soviet Union are "little known outside its national borders" (Takooshian & Trusov, 1992, p. 54). Alexei N. Leontyev, Sergei L. Rubinstein, and Boris G. Ananiev are the most frequently cited Soviet psychologists in Russian-language psychology texts, yet their names are entirely absent from Western psychology texts, especially those that are used in the United States (Takooshian & Trusov, 1992). We doubt that there are many Western readers who could describe the work of these most famous Soviet psychologists. There are many possible reasons for this near total ignorance on the part of Western psychologists.

Very few Western academics are fluent enough in Russian to read the technical literature in psychology that is replete with a specialized jargon and written with the Cyrillic alphabet. Many psychological concepts are abstract with specialized terms that refer to the mind, emotions, and personality constructs. With exchanges between Russian-speaking republics and the West almost impossible for academics, it was a very rare Western psychologist who was able to acquire the language facility necessary to understand the original Russian psychological literature. The lack of language proficiency is self-perpetuating because Western libraries will not subscribe to journals that are rarely read and few teachers are able to provide the high level of language instruction that would be needed to read them. Therefore, few Russian-language books and journals in psychology have been available, even for those with the ability to read them. Few Western libraries subscribed to the Russian-language journals in translation, and many of the translations by Soviet publication houses were of poor quality and therefore very difficult to read. Russian scholars in the West were more likely to specialize in literature, history, or political systems than in the dubious field of psychology.

Westerners also tended to be distrustful of the published literature that came from the Soviet Union. With the knowledge that certain areas of investigation were off-limits and dissident views could not be freely expressed, there seemed to be little reason to read or believe the official Soviet publications. Psychological research that made its way from the Soviet Union to the West had a familiar propagandistic content and tone. There was no way to know if the printed material expressed the true views of the researcher or if the most interesting and reliable work by Soviet psychologists was being published or suppressed.

The first author (Halpern) had a firsthand experience with the effective suppression of information in modern Russia. While living in Moscow on a Fulbright Fellowship in 1994, she attended a meeting of government officials at which it was announced that the formerly secret records of the KGB concerning informants during the Stalinist era would now be available for public scrutiny. This was incredible! There are no official estimates of the number of Russians who were sent to the secret labor camps during this period. And, although it was often suspected that neighbors informed on each other, few people ever knew who was responsible for their deportation. There was, however, a catch to obtaining access to these records. In fact, there may have been as many as 22 catches. Information that was essential to national security would not be released, so some unknown portion of the secret documents would remain secret. If anyone wanted to obtain information from this formerly secret cache, the information would have to be requested by the name that appeared on the KGB file. There would not be open access to all of the files; only to those files that were specifically requested by their official name would be supplied. But, given that the files were all secret, it was impossible to know what to ask for by name! As far as I know, these now open files are still inaccessible despite their official declassification. So much for glasnost.

There was also the general impression among Western psychologists that Soviet psychologists engaged in "strange" work in parapsychology that did not rely on the usual rules of scientific evidence or adhere to the rigorous standards of traditional research methods. While this perception surely was true, at least in part, the same could be said about some research conducted in the West. We do not know if stories about Russian military research into extrasensory perception and communication with plants were exaggerated because such work would surely have been classified at the time and has not been made public, if, in fact, it ever occurred.

The Western press also carried many stories about the abuse of psychiatric and psychological diagnoses as a way of silencing political dissidents. A diagnosis of mental illness meant that a person could be kept incommunicado for an indefinite period of time, without a public trial or access to legal counsel. Although Western psychologists attributed this blatant misuse of diagnoses to psychiatrists (medical doctors), the mistrust extended to psychologists as well. The most flagrant violation was the convenient use of a supposed mental disorder known as "asymptomatic schizophrenia"—literally, serious mental illness without symptoms—a category that fortunately had no counterpart in the West. It was easy to conclude that not much that was useful could be learned from a system that supported such abuse.

The chapters in this text are a marked departure from the not-so-distant past. The authors describe current work in new areas of inquiry—areas that had been forbidden or discouraged under the Soviet system. They talk honestly about research that was not published in past decades, and look forward as they predict the future of psychology.

New Frontiers

Why should we care? Why should Western psychologists and their counterparts from the 15 republics that were the Soviet Union begin an open dialogue and share each other's past, present, and future? There are, of course, the usual reasons given for learning history or geography. We can only know about ourselves by seeing the world through the eyes of other people. But there are other reasons that are peculiar to these two traditions, to psychology, and to this time in history. The editors were children of the Cold War, born after World War II (known as the Great Patriotic War in the Soviet Union). We recall a time when missiles were pointed at each other's country and school drills included "duck and tuck" exercises during which we would scurry under our desks at school in preparation for nuclear attack. In hindsight, these drills seem as silly as the prefabricated bomb shelters that were available for purchase, but at the time they were a serious exercise. (We have no idea why anyone would believe that a desk top would provide protection in the event of a nuclear attack.) We both recall the successful launching of *Sputnik* (or perhaps we are really recalling tales of *Sputnik*—it's hard to know). Halpern recalls pictures of Russian schoolchildren wildly waving flags on national holidays as Russian tanks and troops marched proudly through public squares, and Voiskounsky recalls waving the flags, half-heartedly, but nonetheless waving them. It's an image of the two mightiest powers on earth, whose relationship might best be captured in the picture of Nikita Khrushchev banging his shoe on a table at the United Nations. (Voiskounsky reports that this scene never appeared on Soviet television or in the Soviet press, but tales of this incident were passed around like other political gossip.) They were the enemy. And "they" were the other major power halfway around the world.

Although Russia is no longer a major economic power, it has the potential to once again assume that role. It is a vast country that is rich in natural resources. It has a highly educated population and a long tradition of respect for education and a national love of poetry that is probably unparalleled in the world. The countries of the West are experienced in the ways of free enterprise and democracy, and they maintain an appreciation of the critical importance of a free press and freedom of speech. There are obvious advantages to understanding how the hundreds of millions of people in these two massive world regions think and act.

In selecting the topics to include in this volume, we decided not to include those areas in which a long and mutually respected tradition of research and theory already exists—areas like child development and learning and physiological psychology. Instead, we decided to concentrate on newly evolving areas of study that are particularly important at this time in history. The areas of political psychology and the psychology of persuasion are relatively new to the former Soviets because they were not permitted under communism. How do people decide which candidate to support, which political party to join, or which product to purchase? These are important questions in a democracy and in a free economy. The long tradition in the West can be compared to the developing tradition in the former Soviet countries so that both sides can learn from each other.

Our neighbors on the other side of the globe also face many of the same persistent problems. Alcoholism and other forms of drug abuse know no boundaries. The toll in human lives claimed by alcoholism is as massive as that lost in any war. In 1944, Gunnar Myrdal wrote about the "American dilemma," which was his term for the problem of prejudice. Unfortunately, there is nothing uniquely American about prejudice, and it has reared its ugly head numerous times during this century and throughout history. A related topic is ethnic psychology. Can we use our knowledge about differences and similarities between ethnic groups in ways that are constructive? No part of the globe has been free from the devastation of war and its long-lasting aftermath. Studies of Vietnam War veterans can be compared to those of veterans from the war in Afghanistan (and more recently to conflicts in the Persian Gulf and Chechnya) to understand the psychological sequelae of severe trauma. These findings could also be extended to victims of natural disasters such as earthquakes and floods and to victims of domestic violence and debilitating diseases.

The former Soviet countries and the West face similar contemporary challenges that could benefit from mutual psychological research and understanding. Environmental problems are world problems because air, water, and soil have no regard for national boundaries. Pollution is an international problem that requires worldwide coordination and cooperation, not nationalism or regionalism. Similarly, changes in demographics and emerging technologies have the same effects on both sides of the globe. The countries of the former Soviet Union and the Western countries have an increasing number and proportion of old persons. The many questions concerning the elderly are the same no matter what language is used to pose them.

The technological revolution may be more responsible for the new "openness" than the political powers that have heralded the changes. New technologies have changed forever the way we must think about the ever-shrinking earth. Electronic messages can be sent with the same ease that was once possible only by slipping a note under a neighbor's door. Today the neighborhood is planet earth, and emerging technologies pose new opportunities and challenges to all citizens of our small planet. Isolationism is no longer possible, which means that we must learn how to cooperate and see the world from other points of view.

It is not possible to understand other worldviews without an open dialogue that includes a free exchange of ideas and information. We now have the opportunity to assume a perspective on psychological issues that is different from our own and to see what the world looks like when our feet are firmly planted on the soil that defines a mighty former enemy. That is the purpose of this book. We invite you to join the discussion as outstanding psychologists present their personal views of their area of expertise so that their counterparts halfway around the world can view a portion of the psychological landscape from a new vantage point.

References

Myrdal, G. (1944). *An American dilemma: The Negro problem and modern democracy.* New York: Harper & Row.

Takooshian, H., & Trusov, V. P. (1992). Post-Soviet psychology. In U. P. Gielen, L. L. Adler, & N. A. Milgram (eds.), Psychology in international perspective: 50 years of the International Council of Psychologists (pp. 54–69). Amsterdam: Swets & Zeitlinger.

PART ONE

POLITICS AND

PERSUASION

The major difference between the United States and other Western countries and the former Soviet countries is in the political principles that serve as the legal and philosophical foundation for how we should live, think, feel, and behave. Not surprisingly, the study of political psychology is conceptualized in different ways in each political tradition. Under communism, there were no studies of the way people thought about and reacted to political issues. To the extent that political thought and actions were studied at all, these studies were under the exclusive purview of the Communist Party, which was not likely to make the findings public unless they were supportive of Communist principles. Now that Russia has been transformed from a Soviet republic into a free-market economy, a bewildering array of choices face the "new" Russians. The most fundamental choice is that of selecting the political party to lead Russia out of its staggering economic woes and into the 21st century as a major world leader. Literally hundreds of parties have emerged from the maelstrom that followed the political coup of 1991. The immediate task for the new field of Russian political psychology is to find ways to understand and predict how and what Russian citizens think about this vast array of political parties.

Victor F. Petrenko and Olga V. Mitina, authors of the chapter on post-Soviet political psychology, describe a statistical approach that they have used to investigate how people make judgments about various parties and the political promises and slogans they espouse. Petrenko and Mitina have adopted the method of psycho-semantics to gain insights into the meaning that people ascribe to the varied political goals and parties that have sprung up in Russia in the last several years.

Their results are then analyzed with multivariate techniques so that a meaningful picture of what each party represents and its similarity to other parties can be seen. Experimental techniques like these offer great potential because they can be used to predict voting behaviors, to understand how the electorate thinks about "fuzzy" and controversial issues, and to foresee how voters will respond when a particular party disappears or is added to the political array.

By contrast, contemporary political psychology in the United States has been more concerned with international affairs, especially the prediction of how leaders will make decisions about significant international issues. This theme is seen in the chapter by Philip E. Tetlock, who has applied many of the general principles of cognitive and social psychology to the field of international decision making. He offers insights and caveats for those in the high-stakes arena of international relations and those who study the successes and blunders of the decision makers. Tetlock's analysis of the psychology of international conflict and cooperation should be of interest to politicians, political scientists, psychologists, and concerned citizens throughout the world. He offers ways to recognize and avoid common errors when making political decisions and provides sound advice for interpersonal and international dialogue.

The pair of chapters on political psychology is followed by two perspectives on the psychology of truth and lies. In the post-Soviet chapter, Victor Znakov explains how Soviets developed a unique perspective on receiving and telling lies. The loss of religious-ethical proscriptions against lying combined in a peculiar way with the belief that lies serve a valuable purpose when they further communist ideals to create a society in which truth telling was not as sacrosanct as in other countries that had strong religious sanctions against lying. In Znakov's chapter, the influence of the sociopolitical environment on everyday beliefs is clearly delineated.

Of course, the Soviet/Russian government has no monopoly on the telling of lies, and the Russian people are not unique in their suspicions that officially communicated information is not truthful. A growing number of loosely organized groups in Western countries believe in government conspiracy theories. Paul Ekman, Znakov's American counterpart, explains some of the differences among types of lies and shows that although most of us believe we can discern when someone is lying, in fact we are very poor at this task.

The third pair of chapters in this section ties the other two together by reviewing the relevant findings on mass-media communication and advertising. These are two examples of attempts to persuade citizens to buy something, whether a political philosophy or goal, a product, or a political party. Dmitry Leontiev explains the origins of studies about mass media and advertising. During the Soviet era, any researcher interested in this topic had to show that the research was being conducted for the betterment of propaganda. Every Soviet institution (e.g., trade unions, educational units, and work sites) was required to carry out a program of propaganda that would help maintain a high level of commitment to communism. Official propagandists spoke at group meetings at various work sites where attendance was mandatory. The speaker's job was to "explain" foreign and national politics and to help Soviet citizens understand new technologies such as space conquests and the use of atomic energy in ways that were favorable to the party. For the most part, attendees disliked these propaganda sessions. A particular kind of jelly candy was sometimes served when the speaker finished, a fact that led to many jokes about the candy, which was considered to be very cheap and tasteless. Voiskounsky recalls a humorous story in which an official speaker explained to *kolkhosniks* (peasants or collective farmers) the Soviet position on nuclear energy, which included an overview of the principles of nuclear energy. At the conclusion of the presentation, he asked if there were any questions. An old man raised his hand and asked, "I understand the part about nuclear energy, but what I don't understand is how you get the jelly inside the candy!"

The party also provided training in how to make persuasive presentations. This training typically consisted of reading from Lenin's speeches as a model of effective persuasion. As Leontiev shows, this field is changing very rapidly from the Soviet model and is already moving at full steam as Russia races toward a market economy.

The mass media in the United States and other Western countries are truly massive. Anthony R. Pratkanis presents the American perspective. Many American children spend more time watching television that they do in school, and thus they are bombarded with more advertising and other mass-media messages than could have been imagined a generation or two ago. An advertisement-free zone doesn't seem possible. We have noticed the not-so-subtle increase of advertisements beaming across the Internet, playing at movie theaters, obscuring formerly pristine landscapes, decorating shopping carts, and in other places where they did not exist before. Pratkanis reviews the theories and research about what makes these messages effective and how we are persuaded to buy and believe in products and policies that we have little knowledge of, can ill afford, and do not need.

Political Psychology

The Psychosemantic Approach to Political Psychology

Mapping Russian Political Thought

Victor F. Petrenko & Olga V. Mitina

How can we understand Russian political thought? What can we learn from the weltering array of newly created political parties, strident groups with demands that range from a return to the monarchy to the return of the Stalinists, and a myriad of critical problems that modern Russians face? As political psychologists and other scholars and observers of the political scene in other parts of the world already know, there are no easy answers to complex questions about how and why masses of people think or act as they do.

Most of the world was surprised by the suddenness of the switch from an officially communist country to a multiparty system, but there were ample signs of the changing political climate within the Soviet Union. In this chapter we describe two experiments in which we assessed political thought: the first was conducted just prior to the political earthquake that shook the Soviet Union and the rest of the world in 1991, and the second was done just prior to the attempted coup in Moscow in 1993.

Political Psychology in Russia

Political psychology is a wholly new field for psychologists in Russia. The Russian analogue to freedom of speech can be dated from 1990, when Gorbachev renounced Article 6 of the Soviet Constitution. Article 6, the primary declaration "On the Leading and Guiding Role of the Communist Party in the Soviet

Union," stated that the Communist Party was the sole political force for the Soviet Union. Prior to the rejection of Article 6, and the perestroika (restructuring) and glasnost (openness) that accompanied it, only "competent bodies," a euphemism for the KGB, were permitted to investigate the political mentality of Soviet citizens. The lifting of the ban on political activities resulted in the rapid appearance of numerous informal political associations, popular movements with political orientations, political clubs, ecological and national-religious societies, independent trade unions, and an assortment of groups with political agendas. The multiparty system that erupted under perestroika reflected a genuine pluralism in social consciousness. Sociopsychological research into the political mentality of the Russian people was now both urgently needed and, even more important, practically possible.

At the beginning of the epoch of perestroika and glasnost (somewhere around 1985), the many-voiced chorus intoxicated with the freedom of speech and the opportunity to write political articles included the loud voices of men of letters, philosophers, economists, historians, and representatives from academic fields that were far from political policy, such as mathematics and linguistics. At first, few psychologists contributed to the chorus of political commentary.

Many memorable articles appeared in the popular press at this time, but, as might be expected, the contents and conclusions were not based on research findings. Russian society was at a crossroads, in the center of the bifurcation, and printed words were the raw data of political thought at this time rather than a means of conveying the results of an empirically based investigation. Some psychologists, like L. Radzikhovsky, left psychology and became political journalists, and other psychologists, notably L. Gozman, B. Kochubei, and A. Etkind, published their initial and informal evaluations of the political battlefield, but these contributions were for general audiences and were not grounded in the research methodology of psychological science.

Research articles in the area of political psychology did not appear in the two leading Russian journals in psychology, *Psihologicheskij Zhurnal* (Journal of psychology) and *Voprosy Psihologii* (Questions of psychology), until 1991. A flurry of work was then published, including a series of articles dealing with an analysis of political thinking (Mitina & Petrenko, 1995; Petrenko & Mitina, 1991; Petrenko, Mitina, & Shevchuk, 1993), the political ideas of populations (Kl'amkin, 1994; Shepoval, 1995), the emerging field of political psychology (Gozman, 1994; Roschin, 1990), the study of personal characteristics and psychodiagnoses of politically active groups (Ganina & Etkind, 1991; Shmelev, 1992), and perceptions about the personalities of political leaders (Dubov & Pantileev, 1992; Egorova, 1988; Ol'shanskij, 1992). Related papers covered topics like the psychology of political negotiations (Lebedeva, 1993; Sosnin, 1994) and an analysis of political speeches (Latypov, 1994). Other highly political work by psychologists also appeared for the first time, such as an analysis of in-depth interviews concerning the effect of Stalin's repressive regime on three generations of Russian families (Baker & Gippenreiter, 1995).

Mapping the Terrain of Political Thought

A primary task for the new field of political psychology in Russia is to understand how people think about political issues. One way of understanding how people think is to examine their categorization of events. The structure of the categories that people use and the positive and negative feelings that they attach to these categories provide a way of studying how meaning is assigned to an event.

Categorization is a "system of meanings" that psychologists can take advantage of as a technique for understanding cognitive processes (Leontiev, 1977). The study of how people organize concepts into categories reveals the way they structure meaning because concepts and the labels people use for them are the building materials of consciousness. The origin, content, and structure of the way individuals store information in categories of meaning is the framework for the research method known as *psychosemantics*. As its name literally implies, psychosemantics is a way of studying the psychology of meaning (Petrenko, 1983, 1988; Shmelev, 1983).

Psychosemantics has a long history in psychology and includes concepts and techniques developed by the American psychologists Osgood (Osgood, 1971; Osgood, Suci, & Tannenbaum, 1957) and Kelly (1955). Russian psychosemantics is based on the methodological and theoretical foundations introduced by Lev Vygotsky, Alexei Leontiev, and Alexander Luria. The contemporary American psychologist Michael Cole (1993) described our work in psychosemantics this way: "Petrenko uses techniques developed in the United States to address a classic problem in Russian psychology. More than half a century ago, L. S. Vygotsky proposed word meanings as the basic unit of analysis for the study of human thinking. . . . Petrenko applies the method of factor analysis to this problem" (p. 3). Psychosemantics is based on a system of word meanings (including nonverbal meanings) that is analyzed with multivariate mathematical procedures such as factor analysis, cluster analysis, and other multidimensional scaling techniques.

Groups of individuals who think in similar ways share a particular mental picture of the world. According to this model, members of the same political party organize their meaning structures in similar ways. They use their "picture" or understanding of events that occur in the world to make decisions. This anthropomorphic metaphor of society as a single subject with a collective social consciousness can be found in the writings of Marx and Engels (1957). Early in this century, Spengler (1918–1922) wrote that different civilizations had different models of meaning and that this was one way of understanding essential differences among ancient Egyptian, Roman, Judaic, Arab, and Christian societies. These examples show that the construct of meaning structures was used in early communist writings and in more recent studies of thought.

The psychosemantic approach is consistent with the principles of the psychological theory of constructivism. Exponents of constructivism believe that individuals build their own images of the world—that is, knowledge is constructed by fitting new concepts into existing knowledge structures. These images are influenced by cultural and historical beliefs and other sorts of sociopolitical knowledge that we use to comprehend events. We are only consciously aware of some of the many influences on how we construct meaning. The understanding or pictures that we build depend on multiple kinds of influences that come from different layers of consciousness, such as scientific and conceptual knowledge, religious experiences, virtual constructions of art, ideological principles, and deep layers in the unconscious that could include the mythical and collective unconscious as proposed by Jung (1953).

Kelly (1955) introduced the notion of *personal construct* to refer to the way individuals construct their own implicit theories of personality. This notion can be expanded to describe the meanings that groups members have in common with each other. For example, sayings like "The great wisdom contains the great sorrow" and "One who doesn't work doesn't eat" form the cognitive scaffolding for those groups who believe in the message that is contained in these sayings. The meaning assigned to new experiences is shaped by existing knowledge structures.

Consider, as an example of the way groups share meaning, the conceptualization of the poor and rich in common adages. The idea that "a camel [in some translations it is a rope] can more easily pass through the eye of a needle than a rich man can find himself in paradise" provides information about the "vector of meaning" that people attribute to the rich-poor dimension. If you are closer to the rich end, then according to anyone who shares this meaning vector, you are also not likely to be virtuous (and therefore won't make it into paradise). Add to this set of meanings the idea that "richness obtained through labor is pleasurable to God." Now richness is further understood with another "vector of meaning" that links richness obtained from hard work to godliness. If hard work is "pleasurable to God," how should people who maintain these vectors think about those who don't work? In Victorian England, where these Protestant sayings were common, beggars were condemned to prisons and workhouses. If psychologists had been able to map the meaning space of middle-class citizens in Victorian England, they might have discovered that a system of meanings would lead to the belief that the idle were deserving of a harsh fate. Ideally, they might even have been able to predict the harsh fate that was meted out to the unemployed before the practice of sending beggars to workhouses began.

The task for modern experimental psychosemantics is to map the structure of meaning that individuals and groups use so that we can understand the way people think about political issues and predict how they are likely to act. We are still a long way from the goal of making accurate predictions about anything as complex as how people will act or react, especially in times of great change, such as those we are currently experiencing on the political scene.

In the studies we report here, we use the idea of personal construct in ways that are different from those originally proposed by Kelly (1955). For Kelly, constructs were bipolar dimensions. Meaning was assigned by aligning a concept on multiple scales that were marked with opposite descriptions on either end. In the bipolar model, any idea—for example, democracy—could be described by finding where it lies along multiple bipolar dimensions such as good–bad, just–unjust, many–few, open–closed, beautiful–ugly. The model of constructs that we use in this chapter conceptualizes meaning as a correlation between descriptions of the construct and underlying dimensions that are important in determining how we organize information. This conceptualization is contained in the mathematical models that we use to analyze our data.

Multidimensional Scaling

Like any cartographer mapping an unknown region, we need appropriate tools to make accurate measurements. When the unknown region is semantic space, the tools are the advanced mathematical procedures of multidimensional scaling. More direct methods are not used because individuals do not have access to or knowledge of the dimensions that shape the way they understand. People are simply not aware of the cognitive dimensions of meaning even though the dimensions of meaning that we have for every concept influence the judgments we each make. The methods of experimental psychosemantics allow the researcher to gain access to knowledge of how people think that is not available to the subjects themselves.

In psychosemantics, the task for the individual subject is to provide some classification about a topic. The response could be a judgment of similarity, an indication of the extent to which he agrees or disagrees with a statement, or some other association. Many different types of responses are possible with this technique. On the basis of numerous responses to a range of stimuli, a matrix of data is obtained from each subject. The matrix can then be used with any analytic technique that is based on matrix algebra. There are many possible ways to analyze these matrices, including a variety of multidimensional procedures such as factor analysis, cluster analysis, latent variable modeling, and others familiar to those with a good background in data analytic techniques.

The structures that are found in a data matrix are interpreted as the categorical structures of the subjects' semantic space. These structures are the frameworks or skeletons of the mind that are not available for self-observation or introspection, just as the rules of grammar that adults use so easily cannot be articulated but nevertheless guide the use of a language.

Factor analysis allows the researcher to find "bundles" of interconnected meaning that form the coordinate axes of semantic space. The number of independent factors that emerge from an analysis defines the number of dimensions that are used to locate meanings in semantic space. According to this geometric model of the mind, the greater the number of independent factors that emerge from an analysis, the greater the cognitive complexity of the individual. For any person, the degree of cognitive complexity will vary among spheres of knowledge such that experts in a field will represent their knowledge with many independent factors but may have a simple cognitive representation of some other area in which they have little knowledge.

An example should help to clarify these highly abstract concepts. In a study of the semantic space that defines political parties, Osgood (1962, cited in Osgood, 1971) found that for the "average American man" in the early part of the 1960s, one factor was all that was needed. Osgood labeled the two poles of this factor "benevolent/dynamism–malevolent/impotence." Thus, when this hypothetical average American man thought about political parties, he assessed them according to how they aligned along this dimension—that is, how close he perceived them to being good and effective or bad and ineffective. The subjects whose responses were used to derive this single factor probably could not have told you that this was the single dimension they were using when they thought about political parties, but Osgood was able to extract this single factor from their data. Of course, a more politically sophisticated group of individuals, such as professors of political science, would be expected to have their knowledge and judgments of political issues defined by many dimensions instead of the single dimension identified with the thinking of the average American man in the 1960s.

The identification of a single dimension underlying the assessment of political parties reminds us of the reporting of television news by a "news anchor" named A. Nevzorov. Nevzorov interprets all news stories by where they fall along a dimension whose poles can be described as "our people–not our people." Every news item seems to depend on whether the people in the news have political beliefs that are similar to his (good beliefs) or dissimilar to his (not good beliefs).

Another parameter of semantic space, in addition to the number of factors or dimensions, is the importance of the factor. Some factors are stronger determinants of how people think than others. (Mathematically, the power of a factor is the proportion of the variability in the responses that can be accounted for by the factor.) Consider, for example, a recent study we conducted in which we compared the semantic space of female college students in Azerbaijan with that of Russian female students. Both groups of girls rated statements pertaining to their family and home life, and for both groups of girls the dimension with its poles labeled "emancipation–traditionalism" emerged as important. But "emancipation–traditionalism" was a much more salient (important) dimension for influencing the way the Azerbaijan girls made judgments about their family and home life than for the Russian girls. This means that judgments about emancipation and traditionalism are more central to the way the girls from Azerbaijan think, but the importance of this dimension is not part of their conscious awareness. In addition, for the Azerbaijan girls, their ideal self lay closer to the traditional end of the dimension than for the Russian girls, whose ideal self lay closer to the emancipation end of the dimension.

It is also possible that a dimension can emerge as equally strong for two groups, but each is situated at different ends of the dimension. For example, groups of religious fanatics and militant atheists will both show that their thinking about religious issues is strongly influenced by the dimension of "religiosity," but each will see their favored position at opposite ends.

Changing Boundaries in Semantic Space

People are constantly reconstructing the meanings that they assign to "events." It is hoped that education also causes changes in semantic space. New information should alter what and how people think. In the sphere of political understanding, the realities of political life are expected to have a profound effect on the way Russians construct categories of knowledge about politics, especially because it is developing against a background fairly simple in terms of its underlying dimensions prior to glastnost. The information that is used to create dimensions comes from a variety of sources: public declarations by political leaders, benedictions and curses, malignant gossip and praise, congratulations, glorifications, compliments and insults, and other official and unofficial sources of information. This idea was included in the origin of the word *categories*, which comes from the Greek word *kategoresthai*. Loosely translated, the original word meant to "denounce publicly," which is one way that categories were formed.

Given the background information that was just provided and the explanation of the experimental techniques and how the results are interpreted, we turn now to a description of two studies in which we used these techniques to provide a picture drawn from inside the Russian mind of how Russians think about politics.

The 1991 Experiment: A Map of the Political Mindscape Immediately prior to the Disintegration of the USSR

We began our studies of Russian political consciousness just prior to the disintegration of the USSR and formation of the independent republics that began in August 1991. (Additional information about these studies can be found in Russian-language articles by Petrenko & Mitina, 1991). The subjects were 299 individuals living in and around Moscow who were selected on the basis of their identification as a leader in one of the 32 political parties and political groups in existence during the spring and summer of 1991, prior to the August 1991 "revolution." The number of respondents from each of the parties is shown in table 1.1. These parties are described in more detail by Pribylovsky (1993). A complete list of the 32 political groups, some with the names of their leaders, is presented in table 1.1.

Procedure

Respondents were offered questionnaires consisting of 212 political statements. They were asked to indicate the extent to which they agreed or disagreed with each statement by marking it "+1" if they agreed, "–1" if they disagreed, and "0" if they neither agreed nor disagreed. If the respondents did not understand a statement or did not want to respond to a particular statement, then "–" was used as the response.

Table 1.1. Russian Political Groups Participating in 1991 Study

Unity Value	Party Name	Abbreviation	Number of Respondents
1.6	Democratic Russia Movement	DemRus	95
2.0	Democratic Party of Russia (Travkin)	DPR	19
2.1	Party of Constitutional Democrats (Zolotarev)	ConstDem	13
1.7	All-Union Memorial Society	Memorial	14
2.0	Republican Party of Russia (Shostakovski, Lysenko)	RPR	15
2.6	Social Democratic Party of Russian Federation	SDPR	10
1.8	Russian Union of Young Christian Democrats	ChDU	12
2.6	Moscow Branch for the Establishment of Youth Solidarity "Echo"	Echo	13
1.7	Democratic Union (Novodvorskaya)	DU	13
1.4	Confederation of Anarcho-Syndicalists Anarchists	Anarchists	13
1.7	Russian Greens Party	Green	9
2.0	Association of Socialist-Populists Narodniks	SocPop	5
1.8	Socialist Party	Soc	12
1.3	Communistic Party of the Soviet Union	CPSU	63
1.4	Communists for Democracy (Rutskoy)	CPDem	12
1.7	Communist Initiative	CPInitiative	13
1.7	Marxist Platform in CPSU	CPMarx	12
1.4	CPSU-Neutrals	CPNeutr	10
1.3	Communist Party of the RSFSR	CPRus	9
1.5	The CPSU supporters of M. Gorbachev's CPSU-Center	CPCenter	7
1.7	Liberal Democratic Party (Zhirinovsky)	LDP	13
1.5	Socio-Political Council "Civil Consensus"	SPS	13
1.7	All-Union Society for Protection of Historical and Cultural Monuments	AUSPHCM	6
1.7	Russkaya Academy of Sciences[a]	RussAS	3
1.6	United Workers Front	UWF	11
1.8	Christian Regeneration Union	Monarchists	8
2.3	Pamyat National-Patriotic Front (Vasilyev)	Pamyat	6
	Democratic Party of Soviet Union (Semenov)	DPSU	
	Russian Movement (nationalistic movement)	RusMov	
	Moskva United Republican Committee (nationalistic group)	URC	
1.2	Academy of Ministry of Internal Affairs	MIA	26
1.5	World War II Veterans	Veterans	10

[a]Not to be confused with the Academy of Sciences of Russia.

The 212 statements on the questionnaire were selected from a variety of political sources and covered the spectrum of political thought. They were taken from political declarations from the various parties and movements, the United Nations Universal Declaration on Human Rights, excerpts from political speeches (given between 1988 and February 1991), and presentations made before the Supreme Soviet. The source of each statement was not indicated on the questionnaire. Topics concerned foreign policy, new political thinking, arms reduction and withdrawal from Eastern Europe, understanding of the multiparty system, attitudes toward Marxist-Leninist ideology, religion, economic reforms, private ownership, and private and collective farming. Some of the statements reflected problems in the state structure of the Soviet Union, sovereignty of the republics, national self-awareness, national language and cultures, and the inviolability of personal and human rights. The statements were selected to cover a wide range of political viewpoints and contained opposing opinions.

Questionnaires regarding political opinions are new in the Soviet Union/ Russia, so the respondents' attitudes toward the task were interesting. Some respondents wished the experimenters well and offered advice, comments, and thanks for the opportunity to reflect upon a wide spectrum of problems and political approaches. Other responses ranged from guarded to open hostility. Some avoided the task with the following explanations: "I must speak first to the party's leaders, and if they approve, we'll permit you to take the poll"; "We'll fill in the questionnaire on behalf of the whole party, and as for individual opinions, we know those Bolshevik tricks too well"; "I have filled in the questionnaire but I am not going to submit it to you, for you are likely to misinterpret it." Despite some hostility, mistrust, and suspicion, we were able to receive 299 completed questionnaires, and most of the respondents wished us success with the project.

Data Analysis

Data were tabulated on the basis of party affiliation, with the mean response for each statement computed for each of the 32 parties. These data are presented in appendix 1.1. A "unity" value was also computed for each of the political parties that indicates the degree to which the responding members of the party maintain similar views. These values are also presented in table 1.1. The table shows that the political parties who are most unanimous in their thinking are the Social Democrats, the Constitutional Democrats, and members of the Democratic and Republican parties of Russia. The political groups with the most heterogeneity in the way they think are the Anarchists, the cadets of the Academy of the Ministry of Internal Affairs, and World War II Veterans. The wide range of opinions for these groups would be expected because their affiliation is based on their social community rather than their political perspectives.

Factor Structure

The mathematical model that was used to determine the factor structure of semantic space is the method of principal components with varimax factor axis rotation (Uberla, 1977). Based on these methods, we identified four factors that account for 37, 18, 12, and 7 percent of the variability in responses. Statements that loaded on each of the factors and the factor loadings are listed in appendix 1.1. The term "factor loading" has a specific mathematical meaning, which can be thought of as the degree to which the meaning of the statement and the meaning represented by the factor are the same. The highest possible loading is 1, and the lowest is 0, but statements with small loadings are not included in the table. The sign of the factor loadings show which of two opposite poles of a factor the statement refers to.

The statements that load on the first factor seem to share a concern with issues of unity in a single state or a confederation of sovereign states. We point out that preparations for a referendum on the preservation of the USSR were occurring during the time the questionnaire was being administered (1991). Not surprisingly, this dimension of political thought emerged as the primary factor in the structural organization of thoughts about statehood.

The second factor is defined by acceptance–rejection of communist ideology. The joint representation on one factor of ideological and economic concerns is probably because economic issues are largely determined by ideology for communists, so they coexist as a single dimension of meaning. Also grouped under this factor are statements concerning religious ideology and the demands of a free economy, such as the right to individual farming and reduced aid to foreign countries. It is noteworthy that, based on these results, we find that in purely ideological terms, the pole marked by Marxism-Leninism ideology is opposite to the pole representing religious orientation. In the minds of the respondents, religious beliefs and actions are the antithesis of communist ideology. The apparent absence of an identifiable ideology that has a meaning opposite of that of communist ideology (other than religion) is probably due to the fact that democrats do not present a clearly articulated alternative ideology except for their support of freedom in political, economic, and intellectual spheres.

The relative position of the political parties in 1991 on these two dimensions is shown in the upper plot in figure 1.1. Because four dimensions emerged from the data analysis, the depiction of the political parties in four-dimensional space is shown with two two-dimensional plots. In figure 1.1, the coordinates of each party in "semantic space" is coincident with the location of the initial letter in the party name.

In interpreting figure 1.1, we see that parties close to each other in the graph are similar in the ways their leaders think (the respondents in the study were party leaders) and those that are far from each other are dissimilar. The fact that the quadrant defined by F1+ and F2– is empty shows that there are no parties whose leaders show the logically inconsistent positions of both supporting a unitary state and opposing communist ideology. As might be expected and can be seen in figure 1.1, the most polar views on the second (ideological) factor were exhibited by the Communist Initiative, the Marxist Platform in the CPSU, World War II Veterans, the United Workers' Front, and the Communist Party of the RSFSR on one end and the representatives of the Memorial Society, the Social Democratic and the Republican parties of Russia, members of the Christian Democratic Union, and Socialist-Populists-Narodniks on the other. In addition to the democratic bloc, the communist ideology was rejected by National-Patriots: Monarchists, the Democratic Party of the Soviet Union, the Moskva United Republican Committee, and the Pamyat Front. It is interesting to note

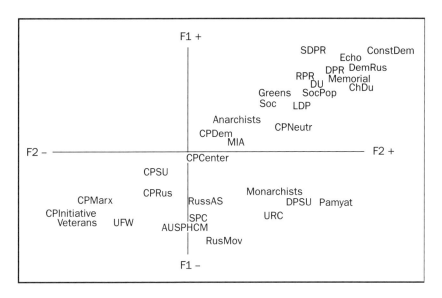

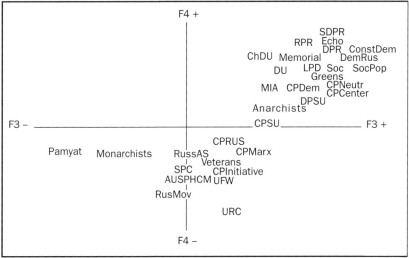

Figure 1.1. Four-Dimensional Semantic Space for Russian Political Parties in 1991

Note: Factor 1: Confederation of Sovereign States– Unity Statehood
    (+): support for decentralized political power
    (–): support for a unitary state
    Factor 2: Rejection of Communist Ideology– Acceptance (especially economic aspects)
    (+): rejection of communist ideology
    (–): acceptance of communist ideology
    Factor 3: Importance–Unimportance of Human Rights
    (+): acknowledge the priority of human rights
    (–): refute the priority of human rights
    Factor 4: Advocates—Opponents of Democratic Forms of Government
    (+): support for democratic government
    (–): opposition to democratic government

that the Communists for Democracy and the CPSU-Neutrals—the party for those who were tired of political parties—were discreet in their rejection of communist ideology, as expressed in the pro-communist statements made by traditionalist communists and included in the questionnaire.

The third factor derived from the data matrix has been defined as "human rights." The statements that load on this factor concern the "third basket" of the Helsinki Conference on Security and Cooperation in Europe. This "basket," or theme, comprises some of the items from the United Nations Declaration on Human Rights. The "pro-human rights" position is represented by the positive pole of factor 3, with the rejection of human rights at the opposite end.

Factor 4 appears to represent statements about a general set of democratic tenets (at its positive pole) and the opposing authoritarian, antimarket sentiments (at its negative pole). Many of the statements that have significant loadings onto factor 4 have also loaded onto other factors, creating cross-associations with the basic characteristics of these factors.

The lower plot of figure 1.1 shows a graph of semantic space as defined by factor 3 (human rights) and factor 4 (support for or rejection of democratic forms of government). Notice that most of the parties load positively on human rights, showing that most parties advocate a pro-human rights position. The most pronounced in their protection of human rights are the Constitutional Democrats, the Democratic Party of Russia, and the Socialists (Populists). The members of CPSU supporting Gorbachev are also among the parties with most extreme loadings on factor 3. A negative attitude regarding human rights was exhibited by the national-patriotic movements, including the Russian Movement, the All-Union Society for Protection of Historical and Cultural Monuments, the Socio-Political Council "Civil Consensus," Monarchists, and especially the Pamyat Front. Thus, rejection of human rights under current conditions manifests itself primarily in the nationalistic political parties.

The Communist Party of the Soviet Union split into Democrats (Communists for Democracy and supporters of Gorbachev) and those opposed to democratic reforms (the Communist Party of Russia, Marxist Platform, and Communist Initiative) in the way it loaded onto factor 4—the factor whose pole can be labeled "rejection" or "support" of democratic forms of government. According to Yanov (1991), professor of political science at New York University and our former compatriot, "the real front-line passes between those striving for democratic reforms and isolationists. The latter may be socialist isolationists claiming that they 'can't give up their principles.' Or they may be patriotic isolationists discoursing upon unique national specifics and inadmissibility of Europeanization. It all starts with philosophical reasoning, like it was with the Slavophiles, and then comes down to politics." Although on the whole we agree with this opinion, we nevertheless resent the rigid term of *front-line*, which is tinged with a civil war connotation. As citizens of this country, we believe that a democratically minded respondent in our poll would have found it extremely painful to appear "on the other side of the barricades" from his father or grandfather. Each factor is a probable line of opposition between the parties, but at the same time each factor presents an opportunity for possible association and unification on basic meanings and basic values. Thus, the acceptance of personal values and human rights (factor 3) by the majority of the respondents (including officers and war veterans) is a hopeful sign of getting consensus on the other political aspects, too.

Cluster Analysis

Data were also analyzed using the statistical techniques of cluster analysis. In cluster analysis, we used the responses of the party leaders to determine a Euclidean metric that reflects the similarity among the political parties. The result is a tree of similarity such that parties that are near to each other are more similar in their belief systems than parties that are far from each other. The mathematical procedure we used to form clusters of similar parties is a standard method known as *minimal contrast* (Duran & Odel, 1974; Ryzin, 1977). The resulting tree of similarity is a semantic mapping of similarity among the parties that should correspond to patterns of partnerships and rivalries as they exist in real life. The similarity tree is shown in figure 1.2.

Perusal of figure 1.2 reveals several striking facts about the structure of political parties in 1991. First, key blocs of parties can be found in the tree structure. In understanding the tree structure shown in figure 1.2, begin with those parties that are grouped in the top third of the figure. Those parties that appear closely linked to the Democratic Russia Movement, in fact, are close in terms of their political guidelines. As shown in figure 1.2, there are many different organized parties that are linked to the Democratic Russia Movement, and these parties are similar in political spirit. On another branch, but still nearby, are the Anarchists and the Greens Party. Although the names of the parties may suggest that they are ideologically distant from each other, in fact these two parties have had the same leaders at different times, so their appearance on close branches of this tree reflects this similarity.

Findings with regard to the various communist parties also reflect realities. The traditionalist Communists (Communist Party of Russia, Marxist Platform, and Communist Initiative) form a compact bloc in their unanimity, which is closely related to the United Workers Front and World War II Veterans parties. A high degree of unanimity, both within the party platforms and the cluster that resulted from our analysis, points to a stable political formation with its own vision and approach to political developments.

Finally, a bloc of national-patriots (the Socio-Political Council "Civil Consensus," Russkaya Academy of Sciences, Monarchists, Moskva United Republican Committee, Democratic Party of the Soviet Union, and Pamyat National-Patriotic Front) is characterized by a rather fuzzy structure reflecting its heterogeneity and the absence of common leaders and orientations.

The categorical structure of political parties as represented by the cluster analysis is a cognitive reality that characterizes the affinity of the party leaders. It reflects the existing political groupings and alliances among the political par-

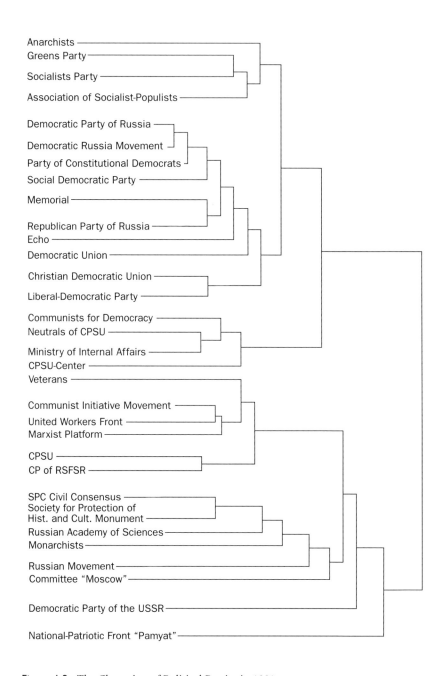

Figure 1.2. The Clustering of Political Parties in 1991

ties. These structures allow us to predict the dynamics of political processes and social development. For example, new political parties often have short lives. By using the results of cluster analysis, we can predict which party will gain in membership when some other party disappears or whether two or more parties are sufficiently similar in their ideologies so that mergers would be successful.

Finding Locations in Semantic Space

Our maps of semantic space that allow us to understand and predict political thought are dependent on the way respondents make judgments about the political statements on the questionnaires. The statements came from a variety of sources in the real world outside of the laboratory, a fact that is important for the ecological validity of our study. However, many respondents expressed their discontent with the wording of some statements, pointing out perceived errors and sometimes trying to paraphrase a statement that they did not like. We had to remind them that the authorship of these statements belonged to someone else, and we had just selected excerpts from the speeches of various politicians. But we had a persistent problem with the fact that persons from different political orientations expressed their discontent with the way statements were worded, and what was acceptable to respondents from one party was disagreeable to those from other parties. Psycholinguists know that perception of reality and expression of thoughts are carried through a prism of categorical structures of the mind that are mediated by language, and that thought is influenced by the language used to communicate it.

Political language is a system of notations and methods of reasoning and furnishing proof, and both the language and the system vary in different political circles. Even after reaching an understanding, the problem known as Sapir-Whorf linguistic relativity arises. According to its spiritual forerunner, Humboldt (1903–1936), "different language are not different definitions of one and the same object, but different visions of it." Therefore, perception of the same fact or event can be radically different for people with divergent political labels and different political views.

Although all of us are evidently inhabiting the same physical space, people with different beliefs, particularly in the political sphere, seem to be living in different worlds, with different axioms and nonconverging laws of cause and effect. For instance, a Monarchist firmly convinced of a singular road of development for Russia needs no pragmatic grounds to prove the aggressive insidiousness of Westerners, that evil force trying to harm Russia because of its special God-chosen Orthodoxy. The laws of logic and rational thinking are untenable to this individual, and a study of political consciousness calls for using structural mythology, clinical notions of changed mental states, and the theory of Freudian defense mechanisms of human personality.

To be able to compare political guidelines and build a common semantic space, we selected statements from a wide political spectrum, with the vocabulary used by different political movements. In this way, we produced a language mediator, a kind of "political Esperanto." By forcing representatives from different political groups to make judgments about phrases and wording alien to them, we may have caused some of the respondents much stress. Some of the respondents found the task to be very upsetting.

The dimensions of semantic space reflect the cognitive complexity of the respondents' knowledge and thinking about the topics described in the statements. The totality of personal meanings and values can be inferred from the way they categorized topics and the location of topics within their semantic space. The study of political consciousness within the framework of a psychosemantic approach allows us to reconstruct the world as it is perceived by various political communities.

We can use this approach to make predictions about the political thinking of single individuals. A new domain of study, which can be called politicodiagnostics, can be used to infer any individual's political affiliation by determining the pattern of responses the individual gives to statements that have been used to identify underlying factors. Thus, the computer program that we developed jointly with M. Gambaryan makes it possible for any person to check his political orientation by responding to the statements on the questionnaire we have previously described. Once completed, individuals can locate their response patterns in the semantic spaces shown in figure 1.1 to find the parties of kindred spirit. In this way, voters who are uncertain as to which of the political parties is closest in philosophy to their own can make this determination by using the new methods of politicodiagnostics.

The 1993 Experiment: A Map of the Political Mindscape
Immediately prior to the Attempted Parliamentary Coup

Unprecedented changes in Russian political life occurred in the years immediately following 1991. To capture the structure of the changes in political thought, we conducted a second experiment in 1993 just prior to the attempted coup by Parliament against President Yeltsin. The timing of the second experiment, like that of the first, may seem fortuitous to those outside of Russia, but there were ample signs of change within Russia, so the timing was not merely "lucky." To assess political thinking in 1993, we used the same methods as in the 1991 study, but the content of the stimulus materials was, in part, changed to reflect all of the changes in the political scene. Those statements from the 1991 questionnaire that still represented major issues were retained.

A second questionnaire was drawn up with statements relevant to the current political situation in 1993. These statements included such topics as the constitution and state system, problems of foreign and home policy, attitudes toward the reform of the armed forces, juridical aspects of the economy, private property, political freedom and civil rights, questions of national policy and interethnic relations, problems of culture, language, religion, and selected topics from the All-Russian referendum of April 1993 concerning trust in the president (Yeltsin) and support for the policy of reform.

The respondents were 1,059 persons selected from 67 political parties or groups that were active in Russian in 1993. Respondents were selected on the basis of their active participation in the various parties, and all were in the Moscow area at the time of the administration. As seen from these statistics, the number of political parties and groups mushroomed in the two years following the "revolution." A much larger sample of respondents was needed for the second study to capture the diversity in all of the new political parties.

As in the previous study, respondents indicated their agreement or disagreement with the statements by marking each statement with "+1" to indicate agreement, "–1" to indicate disagreement, "0" to indicate neither agreement not disagreement, and "–" to indicate that they did not understand the statement or they did not wish to respond.

Charting Semantic Space in 1993

The data were analyzed with factor analytic techniques. Four independent factors emerged accounting, respectively, for 21, 17, 13, and 6 percent of the variance. Figure 1.3 shows the relative position of the major parties in 1993 in the four-dimensional space defined by these factors. The factors are described as: F1, support for Yeltsin's reforms–rejection of Yeltsin's reforms; F2, free market economy–planned economy; F3, human rights are of primary importance–a strong unitary state is of primary importance; and F4, accept communist ideology–reject communist ideology. As explained in the prior sections of this chapter, each political party or group can be located in this four-dimensional space based on the way representatives from the parties responded to the statements in the questionnaire.

Clusters of Parties

Data were also analyzed with the methods of cluster analysis to find meaningful groupings of the 67 political parties. As shown in figure 1.4, in 1993, parties grouped into branches with a primary division along the dimension of whether or not they supported Yeltsin.

Among the strongest supporters were the Anti-Fascist Center, Russia's Choice, and Democratic Russia, 3 of the 67 political parties included in the 1993 study. Another grouping consisted of those parties that offered "constructive and gentle" opposition to Yeltsin's reforms. This was a heterogeneous group with some parties opposing the economic and social consequences of the abrupt transition to a free market, such as the United Fraction of Social Democratic Party of Russia, Civil Union, and Democratic Party of Russia. Other parties in this middle group denounced President Yeltsin for his authoritarianism; the Union of Rebirth of Russia, Young Christian Democrats, and others denounced Yeltsin because they believed that greater authoritarianism was needed because of the dangers in superfluous social democratization, "Pamyat." A third cluster consisted of parties that denied state power in any form, including the power of the president. This group included the Anarchists and several informal political organizations.

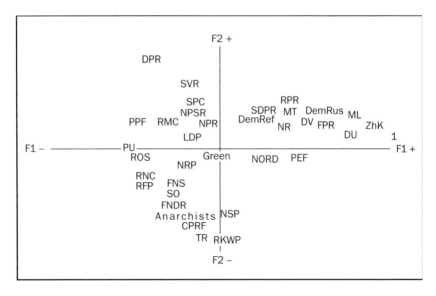

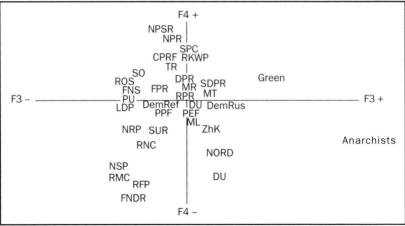

Figure 1.3. Four-Dimensional Semantic Space for Russian Political Parties in 1993

Note: Factor 1: Advocates–Opponents of Yeltsin's Reforms
   (+): support for Yeltsin's reforms
   (−): opposition to Yeltsin's reforms
Factor 2: Free Market–Planned Economy
   (+): support for free market economy
   (−): support for planned economy
Factor 3: Human Rights–Unilateral Nationalism
   (+): support for human rights
   (−): support for nationalism
Factor 4: Acceptance–Rejection of Communist Ideology
   (+): acceptance of communist ideology
   (−): rejection of communist ideology

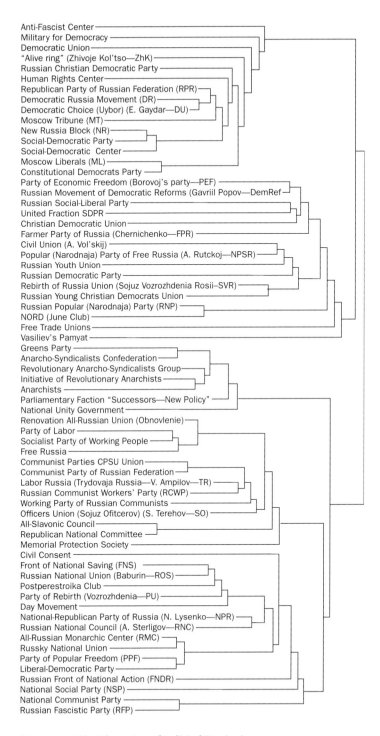

Figure 1.4. The Clustering of Political Parties in 1993

37

As many readers might predict, the fourth branching of parties was composed of those with strong socialist orientations that are in "irreconcilable opposition" to Yeltsin's reforms. These include the Party of Labour, the most strongly identified communist political party. This branch of the political tree can be thought of as ranging in color from red to brown to black, as the parties aligned in continuous gradations with communists at one end and avowed fascists at the other (Fascist Party).

The Dynamics of Political Mentality: Assessing Changes in Political Thought

The two studies described in this chapter provide two pictures in time of political thinking among representatives from Russia's political parties. But political thinking is in a state of flux, and the two political "snapshots," while revealing in their own right, are static and cannot capture the movement and changes inherent in a swiftly shifting system of meanings. One way of examining the shift is by comparing the two pie charts shown in figure 1.5. The upper chart shows the proportional contribution of different sorts of semantic factors to political thinking in 1991; the lower chart shows the same data for 1993.

In the years between 1991 and 1993—short in terms of history but long in the amount of political activity that influenced and reflected Russian political thought—the problems facing Russia underwent radical alterations. The statements in the two questionnaires had to be changed to reflect changes in the real world. However, the process by which change is achieved is important in its own right. We need to understand and predict how and in which directions political thoughts will be altered in order to use our data to make political predictions.

How did the political parties change during the two-year period of political frenzy between the 1991 revolution and 1993 attempted coup? What dimensions emerge when this period is treated as though it were a single point in time? To answer these questions, we combined the data from the two studies and reanalyzed them to create a new semantic space that was representative of political thought in the period between these two historical events.

To combine the data from the 1991 and 1993 studies, we had to make the assumption that the parties that were in existence at both times were stable enough to consider them as bearers of the particular social and political values that they advocated. This assumption is inherent in the individual studies; without it, analysis of party positions would not be meaningful. Those statements that appeared on both questionnaires and those parties and groups that responded to them in 1991 and 1993 formed the data matrix that allowed us to investigate changes in the structure of political thinking during this tumultuous time.

Based on the methods of factor analysis and axis rotation that were described in the earlier studies, we extracted six factors from the combined data set from 1991 and 1993. The six factors accounted for 27, 25, 16, 8, 6, and 5 percent, respectively, of the total variability in the data. These six factors and their polar descriptors in 1991 and 1993 are shown in figure 1.6.

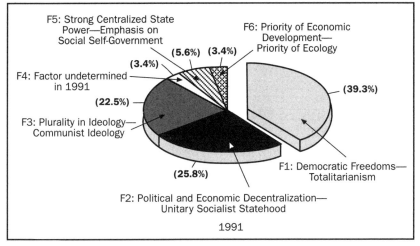

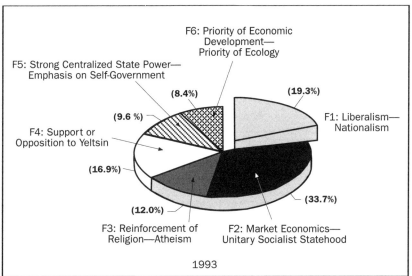

Figure 1.5. The Relative Contribution of Different Factors to Russian Political Thought in 1991 and in 1993

In analyzing the shift in political thinking in the period between 1991 and 1993, consider factor 1. The primary shift was from a dimension that corresponded to democratic freedoms–totalitarianism in 1991 to a dimension that corresponded to liberalism–nationalism in 1993. In the two years between the revolution and the 1993 attempted coup, the struggle against totalitarianism and suppression of democratic freedoms changed to more individually oriented liberal values. The conceptual importance of totalitarianism limitations on human rights was replaced by the concern about nationalism. (*Concern* is meant to have

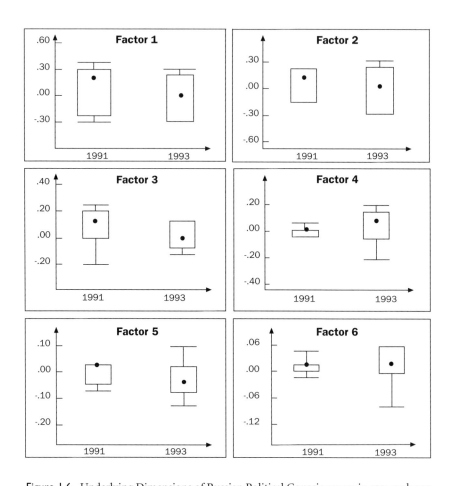

Figure 1.6. Underlying Dimensions of Russian Political Consciousness in 1991 and 1993

Note: The box region in each plot represents the second and third quartiles. The dot in each box is the median score.

Factor 1 (27% of the variance)
1991:   Democratic Freedoms–Totalitarianism
1993:   Liberalism–Nationalism

Factor 2 (25% of the variance)
1991:   Political/Economic Decentralization–Unitary Socialist Statehood
1993:   Market Economics–Unitary Socialist Statehood

Factor 3 (16% of the variance)
1991:   Plurality in Ideology–Communist Ideology
1993:   Reinforcement of Religion–Atheism

Factor 4 (8% of the variance)
1991:   [Doesn't exist in 1991]
1993:   Support of Yeltsin–Opposition to Yeltsin

Factor 5 (6% of the variance)
1991:   Strong Centralized State Power–Emphasis on Social Self-Government
1993:   [Same factor as in 1991]

Factor 6 (5% of the variance)
1991:   Priority of Economic Development–Priority of Ecology
1993:   [Same factor as in 1991]

both positive and negative connotations because the importance of a dimension does not indicate its preferred pole.)

The second major dimension of semantic space is shown by a transition from the political/economic decentralization–unitary socialist statehood to market economy–unitary socialist statehood. The demands for decentralization of political power shifted, so the greater emphasis was on a market economy two years later. Conceptually, the opposite of market economy was the unitary socialist state, and that is implied within the concept of a single source of political control.

The idea of multiple versus communist ideologies was replaced with a religiosity–atheism dimension. The religious aspects of meaning assumed greater significance during this period when there was a great deal of religious activity in Russia. The phenomenal growth in church attendance during this time shows that it had become a major dimension in political thought.

The fourth factor had no counterpart in 1991. In the period just prior to the attempted overthrow of President Yeltsin by some members of Parliament, most notably Alexander Rutskoi, pro- and anti-Yeltsin forces became polarized. Yeltsin, of course, was associated with the government's actions with regard to problems in Russia and abroad. In general, those respondents who showed support for reform also showed support for Yeltsin, but these variables were only moderately correlated because it was possible to support reform and oppose the specific course of action that Yeltsin took in obtaining that reform.

The fifth and sixth factors showed little change between 1991 and 1993. The polarization of self-government and maintenance of a strong central government and the economic versus ecological development underwent little change, but they also accounted for much smaller portions of the variance in responses. Although separate chapters on environmental/ecological psychology appear later in this book, we note here that the ideas of ecology were already in the public consciousness in 1991, but they were still relatively unimportant when compared to issues of the economy, religion, and ideology.

The Investigation of Russian Political Thought

We presented here the data from two separate studies in which we analyzed the judgments of leaders from multiple political parties to see the way they think about politics in Russia. The picture that we drew is a fascinating perspective on political issues from inside the Russian mind. We created a landscape of meaning about contemporary political thought at two critical points in Russian modern history and the changes that occurred between them. We believe that the approach we used offers great potential for anyone who wants to understand or predict how Russians think about politics. The dimensions that have emerged show that relatively few themes dominate the processes of making judgments about political life. The technique of politicodiagnosis also permits psychologists to predict how an individual will select a political party and how successful various party rivalries and mergers are likely to be, making this a potentially powerful approach.

Appendix I.I.   Statements from the Questionnaire Administered in 1991

Statements are listed by their number on the questionnaire and their factor loadings.

Statements at One Pole of Factor 1: Confederation of Sovereign States

116. I favor the idea of dissolving the USSR and setting up a new confederation of independent national states based on the supremacy of republican legislation over the Union laws 0.91
18. It is necessary to disband the political police, the KGB 0.91
125. A republic may have its own monetary system along with the Union currency ... 0.91
190. Under the disguise of idle talk on the republics' sovereignty the center tries its worst to concentrate as much power as possible in its own hands 0.90
93. Citizens should be able to come back to their homeland without any restrictions ... 0.88
176. National republics as independent states must have their own armed forces ... 0.85
6. The national officers cadres must be revived, and recruits should have an opportunity to do their army service in their own republics 0.84
94. I'm for the priority of human rights over state interests as the basic principle of the legal system 0.83
129. The laws of a Union state (republic) should be given priority over the All-Union legislation 0.82
108. I'm for a society wherein the key priority is given to the interests of an individual and not the state, while the rights of the state and not of an individual are restricted in the first place 0.80
92. Foreign passports should be issued to citizens immediately upon request without clearing up the reasons, aims, dates and destination 0.79
6. The numerical strength of armed forces should be cut down 0.79
131. The rights of the native population of a republic should be guaranteed through constitutional acknowledgment of its language, legalization of republican citizenship and protection of national symbol 0.77
128. The best solution to interethnic problems is to sign a new Union Treaty, with the USSR to be transformed into a confederation of sovereign states 0.76
164. It is necessary to authorize the establishment of nongovernmental banking structures enjoing the right to currency operation with foreign banks and firms ... 0.73
126. The republics must have complete economic independence 0.71
32. It is necessary to authorize the functioning of non-governmental television and radio and grant the independent political associations and public spokesmen the right to use the state mass media for free exposition of their views 0.71
97. The whole structure of human life should be adapted to the laws of personality development, with human individuals organized in free associations, while the state should be eliminated 0.66

Statements at the Opposite Pole of Factor 1: Unitary Statehood

134. I'm for the unity and territorial integrity of the USSR .... −0.91
189. The key issue today is to consolidate power, discipline and legal order ...... −0.91
171. Any projects to divide Russia into economic zones should be decisively repulsed
133. I support the internationalist movements in the Baltic republics and Moldova in their struggle for the unity of the Soviet Union, against restoration of the bourgeois structure, fomenting interethnic enmity and breakdown of the CPSU republican organization .... −0.90

10. Service in the army is an honored duty and a sacred obligation of each citizen of the USSR — −0.90

11. We insist on reinforcement of the army, a bulwark of our security, and categorically protest against its reduction and turning a people's army into a mercenary army of professional killers — −0.90

7. It is imperative to strengthen the bond of the Armed Forces with the working people, to repulse attacks at the universal military service and bringing up the Soviet people in the spirit of defenders of their single socialist Motherland — −0.89

83. In the current conditions of general looseness and slackness in this country the order should be enforced by an iron hand — −0.89

24. Some Soviet periodicals are seething with poison against the USSR itself and socialism. You can't help feeling in it the hidden hand of imperialism, reaction and counterrevolution — −0.89

113. A concrete and effective program of consolidating the Soviet federation and overcoming its centrifugal tendencies threatening the state structure would meet the interests and aspiration of all Soviet people — −0.89

188. A parade of sovereignties declared by the Union republics down to rural Soviets, and a war of laws gave rise to an unprecedented lawlessness in this country — −0.89

72. I believe that the new thinking in the sphere of international relations, the political changes in East European countries and reduction of the armed forces actually weaken the USSR and make it more vulnerable in military matters — −0.89

194. I'm for free movement of citizens over their national territory, the common armed forces, and participation in international affairs in the status of an integral state

163. The state must control private ownership — −0.89

127. I believe it expedient to leave the enterprises of Union subordination in the territory of the republics — −0.86

65. Some of our pseudo-leaders sell out the Soviet territory during their foreign trips, having expended neither sweat nor blood on it. And this is going on when the NATO countries do not reduce but build up their war potential, when with the approving praises of the West a hasty conversion of our war industry is being carried out, when owing to the dismantling of the armed forces of our allies and a speedy withdrawal of Soviet troops from Europe the strategic parity in the world is being changed — −0.86

17. We should ban the use of national mass media for subversive propaganda aimed at elimination of the constitutional structure in this country and the breakdown of the CPSU — −0.85

173. I think we should carry out a monetary reform, fix the economically valid prices, rigidly control the fulfillment of production plans and, most probably, introduce the state rationing of food staples. And wherever the traditionally governmental measures fail, we should resort to Party and political responsibility — −0.83

47. While we streamline the forms and methods of Party work to make them more flexible and diverse, we must preserve and, moreover, strengthen the principle of democratic centralism — −0.78, −0.71

201. I'm for promotion of the national economic complex and formation of a common Union market — −0.76

162. A planned economy has many potential advantages — −0.74

188. We believe that the USSR is a multinational state and stand for the establishment of common union citizenship throughout its territory — −0.71

Statements at One Pole of Factor 2: Rejection of Communist Ideology

41. In my view, we should look truth in the eye and give up primarily the outdated idea of communism — 0.92

42. If we are to ever consider what exactly our great leader and founding father had laid the foundation for, it must be mass-scale violence and terror elevated to a principle of state policy — 0.92

33. Compulsory study of the Marxist-Leninist disciplines must be cancelled — 0.91
19. Stalinism and Leninism are the foundations of the totalitarian ideology — 0.90
157. All legislative acts on persecution for private enterprise should be abrogated — 0.90
141. The Church should be granted the right to publish religious literature and make regular appearances on TV and radio — 0.84
140. All building of religious worship should be given back to the Church and used for their original purpose — 0.83
110. The establishment of cooperative and private secondary and higher schools, including those of religious orientations should be authorised — 0.83
167. I'm for development of agriculture on the basis of various ownership — 0.83
175. The peasant should be given the right to individual ownership of land, irrespective of his work in a collective, state, or cooperative farm, or individual farming — 0.82
152. The monopoly in the national economy should be eliminated on the basis of multiple forms of property — 0.80
31. The KGB activities during the period of Brezhnev–Andropov rule should be made known to the wide public — 0.80
68. We should cardinally reduce our financial aid to other countries in view of numerous unresolved domestic problems — 0.75
139. The parents willing to give their children religious education should get such opportunity — 0.74
52. The Communist Party can't yet give up its aspirations for seizing and keeping all governmental power in its hands at any cost — 0.86
29. Ours is a totalitarian state-bureaucratic exploiting system based on the power monopoly of the Communist Party and exploitation of all sections of society by the class of bureaucracy — 0.67

Statements at the Opposite Pole of Factor 2: Acceptance of Communist Ideology

135. I believe that class differences are more vital than nationality distinctions — −0.95
144. Religion is the opium of the people — −0.88
137. Abolition of religion as an illusory happiness of the people is a demand for its actual happiness — −0.87
123. The victory of the October revolution has forever done away with national oppression and inequality of nations — −0.85
182. The revival of religion in our country is a factor hampering scientific progress — −0.85
38. Lenin's ideas, devoid of dogmatic interpretation and enriched by the modern thought and experience in socialist and world construction, serve a reliable foundation for perestroika — −0.80
43. Our goal at the current stage is a revolutionary renovation of socialism, but not renunciation of the choice made by Lenin, the Bolsheviks and the people in October 1917 — −0.79
37. We must promote the study of the Marxist-Leninist teaching by the younger generation their labor and military-patriotic education in the public education system — −0.79
138. Religion is the art of stupefying people to detract their thoughts from the evil done to them by the powers that be — −0.78
50. In all its activities the CPSU sets an example of serving the people's interests and observing the principles of socialist democratism — −0.77
70. International politics have always been of class character and will remain to be so — −0.77
143. The Church must not take part in the upbringing of the younger generation — −0.73
166. I think it is wrong to hand over the land to individual owners — −0.68
158. Private ownership engenders inequality and therefore it is unacceptable for our state — −0.68
23. You can't streamline socialism by giving up the elementary principles of Marxism-Leninism — −0.68

199. I'm against hired labor: private enterprise should be limited to one's own labor or that of family members — −0.62

82. We have forever gotten rid of the power of the privileged minority and poverty of millions of people — −0.61

51. We are sure that at present we have no other force except for the CPSU capable of uniting the people, raising them for overcoming the difficulties of the transitional period and getting the country out of the crisis — −0.61

Statements at One Pole of Factor 3: Acceptance of Human Rights

34. All cultural values, irrespective of their ideological orientation, should be easily accessible to any Soviet citizen — 0.89

16. Soviet people should have a real opportunity to get information from any source, including foreign mass media — 0.89

55. The existence of a democratic opposition is an imperative for national regeneration — 0.79

121. I want to partake of cultural values of all nations — 0.79

69. Cooperation of states should be based on universal legal values devoid of any ideological tinge — 0.75

78. We should set up independent public structures on a democratic basis as opposed to totalitarianism — 0.74

67. Let us not push away the kind hands outstretched toward us from the overseas, which is mostly thanks to the fact that many people over there came to realize through Gorbachev's personality that ours is not at all "an empire of evil" — 0.73

109. The freedom of meetings, demonstrations and street processions should be guaranteed and secured — 0.73

99. No one can be arbitrarily deprived of his citizenship or the right to change it — 0.70

88. The threat of extremism comes primarily from nationalist groupings — 0.67

58. I'm sure that the development and stability of political democracy are possible only under a multiparty system — 0.66

146. By his social and political activities Andrei Sakharov made a great contribution to our perestroika, the assertion of human dignity and rights, and democratization of society — 0.66

101. Parents have the priority right to choose an education for their children — 0.66

81. I believe the democratic road of development to be the only favorable one for any country — 0.63

150. While solving ecological and production problems both sides should be ready to make a compromise — 0.63

151. If we give up all the achievments of human civilization because of ecological hazards, it could lead to regression in social development — 0.61

204. Discussion of a Union Treaty should start with adoption of the Law on personal sovereignty and human rights of Soviet citizens — 0.60

Statements at the Opposite Pole of Factor 3: Rejection of Human Rights

186. Interethnic marriages lead to spiritual degeneration — −0.76

205. The rights of a nation are superior to the human rights — −0.69

60. Democracy hampers perestroika, since it leads to the appearance of opposition parties and rejection of socialism — −0.64

202. Civil consensus is out of the question with the people holding diametrically opposite views and pursuing opposite aims — −0.60

80. The authoritarian system in the conditions of Orthodoxy was not too bad — −0.59

145. By his social and political activities Sakharov aggravated instability in our society — −0.52

122. Over seventy years the Russian people had to withstand a genocide organized by Zion — −0.50

111. Official crimes should be liable to capital punishment — −0.48

106. All children should be taught according to a common school curriculum specified by the state   −0.48

Statements at One Pole of Factor 4: Democracy

30. A free, democratic development of the state can be guaranteed only by ideological
pluralism   0.69
191. I'm for a Union Treaty according to which the republics would grant the rights to
the center, but not vice versa**   0.69
181. The languages of ethnic minorities living in the territory of a national republic
should be acknowledged as state languages on a par with the language of its
aboriginal nationality   0.67
95. The unconditional acknowledgement of the priority of human rights over state
interests is the fundamental principle of any legal system   0.66
153. The monopoly power of the Party apparatus has led our country to its current
crisis   0.66
21. I deem it my direct duty to decisively oppose the forces striving to block the way
to pluralism   0.62
192. The division into union and autonomous republics is a political nonsense. A Union
Treaty should be signed by all 15 republics making up the Union   0.61
100. Each person should have the individual right to his own property   0.60
91. The system of propiska (domicile registration) should be annuled   0.55
81. I believe the democratic road of development to be the only favorable one for our
country   0.55

Statements at the Opposite Pole of Factor 4: Authoritarianism

64. Most of our current problems were caused by a severe blockade and isolation
imposed on the socialist countries by imperialism and capitalist powers   −0.65
36. The mass media should be controlled by the working people   −0.65
66. We have forgotten the great Lenin's words: "The socialist Motherland is in danger! To neglect the permanent danger threatening us until world imperialism is
in existence is paramount to forgetting about our hard-working republic"   −0.62
59. A multinational state like ours should have a one-party system—the system of the
Communist Party   −0.58
145. By his social and political activities Sakharov aggravated instability in our
society**   −0.56
75. Our army was carrying out its internationalist duty in Afganistan   −0.56
158. Private ownership engenders inequality and therefore it is unacceptable for our
state**   −0.56
56. I believe it inadmissible to have factions and platforms within the party   −0.53
77. Under the disguise of the fine slogan "More Socialism" a handful of irresponsible
persons representing the interests of the world and home-bred bourgeoisie is striving for the restoration of capitalism   −0.51
40. Socialism is a historical achievement of our people, and we can't give it up   −0.50
156. I insist on rejecting any attempts to use economic reforms for breaking up and
eliminating the basis of the socialist economic system—that is, the public
property and economic planning—for implanting private ownership, hired labor
and exploitation and turning our national economy into an underdeveloped
uncontrolled market economy**   −0.50
102. I'm for the existing passport system designed to keep up order in the choice of
residence and movement within the country   −0.50
90. The institution of presidential rule is a threat to democratic reforms in this
country   −0.49

79. The errors can't be corrected in the conditions of spreading slanders about socialism, destroying its values, undermining the Party's authority, demoralizing the
vanguard, denying its leading role, nullifying public discipline and spreading chaos
and anarchy   −0.49

**Items-statements entered, with significant loadings, in several factors.

Acknowledgment   Research was supported by the Russian Humanitarian Foundation
for Fundamental Research.

References

Baker, K., & Gippenreiter, Yu. B. (1995). Vlijanie stalinskikh repressij tridzatykh godov
na semejnuju zhizn v pokoleniyakh. (The influence of Stalin repressions at the end
of the 1930s on family life in three generations.) *Voprosy psikhologii, 2,* 66–84. (In
Russian.)

Cole, M. (1993). Introduction. *Journal of Russian and East European Psychology, 31,* 3–4.

Dubov, I. G., & Pantileev, S. R. (1992). Vosprijatie lichnosti politicheskogo lidera. (Image
of the political leader.) *Psihologicheskij Zhurnal, 6,* 25–33. (In Russian.)

Duran, B. S., & Odel P. L. (1974). *Cluster analysis: A survey.* New York.

Egorova, E. V. (1988). *Psikhologicheskie metodiki issledovanija lichnosti politicheskikh
liderov.* (Psychological methods for researching political leaders' personality.)
Moscow. (In Russian.)

Ganina, N. A., & Etkind, A. M. (1991). Politicheskaya aktivnost intellektualov: Opyt
sotzialno-psikhologicheskogo issledovanija. (Political activity of intellectuals: An
attempt of social-psychological research.) *Psikhologicheskii Zhurnal, 1,* 22–30. (In
Russian.)

Gozman, L. Y. (1994). Psikhologija v politike: Ot ob'yasnenia k vozdejstviyu. (Psychology
in politics: From explanation to influence.) *Voprosy Psikhologii, 1,* 70–80. (In Russian.)

Humboldt, W. (1903–1936). *Gesammelte Schriften.* Berlin. (In German.)

Jung, C. G. (1953). *Archetype and symbol: The collected works of C. G. Jung.* (Ed. H. Read
et al.) London.

Kelly, G. (1955). *The psychology of personal constructs.* New York: Norton.

Kl'amkin, I. M. (1994). *Sovetskoe i zapadnoe; Vozmozhen li sintez?* (The Soviet and the
Western: Is synthesis possible?) Polis. (In Russian.)

Latypov, V. V. (1994). Rechevoje vozdejstvie v usloviyakh publichnoj diskussii (na
materiale parlamentskikh vystuplenij). (The verbal influence in the situation of a
public discussion [on the materials of parlimentary speeches.] *Psikhologicheskii
Zhurnal, 50–59.* (In Russian.)

Lebedeva, M. (1993). *Vam predstoyat peregovory.* (You are expecting negotiations.)
Moscow. (In Russian.)

Leontiev, A. N. (1977). *Deyatelnost, soznanie, lichnost.* (Activity, consciousness, personality.) (2d ed.) Moscow. (In Russian.)

Marx, K., & Engels, F. (1957). *Die Deutsche Ideologie.* (The German ideology.) Berlin.
(In German.)

Mitina, O. V., & Petrenko, V. F. (1995). Dinamika politicheskogo soznaniya kak protzess
samoorganizatzii. (Dynamics of political consciousness as the self-organizing process.) *Obshchestvennye nauki i sovremennost, 5,* 103–115. (In Russian.)

Ol'shanskij, D. V. (1992). B. N. Yeltsin na fone massovogo soznanija (politiko-psihologicheskij portret). (B. N. Yeltsin on the background of public consciousness [a political-psychological portrait.]) *Psikhologicheskii Zhurnal*, 4, 4. (In Russian.)

Osgood, C. E. (1971). Where do sentences come from? In D. A. Steinberg and L. A. Jakobovits (eds.), *Semantics: An interdisciplinary reader in philosophy, linguistics, and psychology* (pp. 497–529). Cambridge: Cambridge University Press.

Osgood, C. E., Suci, G. J., & Tannenbaum, P. H. (1957). *The measurement of meaning.* Urbana: University of Illinois Press.

Petrenko, V. F. (1983). *Vvedenie v experementalnuyu psikhosemantiku: Issledovanye form reprezentatzii v obydennom soznanii.* (Introduction in experimental psychosemantics: The research of representational forms in common mind.) Moscow. (In Russian.)

Petrenko, V. F. (1988). *Psikhosemantika soznania.* (Psychosemantics of the consciousness.) Moscow. (In Russian.)

Petrenko, V. F., & Mitina, O. V. (1991). Semanticheskoe prostranstvo politicheskikh partij Rossii. (Semantic space of political parties in Russia.) *Psikhologicheskii Zhurnal*, 6, 55–77. (In Russian.)

Petrenko, V. F., Mitina, O. V., & Shevchuk, I. V. (1993). Socialno-politologicheskoe issledovanie obschestvennogo soznania zhiteley Kazakhstana i postroeniye semanticheskogo prostranstva politicheskikh partij. (Social-politological research of public consciousness in Kazakhstan and the reconstruction of semantical space of political parties.) *Psikhologicheskii Zhurnal*, 1, 53–88. (In Russian.)

Pribylovsky, V. (1993). *The dictionary of the opposition: New political parties and organizations in Russia.* Moscow.

Roschin, S. K. (1990). Obshchestvenno-politicheskie protzessy perestroyki s pozitzij sotzialnoj psikhologii. (Social-political processes of perestroyka from the point of view of social psychology.) *Psikhologicheskii Zhurnal*, 3, 26–38. (In Russian.)

Ryzin, J. V. (ed.) (1977). *Classification and clustering.* New York.

Shepoval, E. B. (1995). *Modeli politicheskoj sotzializatzii i vospriyatie democraticheskikh tzennostey v sovremennoj Rossii.* (Models of political socialization and comprehension of democratical values in contemporary Russia.) Vestnik MGU, seriya Sotziologii i Politologii. (In Russian.)

Shmelev, A. G. (1983). *Vvedeniye v experementalnuyu psikhosemantiku: Teoretiko-metodologicheskie osnovaniya i psikhodiagnosticheskiye vozmozhnosti.* (Introduction in experimental psychosemantics: The theoretical-methodological foundations and psychodiagnostical perspectives.) Moscow. (In Russian.)

Shmelev, A. G. (1992). Psikhologiya politicheskogo protivostoyaniya. (The psychology of the political opposition.) *Psikhologicheskii Zhurnal*, 5, 26–36. (In Russian.)

Sosnin, V. A. (1994). Uregulirovaniye i razreshenie konfliktov: Problema posrednichestva v prikladnoj issledovatelskoj praktike Zapada. (The resolution of the conflicts: The problem of mediation in applied research practice of the West.) *Psikhologicheskii Zhurnal*, 5, 130–141. (In Russian.)

Spengler, O. (1918–1922). *Der Untergang des Abendlandes.* Munich. (In German.)

Uberla, K. (1977). *Faktorenanalyse.* (Factor analysis.) Berlin. (In German.)

Yanov, A. (1991). Kak-nibud perezimuem: A dalshe? (Maybe we overlive the winter: And then what?) *Ogoniok*, 4, 15–16. (In Russian.)

2

Psychological Perspectives on International Conflict and Cooperation

Philip E. Tetlock

From Freud to Tolman to Maslow, psychologists who study politics have often fallen into a reductionist fallacy. The trapdoor to the fallacy is camouflaged by two truisms: (1) politics is the product of decisions by individual human beings who love or hate, cooperate or compete, trade or negotiate with each other; (2) psychology is the science that explores why individuals think, feel, and act as they do. It would seem to follow, as a matter of logical necessity, that insofar as psychologists succeed in achieving their explanatory goals, they will inevitably also shed light on the causes of political action.

Although not devoid of merit, this argument fails for several reasons. Most important, it fails because reducing one scientific discipline or domain of discourse to another cannot be achieved by mere syllogistic decree. It is necessary to show how the explanatory concepts and methods of the putatively more basic discipline account in detail for the substantive phenomena of the derivative discipline. Politics takes extraordinarily diverse forms—fascism, irredentist nationalisms, Marxism-Leninism, Shi'ite fundamentalism, laissez-faire liberalism, welfare-state capitalism, and so on—and it is far from obvious that these diverse forms can be reduced to a compact set of universal psychological principles. Certainly no one has yet succeeded in doing so.

Political psychology cannot be divorced from its historical or political context. A properly framed political psychological question always presupposes a historical trajectory that brought us to where we are and institutional ground rules that constrain the rage of permissible moves that can be made in the competition for power. Only once the political stage has been so set is it reasonable to entertain hypotheses about the operation of psychological processes. There is no way to understand the political psychology of affirmative action in America of the 1990s without acknowledging the civil rights struggles of the last 50 years, the constitutional complexities of power sharing, the frustrating intractability of racial and, more generally, economic inequality, and the deep-rooted cultural skepticism toward "group rights." In a similar vein, the political psychology of presidential politics in post-Soviet Russia would be equally opaque if we could not invoke the brief history of multiparty democracy in that country, the insecurities produced by the economic collapse of state socialism, and the uncertainties created by fractious identity politics both within Russia and in the "near abroad."

This chapter does not pretend to cover political psychology in its entirety. As the foregoing argument suggests, such an assignment would be impossible. There are, in principle, as many political psychologies as there are polities. In each case, we would have the analytical challenge of mapping out how idiosyncratic historical circumstances and institutional structures have channeled and interacted with universal psychological processes. Instead, this chapter stakes out a distinctive subfield: the psychology of world politics. The focus is explicitly transnational: on the role that psychological processes can play in promoting or impeding conflict and cooperation among national entities (each of which could be the object of inquiry in its own right).

The chapter is divided into three sections. The first section examines the now familiar debates over the rationality of national security policy. Since Thucydides, self-styled realists have argued that world politics obeys a distinctive theoretical logic of its own. There is little leeway for slow learners who allow personal beliefs, needs, or ideals to cloud their vision of looming threats. Accordingly, there is also little need for psychological explanations. National leaders either respond in a timely manner to shifting balances of power (whether calibrated in strategic nuclear warheads or gross domestic products), or they are rapidly replaced by more realistic leaders. The choice is between rational updating of expectations in calculating Bayesian fashion and being selected out of the game in ruthless Darwinian fashion. I argue that this dichotomy is too stark and identify a host of ways in which psychological processes appear to shape security policy, giving special emphasis to generalizations that have multimethod support in the experimental and archival research literatures.

The second section deals with interstate influence. Deterrence theorists—who enjoyed remarkable influence over American foreign policy in the post–World War II period—take an extremely parsimonious view of the workings of diplomacy and negotiation. From this perspective, too much psychological subtlety can be a dangerous thing when it communicates weakness and vacillation to potential aggressors. One prevails by possessing the necessary power and by clearly communicating the resolve to use it under specified circumstances. I examine some psychologically richer conceptions of the influence process that emphasize the need to strike reasonable balances between the goals of deterrence (don't let the other side exploit you) and the goals of reassurance (don't exacerbate the worst-case fears of the other side). I also examine evidence—again, whenever possible, from multiple methods—that clarifies when different influence tactics are likely to elicit desired reactions from the other side.

The first two sections focus on fundamental processes—decision making and social influence—that are a safe bet to play key roles in almost every conceivable scenario for the next century. But world politics is in a state of flux. The nation-state is apparently under siege by both subnational forces of ethnic fragmentation and supranational forces of economic integration. An adequate psychological analysis of world politics can no longer treat the nation-state as the unchallenged decision-making unit. People may direct their loyalties elsewhere. Accordingly, the third section targets psychological theories that may play an increasingly central role in an international system subject to these powerful centrifugal and centripetal forces. The focus shifts to the complexities of applying theories of group identification and of distributive and procedural justice to a rapidly transforming world. Key questions become: "With which collectivities do people identify?"; "What counts as a fair distribution of burdens and benefits of group membership within and across national boundaries?"; and "When should we coordinate the policies of our group with those of others to provide the international equivalent of public goods in such diverse domains as health, commerce, peace, and human rights?"

Psychological Challenges to Rational Actor Models

Traditionally, the most influential theories of world politics have been grounded in "realist" and "neorealist" schools of thought that view rationality as a necessity. Competitive pressures compel states to be clear-sighted in appraising threats, methodical in evaluating options, and unsentimental in forming and relinquishing friendships. States that deviate from security-maximizing rationality are quickly punished and, in extreme cases, are selected out of the system. The most prominent neorealist, Kenneth Waltz (1979), builds on the Darwinian metaphor by explicitly comparing international systems to unregulated economic markets. Both are anarchic or self-help systems in which the component units (nations or firms) must either fend for themselves or enter alliances with powerful protectors.

In anarchic social systems, we should expect a high baseline of competition. Each state is responsible for its own security, which it attempts to achieve by building up its military capabilities, its economic infrastructure, and its alliances with other states. Often other states cannot differentiate defensive from offensive strategies and respond by making their own preparations, which can also be mistaken for offensive preparations, triggering further "defensive activity." The result is the well-known security dilemma in which the quest for security ironically generates greater insecurity.

Most neorealists and game theorists, do, however, allow for the possibility of cooperation. They expect cooperation when that response is indeed prudent—specifically, when the penalties for noncooperation are steep (e.g., violating an arms-control agreement would motivate the other side to develop destabilizing first-strike weapons), the rewards of cooperation are high (e.g., the economic and security benefits of some form of détente), and the "shadow of the future" looms large (it does not pay to cross an adversary with whom one expects to deal over a prolonged period). Some neorealists argue that all three conditions were satisfied by the Soviet Union of the late 1980s. The massive Reagan defense buildup made clear to the Soviets that the penalties for nonco-operation were steep (sharp Western responses to the Soviet buildup of ICBMs, to SS20s in Eastern Europe, and to Soviet interventions in Afghanistan, Ethiopia, and Angola); the prospect of revitalizing the moribund Soviet economy by redirecting scarce resources from defense to economic restructuring enhanced the rewards of cooperation; and the shadow of the future hovered ominously (it seems rash to antagonize adversaries who have decisive technological and economic advantages in long-term competition). Gorbachev, in short, did not have to be a nice guy and political psychologists who made such trait attributions succumbed to one of their own favorite biases—the "fundamental attribution error," which refers to the belief that an individual's actions reflect his or her personality characteristics rather than situational constraints. There is no need to invoke altruism when enlightened self-interest is up to the task.

Cognitive Counterattack

Although theoretically incisive, the neorealist framework is also epistemologically restrictive; it rules out of court a lot of reasonable questions. Just as economic actors sometimes fail to respond in a timely fashion to changing market signals (Thaler, 1991), so foreign policy makers are sometimes slow to respond to changes in the international balance of power. There is a hollow tautological ring to purely structuralist explanations that presume a frictionless capacity of rational national actors to adjust strategy in response to new events. It is too easy to generate geopolitical rationalizations for virtually any policy decision after the fact. For instance, one can counter the earlier argument that the conciliatory Gorbachev policies were dictated by systemic necessity by using "systemic necessity" to explain the opposite outcome—namely, the emergence of a militant, neo-Stalinist leadership in the late 1980s. What better way to hold on to superpower status than by reasserting discipline on the domestic front and by devoting massive resources to defense programs? Indeed, some observers read the situation exactly this way in the mid-1980s (Pipes, 1986).

Systemic constraint is insufficiently constraining. To invoke another example, it sounds platitudinous to claim that, all things being equal, governments persist with policies that yield desired consequences and eventually abandon policies that yield undesired consequences (a political restatement one of the earliest behaviorist laws of learning—Thorndike's Law of Effect). But what counts as a good or bad outcome? The answer is not always obvious. There is still sharp disagreement, for example, over whether the Strategic Arms Limitation Treaties of the 1970s should be categorized as good or bad outcomes. The lessons one draws from the early arms control treaties largely reflect one's overall political outlook. Many liberals viewed the early treaties with the Soviets positively; many conservatives drew the opposite conclusion. There is so much room for disagreement here because there is so much uncertainty concerning the causal connections between policies and outcomes. We do not know which outcomes were the result of the policies adopted and which would have occurred anyway.

From a cognitive perspective, the key failing of neorealism is its inability to specify how decision makers will cope with the causal ambiguity inherent in complex historical flows of events. The feedback that decision makers receive from their policies is often equivocal and subject to widely varying interpretations. Moreover, feedback may often be delayed. A prudent policy at one time may appear extraordinarily foolish at another. Consider this example: In the 1970s, Soviet policy in the Third World seemed to bear fruit, with pro-Soviet governments sprouting up in such diverse locations as Indochina, Afghanistan, Ethiopia, and Nicaragua. The Soviets "were on the march." By the late 1980s, a reappraisal was in order. Geostrategic assets increasingly looked like liabilities.

If this analysis is correct—if what counts as rewarding or punishing consequences in the international environment depends on the ideological assumptions of the beholder—it is no longer adequate to "black box" the policy-making process and limit the study of world politics to covariations between systemic input and policy outcomes. It becomes necessary to study how policy makers think about the international system. Cognitive approaches to world politics rest on a pair of simple functionalist premises: (1) the international environment is extraordinarily complex; and (2) people—limited-capacity information processors that we are—frequently resort to simplifying strategies to deal with the complexity and uncertainty of that environment. Policy makers may act rationally, but only within the context of their simplified subjective representations of reality (the classic principle of bounded rationality; see Simon, 1957).

To understand foreign policy, cognitivists focus on these simplified images of reality that decision makers rely upon in interpreting events and choosing among courses of action (Axelrod, 1976; George, 1980; Herrmann, 1985; Holsti, 1992; Jervis, 1976; Larson, 1994; Sylvan, Goel, & Chandrasekaran, 1990; Vertzberger, 1990a, 1990b). Policies that seem sensible within one framework look foolish, even treasonous, within other frameworks. Neo-Stalinists—who subscribed to the two-camp thesis that conflict between imperialist and socialist states was inevitable—looked with horror in the late 1980s on the policy initiatives of Gorbachev and the rhetoric of interdependence that accompanied those initiatives. Conversely, many liberal advocates of arms control were appalled in the early 1980s as the Reagan administration attempted to dismantle the arms control understandings of the 1970s and escape mutually assured destruction (MAD) via the Strategic Defense Initiative (SDI).

Foreign policy belief systems have enormous cognitive utility. As George (1969) and Holsti (1992) explicated in their seminal analyses of operational codes, and as Herrmann (1985, 1988) has explicated in his innovative image theory, belief systems provide policy makers with ready answers to fundamental questions about the political world. What are the basic objectives of other states? Can conflict be avoided and, if so, how? If not, what form is the conflict likely to take? Foreign policy belief systems also facilitate decision making by providing guidelines for choosing among options. They provide frameworks for estimating the consequences of different options and for assessing the significance of those consequences.

There is, however, a price to be paid for these benefits. In their efforts to maintain stable, internally consistent worldviews, policy makers often oversimplify. In the last 25 years, evidence has accumulated that the price of cognitive economy in world politics is—as in other domains of life—susceptibility to error and bias. The next sections consider some potential errors and biases, paying special attention to those that have received sustained attention from both laboratory investigators and archival investigators who rely on field methods as diverse as comparative case studies and content analysis of text and event data.

The Fundamental Attribution Error

People often prefer internal, dispositional explanations for others' conduct, even when plausible, situational accounts exist (Gilbert & Malone, 1995). Our first reaction tends to be that behavior is under intentional volitional control: that it reflects deep and stable goals of the actor rather than transitory responses to the immediate social context. This judgmental tendency can interact dangerously with political properties of the international environment. Consider, for example, the much discussed security dilemma (Jervis, 1976, 1978). To protect themselves in an "anarchic" environment (there is no viable world government), states must seek security either through costly defense programs of their own or by persuading others to defend them by entering into entangling alliances. Assessing intentions in such an environment is often hard. There is usually no easy way to distinguish between states that are defensively responding to the competitive logic of the situation and states that have expansionist objectives. If everyone assumes the worst, the stage is set for conflict-spiral-driven arms races that no one wanted (Downs, 1991; Kramer, 1988). The fundamental attribution error exacerbates matters by lowering the perceptual threshold for attributing hostile intentions to other states. This tendency—in conjunction with the security dilemma—can lead decision makers to exaggerate the hostile intentions of defensively motivated powers. The security dilemma compels even peaceful states to arm; the fundamental attribution error then leads observers to draw incorrect dispositional inferences. The actor-observer divergence in attributions and self-serving motivational biases can exacerbate matters. National leaders tend to attribute their own military spending to situational pressures (Jervis, 1976). These self-attributions could contribute to a self-righteous spiral of hostility in which policy makers know that they arm for defensive reasons, assume that others also know this, and then conclude that others must be building their military capabilities because they have aggressive designs. At best, the result is a lot of unnecessary defense spending; at worst, unnecessary wars.

The fundamental attribution error can encourage a second form of misperception in the international arena: the tendency to perceive governments as unitary causal agents rather than as complex amalgams of bureaucratic and political subsystems, each pursuing its own missions and goals (Jervis, 1976; Vertzberger, 1990a, 1990b). Careful reconstructions of the Cuban Missile Crisis have revealed numerous junctures at which American and Soviet forces could easily have come into violent contact with each other, not as a result of following some detailed master plan plotted by top leaders but rather as a result of local commanders executing standard operating procedures (Blight, 1990). The organizational analog of the fundamental attribution error is insensitivity to the numerous points of slippage between the official policies of collectivities and the policies that are actually implemented at the "ground level."

Both forms of misperception carry serious risks. Deterrence theorists could note, however, that setting a low threshold for making dispositional attributions can be adaptive. A balanced assessment of overattribution in political settings hinges on our base-rate estimates of how common each error is, as well as on the moral-political value we place on avoiding each error.

Metaphors and Analogical Reasoning

People try to understand novel situations by reaching for familiar metaphors and analogies. Indeed, Lakoff and Johnson (1980) go so far as to argue that metaphors and analogies pervade all forms of discourse. Discourse on deterrence is no exception. Metaphorical preferences are correlated closely with policy preferences. Consider the "ladder of escalation" and the "slippery slope" (Jervis, 1989). The former metaphor implies that just as we can easily climb up and down a ladder one step at a time, so we can control the escalation and deescalation of conventional or even nuclear conflicts (Kahn, 1965); the latter metaphor implies that once in a conflict, leaders can easily lose control and slide helplessly into war (Schelling, 1966). In Cold War days, adherents of the "ladder" metaphor supported a war-fighting doctrine that stressed cultivating counterforce capabilities; although they did not relish the prospect, they believed that nuclear war could, in principle, be controlled. By contrast, "slippery slopers" endorsed MAD—both as a policy and as strategic reality—and they feared that, once initiated, conflicts would inevitably escalate to all-out war. They argued that nuclear powers need to avoid crises. Managing them once they break out is too risky. As President John Kennedy reportedly remarked after the Cuban Missile Crisis, "One can't have too many of these" (Blight, 1990).

Metaphorical modes of thought apparently continue both to influence and to justify policy in the post–Cold War world. Some writers invoke communitarian metaphors in which international relations is undergoing an irreversible transformation: "A community of states united by common interests, values, and perspectives is emerging because of technology and economics. Among the modernist states belonging to that community, new norms of behavior are replacing the old dictates of realpolitik: they reject not only the use of weapons of mass destruction, but even the use of military force to settle their disputes" (Blechman & Fisher, 1994–1995, p. 97). By contrast, other writers such as Christopher Layne (1992) believe that nothing fundamental has changed and rely on the social Darwinist metaphors of self-help, anarchy, and Hobbesian struggle of all against all. We have merely moved from a bipolar system to an increasingly multipolar one ("with a brief unipolar moment" in which the United States enjoyed global dominance at the end of the 20th century). Indeed, it is only a matter of time before previously nonnuclear major powers—Japan and Germany—acquire nuclear weapons now that they no longer depend on extended deterrence protection from the United States.

People also give meaning to new situations by drawing on historical analogies (Gilovich, 1981; Jervis, 1976; May, 1973; Neustadt & May, 1986; Vertzberger, 1990a, 1990b). Although a reasonable response by creatures with limited mental resources to a demanding environment, this cognitive strategy can be seriously abused. One mistake is focusing on only the most obvious precedent—often the most recent crisis or war (Jervis, 1976)—rather than a diverse set of precedents. Consider the range of Third World conflicts that American observers in the elite press compared to Vietnam between 1975 and 1995: Lebanon, Israel's Vietnam; Eritrea, Ethiopia's Vietnam; Chad, Libya's Vietnam; Angola, Cuba's Vietnam; Afghanistan, the Soviet Union's Vietnam; Bosnia, the European Community's Vietnam; Nicaragua, potentially a new American Vietnam; and, of course, Kampuchea, Vietnam's Vietnam. To be sure, there are similarities, but the differences are also marked and often slighted (Tetlock, McGuire, & Mitchell, 1991).

Khong (1991) reports arguably the most systematic study of analogical reasoning in foreign policy. Drawing on process tracing of high-level deliberations in the early 1960s, he documents how American policy in Vietnam was shaped by the perceived similarity of the Vietnamese conflict to the Korean War. Once again, a communist army from the north had attacked a pro-Western regime in the south. This diagnosis led to a series of prescriptions and predictions. The United States should resist the aggression with American troops and could expect victory, albeit with considerable bloodshed. A significant side-constraint lesson drawn from the Korean conflict was that in Vietnam, the United States would have to fight hard but should avoid provoking Chinese entry into the war as it did last time. This lesson argued for "graduated escalation."

This example illustrates a second pitfall in analogical foreign policy reasoning: the tendency to neglect differences between the present situation and the politically preferred precedent. Not only in public but also in private, policy makers rarely engage in balanced comparative assessments of historical cases (Neustadt & May, 1986). From a psychological viewpoint, this result is not surprising. Laboratory research suggests that people often overweight hypothesis-confirmatory information (Nisbett & Ross, 1980). To invoke the Vietnam example again, American policy makers concentrated on the superficial similarities between the Vietnamese and Korean conflicts while George Ball—virtually alone within Johnson's inner circle—noted the differences (e.g., the conventional versus guerrilla natures of the conflicts, the degree to which the United States could count on international support). Whereas doves complained about this analogical mismatching, hawks complained about the analogical mismatching that led decision makers to exaggerate the likelihood of Chinese intervention. China had less strategic motivation and ability to intervene in the Vietnam War in 1965 than it had to intervene in the Korean War of 1950, preoccupied as Beijing was in the mid- to late 1960s by the internal turmoil of the Great Proletarian Cultural Revolution and the external threat of the Soviet Union, which had recently announced the Brezhnev Doctrine (claiming a Soviet right to intervene in socialist states that stray from the Soviet line).

A third mistake is allowing preconceptions to drive the conclusions that one draws from experience. In the United States, for instance, hawks and doves drew sharply divergent lessons from the Vietnam War (Holsti & Rosenau, 1979). Prominent lessons for hawks were that the Soviet Union is expansionist and that the United States should avoid graduated escalation and honor alliance commitments. Prominent lessons for doves were that the United States should avoid guerrilla wars, that the press is more truthful than the administration, and civilian leaders should be wary of military advice. Interestingly, no lesson appeared on both the hawk and dove lists. Sharply divergent lessons are not confined to democracies, as a content analysis of Soviet analyses of the Vietnam War revealed (Zimmerman & Axelrod, 1981). Different constituencies in the Soviet Union drew self-serving and largely incompatible lessons from the American defeat in Asia. "Americanists" in foreign policy institutes believed that Vietnam demonstrated the need to promote détente while restraining wars of national liberation; the military press, by contrast, believed that the war demonstrated the implacable hostility of Western imperialism, the need to strengthen Soviet armed forces, and the feasibility and desirability of seeking further gains in the Third World. In summary, although policy makers often use analogies poorly, virtually no one would argue that they should ignore history; rather, the challenge is to employ historical analogies in a more nuanced, self-critical, and multidimensional manner (Neustadt & May, 1986).

Belief Perseverance

Foreign policy beliefs often resist change (George, 1980). Cognitive mechanisms such as selective attention to evidence that confirms the hypothesis being considered while slighting disconfirming evidence, denial, and biased assimilation of incoming information protect these beliefs from disconfirmation. The classic example is the "inherent bad faith model" of one's opponent (Holsti, 1967; Stuart & Starr, 1981). A state is believed to be implacably hostile: contrary indicators such as concessions are ignored, dismissed as propaganda ploys, or interpreted as signs of weakness. For example, Secretary of State John Foster Dulles held an inherent bad faith model of the Soviet Union (Holsti, 1967), and many Israelis believed that the PLO was implacably hostile (Kelman, 1983) and some still do even after the peace accord. Policies of reassurance only tempt such a foe. Although such images are occasionally on the mark, they can produce missed opportunities for conflict resolution. Belief perseverance can also prevent policy makers from shifting to more successful strategies. In World War I, for example, military strategists continued to launch infantry charges despite enormous losses, leading two analysts to observe wryly that men may die easily, but beliefs do not (Art & Waltz, 1983).

Some scholars hold belief perseverance to be the most pervasive moderator of deterrence success or failure (Jervis, 1983). Aggressors can get away with blatantly offensive preparations and still surprise their targets as long as the target believes that an attack is unlikely (Heuer, 1981). An example is Israel's failure to respond to warnings prior to the Yom Kippur War. Israeli leaders believed that the Arabs would not attack, given Arab military inferiority, and dismissed contrary signals. Similarly, a nation that does not plan to attack, yet is believed to harbor such plans, will find it difficult to convince the opponent of its peaceful intentions.

It is easy, however, to overstate the power of belief perseverance. Policy makers do sometimes change their minds (Breslauer & Tetlock, 1991; Levy, 1994; Stein, 1994). The key questions are: Who changes? Under what conditions? And what forms does change take? Converging evidence from archival studies of political elites (Tetlock & Boettger, 1989) and experimental studies of social cognition (Tetlock, 1992) suggest that self-critical thinkers are more prone to give serious weight to counterattitudinal evidence. It is hard to determine, however, whether such people are truly more open-minded or were always more ambivalent toward the attitude object. For instance, was Mikhail Gorbachev a faster learner than his rival, Yegor Ligachev, about the inadequacies of the Soviet system, or was he less committed all along to the fundamental correctness of the Soviet system? It is often even harder to gauge whether policy makers are being good Bayesians who are adjusting in a timely fashion to "diagnostic" evidence. One observer's decisive clue concerning the deteriorating state of the Soviet economy in 1983 might lead another observer to conclude "disinformation campaign" and a third observer to conclude "interesting but only moderately probative." The problem here is not just the opacity of the underlying reality; one's threshold for belief adjustment hinges on the political value that one attaches to the two possible errors of underestimating and overestimating Soviet potential. For instance, one might see the evidence as significant but opt for only minor belief system revision because one judges the error of overestimation (excessive defense spending) as more serious. Defensible normative evaluations of belief persistence and change must ultimately rest on game-theoretic assumptions about the reliability and validity of the evidence (what does the other side want us to believe, and could they have shaped the evidence before us to achieve that goal?).

Psychological Challenges to Deterrence

Whereas neorealism has been the most influential theory in the academic study of world politics, deterrence has been the most influential theory among the policy elites responsible for statecraft in the second half of the 20th century (Achen & Snidal, 1989; Jervis, 1978). Like neorealism, deterrence theory is perhaps best viewed as a particular kind of psychology theory—one that values conceptual parsimony and that emphasizes the amoral, arguably psychopathic, rationality of foreign policy actors. Although deterrence theory comes in many forms (from thoughtful prose to game theoretic models), certain recurring themes justify the common label:

1. The world is a dangerous place. One is confronted by a ruthlessly rational opponent who will capitalize on every opportunity to expand its influence at one's expense. Whenever the option to attack becomes sufficiently attractive (i.e., has greater expected utility than other available options), the risk of attack rises to an unacceptable level.
2. To deter aggression, one should issue retaliatory threats that lead one's opponent to conclude that the expected utility of aggression is lower than the expected utility of the status quo.
3. To succeed, deterrent threats must be sufficiently potent and credible to overcome an adversary's motivation to attack. Potential aggressors must believe that the defender possesses the resolve and capability to implement the threat. Deterrence will fail if either of these conditions is not met.

Testing, Clarifying, and Qualifying Deterrence Theory

Any serious evaluation of deterrence theory must grapple with the methodological problems of determining whether deterrence worked or failed from the historical record. To be sure, dramatic failures of deterrence as *policy* are easy to identify. Country x wanted to stop country y from attacking it or a third country but failed to do so. The historical data are, however, sufficiently ambiguous to allow researchers to argue endlessly over whether individual cases also represent failures of deterrence theory (see Orme, 1987; Lebow & Stein, 1987). An equally imposing obstacle is presented by cases of deterrence success; no one know how to identify them (Achen & Snidal, 1989; George & Smoke, 1974). When crises do not occur, is it due to the credibility of threats (successes for deterrence theory) or to the fact that the other states never intended to attack? Making causal inferences requires making assumptions about what would have happened in the missing counterfactual cells in the contingency table in which the defender issued no threats.

These issues are not just of academic interest. The events that transpired between 1945 and 1991 in American-Soviet relations underscore both the logical problems in determining who is right and the magnitude of the political stakes in such debates. Although almost no one predicted when, how, and why the Cold War would come to an end (Gaddis, 1993), neither conservative deterrence theorists nor their liberal conflict-spiral opponents were at a loss for retrospective explanations. Conservatives argued that the collapse of the Soviet Union vindicated the policies of containment and deterrence that the United States pursued, in one form or another, since World War II. Partisans of the

Reagan administration argued, more specifically, that the new Soviet thinking was a direct response to the hard-line initiatives of the 1980s and to the perceived technological trump card posed by the Strategic Defense Initiative. By contrast, liberal critics of deterrence argued that the policies of the 1980s (and, for many, earlier policies as well) were a massive exercise in overkill, with many lives lost in unnecessary Third World wars and much treasure wasted in defense expenditures. From this perspective, the Cold War ended because of the internal failures of communist societies. If anything, Gorbachev and his policies emerged despite, not because of, the Reagan administration (Lebow & Stein, 1994).

Perhaps historians will someday adjudicate this dispute—although the lack of success on the abundantly documented origins of World War I should constrain optimism here. What is most remarkable for current purposes is how easily the disputants could have explained the opposite outcome. If the Soviet Union had moved in a neo-Stalinist direction in the mid-1980s (massive internal repression and confrontational policies abroad), conservative deterrence theorists could have argued and were indeed prepared to argue that the adversary had merely revealed its true nature (Pipes, 1986), and liberal conflict-spiral theorists could have argued and were indeed prepared to argue that "hard-liners beget hard-liners" in the escalatory dynamic (White, 1984). In short, we find ourselves deep in an epistemological quagmire—an example of what Einhorn and Hogarth (1981) aptly termed an "outcome-irrelevant learning situation."

Assessing the efficacy of deterrence is obviously deeply problematic (indeed, the game theorist Barry Weingast [1996] has shown that if deterrence does work, then there will be many contexts in which the correlation between implementing deterrence and war or peace will be zero). Suffice it to say here that, contrary to White (1984), there is no social psychological warrant for concluding that deterrence theory is wrong in general or even most of the time. But the literature does highlight important gaps in deterrence theory. From a social psychological standpoint, deterrence is but one of a variety of instruments of social influence, and the analytic task is to clarify the conditions under which these diverse influence strategies are effective in eliciting desired responses from other states (George & Smoke, 1974; Jervis, Lebow, & Stein, 1985). Excellent reviews of this voluminous literature on bargaining and negotiations exist elsewhere (Druckman & Hopmann, 1989). This chapter offers a condensed summary of work that bears most directly on international influence, with special attention to hypotheses that have been subject to multimethod tests.

Pure Threat Strategies   Threats sometimes work (McClintock, Stech, & Beggan, 1987; Patchen, 1987). Supporting laboratory evidence comes from bargaining games. Threats of defection have led to beneficial joint outcomes when interests do not conflict (Stech, McClintock, & Moss, 1984). In addition, the mere possession of threat capabilities has reduced defection and increased mutual outcomes in games lacking communication between the parties (Smith & Anderson, 1975). The evidence is, however, mixed. Other studies have found that threats impede cooperation and lower joint outcomes (Duetsch & Krauss, 1960;

Kelley, 1965). Threats have also interfered with cooperation when interests were in conflict (Friedland, 1976) and when communication between bargainers was possible (Smith & Anderson, 1975). Brehm's (1972) reactance theory suggests that threats may backfire by provoking counterefforts to assert one's freedom to do what was forbidden.

Evidence from studies of international conflict is equally mixed. Although a bullying strategy may be essential against some opponents, this strategy is counterproductive when directed at nations with limited goals (Kaplowitz, 1984). Several studies of interstate disputes have discovered that even though bullying occasionally yields diplomatic victories, it can also lead to unwanted escalation of severe crises (Leng, 1993; Leng & Gochman, 1982; Leng & Wheeler, 1979). Case studies of American foreign policy have drawn a similar conclusion. A strategy of coercive diplomacy emphasizing military threats is appropriate only when restrictive preconditions are met—for example, when the coercing power is perceived to be more motivated to achieve its objectives, when adequate domestic support can be generated for the policy, when there are usable military options, and when the opponent fears escalation more than the consequences of backing down (George, Hall, & Simmons, 1971).

Positive Inducements Since Munich gave appeasement a bad name, scholars have largely neglected the role of positive inducements in foreign affairs (for exceptions, see Baldwin, 1971; Milburn & Christie, 1989). The primary advocates of positive inducements have been conflict-spiral theorists who emphasize the debilitating consequences of action-reaction cycles in international conflict (Deutsch, 1983; White, 1984). Although these theorists stress conciliatory gestures, few advocate total unilateral disarmament. And for good reason: experimental evidence indicates that in mixed-motive games, such as prisoner's dilemma, unconditional cooperators are ruthlessly exploited (e.g., Stech et al., 1984). In their study of international disputes, Leng and Wheeler (1979) found that appeasers manage to avoid war but almost always suffer a diplomatic defeat. Positive inducements, such as financial rewards for compliance, can also be very expensive if the other side complies (particularly if it quickly becomes satiated and ups its demands for compensation), and they can foster unwanted dependency and sense of entitlement (Leng, 1993). Finally, just as deterrence theorists face difficulties in operationalizing threats, so reward theorists encounter problems in operationalizing positive inducements, which may be perceived as overbearing, presumptuous, manipulative, or insultingly small or large (Milburn & Christie, 1989).

The picture is not completely bleak, however. Komorita (1973), for example, showed that unilateral conciliatory acts by one party in experimental bargaining games resulted in increased communication, perceptions of cooperative intent, and mutually beneficial outcomes. In reviewing studies of American-Soviet arms control negotiations, Druckman & Hopmann (1989) found that concessions by one side were generally met by counterconcessions by the opponent, whereas retractions provoked counterretractions.

For the most part, conflict-spiral theorists have stressed the importance of combining conciliatory policy initiatives with adequate military strength and nonprovocative threats. The next section: Tit-for-Tat turns to these "mixed" strategies.

Mixed-Influence Strategies Spurred by Robert Axelrod's (1984) "evolution of cooperation," a great deal of attention has been directed to firm but fair approaches to resolving conflict. This section focuses on variants of Axelrod's (1984) tit-for-tat (TFT) strategy.

TFT is straightforward. Applied to prisoner's dilemma (PD) games, one begins by cooperating and thereafter simply repeats one's opponent's previous move. If they cooperated, you cooperate; if they defected, you defect. Considerable research demonstrates that TFT is as effective as it is simple. In Axelrod's (1984) round-robin PD computer tournaments in which expert-nominated strategies were pitted against one another, TFT—the simplest entry in the contest—earned the highest average number of points. In a laboratory simulation of an arms race, Pilisuk and Skolnick (1968) found a pre-programmed matching (TFT) strategy elicited the greatest cooperation from subjects. Moving beyond the laboratory, several case studies and event-analytic studies of international crises have found TFT strategies to be more successful than either pure threat (bullying) or appeasement strategies in avoiding both war and diplomatic defeat (Huth, 1988; Huth & Russett, 1993; Leng, 1993; Leng & Wheeler, 1979; Snyder & Diesing, 1977).

Axelrod (1984) argues that TFT works because it is nice (never defects first), perceptive (quickly discerns the other's intent), clear (easy to recognize), provocable (quickly retaliates), forgiving (willing to abandon defection immediately after the other side's first cooperative act), and patient (willing to persevere). Pruitt (1981) attributes the success of the TFT to its ability to communicate two messages: exploitation is futile and cooperation is necessary for higher payoffs. Other researchers believe that TFT works because it triggers a deeply rooted "norm" of reciprocity (Leng & Wheeler, 1979; Snyder & Deising, 1977).

One major drawback of TFT is that the two parties can easily get caught up in a never-ending series of mutual defections. One possible solution is to respond to defection with a smaller defection. Such a move sends the implicit message that "I will retaliate, but I do not want this conflict to escalate." In a computer tournament to test this notion, To (1988) utilized an expanded payoff matrix in which players could respond to cooperation or defection with more or less extreme cooperation or defection of their own. In this tournament, a version of TFT that retaliates with defection one degree less severe than the others' defection achieved the highest average score. Downs (1991) argues that a tit-for-tat strategy might be the best way to demonstrate resolve while preventing an arms race from spiraling out of control.

A second drawback of TFT is that it applies primarily to prisoner's dilemma games in which both sides prefer mutual cooperation to mutual defection. Many international conflicts, however, may best be described as games of "deadlock," in which at least one party prefers unilateral defection or mutual defection to cooperation (Oye, 1985). In such games, TFT will not induce an opponent to cooperate. In arms races, for example, both nations might prefer a mutual buildup to an arms control treaty, especially if trust is low or if there is an opportunity to benefit from the race (a charge often leveled at the "military-industrial complexes" within major military powers).

A third drawback of TFT is that it implies perfect perception and control—the ability to identify cooperation and defection correctly and to respond to an opponent in ways that will not be misconstrued. In PD games, opponents' moves are unambiguous and this condition can be satisfied; in international politics, policy makers must interpret actions that are, to varying degrees, ambiguous. Misperception may be common, and policy implementation is tricky (Oye, 1985). Actors can attempt to disguise their actions and sneak in a few defections (e.g., by secretly developing chemical weapons or surreptitiously deploying missiles or turning a blind eye toward patent pirates). Arms control negotiations illustrate the problems. Difficulties in verifying compliance can prolong some negotiations and effectively stalemate others. In the late 1980s, many Americans, for example, disagreed over whether the Soviet nuclear testing moratorium was a cooperative initiative or a sign of weakness or a propaganda ploy designed to lock in place a Soviet advantage. The effects of misperception on the ability of TFT to promote mutual cooperation can be devastating. Even when misperceptions are rare, Downs (1991) has shown that arms races often escalate out of control.

World Politics in Flux

The previous sections dealt with psychological processes that are likely to play fundamental roles in world politics in the foreseeable future. Cognitive and motivational constraints on rationality will be of recurring concern as long as human beings make decisions that determine the fates of nations. Influence strategies will be focal topics of political debate as long as humanity is divided into nation-states that make conflicting claims over scarce resources. In each section, however, the analysis was remarkably state-centric. Psychological processes influenced political outcomes through the formal institutions of governance of nation-states. Presidents, prime ministers, foreign ministers, and their associates made decisions (under risk and uncertainty) and selected among influence tactics based on bounded-rationality calculations of the likely reactions of other actors, both domestic and foreign.

This analytic framework is ill-equipped to deal with the types of dramatic institutional change that many pundits now anticipate. We can no longer safely assume the nation-state to be the unchallenged decision-making unit. Subnational and supranational actors appear to be playing progressively more prominent roles. On the one hand, existing state structures are subject to increasing challenge by racial, ethnic, linguistic, and religious groups that demand autonomy or outright secession (Horowitz, 1985; Moynihan, 1993). If we assume that each distinct, homogeneous people (a staggering definitional challenge in itself) has a right to political self-determination, even to a state of its own, the number of states could expand exponentially (Tilly, 1993). On the other hand, the same state structures are under strain by the integrative forces of the new global economy as capital markets and technological innovation erode governmental control over budgetary priorities and over what their citizens watch and hear (Fukuyama, 1992; Ohmae, 1995). Jobs, money, and ideas pass increasingly easily across national borders as investors seek higher returns on equity and as people use modern telecommunications to satisfy their curiosities. In brief, there is no guarantee that citizens will continue to commit their primary political loyalties to the nation-states within which they happen to have been born.

These forecasts of radical impending change may well exaggerate the plasticity of group identifications. The forecasts do, however, highlight important societal trends. Laboratory-based theories of group identification can not only enrich our understandings of identity politics but also be enriched by recent historical developments that shed light on when people both transfer allegiances and translate allegiances into action (sometimes, alas, including mass murder [Staub, 1988]). Theories of distributive and procedural justice can not only deepen our understanding of support and opposition to emerging free trade zones but also be deepened themselves by addressing tensions between the unsentimental monetary logic of global capitalism (good investors should maximize after-tax, risk-adjusted return on capital, even if that means investing abroad) and the deeply emotional psycho-logic of nationalism (good citizens should respect the patriotic symbolism of extended kinship and shared language and territory, even if that means forgoing opportunities to make more money by buying foreign goods or moving operations abroad).

I focus here on two promising domains for political psychological exploration: (1) processes of subnational fragmentation, ethnicity, and identity politics; (2) processes of supranational integration, economic interdependence, and judgments of fairness of cross-border transactions.

Subnational Fragmentation

Cursory inspection of history reveals that there is nothing inevitable about nationalism. It is a remarkably recent phenomenon that takes a kaleidoscopic variety of forms: religious, communist, fascist, liberal, conservative, integrationist, separatist, irredetentist and diaspora (Hutchinson & Smith, 1994; van Evera, 1993). But there may well be something inevitable about the fundamental processes of group identification and loyalty. Human beings are group-living creatures who appear to have a basic need to become emotionally attached to other human beings (Baumeister & Leary, 1995). It is reasonable to suppose that loyalty grows as people become more aware of others who are important to them and begin to identify with others in their group (Druckman, 1994). The experimental literature illustrates how easily such group loyalties and identifications could build up into various forms of nationalism (Brewer & Brown, 1996). Once people form social categorizations, numerous effects often follow: (1) a tendency to exaggerate intergroup differences and intragroup similarities ("we" are different from "them" who, in turn, are strikingly similar to each other); (2) a tendency to perceive the behavior of in-group members more favorably than identical acts of out-group members; (3) a tendency to like, trust, and cooperate with in-group members that does not extend to members of out-groups; (4) a tendency for the previously mentioned effects to be more pronounced among people who score high on measures of prejudice and authoritarianism and among people who have recently suffered setbacks to their self-esteem and social identities.

The psychological literature is less helpful, however, in explaining the groups with which people identify and the inclusion-exclusion rules that people use to distinguish their group from others. Of the infinity of possible ways of partitioning the social world into group categories—endless gradations of ethnicity, race, language, class, and region and countless variations in political and religious belief—why do people "choose" certain categories over others? Basic-process explanations may correctly identify the cognitive and motivational functions underlying partitioning strategies. People may indeed draw group boundaries that maximize between-group variance and minimize within-group variance or that maximize self-esteem or that reinforce claims to scarce resources. But such explanations give us little handle on why the nation-state in particular emerged as such a divisive and decisive symbol of group identity over the last few centuries. The more satisfying "explanations" tend to be grounded in historically contingent details of the recent past. By these accounts, nationalism (as opposed to some other "ism") emerged because of the functional requirements of mass mobilization (rulers found it necessary to whip up nationalistic passion to persuade ordinary people to die for their country [Tilly, 1991]), because of the infrastructure requirements of emerging industrial economies (Gellner, 1983), and because of a human need for new transcendental objects of belief amid religious uncertainty and conflict (Anderson, 1983). Whatever the exact reasons, once people perceived the nation-state to be a salient basis for drawing in-group/out-group distinctions, nationalism became a full-blown functionally autonomous motive in its own right (Allport, 1954/1968). Historical accident or not, tens of millions have died in this century to advance or thwart nationalist claims of one form or another.

But group identifications that history has put together history can tear asunder. Ethnic, racial, and religious subgroups that were once content to identify or comply with superordinate nationalist norms have in the last quarter of the 20th century begun to make increasingly assertive demands for autonomy and statehood (Horowitz, 1985). The evidence—from Ethiopia to Canada to Yugoslavia to the former Soviet Union—is indisputable. An adequate psychological framework has yet, however, to be advanced. A major obstacle here is integrating the largely low-stakes experimental literature (preoccupied with testing abstract hypotheses) with the high-stakes historical case-study literature (preoccupied with the ebb and flow of identity politics in particular places and times). Although these two literatures sometimes diverge, the cumulative weight of the evidence suggests an initial explanatory sketch of intercommunal strife that can tear nation-states apart. The key warning signs include the following.

1. The two groups make incompatible claims on scarce resources (LeVine & Campbell, 1971). Although minimal-group experiments have rather conclusively demonstrated that economic competition is not a necessary condition for intergroup conflict (Brewer & Kramer, 1985), case studies suggest that conflicts over jobs, government patronage, subsidies, and control of markets often play a critical catalytic role by convincing elites within the community that they can maintain their status and prerogatives only through concerted collective action organized around ethnocultural symbols and the political goal of asserting ethnocultural autonomy (Horowitz, 1985). Experimental simulations are hard-pressed to capture the magnitude and symbolism of the material stakes in these real-world confrontations.

2. One group or both groups perceive prevailing methods of allocating scarce resources to be unjust (Horowitz, 1985). Groups that have less tend to endorse more external causal attributions for their plight (current discrimination and market exclusion, historical legacy of past oppression), whereas groups that have more tend to endorse internal causal attributions for both their own relative success ("we" are hardworking, entrepreneurial, and smart) and other groups' lower standing ("they" are lazy, apathetic, and dumb). Have-not groups see a pressing need for state intervention to level the playing field and to implement radical redistribution. The well-off often perceive these appeals as self-serving bids to obtain through political means what they had to achieve through individual initiative and hard work. Political activists can play on these diverging attributions, fueling perceptions of bad faith and political polarization.

3. One group or both groups seek to reaffirm damaged social identities (Brown, 1985; Horowitz, 1985; Tajfel, 1980). Groups that have recently suffered losses (or have been vividly reminded by activists of losses suffered long ago) often seem especially susceptible to political appeals that derogate out-groups, idealize the in-group, and call for mobilization around collective symbols (religious texts and instructions, ethnic-racial purity).

4. The two groups do not possess a common enemy or shared objective that motivates searches for integrative solutions to their disputes or at least suppresses expressions of enmity.

Although useful, these warning signs are still not sufficient to distinguish ethnonationalist rivalries that are resolved through peaceful procedural means from those that descend into civil war and genocidal barbarism. Advocates of "preemptive diplomacy"—who seek to prevent mass murder—need to draw upon a wider network of psychosocial indicators to keep their false-alarm rate at a credibility-maintaining minimum. Drawing on van Evera (1993) and Staub (1988), additional warning signs include: (1) political leaders who explicitly dehumanize out-groups (the appearance of insect and animal imagery—vermin, cockroaches, running dogs, pigs—is especially ominous); (2) bitter grudges rooted in collective memories of atrocities that "they" committed against "us"; (3) widespread lack of public confidence in national institutions of order and justice; (4) the emergence of security and military units whose primary loyalty is to one or another of the contending groups.

Answering exact questions about the timing and intensity of interethnic conflict requires the full complement of levels of analysis. For instance, one influential explanation for the violent disintegration of Yugoslavia invoked the combination of: (1) the death of Tito and the institutionalization of a rotating Collective Federal Presidency, which created strong incentives for local political elites to advance regional causes at the expense of broader national interests (Gagnon, 1994); and (2) the death of the Soviet Union, which eliminated a massive external threat that contributed to Yugoslav cohesion and permitted ancient rivalries to resurface (Mearsheimer, 1990). This explanation, however, still fails to account for the differences between the violent breakup of Yugoslavia and the peaceful "velvet divorce" of the Czechs and Slovaks. At this juncture, political observers resort to a mixture of historical explanations that invoke the long-standing enmity among Catholic Croatians, Orthodox Serbs, and Bosnian Muslims (a dreary legacy of mass murder and dehumanizing stereotypes) and contemporary explanations that invoke key political personalities (the Czech leader was a sophisticated, integratively complex humanist who sought peace, prosperity, and democracy, whereas the Serbian and Croatian leaders were authoritarian demagogues who nurtured intergroup hostilities and irredentist claims). Yugoslavia, from this perspective, is a sad story in which too many predisposing causes for intergroup violence happened to be activated at the same time.

Supernational Integrative Forces

Since the 18th century, prominent economists have expounded the thesis that trade leads inexorably to peace. The earliest proponents of this view, such as Smith, Ricardo, and Mill, were sharp critics of beggar-thy-neighbor mercantilist policies that nurtured domestic monopolies by excluding foreign goods. In addition to articulating the still deeply influential doctrine of comparative advantage, these early economists specified the concrete ways in which economic interdependence could transform a world of warring nation-states into one of peaceful commerce: by stimulating countries to work out basic rules of commerce to regulate exchange, by opening up new export markets (stimulating employment) and making low-cost imports available (checking inflation), and by creating powerful domestic constituencies interested in expanding international commerce and in averting costly wars. To be sure, there is no guarantee of peace and there have been some embarrassingly premature prophecies of the end to war (most notably, Norman Angell's ill-timed argument in 1911 that Europeans were now too interconnected by commerce to go to war). Nonetheless, it seems reasonable to hypothesize that commerce and interdependence raise the threshold for rational actors to go to war. The presumed benefits of conflict must now at least outweigh the costs, including the forgone gains from trade.

With the passing of the Cold War, conflicts over trade loom large once again on the international agenda. From a psychological perspective, however, trade can trigger conflict as well as cooperation. Indeed, the very success in lowering tariffs among nations and the resulting growth in world trade can highlight new tendentious issues (Stein, 1991). Whenever the regulatory, fiscal, and monetary policies of countries diverge, critics of open trade can argue that the playing field is not even and their country has been unfairly handicapped because, for example, it has a higher minimum wage or more stringent antipollution laws or higher health and safety standards or even an inappropriately valued currency. These debates can be fueled by ethnocentric attributional biases, domestic producers seeking protection from stiff foreign competition, nationalist concerns about loss of sovereignty from excessive dependence on foreign goods and increased reliance on international forms of adjudication, egalitarian concerns about the impact of free trade with low-wage nations on the distribution of income within the importing country, and environmentalist concerns about the impact of free trade with nations that have lax regulatory policies. The intense debate within the United States over the entry of Mexico into NAFTA illustrates the unusual confluence of political forces that can mobilize against free trade, with right-wing nationalists, left-wing egalitarians, environmentalist organizations, and assorted industrial groups fearing Mexican competition uniting in opposition to the treaty.

Concluding Thoughts

Fifteen years ago, we confronted a " bipolar" world dominated by two nuclear-armed ideologically antagonistic superpowers. The debates that dominated the political psychological literature of the time revolved around challenges to the intellectual hegemony of the rational-actor model and deterrence theory. As this review attests, these debates continue, but we have learned a great deal in the intervening years. The literature offers much more nuanced analyses of psychological obstacles to, and facilitators of, thoughtful policy analysis. Scholars are now more appropriately circumspect about their epistemic warrants to label particular judgmental tendencies as error and biases. There is growing recognition of the difficulties of specifying how policy makers should have thought or acted in specific situations. So much depends on assumptions about the marginal utility of further information search and analysis, which, in turn, hinges on speculative counterfactual assumptions about what would have happened if policy makers had given more weight to this argument and adopted this alternative policy. And, although some advocates of deterrence and conflict-spiral theory still insist that their prescriptions are unconditionally best, there is now widespread recognition that such claims are wrong—wrong because the outcomes of influence attempts are inevitably highly sensitive to the other side's intentions, beliefs, and capabilities, which are both difficult to assess and prone to vary from one geopolitical circumstance to another.

Today we confront a multipolar world, and expert opinion has fractionated into a cacophony of discordant diagnoses. Old arguments—over the rationality of leaders and the effectiveness of strategies—persist, albeit in new forms as some American hawks from the Cold War era have been transformed into doves who now favor a quasi-isolationist stance and some American doves have been transformed into hawks who support humanitarian military interventions in places such as Bosnia, Somalia, and Rwanda and aggressive tariff retaliation against "unfair" trading practices (cf. Holsti, 1992). And new arguments have arisen. Perhaps the most profound cleavage in expert opinion is now between pessimists and optimists. At the pessimistic end of the continuum are the neo-Malthusians, who foresee an exponentially expanding population that will make impossible demands on the finite resources of the planet (Ehrlich, 1979; Kennedy, 1993). These observers also foresee new, unprecedented threats to the planetary ecosystem, such as global warming and ozone depletion, that international institutions are still far too weak to check. When we combine these ominous demographic and ecological trends with growing inequality in the distribution of wealth (affluent, older countries versus poor, younger countries) and an apparent resurgence of religious fundamentalism and ethnic chauvinism, we have a recipe for disaster on an apocalyptic scale. Weapons of mass destruction will inevitably slip into the hands of some very angry and desperate people. At the optimistic end of the continuum, we find cornucopians who foresee long-term trends toward greater prosperity, more widespread educational opportunities, improved health, longer life spans, and ever-expanding access to the amenities of middle-class life. Whereas the neo-Malthusians emphasize growing demands on dwindling resources, the cornucopians—often free-market economists (Simon, 1987)—emphasize the ingenuity with which people find cost-effective substitutes for scarce resources and invent ways of improving standards of living (from electricity to computers to biotechnology). The optimists stress the planful, rational, and constructively competitive aspects of human nature coupled with favorable macro trends that mutually reinforce each other (Fukuyama, 1992; Ohmae, 1995). Accelerating economic development leads to demands for democracy and individual autonomy (reducing the likelihood of war as the democratic-peace hypothesis predicts); instant worldwide communications further undercut oppressive regimes; increasing education promotes more tolerant, open-minded, and cosmopolitan outlooks on the world and increased skepticism toward would-be demagogues. The dominant forces of the 21st century are moving us toward a peaceful global federation of democratic, capitalist societies. Bartley (1993) suspects that future generations will look in bemused befuddlement at the "crabbed pessimism" of environmental and egalitarian doomsayers. Kennedy (1993) returns the compliment. He suspects that the boomster optimists of the late 20th century are as blind to the imminent peril confronting them as were those thinkers of the early 20th century who confidently declared that humanity had achieved a degree of economic interdependence and moral sophistication that made war unthinkable.

In one set of scenarios, humanity progresses inexorably toward a new millennium of peace, prosperity, and happy long lives; in the other set, humanity slips inexorably into a nightmare world of war, famine, and ecological disaster in which life is nasty, brutish, and short. Underlying these radically different visions of our future, it is possible to identify a tangle of competing assumptions about the nature of the physical world (Is nature fragile or robust?), human nature (How capable are we of recognizing our common interests as a species and transcending more narrowly defined identifications? How inventive, rational, and resilient are we?), and the nature of world politics (How locked are we into an "anarchic" international system?). It is, of course, possible to identify midpoints along the continuum in which various mixes of "boomster" and "doomster" scenarios come to pass. Whatever directions events might take in the next generation, however, it is a good bet that true-believer boomsters and doomsters will demonstrate the power of belief perseverance and claim at least partial vindication of their contradictory prophecies. The dramatic end of the Cold War—unexpected by almost everyone only ten years ago—certainly does not seem to have changed many minds (Gaddis, 1993).

What roles might psychologists play in the changing world scene? A reasonable answer is that they might play all the roles they have played up to now but exercise more systematic self-scrutiny in preventing their own value priorities from influencing the standards used in evaluating causal claims. Psychologists—aware as we are of judgmental bias—should be attuned to the danger that our applied work in a complex, ambiguous, and emotionally involving domain such as world politics can easily become an extension of our partisan preferences rather than of our scientific research programs. Like most social scientists, psychologists have for several decades been largely liberal in our political sympathies. Some found it tempting during the Cold War to characterize conservative advocates of deterrence as cognitive primitives ("Neanderthals") who had failed to adjust to the new strategic realities of nuclear weapons or as biased social perceivers who overattributed Soviet foreign policy to dispositional causes or even as emotionally unstable individuals who were projecting worst-case motives onto the other side (Mack, 1985; Osgood, 1961; White, 1984). Such arguments veer dangerously close to the *ad hominem*. Some social psychologists were also sharply critical of the Bush administration's decision to go to war to reverse the Iraqi invasion of Kuwait, accusing it of relying on crude enemy imagery and simplistic historical analogies (White, 1991a, 1991b). Indeed, one writer confidently assigned a biomedical cause—thyroid malfunctioning—for Bush's decision to resort to force against Saddam Hussein (Abrams, 1992).

As citizens, social scientists obviously have every right to take whatever policy positions they wish, but when we write as social scientists, we have a special responsibility to acknowledge the holes in the evidence. And there have been plenty of holes. Our understanding of why the Cold War ended—and of the role played by American policy in the mid-1980s—remains imprecise, to say the least. Our understanding of the role played by nuclear deterrence in averting a third "conventional" world war is highly conjectural. The strategic wisdom of routing Saddam Hussein's army from Kuwait hinges on speculative counter-factual reconstructions of what would have happened if the Western allies had relied purely on economic sanctions and diplomatic blandishments (Tetlock & Belkin, 1996). Did the West prevent the emergence of Iraq as an oil-wealthy, nuclear-armed regional hegemon? Or did the West sow seeds of hatred and resentment that will contaminate relations with the Arab world well into the future? Dissonant though it is not to be able to answer such important questions, acknowledging uncertainties about what would or could have happened is an integral part of sound scholarship and of checking belief perseverance. In this author's opinion, psychologists are well advised to resist the temptation of claiming to know more than they can properly justify, even if that means disappointing journalists looking for quotable statements with agnostic demurrals. The long-term credibility of the fledgling discipline of political psychology hinges on maintaining higher standards of evidence and proof than do the political partisans whom we study.

Acknowledgments   Comments are welcome and should be sent to the author at the Department of Psychology, 1885 Neil Avenue, 142 Townsend Hall, The Ohio State University, Columbus, Ohio 43210. Preparation of this chapter was assisted by a National Science Foundation research and training grant to the political psychology program of The Ohio State University, as well as by grants from the MacArthur Foundation and the Institute on Global Conflict and Cooperation. I thank Mike Sinatra, Deborah Haddad, Mike Boetcher, and Blair King for helpful comments on an earlier version of this chapter.

References

Abrams, H. (1992). Desert storm or thyroid storm? An inquiry. *Physicians for Social Responsibility Quarterly, 2,* 26–38.

Achen, C. H., & Snidal, D. (1989). Rational deterrence theory and comparative case studies. *World Politics, 41,* 143–169.

Allport, G. W. (1954/1968). *The nature of prejudice.* Cambridge, Mass.: Addison-Wesley.

Anderson, B. (1983). *Imagined communities: Reflections on the origin and spread of nationalism.* London: Verso.

Art, R. J., & Waltz, K. N. (1983). Technology, strategy, and the uses of force. In R. J. Art & K. N. Waltz (eds.), *The use of force* (pp. 3–52). Lanham, Md.: University Press of America.

Axelrod, R. M. (1976). *Structure of decision.* Boston: Little, Brown.

Axelrod, R. M. (1984). *The evolution of cooperation.* New York: Basic Books.

Baldwin, D. A. (1971). The power of positive sanctions. *World Politics, 24,* 19–38.

Bartley, R. (1993). The case for optimism: The West should believe in itself. *Foreign Affairs, 72,* 15–21.

Baumeister, R., & Leary, M. (1995). The need to belong: Desire for interpersonal attachments as a fundamental human motivation. *Psychological Bulletin, 117,* 497–529.

Blechman, B., & Fisher, C. (1994–1995). Phase out the bomb. *Foreign Policy, 99,* 79–96.

Blight, J. (1990). *The shattered crystal ball: Fear and learning in the Cuban Missile Crisis.* New York: Rowman & Littlefield.

Brehm, J. (1972). *Response to loss of freedom: A theory of psychological reactance.* Morristown, N.J.: General Learning Press.

Breslauer, G. W., & Tetlock, P. E. (eds.) (1991). *Learning in U.S. and Soviet foreign policy.* Boulder, Colo.: Westview.

Brewer, M. B., & Brown, R. J. (1996). Intergroup relations. In D. Gilbert et al. (eds.), *Handbook of social psychology* (pp. 219–243). New York: McGraw-Hill.

Brewer, M. B., & Kramer, R. M. (1985). The psychology of intergroup attitudes and behavior. *Annual Review of Psychology, 36,* 219–243.

Brown, R. (1985). *Social psychology.* New York: Free Press.

Bueno de Mesquita, B. (1985). The war trap revised: A revised expected utility model. *American Political Science Review, 79,* 156–177.

Bueno de Mesquita, B., & Lalman, D. (1992). *War and reason.* New Haven: Yale University Press.

Dahl, R. (1989). *Democracy and its critics.* New Haven: Yale University Press.

Deutsch, M. (1983). The prevention of World War III: A psychological perspective. *Political Psychology, 4,* 3–31.

Deutsch, M., & Krauss, R. M. (1960). The effect of threat on interpersonal bargaining. *Journal of Abnormal and Social Psychology, 61,* 181–189.

Downs, G. W. (1991). Arms races and war. In P. E. Tetlock, R. Jervis, P. Stern, J. L. Husbands, & C. Tilly (eds.), *Behavior, society, nuclear war* (vol. 2, pp. 73–109). New York: Oxford University Press.

Druckman, D. (1994). Nationalism, patriotism, and group loyalty: A social psychological perspective. *Mershon International Studies Review* (Supplement to ISQ), *38,* 43–68.

Druckman, D., & Hopmann, P. T. (1989). Behavioral aspects of international negotiation. In P. E. Tetlock et al. (eds.), *Behavior, society, nuclear war* (vol. 1, pp. 85–183). New York: Oxford University Press.

Ehrlich, P. (1979). *The population bomb.* New York: Doubleday.

Einhorn, H., & Hogarth, R. (1981). Behavioral decision theory. *Annual Review of Psychology, 32,* 53–88.

Friedland, N. (1976). Social influence via threats. *Journal of Experimental Social Psychology, 12,* 552–563.

Fukuyama, F. (1992). *The end of history and the last man.* Toronto: Maxwell MacMillan.

Gaddis, J. L. (1993). International relations theory and the end of the Cold War. *International Security, 17,* 5–58.

Gagnon, V. (1994). Serbia's road to war. In L. Diamond & M. Plattner (eds.), *Nationalism, ethnic conflict, and democracy* (pp. 117–131). Baltimore: Johns Hopkins University Press.

Gellner, E. (1983). *Nations and nationalism.* Oxford: Basil Blackwell.

George, A. L. (1969). The operational code: A neglected approach to the study of political leaders and decision-making. *International Studies Quarterly, 13,* 190–222.

George, A. L. (1980). *Presidential decision making in foreign policy: The effective use of information and advice.* Boulder, Colo.: Westview.

George, A. L. (1983). *Managing U.S.-Soviet rivalry: Problems of crisis prevention.* Boulder, Colo.: Westview.

George, A. L., Hall, D. K., & Simmons, W. (1971). *The limits of coercive diplomacy.* Boston: Little, Brown.

George, A. L., & Smoke, R. (1974). *Deterrence in American foreign policy: Theory and practice.* New York: Columbia University Press.

Gilbert, D., & Malone, P. S. (1995). Correspondence bias. *Psychological Bulletin, 117,* 21–38.

Gilovich, T. (1981). Seeing the past in the present: The effect of associations to familiar events on judgments and decisions. *Journal of Personality and Social Psychology, 40,* 709–808.

Herrmann, R. K. (1985). Analyzing Soviet images of the United States. *Journal of Conflict Resolution, 29,* 655–697.

Herrmann, R. K. (1988). The empirical challenge of the cognitive revolution: A strategy for drawing inferences about perceptions. *International Studies Quarterly, 32,* 175–203.

Heuer, R. J. (1981). Strategic deception and counterdeception: A cognitive process approach. *International Studies Quarterly, 25,* 294–327.

Holsti, O. R. (1967). Cognitive dynamics and images of the enemy. In R. Fagan (ed.), *Enemies of politics* (pp. 25–96). Chicago: Rand McNally.

Holsti, O. (1992). Public opinion and foreign policy: Challenges to the Almond-Lippman consensus. *International Studies Quarterly, 36,* 439–466.

Holsti, O. R., & Rosenau, J. N. (1979). Vietnam, consensus, and the belief systems of American leaders. *World Politics, 32,* 1–56.

Horowitz, D. L. (1985). *Ethnic groups in conflict.* Berkeley: University of California Press.

Hutchinson, J., & Smith, A. (1994). *Nationalism.* New York: Oxford University Press.

Huth, P. K., & Russett, B. (1993). General deterrence between enduring rivals: Testing three competing models. *American Political Science Review, 87,* 61–73.

Jervis, R. (1976). *Perception and misperception in international politics.* Princeton: Princeton University Press.

Jervis, R. (1978). Cooperation under the security dilemma. *World Politics, 30,* 167–214.

Jervis, R. (1983). Deterrence and perception. *International Security, 7,* 3–30.

Jervis, R. (1989). Rational deterrence: Theory and evidence. *World Politics, 41,* 183–207.

Jervis, R., Lebow, R. N., & Stein, J. G. (1985). *Psychology and deterrence.* Baltimore: Johns Hopkins University Press.

Kahn, H. (1965). *On escalation: Metaphors and scenarios.* New York: Praeger.

Kaplowitz, N. (1984). Psychopolitical dimensions of international relations: The reciprocal effects of conflict strategies. *International Studies Quarterly, 28,* 373–406.

Kelley, H. H. (1965). Experimental studies of threats in negotiations. *Journal of Conflict Resolution, 9,* 77–105.

Kelman, H. C. (1983). Conversations with Arafat: A social-psychological assessment of the prospects for Israeli-Palestinian peace. *American Psychology, 38,* 203–216.

Kennedy, P. (1993). *Preparing for the twenty-first century.* New York: Random House.

Keohane, R. O. (1986). *After hegemony: Cooperation and discord in the world political economy.* Princeton: Princeton University Press.

Khong, Y. F. (1991). *Analogies at war.* Princeton: Princeton University Press.

Komorita, S. (1973). Concession-making and conflict resolution. *Journal of Conflict Resolution, 17,* 745–762.

Kramer, R. (1988). Windows of vulnerability or cognitive illusions: Cognitive processes and the nuclear arms race. *Journal of Experimental Social Psychology, 25,* 79–100.

Lakoff, G., & Johnson, M. (1980). *Metaphors we live by.* Chicago: University of Chicago Press.

Larson, D. (1994). The role of belief systems and schemas in foreign policy decision-making. *Political Psychology, 15*, 17–32.

Layne, C. (1992). The unipolar illusion. *International Security, 17*, 5–51.

Lebow, R. N., & Stein, J. G. (1987). Beyond deterrence. *Journal of Social Issues, 43*, 5–71.

Lebow, R. N., & Stein, J. G. (1994). *We all lost the Cold War.* Princeton: Princeton University Press.

Leng, R. J. (1993). Influence techniques. In P. E. Tetlock et al. (eds.), *Behavior, society, nuclear war* (vol. 3, pp. 71–125). New York: Oxford University Press.

Leng, R. J., & Gochman, C. S. (1982). Dangerous disputes: A study of conflict behavior and war. *Journal of Conflict Resolution, 26*, 664–697.

Leng, R. J., & Wheeler, H. G. (1979). Influence strategies, success, and war. *Journal of Conflict Resolution, 23*, 655–684.

LeVine, R. A., & Campbell, D. T. (1971). *Ethnocentrism: Theories of conflict, ethnic attitudes, and group behavior.* New York: Wiley.

Levy, J. S. (1994). Learning and foreign policy. *International Organization, 48*, 209–333.

Mack, J. (1985). Toward a collective psychopathology of the nuclear arms competition. *Political Psychology, 6*, 291–321.

May, E. R. (1973). *Lessons of the past: The use and misuses of history in American foreign policy.* New York: Oxford University Press.

McClintock, C. G., Stech, F., & Beggan, J. (1987). The effects of commitments to threats and promises upon bargaining behavior and outcomes. *European Journal of Social Psychology, 17*, 447–464.

Mearsheimer, J. (1990). Back to the future: Instability in Europe after the Cold War. *International Security, 15*, 5–56.

Milburn, T. W., & Christie, D. J. (1989). Rewarding in international politics. *Political Psychology, 10*, 625–645.

Moynihan, D. (1993). *Pandemonium.* New York: Oxford University Press.

Neustadt, R. E., & May, E. R. (1986). *Thinking in time: The uses of history for decision-makers.* New York: Free Press.

Nisbett, R. E., & Ross, L. (1980). *Human inference: Strategies and shortcomings of social judgment.* Englewood Cliffs, N.J.: Prentice-Hall.

Ohmae, K. (1995). *The end of the nation-state.* New York: Free Press.

Olzak, S. (1992). *The dynamics of ethnic competition and conflict.* Stanford: Stanford University Press.

Orme, J. (1987). Deterrence failures: A second look. *International Security, 11*, 96–124.

Osgood, C. E. (1961). *An alternative to war or surrender.* Urbana: University of Illinois Press.

Oye, K. (1985). Explaining cooperation under anarchy: Hypotheses and strategies. *World Politics, 38*, 1–24.

Patchen, M. (1987). Strategies for eliciting cooperation from an adversary: Laboratory and international findings. *Journal of Conflict Resolution, 31*, 164–185.

Pattee, H. (1973). *Hierarchy theory.* New York: George Braziller.

Pilisuk, M., & Skolnick, P. (1968). Inducing trust: A test of the Osgood proposal. *Journal of Personality and Social Psychology, 8*, 121–133.

Pipes, R. (1986). Gorbachev's party congress: How significant for the United States? Miami, Fla.: Soviet and East European Studies Program Working Paper Series.

Pruitt, D. (1981). *Negotiation behavior.* New York: Academic Press.

Pruitt, D., & Rubin, J. (1986). *Social conflict.* Reading, Mass.: Addison-Wesley.

Russell, J. L. (1996). Influence techniques among nations. In P. E. Tetlock et al. (eds.), *Behavior, society and international conflict* (vol. 3, pp. 171–186). New York: Oxford University Press.

Schelling, T. C. (1966). *Arms and influence.* New Haven: Yale University Press.

Simon, H. A. (1957). *Models of a man.* New York: Wiley.

Simon, J. (1987). *Effort, opportunity, and wealth.* Oxford: Basil Blackwell.

Smith, W., & Anderson, A. (1975). Threats, communications, and bargaining. *Journal of Personality and Social Psychology, 32,* 76–82.

Snyder, G. H., & Diesing, P. (1977). *Conflict among nations: Bargaining, decision making and system structure in international crises.* Princeton: Princeton University Press.

Staub, E. (1988). *The roots of evil.* New York: Cambridge University Press.

Stech, F., McClintock, C. G., & Moss, B. (1984). The effectiveness of the carrot and the stick in increasing dyadic outcomes during dupolistic bargaining. *Behavioral Science, 29,* 1–12.

Stein, J. (1991). Deterrence and reassurance. In P. E. Tetlock at al. (eds.), *Behavior, society, nuclear war* (pp. 8–72). New York: Oxford University Press.

Stein, J. (1994). Political learning by doing: Gorbachev as uncommitted thinker and motivated learner. *International Organization, 48,* 155–183.

Streufert, S., & Streufert, S. (1978). *Behavior in the complex environment.* Washington, D.C.: Winston and Sons.

Stuart, D., & Starr, H. (1981). The inherent "bad faith" model reconsidered: Dulles, Kennedy, and Kissinger. *Political Psychology, 2,* 1–33.

Sylvan, D. A., Goel, A., & Chandrasekaran, B. (1990). Analyzing political decision making from an information processing perspective: JESSE. *American Journal of Political Science, 34,* 74–123.

Tajfel, H. (1980). *Human groups and social categories.* Cambridge: Cambridge University Press.

Tetlock, P. E. (1992). The impact of accountability on judgment and choice: Toward a social contingency model. In M. P. Zanna (ed.), *Advances in experimental social psychology* (vol. 25, pp. 331–376). New York: Academic Press.

Tetlock, P. E., & Belkin, A. (1996). *Counterfactual thought experiments in world politics.* Princeton: Princeton University Press.

Tetlock, P. E., & Boettger, R. (1989). Cognitive and rhetorical styles of traditional and reformist Soviet politicians: A content analysis study. *Political Psychology, 10,* 209–232.

Tetlock, P. E., & McGuire, C. B. (1986). Cognitive perspective on foreign policy. *Political Behavioral Annual, 1,* 147–179.

Tetlock, P. E., McGuire, C., & Mitchell, G. (1991). Psychological perspectives on nuclear war. *Annual Review of Psychology, 42,* 239–276.

Thaler, R. (1991). *Quasi-rational economics.* New York: Free Press.

Tilly, C. (1991). *Silver, sword, and capital accumulation.* New York: Oxford University Press.

Tilly, C. (1993). National self-determination as a problem for all of us. *Daedalus, 122,* 29–36.

To, T. (1988). More realism in the prisoner's dilemma. *Journal of Conflict Resolution, 32,* 402–408.

Tyler, T. (1991). *Why people obey the law.* New Haven: Yale University Press.

van Evera, S. (1985). Why cooperation failed in 1914. *World Politics, 38,* 80–117.

van Evera, S. (1993). Hypotheses on nationalism and war. *International Security, 18,* 5–39.

Vertzberger, Y. (1990a). Foreign policy decision makers as practical-intuitive historians: Applied history and its shortcomings. *International Studies Quarterly, 30,* 223–247.

Vertzberger, Y. (1990b). *The world in their minds.* Stanford: Stanford University Press.

Wallerstein, I. (1984). *The politics of the world economy.* Cambridge: Cambridge University Press.

Waltz, K. N. (1979). *Theory of international politics.* Reading, Mass.: Addison-Wesley.

Weingast, B. (1996). Counterfactuals and off-the-path behavior. In P. E. Tetlock & A. Belkin (eds.), *Counterfactual thought experiments in world politics* (pp. 230–246). Princeton: Princeton University Press.

White, R. K. (1984). *Fearful warriors: A psychological profile of U.S.-Soviet relations.* New York: Free Press.

White, R. K. (1991a). Empathizing with Saddam Hussein. *Political Psychology, 12,* 291–308.

White, R. K. (1991b). Nuclear policies: Deterrence and reassurance. In P. Suedfeld & P. E. Tetlock (eds.), *Psychology and social advocacy* (pp. 71–82). Washington, D.C.: Hemisphere.

Zimmerman, W., & Axelrod, R. M. (1981). The "lessons" of Vietnam and Soviet foreign policy. *World Politics, 34,* 1–24.

The Psychology of
Truth and Lies

Let us set up a monument
in the city, at the end of the long avenue,
or at the center of the big square,
a monument
that will stand out against any background
because it will be
quite well built and very realistic.
Let us set up a monument
that will not disturb anybody.

We will plant flowers
around the pedestal
and with the permission of the city fathers
we will lay out a little garden
where our children
will blink
at the great orange sun
and take the figure perched above them
for a well-known thinker
a composer
or a general.

I guarantee that flowers will appear
every morning
on the pedestal.
Let us set up a monument
that will not disturb anybody.
Even taxi drivers
will admire its majestic silhouette.
The garden will be a place
for rendezvous.
Let us set up a monument,
we will pass under it
    hurrying on our way to work,
foreigners will have their pictures taken
    standing under it,
we will splash it at night with the glare
    of floodlights.

Let us set up a monument to The Lie.

3

Comprehension of Lies

A Russian View

Although the study of the psychology of lies is a firmly established area of research in the West, few readers will be surprised to learn that it is a new and poorly understood topic of academic inquiry in Russia. As former Soviets know and Westerns can probably guess, any scientific work that concerned untruthfulness among Russians could not be published in the Soviet Union, and consequently there was little interest in the topic. The psychology of lies is now a topic of great practical urgency as Russia leaps into a competitive economy with multiple political parties and a bewildering array of ideological and consumer choices affecting virtually every sphere of daily living.

Russian psychologists now have access to much of the psychological literature on truth and lies that comes from the West—enough to confirm the supposition that Russians have developed attitudes toward truth and lies that differ from those of Westerners (Znakov, 1993, 1995). Russians and Westerners have had very different day-to-day experiences with telling and receiving truth and lies, and they have received very different social messages about if and when lying is acceptable or even desirable. That there is a difference between Western and Russian understandings of lying is partly because the telling of lies by Russians to their government was an equitable way of dealing with a government that had little regard for the truth. However, the greatest influence on the way Russians experienced truth and lies was not from the official sources of disinformation but from the commonly accepted practice of lying as part of everyday interpersonal relations.

The Russian intelligentsia had an expression for the practice of multiple layers of lies. They coined a new word that was extrapolated from the psychiatric diagnosis of schizophrenia. Although schizophrenia is a complex disorder, the word suggests a schism, or splitting in two, of the psyche. Russians humorously decided that their most common way of existence could be named "tripto-phrenia"—a splitting of the psyche into three parts: We think one thing; we say another; and we do a third. It was a world in which thoughts, words, and actions bore no relationship to each other. Following his trips to the Soviet Union in 1979 and 1990, Ekman (1993), in the introduction to the Russian edition of his book, commented on the universal practice of concealing one's thoughts and actions: "For decades Soviet people learned that if they wanted to achieve something they had to act to evade orders. Tricks and deception became a standard in this country. Everybody knows that laws are unfair, the system vicious, and if you want to survive you have to outwit the system" (p. 10).

Two Psychologies of Truth and Lies

There is an old Marxist saying that is deeply rooted in the minds of Russians that roughly translates to "being makes conscious." Like all literal translations, it is difficult to extract the intended meaning from the separate words. It conveys the idea that if you have lived something, it becomes part of who you are. It is shorthand for saying that people grow in a sociohistorical context that influences how they think and feel. This sentiment leads us to expect that Russians and Westerners have qualitatively different attitudes toward truth and lies because they live in societies in which the overt and covert messages about lying and truth telling differ in many fundamental respects.

The Sociohistorical Context for a Russian Psychology of Lies

Unlike the old czarist society, the new society that replaced it early in this century was based on the ideals of communalism. Religion was officially abolished, social class was no longer dependent on lineage, and new laws and customs were often the opposite of the ones that formerly existed. What was the effect of these profound changes on the way people comprehended the idea of lying? The most respected Russian-language dictionaries, such as the ones by Dal (1979) and Slovar (1957), provide definitions that give no hint of change in the use and meaning of terms that pertain to lying. It is possible that these references are out of date or that the entries have been deliberately falsified, so scholars cannot rely on sources such as these when they want to know about sensitive issues such as functional changes in the use and meaning of sensitive words.

The Russian tradition, which grew from a long history, treated lying as a moral sin, one that is close to betrayal (Ilijin, 1993). The Russian philosopher Soloviev (1896) defined a lie as a conscious contradiction of the truth. This idea is common in all dictionaries of Russian language. A liar is someone who is opposed to the truth, not to the person he lies to. By intentionally twisting the truth, a liar is morally blamed. For the purposes of this paper, I label the old Russian tradition of perceiving lies as a serious sin as the "moral-sin" notion of lying.

Morals have changed dramatically in 20th-century Russia. It is meaningful to ask whether the moral-sin conception of lies has survived or whether it was replaced by a more modernized idea of lying. The Soviet rulers were highly successful in turning moral ideas to their opposites, so it is reasonable to question whether they had similar success in changing the meaning of lies.

The parents and grandparents of today's older Russian adults grew up as children of the revolution. If they were born into aristocracy, they learned a "code of honor" that was deeply rooted in the culture and history of noblemen and was strictly observed. The code of honor provided clear guidelines for behavior that left no doubt as to what was right and what was wrong. Under this code, every aristocratic man knew that his word must be kept, that integrity was an essential component of one's character.

The power of the code of honor is a major theme in Russian history and literature. The most frequently required remedy for defending one's honor was the duel. It is a sad historical fact that Pushkin, the glory of Russian poetry, was mortally wounded defending his and his wife's honor. A great many examples in classical Russian literature concern the principles of honor, honesty, and sin. Readers are undoubtedly familiar with these themes in Dostoevski's *Crime and Punishment* (1866/1966), Pasternak's *Dr. Zhivago* (1958/1991), and many other literary classics from Russia. The Bolsheviks destroyed society's standardbearers for truth and honor when they slaughtered the aristocracy. A generation later, many of the remaining Soviet intelligentsia who had internalized the principles that were inherent in the code of honor were killed in Stalin's concentration camps. The entire code of honor was destroyed when those who swore to uphold it were put to death.

What about the common people? Where did they learn moral behavior and values that included truthfulness? Prior to the revolution, religion provided a strong moral ethic that included the value of truthfulness. The Bolsheviks destroyed religion and, with it, the idea that lying and dishonesty were sinful. Lying, dissembling, feigning, avoiding, deceiving, and other ways of misleading all became essential for survival. It is not so much that lying soon became an accepted part of everyday life in the Soviet Union as it was that the meaning of what constituted a lie had changed. Certain actions and statements became necessary and repetitive and seemed closer to having no meaning than they were to lying. All citizens would publicly, frequently, and routinely announce their patriotism and support of communist ideals, but the fact that they did not have the same degree of zeal for the party as their words suggested was not perceived as a lie. It became more like some mindless action than an active decision to lie. The experimental question that is investigated in this chapter centers on whether the new practice of automatic and obligatory lying has substituted for the older tradition in which lying was a moral sin.

The Sociohistorical Context for a Western Psychology of Lies

As used in this book, the West refers to the countries of Western Europe and the United States and Canada. Although each of the several countries that fit into this category is somewhat different, all have strong traditions of official or unofficial dominant religions. The (Judeo-) Christian ethic, as it is articulated in the Ten Commandments, and the notion of sin in Catholicism provide strong moral sanctions against lying. These sanctions are deeply rooted in religious beliefs. Westerners interpret notions of truth and lies against this background, but Russians have a wholly different background that gives a different meaning to these terms.

Civil rights is a central theme in Western democracies that confers a legal connotation to ideas about truth and lies. In the United States, the amendments to the Constitution have assumed a sacrosanct status in that they are believed to be inviolable and are guaranteed to all citizens. These are "basic" rights that include the rights of free press, free speech, and freedom from unreasonable search and seizure, among others. The free press and free speech amendments provide a mechanism for determining whether the government was providing truthful information because the press is quick to search for possible dishonesty and free to publish its findings.

Free speech obviates the need to dissemble: there is a legal right to say what one believes, so there is no need to lie. The freedom from unreasonable search and seizure ensures that citizens can expect to maintain their privacy. Thus, the conditions that were amenable to a culture of lying in the Soviet Union are absent from Western societies and have been replaced by a set of legal standards that encourage truthfulness. In Western democracies, sanctions against lying are also rooted in a tradition of civil rights that is protected by law. That is why the Western tradition of comprehending lies is called a *legal tradition* in this paper.

Inherent in the Western comprehension of the concept of lying is the key idea that the civil rights of the person who has been deceived have been violated. The centrality of this idea is seen in Western definitions of the term and in the philosophical writings of such influential luminaries as Immanuel Kant (1980), who believed that any lie was bad for all mankind, and Arthur Schopenhauer (1860), who espoused the opposite view. Schopenhauer believed that an intentional untruth is not a lie if it protects the rights of an aggrieved party. But these opposite points of view regarding lies were both based in the Western tradition of preserving human rights. The idea that lying violates the rights of the deceived (i.e., the person being lied to) is deeply ingrained in democratic morals and is reflected in the consciousness of the people. The idea that the recipient of the lie is having a basic right violated is a core difference between Russian and Western conceptualizations of what it means to lie. This concept of rights violation is not part of the Russian notion of lies.

Of course, I am not so naive as to believe that the legal comprehension of lying has been successful in preventing the telling of lies in Western societies. A recent report from the American Council on Education states that two-thirds of students in college and other institutions of higher education lie and cheat (Saxe, 1991). My emphasis in this chapter is on the substantial differences between Russian and Western cultures with respect to truth and lies, although I also acknowledge that there are commonalities as well (Bok, 1978). The psychology of truth and lies as they exist in the West has already been brilliantly discussed (Ekman, 1991). Instead, I focus here on distinctly Russian notions of these concepts and highlight the cultural differences rather than the similarities.

The Motivation for Lying

There are different reasons for why people lie. The motivation or the reason for the lie is the most important dimension from a psychological perspective because we react very differently to identical actions if we believe that they arise from very different motives. Suppose that I told the police that you committed a crime when I knew that you didn't. You would react to this lie one way if you knew I believed that, because of this lie, you would achieve some benefit, like safety; you would react differently if you knew I believed that you would be immediately electrocuted. A lie that arises from a desire to behave morally is considered justified and is free of any pejorative meaning associated with lying. In a situation like this, the negative value associated with telling a lie is less, in its absolute value, than the positive value that justifies the telling of the lie. When these two values are combined, the telling of the lie assumes a positive value. By contrast, the lie that is told solely for personal gain or to inflict injury on a friend or stranger is wholly negative and therefore reprehensible. Both lies involve the conscious concealment of the truth, but they are different in essential ways and cannot be categorized together. Psychological studies of truth and lies could not meaningfully treat these two types of communication as though they were the same.

Morally correct lies have an overall positive value and can be thought of as "lies for a good reason," or more literally translated from the Russian as "lies in order to save." This was the rationale behind the lies that were so prevalent in the highly secretive Soviet government throughout most of this century. The routine practice of lying by the government was justified with the firmly held conviction that, for the majority of people, it is better to have very limited information about governmental activities and outcomes than to give them truth that might cause them to lose faith in their political system. This idea justified the provision of absolutely no information regarding how well the government or economy was functioning or even of false information (i.e., lies) to the public. This practice was deemed to be in the best interest of the people. Hence, the recipient of the lie was not aggrieved, and the higher good of communism was maintained.

The principle of lying for a good reason was used by the officials who provided information to the public following the explosion of the Chernobyl nuclear power station. The scientists assured the government, and it, in turn, assured the public that there was no danger from the explosion at the plant. If we were to assume that they were motivated by their concern for the public good (you may find this a difficult assumption to make), then they lied in the belief that they could avoid panic and possibly save lives and face. In other words, from their perspective, the lies about Chernobyl were justified lies. The disclosure came in this example only because of the monitors from Scandinavian countries that clearly showed that a major catastrophe had just occurred. Before perestroika, the officials could have been secure in their belief that no open acknowledgment of their lie would occur.

It would be expected that, to most Russians, the use of lies by government officials is perceived to be less of a violation of a basic right and more acceptable than to Westerners because these lies are motivated by the belief that it would be better for most people to be told a lie than to know the truth. The notion that one's civil rights had been violated was not part of the consciousness of the Soviet people. The Declaration on Human Rights from the United Nations was not published in the Soviet Union until the Gorbachev era. The idea that a citizen had a basic right to the truth simply did not exist.

Additionally, the notion of saving face by concealing deficiencies and errors has a long history in Russia. It is exemplified in the story of the Potemkin Villages. This is a frequently told story about the elaborate attempts of the Russian field marshal, Grigori Potemkin, to present a positive image of Russian peasant life to Russia's own ruler! During her reign, Catherine the Great had planned a trip across central Russia, a barren and poor area about which she had little knowledge. In order to make the peasant villages appear more prosperous than they were, Potemkin arranged for the appearance of wealthier villages than what actually existed. A pot containing a boiling hen was deposited near the front door of a home she was to pass. The same pot was then carried from home to home so that when she arrived at each home she saw that everyone was preparing a good dinner for that evening. The planned impression was that the peasants had sufficient food and lived relatively prosperous lives. Given this elaborate ruse, it is little wonder Potemkin was such a favorite of the court.

This story is a good example of the reciprocal nature of lying: the leader would lie to the subordinates, and the subordinates, in turn, would lie back to the leader. Examples of this practice are seen in more recent Soviet history, with officials assuring their leaders that a particular factory had fulfilled its production quotas or a police commissioner announcing that virtually all of the crimes had been solved. Western readers may find the extensive deception of one's own leader to be strange, but this practice was deeply ingrained in the culture. Imagine the efforts that would be justified to appear prosperous before one's enemies.

Untruth, Lies, and Deception

The concepts of truth and lies are only two markers along a psychological dimension defined at one end by some hypothetical ideal of complete honesty and at the other end by its hypothetical antithesis of complete falsehood. My position is that the opposition of truth to lying is highly insufficient. Unlike my American colleague, Ekman, I think that *untruths*, *lies*, and *deceptions* cannot be used as synonyms, and I will emphasize the essential differences among these terms. Although I cannot delineate every type of lie, untruth, or deception, because there are many gradations and combinations of different types, I list some of the ways that these concepts can differ.

Untruth

There are three ways in which an untruth is usually revealed. The first is an untruth that is preferable to the truthful alternative. Consider the situation of a runner who is surprised at the new speed record set by a rival he has competed against on several other occasions. The runner believes that such improvement in performance by the rival must be due to the rival's use of illegal drugs, so, in accordance with this belief, he tells others that the rival is taking illegal drugs. This is an untruth because the rival never ingested drugs, but the drug explanation is preferable to acknowledging that the rival is a better athlete; as long as the runner never checks for evidence, it is possibly true.

The second is an untruth caused by a faulty inference about one's motives. This occurs when an individual has knowledge of an action but not the motivation or reason for the action. It can be thought of as a faulty inference. An example should help to clarify this notion. If you have joined a fascist organization, I might say that you are a supporter of fascist ideals and that you willingly engage in racist activities (e.g., you are anti-Semitic). But suppose you joined the fascist organization as a provocateur or informer. In this case, you are really opposed to racism, a fact that makes inferences from your membership in this group a lie. The motive that I inferred from this action is not your true motive, hence it is one type of untruth.

The third is an allegorical untruth. It is possible to convey a meaning that is opposite from that conveyed in the words that are used by relying on context and the skillful use of allegory, irony, or jokes. Shakespeare's genius at this technique is seen in *Julius Caesar* when Anthony, addressing the citizens of Rome, calls Brutus, Cassius, and other murderers of Caesar "honorable men." In the course of his speech to honor these men, he provides ample evidence of their treachery and ingratitude so that the citizens of Rome recognize the true meaning of his speech and turn in anger to avenge the death of Caesar. Anthony's untruth was through the use of irony that permitted him to convey a meaning that did not reside in the words he selected.

Bold-Faced Lies

"A lie is a deliberate false statement made orally, in writing or some other use of language" (Carson, Wokutch, & Cox, 1989, p. 387). This definition captures my own understanding of lies. If I were to say that I saw you take money when I never did or, alternatively, if I were to say that I did not see you take money when, in fact, I did see this act, I would be telling a bold-faced lie. Another prominent example of the telling of bold-face lies that comes to mind is the Soviet denial of wrongdoing in the 1980s when a Korean plane was shot down by missiles of the Soviet armed forces.

Unlike most researchers, I think that the deceiver does not twist the facts. The complete absence of false information is a peculiar characteristic of deception. Instead, a half-truth is told in order to influence the listener to come to a conclusion that is different from the one he or she would reach if the whole truth had been told. When telling a half-truth, the deceiver intentionally conceals other relevant facts.

Deception

Deception is common in advertising. The advertiser creates a false impression that a product is better than it really is by not mentioning critical deficiencies. The advertisement that boasts that "this cat food contains more phosphorus" may be making a true statement. The concealed piece of information that consumers might be unaware of is that cats do not have any need for phosphorus. Usually the legislation pertaining to advertising prohibits unfair or deceptive ads. Successful deception is usually based on erroneous expectations. The deceived person foresees the events, but knowledge acquired in the half-truth prevents him from reaching the correct conclusions. The deceiver benefits from the twisted interpretations made by the recipient of the half-truth.

Deception is often based on playing a false role (Hopper & Bell, 1984). For example, a lazy student who pretends to be a hard worker is deceiving the professor by creating a false impression. This technique is well known to poker players who confidently raise the ante in poker to give other players the impression that they have a winning hand. Of course, it could be argued further that skillful players know this is as a common bluff, so the action is not deceptive in much the same way that telling a lie when a lie is expected becomes neither lie nor truth but some wholly different category (Carson, Wokutch, & Cox, 1989).

Investigating the Russian Psychology of Lies

The rest of this chapter deals with empirical attempts to understand the psychology of lies from a Russian perspective. The notion that lies often serve a higher good and the absence of the connotation that lies harm the people who are being deceived are important features of Russian thinking that differentiate it from Western thinking on this topic. Such differences, if they exist, are likely to be subtle because no citizen is expected to endorse the notion that lies from the government or its people should be encouraged. These hypotheses were investigated in a series of studies.

It was hypothesized that the Russian psychology of lies is rooted in three basic beliefs. First, the Russian people believe that lying is a frequent occurrence in their society. This is important because if you expect to be told a lie, it takes on a different meaning than if you expect the truth. Second, when Russians discuss the concept of lying, they do not spontaneously include the notion that basic civil rights have been harmed. Third, inherent in the way Russians think about lying is the idea that lies are acceptable when they serve a valid and moral purpose. This concept is important because lying for the higher good is key to understanding how Russians understand truth and lies. The studies described in this chapter support the belief that Russians have developed attitudes toward telling and receiving lies that include these three basic concepts.

Three separate studies conducted by the author are described here, each with subjects from different segments of the Russian population. The studies were designed to assess Russian beliefs about lying and are supported by research from other Russian psychologists.

Study 1: Do Most People Tell the Truth?

The war in Afghanistan was a particularly turbulent time in contemporary Soviet history. (See the chapters on post-traumatic stress syndrome for a longer discussion of the war with Afghanistan.) Among common citizens, those who had the greatest exposure to the discrepancy between what the official government sources were telling the Soviet people and what was truly happening in Afghanistan were the war veterans who had fought in Afghanistan. Their experiences with governmental truths and lies made them ideal subjects for this study.

As part of a longer questionnaire (Buss, 1961), a sample of 62 Soviet veterans from the war with Afghanistan were asked if they agreed or disagreed with the following statement (Znakov, 1990): "I thought before that a majority of people told the truth, but now I do not believe this." Fifty of the veterans (81%) said that they agreed with this statement, showing that the vast majority no longer believed that most people tell the truth. Results from this question agree with the commonly acknowledged belief that the telling of lies is quite common in Russian society.

Study 2: When Do You Lie?

For the second study, 317 adults (172 women and 145 men) were sampled from among students, workers in an employment center, and officers. They responded anonymously to two requests: (1) Give a short definition of a lie; and (2) What are situations in which you can tell lies?

A majority of the subjects (84%) defined a lie in ways that are consistent with the idea that it contradicts a fact often for personal gain, but does not include the idea that the person receiving the lie has suffered a violation of rights. For example, prototypical responses were: "A lie is a discrepancy between what is thought and what is said"; "An intentional twist of the truth to justify one's action or for the sake of one's profit"; and "Obvious twist of the truth." These examples of commonly used definitions are similar to those found in Russian-language dictionaries (Dal, 1979; Slovar, 1957). Only 13 percent of the respondents mentioned the rights of the recipient of the lie. There seems to be excellent agreement on what the term means and the omission of the notion of civil rights from the meaning of the term.

The question about the situations in which respondents could tell lies also elicited a surprising degree of agreement. Only 15 respondents (5%) said that they never lie; 101 respondents (32%) said that they frequently lie to further their own interests. Prototypical answers included reciprocity in lying: an 18-year-old female wrote, "If a man lied to me, I can lie to him, too." A common theme was lying to advance one's self: a military officer of 30 wrote that it was acceptable to lie "in order to raise one's prestige," and a woman of 44 wrote, "If I see that a man is not decent, I lie to cause him embarrassment." Answers also showed that people lied to keep their secrets and thoughts private. The most frequently given response about when one would lie was for the sake of others. As expected, respondents spontaneously mentioned the idea that lying for a moral good was justified.

Approximately two-thirds of the subjects provided responses showing that they would "lie in order to save someone." Here are two typical responses that show how respondents believe lying is sometimes justified: "You might need to conceal a diagnosis from a terminally ill person"; "You might want to be vague about the circumstances under which someone's son died in the army if the circumstances were not heroic." Answers of this sort are in accord with the idea that people are often better off when they don't know the complete truth, and it is in service of a higher good to protect them from the truth. The idea that the person receiving the lie is harmed was absent.

Are these results distinctly Russian? In other words, is the idea of the justified lie inherent in the way people from other cultures think about situations in which they would lie? Or is it a finding that is peculiar to Russians because of their unique experiences with "justified lies"? To answer this question, another sample was selected, this time consisting of 49 Vietnamese (22 women and 27 men) who were temporary residents in Russia. Their definitions of the word *lie* were similar to those provided by the other groups, this time showing good agreement across two cultures: lying is acceptable when it serves a higher good along with the absence of any mention of rights violations. Of the 49 subjects, 5 (10%) said that they never lie. Of the remaining subjects, 31 (63%) provided answers that showed they would "lie in order to save," and 13 (26%) said they would lie to gain a personal advantage. Although this study used a small sample, these results are similar to those obtained with the two Russian samples, showing that Vietnamese living in Russia have the same notion of the justified lie in their belief system. It should be noted that many Vietnamese have also experienced widespread lies from and to their own communist leaders, so while these data show that there is some cross-cultural agreement about lying, we cannot determine if it is related to a semi-official policy of government lies or if it is a universal part of the notion of lies.

Study 3: Would You Lie in Court in Order to Save
Innocent Persons?

In order to understand whether the idea of a justified lie is a salient notion in the Russian comprehension of lies, 196 adult subjects selected from a variety of groups were asked the question: "Would you lie in court in order to save innocent persons?" This is a particularly important question for understanding the concept of the justified lie because it pits the need for honesty in a court of law and the desire to save innocent persons from adverse legal consequences—two conditions in which truth telling is emphasized—against each other. There are strict legal and moral laws about telling the truth in court. This is one setting in which the truth is extremely important. What happens when the legal and moral power of the court would lead to the conviction of an honest person if the truth were told? Does this set of facts justify the telling of a lie? (Additional details about this study can be found in Znakov, 1993).

Given this situation, 123 subjects (63%) said they would lie in court; 73 said they would not (37%). Thus, a majority of the respondents believed that even in court, a lie can be justified if it fulfills a higher moral purpose. Here are typical answers: "If our justice system is as it is, then why not help the poor creature?" "The innocent must not suffer and if the court does not administer justice, although that is its mission, I guess I'll help the innocent. Otherwise, the innocent have no one to rely on." It seems that Russians believe that lying is justified when the system of justice is ineffective. In other words, if you cannot trust the system, then it is right to lie if lying will lead to a just outcome.

Volkov's 1979 Study: Why Did You Provide False Evidence?

A fourth study is included here because of its relevance. It was conducted by the Russian psychologist, Volkov (1979).

Asking people when they would be willing to lie is quite different from examining the motives of those who have actually been convicted for lying. Even when responding anonymously, as in the previously described studies, people may not behave in the real world the way they report that they will. For that reason, I discuss a study of 30 convicted criminals, all of whom had been found guilty of providing false evidence during a legal proceeding (Volkov, 1979). The subjects were asked to explain why they lied in court. Eleven of the 30 (37%) gave answers that conveyed the idea that they lied out of sympathy or pity for someone else; 6 (20%) said that they had lied out of concern for a close relative or friend who would be harmed if the truth had been disclosed; 4 (13%) said that they had been persuaded to lie by close friends or relatives who had convinced them that it was a good idea to lie; 3 (10%) denied that they lied; 6 gave other miscellaneous answers. As can be seen from this small sample, even criminals whose only crime was lying in court said that they had lied for a morally justified reason. Thus, the idea that lying for the common good is justified is important to people when they consider the crime of lying in court.

Russian Attitudes toward Truth and Lies

It has been over 20 years since Alexander Solzhenitsyn made the appeal "not to live in lies." Russian dissidents decided that it was time to stop pretending that the communist political system was working. Such leaders as General Grigorenko, academician Andrei Sakharov, and human rights defender Sergei Kovalyev came out to fight the lie and to insist that the constant barrage of lies stop so that people could live in truth. But the lie is still winning. Official figures for the number of deaths in the war in Chechnya are significantly lower than those coming from other sources, and Russians seem unaccustomed to expecting the truth.

The Western legal notion (enshrined in the democratic system) that lies are a fundamental violation of civil rights is not inherent in the way Russians think about lies. Instead, Russians have saved elements of the traditional moral-sin notion of lies, which is rather complicated and which includes the referential content of the situation, the motivations and intentions of the liar, and his or her background knowledge of the situation.

We cannot have a single transcultural psychology of truth and lies. There are too many differences in meanings and in practice between Russians and the West to generalize freely across cultural borders. As long as there are fundamental cultural differences in the experiences people have with the telling of truth and lies, and their expectations from their government and each other concerning truth telling, we cannot make universal statements about how, when, or why people will lie or tell the truth.

Acknowledgments   Research was supported by the Russian Humanitarian Research Foundation. I thank Chan Thi Lin T'i for collecting the Vietnamese data.

References

Bok, S. (1978). *Lying: Moral choice in public and private life*. New York: Pantheon.

Buss, A. H. (1961). *The psychology of aggression*. New York: Wiley.

Carson, T. L., Wokutch, R. E., & Cox, J. E. (1989). *An ethical analysis of deception in advertising: Contemporary moral controversies in business*. New York.

Dal, V. I. (1979). *Tolkovyi slovar zivogo velikorusskogo yazyka.* (Explanatory dictionary of the living great Russian language.) (4 vols., vol. 2.) Moscow. (In Russian.)

Dostoevski, F. M. (1861/1966). *Crime and punishment*. New York: Modern Library.

Ekman, P. (1985). *Telling lies*. New York: Norton.

Ekman, P. (1991) *Why kids lie*. New York: Penguin Books.

Ekman, P. (1993). *Potchemy dieti lgut.* (Why kids lie.) Moscow: Pedagogika. (In Russian.)

Hopper, R., & Bell, R. A. (1984). Broadening the deception construct. *Quarterly Journal of Speech* 70(3), 287–302.

Ilijin, I. A. (1993). *O lzi i predatelstve. Aksiomy religi-oznogo opyta* (On lie and betrayal: axioms of the religious experience.) Moscow. (In Russian.)

Kant, I. (1980). *O mnimom prave lgat' iz chelovekoljubija: Traktaty i pisma.* (On the imaginary right to lie for the sake of love of mankind [philanthropy]: treatise and letters.) Moscow. (In Russian.)

Pasternak, B. (1958/1991). *Dr. Zhivago*. New York: Pantheon.

Saxe, L. (1991). Lying: Thoughts of an applied psychologist. *American Psychologist, 46*, 409–415.

COMPREHENSION OF LIES 91

Schopenhauer, A. (1860). *Die Beiden Grundprobleme der Ethik, behandelt in zwei akademischen Breischriften.* Leipzig. (In German.)

Slovar (1957). *Sovremennogo Russkogo literaturnogo yazyka v 17 tomakh.* (Dictionary of modern Russian literary language.) (17 vols.; vol. 6.) Moscow-Leningrad. (In Russian.)

Soloviev, V. S. (1896). Loz. Entsiklopedicheskii slovar. (Lie. Encyclopedic Dictionary.) In F. A. Brokqaus and I. A. Efron (eds.), *T. XVIIa.* St. Petersburg. (In Russian.)

Volkov, V. V. (1979). *Primenenie metoda dikhotomicheskoi samootsenki v kriminalno-psykhologicheskom issledovanii lichnosty: Lichnost' prestupnika kak ob'ekt psykholog-icheskogo issledovaniya.* (Application of the method of dichotomic self-assessment in the criminal-psychological investigation of personality.) Moscow. (In Russian.)

Znakov, V. V. (1990). Psykhologicheskoye issledovanie stere-otypov ponymaniya lychnosty uchastnikov voiny v Afganistane. (Psychological investigation of comprehension stereotypes of personalities of the Afganistan war veterans.) *Voprosy Psykhologii, 4.* (In Russian.)

Znakov, V. V. (1993). *Pravda i loz' v soznanii russkogo naroda i sovremennoi psykhologii ponimania.* (Truth and lies in the consciousness of the Russian people and in the modern psychology of comprehension.) Moscow. (In Russian.)

Znakov V. V. (1995). Pochemu lgut amerikantsi i russkie?: Razmyshleniya rossiiskogo psykhologa nad knigoi Pola Ekmana. (Why do the Americans and Russians tell lies?: Speculations of the Russian psychologist over the book by Paul Ekman.) *Voprosy Psykhologii, 2.* (In Russian.)

4

Deception, Lying, and Demeanor

Paul Ekman

The focus of my research has been on how, when, and why demeanor may betray a lie. I will describe my findings near the end of this chapter. First, I describe a number of theoretical issues that must be considered in examining lies. This includes my definition of lying and how I distinguish lies from secrets, self-deception, and other kinds of deceit. I will then discuss some of the difficulties in using that definition, when people believe what is false to be true. Next I will consider the different motives that underlie the decision to tell a lie. Then I will discuss two principal reasons why lies fail. Then I will review some of our most recent research on how difficult it is to judge whether someone is lying or telling the truth. Finally, I describe some of my thinking about what happens when people believe the government is lying to them, using the Soviet Union as an example.

Lying and Self-Deception

I use the intent of the liar as one of the two criteria for distinguishing lies from other kinds of deception. The liar *deliberately* chooses to mislead the target. Liars may actually tell the truth, but that is not their intent. And truthful people may provide false information—bad advice from an investment counselor—but that is not their intent. The liar has choice; the liar could choose not to lie. Presumably, a pathological liar is compelled to lie and by my definition therefore is not a liar.

My second criterion for distinguishing lies from other deceptions is that the target is not notified about the liar's intention to mislead. A magician is not a liar by this criterion, but Uri Geller is a liar since he claimed his tricks were not magic. An actor is not a liar but an impostor is. Sometimes notification of an intention to mislead is implicit in the framing, to use Goffman's (1974) term, of the situation. Let the buyer beware is one example of an explicit warning that products or services may not be what they are presented to be. (Of course, that warning does not appear in advertisements, nearly all of which are designed to convey the opposite message.) In real estate transactions, the potential buyer is implicitly notified that the seller's asking price is not the actual price the seller would accept. Various forms of politeness are other instances in which the nature of the situation notifies the target that the truth may not be spoken. It would not be proper for the host to scrutinize the dinner guest to determine if the guest's claim to have enjoyed the evening is true, any more than the aunt should worry whether the nephew is lying when he says that he appreciated being given a tie for Christmas. Deception is expected; even if the target might suspect that the truth is not being told, it is improper to question it. Poker is still another situation in which the rules of the game sanction and notify the players that deception will occur, and therefore one cannot consider bluffing to be a lie. In some situations only certain types of deception are allowable. The poker player cannot use marked cards, nor can the home seller conceal a known defect.

In some situations, the issue of whether people will deceive or be truthful is ambiguous. Courtship is probably such a case. The saying "All's fair in love and war" would seem to warn lovers not to believe all they are told. Recent public opinion polls suggest that lies that diminish the number of previous sexual partners one has had are common among college-age adults. Yet I expect that lovers want to believe in the truthfulness of their lover and popular songs testify to the betrayal felt when lies are discovered. Poets have brilliantly explained how romance may be considered a form of collusion to develop and maintain myths about each other.

I differ from Bok (1982), who only considers false statements to be lies. I (Ekman, 1985) argued that concealment is just as much a lie as falsification, if there is an expectation that concealment will not occur. My daughter knows that if she gets into trouble at school and the head teacher gives her a "slip," a formal warning that she may be suspended if the offense is repeated, she must tell me about it. If she does not inform me, she is lying. I do not need to ask her each evening, "Did you get into trouble at school?" She is obligated to reveal that information, and to conceal it is to deliberately mislead me without giving notification.

Marriages differ regarding the obligation to report without being asked if an extramarital affair has begun. If there is an explicit agreement to that effect, then I consider the failure to volunteer such information to be a lie. If there is no such agreement, then such a concealment should not be designated a lie. Commonly, partners differ about their expectations, or at least about their memory of their mutual obligations regarding the reporting of such liaisons.

Suppose the president had a minor stroke during the middle of his term of office, and the doctors concealed that fact. They would have committed a concealment lie since the American public expects to be told about a change in the president's health that affects his ability to do his job. Concealment and falsification are two different techniques for accomplishing the same objective. There are many reasons why liars will always prefer concealment to falsification if the situation allows it: the liar does not need to remember the false story; if caught, the liar can always claim she was just about to reveal the truth or didn't because she was certain the target knew what was going on.

Concealment and falsification are not the only techniques of lying, although they are the most common. I (Ekman, 1985) distinguished three other techniques. Telling the truth falsely occurs when the liar speaks the truth in such a way as to seem to mean the opposite of what is said. Consider the situation in which a wife asks her husband whether he met any attractive women on his business trip and he replies, "I sure did, I slept with a different one every night, and sometimes another one during the lunch break." If that was indeed the case, then the philandering husband would be telling the truth, but in a manner that implies he was faithful. Another technique is to tell a half-truth as if it were a whole truth. The wife who is asked by her husband if she is attracted to the next-door neighbor is telling a half-truth if she replies "he's nice" if she indeed is having an affair. What she has said is true, but she is deliberately leaving out the crucial information to mislead her husband. The incorrect inference dodge was identified by a newspaper columnist who recommended it as the solution to the problem of not wanting to be truthful to a friend who puts you on the spot. Suppose your friend has an exhibition of her paintings, and you think her work is terrible. The incorrect inference dodge would be to reply to her question about whether you like the paintings by saying "Incredible. I can't believe it. How did you do that!"

Bok (1982) defines intentional concealment as secrecy. I think that confuses matters, for notification is the issue in distinguishing secrecy from concealment lies. I reserve the term *secrecy* for a situation in which notification is given about the intention not to reveal information. By calling something a secret, we state our right not to reveal, to maintain privacy. Secrets may remain within one individual, or two or more people may maintain information they consider secret from others. To return to earlier examples, if my daughter has not told me about the trouble in school, that is not a secret; it is a concealment lie. When I ask her if she has a boyfriend, she may properly tell me "that's a secret." If she does indeed have a boyfriend, then she has concealed that from me, but because it is acknowledged, it is termed a secret. Suppose I have not asked her about this, but she knows of my interest from past conversations. If she does have a boyfriend but does not tell me, she is engaging in concealment, but it is not a secret because she has not acknowledged her right to conceal the truth, and it is not a lie because she has not agreed that there is an obligation to inform.

Lane and Wegner (1995), like Bok, do not distinguish secrets from other forms of concealment. They do provide a useful distinction between all forms of concealment and nonconcealment lies. In concealment, the truth is not presented, while in more typical lies—what I have termed falsifications—an untruth is presented as the truth. Their research has quite a different focus from my own, showing how what is concealed can turn into an obsession, requiring ever-increasing efforts to suppress. By my reasoning that would not occur for what I define as secrets, only for concealments in which the act of concealing is not revealed to those excluded from knowing the information.

A broken promise is not a lie. A week before President Bill Clinton took office, a reporter charged that he had broken his campaign promise about Haitian immigration since he was now adopting the position of former president George Bush, a policy he had criticized during the election campaign. With a trace of anger, Clinton defended himself, saying that the American people would think he was foolish if he did not change his policies when circumstances change. From my framework, Clinton was lying only if he had known at the time he criticized Bush that he intended to follow the same policy himself. Consider the charge that when President Bush raised taxes near the end of his term of office it showed he had lied when he said during the campaign "no new taxes." He could only be branded a liar if it could be proved he knew when he made the promise that he intended to break it.

The failure to remember is not a lie, although liars will often try to excuse their lies, once discovered, by claiming a memory failure. It is not uncommon to forget actions that one regrets, but if the forgetting truly has occurred, we should not consider that a lie, for there was no choice involved. Often it will not be possible to determine whether a memory failure has occurred or whether its invocation is itself a lie.

If someone provides a false account of what truly occurred, that does not necessarily mean the person intended to mislead, and as I explained earlier, if there is not a deliberate intent to mislead, a false statement should not be considered a lie. Why should it matter what we call a false statement? It is not simply a matter of semantics or definition. If the person is not lying, if the person does not believe he is engaged in deception at the moment he is doing it, then I expect his demeanor will be that of a truthful person. There should be no behavioral clues that the account is untrue if the person giving the account does not believe he is lying at the moment he gives the account. While I have no direct evidence for this prediction, it is consistent with my (Ekman, 1985) general theory of when demeanor will betray a lie, and other evidence (Ekman, Friesen, & O'Sullivan, 1988; Ekman, O'Sullivan, Friesen, & Scherer, 1991) does support that account. There are a number of ways in which people may provide false information that they believe to be true.

People do misinterpret events, especially the meaning of other people's actions and the motives that lead people to act one way or another. The fact that someone interprets matters in a way that reflects well upon her, a way that allows her to engage in actions she finds desirable, does not mean that she is necessarily lying rather than misinterpreting. I would not consider such an occurrence necessarily an instance of self-deception. Not every misunderstanding or misinterpretation is self-deception. Self-deception presumably occurs when the deceiver does not realize he is misleading himself and does not know his own motive for deceiving himself. It is a subtle matter to distinguish self-deception from rationalization—an attempt to excuse bad judgment or repression.

Consider an alleged rapist who claims that his victim wanted to have sex with him. Even though rapists who do know they had totally unwilling victims often make this claim, lying to avoid punishment, the claim itself does not tell us that it is false. Even if it is improbable, it conceivably might be true. Suppose it was a date rape, and the victim was shy or very fearful, protested only once, and not very strongly, and then did not resist. A rapist could misinterpret the initial protest and construe the subsequent lack of protest and passivity as consent. Would that rapist be a victim of self-deceit? Not, I believe, unless it was certain that he had no awareness that his misinterpretation of his victim's behavior was motivated by a wish to gratify his own needs. Did a rape occur? I believe the answer must be yes, although the rapist may not think it did and may be telling his truth when he claims his victim implicitly consented. And one of the reasons why someone who makes such a claim might appear believable in his demeanor is that he believes his claim and does not believe he is lying. (See Cross and Saxe [1992] for a discussion of this problem in the context of their critique of the use of polygraph testing in child sexual abuse cases.)

Of course, that is not the only reason someone may appear totally believable. I initially (Ekman, 1985) used the phrase *natural liar* to designate those people whose lies are seamless, whose demeanor is totally believable when they know they are lying. I have since (Ekman, 1992) changed the phrase to *natural performer*, since my studies suggest that they are not psychopaths or necessarily antisocial. Natural performers have the capacity to become the role they are playing, to nearly instantly believe for a time whatever they are saying, and because they believe they are saying the truth, their demeanor is totally credible.

Misinterpreting is not the only route by which someone may believe his false account is true. A person may initially know he is lying, but over time he may come to believe in his lie. If that happens, once he has come to believe his lie is a faithful account of what transpired, he may appear truthful. Consider a child molester who, when first accused, claimed that he was only cuddling the child, doing nothing that was really wrong, nothing the child did not want and enjoy. Even though he initially knew he was lying in his account, over time, with many repetitions of his lie, a molester could, I feel, come to believe his false story is true. It is conceivable that he could maintain in consciousness both the memory of the true event—that he forcibly abused the child—and the constructed belief that he only cuddled a willing child. Or the true memory might over time become much less accessible than the constructed belief, or perhaps not accessible at all.

Consider a child who deliberately lies, alleging that a teacher molested her, knowing that never occurred. Suppose the lying child was motivated by a wish to punish the teacher for having humiliated the child in class for not having done well on a test. If the child felt entitled to her revenge, she might reason that this was the kind of teacher who might have molested her, probably wanted to molest her, probably had molested other children, and so on. I believe we cannot rule out the possibility that over time, with many repetitions and elaborations, the child could come to believe she had been molested.

These examples are troublesome because we do not know how often they may occur. Nor do we know if children are more vulnerable than adults to believing what is false is true, nor do we know whether there are specific personality characteristics associated with this phenomenon. We have no certain way as yet to determine whether a memory is true, partially or totally constructed. We do have ways, which I will describe later, to distinguish a false account, but only when the person giving that account knows he is giving a false account.

Motives for Lying

My interviews with children (Ekman, 1989) and my data on adults from questionnaires suggest nine different motives for lying:

1. To avoid being punished. This is the most frequently mentioned motive by either children or adults. The punishment may be for a misdeed or for an accidental mistake.
2. To obtain a reward not otherwise readily obtainable. This is the second most commonly mentioned motive, by both children and adults.
3. To protect another person from being punished.
4. To protect oneself from the threat of physical harm. This is different from being punished, for the threat of harm is not for a misdeed. An example would be a child who is home alone telling a stranger at the door that his father is asleep and to come back later.
5. To win the admiration of others.
6. To get out of an awkward social situation. Examples are claiming to have a baby-sitter problem to get out of a dull party or ending a telephone conversation by saying someone is at the door.
7. To avoid embarrassment. The child who claims the wet seat resulted from water spilling, not wetting her pants, is an example if the child did not fear punishment, only embarrassment.
8. To maintain privacy without giving notification of the intention to maintain some information as private.
9. To exercise power over others by controlling the information the target has.

I am not certain that every lie would necessarily fit under one of these nine motives, but these are the motives that emerged from the interview data I collected. There are a variety of trivial deceits—lies of politeness and tact—that are not easily subsumed by these nine motives. By my definition these are not lies because the rules of politeness imply notification. A more difficult case is the lie required to maintain a surprise birthday party. Perhaps it should fit under the privacy motive.

Why Lies Fail

Many lies succeed. It is incumbent upon those interested in detecting lies to account for when lies will fail and when they will succeed. Such an account will not only tell us when behavioral clues may betray a lie, and what we should therefore attend to, but also provide guidelines for deciding which types of experimental deceptive scenarios can provide information relevant to particular real-life settings.

Certainly, it is not the arena that determines the success or failure of a lie. It is not that all spousal lies succeed and all political lies fail. Within every arena of life (and when one begins to consider the matter, there are few arenas in which deception does not occur), some lies fail and others succeed.

Lies fail for a variety of reasons that will not concern us here. For example, many lies are betrayed by someone in whom the liar had confided. Liars may also be betrayed by many other kinds of evidence that expose the liar's claims as false. My focus is not upon these types of betrayal but upon instances in which the liar's own behavior betrays the lie. I omit from such considerations instances in which the liar confesses (although much of my discussion is relevant to predicting when a liar will confess) and instances in which the liar might be judged to have acted in a way so that he or she would be caught. Instead, I am interested in those cases in which some aspect of the liar's behavior, despite his or her best intentions, betrays the liar's false pretense.

To put it briefly, before expanding upon this, there are two reasons why lies fail: one involves thinking and the other involves feeling. Lies fail either because the liar failed to adequately prepare or because of the interference of emotions.

I would predict that, in general (disregarding the type of lie, who is the liar, and who is the target and recognizing that disregarding these issues to make a general assertion is a very risky stance to take), most lies fail because the liar has not adequately prepared the false line he or she intends to maintain. One obvious, if not very interesting, example is when the liar forgets what he has said on one occasion and thoroughly contradicts himself on another occasion. Here, the source of clues to deceit is in the verbal content. One must be cautious about this, since truthful people will contradict themselves. However, I believe it would be possible, although I have not tried to do so, to specify the type of contradictions that are reliable signs of lying.

Another consequence of the failure to adequately prepare is being caught off guard when asked questions the liar had not anticipated and for which the liar has no ready reply. In such a jam, the liar must think of a credible answer on the spot. When doing so, most people will evidence various behaviors that signify they are thinking about what they are saying as they are talking. Pauses, gaze aversion, speech disfluencies, and speech mannerisms may all increase over what is usual for that person. And the use of the hands to illustrate speech (what Ekman and Friesen [1969b] termed *illustrators*) may increase, while voice intonation may flatten. Bear in mind that these are not signs of lying per se. There is no behavioral sign of lying itself, I maintain. But when these signs of thinking about a reply occur in contexts in which answers should be known without thought, they can betray the liar.

Lies are also betrayed by signs of emotions. The simplest case is one in which the liar attempts to fabricate convincingly an emotion that is not felt. Few people are good at this, although most of the time people get away with it since rarely does the target of such a lie care whether the emotion displayed is feigned or real. There are what I call "reliable" behavioral signs of emotion—reliable in the sense that few people can voluntarily display them at all or correctly. Narrowing the red margins of the lips in anger is an example of such a reliable sign of anger, typically missing when anger is feigned because most people cannot voluntarily make that movement. There are ways around this for the inventive liar, such as utilizing a Stanislavski-like technique to create the actual emotion, so that its involuntary signs will then appear unbidden.

More typically, lies about emotions do not simply involve fabricating an emotion but concealing an emotion that is actually being experienced. Often concealment goes hand in hand with fabrication, in which the liar uses a feigned emotion to mask signs of the emotion to be concealed. Such concealment attempts may be betrayed in either of two ways. Some sign of the concealed emotion may escape efforts to inhibit or mask it, providing what Ekman and Friesen (1969a) termed *leakage*. What they called a *deception cue*, which does not leak the concealed emotion but betrays the likelihood that a lie is being perpetrated, occurs when only an undecipherable fragment leaks. A deception clue also occurs when the very effort of having to conceal produces alterations in behavior that do not fit the liar's message.

Even when the lie is not about emotions, the liar's feelings about lying can betray the lie. Chief among these feelings about lying are the fear of being caught, guilt about lying, and what I have called *duping delight*—the pleasure and excitement of putting one over. Not all lies will call forth these emotions. Whether they do will depend upon characteristics of the liar, the target of the lie, and the content of the lie. Elsewhere (Ekman 1985) I have described in some detail a lying checklist that facilitates making a prediction about the likelihood that any of these emotions about lying will occur.

To give just a few examples, the fear of being caught is highest when the stakes for being caught—the reward that is lost and especially the punishment for being caught lying—are very high. The fear of being caught will also be greater if the liar has not practiced the lie and has not had the experience of having succeeded before in this very lie with this target. If the target is known to be both suspicious and of extraordinary acumen, the fear of being caught will be greater. Guilt about lying will be highest when the liar shares values with and respects the target, when the target is not collusively aiding the lie and does not benefit from the lie, and when the lie is in no way authorized by any social group or institution. Duping delight is enhanced when others who are allies of the liar observe the liar's actions.

While the arousal of any strong emotion—fear, guilt, or delight—produces changes in behavior that may be detectable and thereby betray the lie if they do not fit the liar's line, each emotion produces some unique behavioral signs. Elsewhere (Ekman, 1985) I have explained in detail how these emotions, and the very process of managing emotions, are manifest in face, body, voice, and paralinguistic behavior. Perhaps here it would be useful to mention that there is no one channel that is the best or most sensitive source for clues to deceit. Every aspect of behavior can provide such clues. And there are hints of individual differences as well, in terms of what behavioral source may be most profitable to scrutinize.

An astute lie catcher will assess the likelihood of any of these emotions, so as to better know what behaviors to be especially alert to. Also, such an exercise will alert the lie catcher as to when the truthful person may appear to be lying. One must not make Othello's error of presuming that a sign of fear is a sign of lying. The truthful person may, under some circumstances, be afraid of being disbelieved, or being thought guilty, or manifesting delight. The crucial issue is to examine the circumstances and evaluate whether or not a truthful or lying person would be experiencing these emotions.

Why Is It So Hard to Discern Truthfulness from Demeanor?

Our behavioral measurements of facial expressions and voice can distinguish when someone is lying, in a high-stakes lie about emotion felt at the moment, for 85 percent of the subjects (Ekman, O'Sullivan, Friesen, & Scherer 1991). Most observers, however, who are shown the videotapes and asked to judge who is lying do little better than chance, even members of the criminal justice community, such as FBI, local police, or judges, as well as members of the mental health community (Ekman & O'Sullivan, 1991).

I believe there are two reasons why most people are such poor judges of lying. The first reason I have no data to support; nevertheless, I believe that few people obtain corrective feedback about the accuracy of their judgments about who is lying and who is truthful. In workshops in which I try to improve the ability to detect deceit, I provide numerous examples of lying, providing such feedback. The second reason why most people do so poorly in judging deceit is that they rely too much upon what people say and ignore the discrepancies between the expressive behaviors and what is said. I have three kinds of evidence consistent with this explanation.

We have consistently (Ekman & O'Sullivan, 1991; Frank, Ekman, & Friesen, 1993) found that those observers who are accurate in identifying facial expressions when they are shown in a fraction of a second are more accurate in judging lying. The second type of evidence is that patients with left hemisphere damage, rendering them more impervious to the content of speech, are more accurate than normal subjects in detecting lying (Etcoff, Ekman, Frank, Torreano, &

Magee, 1992). The third type of evidence comes from a set of studies in which separate groups of observers were shown the face only, the body only, the voice (speech frequencies filtered out), and typescripts of what was said during the lying and truthful interviews. We then correlated our behavioral measurements with the judgments made by the observers who had seen either the full audio-video or the separated channels. The overall finding was that when the subjects were lying, the observers' judgments correlated only with the text measures. Duchenne's smile, leakage smiles, illustrators, and pitch—all of which differentiated the deception from the honest interview—were not correlated with the judgments of the deception interview made by the observers who were exposed to the full audio-video record.

It is not that the other nonverbal and vocal behaviors are not detectable. When we examined the judgments made by observers who only saw the face, we found that Duchenne's smiles were correlated with judgments. Similarly, when we examined the judgments made by observers who saw only the body, illustrators correlated with judgments of those who saw only the body, and changes in pitch were correlated with the judgments made by observers who heard only the speech.

In contrast to the nonverbal measures that were not correlated with the judgments of the audio-video presentation of the deception interview, nearly every measure of the verbal text and many of the vocal measures were correlated with observers' judgments of the audio-visual version of the deception interview. The only text measure not correlated with observers' judgments (the number of I's) and the only vocal measure not correlated with observers' judgments (pitch) were the only text and vocal measures that differentiated the honest from deception interviews.

To sum up these findings, the face, body, voice, and text clues that are most relevant to spotting deceit were ignored. Those behaviors that were least useful for differentiating when someone was lying were most relied upon when the observers responded to the audio-visual presentation of the deception interview. (These findings are reported in detail in Ekman, O'Sullivan, Friesen, & Scherer [1991]). This apparent failure of the observers to make use of the behaviors most relevant to detecting deceit fits with my (Ekman, 1985) notion that, in social life, people unwittingly collude in maintaining rather than uncovering deception.

Lies by Government

In 1990 I spent five weeks in Russia as an exchange professor at Leningrad State University, where I had earlier been a Fulbright lecturer in 1979. I found that everything was different and everything was the same. Now conversation was easy, criticism and discussion open, but there was much of the same bureaucracy and many of the same intimidating and unjust officials still in power. People were no longer afraid to talk to an American or to criticize their own government. "You have come to the right country," I was often told. "This is a country of lies! Seventy years of lies!" Again and again I was told by Russians that they had always known how much their government had lied to them. Yet in my five weeks there, I saw how stunned they were to learn about new lies they had not earlier suspected and the disillusionment many Russians felt because they believed that Gorbachev had lied to them, not revealing the truth about the extent of the Chernobyl disaster.

My long conversations with many different Russians caused me to think anew about the importance of trust in a democratic society. Although I recognize that there are occasions when political leaders must lie (e.g., former president Jimmy Carter's lie that we were not attempting to rescue the hostages at the American embassy in Iran), it is dangerous for governmental leaders to maintain a lie for long or engage in a pattern of widespread lying.

For decades Soviets learned that to achieve anything they had to bend and evade the rules. It became a country in which lying and cheating are normal, where everyone knows the system is corrupt and the rules unfair, and survival requires beating the system. Social institutions cannot work when everyone believes every rule is to be broken or dodged. I am not convinced that any change in government will quickly change such attitudes. No one now believes what anyone in the current government says about anything. Few I met believed Gorbachev, and that was a year before the coup. A nation cannot survive if no one believes what any leader says. This may be what makes people willing, eager perhaps, to give their allegiance to any strong leader whose claims are bold enough, and actions strong enough, to win back trust.

Americans joke about lying politicians—"How can you tell when a politician is lying? When he moves his lips!" My visit to Russia convinced me that, by contrast, Americans still expect their leaders to be truthful even though they suspect they will not always tell the truth. Laws work when most people believe they are fair, when it is a minority, not the majority, who feel it is right to violate any law. In a democracy, government only works if most people believe that most of the time they are told the truth and that there is some claim to fairness and justice.

No important relationship survives if trust is totally lost. If you discover your friend has betrayed you, lied to you repeatedly for his own advantage, that friendship cannot continue. Neither can a marriage be more than a shambles if one spouse learns that the other, not once but many times, has been a deceiver. I doubt any form of government can long survive without using force to oppress its own people if the people believe its leaders always lie.

Trust and truthfulness are not the only requirement. The political structure of the government is crucial. It is hard to establish trust unless people believe they have some control over the policies followed by their government.

It is a mistake to think that the relationship between nations is very similar to the relationship between individuals. The forces at work and the type of social institutions that generate decisions, policies, and actions are vastly different. Even when we consider what happens within a nation—the relationship between the government and the people—I believe it is misleading to use the concepts that are useful for characterizing the relationship between parent and child, husband and wife, or friends. It is easy to make such a mistake, to personalize the nature of government, because government is often symbolized by some representation of the personality of the leader. In a democracy, however, no leader has unchecked power; the network of forces that must be considered is far different from the factors that must be considered to understand the actions of an individual. Even in a dictatorship, the leader's power is not unbridled.

Yet some of the issues involved in lying—that it is not always wrong, that it may destroy trust, that trust may not always be repaired, that most lies eventually are detected—do apply to lies between individuals, lies between government and citizenry, and lies between nations. Some of the lessons we can learn about lying between nations are relevant to understanding lies that occur in friendships and within a family, and vice versa. There is still another reason why trust and lying within the family are relevant to the establishment of a just and decent public climate. Our attitudes about the morality of lying begin within the family, but they extend to all other types of interactions and relationships, even those between a government and its people.

Acknowledgments   Much of what I cover has been published in the second edition of my book *Telling Lies*, my book *Why Kids Lie*, and in articles listed in the reference section of this chapter. An exception is new distinctions between concealment lies and secrets I introduce in this chapter. Much of this material also has appeared in *Memory for Everyday and Emotional Events*, edited by N. L. Stein, P. A. Ornstein, B. Tversky, and C. Brainerd (Hillsdale, N.J.: Lawrence Erlbaum, 1996). The preparation of this chapter was supported by a Research Scientist Award from the National Institute of Mental Health (MH06092).

References

Bok, S. (1982). *Secrets*. New York: Pantheon.

Cross, T. P., & Saxe, L. (1992). A critique of the validity of polygraph testing in child sexual abuse cases. *Journal of Child Sexual Abuse*, 1, 19–33.

Ekman, P. (1985). *Telling lies: Clues to deceit in the marketplace, marriage, and politics*. New York: W. W. Norton.

Ekman, P. (1989). *Why kids lie*. New Uprl: Charles Scribner's Sons.

Ekman, P. (1992). *Telling lies: Clues to deceit in the marketplace, marriage, and politics* (2d ed.). New York: W. W. Norton.

Ekman, P., & Friesen, W. V. (1969a). Nonverbal leakage and clues to deception. *Psychiatry*, 32, 88–105.

Ekman, P., & Friesen, W. V. (1969b). The repertoire of nonverbal behavior: Categories, origins, usage, and coding. *Semiotica*, 1, 49–98.

Ekman, P., Friesen, W. V., & O'Sullivan, M. (1988). Smiles when lying. *Journal of Personality and Social Psychology*, 54, 414–420.

Ekman, P., & O'Sullivan, M. (1991). Who can catch a liar? *American Psychologist, 46,* 913–920.

Ekman, P., O'Sullivan, M., Friesen, W. V., & Scherer, K. R. (1991). Face, voice, and body in detecting deception. *Journal of Nonverbal Behavior, 15,* 125–135.

Etcoff, N. L., Ekman, P., Frank, M., Torreano, L., & Magee, J. (1992). Detecting deception: Do aphasics have an advantage? Paper presented at meeting of International Society for Research on Emotion, Pittsburgh, August.

Frank, M. G., Ekman, P., & Friesen, W. V. (1993). Behavioral markers and recognizability of the smile of enjoyment. *Journal of Personality and Social Psychology, 64,* 83–93.

Goffman, E. (1974). *Frame analysis.* New York: Harper and Row.

Lane, J. D., & Wegner, D. M. (1995). The cognitive consequences of secrecy. *Journal of Personality and Social Psychology, 69,* 237–253.

Advertising and Media

5

Russian Advertising in Search of Psychology

Dmitry A. Leontiev

A Brief History of Advertising in Russia

Western readers may be surprised to learn that advertising is not a new field for Russian psychologists. Its history in Russia, however, has been uneven with several separate periods that are loosely connected to each other.

The first period in the history of Russian advertising coincided with the extensive development of the advertising business all over the world—in the 1900s, before the revolution. This brief period of economic growth was heralded as the start of a New Economic Policy for Russia. It was marked with a burst of capitalist activity fueled by a newly convertible currency known as the "golden ruble." A variety of businesses grew in the periods before and immediately following the revolution, creating a short-lived but intense need for advertising.

No scientific bases were applicable to advertising or the delivery of other persuasive messages at that time. The first psychological institute was not established in Russia until 1911, and there was nothing like consumer advertising or mass-media communication in its research programs. The only psychological research program in 1920s that was relevant to this applied field was Vladimir Bekhterev's collective reflexology, a school of thought that he developed at the Leningrad Psychoneurological Institute. Although the theory of collective reflexology was potentially applicable to the field of advertising and other mass communication, Bekhterev never made the necessary links to develop this application.

There were few psychologists in Soviet Russia in the first quarter of the 20th century. Despite this fact, a review of the literature published in Russia/USSR in the 1920s shows that there were many books with recommendations on how to advertise. Some of them even have the word *psychology* in the title, demonstrating that the importance of psychology was well acknowledged by the authors in this field early in the century. Nevertheless, the authors were not psychologists; they did not have a basic psychological education and did not belong to the scientific community. They were amateurs with no formal study of the field, and all the psychological data given in these books were eclectic collections of separate facts gleaned from Western sources, such as references to Starch's (1923) work.

By 1930 the New Economic Policy was "killed," and the complete monopoly by the totalitarian state of all goods and services made advertising irrelevant. There was no competition or consumer choice in the Soviet-style planned economy. The task for the state-run businesses was to make the quantity of goods consumed equal to the quantity that was being produced. Feedback from the consumers consisted only of complaints. People had to buy inferior goods of all sorts because quality products were rare and nearly impossible to obtain. It soon became difficult for consumers to find even poor-quality products. Under this system, manufacturers had no incentives to improve the quality of their products because there were no negative consequences for producing poor-quality goods.

This does not mean that advertising did not exist in Soviet times but merely that there was no true advertising in the usual sense of the term. A new type of quasi-advertising was developed for the planned economy. The goal of quasi-advertising was to sell goods and services for which there was a surplus, either because they were too expensive or because people did not know the goods or services well enough to consider purchasing them. Classic examples of this can be seen in some early advertisements for perfumes and Aeroflot, the Soviet airline. All the big Soviet advertising sites in the 1970s were covered with large billboards and other signs bearing the slogan: "Fly Aeroflot!" This proclamation was especially curious because no other foreign or national air company could function in the Soviet Union. At the same time, many billboards promoted the taxi service in Moscow. In this case, as in many others, it was not necessary to state concretely what kind of taxi service was being advertised. One could write "Fly planes" instead of "Fly Aeroflot" because the meaning was the same since all goods and services belonged to one owner—the state.

I recollect a newspaper advertisement from the mid-1970s that exemplifies a second type of quasi-advertising. It was meant to persuade us to eat squid. A long and boring text described the many healthy substances—vitamins, minerals, and whatever else—squid contains. After this text on the nutritional value of squid, one more sentence followed: "Squid meat is not only healthy but also tasty."

After several decades without formal studies in advertising and mass communication, the professional journal *Reklama* (Advertising) was established in

1971, and a couple dozen books on advertising were published in the Soviet Union during the 1970s and 1980s. There were even some translations of Western sources on this topic (e.g., Reeves, 1961). Readers with some knowledge of the intellectual climate in the USSR at this time will not be surprised to learn that most of the translated books opened with the warning that advertising is of Western origins and for that reason, the reader should clearly differentiate the wrong, Western, capitalist advertising from the morally correct socialist advertising. The warnings went on to explain that socialist advertising is governed by the principles of party spirit and "planned character" and therefore represents the just use of methods of mass communication.

The only sphere where true advertising was needed at that time was foreign trade. In the 1960s, the Soviet state began to develop foreign trade with several different countries, which put it in direct competition with Western companies. Although foreign trade affairs were never independent of political affairs, in many cases there was real trade and real competition that required real advertising, as well. Specialized state-run foreign trade companies, such as Avtoexport, Tractoroexport, and others, invited professional psychologists to consult with them about how to frame their advertisements in ways that would result in more sales to foreign markets.

It was at the same time that new branches of fundamental and applied psychology—quite relevant to the problems of advertising—emerged in Russia. These were social psychology and communication research, revived after a 30-year blockade, and psycholinguistics and psychosemantics, fields of psychology that developed in the USSR in an original and creative way independent of research in the West. A new research group in psycholinguistics and communication theory was established in the mid-1960s at the Institute of Language Studies of the USSR Academy of Sciences. It immediately became the main source of psychological support for advertising, even though this support was weak. As I mentioned, this research group supported the foreign advertising efforts of the state with consultations and the publication of books and conference proceedings on somewhat related topics. The material in these publications was based mainly on Western sources, for there were still no systematic research programs connected with advertising. Only one book on the issues relevant to persuasive messages was written and published by psychologists from this group, *The Language of the Street* by Leonid Shkolnik and Evgenyi Tarassov (1977).

However, a closely related applied field—party propaganda—showed great interest in the psychology of persuasive communication, and many valuable studies were conducted and brilliant theoretical ideas developed under the aegis of support for the propaganda industry. It is doubtful whether these data and theories were ever used in creating or disseminating propaganda, but they greatly contributed to the development of Soviet social and general psychology, as well as advertising psychology. Some of the psychologists who contributed to the research in mass communication in the 1960s and 1970s—Leonid Shkolnik, Juri Sherkovin, and Olga Melnikova—are currently employed in the Russian advertising business.

Recent Developments

A newly revised psychology of advertising and mass communication was begun in the late 1980s, an immediate beneficiary of perestroika, when the authorities permitted establishment of private businesses. Newly established firms faced an enormous empty marketplace, one that was almost totally bereft of goods and services. Any more or less reasonable business proposal was destined to succeed without competition; its degree of success was limited only by consumer solvency. In this sort of no-lose market, the goal of advertising was reduced to providing publicity and spreading information about the availability of consumer goods so that the seller and buyer could find each other. There was no need to persuade consumers to purchase the products because they were desperate for almost any type of goods.

The slogan of these first years of the new era in Russian advertising (1988–1992) was "Everybody knows us!" Ironically, this became the real slogan of one of the most aggressive Russian trade companies, MMM, a company that swindled thousands of trusting Russians out of their life savings in the mid-1990s. As I write this chapter (1996), the president of MMM is promising that Russians who vote for his political party in the upcoming election will move ahead in the queue to get some of their money returned. Apparently, many cash-strapped Russians have promised to sell their vote to MMM. In another advertising move that divorced information about a product from a general plan to make the product name well known, MMM sometimes surprises metro riders with free tokens and other gimmicks so that their company name becomes associated with an image of generous gift giving. It does seem that everyone, at least in modern Russia, knows the company.

The tasks of publicity in an empty marketplace have nothing to do with the issue of quality, corporate image, or the competition of proposals. The concept of "unique trade proposal" (Reeves, 1961) explains the guaranteed success of all the advertising at the dawn of perestroika: when there is no competition, any proposal becomes unique, and the only "bad" advertisement is a missed opportunity to advertise. Media buying was the only real job of the people engaged in the advertising business. Almost all the advertising agencies established in the early years of perestroika grew from advertising departments of mass media— newspapers, television channels, and broadcasting stations. Not surprisingly, there is much conceptual and actual overlap between advertising and other forms of mass-media communication.

The second stage in the contemporary period for advertising began in 1992. The competition was growing at an exponential rate, and even though the market is still far from being satiated, some market sectors now provide consumers with the possibility of choice. There are still enough consumers for every product on the market, so competition among manufacturers and other types of producers has not reached a level in which businesses actually have to compete for their share of the consumer market. Now that the Russian public has some real choices among brands and types of products for the first time in their lives, another dominant goal for advertising has been created—namely, to stand out. Advertising has proliferated and intruded into the everyday life of most Russians. The steady stream of commercials on television, in the metro, on billboards, and in the newspapers has become irritating to most Russians, for whom this is a new phenomenon. The prime task of every advertisement in this flood of advertisements is to draw the consumer's attention to the message.

Russian businesspeople have begun to understand that effective advertisement is an art. They have become mindful of their public image and are developing public relations departments and long-term advertising plans. The second generation of advertising agencies grew from groups producing advertisements of high quality, often working in specialized design and video studios, printing businesses, and allied companies that are prevalent in the West. Several professional periodicals have been recently established: *Greatis* (since 1993), *Reklamnyi Mir* (The advertising world; since 1994), *Kampaniya* (Campaign; since 1994), and *Reklamist* (Advertising man; since 1994).

This change of emphasis from quasi-advertising in a planned economy to true advertising for a competitive marketplace generated a significant demand for professional psychologists in the advertising business, where they serve as researchers, trainers, professors, and consultants. Graduates of the department of psychology at Moscow State University from the mid-1980s are now heads of research and creative departments of the largest Moscow advertising agencies: Avrora and Premiere-SV. Psychologists at universities and research institutes have also started to pay more attention to the field of advertising psychology. They are planning independent research and proposing direct services for advertising agencies and other firms. The interest among academic psychologists is understandable given the inequities in salary that have been created by the capitalist system. The salaries of faculty and research staff in Russia are still very low, equivalent to $100 a month, so many academic psychologists see the advertising business as a solvent second employer. Psychology students are designing their programs of study to find profitable and creative employment in the advertising business after graduation. The demand for psychological support in the advertising industry is still in its earliest stages. It seems likely that demand will increase exponentially in the next years.

The signs of the new shift in emphasis for advertising have become noticeable. A competitive market is now the rule, and to stand out among one's competition is necessary but not enough to be chosen. What is needed at this third stage of development in Russian advertising is to provide the optimal, planned effect on consumers. Agencies have begun to understand that advertising is as much a science as an art and that this science is psychology more than anything else.

It is quite natural that the psychologists who have gained recognition as specialists in the field of advertising psychology moved to this field from related branches of psychology, especially the social psychology of communication and mass media (e.g., Juri Sherkovin, Olga Melnikova, Lidia Matveyeva), psycholinguistics (Leonid Shkolnik), cognitive psychology of perception (Viktor

Belopolskii), psychosemantics and empirical aesthetics (the present author). Today, however, still relatively few professional psychologists work in the advertising field—perhaps no more than 100 in Moscow and hardly more than 100 in all other cities of Russia taken together; the number of true experts of universal competence in this field does not exceed a dozen.

Psychological Techniques that Work in Advertising

Seven types of psychological processes are directly relevant to the process of creating advertisements. Correspondingly, seven psychological technologies must be used to create an effective advertisement (Leontiev, 1995). Despite the potential benefit, currently only two or three of them have been mastered and are used in practice.

1. Control attention. In order to stand out, an advertisement must attract and keep the attention of the reader or viewer. The devices to reach this goal are numerous and relatively well established, although they are often misused. What I mean by misuse is what Reeves (1961) called "vampire images," advertisements that draw the reader's or viewer's attention to the advertisement itself but not to the object of the advertisement. A comprehensive psychological analysis of this aspect of advertising was given in a recent paper by Belopolskii (1995).

2. Provide optimal perception. In order to be perceived effectively, an advertisement or other type of commercial must be designed in a way that considers the normal functioning of the human visual and auditory systems. An advertisement must not create strain for the vision and/or auditory systems; it must be comfortable for normal perceptual processes. Many principles in perception need to be considered for this aspect of advertising. These principles constitute the ergonomics of advertising and include such factors as the density of text in an advertisement, the size of fonts, the quantity of text in billboards, the speed and brightness of electronic signs, and the speed and volume of radio spots. Some of these principles are listed and analyzed in the paper by Belopolskii (1995), referenced above. A large portion of the information provided in advertisements will be lost if the designer is not mindful of the operating principles of the perceptual systems. Despite the obvious importance of this factor, it is still unusual to use these regularities consciously in present-day advertising practice.

3. Create a semantic charge. It is now well known that people can have definitive impressions about a company or product about which they have no relevant information: people may unconsciously experience a company or product as large or small, intellectual or stupid, modern or archaic, reliable or unreliable. This impression is referred to as the "semantic charge" of the firm's or product's name, its logo, color palette of advertisements, voice timbre of its public speakers, and other factors that are not relevant to product quality. Experimental psychosemantic laboratories all over the world have created a large

repertoire of techniques to assess the unconscious semantics of an advertising image. This information is then used to understand the semantic charge of an advertisement and the product it is touting. These regularities created by the advertisment are not yet used in advertising practice, but there are several interesting studies of semantic charge that can contribute to the psychological investigation of advertising.

It is worth noting that Russian psychosemantics is quite different from the field as practiced in the West. We have developed several original approaches that are, in my opinion, far ahead of Western developments in this field. One of them is the study of phonosemantics that was developed by Alexander Zhuravlev, a Russian professor who works now in New York. Zhuravlev discovered that the sounds of speech each have a stable semantic charge—that is, a meaning and emotion attached to them. After a long series of experiments, he succeeded in deriving formulas that allowed him to calculate the phonosemantic charge of any word or speech sound. He discovered the rule of correspondence between meaning and phonosemantic charge for meaningful words. Interested readers can learn more about his methods from his principal book, *Sound and Meaning* (1991). He used the mathematical formulas to analyze the historical development of the Russian language according to the rule of correspondence. Later, he successfully used the phonosemantic regularities of speech sounds to assess the emotional state of a text. He was even able to determine the emotional state of cosmonauts by applying his method of phonosemantic analysis to a radio communication that was recorded during a prolonged flight.

Another original approach that relies on the psychosemantic analysis of a message is the psychology of subjective semantics developed by Yelena Artemyeva. I explain the underlying concepts in greater detail in a later portion of this chapter.

4. Construct an aesthetic advertisement. An advertisement must be beautiful and expressive from the aesthetic viewpoint. Many of the regularities of empirical aesthetics can be directly applied to the construction of an advertisement. It seems that the aesthetic side of advertising is well mastered and exploited in television commercials, but daily newspaper advertisements are far from being aesthetically satisfactory. There is a body of interesting and relevant psychological research that pertains to the aesthetics of advertising. Much of the research in this field was conducted for the purpose of designing effective ideological propaganda (e.g., Kudin, Lomov, & Mit'kin, 1987). Nevertheless, the findings are directly applicable to the general field of advertising and need to be considered when an advertisement is being planned.

5. Consider the language structure of advertisements. Some psycholinguistic regularities are important in writing the text portion of an advertisement: the rules of text readability that depend on the length of the words and sentences; common barriers to understanding, which include the lexical match between the text and the target population; foreseen and unforeseen ambiguities; and many other similar factors. There is a large body of psychological data on all of these issues, most of which was collected in fields other than advertising.

6. Use neurolinguistic programming. This branch of psychological technology is at the peak of fashion in Russia. The neurolinguistic programming techniques are aimed at increasing confidence in the source of information. In my opinion, this psychological aspect of advertising is the least important among the seven because an advertisement can be very effective without considering these techniques. Many Russian psychologists believe that its presence provides benefits, but its absence does not cause losses in the effectiveness of an advertisement. [Note from the American editor: Independent studies sponsored by the U.S. government have shown that neurolinguistic programming is not effective in enhancing learning and memory, a result that is likely to be challenged over the next few years.]

7. Use sense technology. This special term is connected with one of the central concepts of the activity theory approach in Russian psychology, the concept of personal sense. The term refers to the use of human motivation to create an attractive personal sense (motivation-based significance, or incentive) of the goods and services being promoted. Sense technology is relevant in creating trade proposals and slogans. Motivational research is rarely considered by psychologists who work in advertising. A popular Western book on this topic was written by Packard (1957) nearly forty years ago; for most Russian psychologists who are still at the beginning stages in this area of inquiry, it would be something completely new.

It is against this background of the social and scientific context of advertising psychology in Russia that I now present some of the ideas underlying my research and applied work in this field, along with relevant experimental data.

Psychosemantics and Subjective Semantics

There is a long-established paradigm in psychosemantics used to measure advertisements in terms of their subjective meaning. This paradigm was developed over the last three decades and has been used successfully to generate important results that bear on advertising. I refer, for example, to the data obtained in the study Advertising in the Worldview, performed for the bimonthly newspaper *Reklamist* by Mikhail Dymshits and Galina Berkausova (1995). Several samples (top managers of large Russian and Western advertising agencies, top managers of Russian companies not involved in advertising, schoolchildren in Moscow from the 5–6th and 10–11th grades) used 20-scale semantic differentials to evaluate the following notions: "me"; "advertising as I see it in media"; "the business of advertising as I see it"; "modern art"; and "modern business." In a semantic differential paradigm, subjects are given several different scales with the end of each scale labeled with a word that is the opposite of the word found at the other end. For example, a series of lines could be marked at each end with the following pairs of opposites: near–far, pretty–ugly, like me–not like me, silly–serious, and so on. Subjects place a mark on each line to show where the concept they are judging falls between the two opposite poles. If a subject saw herself as moderately pretty, for example, she would mark the line labeled "pretty–ugly" close to the end labeled "pretty." She would then go on and make similar judgments about herself on each of the other lines.

Results of this study showed that all of the samples of subjects, except for the youngest children, conceptualized advertising as very far from all the other notions and describe it as "silly," "merry," "loud," and "distant." Only the children perceived advertising as something "close" and "of their own."

Another example of using psychosemantic methods to advance the goals of advertising comes from an applied study by Valery Busin (1993). The task for the researcher in this study was to assess the image of four sorts of perfume oils in order to design effective advertisements. A special version of the technique of semantic differential was construed to describe the scents. The subjects smelled each of the perfume oils and then completed the semantic differential scales based on their feelings about the scent. Basin found that the profiles for two of the perfumes, Chanel No. 5 and Poison, were very similar. Beautiful (another perfume) differed from both Chanel No. 5 and Poison, and White Linen (the fourth perfume) differed most among these four perfumes. The scale whose end points were labeled "morning–evening" was the one that discriminated best among these four perfumes.

In traditional psychosemantic paradigms, researchers examine the subjective representations and judgments of advertisements rather than the overall psychological effect created by the advertisements. A new approach based on the psychology of subjective semantics seems to offer more possibilities beyond those available with standard psychosemantic measurement. The theory and methodology of subjective semantics were elaborated in the 1980s at Moscow State University. Artemyeva (1980, 1986a, 1986b) stated that human experience conserves the traces of one's encounters with different objects of the world in the form of amodal semantic codes of the objects. A semantic code describes an object in terms of its emotional values rather than its objective properties, providing the fast recognition and discrimination of different objects by their personal sense and regulating the subject's interaction with the objects. A semantic code can be explicated with several different procedures involving both verbal and nonverbal responses and direct and metaphorical semantic descriptions. Studies of semantic code use a version of semantic differential with either/or dichotomies and do not permit the subject to provide intermediate responses. For example, instead of deciding where a particular concept falls on the scale "pretty–ugly," the subject must select only one of the two categories of "pretty" or "ugly" when responding. In standard semantic differential paradigms, several different dimensions are combined to yield an underlying dimension, such as several different pairs of labels that would denote some aspect of being attractive or unattractive. Studies of semantic code do not combine measures in this way.

Artemyeva (1980) devised a method for measuring the intensity or saliency of the semantic code of an object. This concept was then tested in an applied setting by comparing the intensity of the semantic code for the unique jewelry of the 18th century shown at a museum exhibition, the jewelry of the 19th century selected from a private collection, and more ordinary present-day jewelry (each group consisted of three objects). Artemyeva (1986a) found a significant decline in the intensity of the semantic code for the jewelry in the second group when compared with the unique collection in the first group and an even larger decline in intensity for the jewelry in the third group. In another study, subjects showed a significantly higher intensity of semantic code for the Uspensky cathedral in Kondopoga (northern Russia) when seen as a real object than when shown in a photo. Numerous other studies have shown the value of this approach.

The methods of subjective semantics have been successfully applied by the present author to study aesthetic impressions of works of art (Leontiev, 1991; Leontiev & Yemelyanov, 1994; Leontiev, Delskaya, & Nazarova, 1994). To summarize the main results from this series of studies, my colleagues and I managed to access semantic codes not only for separate works of art but also for the way subjects anticipated them (such as an evaluation of a forthcoming play before it opened) and of their elements (evaluation of a sound shape of a poem recited in an unknown language). All semantic codes show a significant degree of intragroup invariance, although in different samples somewhat different scales contribute to the semantic code of a given object. These differences, however, never show contradictions. In other words, if one group defines the salient attributes of an object as beautiful or smooth, another group may list other dimensions as salient, such as big or slow, while beauty and smoothness are less significant to the second group, but it would be extremely rare for another group to select opposite attributes, such as ugly or rough.

We have shown that it is possible to use nonverbal scales to assess the semantic codes of significant objects. We used, for example, the Color Attitude Test (Etkind, 1987), which is a modification of the Luscher Color Test. It allowed us to capture a subjective representation of an object using a succession of colors that subjects found to be associated with this object. The Color Attitude Test shows individual peculiarities of different objects better than the semantic differential. Correspondingly, it is not as good as the semantic differential at picking up similarities in the semantic nature of objects. Color associations to different objects proved to be consistent among different subjects; a special measure of their congruence analogous to the intensity of a semantic code has been calculated and applied successfully. The most recent study using the Color Attitude Test (Leontiev, Chugunova, & Zherdeva, 1995) was devoted to the analysis of semantic codes of several genres of mass literature—criminal novels, science fiction, and books for children—and specific examples of books selected from these genres and rated by subjects who had not read the books. These studies show that people attach strong "meanings" to objects about which they have little or no knowledge. Among the many results from this large study with six different samples of subjects, I want to highlight the finding that judgments often depend on whether the subject likes a particular genre of literature, but the dimension of liking is not always relevant to the meaning that is attached to the object being judged.

Psychological Conceptions of the Images Used in Advertising

It follows from the theory of subjective semantics that every object in our environment, concrete or abstract, has some semantic charge. Feelings and meanings are attached to the objects with which we interact, and these feelings and meanings (charge) are relatively stable and shared, for the most part, by other people. The methodological tools of subjective semantics make it possible to assess and describe the semantic charge of any given set of objects within a unified frame of reference. From the viewpoint of advertising, this statement means that, for instance, the name of a firm, its logo, corporate colors, television commercials, newspaper advertisements, radio spots, outdoor posters, and office interior can be compared as to whether they carry the same or similar semantic charge, whether this charge is favorable for the goals of a firm, and whether the charge corresponds to the corporate conception of the desired image. A steel company, for example, may want to convey a hard, strong image. The techniques described here allow an investigator to determine whether the firm's advertisements, logos, and packaging are all conveying this same charge of a strong company.

The research possibilities of semantic charge have manifold consequences for the theory and practice of image formation in advertising. It is widely acknowledged that besides, or sometimes instead of, a rational trade proposal in advertisements, there must be a favorable irrational image that would unconsciously attract customers. The point is that a firm inevitably has some image among the public, even if it does not design its advertising and public relations in accord with a specific plan to create an image and whether it wants one or not. This image may not be clear or highly detailed, but it exists and can be revealed. It cannot be reduced to the general evaluation of "good versus bad" but includes many other dimensions such as "national–international," "modern–traditional," "strong–weak," "fast–slow," "sweet–sour," and so on. Semantic charge is the psychological basis of the image.

Given the reality that every firm has an image, how can we use these data to construct a desirable image? Image construction is based on two key principles: the design and unity of the image. The design principle requires that any advertising activity of a firm must begin with an elaboration of the desired image for the firm in terms of the semantic differential dichotomies (e.g., strong, not weak; efficient, not inefficient). The unity principle means that all of the advertisements and all of the various forms in which the firm presents itself to the outside world (interior design, windows, logo, etc.) must carry the same underlying image—that is, the same semantic charge. This last point allows us to give a new interpretation to the old rule of repetition. The role of repetition in advertising has been acknowledged since its early years. If you want to have your advertisement rooted in your audience's minds, you must continue to repeat your message. But it is not only your text that must be repeated but also the underlying image, the semantic charge that you want associated with your firm. If different advertisements for your firm carry different images, even though the explicitly stated message may be the same, they will not penetrate the customer's memory because he or she will not be able to catch a consistent image. On the other hand, if different advertisements carry the same underlying image, they will be experienced with recognition even if the texts are different. The task for psychologists is to test the underlying images of all the elements of a firm's public manifestations and to charge them with the semantic code that is in line with the firm's conception of the desired image.

In the work conducted in my research group, we developed instruments to assess underlying images as fully as possible, beginning with the main image carriers: names and logos. All of the following studies were conducted as part of a research agenda and were not performed under contract to private agencies.

The first study (Olefirenko, 1992) was aimed at investigating the possibilities of using free associations to assess an underlying image. We studied the contribution of "titles" like "joint venture," "small venture," "Ltd.," "firm," and "Co." to determine the general image created by each. Twenty psychology students served as subjects. They were presented the names of five firms, each with one of these five titles in random combinations. The subjects were asked, first, to give free associations to each of the names combined with one of the five titles; second, to guess the sphere of its business; and third, to judge it using the Color Attitude Test. Then we analyzed the structures of free associates to each of the names, the differences determined by the titles, and the congruence of color associations to names and titles independently, as well as to their combinations.

The five names fell into two distinct groups based on responses to the free associations and guesses about the nature of the business in which each company engaged. Titles such as "Russkii ekspress" (Russian Express) and "Smysl" (Meaning) provided a limited number of clearly differentiated bundles of associations and guesses: transportation, mail, tourism, or fast food in the first case and publishing, psychological counseling, or intellectual services in the second case. The combination "Russian Express Co." gives much more favorable and congruent color estimates than all the other combinations. For "Smysl," on the contrary, the title "Co." is quite unfavorable, like "Ltd."; it is assessed most favorably when it is combined with the title "firm."

In a more recent study (Leontiev & Olefirenko, 1994), the objects of assessment were names and logos of ten Moscow banks. Forty subjects with no connections to psychology or banking gave free associations to each of the logos, to each of the names, and then to judgments about them using a specially construed 27-scale semantic differential with either/or choice.

Most of the names yielded up to four bundles of associations, each either directly connected with banking activity or more or less appropriate to it: "Technobank"—techno music, technology, technical progress; "Unicombank"—universal, unique; "Incombank"—income, international, foreign, and so on. Several names, such as "Vostok Bank" (East Bank), "Elbim Bank," "Sinektika Bank," gave very fuzzy associations unrelated to banking. Quite a peculiar associative field was elicited to the name "Gloria Bank." Its strongest bundle of associations was connected with a woman and womanly traits. Female subjects described it as beautiful, coquettish, and refined; male subjects described it as beautiful, insidious, coquettish, and "light." Many other associations conformed to this image, including a flower, a horse, and a perfume scent. Many subjects said that it was a nice name but not a solid name for a bank. It was judged as more appropriate for a boutique than for a bank.

The structure of free associations aroused by the logos is somewhat more complicated (the subjects did not know that the logos belonged to banks). Many of the associations were direct emotional impressions of the pictures themselves. These impressions were never positive, in four cases they were neutral, and in six cases they were negative. Guesses about the spheres of activity were never close to reality. The logo for Technobank reminded subjects of an architecture firm; the logo of Mezhcombank, of a drug store or hairdressing salon; and that of Vostok Bank, of transportation and medicine. Some of the free associations were connected with a cultural context: Ancient Egypt for Unicombank, which had a stylized lion in its logo; and the Soviet state for Technobank and Elbim Bank.

The results of the semantic differential were tallied for male and female subjects separately. In order to obtain a content description of the underlying images, we included in it the semantic differential judgments shared by at least 80 percent of the sample. The results make it possible to infer regularities:

1. It was possible to identify the underlying image for almost every object that was studied.
2. In general, logos give more definite and more congruent estimates than names.
3. The results of male and female subjects significantly differ in many respects. Male subjects tend to give more negative judgments than female subjects. Here is an example illustrating these regularities:

    Technobank logo
        males: pragmatic, cool, foreign, faceless, ugly, wicked, distant
        females: distant, pragmatic, correct
    Technobank name
        males: no congruent estimates
        females: ordinary

We tried also to find the correspondence between the names and the logos using the mathematical techniques of cluster analysis. In the female sample, the names and logos of only three banks (Incombank, Elbim Bank, and Sinektika Bank) were fairly congruent, and those of two (Technobank and Orbita Bank) were somewhat less congruent. This means that there were no contradictions between the underlying images associated with the name and the logo, but some logos of other banks provided a better fit to the names of other banks than their own name.

We see that Russian experimental psychological research in advertising is extremely interesting in both its applied and academic aspects. The approach based on the psychology of subjective semantics has considerable potential that has not yet been realized in the psychology of advertising, as well as in other branches of psychology. To be sure, this is not the only approach of value. In the final section of this paper, I describe other interesting types of research.

Other Research Paradigms

The possibility of using expert judgments with direct verbal impressions and other indirect methods was investigated in a pilot study by the present author and Alexander Shmelev, a colleague at Moscow State University (1994). Nineteen subjects, all psychology students, watched 11 television commercials, which they were to evaluate using 50 criteria, half of which reflected some aspects of their subjective impressions and half using objective parameters. A sample of expert subjects evaluated each "spot" immediately after watching it once, using a 5-point scale. The data were collected with the computer program Expan (Human Technologies agency, Moscow).

Factor analysis revealed 6 significant factors after rotation. The first, accounting for 10.1 percent of the variance, is almost unipolar: 16 variables describing various aspects of creative commercials are opposed to the single variable, official. This factor was labeled creativity. The second factor is also nearly unipolar and includes variables such as modern style, technology, concrete proposal, pragmatism, aggressiveness, and 16 other variables. On the opposite pole we find two variables: narrative and originality. This factor was called modern style. The third factor is completely unipolar and includes 10 variables reflecting different aspects of positive evaluation: range, activity, success, honesty, aggressiveness, originality, arrangement, optimism, attractiveness, dynamism. This is evidently a factor representing a general evaluation. Factor 4 is purely technical: montage and animation versus narrative. Factor 5 is composed of such variables as patriotism, conservatism, high spirituality, intellectuality, retro-style, official style, well-known music, arrangement, humanism, elite spirit, intrigue, as opposed to the single variable: original music. This factor was labeled social values. A final factor covers the single-pole 11 variables that refer to originality. In this way, we found the sorts of judgments that subjects were using when they were watching the television advertisements.

In a series of experiments performed with Nadezhda Astakhova (Leontiev & Astakhova, 1994), we investigated the conditions favorable for a newspaper advertisement to stand out. Several ecologically valid experiments with different designs provided similar results: a close to zero correlation between the size of the advertisement and the probability that it will be noticed by the subjects. What differentiated the well-noticed advertisements from the scarcely noticeable ones was that the well-noticed advertisements began with the information being conveyed rather than with the firm's name, they were characterized by an absence of redundant text, and the ergonomics of well-noticed advertisements made them easy to read.

Some very subtle mechanisms in the perception of television commercials have emerged from a refined experiment by Leonid Radayev (1993). Radayev tried to find out which elements of televised commercial are crucial for their recognition. He created different degrees of distortion of the video and/or soundtrack and then checked for how well they were recognized. It turned out that the best objects for identification are human characters because they are recognizable under various degrees of distortion. The best spots are usually recognized in the first sequence; ordinary spots take longer to be recognized.

This paper is the first review of Russian post-Soviet advertising psychology. Even a year ago, one could not find enough material even for a single review paper. Nowadays, though this applied branch of psychology cannot be called developed, it surely is developing very quickly. A new generation of professionals, educated in the new economic conditions, will soon play the major roles in the psychology of advertising. There is lack of experience, lack of engaged people, lack of finances, lack of tested technologies, but no lack of interest or creative ideas.

There are obvious cultural influences on the effectiveness of advertisements and other types of mass communication that still need to be understood. It is well known that the same advertising is perceived differently in different countries and cultures. Russian professionals know that Western advertisements often do not work in Russia without special transformations. I do not know, however, of any cross-cultural studies in the psychology of advertising that include Russia. It would be especially interesting to investigate the reasons for these differences in the effectiveness of an advertisement because advertising is directly connected with the mentality of a culture. The devices and tricks that are effective for selling correspond to subtle mechanisms of human consciousness, and this makes the field of advertising a very important proving ground for the so-called nonclassical psychology (see Sobkin & Leontiev, 1992), which studies the human psyche through cultural objects and constructions such as art. Lev Vygotsky, the great Russian psychologist, called art "the social technique of emotion" (1971, p. 249). But this definition fits advertising as well, doesn't it? These considerations underlie my vision of the psychology of advertising: it will always be an applied discipline, but it must become an academic discipline as well, revealing our most intimate mechanisms of waking up and moving the human soul.

References

Artemyeva, Ye. Yu. (1980). *Psikhologiya subyektivnoi semantiki.* (The psychology of subjective semantics.) Moscow: Moscow University Press. (In Russian.)
Artemyeva, Ye. Yu. (1986a). Psikhologiya subyektivnoi semantiki. (The psychology of subjective semantics.) Dr. sci. thesis, Moscow State University. (In Russian.)
Artemyeva, Ye. Yu. (1986b). Semanticheskie aspekty izucheniya pam'atnikov kultury. (Semantic aspects of studying cultural memorials.) In *Pam'atnikovedenie: Teoriya,*

metodologiya, praktika (Monumentology: Theory, methodology, practice) (pp. 62–75). Moscow: Institute for Culture Studies. (In Russian.)

Bekhterev, V. M. (1991). *Kollektivnaya refleksologiya* (Collective reflexology.) Moscow-Petrograd: Kolos Publishers. (In Russian.)

Belopolskii, V. I. (1995). Psikhologicheskie osnovy vospriyatiya pechatnoi reklamy. (Psychological bases of perception of printed ads.) In V. A. Bodrov (ed.), *Psikhologiya predprinimatelskoi deyatelnosti* (The psychology of business activity) (pp. 152–173). Moscow: Institute of Psychology of Russian Academy of Sciences. (In Russian.)

Busin, V. N. (1993). Psikhosenticheskij analiz kosmeticheshkikh zapakhov. (Psycho-semantic analysis of perfume scents.) Unpublished report. Moscow State University. (In Russian.)

Dymshits, M., & Berkausova, G. (1995). Reklama i obshestvo: Vavilonskaya bashnia ili beg navstrechu? (Advertising and society: Babilon tower or meeting together?) *Reklamist*, 2(5), 15. (In Russian.)

Etkind, A. M. (1987). Tsvetovoi test otnoshenii. (Color attitude test). In A. Bodalyov and V. Stolin (eds.), *Obshchaya psikhodiagnostika* (General psychological assessment) (pp. 221–227). Moscow: Moscow University Press. (In Russian.)

Kudin, P. A., Lomov, B. F., & Mit'kin, A. A. (1987). *Psikhologiya vospriyatiya i iskusstvo plakata.* (Psychology of perception and the art of the poster.) Moscow: Plakat. (In Russian.)

Leontiev, D. A. (1991). Measuring the effects of art. In *Metrum of art: Third international conference on aesthetics* (pp. 82–88). Krakow: Jagiellonian University.

Leontiev, D. A. (1995). Kakaya reklama nuzhna banku? (What kind of advertising is needed for a bank?) *Noveishiye Bankovskie Technologii* (Newest Banking Technologies) 5, pp.53–55. (In Russian.)

Leontiev, D. A., & Astakhova, N. (1994). *Dumaite o psikhologii, yesli vas interesuyet resultat.* (Consider psychology if you are interested in results.) *Reklami Mir*, 7, 5. (In Russian.)

Leontiev, D. A., with Chugunova, I., & Zherdeva, N. (1995). Unconscious mechanisms of shaping impressions and evaluations of mass fiction. Unpublished report. Moscow State University. (In Russian.)

Leontiev, D. A., Delskaya, T. A., & Nazarova, M. (1994). Images of a theater play: Expectations, impressions, and group differences. In C. Dreyer et al. (eds.), *Life world: Sign world* (vol. 2, pp. 799–814). Lueneburg: Jansen-Verlag.

Leontiev, D. A., & Olefirenko, L. V. (1995). Nazvniya I logotipy kak nositeli obraza. (Names and logos as image carriers.) In *Zhurnalistike v 1995 gody: Tezisy konferentsii* (Journalistics in 1995: Conference abstracts) (part 4, 53–55). Moscow. (In Russian.)

Leontiev, D. A., & Shmelov, A. G. (1994). Factor structure of the evaluation of TV commercials. Unpublished report. Moscow State University. (In Russian.)

Leontiev, D. A., & Yemelyanov, G. A. (1994). Catching psychological effects of poetic form: Experiments with patodies and translations. *SPIEL*, 13(1), 101–113.

Olefirenko, L. (1992). Impressiveness of firms' names and titles: Students' yearly research report. Unpublished report. Moscow State University. (In Russian.)

Packard, V. (1957). *The hidden persuaders.* New York: Pocket Books.

Radayev, L. V. (1993). The problem of adequacy of influence and means by the creation of complicated images in advertising. Unpublished graduate student report. Moscow State University. (In Russian.)

Reeves, R. (1961). *Reality in advertising.* New York: Knopf.

Shkolnik, L. S., & Tarassov, E. F. (1977). *Jazyk ulitsy.* (The language of the street.) Moscow: Nauka. (In Russian.)

Sobkin, V. S., & Leontiev, D. A. (1992). The beginning of a new psychology: Vygotsky's psychology of art. In G. Cupchik and J. Laszlo (eds.), *Emerging visions of the aesthetic process* (pp. 185–193). Cambridge: Cambridge University Press.

Starch, D. (1923). *Principles of advertising.* Chicago: A. W. Shaw.

Vygotsky, L. S. (1971). *The psychology of art.* Cambridge, Mass.: MIT Press.

Zhuravlev, A. P. (1991). *Zvuk i smysl.* (Sound and meaning.) (2d ed., rev.) Moscow: Prosveshchenie. (In Russian.)

6

The Social Psychology of Mass Communications

An American Perspective

Anthony R. Pratkanis

Whether it is the genes of royalty, the ritual of tradition, or the force of a dictator, every society must have a way to make decisions. Early in its history, the United States opted for persuasion—debate, discussion, exhortation, and argument—as a means of deciding which course of collective action to take. Early American institutions promoted persuasion and discourse (Holifield, 1989). For example, in contrast to the elaborate cathedrals of Europe, where elite clergy performed rituals before a distant congregation, colonial churches were small, simple structures with a pulpit placed close to the people; such architecture is ideal for sermons exhorting townsfolk to morality or for a political rally to debate the course of a revolution. Many towns developed around a village green featuring a hall for holding town meetings and a market where consumers could decide the best products to buy. When the new Americans ratified the U.S. Constitution and later the Bill Rights, they ensured that persuasion would remain at the heart of U.S. decision making by guaranteeing freedom of speech, freedom of the press, and the rights of assembly and of petitioning the government. The U.S. government, with its three branches and its two legislative houses, is a system of checks and balances that demands debate, argument, and compromise. The U.S. legal system is adversarial and requires the government to prove, beyond a reasonable doubt, that a crime was committed by a citizen. Persuasion in early America tended to be local and interpersonal (occurring in churches, town-halls, marketplaces, and court rooms) with an emphasis on long discourse (e.g., sermons and political speeches) and debate (e.g., consumers arguing with sellers).

However, beginning in the 19th century, the nature of persuasion changed dramatically as the United States experienced the industrial revolution. New manufacturing techniques created more and more goods; new transportation technologies simplified travel and distribution. Business and industry increasingly saw their markets not as their local communities but as the entire nation and world. To communicate with these mass markets, manufacturers came to rely on mass media such as nationally distributed magazines and radio and television networks. Ad agencies, market research firms, polling organizations, and academic research developed to assist industry in their communications efforts. The result is a set of institutions that can quickly convey consumer, political, and social information to every household in America. The rise of this mass communications system brought with it persuasion that tends to be immediate, impersonal, and national and international in scope; often this persuasion takes the form of propaganda—the use of short messages, images, and slogans that play on emotions and prejudices to move a recipient to a point of view.

The purpose of this article is to describe the social psychology of American mass media. To do this, we describe how the institutions of mass media operate, and we discuss the effects of these institutions on the audience for mass media. We conclude by looking at the future of mass media research. However, before looking at American mass media and its effects, it is fruitful to understand what Americans consider "ideal" communications.

Ideal Persuasion in Three Postindustrial Cultures

During the 20th century, the nature and function of persuasion has received prominent treatment in three regimes—American, Soviet, and Nazi. Each of these regimes developed its own beliefs about how persuasion should be used. It is useful to look at the guiding metaphors of ideal communications in each of these regimes to reveal hidden assumptions we may have about persuasion. By doing so, we are in a better position to understand some of the choices each regime makes about its mass media, and, perhaps most important, we can look at the assumptions about ideal persuasion using the light of research to discover what is typical and what is possible. Table 6.1 summarizes how each regime answers seven important questions about persuasion and the mass media.

The American ideals of persuasion are based in the colonial experience. As a nation of mostly newcomers with few shared traditions, Americans had few agreed-upon rules for what was right and what was wrong. Truth was not invested in any given person (such as a king or queen) or institution (such as the church), as was the case in Europe at the time. How then does a community arrive at decisions? The solution was to argue it out (and sometimes even fight it out). The town meeting became a forum for debate and discussion; since no one had the truth, all points of view had the right to be expressed freely with

Table 6.1. Ideal Persuasion in Three Post-Industrial Societies

Question	United States	Soviet Union	Nazi Germany
What is the guiding metaphor?	Town meeting	Schoolroom	The rally
Who knows the truth?	No one	Communist Party	Nazi elite
What should be the structure of media institutions?	Decentralized; value-pluralism	Centralized; party informs members	Centralized; party dictates to masses
What is the role of persuasion?	Discover what to do through argument	Education of the masses	Communicate elite opinions/mobilize the masses
How capable are citizens?	Thoughtful and self-reliant	Capable of becoming the New Soviet	Stupid and require emotional appeals
What is fair persuasion?	State should not regulate persuasion as free speech	Truth of party ideology is self-evident and not in need of propaganda to convince	All is fair if it promotes Nazi goals
What is the role of the press and news media?	Report on events and serve as gadfly to stimulate debate and uncover wrongdoing	Assist party in its educational function; stimulate debate within party framework	Promote the Nazi Party

few limitations. Through debate and discussion, thoughtful and self-reliant citizens could discover the best course of action. The duty of the local press was to stimulate this debate and investigate wrongdoing. From this history has come a desire by many Americans for the mass media to serve as the modern town hall, presenting many sides to an issue, providing thoughtful analysis, accurately reflecting the views of citizens, and investigating the corrupt.

In contrast, the Soviet regime was clear on the source of the truth—the Communist Party. According to the party, workers and proletariat were duped by a bourgeoisie bent on protecting their own riches; however, workers and proletariat were capable of learning the truth as they confronted their oppressors and became the New Soviet. It was the role of persuasion to educate the masses, with the mass media serving as schoolrooms and reporters as teachers. The party served to coordinate this education effort and to stimulate debate on how to better serve the nation's and party's goals.

Finally, the Nazi regime led by Hitler and Goebbels believed, as did the Soviets, that there was a single source of absolute truth—in this case the Nazi Party. However, unlike the Soviets, the Nazis believed that the great mass of people would remain ever stupid and in constant need of simple and emotional propaganda if they were ever to grasp the truth of the Nazi Party. The task of the party was to promote Nazi goals at all costs and with any tactic that worked.

The mass media were like a giant political rally—useful for whipping up the nation and mobilizing the masses for Nazi purposes.

Which of the assumptions made by these regimes is closest to the truth? Are people capable of thoughtful deliberation and human development (as assumed by Americans and Soviets) or are they forever doomed to be manipulated (as assumed by the Nazi Party)? Can the mass media inform and educate? Or do they move only by playing on emotions and prejudices? How do American media compare to their ideals? We now turn to look at the answers American social psychologists have given to such questions.

Institutions of Mass Communications in the United States

What Are the Mass Media?

The term *mass media* refers to a system of organizations with the primary purpose of delivering communications (such as information, entertainment, or advertisements) to consumers. In 1992, communications was a $400 billion industry with $206 billion spent on mass communications—that is, communications produced and distributed in identical form to people in different locations (Bogart, 1995). In the United States, the mass media include (numbers in parenthesis are dollars spent for a given medium in 1992, according to Bogart, 1995) 1,449 television stations and four major networks ($46.9 billion); 10,688 radio stations ($8.6 billion); 1,688 daily and 7,047 weekly newspapers ($44.2 billion); over 17,000 magazines and newsletters ($29.8 billion); 9 major film studios ($4.9 billion); numerous producers of records ($9 billion), videotapes ($12 billion), and books ($21.1 billion); and distributors of direct mail advertisements ($25.5 billion), telephone directories ($9.3 billion), and outdoor billboards ($1.2 billion). To support the mass media, numerous firms create consumer and political advertising, conduct opinion and market research, and perform public relations.

Americans eagerly consume the products of the mass media (Pratkanis & Aronson, 1992). Each year each American watches an average of 1,550 hours of television (4 hours per day), listens to 1,160 hours of radio on one of 530 million radio sets, and spends 180 hours reading 94 pounds of newspapers and 110 hours reading magazines. Each American sees an average of about 400 advertisements per day. With 6 percent of the world's population, the United States consumes 57 percent of the world's advertising; it spends more money on advertising than any other country—2.2 percent of its gross national product (compared to .95% in Japan and .9% in Germany).

What is the nature of these mass media? Although each medium differs in its characteristics, eight generalizations appear to describe American mass media at the end of the 20th century (see Bogart, 1995; DeFleur & Ball-Rokeach, 1989; Graber, 1993; Jamieson & Campbell, 1992; for an international comparison, see Murray & Kippax, 1979).

1. The mass media are profit-making enterprises. With the exception of a few public broadcasting television and radio stations, the primary purpose of mass-media organizations is to make a profit. Mass-media revenues come from two sources: consumers who pay for a media product directly by buying a newspaper, a cable TV subscription, a ticket to the movie, and so forth (43.5% of revenues), and advertisers who purchase media time and space to sell products and services (56.5% of revenues). To make a profit, mass-media organizations must sell media time and space for more money than it takes to produce the content of that time and space. The implication of the profit orientation is straightforward: much of the mass media is a vehicle for securing an audience for advertising; mass-media organizations are continually looking for programs that are appealing to consumers and cheap to produce.

2. Media access is expensive and thus limited. An hour of prime-time television costs between $1 and $1.5 million to produce. The average feature-length movie costs $23 million to make and $8 million to advertise it. The average national advertiser spends $200,000 to produce an advertisement and can spend upwards of $1 million per 30 seconds of television time to show it. With such high costs, only a few Americans can afford to appear in the mass media.

3. Media ownership is concentrated among a few corporations. For the last decade or so, media ownership in the United States has become concentrated in the hands of a few organizations (Bagdikian, 1992). Today, 23 corporations control most of television, newspapers, magazines, books, and movies: 60 percent of local daily newspapers belong to 1 of 14 corporate chains, 3 corporations dominate the magazine industry, and 6 major record companies control 80 percent of the market for recorded music.

4. Information sources for the mass media are oligopolistic. The mass media rely on a limited number of sources for the information they convey. Nine major film studios produce 70 percent of network television's prime-time schedule. Almost 95 percent of local newspapers are dependent on major wire services such as AP or UPI for their national and international news. News gatherers typically rely on a limited set of sources for information, primarily government officials, media celebrities (actors, sports figures, and other news gatherers), experts, corporate leaders, and police officials. The result is mass media that tend to present a consistent view of reality—the one espoused by the specific sources used by the media.

5. The mass media serve as a pastime and entertainment for most Americans. Although Americans consume mass media to satisfy a variety of needs, they frequently turn to the media for entertainment and to pass the time. For example, studies of media usage find that Americans typically decide first to consume media (i.e., watch TV tonight, go to a movie this weekend) and then decide what to watch specifically from the choices available in a given medium (Bogart, 1995). Surveys reveal that Americans list many reasons for consuming a given medium, including diversion, escape, emotional release, relaxation, companionship, pass time, and entertainment (Rubin, 1994). Thus, to guarantee high ratings and revenues, mass-media content tends to be agreeable and requires little effort to consume yet is arousing, emotionally engaging, and entertaining.

6. Mass media reach general and specific audiences. Much of the mass media reaches a mass audience. On a typical evening between 8:00 and 9:00, 98 million Americans (almost half the nation) are watching television. With such reach, a story on the evening news or a fictional character on a popular prime-time TV show or an ad repeated on different media will quickly become known by most Americans. This gives mass media the potential to create popular culture and to formulate a civic agenda. In addition, some mass media reach very specific audiences (termed market segmentation). For example, each medium vehicle (TV program, magazine, etc.) is targeted toward a given group of people (e.g., *Redbook* magazine is for women who work exclusively in the home, *Late Night with David Letterman* is for males between the ages of 20 and 35). This allows individuals and groups of individuals to develop unique perspectives within the framework of the media they consume.

7. The information presented in the mass media is selective. Given the pressures of limited access and producing entertaining fare at a profit, the mass media present a selective and partial view of America. For example, studies of what appears on the news find that it consists mostly of stories about famous people such as the U.S. president, major federal officials, opposition leaders, local leaders, sports and entertainment figures, and notorious individuals (Croteau & Hoynes, 1994; Gans, 1979). A premium is placed on dramatic stories such as hijackings, murders, and the O. J. Simpson trial and on entertainment (e.g., local news devotes eight times more space to sports than to community problems such as school financing or housing [Ernst, 1972]). Although newsworthy events may be covered, the underlying causes and consequences of social issues are often neglected. Since 1967, George Gerbner and his colleagues (Gerbner, Gross, Morgan, & Signorielli, 1986) have been tracking what appears on television. They find that in prime-time programming, males outnumber females 3 to 1 and nonwhites, young children, and the elderly are underrepresented; most prime-time characters are professional and managerial workers, with only 10 percent holding blue-collar or services jobs (compared to 67% of the American workforce). Crime on television is ten times more prevalent than it is in real life.

8. The mass media create a message-dense environment for most Americans. The advertisers Ries and Trout (1981) call America the overcommunicated society. The average American will see or hear more than 7 million advertisements in a lifetime. Every day Americans watch, hear, or read a medium that is populated with short, catchy, and often visually oriented messages. A typical television ad runs for 30 seconds or less. Magazine ads consist of little more than a brand name, picture, and phrase. News comes in short sound bites and news snippets. This message-dense environment places a burden on both the communicator and the recipient of a message. The communicator must design a message that not only will be appealing but also will attract special notice in the cluttered environment. The recipient is so deluged by messages that it becomes difficult to devote the mental energy necessary to make sense of many of the important issues of the day.

How Do the Mass Media Operate?: Two Examples

To illustrate how the mass media work (and how our eight generalizations operate), we now take a closer look at two media institutions—newsrooms and advertisers (for other media, see Bogart, 1972, 1981; Cantril & Allport, 1935; Comstock, 1980; Jowett & Linton, 1989; Tebbel & Zuckerman, 1991). Our purpose is to understand how and why things appear in the American mass media.

How Is News Space Filled?   On any given day, the world is full of happenings such as wars, riots, consumer frauds, spelling bees, family violence, scientific achievements, Presidential speeches, and human sorrows and happiness. Obviously, the news media cannot cover all these events. How do they decide what will fill the news space and time—the space and time left over in a newspaper, magazine, or on television after the ads are scheduled? To answer that question, we need to look at how news organizations go about gathering information and constructing news stories (for more details, see Fishman, 1980; Gans, 1979; Jamieson & Campbell, 1992; Kaniss, 1991; Tuchman, 1978).

The principal news gatherer is the reporter. Reporters have the job of going out and finding the news and then preparing stories to convey that news to readers or viewers. They obtain their assignments from an editor who is responsible for coordinating the activities of reporters and for ensuring the financial success of the organization (i.e., the product is of interest to consumers and advertisers). Reporters typically work beats or a set of institutions that must be covered, such as the local criminal justice system (police and courts), the White House, or sports teams. For the reporter, a beat makes news gathering a routine process, specifying where to look and whom to talk to about news. However, beats also ensure that the news will consistently select certain types of stories. Beats have routine contacts that include some citizens (typically government officials and representatives of bureaucracies) and exclude many others. Further, things that happen off or between beats have a lower chance of being covered (unless it is a major disaster or other newsworthy event). For example, almost 60 percent of the stories appearing in the *New York Times* and the *Washington Post* were from routine channels and beats (Sigal, 1973).

Reporters must generate a number of stories (as determined by their editor) from their beat on deadline. For example, newspaper and television reporters typically must prepare articles and newsclips by early afternoon (around 1:00 P.M.) for inclusion in the evening news. Events that happen after the deadline have a lower chance of being covered. In preparing the news, reporters must work quickly, thus placing a premium on sources that can be easily contacted (i.e., bureaucrats) and trusted (i.e., ones the reporter has contacted previously). Reporters generally generate the same number of stories each day regardless of what happens on their beats. This means that on slow news days trivial incidents may receive major coverage and on days with major news stories other important incidents are not covered.

On every beat, there are many things that reporters could potentially cover. Two factors influence what stories reporters will file. First, reporters have a general knowledge (or script) of what happens on their beat. For example, a reporter covering the crime beat "knows" that crimes follow a certain sequence: first it occurs, then police investigate and charge an individual with the crime; next there is a preliminary hearing, a trial, and a sentence. This crime script tells the reporter where to look for information (i.e., police crime reports, victims, trial calendars) and where not to look for information (i.e., academic critiques of the justice system; welfare agencies, churches, the homeless, or others who might shed light on the causes of crime). This gives many news stories what Iyengar (1991) calls an episodic frame or perspective (event-oriented report of a concrete instance) as opposed to a thematic frame (an abstract report directed at general outcomes and conditions). Iyengar (1991) finds that episodic framing tends to evoke individualistic rather than societal attributions of responsibilities for a given issue.

Second, reporters have a general knowledge of what makes a "great" story—what stories appeal to an audience and thus increase circulation and ratings. In general, reporters tend to look for stories that (1) are new and timely, (2) involve conflict or scandal, (3) concern strange and unusual happenings, (4) occur with familiar or famous people, (5) are capable of being made dramatic and personal, (6) are simple enough to convey in short space or time, (7) contain visual elements (pictures to illustrate a story, especially for television), (8) fit a theme that is currently prominent in the news or society, and (9) are consistent with reporters' norms of objectivity (i.e., facts can be documented; both sides presented). These factors also result in selective news coverage. For example, a story about a trade imbalance probably won't make the news unless there is a conflict or scandal involved (e.g., a famous person doing something wrong) or consequences can be made personal (e.g., includes an interview with a neighbor who might lose a job) or has some other hook to involve the reader.

Given that news gathering is a routine process, it can be influenced by anyone who knows the routine and has the resources to do so. For example, government officials have learned to announce negative news after deadline, on holidays, or on busy news days. One common way to manipulate news coverage is by creating a pseudo-event—a planned event for the immediate purpose of being reported by the news media (Boorstin, 1961). For example, a president may visit a veterans group (to win support for military spending) or a school cafeteria (to illustrate the need for a school lunch program), thus providing the news media with a "photo op" (opportunity to gather visual elements) to create a story that reinforces the government's agenda. Some other common ways that government and business ensure coverage of a given event is through news leaks ("insider" reports of what an organization is doing) and press releases (prepared stories that reporters may edit and submit as part of their quota of stories).

How Does an Ad Become an Ad? Suppose we wish to advertise a consumer product (or political candidate) to a national audience. How would we do it (for advice, see Aaker & Myers, 1987; Bogart, 1990; Kleepner, 1973; Ogilvy, 1983)? The first thing we would need is lots of money. For example, in 1992, the two top U.S. national advertisers—Procter & Gamble Co. and Philip Morris Cos.—each spent around $2 billion on advertising. Some typical advertising expenditures in 1992: $329 million on AT&T's long-distance telephone services, $125 million on Budweiser beer, $106 million on Coca-Cola Classic, $100 million on Visa credit card, and $33.5 million on Kellogg's Frosted Flakes (Jacobson & Mazur, 1995).

The second thing we need is a set of communication objectives. The purpose of advertising is, of course, to sell the product. However, this objective is difficult to measure and provides little direction on how to create an ad. Thus, advertisers frequently establish specific communication goals. For example, one approach called DAGMAR (Defining Advertising Goals for Measured Advertising Results; see Colley & Dutka, 1995) lists 52 possible communication objectives including creating brand awareness, creating a brand image, reminding the consumer to buy, aiding a sales force in opening new accounts, and stimulating impulse sales.

The selection of specific communication objectives is generally based on three considerations. First, market research is conducted to understand consumer behavior: Are consumers aware of the product? Do they like it? How, when, and why do they buy it? Second, although some products seek mass appeal, most brands are designed for a specific segment of the population called the target market (Piirto, 1991; Weinstein, 1987; Weiss, 1988). Markets can be segmented on a number of criteria, including product-related factors (e.g., benefits sought by the consumer, past usage rates, brand loyalty) and general consumer characteristics (e.g., demographics, social class, geographic residence, psychographics). Finally, communication objectives depend on the competition. The brand must be positioned against the competition in such a way that consumers select it over other brands; advertising is one way to communicate, in simple terms, what this advantage is (Ries & Trout, 1981).

Third, we would probably hire an ad agency to help in the preparation of a communications campaign. One of the most important functions of an ad agency is the creative process—the translation of communication objectives into a specific campaign with theme, copy (content), and visual elements. Ad agencies also help with the execution of the campaign, including creating the actual physical ad, purchasing media space, and setting the media schedule (when and where the ad will be placed). The media schedule is important for determining who sees an ad and thus for reaching the target market.

The ad agency faces considerable obstacles in preparing a campaign. For example, research shows that consumers pay minimal attention to ads, do not process more then a few pieces of information per ad, and rapidly forget the main points of an ad. In the face of these obstacles, advertisers have advanced some ideas of what makes an effective ad. For example, Rosser Reeves (1961) argues that an ad should have a "unique selling proposition"; Leo Burnett (1961) believes an ad should portray the inherent drama of the product; John Caples (1974) and David Ogilvy (1983) have developed guidelines for creating effective ads. In translating a communication objective into an advertisement, ad agencies typically use one of the following formats (Roman & Maas, 1992): demonstrations (to show a product advantage), testimonials (to speak for the advantages of the brand), celebrity or fictitious presenters (to give an image to the brand), slice-of-life (to illustrate how a product solves a typical everyday problem), and comparisons with other brands.

Will our advertising have the desired effect? At any given time many factors can affect a consumer purchase (e.g., marketing efforts of competitors, distribution of product, prior consumer purchases), thus making it difficult to detect the effects of any given ad on consumer behavior. However, recent developments in single-source data can provide an estimate of typical advertising impact (Jones, 1995). Single-source data tracks the television ads watched by a household and the brands of products that household subsequently purchases. Using such data on repeat-purchase package goods, Jones (1995) found that, on average, advertising increases purchase of a brand by 6 percent over the course of a year. However, these effects can vary considerably, with strong campaigns tripling sales and weak campaigns actually cutting purchase rates in half. Jones (1995) found that successful campaigns were typically ones that consumers found likable, that were visual (rather than verbal), and that communicated a benefit relevant to the target market.

However, our advertising can also have some unintended effects for society. Preston (1994; see also Richards, 1990) points out that most brands do not differ much from competitors, making it difficult for advertisers to reach a goal of positively positioning the brand. The result is advertising that can be false and misleading, presents selective facts about a brand, makes trivial differences seem important, and emphasizes nonfacts (e.g., "Coke Is It"). To illustrate the point, my students wrote 99 manufacturers asking them for information backing up the claims they made in their advertising (see Pratkanis & Aronson, 1992). Less than 50 percent of the businesses responded, and only 5 sent information supporting claims; for every 1 page of materials supporting a claim, the students received 86 pages of additional advertising. Social critics (see Jacobson & Mazur, 1995) also point out that advertising can have indirect effects, including maintaining social stereotypes, creating a consumer culture, producing a nation of conformists, and specifying false choices (i.e., Chevy versus Ford as opposed to cars versus mass transportation).

Are American Media American?

Now that we have looked at the institutions of the mass media, we are prepared to answer an important question: How do American media compare to the ideals described in table 6.1? Critics have pointed to a number of shortcomings including:

1. Limited mass-media ownership and access are counter to the American ideal of value pluralism or a free-spirited debate among *all* relevant parties.
2. The mass media's emphasis on entertainment creates a spiral of ignorance that runs counter to the goal of a thoughtful and self-reliant public. Sophisticated news coverage requires an interested and informed public; without an educated audience, journalists and leaders must simplify their message and package it as entertainment, thus reducing further the sophistication of the public at large (Entman, 1989).
3. Short sound bites and news snippets do no provide enough meaningful information to allow for informed debate; propaganda fills the void (Volkogonov, 1986).
4. The selective nature of the news means that some important (but potentially boring) issues will receive little attention whereas trivial (but exciting) events receive widespread coverage.
5. A reporter may be reluctant to fulfill the role of gadfly by attacking those powerful newsmakers capable of providing a steady stream of "news."

The critics' complaints have not gone unanswered. As some have pointed out, the ideal may be unrealistic—mass media were never meant to do the job originally assigned to the local press and community. Despite the mass media oligopoly of ownership and information sources, criticism of American government and leaders still happens. Watergate required a U.S. president to resign, and academics get tenure for writing articles critical of their country. News must be selective; what is trivial to one person may be essential to another. Although some of the criticisms of American media are true, the alternatives of state-controlled media or highly regulated speech are much worse options. And, most important, the American people have the final power to change the mass media, if they so desire; they can demand legislation to prevent mass-media mergers; they can simply stop watching television that is entertaining and start watching shows that are more informative; a rating-driven industry would quickly comply with the public's wishes.

But does the American public have the power to control the media, or is it the public that is manipulated by the media? This is the issue we turn to next when we look at the effects of the mass media on the American public. We will find that, as far as the mass media are concerned, the American public, as Schattschneider (1960) termed it, is semisovereign (capable of making free choices within well-defined alternatives); the public is sometimes capable of living up to its democratic ideal of being thoughtful and self-reliant and is sometimes unthinking and vulnerable to propaganda appeals.

Audience Response to Mass Communications

A Tale of Two Myths

Myth 1: The Mass Media Are All Powerful.   By the end of the 19th century, the industrial revolution had brought about dramatic changes in American society, including the rise of mass media that some feared would come to control and dominate a mass public. As Toennies (1887/1971) observed, Western societies were experiencing a change in the nature of social relationships—from small, cohesive communities emphasizing personal relationships (or what he termed *Gemeinschaft*) to a web of impersonal, secondary relationships in which the individual was socially isolated and in tension with others (or *Gesellschaft*). Cut from their social roots, individuals would be dependent on the mass media for information and thus defenseless against propaganda. In other words, the mass media could fire *magic bullets* of information capable of shaping public opinion and swaying the masses toward any point of view advocated by a communicator (see DeFleur & Ball-Rokeach, 1989, for an excellent review of the magic bullet theory, which has also been called the hypodermic needle or transmission belt theory).

Early mass communications scholars pointed to a number of pieces of evidence in support of a magic bullet thesis. For example, during World War I, British and American governments successfully used the mass media to disseminate atrocity stories about the Germans and to mobilize their citizens for the war effort. After the war, scholars dissected these tactics to show the power of mass-media propaganda in influencing one of the most important decisions a person can make—the decision to take another's life (Lasswell, 1927). The propaganda of Hitler and Goebbels during World War II merely reinforced the point. The 1920s was a period when American advertising had some of its strongest effects as advertisers coined new terms such as B.O. (body odor), athlete's foot, and halitosis (bad breath) to create new needs and to sell new brands of products (Fox, 1984). In addition during the 1920s, the first empirical investigation of movies (the Payne Fund studies) yielded preliminary results showing that motion pictures had direct and immediate effects on children's attitudes and beliefs.

The two dominant psychological theories of the early 20th century—behaviorism and psychoanalysis—also lent support to the magic bullet thesis. Behaviorist J. B. Watson boasted that he could take any infant at birth and, with the application of learning principles such as classical conditioning, create any sort of human being he desired. As the mass media sought to employ these techniques, popular imagination saw visions of a media-controlled society such as that in *Brave New World* or *Clockwork Orange*. Similarly, psychoanalytic theory suggested that the mass media could have strong effects if their messages bypassed the conscious mind (which was capable of scrutinizing claims) and appealed directly to the unconscious. Advertisers were accused of using powerful techniques such as motivation research to develop hidden messages (often sexual in nature) and subliminal messages (slogans presented below the threshold of awareness) to reach the unconscious and to sell unwanted products (Packard, 1957). Psychoanalysis suggested a metaphor of the mass media as a mass hypnotherapist turning viewers into a passive mass awaiting the commands of leaders and advertisers. However, empirical research beginning in the 1940s soon demonstrated that the myth of pervasive media effects doesn't hold, and in the 1950s an opposite myth formed—that the media are of little consequence.

Myth 2: The Mass Media Produces Minimum Effects.   One of the first studies to question the belief that mass media are all-powerful was conducted by Lazarsfeld, Berelson, and Gaudet (1948) during the 1940 presidential campaign. At the beginning and end of the campaign, the voters of Erie County, Ohio, were interviewed about their preferences, party affiliation, media habits, and so on. The results showed that few citizens changed their voting intentions from one candidate to another and that political party (Republican or Democrat), not the mass media, was the most significant determinant of voting. Indeed, party preference appeared to serve as a screen to avoid conflicting information from the mass media. Voters tended to vote consistently with those they worked, played, or prayed with—that is, consistently with their reference groups.

Other studies followed that showed that the mass media had limited, if any, effects on behavior. For example, Berelson, Lazarsfeld, and McPhee (1954) found that those who followed mass-media coverage of a presidential campaign extensively were the least affected by the media. In general, econometric time-series studies of advertising have found small or no effects of the amount a firm spends on advertising on either growth in market share or total product-category sales. Similarly, experimental investigations of single exposures to ads find that few people pay attention to any specific ad exposure and what little effects are created usually dissipate quickly (see McGuire, 1986, for a review).

The psychological underpinnings of the magic bullet model of mass media also did not fare well. Empirical research found little support for hypotheses derived from psychoanalytic theory. For example, attempts to use hypnosis to manipulate behavior failed (Marks, 1979; Spanos & Chaves, 1989). The use of motivation research to identify hidden persuaders proved to be unreliable (Politz, 1957). Despite over 100 years of investigation, a reliable demonstration that a subliminal message can influence motivation or behavior has not yet been made (Moore, 1982; Pratkanis, 1992; Pratkanis, Eskenazi, & Greenwald, 1994; Pratkanis & Greenwald, 1988). Although many of the basic findings of behavioral learning theories have been supported, subsequent research found that such effects were often limited in nature (e.g., Garcia & Koelling's 1966 finding that not all stimuli could be paired with equal success in classical conditioning) and did not hold in all cases (Festinger & Carlsmith, 1959).

In the 1950s, such evidence led some scholars to conclude that the effects of the mass media are minimal and limited. The dominant psychological model of mass-media effects became the information processing or learning model (Hovland, Janis, & Kelley, 1953; McGuire, 1968). According to this model, a persuasive message is processed in a series of sequential stages: first, the message must attract attention; second, it must be understood and comprehended; third, the recipient must learn the arguments of the message and accept them as true; finally, the recipient acts on this learned knowledge and belief. Given that later stages of the processes are dependent on completion of earlier stages, the chances of any given persuasive communication passing to the final stage are quite low, and thus minimal effects abound.

Cognitive Response Model of Persuasion

As with many opposing myths, the truth lies somewhere in the middle. As we saw earlier with the research using scanner data to evaluate advertising effects (Jones, 1995), and as we will see later when we discuss such issues as televised violence and mass-media politics, the media can have consistent, predictable, and sometimes large effects on human behavior. And they can sometimes have minimum or even opposite effects. The resolution to our opposing myths has been a new model of persuasion—termed the cognitive response approach—and the specification of conditions under which the mass media will have their greatest (and least) impact.

The origins of the cognitive response approach lay in an empirical anomaly. According to the information-processing model, attitude change should be correlated with the learning of the message. However, studies found only weak and variable correlations between persuasion and message retention. This evidence prompted Greenwald (1968) to propose a cognitive response analysis of persuasion—the important determinant of persuasion is the respondent's cognitive reaction to the message as he or she attempts to relate the message to existing attitudes, feelings, knowledge, and so on. Psychologists familiar with early Eastern European research will recognize the cognitive response model in Nikolai Rubakin's 1929 work on bibliopsychology or the psychology of reading (see Benn, 1989, for a discussion). Rubakin's general thesis was that, regardless of the author's intent, each reader puts her or his own meaning into what is read (i.e., generates cognitive responses). Interestingly, later Rubakin went on to study communications and propaganda; unfortunately, his work in this area remains unpublished, providing scholars with limited access.

To test the cognitive response model, Greenwald (1968) conducted a set of experiments measuring retention of arguments, cognitive response (as assessed by subjects listing their thoughts about a message), and persuasion. The results showed little relationship between retention and persuasion; however, the evaluative nature of cognitive responses (the amount of support versus counterarguing of the message) was highly related to attitude change. In addition, Greenwald (1968) identified a number of dimensions on which cognitive responses could vary, including evaluative (support versus counterargument), intensity of response, and source of response (self, message, or other). Subsequent research has found considerable support for the cognitive response model and has applied it to such issues as distraction and persuasion, involvement, source of message, and forewarning of persuasive intent (see Petty & Cacioppo, 1981; Petty, Ostrom, & Brock, 1981).

The cognitive response model is important for understanding mass-communication effects for at least three reasons. First, it gives us a methodology (thought listing and experimental manipulation of thoughts) to investigate mass-media effects. Second, the cognitive response model argues that the recipient of a communication is an active participant in the persuasion process—not a passive vessel as suggested by the magic bullet theory. On the other hand, it suggests that on occasion cognitive responses can be quite limited and that message recipients may not be as vigilant in their evaluation of persuasive appeals as suggested by the limited effects model. Finally, the cognitive response approach begs the question, Where do cognitive responses come from? The answer to that question will be the focus of the following sections.

Developing the Pictures in Our Heads

In 1965, Herbert Krugman made an important observation about television advertising: viewers typically find advertising to be of little interest and thus pay little attention to it. Ironically, this lack of interest can result in effective mass communications because recipients often fail to scrutinize and counterargue ads. Through repetition of simple slogans and images, advertising alters the structure of perceptions about a product and shifts the relative salience of product attributes. Advertising can best be described as "low-involvement" learning. In other words, mass communications create the picture we have of the world by creating our images of what is good and bad, what to expect and assume, what is important to talk about, and how things work. Pratkanis and Aronson (1992) term this "pre-persuasion," the construction of the persuasion landscape in such a way to favor certain positions. A growing body of evidence suggests that the mass media can produce such indirect effects (that is, draw the ground in the figure-ground). Let's look at two programs of research illustrating this pre-persuasion process: cultivation and agenda-setting.

The Cultivation Hypothesis.   According to George Gerbner and his colleagues (see Gerbner, Gross, Morgan, & Signorelli, 1986), the mass media (in particular television) *cultivate* our image of the world by transmitting shared images and messages that influence viewers' conceptions of social reality. What is the evidence for this hypothesis? Recall that the information presented in the mass media is selective—white males outnumber nonwhites and females, crime is prevalent, few blue-collar workers appear, and so on. To demonstrate the effects of a steady diet of selective television fare, Gerbner et al. (1986) surveyed heavy and light television viewers as to their perceptions and beliefs about the social world. They found that heavy viewers of television express more racially prejudice beliefs; overestimate the number of people employed as physicians, lawyers, and athletes; perceive women as having more limited abilities and interests than men; and hold exaggerated views of the prevalence of violence in society. In other words, the selective content of television led heavy viewers to a distorted reality of the social world in which they live.

Agenda Setting.   In an impressive set of studies, Iyengar and Kinder (1987) demonstrated the power of the mass media to set agendas—to determine what issues are important and which ones the nation should address. In their experiments, Iyengar and Kinder (1987) edited the evening news so that participants received a steady dose of news about a specific problem facing the United States. For example, in one experiment, some participants heard about the weakness of U.S. defense capabilities; a second group watched shows emphasizing pollution concerns; a third heard about inflation and economic matters. The results showed that after a week of viewing the programs, participants emerged from the study more convinced than they were before that the target problem—the one receiving extensive coverage in the shows they watched—was a more important one for the country to solve. In addition, the participants acted on their newfound perceptions, evaluating the current president's performance on the basis of how he handled the target issue and evaluating more positively those political candidates who took strong positions on the target problem. Iyengar and Kinder's (1987) research is not a fluke. For example, McCombs and Shaw (1972) found that, in a political campaign, the more the media cover an issue, the more likely citizens will find that issue to be important. (For another example of pre-persuasion, see Iyengars (1991) on news framing and intentions of responsibility described above.) Taken as a whole, the work on cultivation processes and on agenda setting provide support for Schattschneider's (1960) description of democracy in America as "the semisovereign people": the freedom to make choices within the range of alternatives provided—in this case, by the mass media.

Elaboration Likelihood Model of Persuasion

The intention of much of the mass media is to produce direct effects—to persuade the target to buy this product or vote for that candidate—as opposed to the indirect cultivation of conceptions of reality (although those conceptions can help with the task of persuasion). How do audiences cognitively respond to mass-media persuasion? According to Petty and Cacioppo's (1986) Elaboration Likelihood Model (ELM), there are two routes to persuasion: peripheral and central. In the peripheral route a message recipient devotes little attention and effort to processing a communication; persuasion is determined by simple cues such as the attractiveness of the communicator, whether or not other people agree with the position, or the confidence of the communicator. Such cues can be very effective persuasion devices in the short term. In contrast, in the central route, a message recipient engages in a careful and thoughtful consideration of the true merits of the information presented; the person may actively argue against the message, may want to know the answers to additional questions, or may seek out new information; persuasion is determined by how well the message can stand up to this scrutiny. Attitude change in the central route can be long-lasting. What determines the route of persuasion? Petty and Cacioppo (1986) identify two general factors: (1) the motivation to think about an issue (for example, the issue is personally relevant or the message is presented in an unusual manner) and (2) the ability to process a message (for example, the cognitive capacity of the message recipient or the ease with which information can be processed).

An experiment by Petty, Cacioppo, and Goldman (1981) can serve to illustrate the ELM. In this study, students at the University of Missouri heard a message advocating that their university adopt a senior comprehensive exam that all students would need to pass in order to graduate. For half of the students, the message was made personally relevant by informing them that the university's chancellor was considering adopting the plan for next year (and thus they would need to take the exam); the other half of students were told that the changes would not take place for ten years. The students then received one of four messages. Half of the messages were attributed to a source low in expertise (a local high school class), whereas the other half were attributed to an expert source (the Carnegie Commission on Higher Education). The researchers also varied the quality of arguments in the message, with half of the messages containing weak arguments and the other half consisting of strong evidence for senior exams. What were the results? The personal relevance of the message determined the route to persuasion. For those students for whom the issue of the comprehensive exam was personally relevant, the strength of the message was the most important factor in determining persuasion. In contrast, for those students for whom the issue of the exam was not personally relevant, the source of the message mattered—the source high in expertise convinced whereas the high school class did not.

Petty and Cacioppo's research is important for a number of reasons. First, the ELM specifies what types of messages are most likely to be effective in the mass media. Given that much advertising is of little consequence and that the message-dense environment of the mass media hinders thought, we should expect that peripheral persuasion cues should be effective (i.e., an attractive athlete promoting a razor as opposed to a university professor explaining in detail why a given razor is better). Second, it specifies the conditions under which an audience member will process detailed information about an issue (i.e., when a purchase decision is personally relevant; when an election has important consequences and receives extensive coverage). Finally, the elaboration likelihood model has important implications for how to conduct a democracy in an age of mass media (see Pratkanis & Turner, in press). According to the ELM, the American ideal of persuasion as discussion, debate, and argument (that is, central route persuasion) can be accomplished under certain conditions. However, in the mass media, peripheral route propaganda will predominate unless steps are taken to ensure thoughtful processing.

The Self and Mass-Mediated Rationalization

Although much of the content of the mass media is processed in a low-involvement and passive state, on occasions the information presented can be so arousing that it involves the self. For example, advertisers may remind viewers of their inadequacies by showing beautiful bodies that we all wished we had; public service announcements can advocate behavior (e.g., practice safe sex; don't litter) that makes us feel guilty or inferior because we rarely measure up. The news can show graphic footage of young American men and women destroying people in other lands as an act of war. Each of these incidents can create a state of cognitive dissonance—a tension state where an individual holds two discrepant cognitions and this discrepancy is painful for the self (Aronson, 1969; Festinger, 1957).

How can a member of the mass-media audience reduce dissonance? Simply put, the need to reduce dissonance changes the goal of processing a message from one of trying to think rationally about an issue to one of trying to rationalize one's self. Practically speaking, one of the easiest ways to reduce dissonance is to avoid the dissonance-arousing message. For example, when a dissonance-arousing public service announcement comes on urging the practice of safe sex, a viewer can simply turn the channel or go to the bathroom. If that option isn't available, the viewer can selectively interpret the communication— that information is for others, not me. The tendency to avoid dissonance information identifies a condition when the mass media are likely to have minimum effect: when its message threatens the viewer's self (see the later discussion of information campaigns). Conversely, the clever propagandist can use dissonance to motivate behavior by first arousing dissonance and then offering a simple means for reducing it. This is what happens in many ads for diet products and gym equipment; the ad makes viewers feel inferior about their body and then offers a quick solution—buy the product. Similarly, war propaganda is designed to make us feel that our nation's actions are justified—atrocities perpetrated by the enemy to lend justice to the cause, sterile terms such as *collateral damage* (for innocent dead women we didn't mean to kill) to reduce the disturbing nature of war, and flag waving to bolster our national self-esteem.

The Social Structure Mediates Mass-Media Content

Individuals often turn to their friends, neighbors, and acquaintances for help in understanding mass-media content. Research in this area has looked at how an individual's social groups serve to filter official information (diffusion) and how those groups create unofficial information (rumors). In general, this research has reached the following conclusions (see Kapferer, 1990; Katz, 1957; Katz & Lazarsfeld, 1955; Rogers, 1983; Rosnow & Fine, 1976; Weimann, 1994):

1. Americans live in social or communication networks; information is passed and discussed within these networks depending on the nature of the communication channels.
2. Most Americans consult with others about consumer and political decisions.
3. The diffusion of mass-media information depends on local opinion leaders— locally recognized experts in a specific domain (political, fashion, consumer goods, etc.); opinion leaders rely heavily on the mass media as well as other sources for their expertise.
4. Information in social channels tends to be leveled (irrelevant details deleted) and sharpened (addition of information) depending on the needs and common knowledge of the community.

5. Rumors increase when people are uncertain; rumor creation is a means of dealing with that uncertainty.

In sum, social groups can amplify, modify, or diminish the effects of the mass media.

Soviet leaders also understood the power of the local group to mediate mass-communicated messages in ways that might run opposite to the goals of the leaders. To counter such possibilities, they instituted agitation or the transmission of political information by party members to small groups of co-workers (Benn, 1989; Inkeles, 1950; Mickiewicz, 1989). In the United States, leaders adopted a number of tactics to enlist the support of local groups, including local affiliates of political parties, detailed study of special groups such as physicians and pharmacists to understand new product adoption decisions (Katz, 1957), and complex psychographic techniques for understanding clusters of consumers who share certain attitudes and lifestyles (Piirto, 1991; Weinstein, 1987; Weiss, 1988).

Tactical Analysis of Mass Communications

Finally, both early (Lasswell, 1927; Lee & Lee, 1939) and contemporary (Cialdini, 1984; Pratkanis & Aronson, 1992) researchers have sought to understand the power of the mass communications by investigating the persuasion tactics commonly appearing in the media. This approach has used what Cialdini (1980) calls full-cycle social psychology: first, scout for persuasion tactics used in the mass media and then capture the phenomenon in the laboratory to understand when and how it works. Table 6.2 presents some of the fruits of this work—13 common (and effective) mass-media persuasion tactics that have been studied by social psychologists. It should be noted that all of these tactics rely on what can be called the cognitive response law of influence (Pratkanis & Aronson, 1992): The successful persuasion tactic is one that directs and channels thoughts so that the target thinks in a manner agreeable to the communicator's point of view; the successful tactic disrupts any negative thoughts and promotes positive thoughts about the proposed course of action.

Selected Issues in Mass Communications

In this section, we look at five topics—social issues of considerable importance in American democracy—that have received extensive research attention.

The Nature of Public Opinion

We have seen that the mass media are capable of selectively influencing perceptions, beliefs, and attitudes. What is the result of this influence? Such a question is of particular importance in democracies that ostensibly rely on public

Table 6.2. Common Persuasion Tactics Used in U.S. Mass Media

Authority. Linking a message with a source that is likable, attractive, or appears to be an expert (Cialdini, 1984; Pratkanis & Aronson, 1992).

Bandwagon. Making it appear that everyone supports a position or wants a desired option (Cialdini, 1984; Lee & Lee, 1939; Pratkanis & Aronson, 1992).

Commitment trap. Securing a commitment (either a small commitment or a false one) from a target and then insisting that the target act consistently with that commitment (Cialdini, 1984).

Decoy. An inferior option that makes other options appear superior by comparison (Pratkanis & Aronson, 1992; Tyszka, 1983).

Fear appeal. An appeal that arouses intense fear and offers a specific recommendation for overcoming the fear that the target believes will be effective (Pratkanis & Aronson, 1992).

Granfalloon tactic. Linking an advocated course of action with a target's social identity; to maintain a social identity, the target must perform the desired behavior (Pratkanis & Aronson, 1992).

Inoculation. To prevent persuasion, a target receives a brief, opposing message that can be easily refuted and thus immunizes against a subsequent attack (McGuire, 1964).

Norm of reciprocity. Giving a target a gift or performing a favor with the expectation that the target will be obliged to follow social norms and reciprocate by doing what you want him or her to do (Cialdini, 1984).

Pique technique. Disrupting a mindless refusal script with a strange or unusual request that induces the target to think positively about compliance (Santos, Leve, & Pratkanis, 1994).

Repetition with variation. The repetition of a message increases its familiarity, liking (Zajonc, 1965), and perceived validity (Boehm, 1994).

Scarcity. Making an alternative appear rare or unavailable in order to increase its value (Cialdini, 1984).

Self-generated persuasion. Subtly designing the situation so that a target generates arguments in support of a position (Lewin, 1947) or imagines adapting an advocated course of action (Gregory, Cialdini, & Carpenter, 1982).

Vivid appeals. Making a message emotionally interesting, concrete and image-provoking, and immediate (Nisbett & Ross, 1980).

opinion (see Price, 1992, for discussion). Researchers have looked at two issues: the societal consequences of public opinion (Glasser & Salmon, 1995) and the structure and function of individual attitudes (Pratkanis, Breckler, & Greenwald, 1989).

The Role of Public Opinion in Society. According to traditional democratic theory, public opinion is the aggregate opinion of citizens arrived at through the thoughtful consideration of the facts. Key (1967) has identified some common forms that public opinion may take: consensus (widespread agreement in the population on an issue that receives little debate), conflict (public opinion is divided on an issue that is hotly contested), and concentration (only a few citizens know and care about an issue). The role of the press (mass media) is to stimulate debate so that citizens can be better informed and reach a wise opinion. The primary purpose of public opinion is to convey to the governing the wants and feelings of the governed—a task accomplished in a mass society by opinion polling and market research.

In contrast to this traditional theory, Noelle-Neumann (1984, 1995) has proposed that the primary function of public opinion is social control through a spiral of silence. According to Noelle-Neumann, all societies threaten their members who deviate from consensus with isolation and individuals fear this isolation. Thus, citizens constantly survey the environment in order to see which opinions will win the approval of society and which will lead to isolation. The mass media reinforce a spiral of silence by describing what issues can be safely talked about and what issues and positions are taboo. When an issue is portrayed as acceptable, other individuals adopt that position, thus giving the impression that everyone thinks that way. On the other hand, when there is low support for an issue, people tend to conceal their positions, making the position appear weaker than it really is.

Which of these two views is correct? The traditional model emphasizes the feedback loop from citizens to leaders; leaders' actions are constrained by public opinion. The spiral of silence emphasizes conformity to public consensus conveyed, in part, by the mass media—a consensus that can be engineered by elites. As we noted above, the people are semisovereign and thus both positions have merit under certain conditions—leaders need to consider public opinion to stay in power, but they also have the ability to specify the range of thinking on a given issue.

The Sociocognitive Model of Attitudes.   How is public opinion represented in the individual? One answer is given by Pratkanis (Pratkanis, 1989; Pratkanis & Greenwald, 1989), who has proposed a sociocognitive model to describe the structure and function of attitudes. According to this model, attitudes are cognitive representations that serve to relate a person to the social world. When someone holds an attitude, three types of information can be stored in memory. First, there is an object label (e.g., abortion, the Furhman tapes, racial equality), along with rules for applying that label. Second, there is an evaluative summary of the object (e.g., Furhman is a racist). Third, there can be an organization of knowledge about the object and its evaluation (e.g., Furhman was an LAPD officer; why wasn't he fired?). Attitudinal knowledge may include arguments for or against a proposition, technical information about the object, guidelines for how to behave, and the social implications of adopting a belief. Three common organizations of attitudinal knowledge are cultural truism (an evaluation of an object with limited supporting knowledge), bipolar evaluation (an evaluation along with knowledge of arguments supporting and opposing this evaluation), and unipolar evaluation (an evaluation with knowledge on only one side of an issue). Attitudes as cognitive representations serve two important functions. First, they help the individual make sense of the social world (knowing function) by serving as a heuristic (use of stored evaluation to quickly appraise an object [Pratkanis, 1988]) and as a schema (use of attitudinal knowledge to organize and guide memory and complex action). Second, attitudes serve to maintain self-worth (self-functions); holding and expressing an attitude can generate approval from the private self (value expressive function), from generalized others (social adjustment function), or from a valued collective or reference group (social identity function). The sociocognitive model is useful for understanding mass media and public opinion on at least three accounts.

First, the sociocognitive model provides the psychological underpinnings for research on public opinion. For example, Key's (1967) three types of public opinion correspond to cultural truisms (consensus), bipolar attitudes (conflict), and unipolar attitudes (concentrated). Noelle-Neumann's (1995) position that public opinion is based on a desire to avoid isolation is consistent with the proposition that attitudes serve a self-function (in particular, social adjustment and social identity).

Second, the sociocognitive model provides a framework for understanding mass-media effects. We have seen that the media tell us what to think about and how to think about it but not necessarily what to think. In other words, the mass media produce their strongest effects in the formation of object labels (what is the issue? which ones are important to think about?) and on attitudinal knowledge (teaching how to behave and what other people think) and their weakest impact on the evaluative component. The sociocognitive model also predicts which types of attitudes will be the hardest to change—ones supported by bipolar knowledge (since the recipient has a store of knowledge to argue against any attack; see inoculation in table 6.2) and ones linked to the self (since an attack may result in the need for dissonance reduction).

Finally, one important concern is when individuals will act on the attitudes formed by the mass media. Early research on this issue found little relationship between attitudes and behavior (LaPiere, 1934; Wicker, 1969); however, recent work has established conditions under which attitudes will be predictive of behavior (see Ajzen & Fishbein, 1977; Fazio, 1986, for summaries). The sociocognitive model lists six conditions that increase the likelihood that an attitude will be predictive of overt behavior (Pratkanis & Turner, 1994): (1) the attitude object is well defined and salient for the person (or else it is difficult to access the evaluation of that object in order to act); (2) the evaluation is strong and comes quickly to mind (thereby influencing subsequent perceptions and judgments); (3) the person knows how to behave in support of an attitude; (4) the attitude is strongly linked to the self; (5) the behavior is self-consistent; and (6) the environment allows enough freedom to act on the attitude.

Mass-Media Politics

In 1952, presidential candidate Dwight D. Eisenhower hired famed advertiser Rosser Reeves to create a series of ads entitled Eisenhower Answers America. In these first televised political ads, Eisenhower answered seemingly spontaneous question posed by everyday Americans about issues such as taxes, the spread of communism, and U.S. involvement in Korea. Since that time presidential candidates have attempted to gain an advantage by creating ads that have used a little girl pulling the petals of a daisy to explode a nuclear bomb (Johnson versus Goldwater in 1964), shown upbeat pictures of America (Reagan versus Mondale in 1964), and featured an escaped black convict named Willie Horton (Bush versus Dukakis in 1988). In 1960, many Americans believed the election turned when John Kennedy successfully debated Richard Nixon on television (although radio listeners were likely to view Nixon as the winner). These incidents raise an important question: How has today's mass media—with their immediate coverage, message-dense environment, and entertainment emphasis—influenced political campaigns? Research has identified seven trends in current political campaigning (for discussions, see Ansolabehere, Behr, & Iyengar, 1993; Diamond & Bates, 1984; Graber, 1993; Kern, 1989; Jamieson, 1984, 1988; West, 1993; for an analysis of the 1992 presidential campaign, see Pratkanis, 1993).

1. In the 1940s, Lazarsfeld, Berelson, and Gaudet (1948) found that voters relied on party identification to make their political choices, either by using party as a simple decision rule (i.e., vote for my party) or through the interpersonal influence of party leaders. The rise of televised campaigns has changed the emphasis to those aspects that can be easily communicated in the mass media—the candidate's image and the position he or she takes on a few key issues (Abelson, Kinder, Peters, & Fiske, 1982; Boiney & Paletz, 1991; Graber, 1993; Sniderman, Brody, & Tetlock, 1991). In other words, candidates must now televise well.

2. The news media tend to cover elections as horse races (which candidate is ahead? will this change?) at the expense of an in-depth analysis of candidates and issues. The reason for this type of coverage is straightforward: ratings and circulation. A horse race is interesting, entertaining, and involves conflict and thus will generate viewers and readers; a discussion of issues is boring.

3. A major goal of a political campaign is to gain access to the media. Candidates can do this by purchasing media time for advertising or by trying to influence the news media to cover their campaign. Thus, campaigns attempt to create images and pithy sound bites for the media to cover.

4. Given the cost of media time, campaign funding-raising increases in importance. During the 1992 presidential campaign, Clinton spent $1.26 per vote (or $55 million), Bush spent $1.44 per vote (or $55 million), and Perot spent $3.12 (or $60 million) per vote (Pratkanis, 1993). A typical candidate for the U.S. Senate spends $2.5 million; a candidate for the House of Representatives spends $350,000 (Ansolabehere et al., 1993). And winning may depend on raising money. Typically, winners spend double the amount of losers—for example, $3.4 million to win a Senate seat (versus $1.9 million for a loser) and $410,000 to win a House seat (versus $200,000 for a loser [Ansolabehere et al., 1993]). Political advertising is especially effective when the candidates are relatively unknown, as in local elections. Thus, a premium is placed on satisfying those individuals and institutions that can contribute large amounts to a campaign.

5. We have seen that audience responses to the mass media tend to be via the peripheral route, and thus extended discourse on a range of topics is diffi-

cult. Because of this tendency, campaigns select a few key issues, develop images and slogans to address those issues, and then repeat those messages consistently (see Jamieson's 1984 analysis of winning political advertising). Unfortunately, such campaigns tend to do little to increase political knowledge (Entman, 1989).

6. Campaigns tend to be divisive, using negative character assassination (West, 1993) and wedge issues. One of the easiest ways to prevent another candidate from developing a positive image or destroying one that is already established is to attack his or her character through innuendoes (Wegner, Wenzalaff, Kerker, & Beattie, 1981). Given that only a few issues can be emphasized during the mass-media coverage of an election, campaigns try to emphasis wedge issues or issues that will splinter support for the opposition. For example, Republicans frequently use race to separate lower income whites from blacks in the Democratic Party, whereas Democrats use abortion rights to separate moderate Republican women from the rest of the party. Innuendo and wedge issues are popular with the media because they emphasis conflict and are entertaining.

7. Local campaigns are frequently ignored since the audience is often not large enough to support the expense of news coverage, despite the fact that many important decisions about the quality of life (schools, taxes, community development) are made at this level.

The Effects of Television Violence

American television, by any standard, is violent (for reviews, see National Institute of Mental Health [NIMH], 1972; Berkowitz, 1993; Comstock, 1980; Liebert & Sprafkin, 1988). The typical prime-time television show has 5 to 6 violent acts per hour; a typical children's cartoon has 21 violent acts per hour. Over 70 percent of all prime-time television contains at least one violent episode; 95 percent of all children's programming features violence.

Does all this aggression in the media have an effect? The answer is yes—watching violent television increases the likelihood of aggression among viewers (NIMH, 1972). What is the evidence for this conclusion? First, laboratory studies find that subjects who are shown violent television material are more likely to aggress later in the study (for example studies, see Bandura, 1973; Berkowitz, 1964; for reviews, see Andison, 1977; Wood, Wong, & Chachere, 1991). Second, natural experiments find that increases in televised violence results in increased violence. For example, Phillips (1986) found that homicide rates rose significantly on the third and fourth day after televised heavyweight championship prize fights. Third, correlational studies find that those children who are heavy viewers of violent television are more aggressive in school than their peers. For example, Eron (1963, 1987; Eron, Walder, & Lefkowitz, 1971) found that the more hours of television a child watched per week and the more violence in the child's three favorite television programs, the more likely other children were to rate that child as aggressive. Finally, longitudinal research has found that heavy doses of television violence as a child will make for a more aggressive adult. For example, a subset of those subjects who participated in the Eron (1963) study were contacted 10 and 20 years later and completed measures of adult aggression including self-reports and peer reports of aggression and legal offenses (Eron, Huesmann, Lefkowitz, & Walder, 1972; Huesmann, 1986). The results: third grade boys who exhibited the strongest preferences for violent television shows were the most aggressive men at age 19 and had the highest criminal conviction rates at age 30. These results have been replicated in the United States, Poland, and Finland and in Israeli cities (Huesmann & Eron, 1986; see also Murray & Kippax, 1979).

Indeed, the link between televised violence and aggression is so established that most researchers have turned their attention to the question of why. Three general answers have been supported by the literature. First, televised violence can serve as a model for how to respond to everyday situations (Bandura, 1973). Second, violent programs prime aggressive responses; in other words, heavy doses of television violence increase the likelihood that aggressive thoughts and responses will come to mind in a variety of situations and then be acted upon (Berkowitz, 1984). Finally, aggressive television teaches how violence (as opposed to alternative approaches) can be used to resolve social conflicts (Huesmann, 1986).

Can anything be done to reduce the effects of watching violent television? One obvious approach is to change the content of programming to feature less violence and more prosocial models. The evidence shows that such programming does reduce violence and promotes prosocial behavior. However, such proposals have not met with widespread acceptance among television executives, who view violent programming as an inexpensive way to maintain ratings. Alternatively, parents and teachers can instruct children on how to respond cognitively to television violence. For example, in one study, schoolchildren were induced to self-generate and then think about reasons why television violence is bad (Huesmann, Eron, Klein, Brice, & Fischer, 1983). Four months later, these children were less aggressive than their classmates, and, most interesting, there was no correlation between how much television violence these students watched and their level of aggression.

Children and Advertising

Children's advertising is big business. In 1992, children between the ages of 4 and 19 spent $102 billion and directly influenced their families to spend another $130 billion (Jacobson & Mazur, 1995). U.S. businesses spend an estimated $6.8 billion a year on marketing communications directed toward children (McNeal, 1992) through a wide range of media, including Saturday morning and early afternoon television (Schneider, 1987), Channel One (a commercial television channel delivered to schools), and magazines and newspapers designed for children.

How do children respond to mass communications? The research to date has found the following (see Comstock, 1980; Comstock & Paik, 1991; Goldberg & Gorn, 1978; Liebert & Sprafkin, 1988; Murray & Kippax, 1979):

1. Children below the age of 8 demonstrate very good recognition of advertised brand names but poor recall of the specifics of advertised claims.
2. Young children do not understand the persuasive intent of advertising.
3. Children who frequently watch children's programs on television are more likely to request and consume advertised snacks, cereals, and fast food.
4. Over 90 percent of children (in one study) asked for toys and food they saw advertised on television.
5. Children who watch advertising increasingly accept materialistic values. One study showed that 4- and 5-year-old children, after watching an ad for a toy, were twice as likely to say that they would rather play with a "not so nice boy" with the toy than a "nice boy" without the toy.

The susceptibility of children to persuasive appeals has results in calls for the government regulation of children's advertising—for example, to reduce the number of ads per hour on children's shows, to require clear separation between ads and programs, and to prohibit certain types of appeals (e.g., those suggesting that product ownership will enhance a child's social standing). The implementation of such regulations is a political matter and has varied as a function of the agenda of government leaders (with regulations reaching a peak in the 1970s and declining in the 1980s).

Prosocial Uses of the Mass Media

Can the mass media be used to obtain prosocial goals such as promoting world peace, increasing safe driving, improving health, and cultivating academic achievement? The answer is yes, but only under certain conditions. Some of the first uses of American mass media to promote prosocial goals employed what can be termed an information campaign. These campaigns featured a highly intelligent discussion of an issue at hand (say, U.S.–Russia relationships or the need for health-care reform) with a detailed presentation of the problem and a careful weighing of options. Such critical discussions should be valued in democracies that place considerable emphasis on an informed populace. However, information campaigns of this nature routinely failed to inform and convince. As Hyman and Sheatsley (1947) noted, large segments of the American population find such shows to be of little interest and often avoid or reinterpret information that is disagreeable. (Interestingly, during the 1970s, some Russian researchers reached the same conclusion about Soviet news and information affairs programming; see Benn, 1989; Mickiewicz, 1989).

Nevertheless, some information campaigns do work (Kotler & Roberto, 1989; Mendelsohn, 1973). For example, during World War II, a radio program hosted by the singer Kate Smith was highly successful in strengthening American commitment to the war effort and sold $39 million worth of bonds to finance the war (Merton, 1946). In 1965, CBS television sought to promote safe driving by airing *The National Drivers' Test*, a show in which drivers were given a quiz about how to handle various road situations. The show was viewed by 30 million Americans, of whom 1.5 million wrote CBS for more information and at least 35,000 enrolled in driver-improvement courses (Mendelsohn, 1973).

Why did these campaigns succeed where others failed? Four principles of successful campaigns can be identified. First, make the program entertaining. Kate Smith was a very popular singer of her time, and *The National Drivers' Test* was intriguing (just what is the right thing to do?). Entertainment gives viewers a reason to watch and not change the channel—a principle clearly understood by Nazi propagandist Joseph Goebbels, who made sure Hitler spoke on the radio after the appearance of popular singers. Second, do not directly attack a viewer's attitudes and beliefs and thus encourage the listener to tune out. Smith linked the war effort with American values. *The National Drivers' Test* allowed viewers to discover what they know about safe driving on their own instead of being scolded to "practice safe driving" or told they were "bad drivers." Third, use influence tactics, as listed in table 6.2. Kate Smith used such tactics as repetition with variation (stating reasons to "buy bonds" in different ways) and granfallooning (we are in this war together). *The National Drivers' Test* employed self-generated persuasion as viewers sought to find the correct answer to each question. Finally, request a simple, straightforward, and doable response from the audience: buy war bonds and take courses to improve driving skills.

One of the most ambitious attempts at using the mass media to obtain prosocial goals with children has been the use of television to encourage academic achievement through shows such as *Sesame Street* and to promote positive social relations through shows such as *Mr. Roger's Neighborhood*. The logic is clear: by the time a typical American child graduates from high school, he or she will have spent more time in front of a television set (17,000 hours) than in a classroom (11,000 hours). Why not use television to teach?

In general, the results have been positive. For example, *Sesame Street* has been on the air since 1969 and is watched on a weekly basis by about half of all preschoolers in America (Liebert & Sprafkin, 1988). The program teaches such skills as counting, letter and number recognition, and vocabulary through fast-moving, attention-grabbing segments featuring characters such as Bert and Ernie, Big Bird, and Oscar the Grouch. (Note the adherence to our formula given above.) Early tests of the program found that preschoolers who watched *Sesame Street* showed significant gains on education tests measuring knowledge of letters and numbers and matching, sorting, and classifying skills (Ball & Bogatz, 1970; Bogatz & Ball, 1972). However, there is a fly in the ointment—in natural settings not all children watch *Sesame Street*. In particular, children from advantaged homes are more likely to watch *Sesame Street* than those from disadvantaged homes, and thus the program (opposite to its original intentions) may increase the knowledge gap between rich and poor children (Cook et al., 1975). Positive results have been obtained for shows such as *Mr. Roger's Neighborhood*, which attempt to promote altruism, cooperation, and other prosocial behavior; children who watch such shows on a regular basis are more likely to engage in prosocial behavior (Stein & Friedrich, 1972; Friedrich & Stein, 1975; Hearold, 1986; Murray & Kippax, 1979; Rushton, 1979).

The Importance of the Next Wave of Mass Communications Research

In 1991, over 1 billion people in 108 nations tuned in to CNN to watch its coverage of the Persian Gulf War. Mass-media entertainment is the United States' second largest export in what is mostly a one-way exchange. (For example, international sales of movies make up half of Hollywood's revenues, whereas foreign films make up only 2% of the U.S. market.) Mergers and buyouts in the 1980s have created cross-national, interlocking media giants such as Time-Warner, Paramount, Newhouse, Capital Cities/ABC, and others that have the ability to disseminate information worldwide. Mass communications are becoming increasingly global in their scope, giving worldwide significance to research on the mass media and especially American-style media, which currently dominate world markets. What will the next generation of mass communications research tell us?

Although research trends are hard to predict, we can expect the next generation of communications research to get its inspiration from one of two sources. First, researchers will continue to pursue the questions raised by their theoretical models and past empirical findings. For example, researchers will continue to look for new persuasion tactics, attempt to understand the implications of the ELM, explore how mass-media attitudes develop and with what impact, and continue to address issues such as television violence and consumerism.

Second, communications researchers study a dynamic set of phenomena; these changes will motivate research from two perspectives. Some researchers will take the perspective of those who own and use the mass media and investigate the question of how to use the mass media more effectively. Such researchers are likely to be interested in the development of new forms of mass media (such as the Internet, virtual reality, and homes wired for over 500 cable channels) and to continue their interest in refining mass-media technique. Other researchers will take a perspective that is critical of the media. These researchers will be interested in documenting the unintended consequences of the media, observing trends that may have an adverse impact on society and discovering ways to correct what are perceived to be mass-media abuses and problems. Of particular importance is the issue of how to conduct a democracy in a mass-media environment (see Pratkanis & Turner, in press).

With the globalization of mass communications, it becomes increasingly important to study the mass media and how they operate in different social environments—a goal promoted by the present volume. Cross-cultural comparisons of mass media can show us what we share in common. For example, many of the persuasion tactics described in table 6.2, the finding that televised violence promotes aggression, the way that social networks buffer mass-media effects, and the importance of cognitive responses in persuasion are not limited to the United States. Our differences are important, too. If we view the way each culture structures and uses its mass media as a social experiment, then we can gain much-needed knowledge about what works and what doesn't work in our attempt to obtain persuasion and communication that live up to our ideals.

References

Aaker, D. A., & Myers, J. G. (1987). *Advertising management*. Englewood Cliffs, N.J.: Prentice-Hall.

Abelson, R. P., Kinder, D. R., Peters, M. D., & Fiske, S. T. (1982). Affective and semantic components in political person perception. *Journal of Personality and Social Psychology, 42*, 619–630.

Ajzen, I., & Fishbein, M. (1977). Attitude-behavior relations: A theoretical analysis and review of empirical research. *Psychological Review, 84*, 888–918.

Andison, F. S. (1977). TV violence and viewer aggression: A cumulation of study results, 1956–1976. *Public Opinion Quarterly, 41*, 314–331.

Ansolabehere, S., Behr, R., & Iyengar, S. (1993). *The media game*. New York: Macmillan.

Aronson, E. (1969). The theory of cognitive dissonance: A current perspective. In L. Berkowitz (ed.), *Advances in experimental social psychology* (vol. 4, pp. 1–34). New York: Academic Press.

Bagdikian, B. H. (1992). *The media monopoly*. Boston: Beacon.

Ball, S., & Bogatz, G. A. (1970). *The first year of Sesame Street*. Princeton, N.J.: Educational Testing Service.

Bandura, A. (1973). *Aggression: A social learning approach*. Englewood Cliffs, N.J.: Prentice-Hall.

Benn, D. W. (1989). *Perusasion and Soviet politics*. New York: Basil Blackwell.

Berelson, B., Lazarsfeld, P., & McPhee, W. (1954). *Voting*. Chicago: University of Chicago Press.

Berkowitz, L. (1964). The effects of observed violence. *Scientific American, 210*, 35–41.

Berkowitz, L. (1984). Some effects of thoughts on anti- and prosocial influences of media events: A cognitive-neoassociation analysis. *Psychological Bulletin, 95*, 410–427.

Berkowitz, L. (1993). *Aggression*. New York: McGraw-Hill.

Boehm, L. E. (1994). The validity effect: A search for mediating variables. *Personality and Social Psychology Bulletin, 20*, 285–293.

Bogart, L. (1972). *The age of television*. New York: Frederick Ungar.

Bogart, L. (1981). *Press and public*. Hillsdale, N.J.: Lawrence Erlbaum.

Bogart, L. (1990). *Strategy in advertising*. Lincolnwood, Ill.: NTC Business Books.

Bogart, L. (1995). *Commercial culture*. New York: Oxford University Press.

Bogatz, G. A., & Ball, S. (1972). *The second year of Sesame Street*. Princeton, N.J.: Educational Testing Service.

Boiney, J., & Paletz, D. (1991). In search of the model model: Political science versus political advertising perspectives on voter decision making. In F. Biocca (ed.), *Television and political adverting* (vol. 1, pp. 3–25). Hillsdale, N.J.: Lawrence Erlbaum.

Boorstin, D. J. (1961). *The image: A guide to pseudo-events in America*. New York: Atheneum.

Burnett, L. (1961). *Communications of an advertising man*. Chicago: Leo Burnett.

Cantril, H., & Allport, G. W. (1935). *The psychology of radio*. New York: Harper Brothers.

Caples, J. (1974). *Tested advertising methods*. Englewood Cliffs, N.J.: Prentice-Hall.

Cialdini, R. B. (1980). Full-cycle social psychology. In L. Berkowitz (ed.), *Applied social psychology annual* (vol. 1, pp. 21–47). Beverly Hills: Sage.

Cialdini, R. B. (1984). *Influence.* New York: William Morrow.

Colley, R., & Dutka, S. (1995). *DAGMAR: Defining advertising goals for measured advertising results.* Lincolnwood, ILL: NTC Business Books.

Comstock, G. (1980). *Television in America.* Beverly Hills: Sage.

Comstock, G., & Paik, H. (1991). *Television and the American child.* San Diego: Academic Press.

Cook, T. D., Appleton, H., Conner, R. F., Shaffer, A., Tabkin, G., & Weber, J. S. (1975). *Sesame Street revisited.* New York: Russell Sage.

Croteau, D., & Hoynes, W. (1994). *By invitation only.* Monroe, Maine: Common Courage.

DeFleur, M. L, & Ball-Rokeach, S. (1989). *Theories of mass communication.* White Plains, N.Y.: Longman.

Diamond, E., & Bates, S. (1984). *The spot.* Cambridge, Mass.: MIT Press.

Entman, R. M. (1989). *Democracy without citizens.* New York: Oxford University Press.

Ernst, S. W. (1972). Baseball or brickbats: A content analysis of community development. *Journalism Quarterly, 49,* 86–90.

Eron, L. D. (1963). Relationship of TV viewing habits and aggressive behavior in children. *Journal of Abnormal and Social Psychology, 67,* 193–196.

Eron, L. D. (1987). The development of aggressive behavior from the perspective of a developing behaviorist. *American Psychologist, 42,* 435–442.

Eron, L. D., Huesmann, L. R., Lefkowitz, M. M., & Walder, L. O. (1972). Does television violence cause aggression? *American Psychologist, 27,* 253–263.

Eron, L. D., Walder, L. O., & Lefkowitz, M. M. (1971). *Learning of aggression in children.* Boston: Little, Brown.

Fazio, R. H. (1986). How do attitudes guide behavior? In R. M. Sorrentino & E. T. Higgins (eds.), *Handbook of motivation* (pp. 204–242). New York: Guilford.

Festinger, L. (1957). *Theory of cognitive dissonance.* Stanford, Calif.: Stanford University Press.

Festinger, L., & Carlsmith, J. M. (1959). Cognitive consequences of forced compliance. *Journal of Abnormal and Social Psychology, 58,* 203–210.

Fishman, M. (1980). *Manufacturing the news.* Austin: University of Texas Press.

Fox, S. (1984). *The mirror makers.* New York: William Morrow.

Friedrich, L. K., & Stein, A. H. (1975). Prosocial television and young children: The effects of verbal labeling and role playing on learning and behavior. *Child Development, 46,* 27–38.

Gans, H. J. (1979). *Deciding what's news.* New York: Pantheon.

Garcia, J., & Koelling, R. A. (1966). Relation of cue to consequence in avoidance learning. *Psychometric Science, 4,* 123–124.

Gerbner, G., Gross, L., Morgan, M., & Signorielli, N. (1986). Living with television: The dynamics of the cultivation process. In J. Bryant & D. Zillman (eds.), *Perspectives on media effects* (pp. 17–40). Hillsdale, N.J.: Lawrence Erlbaum.

Glasser, T. L., & Salmon, C. T. (eds.) (1995). *Public opinion and the communication of consent.* New York: Guilford.

Goldberg, M. E., & Gorn, G. J. (1978). Some unintended consequences of TV advertising to children. *Journal of Consumer Research, 5,* 22–29.

Graber, D. A. (1993). *Mass media and American politics.* Washington, D.C.: Congressional Quarterly.

Greenwald, A. G. (1968). Cognitive learning, cognitive response in persuasion, and attitude change. In. A. G. Greenwald, T. C. Brock, & T. M. Ostrom (eds.), *Psychological foundations of attitudes* (pp. 147–170). New York: Academic Press.

Gregory, W. L., Cialdini, R. B., & Carpenter, K. M. (1982). Self-relevant scenarios as mediators of likelihood estimates and compliance: Does imagining make it so? *Journal of Personality and Social Psychology, 43,* 89–99.

Hearold, S. (1986). A synthesis of 1,043 effects of television on social behavior. In G. Comstock (ed.), *Public communication and behavior* (vol. 1, pp. 66–133). San Diego: Academic Press.

Holifield, E. B. (1989). *The era of persuasion: American thought and culture, 1521–1680.* Boston: Twayne.

Hovland, C. I., Janis, I. L., & Kelley, H. H. (1953). *Communication and persuasion.* New Haven: Yale University Press.

Huesmann, L. R. (1986). Psychological processes promoting the relation between exposure to media violence and aggressive behavior by the viewer. *Journal of Social Issues, 42,* 125–140.

Huesmann, L. R., & Eron, L. D. (eds.) (1986). *Television and the aggressive child: A cross-national comparison.* Hillsdale, N.J.: Lawrence Erlbaum.

Huesmann, L. R., Eron, L. D., Klein, R., Brice, P., & Fischer, P. (1983). Mitigating the imitation of aggressive behaviors by changing children's attitudes about media violence. *Journal of Personality and Social Psychology, 44,* 899–910.

Hyman, H. H., & Sheatsley, P. B. (1947). Some reasons why information campaigns fail. *Public Opinion Quarterly, 11,* 412–423.

Inkeles, A. (1950). *Public opinion in Soviet Russia.* Cambridge, Mass.: Harvard University Press.

Iyengar, S. (1991). *Is anyone responsible?: How television frames political issues.* Chicago: University of Chicago Press.

Iyengar, S., & Kinder, D. R. (1987). *News that matters.* Chicago: University of Chicago Press.

Jacobson, M. F., & Mazur, L. A. (1995). *Marketing madness.* Boulder, Colo.: Westview Press.

Jamieson, K. H. (1984). *Packaging the presidency.* New York: Oxford University Press.

Jamieson, K. H. (1988). *Eloquence in an electronic age.* New York: Oxford University Press.

Jamieson, K. H., & Campbell, K. K. (1992). *The interplay of influence.* Belmont, Calif.: Wadsworth.

Jones, J. P. (1995). *When ads work.* New York: Lexington Books.

Jowett, G., & Linton, J. M. (1989). *Movies as mass communication.* Newbury Park, Calif.: Sage.

Kaniss, P. (1991). *Making local news.* Chicago: University of Chicago Press.

Kapferer, J. N. (1990). *Rumors.* New Brunswick, N.J.: Transaction.

Katz, E. (1957). The two-step flow of communication: An up-to-date report on an hypothesis. *Public Opinion Quarterly, 21,* 61–67.

Katz, E., & Lazarsfeld, P. F. (1955). *Personal influence.* New York: Free Press.

Kern, M. (1989). *30-second politics.* New York: Praeger.

Key, V. O. (1967). *Public opinion and American democracy.* New York: Knopf.

Kleepner, O. (1973). *Advertising procedure.* Englewood Cliffs, N.J.: Prentice-Hall.

Kotler, P., & Roberto, E. L. (1989). *Social marketing.* New York: Free Press.

Krugman, H. E. (1965). The impact of television advertising: Learning without involvement. *Public Opinion Quarterly, 29*, 349–356.

LaPiere, R. T. (1934). Attitudes versus action. *Social Forces, 13*, 230–237.

Lasswell, H. (1927). *Propaganda technique in the world war.* New York: Knopf.

Lazarsfeld, P., Berelson, B., & Gaudet, H. (1948). *The people's choice.* New York: Columbia University Press.

Lee, A. M., & Lee, E. B. (1939). *The fine art of propaganda.* New York: Harcourt, Brace, & Co.

Lewin, K. (1947). Group decision and social change. In T. M. Newcomb & E. L. Hartley (eds.), *Readings in social psychology* (pp. 330–344). New York: Holt.

Liebert, R. M., & Sprafkin, J. (1988). *The early window.* New York: Pergamon.

Marks, J. (1979). *The search for the "Manchurian candidate."* New York: W. W. Norton.

McCombs, M. E., & Shaw, D. L. (1972). The agenda setting function of mass media. *Public Opinion Quarterly, 36*, 176–187.

McGuire, W. J. (1964). Inducing resistance to persuasion: Some contemporary approaches. In L. Berkowitz (ed.), *Advances in experimental social psychology* (vol. 1, pp. 191–229). New York: Academic Press.

McGuire, W. J. (1968). Personality and attitude change: An information-processing theory. In A. G. Greenwald, T. C. Brock, & T. M. Ostrom (eds.), *Psychological foundations of attitudes* (pp. 171–196). New York: Academic Press.

McGuire, W. J. (1986). The myth of massive media impact: Savagings and salvagings. In G. Comstock (ed.), *Public communication and behavior* (vol. 1, pp. 175–257). San Diego: Academic Press.

McNeal, J. U. (1992). *Kids as customers.* New York: Lexington Books.

Mendelsohn, H. (1973). Some reasons why information campaigns can succeed. *Public Opinion Quarterly, 37*, 50–61.

Merton, R. K. (1946). *Mass persuasion: The social psychology of a war bond drive.* New York: Harper & Brothers.

Mickiewicz, E. (1989). *Split signals.* New York: Oxford University Press.

Moore, T. E. (1982). Subliminal advertising: What you see is what you get. *Journal of Marketing Research, 46*, 38–47.

Murray, J. P., & Kippax, S. (1979). From the early window to the late night show: International trends in the study of television's impact on children and adults. In L. Berkowitz (ed.), *Advances in experimental social psychology* (vol. 12, pp. 254–320). New York: Academic Press.

National Institute of Mental Health (1972). *Television and growing up: The impact of televised violence.* (DHEW Publication No. HSM 72–9090.) Washington, D.C.: U.S. Government Printing Office.

Nisbett, R. E., & Ross, L. (1980). *Human inference: Strategies and shortcomings of social judgment.* Englewood Cliffs, N.J.: Prentice-Hall.

Noelle-Neumann, E. (1984). *The spiral of silence.* Chicago: University of Chicago Press.

Noelle-Neumann, E. (1995). Public opinion and rationality. In T. L. Glasser & C. T Salmon (eds.), *Public opinion and the communication of consent* (pp. 33–54). New York: Guilford.

Ogilvy, D. (1983). *Ogilvy on advertising.* New York: Crown.

Packard, V. (1957). *The hidden persuaders.* New York: MacKay.

Petty, R. E., & Cacioppo, J. T. (1981). *Attitudes and persuasion: Classic and contemporary approaches.* Dubuque: Wm. C. Brown.

Petty, R. E., & Cacioppo, J. T. (1986). *Communication and persuasion: Central and peripheral routes to attitude change.* New York: Springer-Verlag.

Petty, R. E., Cacioppo, J. T., & Goldman, R. (1981). Personal involvement as a determinant of argument-based persuasion. *Journal of Personality and Social Psychology, 41,* 847–855.

Petty, R. E., Ostrom, T. M., & Brock, T. C. (eds.) (1981). *Cognitive response in persuasion.* Hillsdale, N.J.: Lawrence Erlbaum.

Phillips, D. P. (1986). Natural experiments on the effects of mass media violence and fatal aggression: Strengths and weaknesses of a new approach. In L. Berkowitz (ed.), *Advances in experimental social psychology* (vol. 19, pp. 207–250). New York: Academic Press.

Piirto, R. (1991). *Beyond mind games.* Ithaca, NY: American Demographics Books.

Politz, A. (1957). Motivational research from a research viewpoint. *Public Opinion Quarterly, 20,* 663–673.

Pratkanis, A. R. (1988). The attitude heuristic and selective fact identification. *British Journal of Social Psychology, 27,* 257–263.

Pratkanis, A. R. (1989). The cognitive representation of attitudes. In A. R. Pratkanis, S. J. Breckler, & A. G. Greenwald (eds.), *Attitude structure and function* (pp. 71–98). Hillsdale, N.J.: Lawrence Erlbaum.

Pratkanis, A. R. (1992). The cargo-cult science of subliminal persuasion. *Skeptical Inquirer, 16,* 260–272.

Pratkanis, A. R. (1993). Propaganda and persuasion in the 1992 U.S. presidential election: What are the implications for democracy? *Current World Leaders, 35,* 341–362.

Pratkanis, A. R., & Aronson, E. (1992). *Age of propaganda: The everyday use and abuse of persuasion.* New York: W. H. Freeman.

Pratkanis, A. R., Breckler, S. J., & Greenwald, A. G. (eds.) (1989). *Attitude structure and function.* Hillsdale, NJ: Lawrence Erlbaum.

Pratkanis, A. R., Eskenazi, J., & Greenwald, A. G. (1994). What you expect is what you believe (but not necessarily what you get): A test of the effectiveness of subliminal self-help audiotapes. *Basic and Applied Social Psychology, 15,* 251–276.

Pratkanis, A. R., & Greenwald, A. G. (1988). Recent perspectives on unconscious processing: Still no marketing applications. *Psychology & Marketing, 5,* 339–355.

Pratkanis, A. R., & Greenwald, A. G. (1989). A socio-cognitive model of attitude structure and function. In L. Berkowitz (ed.), *Advances in experimental social psychology* (vol. 22, pp. 245–285). New York: Academic Press.

Pratkanis, A. R., & Turner, M. E. (1994). Of what value is a job attitude?: A socio-cognitive analysis. *Human Relations, 47,* 1545–1576.

Pratkanis, A. R., & Turner, M. E. (in press). Persuasion and democracy: Strategies for increasing deliberative participation and enacting social change. *Journal of Social Issues.*

Preston, I. L. (1994). *The tangled web they weave: Truth, falsity, and advertisers.* Madison: University of Wisconsin Press.

Price, V. (1992). *Public opinion.* Newbury Park, Calif.: Sage.

Reeves, R. (1961). *Reality in advertising.* New York: Knopf.

Richards, J. I. (1990). *Deceptive advertising.* Hillsdale, N.J.: Lawrence Erlbaum.

Ries, A., & Trout, J. (1981). *Positioning.* New York: Warner.

Rogers, E. M. (1983). *Diffusion of innovations.* New York: Free Press.

Roman, K., & Maas, J. (1992). *The new how to advertise.* New York: St. Martin's.

Rosnow, R. L., & Fine, G. A. (1976). *Rumor and gossip.* New York: Elsevier.

Rubin, A. M. (1994). Media uses and effects: A uses-and-gratifications perspective. In J. Bryant & D. Zillman (eds.), *Media effects*. Hillsdale, N.J.: Lawrence Erlbaum.

Rushton, J. P. (1979). Effects of prosocial television and film material on the behavior of viewers. In L. Berkowitz (ed.), *Advances in experimental social psychology* (vol. 12, pp. 321–351). New York: Academic Press.

Santos, M. D., Leve, C., & Pratkanis, A. R. (1994). Hey buddy, can you spare seventeen cents?: Mindful persuasion and the pique technique. *Journal of Applied Social Psychology*, 24, 755–764.

Schattschneider, E. E. (1960). *The semisovereign people*. Hinsdale, Ill.: Dryden.

Schneider, C. (1987). *Children's television*. Lincolnwood, Ill.: NTC Business Books.

Sigal, L. V. (1973). *Reporters and officials: The organization and politics of newsmaking*. Lexington, Mass.: D. C. Heath.

Sniderman, P. M., Brody, R. A., & Tetlock, P. E. (1991). *Reasoning and choice*. New York: Cambridge University Press.

Spanos, N. P., & Chaves, J. F. (eds.) (1989). *Hypnosis*. Buffalo, N.Y.: Prometheus.

Stein, A. H., & Friedrich, L. K. (1972). Television content and young children's behavior. In J. P. Murray, E. A. Rubinstein, & G. A. Comstock (eds.), *Television and social behavior* (vol. 2, pp. 202–317). (DHEW Publication No. HSM 72–9057.) Washington, D.C.: U.S. Government Printing Office.

Tebbel, J., & Zuckerman, M. E. (1991). *The magazine in America*. New York: Oxford University Press.

Toennies, F. (1887/1971). *On sociology: Pure, applied, and empirical*. Chicago: University of Chicago Press.

Tuchman, G. (1978). *Making news*. New York: Free Press.

Tyszka, T. (1983). Contextual multiattribute decision rules. In L. Sjoberg, T. Tyszka, & J. Wise (eds.), *Human decision making*. Lund, Sweden: Doxa.

Volkogonov, D. (1986). *The psychological war*. Moscow: Progress Publishers.

Wegner, D. M., Wenzalaff, R., Kerker, R. M., & Beattie, A. E. (1981). Incrimination through innuendo: Can media questions become public answers? *Journal of Personality and Social Psychology*, 40, 822–832.

Weimann, G. (1994). *The influentials*. Albany, N.Y.: State University of New York Press.

Weinstein, A. (1987). *Market segmentation*. Chicago: Probus.

Weiss, M. J. (1988). *The clustering of America*. New York: Harper & Row.

West, D. M. (1993). *Air wars*. Washington, D.C.: Congressional Quarterly.

Wicker, A. W. (1969). Attitudes versus action: The relationship of verbal and overt behavioral responses to attitude objects. *Journal of Social Issues*, 25, 41–78.

Wood, W., Wong, F. Y., & Chachere, J. G. (1991). Effects of media violence on viewers' aggression in unconstrained social interaction. *Psychological Bulletin*, 109, 371–383.

Zajonc, R. B. (1968). The attitudinal effects of mere exposure. *Journal of Personality and Social Psychology*, Monograph Supplement, 9, 1–27.

PART TWO

CONTEMPORARY CRISES

in MENTAL HEALTH

Many people who are not familiar with the field of psychology believe that psychology is primarily about mental health. In fact, mental health or illness is only one of several different areas of study in psychology. In this part, we focus on three different areas of mental health rather than tackling the entire field. The three areas were selected because they are especially critical at this time in history, and we believe that they will continue to be critical issues as we enter the next millennium.

Readers may be surprised at the choice of alcoholism as a contemporary problem in mental health because it is certainly not a new problem in either the United States or the former Soviet countries. Alcoholism is a national tragedy in modern Russia and in many areas of the West and other places in the world. Although no country has a monopoly on the pain caused by excessive alcohol use, modern Russia seems to be particularly hard hit. Recent surveys show that Russia has the highest alcohol consumption rate in the world and that it is still rising (Specter, 1995). Not only are more Russians drinking excessively, but they are drinking larger quantities than in any other country, with an average of 14.5 liters of pure alcohol per capita, a number that many believe is a serious underestimation because it does not include "home brews," which are popular in Russia (Efron, 1995). The Russians and later the Soviets imported this tragedy to Siberia, where it has decimated the native population. In this regard, the spread of alcoholism to Siberian natives is analogous to the death and depression suffered by Native North Americans in the United States and Canada when alcohol was brought to them by the European Americans who had settled on their land.

Soviet propaganda was fond of presenting American alcoholics and drug abusers as an example of the decadence, despair, and decline in moral values caused by market economy systems. Outside the Soviet Union, alcohol and drug abuse were presented as social problems. Not so inside the country. Considering that alcoholics needed medical treatment, this treatment was administered in a characteristically totalitarian way. Treatment for alcoholics was a task officially assigned to the militia. Military treatment of alcoholics consisted of mandatory stays in harsh facilities (a sort of imprisonment) and some experimental treatment with aversion therapies, such as those that would cause the alcoholics to vomit if they ingested alcohol. In fact, there were no effective treatment programs for any type of drug abuse in the Soviet Union because the existence of such programs would mean that the authorities would have to admit that Soviets abused alcohol and other drugs. Such an admission was unthinkable, or at least unspeakable, because it would show communism to be imperfect.

Voiskounsky, the Russian editor, has reflected on the reasons why alcoholism has been such a major problem in the Soviet Union. He believes that it reflects the hopelessness and powerlessness that many Russians (in prerevolutionary Russia) and Soviets felt and contemporary Russians still feel. When people consume alcohol, they often gain self-confidence; they believe that they are wittier, more confident, and more popular than they are when they are sober. Drinking is also a social activity, especially for Soviet/Russian men. It represents a kind of community. Being a drunkard is seen as a philosophical approach to life and a type of escapism. Escaping from the sober and always unfriendly reality is common for the most gifted Russians. Among those who have died most recently are Venedikt Yerofeev, writer; Evald Ilyenkov, philosopher; and Anatoly Zverev, artist. Escape into alcoholism is a common theme in classic and modern literature. An expression in Russian roughly translates to "Drink a lot to forget yourself." It is a problem that is centuries old— every bitterly cold morning, alcoholics who had passed out in the streets the night before and died because they could not survive a night in the extreme cold were hauled off to the morgue.

The moral sanctions against women alcoholics are even stricter than against men with the same problem. Alcoholic men are frequently seen in public places, and many prominent families have male family members with serious alcohol problems. The visibility and widespread prevalence of alcoholism among males both reflects and creates a more tolerant attitude toward males, but alcoholic women are thought of as a disgrace. When asked about this sex-differentiated evaluation of the same problem behavior, most Russians explain that women are mothers and wives, and this is no way for a woman to behave. The idea that men are fathers and husbands does not seem at all comparable. Alcoholism is but one area in which women and men are held to very different standards of behavior. Despite the strong sanctions against alcoholism for women, many indicators suggest that alcohol is a terrible problem for women. For years, large numbers of abandoned children have been reared in orphanages, many of them with obvious health problems caused by fetal alcohol syndrome (Efron, 1995). Women also suffer when they have alcoholic husbands or fathers who beat them, cannot keep a job, or die a premature death.

The toll that alcohol exacts from every segment of the Russian population is enormous.

Alcoholism has become an even greater problem in the last several years. For some periods under communism, the sale of vodka was restricted, so that it was difficult to obtain large quantities at any one time. There are no restrictions under the new market economy. Single-serving plastic cups of vodka are now available on most street corners from vendors, prepackaged in small cups covered with foil, like single servings of juice or other beverages. Most men drink it on the spot and can get their much-needed drink without purchasing an entire bottle at one time. Such convenience will only worsen an already bad problem.

We are very fortunate to include the chapter written by Boris S. Bratus, a leading authority on alcoholism. Bratus describes an extensive social network that supports excessive consumption of alcohol. Children learn at a very young age that drinking alcohol is as much a part of Russian life as snow in Moscow. All of life's significant events are celebrated with drinking, and to refuse to drink, especially by males, is considered rude and even arrogant. It numbs the pain when life is hard. Alcohol satisfies so many needs that it is easy to understand why it is abused.

The American chapter on alcoholism, written by Peter Nathan, shows that alcohol abuse is also a major problem in the United States. Nathan is a prolific author and an expert in the area of alcoholism. He presents information about its prevalence, diagnostic criteria, types of treatment, and major problems that are associated with this cruel problem. Data are presented on controversial issues, such as the heritability of alcoholism and comparisons of treatment programs that permit or do not permit moderate drinking. Alcoholism and other types of drug abuse are likely to remain a major health problem for much of the world well into the 21st century.

Psychological trauma is the second topic addressed in this trilogy of crises in mental health. Psychological trauma is as old as humankind because humans have always had to cope with devastating disasters, of both natural and human origin. Post-traumatic stress syndrome is the official label for the psychological sequelae of traumatic events. Teresa L. Kramer and Bonnie L. Green discuss this complex phenomenon, including the defining symptoms, treatment options, and prognoses. Madrudin S. Magomed-Eminov has written the corresponding chapter based on post-Soviet nosologies and experiences. Although the recognition of this problem and theories of its origin are quite different in the Western and post-Soviet societies, the syndrome itself seems to be remarkably similar in both cultures. The post-Soviet perspective is more existential in its approach than the Western perspective, which seems to be more empirically based. Much can be learned by comparing these two perspectives.

There are many reasons why psychological studies of trauma are critically important. Former war veterans, especially heroes, often find their "reward" to be a high-level position in government. Universally, a disproportionate number of war heroes have become heads of government. How have their experiences with the horrors of war affected the way they think and the decisions that they make? For example, as we are writing this section, all of the high-level defense department officials in Russia had been officers in the war in Afghanistan, which ended in 1989, and they all have supported the subsequent use of Russian military force in Chechnya. Is their position on Chechnya a reflection of their war mentality? Can future wars or other types of aggression be avoided if psychologists and others can understand the effects of trauma on the people involved? Can we alleviate some of the intense psychological pain that follows disasters of all sorts? Questions like these are the reason we included post-traumatic stress syndrome in this volume, which looks at topics in psychology that affect the present and the future.

The psychology of aging is the final topic in this section. Of course, growing old is not a new phenomenon, but the rapidly increasing proportion of the population that is old represents a major shift in demographics. On average, people are living much longer than ever before, at least in Western countries. For those in the United States, Canada, and many countries in Western Europe, the expected life span has increased by several decades since the turn of the century. The data on expected life span are less optimistic in the countries that once constituted the Soviet Union. The average life span for males in the former Soviet countries has fallen from 64 in 1990 to 62 in 1992 to 59 in 1996 and is still falling. By contrast, the same value for males in the United States is in the mid-70s and increasing. Women are living longer than men, with an average advantage of 6 to 7 years, but this value is falling in the former Soviet Union and rising in the West.

These alarming figures for the former Soviet countries are even more significant because over one-third of the Russian population is over 60 years old. Health care in Russia and many of the other former Soviet countries is abysmal, so the trend toward an earlier death is not going to be easy to reverse. According to a recent report by the Russian Health Ministry, half of Russia's 21,000 hospitals have no hot water, one-fourth have no sewage system, and several hundred have no indoor plumbing (Specter, 1995). Small remote regions of the Soviet Union were renowned for the long lives of their citizens, but accurate current statistics are hard to verify. There is also considerable concern that the crisis in health care in the former Soviet countries, combined with recent increases in the numbers who maintain a poor diet and smoke cigarettes, will significantly decrease expected life spans.

A major concern of the elderly is maintenance of their cognitive abilities. Timothy A. Salthouse, the author of the American chapter on psychogerontology, notes that much of psychological research in Western countries has been concerned with aging and cognition, although related issues, such as work and perception, have also been hot topics in research with older adults. The post-Soviet chapter written by Vera A. Kol'tsova, Natasha B. Meshalkina, and Yury N. Olegnik explains why under communism little research was conducted in the psychology of aging. These authors show the interplay between official government policies and psychological research and the way this dance continued for much of the 20th century. The need for useful information about the psychology of growing old has created recent interest in this topic. Journals are now looking for high-quality research to publish and psychologists are specializing in old age.

Kol'tsova, Meshalkina, and Olegnik discuss the work of Ivan Sikorsky, the prominent psychologist in the fields of pedagogical (educational) psychology and psychogerontology. Voiskounsky notes that despite Sikorsky's successful career as a respected psychiatrist and psychologist, he was unable to achieve high moral standards in his own old age. The influence of the sociohistorical context is clearly seen in an ignoble event that occurred in Kiev, Ukraine, in 1913. It was a time of virulent anti-Semitism, and M. Beilis, a Jew, was on trial, accused of the ritual murder of a young Christian boy. The alleged motive was to use the young boy's blood for the baking of Passover matzos for the Jewish holy day. The anti-Semitic accusation was wholly false; there has never been any evidence that Jews used the blood of Christians in their holiday recipes, although the Nazis later continued to make this claim as a rationale for the mass extermination of Jews. After fierce debate about this alleged crime, the final verdict was that the accused man was not guilty. During this Russian equivalent of the 1894 Dreyfus Trial (a notorious trial that took place in France, in which numerous officials blatantly provided anti-Semitic false testimony against Dreyfus, a Jew, who was wrongly convicted of treason), the esteemed professor Sikorsky provided "expert" evidence that Jewish rituals required cooking with the blood of Christians. In this particular case, it is clear that the professor overstepped the limits of his qualifications and defamed his reputation.

The reputation of the Russian medical and psychological professional communities was saved by other specialists, including the world-famous psychologist Vladimir Bekhterev, whose evidence in court was contrary to that of Sikorsky's. Perhaps Sikorsky's prejudice needs to interpreted within the social, political, and historical context. Nevertheless, Sikorsky provides an example of the way science and one's scientific reputation can be misused in the service of prejudice, the topic discussed in part III.

References

Efron, S. (1995). A country besieged by the bottle. *Los Angeles Times*, 12 November, pp. A1, A6–A7.
Specter, M. (1995). Russia's declining health: Rising illness, shorter lives. *New York Times*, 19 February, pp. 1, 12.

Alcoholism

7

Alcoholism in America

Extent, Diagnosis, Etiology, Treatment, and Prevention

Peter E. Nathan

How Many Americans Suffer from Alcohol-Related Disorders?

Between 5 and 7 percent of the U.S. population, or between 14 million and 16 million people, meet *DSM-IV* criteria for alcohol abuse or dependence (NIAAA, 1993). Annual per capita alcohol consumption in America has remained generally steady over the past 150 years, with two exceptions: during the 14 years of Prohibition from 1919 to 1933 and since about 1960, which first saw a rise in alcohol consumption and then a fall. Rates of alcohol abuse and dependence have probably remained steady over the same time span (Horgan, 1993).

Rates of alcohol abuse and dependence vary with age, gender, and ethnicity (Horgan, 1993; NIAAA, 1993). Rates of abuse and dependence among men between the ages of 18 and 44, for example, are more than double the overall rates; women's rates at the same ages are about one-fourth those of men. Between 45 and 64 and especially at 65 years and beyond, rates of abuse and dependence for both men and women plummet to half the overall rates. African Americans and Hispanics of both genders demonstrate slightly higher rates of abuse and dependence than their white counterparts at most ages.

Polydrug abuse, most often involving alcohol and one or more other substances, is more the rule than the exception nowadays in the United States, making it very difficult to attain accurate numbers of the nation's alcohol and drug abusers. The latest National High School Senior Survey, conducted for the National Institute on Drug Abuse (NIDA, 1991), indicated that almost 20 percent of high school seniors surveyed had used marijuana during the month preceding the survey, more than 60 percent had used alcohol, and almost 30 percent had smoked cigarettes. No other drugs were used by more than 5 percent of the seniors during the same time period.

Diagnosis of Alcohol-Related Disorders

Early Diagnostic Conceptions

Alcohol and drug addiction were included in both the first and second editions of the *Diagnostic and Statistical Manual of Mental Disorders*, the most widely accepted psychiatric nomenclature in use in the United States. However, neither in *DSM-I*, published in 1952, nor in *DSM-II*, which appeared in 1968, were these conditions included as independent diagnostic conditions. Instead, they were considered varieties of sociopathic personality disturbance, a catchall diagnostic category that also covered antisocial behavior and sexual deviations. The implication was that persons diagnosed with alcoholism, drug addiction, antisocial behavior, or one of the sexual deviations threatened society's moral fabric by virtue of their intemperate or immoral behavioral choices.

 DSM-III (American Psychiatric Association, 1980) accorded the alcohol- and drug- related disorders their own separate identity as substance-use disorders, thereby avoiding the "guilt by association" implicit in the 1952 and 1968 diagnostic manuals. The 1980 manual highlighted new research findings implicating sociocultural and genetic factors in the etiology of the conditions, which led it to assign tolerance and withdrawal symptoms key diagnostic roles. *DSM-III* also established a separate diagnosis for substance abuse, to identify persons whose substance use, while problematic, had not reached the proportions of substance dependence. *DSM-III-R* (American Psychiatric Association, 1987) retained many of the diagnostic advances achieved by *DSM-III*.

DSM-IV Substance-Related Disorders

DSM-IV (American Psychiatric Association, 1994) is the current standard American psychiatric nomenclature. The *DSM-IV* Substance Disorders Work Group undertook a very extensive series of field trials and data analyses designed to establish the criteria for substance abuse and dependence on the firmest possible empirical base (Cottler et al., 1995; Schuckit, 1994b). These efforts led the work group to retain many of the criteria developed for *DSM-III* and *DSM-III-R* because of their sound predictive validity (Helzer, 1994; Nathan, 1994). The work group also reaffirmed *DSM-III*'s diagnostic emphasis on tolerance and withdrawal symptoms; they frequently accompanied substance dependence in the field trials. And they reemphasized the valuable role of substance abuse as a diagnosis separate from substance dependence; they identified a unique group of persons who benefit from the clinical attention they receive from this diagnosis (Widiger et al., 1994).

The *DSM-IV* operational criteria for substance dependence shown in table 7.1 illustrate the range of behaviors linked to alcohol dependence in the United States at this time. Tolerance and withdrawal are important symptoms of substance dependence (Nathan, 1994). For that reason, the diagnosis of substance dependence in *DSM-III* required one or both, in the belief that dependence could not develop in the absence of these symptoms. Though the drafters of *DSM-III-R* concluded that a person could be dependent without demonstrating either symptom, the *DSM-IV* work group thought the presence of these symptoms was important enough to distinguish between addicted persons with tolerance or withdrawal symptoms (by labeling their dependence "with physiological dependence") and those who showed neither symptom (by labeling their dependence "without physiological dependence"). This diagnostic distinction implies that the two varieties of dependence may differ in etiology, in disease course, or in response to treatment.

Table 7.1. *DSM-IV* Operational Criteria for Substance Dependence

---

Substance dependence is a maladaptive pattern of substance use leading to clinically significant impairment or distress, as manifested by three (or more) of the following, occurring at any time in the same 12-month period:

1. Tolerance, as defined by either of the following:
    a. A need for markedly increased amounts of the substance to achieve intoxication or desired effect.
    b. Markedly diminished effect with continued use of the same amount of the substance.
2. Withdrawal, as manifested by either of the following:
    a. The characteristic withdrawal syndrome for the substance.
    b. The same (or a closely related) substance is taken to relieve or avoid withdrawal symptoms.
3. The substance is often taken in larger amounts or over a longer period than was intended.
4. There is a persistent desire or unsuccessful efforts to cut down or control substance use.
5. A great deal of time is spent in activities necessary to obtain the substance (e.g., visiting multiple doctors or driving long distances), use the substance (e.g., chain-smoking), or recover from its effects.
6. Important social, occupation, or recreational activities are given up or reduced because of substance use.
7. The substance use is continued despite knowledge of having a persistent or recurrent physical or psychological problem that is likely to have been caused or exacerbated by the substance (e.g., current cocaine use despite recognition of cocaine-induced depression or continued drinking despite recognition that an ulcer was made worse by alcohol consumption).

Specify if:
With Physiological Dependence: evidence of tolerance or withdrawal (i.e., either item 1 or 2 is present).
Without Physiological Dependence: no evidence of tolerance or withdrawal (i.e., neither item 1 nor 2 is present).

Source: American Psychiatric Association, 1994, p. 181.

Tolerance occurs at both the cellular and the psychological levels (Chiu et al., 1994; Nathan, 1994). Cells adjust to the long-term presence of alcohol and other drugs in the bloodstream by altering certain biochemical processes to achieve physiological balance with the substance, just as long-term substance-abusing humans learn to adjust to certain psychological and behavioral consequences of regular alcohol or drug ingestion (we discuss learned tolerance later in this chapter). Tolerance requires substance abusers to use more of the substance to maintain its original reinforcing effects. Tolerance also induces a gradual decline in those feelings if the dosage of the substance is not increased.

Withdrawal refers to the physical and psychological events that accompany cessation of drug or alcohol intake after use for a long enough period of time to induce dependence (Hughes, 1994a, 1994b). Symptoms include nausea, vomiting, restlessness and agitation, and sleeplessness. In severe withdrawal states, like delirium tremens, withdrawal may actually be life threatening. The symptoms of withdrawal, like those of tolerance, are influenced by both psychological and cellular factors (Crowley, 1994).

Nature of Alcohol Abuse and Dependence

Once it enters the stomach and small intestine, following ingestion, alcohol is quickly absorbed into the blood. In turn, alcohol is carried in the bloodstream to the brain, where its effects on behavior take place. At moderate doses, alcoholic beverages initially produce a mild sense of stimulation and enhanced well-being, followed by relaxation and calm. At higher concentrations, alcohol interferes with cognitive functioning, balance and coordination, judgment, memory, and perception. At extremely high levels, alcohol's sedative effects can impair respiration and breathing and lead to death from respiratory failure.

The negative impact of alcohol intoxication on the health and welfare of American citizens is striking (Klatsky & Armstrong, 1993). It includes a heightened risk of automobile accidents (in 1991, 47.9% of traffic-related deaths were alcohol related [U.S. Department of Transportation, 1992]) and of alcohol-related accidents and injuries on the job and at home (Trice, 1992). High blood alcohol levels are also associated with crimes of all kinds (almost 80% of crimes involving possession or sale of drugs were alcohol or drug related in 1992 [U.S. Department of Justice, 1993]; between 40 and 60% of violent crimes in this country in 1991 were alcohol related [Martin, 1992]), with high-risk sexual behavior (Leigh, 1990), and with family violence and spouse and child abuse (overall, battered women report that approximately 50% of their husbands have long-term alcohol problems [Leonard, 1993]).

The long-term effects of alcohol are at least as devastating as its shorter term effects. Chronic alcohol abuse is associated with permanent, disabling changes in brain function that reflect alcohol's toxic effects on brain tissue (Hunt & Nixon, 1993), as well as a variety of alcohol-related birth defects (Michaelis & Michaelis, 1994; Streissguth, 1994). Long-term alcohol abuse is also responsible for life-threatening physical disorders affecting the brain, heart, liver, and gastrointestinal system. Chronic abuse of alcohol is a major cause of premature death in the United States; on average, people dying from alcohol-related causes lose 26 years from their normal life expectancy (Horgan, 1993).

Causes of Alcohol Abuse and Dependence

Genetic/Biological Factors

It has long been recognized that alcoholism runs in families. Is this because a genetic predisposition to alcohol abuse or dependence is transmitted from alcoholic parent to child, because the environment an alcoholic parent creates conveys psychological and behavioral factors leading to abuse and dependence to their children, or both? We review here the substantial data supporting the view that a genetic predisposition to abuse and dependence is transmitted from parent to child.

Concordance Rates for Alcoholism in Twins　If there is a genetic component in the risk for alcoholism or drug dependence, then identical twins, who share identical genes, should exhibit similar use and abuse histories. Fraternal twins, who are genetically different individuals born at the same time, would be more likely to differ in their tendencies to develop abuse and dependence. In general, researchers using the twin method to study the genetics of alcoholism (the twin method has not been used to study the genetics of other substance abuse and dependence) have confirmed these expectations.

In an early, influential study, Kaij (1960) reported that the concordance rate for alcohol abuse among Swedish monozygotic (identical) twins was 54 percent, whereas among dizygotic (fraternal) twins, it was 28 percent. In a study of 850 pairs of American like-sex twins who were high school juniors at the time, Leohlin (1977) observed that identical twins were significantly more often concordant for heavy drinking than fraternal twins. And in a recent study of 1,030 female-female twin pairs in Virginia, concordance for alcoholism was consistently higher in monozygotic than in dizygotic twin pairs; overall, 58 percent of the identical twin pairs were concordant for alcoholism while only 29 percent of the fraternal twin pairs were concordant for the disorder (Kendler et al., 1992). Commenting on his findings, Kendler cautioned, "Women with relatives who have been alcoholic should be warned early in life to watch for early signs of alcohol dependence, like repeatedly finding yourself drinking more than you want to" (Goleman, 1992b).

Adoption Studies of Children of Alcoholics　Adoption studies hold environmental influences constant—which twin studies may not—while systematically varying genetic factors. As a consequence, many behavioral scientists believe they provide the best perspective on the role of genetic factors in mental disorders.

The most influential adoption studies of alcoholism were a series of Danish studies by Goodwin (1976, 1979, 1985) that compared four groups of young adult children of alcoholics. The groups included sons of alcoholics raised by nonalcoholic foster parents, sons of alcoholics raised by their biological parents, and daughters of alcoholics raised, respectively, by nonalcoholic foster parents and by their biological parents. Paired with each of these four groups was a control group matched for age, gender, and adoption status. All adoptees had been separated from their biological parents during the first few weeks of life and then adopted by nonrelatives. These extensive studies yielded two principal findings: (1) sons of alcoholics were about four times more likely than sons of non-alcoholics to become alcoholic adults regardless of whether they had been raised by their own alcoholic biological parents or by nonalcoholic adoptive parents; and (2) the influence of genetics on the daughters of alcoholics was not as strong as on the sons of alcoholics.

Subsequent Swedish research on adopted children has confirmed Goodwin's initial conclusions on the role of genetic factors in male alcoholism (Bohman, Cloninger, von Knorring, & Sigvardsson, 1984). It has also shown more strongly than did Goodwin that genetic factors significantly affect female alcoholism as well. The Swedish research also suggested the existence of at least two forms of inherited alcoholism. On analyzing data from 2,000 Swedish adoptees, these researchers (Bohman, Sigvardsson, & Cloninger, 1981; Cloninger Bohman, & Sigvardsson, 1981) identified two groups of alcoholics differing in alcoholism heritability. The more common, lower heritability, Type I alcoholics begin drinking in their mid-twenties to thirties, although they typically do not develop alcohol problems until middle age; they have a high risk of liver disease and show little antisocial behavior and relatively few social and occupational problems. Children of Type I alcoholics are twice as likely to develop alcoholism themselves as are children without a family history of alcoholism; sons of Type I alcoholics raised in troubled adoptive homes are at even greater risk to develop alcoholism. In contrast, the higher heritability Type II alcoholics, whose alcoholism begins very early, experience profound social and occupational problems but relatively few medical difficulties. Their biological sons—but not their biological daughters—are nine times more likely to become alcoholics, regardless of environmental influences.

Electrophysiological Studies of Children of Alcoholics   Two electroencephalographic (EEG) techniques commonly used to study the brain's electrical activity—the evoked potential (EP) and the event-related potential (ERP)—have also been employed in the United States to study genetic influences on alcoholism. EP techniques measure the brain's electrical response to external stimuli, such as flashes of light or loud sounds. ERP techniques measure electrical events that arise during the brain's processing of information.

Noting substantial evidence that EP and ERP waveforms are genetically determined, Begleiter, Porjesz, Bihari, and Kissin (1984) hypothesized that a specific ERP response, the P300 wave deficit, may be a genetically determined antecedent of alcoholism rather than its consequence, as had previously been believed.

Begleiter and his colleagues tested this hypothesis by comparing the ERPs of 25 12-year-old boys with alcoholic fathers with those of 25 boys with no history of paternal alcoholism. Significant differences in P300 voltage were found between the two groups. Interestingly, the boys with a paternal history of alcoholism showed a pattern of significantly reduced P300 voltage similar to a pattern previously seen in abstinent chronic alcoholics (Porjesz & Begleiter, 1983). This coincidence strengthened the case for this deficit's role in the development of alcoholism. Data from two recent reports of reduced P300 voltage in groups of boys and girls with a family history of alcoholism (Hill & Steinhauer, 1993; Steinhauer & Hill, 1993) strengthen the likelihood that the ERP may reflect a central nervous system–based genetic predisposition to alcoholism.

A Genetic/Biological Basis for Alcohol Abuse and Dependence? Do these findings prove that the children of alcoholics are doomed to follow in their parents' footsteps? Absolutely not. Despite what some believe about the extra burden of adult children of alcoholics, most children of substance abusers do not themselves become substance abusers, and most substance abusers are not the children of substance abusers, proving how important environmental factors are in the development of substance abuse (Prescott et al., 1994; Schuckit, 1994a). A genetic basis for alcoholism and drug dependence simply implies a heightened predisposition to develop the disorder—an increase in the chances of developing it—if one's father or mother was or is a substance abuser.

However, American alcoholism workers believe that if a person is the child of an alcoholic, that person owes it to himself or herself to be aware of the increased risk of developing alcoholism he or she bears. How? By taking more care than persons who do not share the heightened risk in how alcohol is used; abusive drinking will develop more readily if the person at risk drinks heavily. American alcoholism workers believe that persons with a family history of alcoholism have an obligation to treat alcohol with even greater care and respect than persons without such a history.

Sociocultural Factors

The groups of which we are members—the racial, religious, national, and/or ethnic groups which constitute the American melting pot—as well as our gender, profession, education, and age influence who we are, including how we behave. This is hardly surprising since our parents' group membership influenced the child-rearing patterns that in turn affected us. Group identification also directly affected our behavior during childhood as well as now since we doubtless wanted to behave like our elders and others we admired. Whereas group membership influences many kinds of human behavior, its impact on alcohol use and abuse appears to be especially strong (Johnson, Nagoshi, Danko, Honbo, & Chau, 1990).

The widely differing rates of alcohol consumption across this country's nine census regions summarized in table 7.2 illustrate the effects of group membership on alcohol consumption. These differences in per capita consumption (and,

Table 7.2. Per Capita Consumption of Ethanol in Nine Census Regions of the United States, 1940, 1964, 1979, and 1988

	Per Capita Consumption				Rank Order on Per Capita Consumption			
Region	1940	1964	1979	1988	1940	1964	1979	1988
Pacific	1.9	2.6	3.4	2.8	1	1	1	2
Middle Atlantic	1.8	2.4	2.7	2.4	2	3	5	6
East North Central	1.8	2.3	2.7	2.4	3	4	5	5
New England	1.7	2.5	3.1	2.9	4	2	3	1
Mountain	1.3	2.1	3.3	2.8	5	5	2	3
West North Central	1.2	1.8	2.5	2.2	6	7	8	8
South Atlantic	1.1	1.9	2.8	2.5	7	6	4	4
West South Central	0.9	1.7	2.6	2.3	8	8	7	7
East South Central	0.6	1.0	2.0	1.9	9	9	9	9

Source: Alcohol Health and Research World, 16(3), 185.

in turn, rates of alcoholism, which are closely related to consumption rates) reflect regional population differences in the religious, ethnic, and racial makeup of the American melting pot. For example, in New England, a region with large numbers of northern Europeans whose parents and grandparents came from countries with high alcoholism rates, per capita consumption is much higher than in the three southern census regions, in which a substantial number of Southern Baptists, for whom drinking is proscribed, live. Moreover, the shifts over time in rank order of per capita consumption shown in the table likely reflect geographic shifts in population groups. More individuals from groups with lower rates of drinking have moved up north to the Middle Atlantic region since 1940 in search of employment, just as more persons from groups with higher rates of drinking have moved to the South Atlantic region for the same reason.

Earlier in this chapter, we reviewed data indicating that age and ethnicity, as well as gender, affect rates of alcohol and drug consumption. A recent study (Harford, Parker, Grant, & Dawson, 1992) suggests that the occupations we choose also affect both whether we drink at all and if our drinking is likely to lead to alcohol dependence. Harford and his colleagues found, for example, that while more than 70 percent of men holding managerial, administrative, or professional positions drank, putting them at the top of the list, the men in these job categories were also least likely to develop alcohol dependence. Conversely, men working in transportation-related jobs, on railroads and as truck drivers, for example, were least likely to drink but most likely to develop alcohol dependence.

A population survey of alcohol abuse and addiction in five sites across the globe in the late 1980s—in St. Louis, Missouri; Edmonton, Alberta, Canada; Puerto Rico; Seoul, South Korea; and Taipei City, Taiwan—confirms that gender is a major risk factor for alcoholism (Helzer et al., 1990), just as it is for drug abuse and disorders like depression and antisocial personality disorder. The study revealed marked disparities in lifetime prevalence between men and women in all five geographically diverse sites, confirming in every instance that men are at markedly higher risk for alcoholism than women. As an example, the survey found lifetime prevalence rates for alcoholism in St. Louis to be 29 percent for men and only 4 percent for women. These cross-national findings confirm studies reviewed earlier that reported substantial differences in alcoholism rates in the same direction for men and women in the United States.

Two theories explaining these marked differences between men and women in alcohol abuse and dependence have become most widely accepted in the United States. First, many observers point to our society's lower tolerance for heavy alcohol use by women because of women's traditional child-care role. Second, recent empirical data on differential rates of metabolism of alcohol by men and women (Frezza et al., 1990) suggest that women may possess smaller amounts than men of a crucial enzyme that detoxifies alcohol in the stomach and small intestine. Such a gender-based metabolic difference would explain why alcohol consumed in equivalent doses by men and women has greater behavioral and physiological effects on women (Gallant, 1987). Simply put, fewer women than men may drink to excess because alcohol in large quantities produces aversive behavioral and bodily consequences for women.

Learning-Based Factors

Classical Conditioning   Classical conditioning mechanisms have been implicated in such common symptoms of dependence as craving and tolerance. A series of experiments with alcohol (Crowell, Hinson, & Siegel, 1981) and morphine (Siegel, 1978) demonstrated that substance-dependent rats that had developed drug tolerance maintained it only when they were tested under the environmental conditions originally associated with drug or alcohol administration. Tolerance was not observed when the drug was given in a novel environment. These experiments led Siegel and his colleagues to propose the conditioned compensatory response model, a classical conditioning model of drug tolerance. Siegel (1978) argued that environmental stimuli associated with drug intake link with the drug's effects on the body to elicit a conditioned response opposite to the drug's effect, a compensating response designed to maintain bodily homeostasis. As this conditioned response increases in magnitude with continued drug intake, the drug's effects continue to decrease and tolerance increases.

The conditioned appetitive motivational model is a classical conditioning model of craving (Stewart, deWit, & Eikelboom, 1984). According to this theory, the conditioned stimuli associated with the positive reinforcing effects of drugs (for example, the smell, sounds, and lighting of the place where heroin is most often injected) become capable of eliciting a positive motivational state similar to the one elicited by the drug itself. This state, in turn, creates strong, continuing urges to seek and use the drug. This theory helps explain the great difficulty former abusers have maintaining abstinence when they must return to the environments in which they developed their addictions.

Operant Conditioning One of the first studies of the operant-conditioning mechanisms involved in alcohol self-administration by humans was reported by Nathan and O'Brien (1971), who studied alcoholic subjects living in an experimental environment on a Boston City Hospital ward during 33-day studies. The social behavior, mood, and drinking behavior of matched groups of alcoholics and nonalcoholics were compared over this prolonged period. Operant procedures were used to assess the differential reinforcement value of alcohol and social interaction, both of which are extremely powerful reinforcers for these subjects. All subjects had to press an operant panel's push-button repeatedly, on a high fixed-ratio schedule, to earn points to "purchase" alcohol, time out of their rooms in a social area, or both.

Comparisons of the operant behavior of the alcoholic and nonalcoholic groups revealed the following:

- Alcoholics worked much longer and harder to earn points to purchase alcohol. As a result, though both alcoholics and nonalcoholics reached the same high blood-alcohol levels early in drinking, the alcoholics remained at these levels longer, and they returned to them more frequently. They drank almost twice as much as the nonalcoholics.
- Nonalcoholics worked much longer and harder to earn points that permitted them to leave their rooms and spend time with each other in a social area. By contrast, the alcoholics remained social isolates before, during, and after drinking.
- Once drinking began, the alcoholics became significantly more depressed and less active and demonstrated significantly more psychopathology (including anxiety, manic behavior, depression, paranoia, and phobic and compulsive behavior) than the nonalcoholics.

This research program ultimately led a number of other clinical researchers to explore operant programs designed to reinforce alcoholics for reducing or stopping their drinking. Bigelow and his colleagues (Bigelow, Cohen, Liebson, & Faillace, 1972; Bigelow, Liebson, & Griffiths, 1974), for example, reported marked reduction in alcoholics' drinking when subjects were reinforced with money and other rewards for maintaining limited periods of abstinence in a laboratory setting.

Alcohol Expectancies In a 1985 study of adolescent alcohol expectancies, Christiansen, Goldman, and Brown found that as adolescents age, they become increasingly convinced that alcohol improves social behavior, increases arousal, and decreases tension. Subsequently, the same investigators (Goldman, Brown, & Christiansen, 1987) reported that adolescent alcohol abusers differ from nonabusers in what the two groups expect alcohol to do for them. When 116 adolescents—alcohol abusers and nonabusers with and without a family history of alcoholism—completed the Alcohol Expectancy Questionnaire, striking differences in expectancies distinguished these four groups. Adolescent alcohol abusers anticipated significantly more pleasure from drinking than their nonabusing peers. Moreover, adolescents with an alcohol-abusing parent expected more cognitive and motor enhancement from alcohol than did those without a family history of alcoholism. These finding confirm that adolescents' alcohol use patterns and family history of alcoholism affect their attitudes toward drinking. They also suggest that alcohol expectancies may affect the adolescents' chances of developing more serious drinking problems as adults.

Derman and Cooper (1994) have developed a questionnaire designed to explore sex-related alcohol expectancies that will permit them to examine the role of drinking and drinking expectancies on sexual risk taking, a timely topic in our AIDS era. Table 7.3 shows some of the items included within each of the questionnaire's three item factors, Enhancement, Sexual Risk-Taking, and Disinhibition.

When the questionnaire was administered to 916 sexually experienced adolescents between the ages of 13 and 19, males, African Americans, and older respondents were found to be more likely than females, Caucasians, and younger respondents to expect sexual risk taking and disinhibition to increase when they drank (Derman & Cooper, 1994).

Psychopathological and Personality Factors

Comorbidity   Psychopathological explanations of substance abuse assume that it occurs, at least partially, because of comorbidity—the presence of two or more psychiatric disorders in a single person. Alcohol-dependent persons are more likely than persons with any other *DSM* disorder to suffer from other psychiatric conditions (Neighbors, Kempton, & Forehand, 1992; Sher & Trull, 1994). The

Table 7.3. Selected Items from Derman and Cooper's Sex-Related Alcohol Expectancy Questionnaire

After a few drinks of alcohol . . .

Factor 1: Alcohol enhances a sexual experience.
• I feel closer to a sexual partner.
• I am *more* sexually responsive.
• I am *less* nervous about sex.
• I enjoy sex *more* than usual.

Factor 2: Alcohol increases sexual risk-taking.
• I am *less* likely to use birth control.
• I am *less* likely to take precautions before having sex.
• I am *less* likely (to ask a partner) to use a condom.
• I have sex with people whom I wouldn't have sex with if I were sober.

Factor 3: Alcohol reduces sexual inhibitions.
• I am *more* likely to do sexual things that I wouldn't do when sober.
• I find it harder to say no to sexual advances.
• I am *more* likely to have sex on a first date.

Source: Derman & Cooper, 1994, p. 156.

conditions that most often accompany alcohol dependence are depression and antisocial personality disorder, followed by schizophrenia, anxiety disorders, and sleep disorders (Schuckit, 1994c). When alcohol abuse follows the onset of other disorders, alcohol is probably being used in many instances to dampen symptoms of the other conditions.

Personality Factors   The psychodynamic model of alcoholism portrayed it as an ultimately unsuccessful effort to satisfy strong dependency needs in adulthood that were unmet in infancy and early childhood. According to this view, the alcohol abuser has substituted substance abuse to satisfy oral dependency needs that went unsatisfied much earlier (Khantzian, 1985). The psychodynamic explanation for substance dependence is much less influential in the United States than it was several decades ago, largely because efforts to confirm it empirically have not been successful.

What about the addictive personality? Has it been established that alcoholics and drug addicts share a set of personality characteristics that make them different from those of us who do not suffer from these conditions? Put another way, have behavioral scientists been able to identify a personality pattern that predicts substance abuse? Supporters of this position point to indications that many alcoholics share certain behaviors and personality characteristics, like antisocial and depressive tendencies, that differentiate them from nonalcoholics (Morey & Skinner, 1986; Sutker & Allain, 1988). Nathan (1988), however, claims that the personality factors that appear to distinguish substance abusers from others (like antisocial and depressive traits) are consequences, rather than causes, of these disorders, so they are unlikely to have played a role in the development of the substance abuse. Sher and Trull (1994), who also reject the idea of the addictive personality, nonetheless believe that personality factors play a role in the etiology of both alcoholism and antisocial personality disorder and that the same factors (they refer to them as "broad-band personality trait dimensions" that mediate disinhibitory behavior) might be responsible for both conditions.

Cloninger's biopsychosocial theory of neurogenetic adaptive mechanisms (1987) is one of the most interesting developments in this dialogue. According to Cloninger, genetic and neurobiological factors, personality factors, and environmental factors interact to yield persons at substantially higher risk to develop alcohol dependence than persons without these predisposing factors. This theory, if confirmed empirically, would represent strong support for a role for personality factors in alcoholism.

Treatment of Alcohol Abuse and Dependence

Group and Family Therapy

Group therapy first gained popularity because it offered therapists a way to confront their patients' denial of the seriousness of their alcohol abuse problem. Fellow substance abusers can often confront fellow patients who deny their abuse with greater effectiveness than therapists can.

During the past decade, family therapy has also become a popular treatment for alcoholism in the United States (e.g., Bowers & Al-Redha, 1990; McCrady, Stout, Noel, Abrams, & Nelson, 1991). An appealing feature of family therapy is its assumption that substance abuse is not the abuser's problem alone. Because it affects every member of the family, family therapists are convinced it is everyone's problem and that all family members must participate in treatment.

Family therapy enables family members to share with their alcohol-abusing loved one the negative impact of his or her abuse on the family. The supportive atmosphere of the family therapy session makes it easier for family members to share these feelings with the abuser, thereby confirming a deeply felt, long-hidden truth. This difficult sharing of feelings is as important for abusers as for the abused since afterward it becomes more difficult for them to deny the impact of the behavior on those they claim to love.

American family therapists are convinced that alcohol and drug abuse is a "family disorder," created and maintained by disordered family relationships. The wife who drinks so she can forget her husband's infidelity, the husband who drinks to dampen the stress of his job, and the adolescent who drinks to deal with feelings brought on by having been made the family scapegoat for his older brother's failures represent family patterns that family therapists believe lead to abusive substance use.

McCrady and her colleagues (1986, 1991) reported the results of a trial of outpatient behavioral therapy for couples. Alcoholics and their spouses were assigned to one of three conditions: (1) minimal spouse involvement; (2) alcohol-focused spouse involvement, in which the spouse's involvement was restricted to discussions of how the alcoholic spouse could gain control over his or her drinking; and (3) alcohol-behavioral marital therapy (ABMT), in which the spouse became involved in all aspects of his or her alcoholic partner's treatment, including efforts to improve skills in communicating feelings. No differences in alcohol use were found among the three treatment groups at a six-month follow-up. At an 18-month follow-up, however, the number of abstinent days for the ABMT patients had increased while the number of abstinent days had decreased for the alcoholic spouses in the other two treatment groups. Moreover, the ABMT patients reported improved marital satisfaction, unlike their counterparts in the other two groups.

Behavior Therapy

Aversive Procedures   Chemical aversion, based on classical conditioning principles, was developed in the late 1930s (Voegtlin, 1940). Today it is an accepted, though still controversial, treatment. Chemical aversion conditioning for alcoholism involves the repeated pairing of the sight, smell, and taste of the patient's preferred alcoholic beverage with drug-induced nausea and vomiting to establish a conditioned aversion to alcohol. When the conditioned aversion has been established, patients will reexperience strong feelings of nausea and disgust at the sight, taste, and smell of alcohol. They can then enjoy a "craving-free" interval for as long as the aversion persists (generally, a few months), during which they can work toward a more lasting solution to their substance abuse.

The data on outcomes of chemical aversion treatment have consistently been among the most promising of all approaches to the treatment of alcoholism (Smith, Frawler, & Polissar, 1991). However, because it is extremely unpleasant and demanding (it requires the repeated experiencing of nausea and vomiting during conditioning sessions), it requires patients to be strongly motivated; that level of motivation alone probably accounts for a substantial part of the success rate of chemical aversion treatment (Nathan & Skinstad, 1987).

Broad-Spectrum Behavioral Treatment for Alcoholism with Nonabstinent Treatment

Goals   Several behavioral treatment programs developed in the United States over the past 25 years focused simultaneously on the abusive drinking of alcoholics and its negative vocational, interpersonal, and emotional consequences; their ambitious treatment focus explains why they were termed broad-spectrum treatments. Several of these programs (e.g., Alden, 1988; Miller, Leekman, Delaney, & Tinkcom, 1992; Pomerleau et al., 1978; Sobell & Sobell, 1973, 1976) also tested a revolutionary concept: nonabstinent treatment goals.

Individualized behavior therapy for alcoholics (IBTA) was one of the first and remains the best-known of these programs (Sobell & Sobell, 1973, 1976). Until the IBTA study, virtually all alcoholism treatment programs had tended to emphasize nonspecific treatment goals like "personality change" or "increased psychological maturity," in hopes that those nonspecific changes would somehow lead to a change for the better in drinking. The IBTA program, however, was targeted; its interventions were designed (1) to modify its subjects' abusive drinking by providing them social drinking skills; and (2) to redress abuse-related deficits in social, interpersonal, and emotional skills. A fundamental assumption of the IBTA program was that addressing abusive drinking alone or its consequences alone represented incomplete treatment.

The success of the IBTA program was assessed by determining which group of patients drank less at the follow-up intervals—patients receiving IBTA or those receiving standard treatment. Patients presented the IBTA treatment package did drink less—and less often—over six-month and two-year follow-up periods than patients receiving standard treatment. The patients who did best of all during the follow-up period, however, turned out to be those who had received both IBTA treatment and the assigned treatment goal of controlled social drinking—a nonabstinent treatment goal, rather than the traditional goal of abstinence. This finding was extremely controversial, engendering heated debate that has only in recent years begun to diminish.

Although controlled drinking goals for chronic alcoholics are rejected by most American alcoholism workers nowadays on the basis of the weight of research findings, nonabstinent drinking goals for drinkers who have just begun to have problems with their drinking enjoy stronger research support in this country. Drinkers who have just begun to experience problems with their drinking tend to be unwilling to stop drinking altogether. If they can be helped to see that they do have a problem, however, they might be willing to participate in a program designed to help them achieve a moderate drinking pattern and avoid future drinking-related problems. That's why the studies of early-stage problem drinkers testing nonabstinent treatment goals that have been reported (e.g., Kivlahan, Marlatt, Fromme, Coppel, & Williams, 1990) encourage the view that controlled-drinking goals for early-stage problem drinkers, unlike those for chronic alcoholics, appear to be feasible. Behavioral treatments for early-stage problem drinkers typically include self-control training to help set limits on drinking; concentrated efforts to identify rewarding alternatives to heavy drinking; and cognitive restructuring to alter the frequent mind-set that moderate drinking isn't possible for someone who's already had a problem with alcohol.

Relapse Prevention

Marlatt, Gordon, and their colleagues (e.g., Larimer & Marlatt, 1994; Marlatt & Gordon, 1985) argue convincingly that treatment for substance abuse should not end when formal treatment ends for the newly sober patient. At that point, he or she is in the midst of confronting the many risky environmental situations that can induce a return to substance abuse. These risks are maximized when the newly abstinent person returns to job, neighborhood, friends, and family, all of which may have been associated with abusive drinking before treatment.

Marlatt and Gordon's relapse prevention model stresses the importance of identifying the cues in the recovering person's environment associated with relapse (for example, situations that elicit the anger, depression, and anxiety that typically precede relapse in recovering persons). The model also aims to develop and strengthen coping strategies the recovering person can use to deal with these high-risk situations. These strategies typically involve cognitive restructuring (for example, redefining oneself as strong enough to cope with the risk of relapse) and frequent rehearsal of coping skills to strengthen the ability to confront risky situations without relapsing. Several clinicians (e.g., Annis, 1986; Rankin, 1986) have developed relapse prevention programs designed to extend alcoholism treatment beyond the period of inpatient treatment.

Motivational Interviewing

Miller, a well-known American behavior therapist, has developed a motivational interview to be administered to alcoholic patients just after they enter treatment. The interview provides patients direct feedback on 44 measures of past and present alcohol consumption, abuse, and dependence. It was developed from individual questionnaire items taken from three well-established alcohol screening questionnaires. Miller created the interview because the treatment literature suggests that straightforward feedback on the status and severity of drinking-related problems sometimes increases patients' motivation to change their drinking patterns for the better (Brown & Miller, 1993).

In an initial test of the motivational interview, 14 chronic alcoholic inpatients received it early in their inpatient treatment (Brown & Miller, 1993). They participated more fully in their treatment and showed significantly lower alcohol consumption at a three-month follow-up interview than 14 patients who did not have the motivational interview but did participate in all other treatments in the same setting. While substantial additional research on the usefulness of the motivational interview is clearly called for, this initial finding is nonetheless promising.

Pharmacological Interventions

Alcohol- and Drug-Sensitizing Agents   Antabuse (disulfiram) blocks the chemical breakdown of alcohol. Individuals who have ingested Antabuse cannot metabolize alcohol beyond the point at which it has been metabolized in the bloodstream to acetaldehyde. Because acetaldehyde is toxic to the body in very small quantities, when even the smallest amount of alcohol has been consumed by someone who has disulfiram in the bloodstream, an acetaldehyde reaction takes place (Christensen, Moller, Ronsted, Angelo, Johansson, 1991). The alcoholic quickly experiences nausea, vomiting, profuse sweating, and markedly increased respiration and heart rate. Alcoholics who have had an Antabuse reaction say it is an experience they would do almost anything to avoid.

It is because of the acetaldehyde reaction that Antabuse has been used for several decades in this country to treat alcoholism. Alcoholics taking an Antabuse tablet every day cannot consume alcohol without experiencing an acetaldehyde reaction. They are "protected" from the impulse to drink even if they are tempted to do so by alcohol-related cues. Because of the dangers of the acetaldehyde reaction, however, physicians in the United States prescribe disulfiram only to patients who are physically fit, motivated to stop drinking, and fully able to appreciate the consequences if they drink while they are taking the drug.

Some experienced clinicians swear by Antabuse; others find it ineffective. The data on its effectiveness are equivocal (Wright & Moore, 1989), largely because it works well for some patients and not at all for others; patient differences in sensitivity to the effects of the drug may explain its inconsistent effectiveness. In general, clinicians prescribe Antabuse to give alcoholics a recovery "window" that reduces their risk of succumbing to craving. This grace period permits psychological and behavioral gains to take place that will allow the Antabuse to be discontinued at some point.

Agents for Managing Withdrawal and Maintaining Sobriety   Two decades ago, clinicians in this country routinely gave alcoholics the minor tranquilizers Librium and Valium during withdrawal. It was widely assumed these drugs eased the physical and psychological pains of detoxification and prevented the development of more serious withdrawal phenomena like delirium tremens. Nowadays, however, many clinicians have recognized that relatively few alcoholics experience severe enough withdrawal symptoms to warrant pharmacological intervention (Wartenburg et al., 1990); as a result, many more patients are routinely detoxified nonpharmacologically.

In years past, antianxiety agents were given to alcoholics in hopes the drugs would help them stop drinking by dampening the anxiety for which many alcoholics say they self-medicate. Instead, many alcohol abusers simply added the abuse of Librium or Valium to their abuse of alcohol and other drugs. Both Librium and Valium are dependency inducing; addiction to them tremendously complicates withdrawal from alcohol. As a result, these drugs are now rarely given to persons dependent on alcohol or other drugs.

Anticraving Agents   Over the past decade, investigations of several drug classes acting on neurotransmitters in the brain, including serotonin reuptake inhibitors, dopamine agonists, and opioid antagonists, have led to the development of drugs that may have the potential to decrease craving and the reinforcing effects of alcohol. Accordingly, these drugs would prevent, rather than simply treat the effects of, alcohol abuse and dependence.

Serotonin reuptake inhibitors increase the supply of serotonin at synapses in the brain. They have produced modest decreases in alcohol consumption in male heavy drinkers with mild to moderate alcohol dependence (Naranjo, Kadlec, Sanhueza, Woodley-Remus, & Sellers, 1990), probably because serotonin appears to exert an anticraving effect. Dopamine agonists have also been reported to decrease alcohol consumption and self-reported craving because of their effect on concentrations of dopamine in brain synapses (Dongier, Vachon, & Schwartz, 1991); dopamine appears to increase craving. Finally, the opioid antagonist naltrexone, originally developed to treat opioid dependence by inducing withdrawal in opioid addicts, also appears to have a marked impact on alcohol consumption by alcoholics. O'Malley and her colleagues (O'Malley et al., 1992), for example, have reported that naltrexone led to a marked decrease in alcohol consumption by outpatient alcoholics, largely because the drug appeared to reduce the pleasureable feelings alcohol induces.

Self-Help Groups: Alcoholics Anonymous

> This is not the story of my life. It is the story of how I got drunk, and how I got sober. I have told it before, many times: at A.A. meetings, and to my A.A. sponsor, and to other close A.A. friends gathered in coffee shops—what we in A.A. call "the meeting after the meeting." But I have never before told it in full. By tradition, no speaker leading an A.A. meeting runs over thirty minutes. I will tell it as I would at an A.A. meeting, in the same spirit.
>
> My name is Nan, and I am an alcoholic. (Robertson, 1988, p. 238)

This excerpt is from a compelling first hand account of the workings of Alcoholics Anonymous written by Nan Robertson, at the time a reporter for the

New York Times. A.A.:Inside Alcoholics Anonymous (1988) describes the author's struggles with alcohol and her ultimate recovery with the help of the fellowship of Alcoholics Anonymous.

Alcoholics Anonymous (AA) is the best-known, largest, and most influential of the addiction self-help groups. AA says it serves more than 850,000 alcoholics in this country every year; worldwide, the figure is more than 1.7 million (Alcoholics Anonymous, 1993). The organization has grown dramatically since it was founded in 1935 in Akron, Ohio, by Doctor Bob and Bill W., two alcoholics who came together to share their suffering and find a solution to their misery.

Alcoholics Anonymous seems to work best when people determined to do something about their abusive drinking commit as much time as possible to attending meetings. That's why the prescribed goal for newly sober alcoholics is "90 meetings in 90 days." Members believe that a meeting every night during the crucial initial recovery period is the best way to prevent a return to drinking, partly because AA meetings represent a protected, alcohol-free social environment. The movement's commitment to nonjudgmentalism is particularly helpful for individuals whose drinking has caused family, friends, and themselves to judge their behavior—and themselves—harshly.

Nan Robertson put it this way:

> Soon, I began to see why A.A. members kept going to meetings. They comforted and centered me. The people in them steadied and supported me in ways as small but crucial as an arm around my shoulder. Sometimes my attention wandered for stretches of time while I retreated into my own thoughts. Sometimes I was bored. But a speaker, or even a sentence uttered from the floor, would get through to me. At one meeting, a man said, "I began coming to these basements and I discovered that I was right about myself—I am a decent person." I thought with surprise, "So am I." (Robertson, 1988, p. 250)

Although AA has been a major factor in alcoholism treatment for more than half a century, its impact has been hard to quantify (McCrady & Miller, 1993). This partly reflects the organization's decentralized nature. While broadly conforming to AA traditions, each group develops its own focus, traditions, and helping procedures. Though this philosophy has maintained AA as a vital organization capable of continuous renewal, it has also made the coordinated study of treatment outcomes across AA groups extremely difficult.

The modest amount of research on AA's effectiveness that is available suggests an abstinence rate of between 25 and 50 percent at the one-year mark, which is within the range of outcomes from other treatments (NIAAA, 1993). A recent membership survey (Alcoholics Anonymous, 1993) reports an average sobriety length of 50 months for those attending meetings regularly (defined as an average of four meetings a week by the typical member). The survey also found that about half of those who attend three or four AA meetings do not continue to do so for longer than three months.

In 1991, Walsh and a large number of colleagues reported the results from one of the most important treatment outcome studies of Alcoholics Anonymous.

Industrial workers with newly identified alcohol problems were assigned to one of three treatment groups: compulsory inpatient treatment for alcoholism followed by compulsory AA attendance; compulsory AA attendance only; and free choice of what treatment program, if any, to enter. Forty-six percent of the subjects in the free-choice condition chose to attend AA; 41 percent chose inpatient treatment. Although all three groups showed comparable improvement on measures of job performance, subjects compelled to enter inpatient treatment and attend AA meetings did better than those in either of the other two groups on measures of drinking, leading the authors to conclude that inpatient treatment was more often associated with long-term abstinence than was AA membership. However, AA also seemed to have made a substantial contribution to positive outcomes.

Stages of Change in Addictions Treatment

During the past 15 years, psychologist James O. Prochaska and his co-workers (e.g., Prochaska & DiClemente, 1983, 1986) have studied how people intentionally change addictive behaviors, concluding that modification of addictive behaviors reliably progresses through five stages: precontemplation, contemplation, preparation, action, and maintenance. Substance-dependent persons typically recycle through these stages several times before they achieve stable abstinence (Prochaska, DiClemente, & Norcross, 1992). These researchers have also identified the specific treatments they believe are most effective at each stage of change (Prochaska & DiClemente, 1992).

The first of the stages of change is *precontemplation*, during which the individual has no intention to change behavior in the foreseeable future; in fact, he or she may not be aware of an addiction problem. *Contemplation* is the next stage; in it, the individual is aware that an addiction problem exists, is seriously thinking about doing something about it, but has not yet made a commitment to do so. *Preparation* is the stage that brings together the intention to change with preparations for doing so; small changes may even have been initiated, such as reducing drinking by a few beers a week. It is during the *action* stage that individuals confront their addictions most directly by changing behavior or the environment; abstinence is the most meaningful of these behavior changes. During *maintenance*, the last of the stages of change, the principal task is to prevent relapse and consolidate the gains made in the action stage.

Although much of this research program has focused on smoking cessation, it has also investigated stages of change in persons with histories of alcohol abuse. For example, in a recent study (Snow, Prochaska, & Rossi, 1992), the readiness of current smokers who were also former problem drinkers to stop smoking was assessed. Since so many recovering problem drinkers are or have been regular smokers, understanding the processes by which these two common addictions interact during recovery is important. A group of 191 adults who admitted having once had a drinking problem but were no longer drinking was recruited. Forty-one percent were current smokers; 81 percent had smoked regularly in the past. Mean alcohol sobriety was slightly less than six years. Of the 79 current smokers in the sample, 52 percent were in the precontemplation stage, 34 percent were in the contemplation stage, and 14 percent were in the preparation stage of change. These stage distributions were comparable to the stages of change found in smokers in other studies. The only difference was that women smokers in this sample were at an earlier stage of change (67% of women and 38% of men were in the precontemplation stage).

How Effectively Do We Prevent and Treat Alcohol Abuse?

Preventing Alcohol Abuse

Many alcohol and drug prevention efforts in this country focus on the schools (Hansen, 1992). School-based programs are typically tailored to the age of the students involved, describe the metabolism and physiology of alcohol and drugs, and provide detailed information on the range of potentially dangerous effects of abuse. They may also detail the causes of substance abuse, the impact of parental alcoholism and drug dependence, and the kinds of treatments available. Some combine information on alcohol and drug effects with efforts to teach ways to resist peer pressure to use and abuse alcohol and drugs (Botvin, Filazzola, & Botvin, 1990); parents are sometimes invited to join their children at these discussions (Hawkins, Catalano, & Kent, 1991). All these programs share the goal of inducing children and adolescents to consider more seriously than they might otherwise the negative consequences of the decision to begin drinking or using drugs. In doing so, they attempt to change attitudes of youthful users about alcohol and drugs from symbols of emerging adulthood and sophistication to agents of injury, disease, and death. Most available data on the outcomes of preventive education and attitude change programs in secondary schools and colleges reveal success in increasing information level and changing attitudes on use from positive to less positive but only modest success in changing consumption levels in young people already using alcohol and drugs (Hansen, 1992; Nathan, 1988).

Preventing the Consequences of Alcohol Abuse

Strategies for reducing certain of the negative consequences of alcohol use have been distinctly more successful than efforts to prevent alcohol abuse in the first place. Efforts to limit alcohol's availability to youthful drivers (by raising the legal age for purchase of alcoholic beverages to 21) and to increase the effective enforcement of laws pertaining to alcohol sales to underage individuals have succeeded in substantially reducing the number of fatal automobile accidents involving youthful drinkers (Hingson, 1993; Klitzner, Stewart, & Fisher, 1993). Programs designed to educate pregnant women on the risks of fetal alcohol syndrome (FAS)—which afflicts the children of mothers who drink heavily during pregnancy—have led to significant reductions in the frequency of FAS (NIAAA, 1993). Finally, programs to prevent workplace alcohol and drug problems (Ames, 1993) and alcohol- and drug-related HIV infection (Strunin & Hingson, 1993) have also shown promising results.

Drunken driving and FAS are major public health problems. Drunken drivers kill and injure thousands of Americans and cause millions of dollars of property damage each year. Similarly, victims of FAS number in the thousands in the United States; the loss of their full productivity to the country because of mental retardation and physical and emotional disabilities is enormous. Hence, the success of efforts to this time to reduce drunken driving and the incidence of fetal alcohol syndrome represents an important public health advance. While more difficult to ascertain, the costs of workplace alcohol problems and alcohol-related HIV infection are also very substantial, so increased success in preventing them has also had substantial positive consequences for the country.

Treating Alcohol Abuse

Though the effectiveness of treatment for alcohol abuse remains limited, we anticipate improvement in the future. Before detailing the reasons for our optimism, though, let us briefly review some gloomy statistics.

First, no more than 10 percent of all alcohol-dependent people enter treatment in any given year in the United States (NIAAA, 1993). Adopting the most widely accepted prevalence estimate, between 5 and 7 percent of the U.S. population—around 15 million people—suffers from a significant alcohol problem; a substantial number of those persons abuse drugs as well. These data suggest that over a million alcohol abusers enter treatment during any given year.

The most widely accepted consensus on treatment outcomes for alcoholism is that, on average, only 30 percent of those who begin a treatment program remain abstinent a year after it has ended (Nathan & Skinstad, 1987; NIAAA, 1993). Over 50 percent of patients entering treatment drop out before its conclusion, while a substantial number of patients who complete treatment fail to benefit from it. Because patients in some programs are better prospects for successful outcomes than the average, those groups of patients do better than 30 percent; conversely, programs treating more difficult patients do worse than 30 percent. Multiplying this 30 percent average positive outcome figure by 10 percent—the percent of alcoholics treated in a year in this country—yields a product of 3 percent: only 3 of 100 of our nation's alcohol abusers are helped out of their dependency in any single year.

Judging from these figures, we treat alcoholism dependence with very modest effectiveness. However, the situation is not as bad as it seems, and it will likely become even better in years to come. Why? Largely because the substantial research on treatment outcomes for alcohol abuse undertaken in this country during the past two decades has begun to yield important results.

For example, data reported in recent years suggest that patient variables and, perhaps, therapist variables play important roles in the success of alcoholism treatment, likely more important than the specifics of the treatment itself (McLellan et al., 1994). Patient variables that influence treatment success include such factors as marital status (married people do better), education (better educated people do better), and employment status (employed people do better). Even more important is the patient's drinking history. Predictably, patients whose abusive drinking has not progressed to dependence or led to physical disease, patients who have shown themselves able to abstain from alcohol or control their intake for significant periods in the past, and patients with minimal polydrug involvement are better treatment prospects than patients whose alcohol abuse is of long duration and has long been out of control (Langenbucher, McCrady, Brick, & Esterly, 1993).

Abusers' motivation to change their abusive drinking pattern is an especially important determinant of treatment success (Brown & Miller, 1993; Miller, Benefield, & Tonigan, 1993). For this reason, clinicians have begun to make specific efforts to increase their patients' treatment motivation and to select individuals for treatment who are clearly motivated to benefit from rigorous treatments.

Another promising effort to improve treatment success involves matching patients to both treatment and therapist. This strategy is based on research suggesting that particular patients may be motivated to work hardest in a particular treatment setting with a particular kind of therapist (Litt, Babor, DelBoca, Kadden, & Cooney, 1992; Mattson & Allen, 1991). However, two of the nation's leading researchers on treatment matching caution against imminent breakthroughs (Moos, Finney, & Cronkite, 1990), in large part because the conceptual and methodological problems associated with effective treatment matching are quite formidable.

Research on new alcohol-sensitizing agents and anticraving agents has also been encouraging. While these drugs alone are unlikely to affect substantial numbers of alcoholics, when used in combination with psychological and behavioral interventions, they hold great promise. Both classes of drugs can provide alcohol- and drug-dependent persons an interval of freedom from their addiction that is long enough to enable them to invest in efforts to reorganize and reorder their lives more permanently.

References

Alcoholics Anonymous (1993). *Alcoholics Anonymous 1992 membership survey.* New York: Alcoholics Anonymous World Services.

Alden, L. E. (1988). Behavioral self-management controlled-drinking strategies in a context of secondary prevention. *Journal of Consulting and Clinical Psychology, 56,* 280–286.

American Psychiatric Association (1952). *Diagnostic and statistical manual of mental disorders.* Washington, D.C.: American Psychiatric Association.

American Psychiatric Association (1968). *Diagnostic and statistical manual of mental disorders* (2d ed.). Washington, D.C.: American Psychiatric Association.

American Psychiatric Association (1980). *Diagnostic and statistical manual of mental disorders* (3d ed.). Washington, D.C.: American Psychiatric Association.

American Psychiatric Association (1987). *Diagnostic and statistical manual of mental disorders* (3d ed., rev.). Washington, D.C.: American Psychiatric Association.

American Psychiatric Association (1994). *Diagnostic and statistical manual of mental disorders* (4th ed.). Washington, D.C.: American Psychiatric Association.

Ames, G. (1993). Research and strategies for the primary prevention of workplace alcohol problems. *Alcohol Health & Research World, 17*, 19–27.

Annis, H. M. (1986). A relapse prevention model for treatment of alcoholics. In W. R. Miller & N. Heather (eds.), *Treating addictive behaviors: Processes of change* (pp. 407–433). New York: Plenum.

Begleiter, H., Porjesz, B., Bihari, B., & Kissin, B. (1984). Event-related potentials in boys at risk for alcoholism. *Science, 225,* 1493–1496.

Bigelow, G., Cohen, M., Liebson, I., & Faillace, L. (1972). Abstinence or moderation?: Choice by alcoholics. *Behaviour Research and Therapy, 10,* 209–214.

Bigelow, G., Liebson, I., & Griffiths, R. R. (1974). Alcohol drinking: Suppression by a behavioral time-out procedure. *Behaviour Research and Therapy, 12,* 107–115.

Bohman, M., Cloninger, C. R., von Knorring, A. L., & Sigvardsson, S. (1984). An adoption study of somatoform disorders: III, Cross fostering analysis and genetic relationship to alcoholism and criminality. *Archives of General Psychiatry, 41,* 872–878.

Bohman, M., Sigvardsson, S., & Cloninger, C. R. (1981). Maternal inheritance of alcohol abuse. *Archives of General Psychiatry, 38,* 965–969.

Botvin, Baker E., Filazzola, A. D., & Botvin, E. M. (1990). A cognitive behavioral approach to substance abuse prevention: One-year follow-up. *Addictive Behavior, 15,* 47–63.

Bowers, T. G., & Al-Redha, M. R. (1990). A comparison of outcome with group/marital and standard/individual therapies with alcoholics. *Journal of Studies on Alcohol, 51,* 301–309.

Brown, J. M., & Miller, W. R. (1993). Impact of motivational interviewing on participation and outcome in residential alcoholism treatment. *Psychology of Addictive Behaviors, 7,* 211–218.

Chiu, T.-M., Mendelson, J. H., Woods, B. T., Teoh, S. K., Levisohn, L., & Mello, N. K. (1994). *In vivo* proton magnetic resonance spectroscopy detection of human alcohol tolerance. *Magnetic Resonance Medicine, 32,* 511–516.

Christensen, J. K., Moller, I. W., Ronsted, P., Angelo, H. R., & Johansson, B. (1991). Dose-effect relationship of disulfiram in human volunteers: I, Clinical studies. *Pharmacology and Toxicology, 68,* 163–165.

Christiansen, B. A., Goldman, M. S., & Brown, S. A. (1985). The differential development of alcohol expectancies may predict adult alcoholism. *Addictive Behaviors, 10,* 299–306.

Cloninger, C. R. (1987). Neurogenetic adaptive mechanisms in alcoholism. *Science, 236,* 410–416.

Cloninger, C. R., Bohman, M., & Sigvardsson, S. (1981). Inheritance of alcohol abuse: Cross-fostering analysis of adopted men. *Archives of General Psychiatry, 38,* 861–868.

Cottler, L. B., Schuckit, M. A., Helzer, J. E., Crowley, T., Woody, G., & Nathan, P. E. (1995). The *DSM-IV* field trial for substance use disorders: Major results. *Alcohol and Drug Dependence.*

Crowell, C. R., Hinson, R. E., & Siegel, S. (1981). The role of conditional drug responses in tolerance to the hypothermic effects of alcohol. *Psychopharmacology, 73,* 51–54.

Crowley, T. J. (1994). The organization of intoxication and withdrawal disorders. In T. A. Widiger, A. J. Frances, H. A. Pincus, M. B. First, R. Ross, & W. Davis (eds.), *DSM-IV sourcebook* (vol. 1, pp. 93–108). Washington, D.C.: American Psychiatric Association.

Derman, K. H., & Cooper, M. L. (1994). Sex-related alcohol expectancies among adolescents: I, Scale development. *Psychology of Addictive Behaviors, 8,* 152–160.

Dongier, M., Vachon, L., & Schwartz, G. (1991). Bromocriptine in the treatment of alcohol dependence. *Alcoholism: Clinical and Experimental Research, 15,* 970–977.

Edwards, G. (1992). The history of two dimensions. In M. Lader, G. Edwards, & D. C. Drummond (eds.), *The nature of alcohol and drug related problems* (pp. 1–14). New York: Oxford University Press.

Frezza, M., DiPadova, C., Pozzato, G., Terpin, M., Baraona, E., & Lieber, C. S. (1990). High blood alcohol levels in women: Role of decreased gastric alcohol dehydrogenase activity and first pass metabolism. *New England Journal of Medicine, 322,* 95–99.

Gallant, D. M. (1987). The female alcoholic: Early onset of brain damage. *Alcoholism, 11,* 190–191.

Garvey, A. J., Bliss, R. E., Hitchcock, J. L., Heinold, J. W., & Rosner, B. (1992). Predictors of smoking relapse among self-quitters: A report from the Normative Aging Study. *Addictive Behaviors, 17,* 367–377.

Gawin, F. H., & Ellinwood, E. H. (1988). Cocaine and other stimulants: Actions, abuse, and treatment. *New England Journal of Medicine, 318,* 1173–1182.

Goldman, M. S., Brown, S. A., & Christiansen, B. A. (1987). Expectancy theory: Thinking about drinking. In H. T. Blane & K. E. Leonard (eds.), *Psychological theories of drinking and alcoholism* (pp. 181–226). New York: Guilford.

Goleman, D. (1992a). The children of alcoholics suffer problems that afflict others, too. *New York Times,* 19 February, p. B5.

Goleman, D. (1992b). Study ties genes to alcoholism in women. *New York Times,* 14 October, p. B7.

Goodwin, D. W. (1976). *Is alcoholism hereditary?* New York: Oxford University Press.

Goodwin, D. W. (1979). Alcoholism and heredity. *Archives of General Psychiatry, 36,* 57–61.

Goodwin, D. W. (1985). Genetic determinants of alcoholism. In J. H. Mendelson & N. K. Mello (eds.), *The diagnosis and treatment of alcoholism* (pp. 65–87). New York: McGraw-Hill.

Hansen, W. B. (1992). School-based substance abuse prevention: A review of the state of the art in curriculum, 1980–1990. *Health Education Research, 7,* 403–430.

Harford, T. C., Parker, D. A., Grant, B. F., & Dawson, D. A. (1992). Alcohol use and dependence among employed men and women in the United States in 1988. *Alcoholism: Clinical and Experimental Research, 16,* 146–148.

Hawkins, J. D., Catalano, R. F., & Kent, L. A. (1991). Combining broadcast media and parent education to prevent teenage drug abuse. In L. Donohew, H. E. Sypher, & W. J. Bukoski (eds.), *Persuasive communication and drug abuse education.* Hillsdale, N.J.: Lawrence Erlbaum.

Helzer, J. E. (1994). Psychoactive substance abuse and its relation to dependence. In T. A. Widiger, A. J. Frances, H. A. Pincus, M. B. First, R. Ross, & W. Davis (eds.), *DSM-IV sourcebook* (vol. 1, pp. 21–32). Washington, D.C.: American Psychiatric Association.

Helzer, J. E., Canino, G. J., Yeh, E. -K., Bland, R. C., Lee, C. K., Hwu, H. -G., & Newman, S. (1990). Alcoholism—North America and Asia. *Archives of General Psychiatry, 47,* 313–319.

Hill, S. Y., & Steinhauer, S. R. (1993). Assessment of prepubertal and postpubertal boys and girls at risk for developing alcohol with P300 from a visual discrimination task. *Journal of Studies on Alcohol, 54,* 350–358.

Hingson, R. (1993). Prevention of alcohol-impaired driving. *Alcohol Health & Research World, 17,* 28–34.

Horgan, C. (1993). *Substance abuse: The nation's number one health problem—Key indicators for policy.* Princeton, N.J.: Robert Wood Johnson Foundation.

Hughes, J. R. (1992). Tobacco withdrawal in self-quitters. *Journal of Consulting and Clinical Psychology, 60,* 689–697.

Hughes, J. R. (1994a). Caffeine withdrawal, dependence, and abuse. In T. A. Widiger, A. J. Frances, H. A. Pincus, M. B. First, R. Ross, & W. Davis (eds.), *DSM-IV sourcebook* (vol. 1, pp. 129–134). Washington, D.C.: American Psychiatric Association.

Hughes, J. R. (1994b). Nicotine withdrawal, dependence, and abuse. In T. A. Widiger, A. J. Frances, H. A. Pincus, M. B. First, R. Ross, & W. Davis (eds.), *DSM-IV sourcebook* (vol. 1, pp. 109–116). Washington, D.C.: American Psychiatric Association.

Hunt, W. A., & Nixon, S. J. (eds.) (1993). *Alcohol-induced brain damage.* Washington, D.C.: National Institute on Alcohol Abuse and Alcoholism.

Johnson, R. C., Nagoshi, C. T., Danko, G. P., Honbo, K. A. M., & Chau, L. L. (1990). Familial transmission of alcohol use norms and expectancies and reported alcohol use. *Alcoholism: Clinical and Experimental Research, 14,* 216–220.

Kaij, J. (1960). *Studies in the etiology and sequels of abuse of alcohol.* Lund, Sweden: University of Lund Press.

Kendler, K. S., Heath, A. C., Neale, M. C., Kessler, R. C., & Eaves, L. J. (1992). A population-based twin study of alcoholism in women. *Journal of the American Medical Association, 268,* 1877–1882.

Khantzian, E. J. (1985). The self-medication hypothesis of addictive disorders: Focus on heroin and cocaine dependence. *American Journal of Psychiatry, 142,* 1259–1264.

Kivlahan, D. R., Marlatt, G. A., Fromme, K., Coppel, D. B., & Williams, E. (1990). Secondary prevention with college drinkers: Evaluation of an alcohol skills training program. *Journal of Consulting and Clinical Psychology, 58,* 805–810.

Klatsky, A. L., & Armstrong, M. A. (1993). Alcohol use, other traits, and risk of unnatural death: A prospective study. *Alcoholism: Clinical and Experimental Research, 17,* 1156–1162.

Klitzner, M., Stewart, K., & Fisher, D. (1993). Reducing underage drinking and its consequences. *Alcohol Health & Research World, 17,* 12–18.

Langenbucher, J. W., McCrady, B. S., Brick, J., & Esterly, R. (1993). *Socioeconomic evaluations of addictions treatment.* New Brunswick, N.J.: Rutgers Center of Alcohol Studies.

Larimer, M. E., & Marlatt, G. A. (1994). Addictive behaviors. In L. W. Craighead, W. E. Craighead, A. E. Kazin, & M. J. Mahoney (eds.), *Cognitive and behavioral interventions* (pp. 157–168). Boston: Allyn and Bacon.

Leigh, B. C. (1990). Relationship of substance use during sex to high-risk sexual behavior. *Journal of Sex Research, 27,* 199–213.

Leohlin, J. C. (1977). An analysis of alcohol-related questionnaire items from the National Merit twin study. In F. A. Seixas, G. S. Omenn, E. D. Burk, & S. Eggleston (eds.), *Annals of the New York Academy of Sciences, 197,* 117–120.

Leonard, K. E. (1993). Drinking patterns and intoxication in marital violence: Review, critique, and future directions for research. In S. E. Martin (ed.), *Alcohol and interpersonal violence: Fostering multidisciplinary perspectives* (pp. 253–280). Washington, D.C.: National Institute on Alcohol Abuse and Alcoholism.

Litt, M. D., Babor, T. F., DelBoca, F. K., Kadden, R. M., & Cooney, N. (1992). Types of alcoholics: II. Application of an empirically derived typology to treatment matching. *Archives of General Psychiatry, 49,* 609–614.

Marlatt, G. A., & Gordon, J. R. (eds.) (1985). *Relapse prevention.* New York: Guilford.

Martin, S. E. (1992). The epidemiology of alcohol-related interpersonal violence. *Alcohol Health & Research World, 16,* 230–237.

Mattson, M. E., & Allen, J. P. (1991). Research on matching alcoholic patients to treatments: Findings, issues, and implications. *Journal of Addictive Disorders, 11,* 33–49.

McCrady, B. S., & Miller, W. R. (1993). *Research on Alcoholics Anonymous: Opportunities and alternatives.* New Brunswick, N.J.: Rutgers Center of Alcohol Studies.

McCrady, B. S., Noel, N. E., Abrams, D. B., Stout, R. L., Nelson, H., & Hay, W. M. (1986). Comparative effectiveness of three types of spouse involvement in outpatient behavioral alcoholism treatment. *Journal of Studies on Alcohol, 47,* 459–467.

McCrady, B. S., Stout, R., Noel, N. E., Abrams, D. B., & Nelson, H. F. (1991). Effectiveness of three types of spouse-involved behavioral alcoholism treatment. *British Journal of Addiction, 86,* 1415–1424.

McLellan, A. T., Alterman, A. I., Metzger, D. S., Grissom, G. R., Woody, G. E., Luborsky, L., & O'Brien, C. P. (1994). Similarity of outcome predictors across opiate, cocaine, and alcohol treatments: Role of treatment services. *Journal of Consulting and Clinical Psychology, 62,* 1141–1158.

Michaelis, E. K., & Michaelis, M. L. (1994). Cellular and molecular bases of alcohol's teratogenic effects. *Alcohol Health & Research World, 18,* 17–21.

Miller, W. R. (1993). Behavioral treatments for drug problems: Lessons from the alcohol treatment outcome literature. In L. S. Onken, J. D. Blaine, & J. J. Boren (eds.), *Behavioral treatments for drug abuse and dependence* (NIDA Research Monograph Series; pp. 167–180). Washington, D.C.: U.S. Department of Health and Human Services.

Miller, W. R., Benefield, R. G., & Tonigan, J. S. (1993). Enhancing motivation for change in problem drinking: A controlled comparison of two therapist styles. *Journal of Consulting and Clinical Psychology, 61,* 455–461.

Miller, W. R., Leckman, A. L., Delaney, H. D., & Tinkcom, M. (1992). Long-term follow-up of behavioral self-control training. *Journal of Studies on Alcohol, 53,* 249–261.

Moos, R. H., Finney, J. W., & Cronkite, R. C. (1990). *Alcoholism treatment: Context, process, and outcome.* New York: Oxford University Press.

Morey, L. C., & Skinner, H. A. (1986). Empirically-derived classifications of alcohol-related problems. In M. Galanter (ed.), *Recent developments in alcoholism* (vol. 4, pp. 144–168). New York: Plenum.

Naranjo, C. A., Kadlec, K. E., Sanhueza, P., Woodley-Remus, D., & Sellers, E. M. (1990). Fluoxetine differentially alters alcohol intake and other consummatory behaviors in problem drinkers. *Clinical Pharmacological Therapy, 47,* 490–498.

Nathan, P. E. (1988). The addictive personality is the behavior of the addict. *Journal of Consulting and Clinical Psychology, 56,* 183–188.

Nathan, P. E. (1994). Psychoactive substance dependence. In T. A. Widiger, A. J. Frances, H. A. Pincus, M. B. First, R. Ross, & W. Davis (eds.), *DSM-IV sourcebook* (vol. 1, pp. 33–44). Washington, D.C.: American Psychiatric Association.

Nathan, P. E., & O'Brien, J. S. (1971). An experimental analysis of the behavior of alcoholics and nonalcoholics during prolonged experimental drinking. *Behavior Therapy*, 2, 455–476.

Nathan, P. E., & Skinstad, A. H. (1987). Outcomes of treatment for alcohol problems: Current methods, problems, and results. *Journal of Consulting and Clinical Psychology*, 55, 332–340.

National Institute on Alcohol Abuse and Alcoholism (1993). *Eighth special report to the U.S. Congress on alcohol and health*. Washington, D.C.: U.S. Department of Health and Human Services.

National Institute on Drug Abuse (1991). *Third triennial report to Congress on drug abuse and drug abuse research*. Washington, D.C.: U.S. Department of Health and Human Services.

Neighbors, B., Kempton, T., & Forehand, R. (1992). Co-occurrence of substance abuse with conduct, anxiety, and depression disorders in juvenile delinquents. *Addictive Behaviors*, 17, 379–386.

O'Malley, S. S., Jaffe, A., Chang, G., Witte, G., Schottenfeld, R. S., & Rounsaville, B. J. (1992). Naltrexone in the treatment of alcohol dependence: Preliminary findings. In C. A. Naranjo & E. M. Sellars (eds.), *Novel pharmacological interventions for alcoholism* (pp. 148–157). New York: Springer-Verlag.

Pomerleau, O., Pertschuk, M., Adkins, D., & D'Aquili, E. (1978). Treatment for middle income problem drinkers. In P. E. Nathan, G. A. Marlatt, & T. Loberg (eds.), *Alcoholism: New directions in behavioral research and treatment* (pp. 143–160). New York: Plenum.

Porjesz, B., & Begleiter, H. (1983). Brain dysfunction and alcohol. In B. Kissin & H. Begleiter (eds.), *The pathogenesis of alcoholism* (pp. 415–483). New York: Plenum.

Prescott, C. A., Hewitt, J. K., Truett, K. R., Heath, A. C., Neale, M. C., & Eaves, L. J. (1994). Genetic and environmental influences on lifetime alcohol-related problems in a volunteer sample of older twins. *Journal of Studies on Alcohol*, 55, 184–202.

Prochaska, J. O., & DiClemente, C. C. (1983). Stages and processes of self-change of smoking: Toward an integrative model of change. *Journal of Consulting and Clinical Psychology*, 51, 390–395.

Prochaska, J. O., & DiClemente, C. C. (1986). Toward a comprehensive model of change. In W. R. Miller & N. Heather (eds.), *Treating addictive behaviors* (pp. 3–27). New York: Plenum.

Prochaska, J. O., & DiClemente, C. C. (1992). Stages of change in the modification of problem behaviors. In M. Hersen, R. M. Eisler, & P. M. Miller (eds.), *Progress in behavior* modification (pp. 184–214). Sycamore, Ill: Sycamore Press.

Prochaska, J. O., DiClemente, C. C., & Norcross, J. C. (1992). In search of how people change. *American Psychologist*, 47, 1102–1114.

Rankin, H. (1986). Dependence and compulsion: Experimental models of change. In W. R. Miller & N. Heather (eds.), *Treating addictive behaviors: Processes of change* (pp. 361–374). New York: Plenum.

Robertson, N. (1988). *A.A.: Inside Alcoholics Anonymous*. New York: William Morrow.

Schuckit, M. A. (1994a). A clinical model of genetic influence in alcohol dependence. *Journal of Studies on Alcohol*, 55, 5–17.

Schuckit, M. A. (1994b). *DSM-IV*: Was it worth all the fuss? Presentation at the 7th Congress of the International Society for Biomedical Research on Alcoholism, Queensland, Australia, June.

Schuckit, M. A. (1994c). The relationship between alcohol problems, substance abuse, and psychiatric syndromes. . In T. A. Widiger, A. J. Frances, H. A. Pincus, M. B. First, R. Ross, & W. Davis (eds.), *DSM-IV sourcebook* vol. 1, (pp. 45–66). Washington, D.C.: American Psychiatric Association.

Sher, K. J. (1991). *Children of alcoholics: A critical appraisal of theory and research.* Chicago: University of Chicago Press.

Sher, K. J., & Trull, T. J. (1994). Personality and disinhibitory psychopathology: Alcoholism and antisocial personality disorder. *Journal of Abnormal Psychology, 103,* 92–102.

Siegel, S. (1978). A Pavlovian conditioning analysis of morphine tolerance. In N. A. Krasnegor (ed.), *Behavioral tolerance.* Washington, D.C.: NIDA.

Smith, J., Frawler, P. J., & Polissar, L. (1991). Six- and twelve-month abstinence rates in in patient alcoholics treated with aversion therapy compared with matched inpatients from a treatment registry. *Alcoholism: Clinical and Experimental Research, 15,* 862–870.

Snow, M. G., Prochaska, J. O., & Rossi, J. S. (1992). Stages of change for smoking cessation among former problem drinkers: A cross-sectional analysis. *Journal of Substance Abuse, 4,* 107–116.

Sobell, M. B., & Sobell, L. C. (1973). Alcoholics treated by individualized behavior therapy: One-year treatment outcome. *Behaviour Research and Therapy, 11,* 599–618.

Sobell, M. B., & Sobell, L. C. (1976). Second-year treatment outcome of alcoholics treated by individualized behavior therapy: Results. *Behaviour Research and Therapy, 14,* 195–215.

Steinhauer, S. R., & Hill, S. Y. (1993). Auditory event-related potentials in children at high risk for alcoholism. *Journal of Studies on Alcohol, 54,* 408–421.

Stewart, J., deWit, H., & Eikelboom, R. (1984). The role of unconditioned and conditioned drug effects in the self-administration of opiates and stimulants. *Psychological Review, 91,* 251–268.

Streissguth, A. P. (1994). A long-term perspective of FAS. *Alcohol Health & Research World, 18,* 74–81.

Strunin, L., & Hingson, R. (1993). Alcohol use and risk for HIV infection. *Alcohol Health & Research World, 17,* 35–38.

Sutker, P. B., & Allain, A. N., Jr. (1988). Issues in personality conceptualizations of addictive behaviors. *Journal of Consulting and Clinical Psychology, 56,* 172–182.

Trice, H. M. (1992). Work-related risk factors associated with alcohol abuse. *Alcohol Health & Research World, 16,* 106–111.

U.S. Department of Justice (1993). *1991 drug use forecasting annual report.* Washington, D.C.: U.S. Department of Justice.

U.S. Department of Transportation, National Highway Safety Administration (1992). *FARS: Fatal accident reporting system, annual report, 1992.* Washington, D.C.: U.S. Department of Transportation.

Voegtlin, W. L. (1940). The treatment of alcoholism by establishing a conditioned reflex. *American Journal of Medical Science, 199,* 802–899.

Walsh, D. C., Hingson, R. W., Merrigan, D. M., Levenson, S. M., Cupples, L. A., Heeren, T., Coffman, G., Becker, C. A., Barker, T. A., Hamilton, S. K., McGuire, T. G., & Kelly, C. A. (1991). A randomized trial of treatment options for alcohol-abusing workers. *New England Journal of Medicine, 325,* 775–782.

Wartenburg, A. A., Nirenberg, T. D., Liepman, M. R., Silvia, L. Y., Begin, A. M., & Monti, P. M. (1990). Detoxification of alcoholics: Improving care by symptom-triggered sedation. *Alcoholism: Clinical and Experimental Research*, *14*, 71–75.

Widiger, T. A., Frances, A. J., Pincus, H. A., First, M. B., Ross, R., & Davis, W. (eds.) (1994). *DSM-IV sourcebook* (vol. 1). Washington, D.C.: American Psychiatric Association.

Wright, C., & Moore, R. D. (1989). Disulfiram treatment of alcoholism: Position paper of the American College of Physicians. *Annals of Internal Medicine*, *111*, 943–945.

8

Alcoholism in Russia

The Enemy Within

Boris S. Bratus

It was spring 1985 when Gorbachev assumed the post of general secretary of the Communist Party of the Soviet Union. Neither the Soviet people nor the rest of the world knew that Gorbachev's era would mean the end of the Soviets, the end of socialist rule in Eastern Europe, and the destruction of the Berlin Wall that had come to symbolize the impenetrable Soviet empire. The only major change that Gorbachev announced soon after he assumed office was the start of a rigorous anti-alcohol campaign. Ironically, this was to be the last purely Soviet campaign, and it was launched in traditional Bolshevik style—a sudden and surprise attack of grand scale against a long-time enemy. Students of history will recognize that the anti-alcohol campaign did not originate with Gorbachev. The Central Committee of the Communist Party of the Soviet Union (CPSU) had already planned the campaign before Gorbachev took office. Although in the minds of most Soviet citizens the campaign against the use of alcohol is associated with Gorbachev, most are aware that it was really the brainchild of the secretary of ideology, Egor Ligachev.

News of the campaign was well disseminated. The leading Russian newspaper, *Pravda* (which means "truth"), all of the other media, and millions of brochures published the Resolution of the Central Committee of the CPSU of 7 May 1985. The resolution was titled "On the Ways of Overcoming the Problem of Alcoholism." The directive was clear: alcoholism had become an increasingly urgent problem over the last several years. Strict orders were given to a variety of organizations, including the Soviet of Ministeries (government) of the USSR, the Ministries of Justice, Public Health, Home Affairs, and Education and Culture, the Comsomol (Young Communists' League), all trade unions, public organizations, and courts of law, to "strengthen the struggle with and prepare corresponding directives, decisions, laws, actions, interpretations and elucidations" that would further the fight against the consumption of alcoholic drinks. The response was immediate in all 15 republics of the Soviet Union as newspapers, radio, and television responded with features and shows carrying anti-alcohol themes. Entire "alcoholic" episodes were cut from films. Even well-known movies were altered. The chapter on environmental psychology describes a movie in which the hero boards a plane in error because of his inebriated state and soon finds himself in another city. This popular comedy was "half-prohibited" during the height of the anti-alcohol campaign.

Alcoholic drinks were forbidden at official meetings. Violators of the spirit or the letter of the ensuing laws were quickly reprimanded so as to make a public example of them. A common reprimand was to exclude the violator from the Communist Party, which meant that the violator would never attain the material benefits of party members (e.g., better housing) and could never rise to high-level government positions. Thus, the consequences were harsh and long-lasting.

The anti-alcohol campaign that began in 1985 differed from previous ones, such as the campaign of 1972, in that even intelligent or moderate drinking of low-alcoholic beverages and high-quality wines was strictly forbidden. The whole of the Soviet Union was declared a "zone of sobriety." Every town and village in the massive Soviet Union displayed large signs that read "Fight a Drink" (or more colloquially translated, "No Drinking"). Regional administrators competed to be among the first to inform the leaders in Moscow of their regional success with the anti-alcohol campaign. (The theme of telling government leaders what they want to hear is explained more fully in the chapter on lies.) Experience from previous campaigns of all sorts had taught regional leaders that the first to report success would be praised and the last to report success would be punished, possibly even dismissed from their positions of leadership. In order to spare their own jobs, regional leadership ordered that the production of wine, liquor, vodka, and even beer be stopped immediately. Expensive equipment, even new equipment that was recently purchased with the short supply of foreign currency, was discarded.

The southern republics of the Soviet Union suffered disproportionately from this campaign because they monopolized the vine agriculture. Some of the fine old vines predated the Communist revolution and enjoyed a worldwide reputation for the excellent wines they produced. Most of these agricultural treasures were destroyed during this campaign. Many of the republics that are now independent states (Ukraine, Moldovia, and the Transcaucacus states of Georgia, Azerbaijan, and Armenia) were especially hard-hit. Drinking was banned, swiftly and forever.

Secret Statistics

Was this sudden cavalry raid against alcohol really needed? Was the problem of alcoholism really as urgent as the government documents claimed in pre-perestroika Russia? In order to answer these questions, reliable statistics are needed to decide if alcoholism was decimating the Soviet population as the officials claimed. The relevant data, like most useful information in communist Russia, were secret. I learned of the data through my participation as a psychologist with expertise in the area of alcoholism. I was a participant in a specially formulated commission designed for the "Governmental Complex Program for Prevention and Suppression of Alcoholism." I soon learned that the bureaucrats who headed this commission were not interested in examining the data or listening to scientific forecasting. Instead, they were in a hurry to initiate the anti-alcohol campaign as they had been directed and were not to be delayed or deterred by data or expert opinion. The campaign was initiated with virtually no discussion as to its need or merits; my sole remuneration was access to the secret statistics that had been collected regarding alcoholism in the Soviet Union.

According to the official statistics, alcoholic consumption in the Soviet Union had increased 2.3 times over the amount that was consumed in 1965, 20 years prior to the start of the campaign. In 1980, alcohol consumption averaged 8.7 liters per individual, not counting strong homemade brews that undoubtedly were a major additional source of alcohol. Approximately 21 percent of an average family's budget was spend on alcohol. It was estimated that 40 percent of male workers consumed at least .5 liters of vodka at least three times a week. Treatment for alcoholism usually consisted of the militia's rounding up, transporting, and then dumping drunken men at "sobering stations." These stations were run by a notoriously rude militia-like staff; they served 9 million "patients" per year. In Moscow, the main causes of death for males who were capable of working (i.e., not diagnosed with a debilitating illness) were alcohol-related accidents and alcohol poisoning (overdose). At the start of 1985, 2.1 percent of the population aged 14 and older was registered as addicted to alcohol; the percentage of males 14 and older with this diagnosis was 4 percent. Economic loss owing to missed days (even years) of work is difficult to calculate accurately but is undoubtedly a large number.

It is evident that the Soviet Union had a horrific problem with alcohol. Most Soviets did not need access to these secret statistics to realize the gravity of the situation. People everywhere drank a lot; many drank nonstop; every social layer and every job category was affected. The Soviet people called these years "stagnant" and "hard drinking." In Russian, the two words sound almost identical: *zastoy* (stagnation) and *zapoy* (hard drinking). Why were so many Soviet citizens alcoholics? Why did all of the governmental efforts to reduce alcohol consumption fail? Why did the proportion of the population that was seriously alcoholic increase during the pre-perestroika years? From a purely psychological perspective, why do the Russian people work so hard and then destroy everything that they have worked for with excessive use of alcohol? What are they trying to find or trying to hide in their "bitter drinking"? (In Russian, the direct translation is not literally "hard drinking" as it would be in English but "bitter drinking.")

Why the Russian People Find Alcohol Irresistible

The "need" for alcohol is not the same as the need for water, food, or air. One can live without alcohol but not without the other more basic needs that support life. Alcoholism is created and supported by the social environment. Over a century ago, the Russian psychiatrist V. P. Portugalov (1890) wrote that the "existing habit of drinking breeds in subsequent generations a consistent predisposition, and by way of imitation and learning, it is transferred from one to the other."

In the years following the Second World War, drinking until becoming drunk became more and more acceptable. In fact, it became a behavioral norm that was close to compulsory at many social gatherings. The change in attitudes toward alcohol can be seen in a short novel written by the modern writer Valentin Rasputin (1980). An old woman from Siberia was comparing modern times (in the early 1970s) to the times of her youth. She pronounced, "In previous times, was it like this? . . . Remember, in the village, when Danila, the miller, would drink. Did anyone take him for something? A drunkard—that's all one had to say or think about him. Nowadays, Golubev is the only man in the entire village who is not a drunkard, and you know, he is now taken for nothing. Everyone in the village laughs at him because he does not drink."

The acceptability of alcohol consumption is learned by Russian children at a very young age. It is quite typical in many households to include children in celebrations, where the child is given a glass of some nonalcoholic beverage, such as lemonade, which is labeled the "kids' wine." The ritual of the toast and clinking of the glasses, the praise for the child who participates in these rituals, and the child's perception of the jovial occasion are part of the learning process. The probable quarrels and fighting that follow long bouts of drinking are also observed by the child who comes to see them as a natural and accepted part of family life. In a 1970s study of the way young children learn about social events, preschoolers were asked to play at "a wedding party," "a birthday," or "a visit." The adults were horrified to see that the children mimicked with great accuracy the drinking, followed by unsteady and aimless walking, the drunklike kissing, and other typical scenes that accompany inebriation. In general, these sorts of make-believe are popular with young children and their parents, who frequently ask them to show off their imitations of being drunk for visitors and family members. Typical requests to children might include, "Show how Dad (or Grandfather) sings when he gets drunk." These behaviors are encouraged in even the most remote regions of the former Soviet Union. A. I. Tsaplin (1972) surveyed 100 boys in a kindergarten in Perm, a city in the Urals, where he found that 97 percent could realistically portray the behaviors of alcoholic intoxication.

It is significant that one's first taste of alcohol contrasts in an unexpected manner with its anticipation. Alcohol is expected to cause happiness and easiness; instead, adolescents find that vodka is bitter, it makes their mouth burn, and it leaves their heads swimming and stomachs nauseated. The negative reactions are less severe when the first tastes of alcohol are limited to weaker drinks, such as wine and beer. When Matveev, Kucher, and Lagovsky (1979) asked adolescents to describe their first impressions of alcoholic drinks, 53 percent felt disgusted, 33 percent felt indifferent, and only 24 percent said they felt pleasure. The reasons adolescents continue to drink alcohol even when it initially elicits a response of disgust are easy to understand. In Russia, drinking is an obligatory ritual for adults at weddings, birthdays, funerals, upon entering the army, and many other occasions. Ouspensky (1914/1988) provided an apt description of the process of learning to drink: "The first glass of alcohol is no more pleasing than the first cigarette. One might assume that the first taste will have a continuing effect, but this assumption is mistaken. Grownups keep urging the adolescent boy: 'Drink! Everyone drinks! You are not a man if you have no taste for alcohol.'" Those who drink make drunkards of those who abstain, and it is friendship plus imitation that cause much drinking.

The physical processes involved in becoming inebriated cause the ongoing problem when drinking moves from social functions to private and continual consumption. In general, the effect of alcohol is first characterized by a high or buzz that occurs when cortical activity is depressed and the subcortical areas of the brain are liberated. Later, with increasing doses of alcohol, the subcortical areas also become depressed as activity slows down. The effect of alcohol on higher cognitive activities, such as memory and thought, also goes through distinct phases. I supervised a study by Kharevskaya (1987), in which three phases were identified as a function of the amount of alcohol consumed as a percentage of total body weight. Within 10 minutes of consumption, short-term negative effects were seen. Memory and other intellectual problems could be observed within 30 minutes. From 90 to 120 minutes after drinking a carefully prescribed dose of alcohol, torpor set in, which brought about relaxation and sleepiness. A full-scale case of intoxication is characterized by disrupted motor activity, lack of coordination, and slurring of speech. During the Czarist era, a person was declared drunk based on the way he executed specific tasks, such as the ability to stand up from a lying position, blow out a candle, or smoke a cigarette. It is surely not a desire to lose control of one's speech or motor ability that causes people to drink to excess.

The most frequently given reason for drinking is the desire to be merry and participate in the festive atmosphere that most believe should prevail when friends gather for a celebration. Again, the rich nuances of the Russian language provide a guide for understanding these linkages. One of the meanings of the Russian word for *merry* is "slightly tipsy." The dictionary of the Russian vernaculars of the Arkhangelsk, a northern Russian region close to the Arctic Ocean, defines *merry* as "intoxicating, inebriating, and alcoholic." The following phrase is provided as an illustration: "Shall I give you some merry? Have some merry [vodka]." Special occasions require special party clothing, and while the individual prepares for the anticipated event, he or she begins the unconscious preparation for all that is expected to accompany the event, and this includes drinking alcoholic beverages and the physiological sensations that follow alcohol consumption.

Placebos and Expectancy Effects

The consumption of alcohol causes changes in the nervous system that become associated with joyous occasions. As with all addictive drugs, the subjective experience is caused by a combination of the physiological effects that the drugs have on the body and the individual's beliefs about and learned associations with the drug. One way to separate these two effects is with the use of placebos; generally inert substances that have no physiological effects are administered to individuals who believe they have been (or might have been) giving the drug, and the drug in question is administered to individuals who do not know that they are receiving it. For example, a placebo in a study on alcoholism would look, taste, and smell like an alcoholic beverage, but it would not contain the alcohol that causes inebriation. Subjects would not be aware of the fact that they were not drinking an alcoholic beverage. We know that a number of strong psychological processes come into effect when individuals believe they are receiving a particular drug. For example, medications that are expensive and difficult to obtain always seem more effective than those that are cheaper and more readily available, and the same medication is perceived as being more effective when it is prescribed by physicians with prestigious backgrounds than when it is prescribed by physicians with less prestigious backgrounds. This is why older and more experienced physicians would take the time to tell their patients what sort of beneficial effect to expect from their medication rather than merely handing them a prescription and sending them off to a pharmacy. Patients are more likely to report the desirable effect of the medication when they know what it should be in advance.

Under most circumstances, it would be unethical to conduct a placebo study with alcohol. Fortunately, Sidorov and I (1984) were able to perform such a study during a medical examination of the liver and kidneys. In order to image these body parts with infrared tomography, Sidorov had to inject his subjects (all young males) with a 33 percent alcohol solution. Some of the subjects were told only that they were being injected with a "functional load." These subjects reported an increase in overall level of excitement that was followed by a feeling of relaxation and then sleepiness. No other behavioral components were observed. Other subjects were told that they were being injected with alcohol. These subjects showed the more usual effects of alcohol consumption; in addition to enhanced excitement, they told jokes, used "catchy phrases," and showed other evidence typically associated with alcohol intoxication.

In a second study, adult volunteers with a positive attitude toward alcohol were invited to one of the medical wards at a psychoneurological rehabilitation clinic in order to study the psychological effects of alcohol. They were paid a small amount of money for their participation. After an intake of a specified dose of alcohol, they were asked to describe their subjective emotional experience. The subjects were somewhat surprised to find that the alcohol had not induced the expected effect: sitting in a medical ward under the supervision of the doctor who conducted the experiment, they felt depressed rather than excited. In their reports, the subjects spoke about the physiological correlates of intoxication—they felt hot, sick (with nausea), and so on. This condition was relieved when the effect of alcohol had disappeared.

These studies demonstrate that it is not only the anonymous administration of alcohol that leaves the state of being intoxicated without the characteristics usually attributed to it. The subjective experience of alcohol is destroyed when the specific situation in which the drinking occurs and the circumstances surrounding it are changed. It is true, though, that this parameter changes significantly if drinking becomes increasingly heavier and turns into a disease. At the initial stage of heavy drinking, the social environment plays a very important role. Practicing psychologists know only too well that if a person drinks alone, this points to a case that is not typical. In ordinary cases, even the presence of one or two sober people when others are drinking heavily is regarded as undesirable, and those who are drinking try to make the abstainers drink too, or the drinkers will drive them away. This explains why it is more appropriate to speak not so much about the effect of alcohol but the effect of the entire ritual surrounding the use of alcohol in company.

Studies like these show that at least part of the effect of alcohol on behavior is related to socially mediated expectations and beliefs. This idea can be found in old Russian laws regarding aggressive acts that were committed when the individual was inebriated. Legal documents written in 1649 list alcoholic intoxication as one of the facts that reduce guilt when a crime has been committed. Later, the law was reversed, and the inebriated individual was considered to have an even higher degree of guilt if a crime was committed when he was in this state. Yet even though the law was reversed, in the minds of many people, a drunken individual is less guilty than a sober one when he commits a crime.

The consumption of alcohol is an activity that occupies a unique niche in Russian culture. It is used to mark the significance of both happy and sad events. Its effects on individuals are expected to be in accord with the specific occasion, and its use excuses only some kinds of antisocial behaviors and not others. It can be used to reduce culpability if a crime is committed, but if an intoxicated individual behaves in a euphoric manner at a funeral, the heavy consumption of alcohol does not excuse this unacceptable behavior, which shows disrespect for the deceased. However, its association with boisterous singing and dancing is expected at a joyous occasion, such as a wedding. The subjective reasons for heavy drinking include drinking "for courage," because one feels offended, to relax, to improve a sad mood, and in preparation for a serious discussion. Alcohol serves as a backdrop for both happy and sad events and many other sorts of events that are unrelated to mood.

Influence of Alcohol on Cognition and Confidence

Abundant evidence shows that alcohol impairs one's ability to think and learn. For example, Wutrich (1974) linked a decrease in the ability to perceive new information and a reduction in the length of attention span to the fact that alcoholics believe they are better able to handle cognitive tasks when they are inebriated. They are dealing with less information, a fact that makes them think they are dealing more efficiently with the information. Alcoholics have no awareness of the decrease in the quality of their work when they consume alcohol (Tsaneva & Danev, 1981). Intoxicated individuals are overly optimistic in their assessment of their work. When intoxicated individuals were presented with a series of problems to solve, they reported with complete confidence that their performance was improving, when, in fact, they were solving fewer and fewer problems correctly (Kharevskaya, 1987). Comments included, "It is easier to think now," when performance showed an increase in errors. A report in 1912 (Kraepelin) described a drunk who believed that his brain worked particularly well when he was intoxicated. Thus, the problem of alcoholism is particularly difficult because many people are very confident that it improves their cognitive abilities, a belief that is in direct opposition to performance data.

Understanding Alcoholism in the Context of Activity Theory

One way to understand alcoholism is to view it from the perspective of activity theory, a highly influential theory of human consciousness and action that originated with the Soviet psychologist Alexei N. Leontiev (1978). According to this theory, human activity is associated with a motive, which is triggered by a need. Needs create a sequence of goal-directed actions designed to overcome barriers and obstacles. Graphically, consider a sequence that begins at one end with a need and ends with a motive that is activated (or energized) by an emotional arousal. In order to go from the need to the motive, a series of subgoals are set up, and each subgoal has an act associated with it. This is depicted in figure 8.1.

Consider the specific example of achieving the important goal of self-respect. In order to achieve self-respect, a series of effortful activities is needed. But when an individual is under the influence of alcohol, he has the illusion of self-respect, without all of the difficult work that is normally needed. He is a "winner," who has satisfied a need without having to do any of the work that is usually necessary for self-respect. Alcohol is an easy and cheap way to achieve a goal. But the feeling of achievement is illusionary and short-lived. In order to regain the positive emotional arousal that comes with self-respect, the individual will need to drink heavily once again, establishing a vicious circle in which the quick route

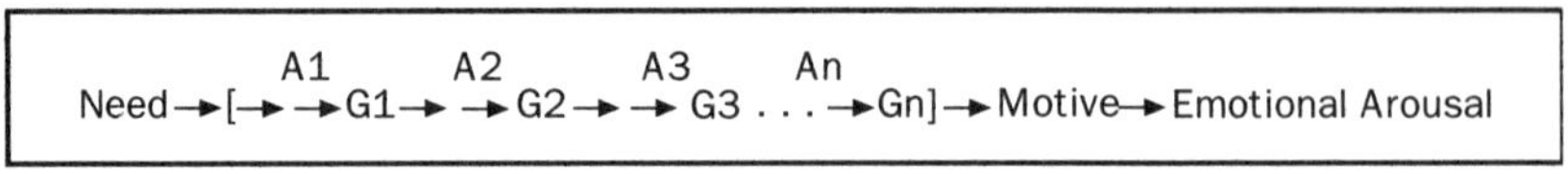

$$Need \rightarrow [\rightarrow \overset{A1}{\rightarrow} G1 \rightarrow \overset{A2}{\rightarrow} G2 \rightarrow \overset{A3}{\rightarrow} G3 \ldots \overset{An}{\rightarrow} Gn] \rightarrow Motive \rightarrow Emotional\ Arousal$$

Figure 8.1. Graphical Depiction of Leontiev's Activity Theory

Note: Actions (A1, A2, A3, . . . , An) are each associated with subgoals (G1, G2, G3, . . . , Gn). These intervene between needs and motives. Motives intervene between needs and emotional arousal.

to an illusory goal is substituted for the more difficult route of achieving real-life goals through a sequence of activities.

The Alcoholic Theater

Metaphorically speaking, what we are faced with is an "alcoholic theater." Essentially, every drinking company represents this kind of theater, with its own cast. This theater is special in that all the characters in it are overdrawn. One person is unnaturally gloomy, another puts on a show of extreme high spirits, still another behaves wildly. The grotesqueness of this sort of behavior is easily evident. Even former alcoholics, when they find themselves at these parties and remain sober, can easily comprehend the unnaturalness of the behavior. Former alcoholics wonder how these behaviors could have made sense for them before and how it could have attracted them.

The view of an alcoholic party from the inside provides an opposite image. Korolenko and Zavyalov (1987) analyzed diverse groups of alcoholics differing in age, profession, and group structure. The researchers concluded that there are common features in all of these groups. In all alcoholic parties, the individual participants have standardized roles, there is an emphasis on identifying with the group, there is the belief that all the "ordinary living problems" are now comprehended, deindividualization occurs ("I am as everyone else"), and group approval is of paramount importance—a motive that is easily achieved because group members freely express praise for each other.

These are some of the activities that are typical of alcoholic parties, but a closer look at the behaviors will show that many of the group members are trying to overcome self-doubts, forget about past offenses, revive hopes that have been dashed, and relive dreams that have not come true. One person typically plays the role of a man who is not appreciated enough, while another is cast in the role of his sole admirer, with statements like "You know, mate, you have talent. You'll show them. Let's have another drink." All of the alcoholic parties represent an attempt to ultimately justify the drinker's feeling that he is not appreciated and to prompt the conclusion that he is a worthy person.

The Play: An Illusory-Compensatory Ritual

Feelings of self-worth are usually facilitated by the specific structure of the alcohol-induced role and the way it is played out. Here is one frequent scenario.

Part one is *condemnation*: "I am a nobody, a villain. I ruined my family. I make everybody's life intolerable. I am a good-for-nothing." The people in the audience sympathize. They are touched by this kind of contrition, and tears well up in their eyes. Then the repenting person suddenly poses the question: "And who is to blame for all this?" And the second part begins, *justification*: "My wife is a bitch. She has ruined my life. The boss is just a bastard. Society does not provide . . ." Having acted it, the person feels expurgated and reconciled with his life. It is true, however, that both the expurgation and the reconciliation with oneself are short-lived and not real because to attain genuine expurgation it is necessary to engage in difficult work in real-life situations, resolve conflicts, face difficulties, and meet with disappointment before one attains the desired objective. But in the alcoholic theater he can receive his rewards on the same night. Therefore, as we have already noted, a sober person is never a welcome guest at a drinking party because he is seen as a reminder of the real world and impedes the acting out of the illusory-compensatory ritual. If drinking is left without its illusory-compensatory component, the drinkers will be deprived of the main reason that brings them together.

The Coaches

The role of those who initiate other people in drinking deserves special mention here. Traditions do not exist by themselves. As a rule, the life of any alcoholic or ordinary drinker can be seen to be dominated by his "alcoholic tutors," who provide role models by demonstrating how a man should actually drink in order to attain the desired state of internal reconciliation with oneself. One of the main premises of psychic development, according to Vygotsky (1978), is that any psychological entity is initially divided between two poles: a child and an adult, a student and a teacher. It is only at a later stage in the developmental sequence that the new behavior is internalized and becomes something possessed by the child/learner. The acquisition of alcoholic emotional experiences proceeds in the same way. Leo Tolstoy (1891/1988) noted that when a drunkard is asked why he drinks, the response is invariably the same: everyone drinks. In part, it is learned from tutors, much as one learns how to read or perform arithmetic.

The Illusory-Compensatory Model of Alcoholism in a Sociohistorical Context

The model of alcoholism that is proposed here is based on activity theory, which posits that individuals engage in activities that will achieve a goal and satisfy a need. When intoxicated, people have the illusion that a difficult goal has been attained, without the hard work of dealing with reality or working through subgoals. The use of alcohol compensates for the inability to achieve these goals through real effort. This illusion is further supported by others who also engage in heavy drinking, a group process that supports the illusion that the inebriate has, in fact, achieved important life goals.

How well does this model fit into the Russian sociohistorical context? From this perspective, it is important to ask, "What is the reality of life in Russia?" A decade ago, when the anti-alcohol campaign was in process, Russian life was so oppressive and suffocating that it is no wonder the people consumed large quantities of alcohol. A great many of those addicted to alcohol stayed in the illusory-compensatory kind of activity because of one simple reason: all the possible ways to the real activities were blocked.

A popular saying from that time may help readers understand the context: one can't achieve the three merits—to be honest, to be a (Communist) Party member, and to be smart (have intellect). The argument went like this: (1) being a smart party member means you are an "old fox"; (2) being an honest party member means you are, sorry to say, a fool; (3) being honest and smart automatically means you are outside the Communist Party. The three merits really are incompatible.

In reality, people were forced to restrict their goal-directed behaviors to illusionary compensations. "Free activity" was limited to the space of their narrow kitchens in panel houses (people named these panel apartment houses after Khrushchev, who was the initiator of separate family dwellings as an alternative to the communal way of living). The kitchens were thought by intellectuals to be the only place where the closest friends expressed themselves freely and did not hide their views. Of course, they had a drink when speaking freely—a popular toast was "To the success of our desperate deeds and hopes." But at the time, it seemed more like a Zen Buddhist riddle, something as impossible as "one hand clapping" but possible to imagine during a good drink with your friends.

"No" was the beloved reaction of Soviet bureaucracy to every position that would allow the Russian people the means to achieve their personal goals. Andrei Gromyko, who retained the position of foreign affairs minister for decades, was informally called "Mister No" because of his permanent refusals and vetoes. But why recall Gromyko's shouts of "No!" in the United Nations? Every Soviet met the same "No!" whenever he entered a bureaucrat's office and tried to ask for something that he needed: "Can I please . . . ?" he whispered, and immediately the bureaucrat shouted back his beloved "No!," having not even heard the essence of what the visitor needed. The answer was always no, no matter what the request.

Recall another "pretty" word from these times: *dostat* (to get). It was used to express the obstacles that had to be overcome in order to get something. *Dostat* was associated with cunning, foxlike behavior and with smartness, patience, and impudence. One had to "get" everything this way: ham and sausages, novels and textbooks, a chance to stay at a sanatorium or rest place in the summer, and a chance to enroll your children in a kindergarten. The whole life of a Soviet was a "getting," an exhausting and desperate struggle for every commodity needed for life. This struggle started with the chance for your mother to get her bed at the maternity hospital, and it finished with your getting a place at a cemetery. It was a society in which the individual was accorded no respect, an important goal that could be achieved only under the illusionary haze of an alcoholic stupor. Thus, the roots of excessive alcoholism are clear.

And what about today? Is the illusory-compensatory model of alcoholism still viable in today's Russia? Throughout much of this century, communism was fighting capitalism, and the Communist Party and KGB led the struggle against dissidents. Are the dramatic political changes of the 1990s expected to change the alcoholic habits of Russians? Today's leading struggle is on the battlefield of privatization, a battlefield in the hands of marauders. They decorate the cities with their flags and slogans and teach us how to live, what music to listen to, what movies to see, how to spend our leisure. They seduce the youth. Everything they touch becomes consumer goods; everything is sold; there is nothing sacred to them. They try to get to the Parliament to gain power. Never in the history of Russia were such favorable conditions given to the so-called new Russians. No one ever noticed these sort of people in Russia. It should be mentioned here that such people always existed in Russia (as elsewhere), but before they stayed in the shadows, careful not to show off in a society that officially eschewed materialism. This situation has changed completely. Now these people are at the center of social life; they are masters of life, big bosses, many of them former criminals. The former ideological leaders of the Soviet Union who survived the coup of August 1991 now have power concentrated in their hands again, forming a very strong union with the new Russian riffraff. Not everyone from the former nomenclature, of course; only those selected in the filters of market economy, those smart party members (during communist times) who necessarily lacked honesty (as captured by the three incompatible merits that were described earlier).

Remember, it was the former Comsomol leaders who were the first to install private companies, open savings banks, invest in erotic show business, and the like. Why not? They are Russian young adults who received training in management. They were smart enough to join the Communist Party and make it a successful career; when it turned out to be the wrong side, they quickly switched to free enterprise. Tomorrow, they will easily abandon this system if it is not profitable.

But enough of new Russians with their obscene display of wealth (the most expensive models of Mercedes-Benz cars are more numerous in Moscow than in any other world capital). What about the people (simple people, as they were always called)? They have become paupers, with more than 40 million Russians now living in extreme poverty. The Russians are dying. On average, only 9 newborns replace every 15 deaths, and the average life span of males decreased to only 57 years at a time when longevity is at an all-time high in many industrialized countries. Robbery and murder have become common occurrences; when surveyed, many people say they do not feel safe, even at home. Those who worked for decades feel themselves deceived and robbed by the governmental authorities, as their small savings dwindle to nothing due to hyperinflation.

And so why not have a drink? How can one fail to drink some alcohol? When drunk, one has a chance to leave for a short while the shameful, desperate, and unloved reality. Taking this position, there is nothing comparable to a heartful Russian party with close or distant friends sitting at a table, peacefully talking and having drinks, feeling (and expressing) mutual understanding and attraction.

Westerners drink just to have a drink. Russians drink to leave reality. We are not satisfied when we have a drink at home or even in a bar. When drunk, a Russian rushes to the street to meet people. This untidy street seems to turn not to the corner but to the heavens—something very distant from reality. A Russian strives to universalize his drinking, to find a way to a final solution of world problems and to unity.

An old woman in Rasputin's *The Last Term* remembers her husband: "He was not drinking, though who knows? It might be better and easier if he did. All the stupid matters in a man are like a scum in sauce-pan that is to be removed; vodka might be a medicine, if not too much of it. And if not too much, one drinks, sings, makes stupid things, after that he is without scum. My old man saved his scum and stupid things inside him for months" (1980, p. 528).

Just try to remove the drinking rituals from the Russian life and a nation-wide way of living might disappear because drinking is the glue that binds the Russian way of life most strongly. To attack the excessive use of alcohol in Russia is needed and justified, based on scientific findings and morals. But in reality all attempts to reduce alcohol consumption in Russia are desperate and have no chance of success. Ten years ago the anti-alcohol campaign was strong and destructive and bore no lasting results. Everything is the same in the new Russia, but for the fact that even more people drink until intoxicated. Isn't it better to leave Russia drinking as it is?

Russia's literary giants knew much about the psychological motivation that made alcoholism a major problem for Russians. As one of the characters in Rasputin's *The Last Term* explains:

> Life has now become totally different, you bet. Everything has changed and these changes have forced people to make another effort. We have grown very tired and I tell you what. It's not so much because of work but rather I don't know from what God damn thing. Only a week has gone by but I can hardly move my feet I feel so tired. But when I take a drink I feel as though I've taken a bath, and I feel as light as a feather. I know I can be blamed for so many things: at home I had a row with my wife, spent all the money we had, was absent from work many days, roamed around the village begging for money—what a shame! But on the other hand it's easier this way. . . . You go to work again asking pardon for your sins. You work one day, two days, five days. You work like a horse, and somehow you feel strong, well, things seem to have settled down and the shame has gone, you can go on living. Only don't drink. . . . But how can you go on without drinking? One, two, three days—or even a whole week you can keep away from it. But if you won't ever drink again until your dying day? Just imagine. Nothing to look forward to. The same old story every day. We are bound hand and foot by so many ropes both at home and work that you can't say a word. You have so many things to do and haven't done any of them. You have to do this and that and that, and the more you live, the more things you have to do. God damn it all. But when you take a drink, you feel like a free man, you have

your freedom and there is not a single thing that you have to do. You've done everything there was to do. (1980, p. 453)

When I think about the problem of alcoholism in Russia, I often recall my years working as a psychologist in a clinic for alcoholics. Sometimes the patients would speak about the positive and pleasant aspects of their addiction—what a pleasure it was to have a drink with friends. But as a psychologist, I had to remind them that their drinking was, in fact, extremely destructive. To make this point, I would simply ask, "And how did these pleasant drinking sessions end?" In this way, I would help them realize that there was a discrepancy between their selective memories of good times spent drinking and the final results of their drunken binges. Their goal was to relax and have fun, and excessive drinking was seen as a way to do this. The results were far from the relaxation and fun that they sought. Instead, they awoke in a strange place with all of their money gone, in the street with their faces bleeding, or in some similar miserable state. Similarly, the simplest question in understanding alcoholism in modern Russia is to ask, "If Russians continue to consume excessive quantities of alcohol, what will happen to our country and to the people of Russia?" The answer to this simple question will be found in a bleak future, if Russians do not slake their thirst for alcohol.

References

Bratus, B. S., & Sidorov, P. I. (1984). *Psikhologiya, klinika i profilaktika rannego alkogolizma.* (Psychology, clinics, and prophylaxis of alcoholism.) Moscow: Moscow University Press. (In Russian.)

Kharevskaya, A. Y. (1987). Fiziologicheskie posledstviya oupotrebleniya alkogolya. (Physiological consequences of alcoholism.) In *Preodolenie alkogolizma u podrostkov i yunoshej: Psikhologo-fizio-logicheskii aspekt.* Moscow: Pedagogika. (In Russian.)

Korolenko, Ts. P., & Zavyalov, V. Ju. (1987). *Lichnost' i alkogol'.* (Personality and alcohol.) Novosibirsk: Nauka. (In Russian.)

Kraepelin, E. (1912). Psikhologiya alkogol'nogo otravleniya. (The psychology of alcoholic intoxication.) *Vestnik Trezvosti, 205,* 36–40. (In Russian.)

Leontiev, A. N. (1978). *Activity, consciousness, and personality.* Englewood Cliffs, N.J.: Prentice-Hall.

Matveev, V. F., Kucher, L. D., & Lagovsky (1979). K voprosu stanovleniya i prognoza alkogolizma. (On the formation and forecasting of alcoholism.) *Sovetskaya Meditsina, 12,* 15–19. (In Russian.)

Ouspensky, S. (1914/1988). Shkola trezvosti. (A school of sobreity.) In *Dlya chego liudi odurmanivaiutsya?* (Why do people get intoxicated?) (pp. 194–195). Moscow: Moskovskii Rabochii Publishers. (In Russian.)

Portugalov, V. (1890). P'yanstvo kak plod vospitaniya. (Drinking as a result of upbringing.) *Vestnik Vospitaniya, 8,* 92–114. (In Russian.)

Rasputin, V. G. (1980). *Poslednii srok.* (The last term.) In *Povesti* (Short novels.) Moscow: Molodaya Gvardiya. (In Russian.)

Tolstoy, L. N. (1891/1988). *Dlya chego liudi odurmanivaiutsya?* (Why do people get intoxicated?) Moscow: Moskovskii Rabochii. (In Russian.)

Tsaneva, L., & Danev, S. (1981). Izmenenie nekotorykh parametrov operatorskoi deyatel'nosti pod vliyaniem alkogolya. (Alcohol-induced transformations of some parameters of operator activity.) *Gigiena Truda i Profzabolevanii*, 5, 19–26. (In Russian.)

Tsaplin, A. I. (1972). Materialy k epidemiologii alkogolizma v rannem detskom vozraste. (Materials on the epidemiology of alcoholism in early childhood.) *Trudy Permskogo Meditsinskogo Instituta* (Proceedings of the Medical Institute in Perm), 110, 160–162. (In Russian.)

Vygotsky, L. S. (1978). *Mind in society: The development of higher psychological processes*. Cambridge: Cambridge University Press.

Wutrich, P. (1974). *Soziogenese der chronisdhen alcoholismus*. Basel: Karger.

Zaehner, R. C. (1972). *Druge, mysticism and make-believe*. London: Collins.

Psychological Trauma

9

Post-Traumatic Stress Disorder

A Historical Context and Evolution

Teresa L. Kramer & Bonnie L. Green

Despite numerous portrayals in classic literature of humankind's psychic struggle over the effects of war, murder, rape, disasters, plagues, and so forth, clinicians and researchers have only recently begun to name, describe, study, and treat post-trauma phenomena. The earliest clinical observations on the effects of trauma were recorded by Charcot, Freud, and Breuer. In *Studies on Hysteria*, Breuer and Freud (1956) offered the following definition: "In traumatic neurosis the operative cause of illness is not the trifling psychical injury but the effect of fright—the psychical trauma. . . . Any experience which calls up distressing affects—such as those of fright, anxiety, shame or physical pain— may operate as a trauma of this kind" (pp. 5–6, as cited by Krystal, 1978). As the reader will see, the term *traumatic neurosis* initially provided the theoretical framework for the study of post-traumatic symptomatology. Eventually, as this area of study progressed, the term *neurosis* was seen as inadequate, as well as biased toward psychoanalytic thinking, and was therefore replaced—first by terminology specific to the type of trauma and then by the current nosology of post-traumatic stress disorder (Scrignar, 1984).

The development of post-traumatic stress disorder as a clinical entity can be traced through three distinct lines of history as the nosology was applied to individuals experiencing interpersonal violence, including rape and domestic abuse, combat, and natural and technological disasters. In each case, symptoms were documented by clinicians who treated the exposed individuals. However, the systematic study and naming of such symptoms could transpire only with societal legitimization of the individual's suffering. As Weisaeth and Eitinger (1991) point out, the diagnosis, understanding, and treatment of post-traumatic stress disorder have been influenced by its place in history more than perhaps any other psychiatric illness.

Combat Trauma

Initially, post-traumatic combat syndrome was a loosely defined constellation of symptoms that varied in name depending on the source. For example, combat stress was first identified in the United States as a clinical entity in the American Civil War. Because the symptoms included palpitations, pain in the cardiac region, headache, vision problems, breathlessness upon exertion, and giddiness but were not caused by any myocardial disease, DaCosta labeled the condition "irritable heart." Later, it also became known as DaCosta's syndrome (Scrignar, 1984).

During the First World War, the psychological casualties of soldiers were again documented. The British psychologist Charles Myers, attributing the symptoms of soldiers in combat to the physical effects of exploding shells, initially called the disorder "shell shock" (Myers, 1940, as cited by Herman, 1992b). Several years later, after treating hundreds of soldiers, Myers wrote that shell shock, "a singularly ill-chosen" and potentially "harmful" term (p. 26), may play no part whatever in the causation of the symptoms. He attributed the origins of shell shock to psychological phenomena: "excessive emotion, e.g., sudden horror or fear—indeed any 'psychical trauma' or 'inadjustable experience'—is sufficient" (p. 26).

The disorder was also referred to as "Soldier's Heart and the Effort Syndrome," by Sir Thomas Lewis. The condition was described in terms similar to that of DaCosta—chest pain, breathlessness, tachycardia, heart palpitations, and fatigue. Consistent with these hypotheses, veterans with shell shock exhibited more significant increases in heart and respiratory rates than normal subjects when exposed to gunfire or sulfuric flame in laboratory studies (Bury, 1918; Campbell, 1918, as cited by Krystal et al., 1989).

Despite the biological evidence that could explain, in part, the manifestation of post-traumatic symptomatology, physiological investigations, as well as behavioral mechanisms, were abandoned in favor of psychodynamic theories of etiology. Consistent with the thinking of the times (including that of Freud), the symptoms induced by trauma, labeled "anxiety," were viewed as a result of neurotic conflicts (Scrignar, 1984). The term *traumatic neurosis* came into popular usage and was applied to the soldiers who developed symptoms on the battlefield (Kaiser, 1968). Concurrent with this conceptual framework was a bias toward viewing the soldier with traumatic neurosis as deficient, someone who was "at best a constitutionally inferior human being, at worst a malingerer and a coward" (Herman, 1992b, p. 21). Rado (1942, as cited by Krystal et al., 1989) describes the social costs of such a view:

The cost of this progress was a misuse of (psychodynamic) terms by writers . . . who took such phrases as "unconscious motivation" to refer to deliberate intent on the part of the patient, rather than to automatic biological reactions not subject to his control. This interpretation lent support to the frequently heard charge of malingering, leading to futile disciplinary measures and need-less cruelty. (p. 362)

During the Second World War, clinicians continued to report and treat numerous psychiatric casualities. In 1952, the American Psychiatric Association (APA) included gross stress reaction in its first *Diagnostic and Statistical Manual of Mental Disorders* (*DSM-I*). The diagnosis was applied in situations involving exposure to "severe physical demands of extreme stress, such as in combat or civilian catastrophe" (p. 40). The *DSM-I* also stated that the diagnosis can apply to previously normal persons who experience intolerable stress (Saigh, Green, & Korol, in press). However, the *DSM-I* did not provide any operational criteria for making the diagnosis. *DSM-II*, which was published in 1968, omitted the term *gross stress reaction* and replaced it with *transient situational disturbance* yet failed to provide any operational criteria, although there were a number of age-related subclassifications for the first time.

Despite the formal recognition of a post-traumatic syndrome, systematic, long-term research into the psychological effects of combat was not initiated until after the Vietnam War (Herman, 1992b). This trend was spurred on by veterans themselves, who formed hundreds of informal rap groups in which the psychological traumas of war were brought to the forefront. Because these veterans' experiences were legitimized by the antiwar movement and the public's dissatisfaction with the outcome of the war, psychological treatment programs and formal research studies were eventually advocated and financially supported.

In 1975, Horowitz and Solomon coined the term *delayed stress response syndrome* to describe the symptoms of veterans, which included "nightmares, painful moods and emotional storms, direct or symbolic behavioral repetitions, and concomitant secondary signs such as impaired social relations, aggressive and/ or self destructive behavior, and fear of loss of control over hostile impulses" (p. 72, as cited by Saigh et al., in press). In their article, Horowitz and Solomon cited earlier works by Breuer (1895/1956) and Freud (1920/1953), as well as later papers by Krystal (1968) and Lifton (1970), in which the post-traumatic syndrome is described as an interrelationship between an intrusive-repetitive tendency (e.g., compulsive repetitions of trauma-related *behavior* and recurrent attacks of trauma-related emotional *sensations*, including intrusive images and nightmares) and an opposite syndrome of denial, repression, and emotional avoidance. They write, "The denial-numbing tendency is thought to be a defensive function that interrupts repetition-to-completion in order to ward off intolerable ideas and emotions" (p. 69).

Since then, numerous studies have documented post-traumatic symptomatology in veterans of war, the most comprehensive and sophisticated being the National Vietnam Veterans Readjustment Study by Kulka et al. (1988), in which 15.2 percent of Vietnam veterans were diagnosed with full post-traumatic stress disorder, or PTSD (at the time of the study) and another 11.2 percent were diagnosed with partial PTSD. Thirty-one percent had met the criteria at some point in their lives since the war. Findings from this study and related research indicate that exposure to combat increases the risk for PTSD, along with other variables, such as lower socioeconomic status, prior psychiatric history, and reports of childhood abuse.

In addition, researchers have begun to study the effects of war on refugees, prisoners of war, and children exposed to combat. For example, in a study of American POWs held in captivity in Japan during World War II, Speed, Engdahl, Schwartz and Eberly (1989) found retrospectively that half experienced PTSD in the year following release from captivity, and 29 percent met full criteria more than 40 years after release. In a study of a Norwegian ship's crew that was captured and tortured for 67 days, Weisaeth (1993) found that 54 percent of the survivors met the criteria for PTSD six months after the event. Finally, in a group of Lebanese children exposed to war-related stress, Saigh (1989) found that 32.5 percent met criteria for PTSD one to two years after the experience. Similar rates have also been found in young survivors of the Pol Pot regime and the Kuwait invasion by Iraq (Kinzie, Sack, Angell, & Mason, 1986; Nader, Pynoos, Fairbanks, Frederick, Al-Ajeel, & Al-Asfour, 1993; Sack et al., 1993). Recent studies have also documented the effects on children who live with PTSD-afflicted parents, most notably fathers who fought in Vietnam (Harkness, 1993). Although symptoms of such children include depression, anxiety, low frustration tolerance, and aggression, specific rates of PTSD in such children have not yet been reported.

Interpersonal Violence

For most of the 20th century, the documentation and study of war trauma dominated the literature in this area. However, the effects of interpersonal violence, most notably the sexual abuse of children, were some of the first traumatic responses to be formally identified and named. In 1896, Freud published *The Aetiology of Hysteria*, in which he argued that "at the bottom of every case of hysteria there are one or more occurrences of premature sexual experience" (Freud, 1896, as cited by Masson, 1984, p. 263). At the time, the significance of Freud's clinical revelation was twofold: he was not only the first clinician to attribute psychopathology to the occurrence of external stressors, but he was also the first to recognize the negative effects that sexual trauma may have on later development (van der Kolk, 1987). However, within a year, Freud had turned away from his original supposition, presumably owing to the sharp criticism he received from the medical community for espousing this view; he concluded that his patients' accounts of sexual abuse were unfounded and that the etiology of hysteria resided in his patients' sexual fantasies and longings.

The role of interpersonal trauma in the development of post-traumatic stress disorder was virtually abandoned in the United States until the second half of the 20th century. This renewed interest appears to be attributable to several developments in the field, including more widespread acceptance by the scientific community that child sexual abuse does occur and that the effects can be deleterious. Most important, the women's movement gained prominence, which heightened interest in the psychology of women; allowed freer communication on sexual issues; recognized the impact of female victimization; and legitimized the study of rape, domestic violence, and incest. In 1974, Burgess and Holmstrom published *Rape Trauma Syndrome*, one of the most significant contributions to the study of trauma and interpersonal violence. In that study of 92 women, they documented the acute psychological sequelae of rape—fear, anxiety, physical trauma, skeletal muscle tension, gastrointestinal irritability, genitourinary disturbance, and emotional stress. Symptoms that may persist up to two to three weeks included increased motor activity, nightmares, fear of being alone or in crowds, and anxiety related to sexual activity. Complicating the symptom picture was the shame the survivor feels as a result of societal stigmatization, unresponsiveness of the legal system, and, at times, insensitive medical interventions (Bard & Sangrey, 1986; Herman, 1992b; Weisaeth & Eitinger, 1993).

With the publication of *DSM-III* (1980), rape trauma syndrome was reconceptualized as post-traumatic stress disorder, resulting in more systematic investigations exploring the epidemiology, etiology, and treatment of rape survivors. For example, Kilpatrick, Saunders, Veronen, Best, and Von (1987b) found in a local sample of rape victims that 16 percent met the criteria for PTSD an average of 17 years after the assault and that 57 percent retrospectively had met the criteria for PTSD at some point in their lives after the assault. In a similarly designed study on the national level, the figures were 11 and 31 percent, respectively. Factors that predicted more severe PTSD symptoms following sexual assault included preassault psychiatric history, low or high levels of preassault stress (as opposed to medium levels of stress), prior victimization, and brutality of the assault combined with a perception of life threat.

Coinciding with these developments in the study of rape was the renewed emphasis on the short- and long-term effects of sexual trauma of children. Until the 1950s, reports of child sexual abuse had been relegated to case histories (Bender & Blau, 1937; Bender & Grugett, 1952). Thereafter, researchers began to more systematically identify symptoms that clinicians had earlier associated with sexual abuse, including anxiety, phobias, nightmares, eating and sleeping problems, excessive and inappropriate sexual behaviors, physical complaints, and delinquency (Conte, 1988; DeFrancis, 1969; Friedrich, Urquiza, & Beilke, 1986; Gomes-Schwartz, Horowitz, & Sauzier, 1985). With the introduction of PTSD into the literature, studies have shown that sexual abuse of children affects 16 percent of all males and 27 percent of all females (Finkelhor, Hotaling, Lewis, & Smith, 1990). Six studies to date have involved the application of *DSM-III* or *DSM-III-R* criteria to child cases of sexual abuse (McNally, 1993). Four of these reported no cases of PTSD (Krener, 1985; Livingston, 1987; Sansonnet-Hayden, Haley, Marriage, & Fine, 1987; Sirles, Smith, & Kusama, 1989). Two of these studies (Kiser et al., 1988; McLeer, Deblinger, Atkins, Foa, & Ralphe, 1988) reported rates of 48 and 90 percent, respectively. In studies of adults who were sexually abused as children, approximately 32 to 100 percent have been diagnosed as having PTSD, although these studies only included individuals seeking treatment (Donaldson & Gardner, 1985; Kramer & Green, in press; Lindberg & Distad, 1985a, 1985b).

In addition, domestic violence, including physical abuse of spouses and children, was recognized as another form of trauma, with severe couple violence estimated at 6 percent per year and severe abuse of children estimated at about 11 percent per year (Straus & Gelles, 1986). Walker (1979), in her landmark book *The Battered Woman*, first described the symptoms associated with spousal abuse—depression, anxiety, general suspiciousness, hypervigilance, and physiological complaints. Though empirical studies have since verified these symptoms in groups of abused women, research on the application of the PTSD diagnosis to this group has been scant, with advances in the field occurring primarily in the last five to six years. For example, Kemp, Rawlings, and Green (1991) found that 84 percent of 77 battered women in shelters met the criteria for PTSD, while Houskamp and Foy (1991, as cited by Kemp & Green, in press) found the figure to be closer to 45 percent in a similar sample. Both studies found the degree of violence and life threat positively correlated with PTSD symptoms. Kemp and her colleagues (1991, in press) also found PTSD to be related to prior abuse, extent of current abuse, disengagement coping strategies, negative life events, and subjective distress experienced by the victim during or immediately following the assault.

Children who are physically abused develop similar symptoms as those discussed above, with the addition of impaired impulse control and frequent episodes of aggression directed toward peers. (See A. Green, 1993, for a review.) Physical abuse has also been associated with cognitive and language impairment and central nervous system dysfunction. However, further studies are needed to determine whether the physical abuse actually contributed to these difficulties or whether such children are more likely to be the victims of such abuse (A. Green, 1993). Although most studies of PTSD in children are likely to include both physically and sexually abused victims, Adams, Everett, and O'Neal (1992, as cited by Saigh et al., in press) examined 98 young outpatients and found that 20 percent of the physically abused children met criteria for PTSD.

Natural and Technological Disasters

The term *post-traumatic neurosis* was also applied by physicians to victims of railway accidents late in the 19th century (Horowitz, 1986). Oppenheim (1889, as cited by Weisaeth & Eitinger, 1991) wrote that the condition may appear following injury or surgery; however, he asserted that traumatic neurosis was clearly different from hysteria, a supposition that was later disputed by other physicians. One of the first actual researchers in disaster psychiatry (Weisaeth & Eitinger, 1991) was a Swiss named Edward Stierlin who published a doctoral dissertation in 1909 focusing on his observations on two disasters, one a technological disaster involving a mine collapse and the other a natural disaster—an earthquake in Messina in Sicily in 1908. Stierlin wrote that violent emotions can give rise to serious psychoneurotic effects as a result of lowered resistance within the nervous system. He singled out the cases of traumatic neurosis and discussed such relevant issues as the resilience of children, the vulnerability of the elderly, and the rarity of classical hysteria. At about the same time in the United States, James (1906/1911) described the reactions of survivors to the San Francisco earthquake. However, he focused primarily on the positive effects the disaster had on the cooperativeness and equanimity of the people: "The hearts concealed private bitterness enough, no doubt, but the tongues disdained to dwell on the misfortunes of self, when almost everybody one spoke to had suffered equally" (p. 224). It is this observation regarding the community's spirit and resolve that will be addressed in later studies as a mediating factor in the subsequent development of psychological symptoms.

Despite these independent forays into the disaster arena, little empirical research was available until 1943, when Adler published her study on 46 survivors of the Cocoanut Grove Night Club fire in Boston, Massachusetts, which killed 491 patrons. In 25 of 46 survivors, post-trauma symptoms were noted, including repetitive memories of being trampled and/or choked by smoke; general nervousness, irritablity, and fatigue; nightmares; fear of fires, nightclubs, and being alone; and depression. Nine months after the fire, 13 individuals still suffered from general nervousness and anxiety neuroses. Adler also used the term *post-traumatic neurosis* to describe the symptoms of these survivors.

In recent years, the literature on disasters has grown considerably, incorporating volcanic eruptions; floods; storms, tornados, and hurricanes; fires; explosions; motor vehicle and train accidents; and earthquakes. The distinction is often drawn between natural and technological (or human-caused) events and, as B. L. Green (1992, 1993) describes, can be conceptualized along a continuum of "deliberateness." Thus, natural disasters are at the low end of the continuum in that they are "acts of God," while technological or human-caused disasters are in the middle to upper end of the continuum because they may be a result of error, mishap, negligence, or intention. Currently, almost no empirical research exists that directly compares the two types of disaster for their effects on the survivor (B. L. Green, in press), although there is some conjecture that those events caused by human negligence or intention may be more harmful. For example, in a study comparing residents exposed to a natural toxic hazard, radon, to those exposed to human-caused events, such as chemical contamination, leaking landfills, and industrial release of toxic chemicals, Baum and Fleming (1993) found that symptoms following exposure to the human-caused events were more severe than those of the radon-exposed group. Comparing across studies, research also suggests that symptoms (particularly anger and irritability) in groups exposed to technological disasters may persist longer than symptoms following naturally occurring events. While further study is needed to confirm this, such comparisons are difficult since disasters rarely differ only on the natural or technological dimensions (B. L. Green, in press).

In an extensive review of the disaster literature since Adler's study in 1943, Smith and North (1993) found 37 articles in which the symptoms of survivors were systematically documented. Thirteen of these studies (the first of which was written in 1984 by Fairley) reported rates of PTSD using *DSM* criteria. Rates ranged from 4 percent to 100 percent, with the highest rates occurring in studies of technological disasters in which structured interviews were not used. Reports on natural disasters in which structured interviews were used showed the lowest rates. Rates also seemed to vary depending on the type of disaster, method of evaluation, and time elapsed since the traumatic event. In addition, more severe symptoms were associated with perceived threat of personal injury or death, experiencing or witnessing grotesque or mutilating events, bereavement, social support, and loss of property or home (Gleser, Green, & Winget, 1981; Lima, Pai, Santacruz, Lozano, & Luna,1987; McFarlane, 1986; Newman & Foreman, 1987; Parker, 1977). Smith and North also concluded that individual characteristics associated with the development of disaster-related PTSD include being female, being elderly, having lower socioeconomic status, and having a prior history of psychiatric problems (Bromet, Parkinson, Schulberg, Dunn, & Gondek,1982; Gleser et al.,1981; Lopez-Ibor, Canas, & Rodriguez-Gamazo,1985; Parker, 1977; Shore, Tatum, & Vollmer, 1986; Weisaeth, 1985). In a similar review of studies published within the last 10 years, B. L. Green (in press) also found that rates of PTSD varied (from 4 to 91%) depending on the traumatic event and time of the evaluation.

Exposure to toxic chemicals and/or radioactivity has also recently been added to the list of disasters that may result in PTSD, although this category continues to evoke controversy. Individuals living in or near areas in which there have been environmental contaminations (e.g., Three Mile Island, Love Canal, Chernobyl) have reportedly developed symptoms similar to post-traumatic stress disorder. The controversy arises in that in the majority of cases, the trauma is a "silent" one in which individuals nearby who are exposed to the chemicals may learn of this exposure only days, weeks, or even years following the incident. As a result, the identifiable stressor (which is information rather than observable effects on the environment) does not evoke the classic feeling of terror or horror as conceptualized by *DSM-IV* (B. L. Green, 1994). The stressor also has a component of "future orientation," in that such exposure poses the risk of cancer, birth defects, and the like at some unknown point in time (B. L. Green, in press).

Nonetheless, studies of individuals exposed to toxic contamination show signs of psychiatric distress, if not complete PTSD, even up to five years after the event. For example, Baum and his colleagues (Baum, Gatchel, & Schaeffer, 1983; Davidson, Fleming, & Baum, 1986) studied the survivors within a five-mile radius of Three Mile Island (TMI), where a nuclear radiation leak had occurred. The individuals exposed to the radiation leak had more symptoms of anxiety, somatic complaints, alienation, obsessive-compulsive thoughts, and sleep disturbance and they performed more poorly on concentration tasks than control subjects. Up to five years after the event, symptoms had actually increased, especially hostility and suspiciousness. Davidson et al. (1986) also studied residents within a one-mile radius of a toxic waste landfill. Symptoms were higher than those reported in the TMI group and included depression, anxiety, fear, and suspicion. In addition, both the TMI and landfill groups showed elevated scores on the Impact of Event Scale (IES), which assesses intrusive and avoidance symptoms included in the PTSD diagnosis. B. L. Green and her colleagues (1994) also found that the news of radioactive leakage from a nuclear weapons production facility resulted in significant symptoms of anxiety, depression, somatic concerns, and belligerence, as well as intrusion and avoidance symptoms of PTSD. Based on their results, the authors proposed a new syndrome, *informed of radioactive contamination syndrome* (IRCS), which is distinguishable from PTSD in that the stressor is ongoing and future oriented. The fact that the trauma is not confined to a single event that can be processed by the senses seems to decrease the potential for intrusive symptoms, such as nightmares and reenactments.

Current Nosology

A number of studies in recent years have shown that up to three-quarters of the general population in the United States have been exposed to a traumatic event in their lifetime, meeting the first criterion for the diagnosis of PTSD, according to *DSM-IV* (Norris, 1992; Resnick, Kilpatrick, Dansky, Saunders, & Best, 1993). Events identified as traumatic now include military combat, violent personal assault (sexual assault, physical attack, robbery, mugging), being kidnapped, being taken hostage, terrorist attack, torture, incarceration as a prisoner of war or in a concentration camp, natural or manmade disasters, severe automobile accidents, or being diagnosed with a life-threatening illness. Witnessed events (such as observing the serious injury or unnatural death of another person) and events experienced by others that are learned about (such as a serious accident, injury, or assault experienced by a family member or close friend) are also included.

A second criterion involving the stressor experience, added to *DSM-III-R* (1987) and maintained in *DSM-IV* (1994), stipulates that the person's response to the traumatic event must involve intense fear, helplessness, or horror. Implicit in this requirement is the assumption that the impact of the event on the individual determines whether or not the event is traumatic (March, 1993). Although no empirical research exists that addresses this topic specifically, studies have shown that higher levels of perceived threat and suffering and perceptions of low controllability exacerbate the risk for PTSD (Frye & Stockton, 1982; B. L. Green, Grace, & Gleser, 1985; Mikulincer & Solomon, 1988; Speed et al., 1989).

Over a period of at least two decades, results from studies of various kinds of trauma have revealed that humans react with similar symptoms to very different situations, from firsthand combat, to rape and physical abuse, to community-wide disasters. Faced with the overwhelming psychological and physical threats of a catastrophe, survivors develop one set of symptoms of an intrusive, repetitive nature (often described as a repetition compulsion) and another set of related but antithetical symptoms, including denial, emotional numbness, and avoidance (Horowitz, 1993). As Horowitz points out, these phases of denial and intrusion may occur in temporal phases that may overlap and vary in sequence but constitute a general stress response to trauma. Clinical studies have also revealed at least nine themes identified with PTSD: fear of repetition, fear of merger with victims, shame and rage over vulnerability, rage at the source and at those exempted, fear of loss of control of aggressive impulses, guilt or shame over aggressive impulses, guilt or shame over surviving, and sadness over losses (Horowitz, 1986).

The current nosology of post-traumatic stress disorder (*DSM-IV*) includes the above-mentioned categories of symptoms, referred to as the reexperiencing and avoidant criteria, as well as the hyperarousal phenomena, all of which must be present in some degree for one month in order for an individual to be diagnosed with PTSD after experiencing a traumatic event. At least one (or more) of the following reexperiencing phenomena must be present: (1) recurrent, intrusive, distressing recollections of the event, including images, thoughts, or perceptions; (2) recurrent, distressing dreams of the event; (3) acting or feeling as if the traumatic event were recurring; (4) intense psychological distress at exposure to internal or external cues that symbolize or resemble an aspect of the event; or (5) physiological reactivity on exposure to internal or external cues that symbolize or resemble an aspect of the event.

At least three of the following avoidant symptoms must be present: (1) efforts to avoid thoughts, feelings, or conversations associated with the trauma; (2) efforts to avoid activities, places, or people that arouse recollections of the trauma; (3) inability to recall an important aspect of the trauma; (4) markedly diminished interest or participation in significant activities; (5) feeling of detachment or estrangement from others; (6) restricted range of affect; or (7) sense of a foreshortened future.

At least two of the following symptoms of hyperarousal must also be present: (1) difficulty falling or staying asleep; (2) irritability or outbursts of anger; (3) difficulty concentrating; (4) hypervigilance; or (5) exaggerated startle response. *DSM-IV* also includes additional symptoms identified as possibly occurring with PTSD, including painful guilt feelings about surviving; phobic avoidance of situations or activities that resemble or symbolize the original trauma; impaired affect modulation; self-destructive and impulsive behavior; dissociation; somatic complaints; feelings of ineffectiveness, shame, despair, or hopelessness; feelings of being permanently damaged; a loss of previously sustained beliefs; hostility; social withdrawal; feeling constantly threatened; impaired relationships with others; or a change from the individual's previous personality characteristics.

Also included in *DSM-IV* is *acute stress disorder*, a new diagnostic category, the symptoms of which develop immediately following the traumatic event and last no longer than four weeks. The disorder is characterized by three of the following dissociative symptoms (numbing, detachment, or absence of emotional responsiveness; reduction in awareness of an individual's surroundings; derealization; depersonalization; or dissociative amnesia), as well as the presence of the reexperiencing, avoidant, and hyperarousal criteria previously discussed under PTSD. This particular diagnostic category resembles combat stress reaction, a term still used in the literature to demarcate post-combat symptoms lasting less than one month (Oei, Lim, & Hennessy, 1990).

Recently, Herman (1992a) proposed a complex form of post-traumatic disorder that was considered for possible inclusion in *DSM-IV* under the name of DESNOS (disorders of extreme stress not otherwise specified). DESNOS applies to survivors of repeated trauma where the victim has been in a state of captivity, unable to flee, and under the control of the perpetrator. Under such conditions, Herman asserts that an individual may develop symptoms that are more complex, diffuse, and tenacious than those of PTSD; characteristic personality changes, (e.g., deformations of relatedness and identity); and increased vulnerability to repeated harm, either self- or other-inflicted. Because the literature offers extensive but unsystematized support for this classification, further research is needed before DESNOS can be accepted as a formal diagnostic category.

Prevalence of PTSD and Related Symptomatology

A number of researchers in recent years have studied the prevalence of PTSD in exposed individuals in the United States. On the average, about a quarter of individuals who have been exposed to an extreme stressor develop PTSD. In a community sample of four southeastern cities, Norris (1992) estimated current rates of PTSD to be 14 percent from sexual assault, 13 percent from physical assault, 12 percent from motor vehicle accidents, 5 percent from disasters, and 8 percent from tragic death. Based on these results, estimated current rates of PTSD range from 5 to 11 percent. Resnick et al. (1993) reported similar rates of current PTSD from a sample of women: 13 percent from sexual assault, 12 percent from rape, 18 percent from physical assault, 2 percent from sexual molestation, 9 percent from homicide of family or close friend, and 3 percent from noncrime trauma, such as exposure to disaster or an accident. They similarly reported that the lifetime prevalence of PTSD was 12 percent, while the current rate of PTSD was approximately 5 percent. In a study that included both men and women, Breslau and colleagues (1991, 1992) reported a 9 percent lifetime prevalence of PTSD. Other studies have found much lower rates of PTSD (e.g., Helzer, Robins, & McElvoy, 1987), which may be due, in part, to differences in evaluation methods for assessing PTSD and exposure to a traumatic event.

In addition, PTSD is often accompanied by other symptoms, including depression and substance abuse in veterans (Kulka et al., 1990); sexual dysfunction, major depression, obsessive compulsive tendencies, and phobias in crime victims (Kilpatrick, Saunders, Veronen, Best, & Von, 1987a, reported in Keane

& Wolfe, 1990); and depression, phobias, and generalized anxiety disorder in disaster survivors (B. L. Green, Lindy, Grace, & Leonard, 1992). Individuals with PTSD were also eight times more likely to have attempted suicide even when controlling for depression (Davidson, Hughest, Blazer, & George, 1991). While these comorbidity studies provide further evidence regarding the pervasive effects of trauma, there is little information as to why such comorbidity exists (B. L. Green, 1994). Whether the symptoms overlap in the various diagnostic categories, whether the pattern of comorbidity is related to the specific stressor or other factors, or whether the other diagnoses are a reaction to the PTSD are questions that deserve further study.

Treatment

A number of treatment interventions have been proposed and discussed extensively in the literature. Most notably are pharmacotherapy, individual psychotherapy (behavioral, cognitive-behavioral, psychodynamic, and crisis oriented), group psychotherapy, and family therapy. In a review of 250 treatment studies in which these various approaches were used, S. D. Solomon, Gerrity, and Muff (1992) found only 11 used randomized, controlled clinical trials. They concluded that drug studies show a modest but clinically meaningful effect on PTSD, while behavioral techniques, though generally successful, may have limited usefulness in individuals with comorbid disorders. In addition, those individuals treated by cognitive, psychodynamic, and hypnotherapy also have shown improvement in symptomatology. A brief description of each treatment approach follows, along with any relevant studies published supporting the efficacy of that particular approach.

There appears to be considerable evidence that PTSD is associated in part with sympathetic hyperarousal, which may be due to a hyperadrenergic state, hypofunctioning of the hypothalamic-pituitary-adrenocortical axis, and dysregulation of the endogenous opioid system (Friedman, 1993). Any medication that can dampen this physiological hyperactivity, relieve the disturbed sleep cycle, or reduce anxiety should consequently be helpful for PTSD. In fact, a number of different pharmacological treatments have been recommended to relieve various symptoms, such as antidepressants for depression, anxiolytics for anxiety, and neuroleptics for flashbacks (Fairbank & Nicholson, 1987, as cited by Oei et al., 1990). However, few controlled pharmacological trials have been published (National Center for PTSD, 1990). In their review of the literature, S. D. Solomon et al. (1992) found only five double-blind, placebo-controlled trials of drug therapies for PTSD, four of which were of antidepressants (three with tricyclics and one with monoamine oxidase inhibitors). Results from these studies were mixed. The fifth study consisted of controlled trials with alprazolam, a triazolo-benzodiazepine with antipanic and antidepressant properties. Braun, Greenberg, Dasberg, and Lerer (1990) found the alprazolam reduced symptoms of anxiety, but no evidence was found for its efficacy in reducing intrusive or avoidant symptoms. In addition to the above-mentioned studies, drug trials with propanolol, carbamazepine, and fluoxetine have also been conducted, again with mixed results (National Center for PTSD, 1990). The medications are often recommended in conjunction with other therapeutic interventions; positive symptoms (e.g., intrusive memories and flashbacks) are generally considered to be a response to pharmacotherapy more than negative symptoms (Marmar et al., 1994).

Horowitz (1986) writes that the work of Lindemann (1944) and Caplan (1964) led to the concept of crisis intervention where the onset of the crisis as a precipitatory event exceeds a person's ordinary coping capacity. The individual comes into treatment because of a "cognitive impasse" in response to a "hazard" (Jacobson, 1974, as cited by Horowitz, 1986), which provides an opening for the therapist to explore with the survivor details of the stressor and the psychological meaning that the survivor may attribute to the event or its consequences. Treatment goals include reduction of anxiety, shoring up of defenses, restoration of safety and coherence of self, and provision of a holding environment aimed a preventing post-traumatic narcissistic regression (Marmar & Freeman, 1988, as cited by Marmar, Foy, Kagan, & Pynoos, 1993). Numerous articles have been published outlining crisis-intervention protocols for specific traumas (e.g., disasters) and providing empirical support for the implementation of such strategies (c.f., Baisden & Quarantelli, 1981; Cohen & Ahearn, 1980).

Time-limited, brief, dynamic psychotherapy for stress disorders was originally developed by Horowitz (1973). In this approach, efforts are directed at modifying preexisting conflicts, developmental problems, and/or defensive styles that render the person vulnerable to traumatization by external stressors. For the trauma survivor who is experiencing a failure of control (resulting in intrusive symptomatology and overwhelming affects), the therapy is directed at resurrecting adaptive defenses. For a survivor who presents with overcontrol, avoidance, and emotional numbing, the therapist strives to create a safe environment in which the warded-off images and feelings can be explored (Marmar et al., 1994). In describing the ultimate goal of such treatment, Horowitz (1973) writes: "The goal is continuity of the traumatic experience with other life memories, and the reintegration of personal aims" (p. 99). Although there currently exists only one published study of psychodynamic psychotherapy using comparison and control groups (Brom, Kleber, & Defares, 1989), numerous case studies have been published that provide rich clinical data as well as formal assessments indicating symptom reduction. (For example, see Horowitz, 1986, and Lindy, 1988.)

Interventions based on behavioral theory reduce anxiety by means of continued exposure to the feared event. Exposure-based therapies include systematic desensitization and imaginal and *in vivo* flooding. In the behavioral studies reviewed by S. D. Solomon et al. (1992), two studies examining systematic desensitization and two studies examining flooding showed decreased symptoms in survivors when compared with survivors who received no treatment (Peniston, 1986; Brom et al., 1989; Keane, Fairbank, Caddell, & Zimering, 1989; Cooper & Clum, 1989). A fifth study reviewed by S. D. Solomon et al. (1993) demonstrated symptom reduction in flooded inpatients when compared with inpatients receiving a program of individual counseling (Boudewyns & Hyer, 1990). Foa, Rothbaum, Riggs, & Murdock (1991) also compared prolonged exposure with stress inoculation training (SIT) (Kilpatrick, Veronen, & Resnick, 1982), supportive counseling, and a waiting list control group and found that SIT was most effective in reducing symptoms immediately following treatment; prolonged exposure was superior to the other therapy in a 3.5-month follow-up.

In contrast to behavioral therapies, cognitive therapies focus on reducing anxiety by providing patients with the skills to control fear, such as progressive muscle relaxation, thought stopping, breathing control, and guided self-dialogue (S. D. Solomon et al., 1992). The previously mentioned SIT program incorporates all of the above interventions and has been found to be highly effective in reducing short-term symptoms (Foa et al., 1991).

Related to systematic desensitization but considered to be a separate category of treatment interventions is eye movement desensitization (EMD), in which rhythmic, multisaccadic eye movements are generated with the assistance of the therapist, while the survivor concentrates on a selected traumatic memory (Shapiro, 1989). Preliminary testing, as well as more controlled studies, has demonstrated that the procedure has the capacity to desensitize a traumatic memory within a short period of time, can produce a cognitive restructuring of irrational beliefs or self-statements, and can cause consequent behavioral shifts (Shapiro, 1989; Silver, Brooks, & Obenchain, 1995).

In addition to the individual therapies discussed previously, many clinicians have recommended the use of group treatment as an adjunct form of intervention (van der Kolk, 1987). For example, Scurfield (1993) writes that peer groups are important in the treatment of Vietnam veterans, owing to the fact that war-related traumas often occurred in the context of a group; the group facilitates expression and helps prevent denial and avoidance; and the sharing of experiences reduces the shame and isolation that the veteran may feel. Other survivor groups for which group treatment has been discussed as an effective therapeutic intervention include children of sexual abuse (Damon & Waterman, 1986), adults with histories of childhood sexual abuse or rape (Dye & Roth, 1991), Holocaust survivors (Danieli, 1993), and disaster workers (Mitchell & Dyregrov, 1993). Family assessment and therapy have also been recommended to minimize the effects a traumatic event may have on the system and, in the case in which only one family member was exposed to the trauma, to provide support for him or her (Carroll, Foy, Cannon, & Zwier, 1991; S. D. Solomon, Bravo, Rubio-Stipec, & Canino, 1993).

Future Research

There is a burgeoning area of research focused on identifying the neurobiological underpinnings of PTSD. Although a full explanation of these studies is beyond the scope of the current chapter, preclinical studies suggest that exposure to extreme stress may result in long-term changes in norepinephrine, corticotropin-releasing factor/hypothalamic-pituitary adrenal axis, dopamine, benzodiazepine, and opiate brain systems (Bremner, Davis, Southwick, Krystal, & Charney, 1994). It is hypothesized that the symptoms of PTSD are a manifestation of physiological processes that were initiated at the time of the original trauma, which, as a result of multiple neurochemical processes, may continue long after the trauma is over. Such studies may lead to advances in treatment for PTSD, including medications that act at the level of each of these systems (e.g., clonidine as a possible intervention to prevent long-term changes in the noradrenergic system). In conceptualizing such research, Pitman (1993) has argued for a differentiation between the phasic features of PTSD (those that appear intermittently and are primarily the reexperiencing phenomenon) and the tonic features of PTSD (those that manifest all or most of the time and include primarily the avoidant phenomenon).

Virtually all the studies on PTSD to date have been retrospective in nature, precluding any statements on the relative effects of a traumatic event and the natural history of PTSD, from prestressor to poststressor adjustment. A number of longitudinal studies (e.g., B. L. Green et al., 1994) have documented variations in rates of PTSD over time, with an overall decrease in symptoms, but either a cyclical or a delayed reaction seen in some survivors. Prospective and longitudinal studies are particularly necessary when children and adolescents are exposed to traumatic events in order to better understand the developmental effects of such stressors. As Pynoos (1994) so aptly describes: "A developmental approach places knowledge about traumatic stress into an intricate matrix of a changing child and environment, and evolving familial and societal expectations, and recognizes the essential linkage between disrupted and normal development" (p. 65).

Additional studies on treatment efficacy with survivors is also an area deserving future attention. Numerous approaches to therapy with survivors have been proposed and briefly discussed above. Although clinical studies and empirical research have demonstrated that each of these can be effective in reducing the symptoms of PTSD, considerable work needs to be accomplished to better understand whether there are differences among survivors' responses to treatment and to differentiate which factors may account for those differences. Such studies should include a larger number of and more diverse (i.e., ethnocultural, age, and stressor criteria) samples, comparison groups, and controlled combinations of treatment models. In addition, research studies have only recently begun to document that early intervention may prevent the development of more severe PTSD symptoms in combat survivors (e.g., L. Solomon & Benbenishty, 1986, as cited by Oei et al., 1990). These studies may indicate that symptoms of other types of survivors may also be minimized by immediate referrals to appropriate intervention programs.

Summary

Approximately 5 to 11 percent of the population in the United States suffers from PTSD. It has been shown through clinical reports and empirical investigations that the responses of these survivors are strikingly similar, regardless of whether the traumatic event to which they were exposed involves war, terrorism, domestic violence, rape and sexual abuse, crime, earthquakes, hurricanes, or floods. The symptoms invariably involve physiological reactivity and intrusive and avoidant phenomena, which fluctuate as the individual attempts to return to his or her previous level of functioning after the event has occurred. The study of PTSD, therefore, involves not only the physical aspects of the disorder but also the cognitive and affective components, particularly the meaning that the individual attributes to the event and the changes that occur in his or her ideas about the world and self. This interaction of affective, cognitive, behavioral, and physiological symptoms as a result of an acute or chronic trauma is what makes this disorder so complex and yet so fascinating. A considerable amount of prevention, research, and treatment remains to be conducted in this ongoing exploration of PTSD, but the healing of survivors has already been advanced significantly in the past three to four decades by the naming and normalization of the disorder and the formal recognition of survivors.

References

Adams, B. S., Everett, B. L., & O'Neal, E. (1992). PTSD in physically and sexually abused psychiatrically hospitalized children. *Child Psychiatry and Human Development*, 23, 3–8.
Adler, A. (1943). Neuropsychiatric complications in victims of Boston's Cocoanut Grove disaster. *Journal of the American Medical Association*, 123, 1098–1101.
American Psychiatric Association (1952). *Diagnostic and statistical manual of mental disorders*. Washington, D.C.: American Psychiatric Association.
American Psychiatric Association (1968). *Diagnostic and statistical manual of mental disorders* (2d ed.). Washington, D.C.: American Psychiatric Association.
American Psychiatric Association (1980). *Diagnostic and statistical manual of mental disorders* (3d ed.). Washington, D.C.: American Psychiatric Association.
American Psychiatric Association (1987). *Diagnostic and statistical manual of mental disorders* (3d ed., rev.). Washington, D.C.: American Psychiatric Association.
American Psychiatric Association (1994). *Diagnostic and statistical manual of mental disorders* (4th ed.). Washington, D.C.: American Psychiatric Association.
Baisden, B., & Quarantelli, E. L. (1981). The delivery of mental health services in community disasters: An outline of research findings. *Journal of Community Psychology*, 9, 195–203.
Bard, M., & Sangrey, D. (1986). *The crime victim's book* (2d ed.). New York: Brunner/Mazel.
Baum, A., & Fleming, I. (1993). Implications of psychological research on stress and technological accidents. *American Psychologist*, 48(6), 665–672.
Baum, A., Gatchel, R., & Schaeffer, M. A. (1983). Emotional, behavioral, and physiological effects of chronic stress at Three Mile Island. *Journal of Consulting and Clinical Psychology*, 15, 562–572.
Bender, L., & Blau, A. (1937). The reaction of children to sexual relations with adults. *American Journal of Orthopsychiatry*, 7(4), 500–518.
Bender, L., & Grugett, A. W. (1952). A follow-up report on children who had an atypical sexual experience. *American Journal of Orthopsychiatry*, 22, 825–837.

Boudewyns, P. A., & Hyer, L. (1990). Physiological response to combat memories and preliminary treatment outcome in Vietnam veteran PTSD patients treated with direct therapeutic exposure. *Behavior Therapy, 21,* 63–87.

Braun, P., Greenberg, D., Dasberg, H., & Lerer, B. (1990). Core symptoms or posttraumatic stress disorder unimproved by alprazolam treatment. *Journal of Clinical Psychiatry, 51,* 236–238.

Bremner, J. D., Davis, M., Southwick, S. M., Krystal, J. H., & Charney, D. S. (1994). Neurobiology of posttraumatic stress disorder. In R. S. Pynoos (ed.), *Posttraumatic stress disorder: A clinical review* (pp. 43–64). Lutherville, Md.: Sidran.

Breslau, N., & Davis, G. C. (1992). Posttraumatic stress disorder in an urban population of young adults: Risk factors for chronicity. *American Journal of Psychiatry, 149,* 671–675.

Breslau, N., Davis, G. C., Andreski, P., & Peterson, E. (1991). Traumatic events and posttraumatic stress disorder in an urban population of young adults. *Archives of General Psychiatry, 48,* 216–222.

Breuer, J., & Freud, S. (1893–1895/1956). *Studies on hysteria* (standard ed., vol. 2). London: Hogarth.

Brom, D., Kleber, R. J., & Defares, P. B. (1989). Brief psychotherapy for posttraumatic stress disorders. *Journal of Consulting and Clinical Psychology, 57,* 607–612.

Bromet, E. J., Parkinson, D. L., Schulberg, H. C., Dunn, L. O., & Gondek, P. C. (1982). Mental health of residents near the Three Mile Island reactor: A comparative study of selected groups. *Journal of Preventive Psychiatry, 1,* 225–276.

Burgess, A. W., & Holmstrom, L. L. (1974). Rape trauma syndrome. *American Journal of Psychiatry, 131*(9), 981–986.

Bury, J. S. (1918). Pathology of war neuroses. *Lancet, 1,* 97–99.

Campbell, C. M. (1918). The role of instinct, emotion and personality in disorders of the heart. *Journal of the American Medical Association, 71,* 1621–1626.

Caplan, G. (1964). *Principles of preventive psychiatry.* New York: Basic Books.

Carroll, E. M., Foy, D. F., Cannon, B. J., & Zwier, G. (1991). Assessment issues involving the families of trauma victims. *Journal of Traumatic Stress, 4,* 25–40.

Cohen, R. E., & Ahearn, F. L. (1980). *Handbook for mental health care of disaster victims.* Baltimore: Johns Hopkins University Press.

Conte, J. R. (1988). The effects of sexual abuse on children: Results of a research project. *Annals of the New York Academy of Sciences, 528,* 310–326.

Cooper, N. A., & Clum, C. A. (1989). Imaginal flooding as a supplementary treatment for PTSD in combat veterans: A controlled study. *Behavior Therapy, 20,* 381–391.

Damon, L., & Waterman, J. (1986). Parallel group treatment of children and their mothers. In K. MacFarlane & J. Waterman (eds.), *Sexual abuse of young children* (pp. 244–298). New York: Guilford.

Danieli, Y. (1993). Diagnostic and therapeutic use of the multigenerational family tree in working with survivors and children of survivors of the Nazi Holocaust. In J. P. Wilson & B. Raphael (eds.), *International handbook of traumatic stress syndromes* (pp. 889–898). New York: Plenum.

Davidson, J., Hughest, D., Blazer, D., & George, L. (1991). Post-traumatic stress disorder in the community: An epidemiological study. *Psychological Medicine, 21,* 713–721.

Davidson, L., Fleming, I., & Baum, A. (1986). Post-traumatic stress as a function of chronic stress and toxic exposure. In C. Figley (ed.), *Trauma and its wake* (vol. 2). New York: Brunner/Mazel.

DeFrancis, B. (1969). *Protecting the child victim of sex crimes committed by adults.* Denver: Children's Division, American Humane Association.

Donaldson, M. A., & Gardner, R. (1985). Diagnosis and treatment of traumatic stress among women after childhood incest. In C. R. Figley (ed.), *Trauma and its wake* (pp. 356–377). New York: Brunner/Mazel.

Dye, E., & Roth, S. (1991). Psychotherapy with Vietnam veterans and rape and incest survivors. *Psychotherapy, 28,* 103–120.

Fairbank, J. A., & Nicholson, R. A. (1987). Theoretical and empirical issues in the treatment of post-traumatic stress disorder in Vietnam veterans. *Journal of Clinical Psychology, 51,* 912–919.

Fairley, M. (1984). Tropical cyclone Oscar: Psychological reactions of a Fijian population. Paper presented at the Disaster Research Workshop, Mt. Macdeon, Victoria, Australia.

Finkelhor, D., Hotaling, G., Lewis, I. A., & Smith, C. (1990). Sexual abuse in a national survey of adult men and women: Prevalence, characteristics, and risk factors. *Child Abuse & Neglect, 14,* 19–28.

Foa, E. B., Rothbaum, B., Riggs, D. S., & Murdock, T. B. (1991). Treatment of posttraumatic stress disorder in rape victims: A comparison between cognitive-behavioral procedures and counseling. *Journal of Consulting and Clinical Psychology, 59,* 715–723.

Freud, S. (1896). The aetiology of hysteria. Paper presented at the meeting of the Society for Psychiatry and Neurology, Vienna. In J. M. Masson, *The assault on truth* (pp. 251–282). New York: Farrar, Straus and Giroux.

Freud, S. (1920/1953). *Beyond the pleasure principle* (standard ed., vol. 19). London: Hogarth.

Friedman, M. J. (1993). Psychological and pharmacological approaches to treatment. In J. P. Wilson & B. Raphael (eds.), *International handbook of traumatic stress syndromes* (pp. 785–794). New York: Plenum.

Friedrich, W. N., Urquiza, A. J., & Beilke, R. L. (1986). Behavior problems in sexually abused children. *Journal of Pediatric Psychiatry, 11,* 47–57.

Frye, S., & Stockton, R. (1982). Discriminant analysis of posttraumatic stress disorder among a group of Vietnam veterans. *American Journal of Psychiatry, 139,* 52–56.

Gleser, G. C., Green, B. L., & Winget, C. N. (1981). *Prolonged psychosocial effects of disaster: A study of Buffalo Creek.* New York: Academic Press.

Gomes-Schwartz, B., Horowitz, M. J., & Sauzier, M. (1985). Severity of emotional distress among sexually abused preschool, school-age, and adolescent children. *Hospital and Community Psychiatry, 36*(5), 503–508.

Green, A. (1993). Childhood sexual and physical abuse. In J. P. Wilson & B. Raphael (eds.), *International handbook of traumatic stress syndromes* (pp. 577–592). New York: Plenum.

Green, B. L. (1992). Assessing levels of psychosocial impairment following disaster: Consideration of actual and methodological dimensions. *Journal of Nervous and Mental Disease, 17*(9), 544–552.

Green, B. L. (1993). Disasters and posttraumatic stress disorder. In J. R. T. Davidson & E. B. Foa (eds.), *Posttraumatic stress disorder: DSM-IV and beyond* (pp. 75–98). Washington, D.C.: American Psychiatric Press.

Green, B. L. (1994). Psychosocial research in traumatic stress: An update. *Journal of Traumatic Stress, 7*(3), 341–362.

Green, B. L. (in press). Traumatic stress and disaster: Mental health effects and factors influencing adaptation. In J. R. T. Davidson & A. McFarlane (section eds.) & F. LiehMac & C. Nadelson (vol. eds.), *International review of psychiatry* (vol. 2). Washington, D.C.: American Psychiatric Association.

Green, B. L., Grace, M., & Gleser, G. (1985). Identifying survivors at risk: Long-term impairment following the Beverly Hills Supper Club fire. *Journal of Consulting and Clinical Psychology, 53,* 672–678.

Green, B. L., Grace, M. C., Lindy, J. D., Gleser, G. C., Leonard, A. C., & Kramer, T. L. (1990). Buffalo Creek survivors in the second decade: Comparison with unexposed and nonlitigant groups. *Journal of Applied Psychology, 20,* 1033–1050.

Green, B. L., Lindy, J. D., & Grace, M. C. (1994). Psychological effects of toxic contamination. In R. J. Ursano, B. G McCaughey, & C. S. Fullerton (eds.), *Individual and community responses to trauma and disaster: The structure of human chaos* (pp. 154–178). Cambridge: Cambridge University Press.

Green, B. L., Lindy, J. D., Grace, M. C., & Leonard, A. C. (1992). Chronic posttraumatic stress disorder and diagnostic comorbidity in a disaster sample. *Journal of Nervous and Mental Disease, 180,* 760–766.

Harkness, L. L. (1993). Transgenerational transmission of war-related trauma. In J. P. Wilson & B. Raphael (eds.), *International handbook of traumatic stress syndromes* (pp. 635–644). New York: Plenum.

Helzer, J., Robins, L., & McEvoy, L. (1987). PTSD in the general population. *New England Journal of Medicine, 317,* 1630–1634.

Herman, J. L. (1992a). Complex PTSD: A syndrome in survivors of prolonged and repeated trauma. *Journal of Traumatic Stress, 5*(3), 377–392.

Herman, J. L. (1992b). *Trauma and recovery.* New York: Basic Books.

Horowitz, M. J. (1973). Phase oriented treatment of stress response syndromes. *American Journal of Psychotherapy, 27,* 506–515.

Horowitz, M. J. (1986). *Stress response syndromes* (2d ed.). Northvale, N.J.: Jason Aronson.

Horowitz, M. J. (1993). Stress-response syndromes: A review of posttraumatic stress and adjustment disorders. In J. P. Wilson & B. Raphael (eds.), *International handbook of traumatic stress syndromes* (pp. 49–60). New York: Plenum.

Horowitz, M. J., & Solomon, G. F. (1975). A prediction of delayed stress response syndrome in Vietnam veterans. *Journal of Social Issues, 4,* 67–79.

Houskamp, B. M., & Foy, D. (1991). The assessment of posttraumatic stress disorder in battered women. *Journal of Interpersonal Violence, 6,* 367–375.

Jacobson, G. F. (1974). The crisis interview. Paper presented to the symposium on Comparative psychotherapies, University of Southern California School of Medicine, Department of Psychiatry, Division of Continuing Education, San Diego, 24–28 June.

James, W. (1906/1911). On some mental effects of the earthquake. In H. James (ed.), *Memories and studies* (pp. 207–226). New York: Longmans, Green.

Kaiser, L. (1968). *The traumatic neurosis.* Philadelphia: Lippincott.

Keane, T. M., Fairbank, J. A., Caddell, J. M., & Zimering, R. T. (1989). Implosive (flooding) therapy reduces symptoms of PTSD in Vietnam combat veterans. *Behavior Therapy, 20,* 245–260.

Keane, T., & Wolfe, J. (1990). Comorbidity in posttraumatic stress disorder: An analysis of community and clinical studies. *Journal of Applied Social Psychology, 20,* 1776–1778.

Kellett, A. (1982). *Combat motivation: The behavior of soldiers in battle.* Boston: Kluwer-Nijhoff.

Kemp, A., & Green, B. L. (in press). Battered women and post-traumatic stress disorder: Research findings. In D. J. Miller (ed.), *Handbook of posttraumatic stress disorders.* New York: Plenum.

Kemp, A., Green, B. L., Hovanitz, C., & Rawlings, E. I. (1995). Incidence and correlates of post-traumatic stress disorder in battered women: Shelter and community samples. *Journal of Interpersonal Violence, 10,* 43–55.

Kemp, A., Rawlings, E., & Green, B. (1991). Post-traumatic stress disorder (PTSD) in battered women: A shelter sample. *Journal of Traumatic Stress, 4,* 137–148.

Kilpatrick, D. G., & Resnick, H. S. (1993). PTSD associated with exposure to criminal victimization in clinical and community populations. In J. R. T. Davidson & E. B. Foa (eds.), *Post-traumatic stress disorder: DSM IV and beyond* (pp. 113–143). Washington, D.C.: American Psychiatric Press.

Kilpatrick, D. G., Saunders, B. E., Veronen, L. J., Best, C. L., & Von, J. M. (1987a). Criminal victimization: Lifetime prevalence, reporting to police, and psychological impact. Paper presented at the meeting of the Association for the Advancement of Behavior Therapy, Boston, Mass.

Kilpatrick, D. G., Saunders, B. E., Veronen, L. J., Best, C. L., & Von, J. M. (1987b). Criminal victimization: Lifetime prevalence, reporting to police, and psychological impact. *Crime & Delinquency, 33*(4), 479–489.

Kilpatrick, D. G., Veronen, L. J., & Resick, P. A. (1982). Psychological sequelae to rape: Assessment and treatment strategies. In D. M. Dolays & R. L. Meredith (eds.), *Behavioral medicine: Assessment and treatment strategies* (pp. 473–497). New York: Plenum.

Kinzie, J. D., Sack, W. H., Angell, R. H., & Mason, S. M. (1986). The psychiatric effects of massive trauma on Cambodian children: I, The children. *Journal of the American Academy of Child and Adolescent Psychiatry, 25,* 370–376.

Kiser, L. J., Ackerman, B. J., Brown, E., Edwards, N. B., McColgan, E., Pugh, R., & Pruitt, D. B. (1988). Post-traumatic stress disorder in young children: A reaction to purported sexual abuse. *Journal of the American Academy of Child Psychiatry, 27,* 645–649.

Kramer, T. L., & Green, B. L. (1991). Post-traumatic stress disorder as an early response to sexual assault. *Journal of Interpersonal Violence, 6,* 160–173.

Kramer, T. L., & Green, B. L. (1995). Post-traumatic stress disorder and borderline personality traits in female survivors of child sexual abuse. Unpublished manuscript.

Krener, P. (1985). After incest: Secondary prevention? *Journal of the American Academy of Child Psychiatry, 24,* 231–234.

Krystal, H. (1968). *Massive psychic trauma.* New York: International Universities Press.

Krystal, H. (1978). Trauma and affects. *Psychoanalytic Study of the Child, 33,* 81–116.

Krystal, J. H., Kosten, T. R., Southwick, S., Mason, J. W., Perry, B. D., & Giller, E. L. (1989). Neurobiological aspects of PTSD: Review of clinical and preclinical studies. *Behavior Therapy, 20,* 177–198.

Kulka, R. A., Schlenger, W. E., Fairbank, J. A., Hough, R. L., Jordan, B. K., Marmar, C. R., & Weiss, D. S. (1988). *National Vietnam veterans readjustment study: Description, current status, and initial PTSD prevalence rates.* Research Triangle Park, N.C.: Research Triangle Institute.

Kulka, R. A., Schlenger, W. E., Fairbank, J. A., Hough, R. L., Jordan, B. K., Marmar, C. R., & Weiss, D. S. (1990). *Trauma and the Vietnam war generation.* New York: Brunner/Mazel.

Lifton, R. J. (1970). *History and human survival.* New York: Random House.

Lima, B. R., Pai, S., Santacruz, H., Lozano, J., & Luna, J. (1987). Screening for the psychological consequences of a major disaster in a developing country: Armero, Colombia. *Acta Psychiatrica Scandinavica, 76*, 561–567.

Lindberg, F. H., & Distad, L. J. (1985a). Post-traumatic stress disorders in women who experienced childhood incest. *Child Abuse & Neglect, 9*, 329–334.

Lindberg, F. H., & Distad, L. J. (1985b). Survival responses to incest: Adolescents in crisis. *Child Abuse & Neglect, 9*, 521–526.

Lindemann, E. (1944). Symptomatology and management of acute grief. *American Journal of Psychiatry, 101*, 141–148.

Lindy, J. D. (in collaboration with Green, B. L., Grace, M. C., MacLeod, J. A., & Spitz, L.) (1988). *Vietnam: A casebook.* New York: Brunner/Mazel.

Livingston, R. (1987). Sexually and physically abused children. *Journal of the American Academy of Child and Adolescent Psychiatry, 26*, 413–415.

Lopez-Ibor, J. J., Jr., Canas, S. F., & Rodriguez-Gamazo, M. (1985). Psychological aspects of the toxic oil syndrome catastrophe. *British Journal of Psychiatry, 147*, 352–365.

March, J. S. (1993). What constitutes a stressor?: The "Criterion A" issue. In J. R. T. Davidson and E. B. Foa (eds.), *Posttraumatic stress disorder: DSM-IV and beyond* (pp. 37–56). Washington, D.C.: American Psychiatric Press.

Marmar, C. R., Foy, D., Kagan, B., & Pynoos, R. S. (1993). An integrated approach for treating posttraumatic stress. In R. S. Pynoos (ed.), *Posttraumatic stress disorder: A clinical review* (pp. 99–132). Lutherville, Md.: Sidran.

Marmar, C. R., & Freeman, M. (1988). Brief dynamic psychotherapy of post-traumatic stress disorders: Management of narcissistic regression. *Journal of Traumatic Stress, 1*, 323–337.

Marmar, C. R., Weiss, D. S., Schlenger, W. E., & Fairbank, J. A. (1994). Peritraumatic dissociation and posttraumatic stress in male Vietnam theater veterans. *American Journal of Psychiatry, 151*, 902–907.

Masson, J. M. (1984). *The assault on truth.* New York: Farrar, Straus and Giroux.

McFarlane, A. C. (1986). Posttraumatic morbidity of a disaster: A study of cases presenting for psychiatric treatment. *Journal of Nervous and Mental Disease, 174*(1), 4–13.

McLeer, S. B., Deblinger, E., Atkins, M. S., Foa, E. B., & Ralphe, D. L. (1988). Posttraumatic stress disorder in sexually abused children. *Journal of the American Academy of Child and Adolescent Psychiatry, 29*, 70–75.

McNally, R. J. (1993). Stressors that produce posttraumatic stress disorder in children. In J. R. T. Davidson & E. B. Foa (eds.), *Posttraumatic stress disorder: DSM-IV and beyond* (pp. 57–74). Washington, D.C.: American Psychiatric Press.

Mikulincer, M., & Solomon, Z. (1988). Attributional style and combat-related posttraumatic stress disorder. *Journal of Abnormal Psychology, 97*, 308–313.

Mitchell, J. T., & Dyregrov, A. (1993). Traumatic stress in disaster workers and emergency personnel: Prevention and intervention. In J. P. Wilson & B. Raphael (eds.), *International handbook of traumatic stress syndromes.* New York: Plenum.

Myers, C. S. (1940). *Shell shock in France, 1914–1918.* London: Cambridge University Press.

Nader, K., Pynoos, R., Fairbanks, L., Frederick, C., Al-Ajeel, M., & Al-Asfour, A. (1993). A preliminary study of PTSD and grief among the children of Kuwait following the Gulf crisis. *British Journal of Clinical Psychology, 32*, 407–416.

National Center for Post-Traumatic Stress Disorder (1990). Biological aspects of PTSD: Laboratory and clinical research. *PTSD Research Quarterly, 1,* 1–8.

Newman, J. P., & Foreman, C. (1987). The Sun Valley Mall disaster study. Paper presented to Society for Traumatic Stress Studies, Baltimore, Md., October.

Norris, G. H. (1992). Epidemiology of trauma: Frequency and impact of different potentially traumatic events on different demographic groups. *Journal of Consulting and Clinical Psychology, 60,* 409–418.

Oei, T. P. S., Lim, B., & Hennessy, B. (1990). Psychological dysfunction in battle: Combat stress reactions and posttraumatic stress disorder. *Clinical Psychology Review, 10,* 355–388.

Oppenheim, H. (1889). *Die traumatischen Neurosen: Nach den in der Nervenklinck der Charité in den letzten 5 Jahren gesammelten Beobachtungen.* (Traumatic neuroses; Collected observations from the last five years in the Nervenklinik der Charité.) Berlin: Hirschwald.

Parker, G. (1977). Cyclone Tracy and Darwin evacuees: On the restoration of the species. *British Journal of Psychiatry, 130,* 548–555.

Peniston, E. G. (1986). EMG biofeedback-assisted desensitization treatment for Vietnam combat veterans post-traumatic stress disorder. *Clinical Biofeedback Health, 9,* 35–41.

Pitman, R. K. (1993). Biological findings in posttraumatic stress disorder: Implications for *DSM-IV* classification. In J. R. T. Davidson & E. B. Foa (eds.), *Posttraumatic stress disorder: DSM-IV and beyond* (pp. 173–190). Washington, D.C.: American Psychiatric Press.

Pynoos, R. S. (1994). Traumatic stress and developmental psychopathology in children and adolescents. In R. S. Pynoos (ed.), *Posttraumatic stress disorder: A clinical review* (pp. 65–98). Lutherville, Md.: Sidran.

Rado, S. (1942). Pathodynamics and treatment of traumatic war neurosis (traumatophobia). *Psychosomatic Medicine, 42,* 362–368.

Resnick, H. S., Kilpatrick, D. G., Dansky, B. S., Saunders, B. E., & Best, C. L. (1993). Prevalence of civilian trauma and posttraumatic stress disorder in a representative national sample of women. *Journal of Consulting and Clinical Psychology, 61,* 984–991.

Sack, W. H., Clarke, G., Him, C., Dickason, D., Goff, B., Lanham, D., & Kinzie, J. D. (1993). A six year follow-up of Cambodian adolescents. *Journal of the American Academy of Child and Adolescent Psychiatry, 32,* 3–15.

Saigh, P. A. (1989). The development and validation of the Children's Posttraumatic Stress Disorder Inventory. *International Journal of Special Education, 4,* 75–84.

Saigh, P. A., Green, B. L., & Korol, M. (1996). The history and prevalence of posttraumatic stress disorder with special reference to children and adolescents. *Journal of School Psychology, 34,* 103–105.

Sansonnet-Hayden, H., Haley, G., Marriage, K., & Fine, S. (1987). Sexual abuse and psychopathology in hospitalized adolescents. *Journal of the American Academy of Child and Adolescent Psychiatry, 26,* 753–757.

Scrignar, C. B. (1984). *Post-traumatic stress disorder: Diagnosis, treatment, and legal issues.* New York: Praeger.

Scurfield, R. M. (1993). Treatment of posttraumatic stress disorder among Vietnam veterans. In J. P. Wilson & B. Raphael (eds.), *International handbook of traumatic stress syndromes* (pp. 879–888). New York: Plenum.

Shapiro, G. (1989). Efficacy of the eye movement desensitization procedure in the treatment of traumatic memories. *Journal of Traumatic Stress, 2,* 199–205.

Shore, J. H., Tatum, E. L., & Vollmer, W. M. (1986). The Mount St. Helens stress response syndrome. In J. H. Shore (ed.), *Disaster stress studies: New methods and findings* (pp. 7–97). Washington, D.C.: American Psychiatric Press.

Silver, S. M., Brooks, A., & Obenchain, J. (1995). Treatment of Vietnam war veterans with PTSD: A comparison of eye movement desensitization and reprocessing, biofeedback, and relaxation training. *Journal of Traumatic Stress, 8,* 337–342.

Sirles, E. A., Smith, J. A., & Kusama, H. (1989). Psychiatric status of intrafamilial child sexual abuse. *Journal of the American Academy of Child and Adolescent Psychiatry, 28,* 225–229.

Smith, E. M., & North, C. S. (1993). Posttraumatic stress disorder in natural disasters and technological accidents. In J. P. Wilson & B. Raphael (eds.), *International handbook of traumatic stress syndromes* (pp. 405–419). New York: Plenum.

Solomon, S. D., Bravo, M., Rubio-Stipec, M., & Canino, G. (1993). Effect of family role on response to disaster. *Journal of Traumatic Stress, 6,* 255–270.

Solomon, S. D., Gerrity, E. T., & Muff, A. M. (1992). Efficacy of treatments for posttraumatic stress disorder. *Journal of the American Medical Association, 268,* 633–638.

Solomon, Z., & Benbenishty, R. (1986). The role of proximity, immediacy and expectancy in frontline treatment of combat stress reaction among Israelis in the Lebanon War. *American Journal of Psychiatry, 143*(5), 613–617.

Speed, N., Engdahl, B., Schwartz, J., & Eberly, R. (1989). Post-traumatic stress disorder as a consequence of the POW experience. *Journal of Nervous and Mental Disease, 177,* 147–153.

Stierlin, D. (1909). Uber psychoneurpathische Folgezustande bei den Uberlebenden der Katastrophe von Courrieres am 10. Marz 1906. (On the psychoneuropathic consequences among the survivors of the Courrieres catastrophe of 10 March 1906.) Doctoral dissertation, University of Zurich.

Straus, M. A., & Gelles, R. J. (1986). Societal change and change in family violence from 1975 to 1985 as revealed by two national surveys. *Journal of Marriage and Family, 48,* 465–479.

van der Kolk, B. A. (1987). *Psychological trauma.* Washington, D.C.: American Psychiatric Press.

Walker, L. E. (1979). *The battered woman.* New York: Harper & Row.

Weisaeth, L. (1985). Posttraumatic stress disorder after an industrial disaster. In P. Pichot, P. Berner, R. Wolf, & K. Thau (eds.), *Psychiatry—The state of the art* (vol. 6, pp. 299–307). New York: Plenum.

Weisaeth, L. (1993). Torture of a Norwegian ship's crew: Stress reactions, coping, and psychiatric aftereffects. In J. P. Wilson & B. Raphael (eds.), *International handbook of traumatic stress syndromes* (pp. 743–750). New York: Plenum.

Weisaeth, L., & Eitinger, L. (1991). Research on PTSD and other post-traumatic reactions: European literature. *PTSD Research Quarterly, 2*(2), 1–2.

Weisaeth, L., & Eitinger, L. (1993). Posttraumatic stress phenomena: Common themes across wars, disasters, and traumatic events. In J. P. Wilson & B. Raphael (eds.), *International handbook of traumatic stress syndromes* (pp.69–78). New York: Plenum.

10

Post-Traumatic Stress Disorders as a Loss of the Meaning of Life

Madrudin S. Magomed-Eminov

War never ends for those who have suffered through it. Those who committed the atrocities of death and destruction, those who witnessed them, and those who suffered at the hands of their enemies are sentenced to a life of recurring memories from which they cannot escape. For these multiple victims, the psychic war continues long after they have returned from the battlefield, their towns have been rebuilt, and their respective governments have resumed trade and promoted tourism. The psychological sequelae of war and other traumatic events show a distinct pattern of symptoms that are known as post-traumatic stress disorder (PTSD). The approach that has been used in the laboratories and clinical settings in the former Soviet countries is to understand the aftermath of traumatic events as an existential crisis.

According to the existential approach, PTSD is caused by the conflict between two different systems that provide meaning to life. Existentialism is an introspective theory in which life is analyzed by examining its critical situations and the feelings of suffering, guilt, and anxiety that accompany and follow them. In critical situations, like war, individuals make decisive judgments; it is these choices that provide meaning in an apparently purposeless and meaningless world. In the studies done in my laboratories and those of other former Soviets, we examined the loss of meaning and the search to regain it among Soviet veterans of the war in Afghanistan and, more recently, Russian Federation veterans of the war in Chechnya.

Existentialism and the Conflict of Meaning

The study of PTSD in the former Soviet countries was influenced by the theories and research of Victor Frankl (1959), a native Austrian, who was also a survivor of Nazi concentration camps. Frankl was a psychotherapist who developed a type of therapy known as *logotherapy*. He formulated his theories based on his work with many other survivors of the Holocaust following World War II. According to Frankl, a sense of meaning always comes from the world in which an individual lives and is never invented by the individual. We each strive to understand the meaning of life based on how we experience the world, but if one is not found, then we will exist in an existential vacuum. People interpret their life by the way they answer three key questions: (1) What is the meaning of the world I live in? (2) How can I live my life in a way that will satisfy my needs and values? and (3) Who am I? The way each of us answers these questions defines our personality. The search for the meaning of life is an inherited necessity that is part of the human condition (Frankl, 1959).

The Loss of Meaning

All humans try to understand their lives. We do this by connecting the present with the past and the future. These connections help us to find our place in the world. Under extreme conditions, the search for meaning fails and existential neurosis results from the conviction that life is essentially meaningless, and we are alone and rootless in a great void (Maddi, 1967). The centrality of the loss of meaning in PTSD is seen in the writing of Janoff-Bulman (1985, 1989; Janoff-Bulman & Frieze, 1983), who believes that the need to attribute meaningfulness to horrific events is an essential component in the psychology of victimization. Lifton (1967, 1973, 1985, 1986), a prominent author in this area, also believes that it is not possible to understand PTSD without understanding the search for meaning that survivors of atrocious life experiences must undergo. The senselessness of the world is a major interpretive event for those who participated in horrors that are of human origin—horrors like war.

Loss of Meaning for War Veterans

The theme of loss of meaning served as a major focus in group psychotherapy sessions with American veterans from the Vietnam War (Egendorf, 1985; Egendorf, Kadushin, Laufer, Rothbart, & Sloan, 1981). Following this unpopular war, numerous veterans reported feelings of extreme emptiness and meaningless. Overwhelmingly, they reported that the loss of meaning was profoundly disturbing. During the war, these men were obsessed with fears of death and being wounded. The world that they had known before the war was irrelevant during periods of fighting in Vietnam. All of their former beliefs about who they were and what was right had become meaningless. Following the war experience, the sense of meaning that they had developed during the war became irrelevant, so once again they had no basis for understanding fundamental questions about the meaning of life.

How can this model of profound disturbance caused by an existential crisis be used to understand PTSD (Lazarus & DeLongis, 1983)? Kobasa (1979) worked out a scheme for differentiating between people who succumb to extreme stress with illness and those who remain healthy. Healthy individuals are able to remain closely connected to the meaning of life and are able to create a personal understanding of the meaning of extremely traumatic events. The preservation of meaning, or the ability to make sense out of life experiences, is a major factor in preventing stress-related illness. It is an important mediator between stress and depression (Ganellen & Blaney, 1984).

Under the severe strains of war, meaning structures change because there is little evidence that life is valued or valuable. The veteran's own life is repeatedly threatened during prolonged periods of war. In this framework, it is believed that the reminiscences of war veterans, which linger long after the veterans have returned from the place and time of war, serve the purpose of forcing the veterans to give meaning to their experiences. Veterans diagnosed with PTSD often report that they suffer from intrusive flashbacks and recurring thoughts that force them to place their memories within a framework that permits an explanation. For example, the death of a close friend, or even a stranger, is difficult to understand or to justify. What is the reason, what is the principle, for which these other people died? If the veteran sustained a permanent injury or extreme hardship of some other sort (e.g., if he was tortured or did the torturing), the haunting question "Why?" needs to be answered. Unless some answer can be found, these losses in understanding the world create a permanent stress in their lives.

Regression as Progress

Regression is only possible when society makes progress. For example, in earlier times, captured enemies were scalped by their victors, who performed this gruesome act with pride and euphoria. It is a sign of societal progress that we now view this act with horror. When the victors question the meaning in these acts, the loss of sense of meaning is progress. Veterans who do not struggle to understand atrocities, but merely accept them as normal, are not as advanced in a moral sense as those who are troubled and in search of meaning. From this perspective, PTSD, although painful for the individual, is a sign of moral development for the society.

Investigations of Existential Loss of Meaning in Vietnam War Veterans

Veterans must find a new sense of meaning (Williams, 1983). Those who left the comforts of home to fight in Vietnam had hostile feelings toward those who opposed the war. The veterans had risked their lives and often endured and committed unspeakable horrors, yet when they returned home they did not find a grateful or admiring reception. Those veterans who had previously believed they were good and honest people came to doubt these earlier assessments of themselves. Sitting in their own living rooms, they could not come to grips with the idea that they had killed other people only a short time before. The pain associated with killing and fears of being killed seemed to intensify after the war ended. The veterans had to find some way to make sense out of the juxtaposition of their view of themselves as good individuals and the fact that they had taken lives. How could they readjust to the life they reentered, one that had made sense before the war but now seemed devoid of meaning?

The meaning of life before the war now conflicted with the new meaning that developed during the war—one that allowed, even required, killing and committing other atrocities (Lifton, 1973). These two sets of values—the ones that were valid for their everyday lives before and after the war and the ones that were valid during the war—were in direct conflict with each other. The predominant conflicts involved questions of life and death and where they appear in one's hierarchy of values.

Meanings of Life and Death

Questions of life and death have absolute values. Unlike other values, these conceptualizations are not relative to other life events. In prewar and postwar values, the idea of death is suppressed or rejected. During times of war, death assumes a conscious and higher position in a value hierarchy as the killing of an enemy is valued and preserving one's own life is an active motivator. It cannot be repressed or ignored when life is being actively threatened.

Who should live? This was a difficult and persistent thought during the war. A wrong decision could cost one's own life or result in the murder of innocent people. This was a predominant problem during the war in Afghanistan. It was very difficult for the Soviet troops to tell the difference between the civilian population they were there to defend and the *modzjaheds*, the enemy they were to vanquish. The inability to distinguish between those whom you are to protect and those whom you are to kill was a source of constant strain that created many moral dilemmas.

The veterans had become moral bookkeepers as they kept an informal ledger of who was to live and who was to die. They were involved in their own personal intrapsychic conflict as their meaning of life prior to the war clashed with the meaning that developed during the war. The change in the meaning of life was not a simple reordering of hierarchies but was instead a major revision of what one knew to be just and moral and what one knew to be base and wrong. Death acquired a new meaning, and as the veterans stayed in situations of war for prolonged periods of time, intrapsychic conflict continued with the unabated intensity of the external war that raged around them. Thus, for every veteran, two wars raged. The one that went on outside was filled with pain, killing, and the death of others, and the one within involved a conflict between the soldier's prewar beliefs about life and those he had to adopt during the war.

It was impossible for two different systems that define the meaning of life to coexist within one person. The conflict of meaning systems led to a "doubling of personality" within each veteran. The two meaning structures were too disparate to be merged, so they had to coexist within each person, who now assumed a new personality. PTSD became increasingly likely as the intensity of the meaning conflict increased. According to this view, it was the failure to create a single meaningful view that would allow the veterans to understand their actions during the war that caused PTSD. To test this hypothesis, researchers in my laboratory conducted an experiment in which they examined differences between those veterans who showed evidence of high or low levels of conflict in their ability to make sense out of the war and the association of these two levels of conflict of meaning with the diagnosis of PTSD.

Experiment 1: The Conflict of Meaning and Its Resolution

In order to assess conflicts in the way in which Soviet veterans of the war in Afghanistan gave meaning to life, 210 veterans were given a 13-item sentence-completion task that was followed by a structured interview. These are standard projective techniques that are used to identify underlying themes or problems not amenable to direct questioning. Their responses were content-analyzed by four independent experts. Thirteen categorical themes emerged from their analysis of these data. Six themes showed evidence of conflicts in the way the veterans interpreted the meaning of life, and seven themes were classified as attempts to overcome or resolve this intrapsychic conflict.

Categorical Themes Showing the Intrapsychic Conflict of Meaning with Verbatim Examples

1. Negative interpretations of one's own deeds—realization that one has acted in ways that are contrary to how one perceives oneself: "How could I have done something like that? What had I done?"
2. Realization and rejection of values based on ideological grounds—no higher good could be used to justify one's actions: "This is not our international obligation. We do not belong here. Why were we fighting in Afghanistan?"
3. Perception of the absurdity of the situation: "It is impossible to justify such as a war. It is moronic."
4. Prolonged cognitive representation of the conflict in the meaning of life: "I became increasingly hesitant. Sometimes at night I couldn't sleep. I kept thinking, why are we in this damn war? All the time, I ask myself why am I alive today if tomorrow I might be killed?"
5. Actively trying not to think about the situation: "I tried not to think about what's going on and what I was doing. I smoked marijuana because it helped me to stop thinking."
6. Feeling of emptiness; closed to feelings: "I lost the ability to feel. I wanted to close my eyes and forget about everything. At the beginning it was very dif-

ficult, but with time I became numb. I felt empty inside. All feeling was dulled as though everything was burned out from inside. I felt that I had no heart, no soul, no strength."

Categorical Themes Showing a Resolution of the Conflict of Meaning with Verbatim Examples

1. Survival as a primary meaning: "The main thing for me was to overcome. I wanted to live. Most important, I had to try to remain alive and not to become an invalid. There was nothing that was as important for me as returning home with my friends. Every day I thought, 'Today I am alive, thank God.'"

2. Preserving one's humanity: "I tried to remain humane, not to turn into a beast. I wanted to return as I had been; what I was most afraid of was that I would lose everything humane in me."

3. Helping others: "The most vivid memory for me was the help of my friends in getting me out of the battlefield when I was injured. Without their help I would not be alive. The main thing for me was that none of my men should get killed."

4. Revengeful aggression as a meaning—death for death: "We had to exchange a death for a death. I knew what I had to do."

5. Focusing on day-to-day living: "I tried to just get from day to day. I would sit around and just try to focus on killing birds or something else to get through the day."

6. Imitation of being a hero: "I imagined myself as a cowboy or other hero as seen in the films."

7. Dreaming about the future: "I tried to imagine what I would be doing when I returned. I wanted to achieve something when I get home. I thought about beautiful girls and a pleasant life."

In scoring these responses, every category that was present in a veteran's response was given 1 point. Thus, the highest scores possible for each veteran were 6 for conflict in meaning and 7 for overcoming or resolving the conflict in meaning. Data were then split along the median scores into two separate groups— those who scored in the top half of the sample in terms of the extent to which they overcame the problem of conflict in meaning and those who scored in the lower half on this measure.

The Afghanistan veterans were then classified for the presence or absence of PTSD using a standard procedure for making this diagnosis that was adapted for them. The number of veterans who scored in each of the four groups defined by the presence or absence of PTSD diagnosis and high or low on whether or not they overcame the meaning crisis is presented in table 10.1.

Perusal of table 10.1 shows a significant relationship between the failure to resolve the conflict in the meaning of life that arose from their war experiences and the diagnosis of PTSD: $x^2 = 107. 170, (fi) = .732$.

These data were supported by comments and discussions among the veterans. A frequently used slogan by those responsible for military propaganda was the appeal to assist Afghanistan, a country that needed assistance from the Soviet

Table 10.1. Afghanistan Veterans, PTSD, and Crisis of Meaning

	PTSD	No PTSD	Total
Overcame crisis of meaning	18	79	97
Failed to overcome crisis of meaning	94	9	103
Total	112	88	210

Union in its struggle to become communist. At that time, there were Soviet officials in charge of maintaining a high level of military spirit in the troops. The Soviet office of war propaganda had been operating since the civil wars in the Soviet Union that followed the revolution of 1917. Their job was to convince young soldiers and the general public that this was a just war and to maintain Soviet support for the war. But the veterans soon came to realize that they had been lied to and that very few of the Afghanis whom they had come to save for communism wanted them there.

The veterans had expected a grateful reception from the Afghanis, but this was not to be the reality. Few of the people whom they were preserving for communism perceived them as allies or defenders. Instead of a supportive populace, they found that the enemy could be anywhere and every setting was potentially hostile. Many veterans also reported that they did not know that they were being sent to Afghanistan until they arrived. They had been herded onto large covered transport vehicles (trucks and trains) much like cattle, with no knowledge of their destination. When they arrived, they felt at a complete loss, both literally and figuratively. Some thought that they were being sent on training expeditions and were startled to find themselves in the midst of a real war.

There are many parallels between the responses of the veterans of the Afghani war and those of the newest generation of veterans, veterans from the Chechen war. Like the responses presented above, many Russian veterans of Chechnya report that they did not know that they were being taken to the Chechen war until they actually arrived.

The Absurdity of Life

It is not difficult to understand how these veterans came to perceive life in all of its absurdities. Psychologists in my laboratory found that the feeling of absurdity is a universal meaning that veterans take from their war experiences. Our most recent work with veterans from Chechnya confirm these findings. Instead of asking "Why am I living?," the predominate question becomes "Why am I killing?" A more literal translation of this question from the Russian is "For what reason am I killing?" All of life's values are reevaluated in the light of these questions. No sense could be gleaned from this war. The dirty work of the war had been done by their own hands for no justifiable reasons. Day and night, they returned to the same questions: "For what reason am I killing? Why am I here? Why did my friends die?" Despair and depression were the only answers.

Not to Think, Not to See, Not to Hear, Not to Feel

Earlier in this century, Freud (1955) observed that not thinking is a characteristic of people suffering from traumatic neurosis. This is the classical Freudian notion of repression, in which traumatic events are unavailable in memory until some time in the future. Instead, we found that horrific memories could not be avoided, even though the veterans did not speak of them and tried to make them disappear. This theme was seen in many stories that the veterans told. After they returned from a battle, they rarely spoke of what had just happened. When handling corpses, peering into the faces of the dying, listening to their anguished screams, and in similar situations, they felt only emptiness. The shutdown of emotional systems is an important characteristic of veterans and other traumatized people for whom life has lost its meaning. The highest value was staying alive. Survival became the only meaning that was left in life. One veteran remembered:

> During a raid on a tank in which we were working, a missile struck it, and the tank burst into flames. The chief and two others were killed almost immediately. I was engulfed with fire as was my friend. I could not see anything because my eyes were burned. My friend and I knew we had to get out of the tank. So together and almost blind, with no weapons, we crawled out of the tank because we knew it would blow up at any moment. We were both wounded, I in my hand, my friend in his side. While we were crawling on the ground, we came across a group of *modzjaheds* who were also without weapons, but they had spades. There was a fight and my friend was killed with a spade. I ran as fast as I could to the site where the fire was raging out of control—a place in the midst of the fire where the *modzjaheds* did not want to follow me. I hid behind a stone in the middle of the fire, and this is how I survived. I had only one desire—to get out of this hell.

Maintaining Humanity

The desire to preserve oneself as a humane person was another overriding theme that was seen repeatedly when the veterans were allowed to talk for themselves:

> Yes, this war was dirty. The main thing was not to lose human dignity. Perhaps I really was cruel. I saw a lot in this war, but no one could understand why there was so much cruelty. I tried not to turn into a beast—to preserve something worthy of a human in spite of everything that was going on around us. Many soldiers tried to overcome what was going on around them—the killing of civilians, the destruction of towns and villages—so some of them were ready to help others, their comrades, their friends, and the villagers. We gave our bread to local residents. When our tour of service ended, we gave help to others. The soldiers

gave their shoulders for others to lean on. Those who were not there, those who never shared their last cigarette or crust of bread, cannot understand.

Revenge as the Meaning of Life

Revenge is also seen as a major theme in the structured interviews. Veterans needed to have an understanding of what the enemy came to mean. This theme is seen in statements taken from the Russian Federation troops that recently returned from Chechnya. Revenge is another type of adaptation to meaning. The massacre and genocide that are occurring in Chechnya can only be understood with this framework. The city of Grozny was turned to ruins. Unlike the war in Afghanistan, the majority of Russian Federation troops in Chechnya did not want to fight, even at the beginning of the war, because they did not understand why they should be there.

Revenge was one reason for fighting—revenge for the death of one's friend, one's fellow soldier. The Chechens declared that they would exact bloody revenge for the deaths that had occurred on their side, so why shouldn't the Russian Federation troops declare the same sort of bloody revenge for their fallen comrades? This was an idea that gave some sense to the war. This idea soon became part of the official military propaganda that provided a reason for killing. The idea of revenge as a motive for continuing the fighting was implanted into the heads of the soldiers, who stated that they were drawn even deeper into an escalating cry for revenge. Ironically, after Afghanistan, when the tide of opinion turned, the Russian veterans said that they would seek revenge on those who had sent them to war. Revenge became a meaning-giving factor that provided the justification for their actions. A new meaning was created: a death for a death. One soldier stated: "We knew that the worst was to be caught by the Afghani peasants because they would skin you alive. I couldn't know if any particular village was fighting against us or not, so it was better to just destroy everyone than to take the risk." Another remembered: "My friends perished and as I was alive, my life was needed to take revenge. They tortured my friend. Now it is all the same for me. I don't know who the enemy is, it might be a child, but it is all the same for me. I'll take revenge. A death for a death."

Meaning as Essential for Survival

No one could leave this situation by choice. Every day the veterans had to get through the war without going mad. One claimed: "I saw how some of these boys couldn't stand it anymore. I saw them crying as children. These were the first to be killed." Survival depended on the veteran's ability to provide some meaning to this inescapable hell. Without some meaning, they could not act in ways that helped them to survive. Being in a situation with no freedom of choice and no chance of escape, the men had to find some meaning in the war in order to stay alive. Motivation for self-preservation depended on their ability to find meaning.

PTSD Is a Conflict in the Meaning of Life

The long-term consequences of exposure to a prolonged severe trauma like war are seen after the veterans return to a world that is different from the one that they left. The veteran is changed; his system that provided the meaning of life during the war does not work in a society at peace, but if he gives up the wartime meaning, then he cannot live with the actions that he committed during the war. Structures that provide the meaning of life cannot be automatically abandoned as one goes off to war or returns home. The nightmares of war follow the participants home. Actions and events cannot be left on the battlefield or in a trench; they return with the veteran as a part of who he is. He must find a way to provide a new meaning to what has happened—one that can be used to guide him through the future and through times of peace. It is this existential dilemma that has come to be known as PTSD.

Experiment 2: The Relationship between Conflicts in the Meaning of Life and PTSD

A second study was conducted with 200 veterans of the Afghanistan war. Data were collected in the period between 1987 and 1988. Clinical interviews were used to determine if the veterans showed evidence of suffering caused by the loss of meaning of life. The veterans were also examined using a 35–item diagnostic questionnaire to determine if they met the criteria that were used for a diagnosis of PTSD. As in the previously described study, diagnoses were confirmed with clinical judgments by mental health professionals.

Veterans were categorized by the presence or absence of PTSD and whether they scored in the top or bottom half of the sample in terms of their loss of life meaning. The number of Soviet veterans from the Afghanistan war that were classified into these categories is shown in table 10.2. As shown in table 10.2, veterans whose responses showed themes of a high level of meaning conflict were overwhelmingly more likely to be diagnosed with PTSD than those who showed few themes of meaning conflict: $x^2 = 49.925$, (fi) = .5000.

Three independent experts content-analyzed the clinical interviews with this group of veterans. Nine themes emerged from these interviews, and they are

Table 10.2. Afghanistan Veterans, PTSD, and Meaning Conflict

	PTSD	No PTSD	Total
High on meaning conflict	103	29	132
Low on meaning conflict	18	50	68
Total	121	79	200

presented here with short verbatim examples so that readers can understand, in the veterans' own words, how the absence of a meaning of life caused great anguish and prolonged problems following their return home from the war.

Themes of Conflict in the Meaning of Life

1. Fluctuations and variations in the meaning of life: "So we were going through a small village in Afghanistan. My friends and I entered a yard to one of the houses. We started to wonder whether there might be *modzjaheds* in the house or in the village. The owner of the house, an old man, looked very frightened. He spoke something that we couldn't understand and gesticulated that we should look around. I think he was trying to tell us that there were no *modzjaheds*. We found in the yard a hole that was covered. In these places, the holes were used for shelter. I took the cover off and I heard some noises coming from the hole. In this case, I took a grenade and threw it into the hole. After that I looked to see what was there. There were several young boys in this underground shelter, the sons or grandsons of the old man. They had no weapons; their bodies were torn to pieces, sprayed all over the shelter. It was just horrible. On the other hand, why were they there, why should they hide there? This question tortures me all the time. I have this picture in front of my eyes. I don't know if I was right or wrong."

2. Negative evaluations of one's morality: "I returned a different man because of what I have done. I cannot finish my studies. I don't think that anyone could give me a job because I am a moral invalid."

3. Negative evaluations of one's actions: "I saw that everything should have been different. I began to make self-assessments and to look at what I had done. I can't return to undo the things that I did in the past. I am embarrassed by my past."

4. Negative assessment of the value of survival: "It was better to die than to return." "I am not glad that I returned alive. I envy those who perished there, even those who became POWs. Why did I return and not a friend of mine? It would have been better for me to be killed there." "I wish I were dead."

5. Disillusioned views of the future—the veterans had expected a better future than the one they experienced when they returned home: "Today I am having a nightmare." "As for the hell in which I existed, any images of home seemed as paradise. During the war I lived in the future, but after I returned my hopes were not fulfilled." "I thought that the moment I returned everything would be quite different, but it was nothing of the kind. After I returned to my motherland, everything seemed strange."

6. Nonunderstanding—feelings that no one could understand who they had become or what they had gone through: "My people met me with some a joy, but nevertheless, they cannot understand me." "I have my third divorce. I can't find a way to make contact with my people. I think that they avoid me, but I might be wrong." "We have different views on death. Only my friends, the other Afghani veterans, can understand me." "There is no one to speak to. No one

can understand the pain in my heart and my soul." "If you were not there, you cannot understand."

7. Loss of meaning—earlier values had become irrelevant and nothing seemed to make sense anymore: "I am hanging between my past experiences and my current life." "I have a crisis of spirit and soul." "I feel like a stranger from outer [cosmic] space."

8. Solitude and avoidance of human contacts—some of it justified by real rejection by others because of their involvement in unpopular wars and some by the expectation of such rejection or even by a wish to escape human contacts: "I don't want to see anyone. People embarrass me." "We hide a stone in our vest pocket [a metaphorical reference to an old Russian saying that suggests hiding the pain that one keeps in one's heart]." "I try not to come close to other people."

9. Search for meaning: "When in Afghanistan, everything was meaningful. We were soldiers and we knew the sense of our lives. I am still there, in my past." "Why was I there?" "For what reason did I suffer?" "For what reason did I kill?"

PTSD Caused by the Conflicts between Making Sense of a World at Peace and a World at War

As shown in these studies and in the words of the Soviet veterans from the war in Afghanistan and the most recent generation of veterans from the Russian Federation troops in Chechnya, the real trauma in PTSD comes from the loss of meaning to life. It was not the traumatic aspects of war per se that have the long-lasting effects that are diagnosed as PTSD, but it is the existential crisis and inability to come to grips with a meaningful theory of life that causes the prolonged pain. Of course, I do not deny that psychopaths and others also fit this description, but they do not suffer PTSD and seem to thrive under conditions of war. These descriptions are not meant to apply to this small and abnormal portion of the veteran population.

Pushkin, the great Russian poet, promised that "you are inspired by the battle." In other words, he believed that troops find zest for their actions in the sight and smell of spilled blood. But the experiences of the veterans do not match these expectations. Instead of finding glory or inspiration, it is far more critical to find meaning in the war experience. Based on these in-depth studies with hundreds of recent veterans using the projective techniques of sentence completion, content analysis, structured interviews, and clinical interviews, I concluded that the real struggle is to find meaning, and our best hope for treating PTSD is to help veterans construct a meaningful theory of life. The conflict among prewar, war, and postwar standards needs to find some resolution or the important questions about life and death will never be put to rest. Veterans and other victims of extreme trauma need to make sense of essentially senseless events and come to grips with the absurdity of life at a time when killing is the dominant activity. We owe it to these suffering souls to help them discover a tolerable meaning of life.

References

Egendorf, A. H. (1985). *Healing from the war: Trauma and transformation after Vietnam.* Boston: Houghton Mifflin.

Egendorf, A., Kadushin, C., Laufer, R., Rothbart, G., & Sloan, L. (1981). Legacies of Vietnam: Comparative adjustment of veterans and their peers. Study prepared by the Center for Policy Research for the Veterans Administration. Washington, D.C.: U.S. Government Printing Office.

Frankl, V. (1959). *Man's search for meaning.* New York: Washington Square Press/Pocket Books.

Freud, S. (1955). *Beyond the pleasure principle* (standard ed., vol. 18). London: Hogarth.

Ganellen, R. J., & Blaney, P. H. (1984). Hardiness and social support as moderators of the effects of life stress. *Journal of Personality and Social Psychology, 47,* 156–163.

Janoff-Bulman, R. (1985). The aftermath of victimization: Rebuilding shattered assumptions. In C. R. Finley (ed.), *Trauma and its wake* (pp. 15–35). New York: Brunner-Mazel.

Janoff-Bulman, R. (1989). Assumptive worlds and the stress of traumatic events: Applications of the schema concept. *Social Cognition, 7,* 113–136.

Janoff-Bulman, R., & Frieze, I. H. (1983). A theoretical perspective for understanding reactions to victimization. *Journal of Social Issues, 39,* 1–17.

Kobasa, S. C. (1979). Stressful life events, personality, and health: An inquiry into hardiness. *Journal of Personality and Social Psychology, 37,* 1–11.

Lazarus, R. S., & DeLongis, A. (1983). Psychological stress and coping in aging. *American Psychologist, 38,* 245–254.

Lifton, R. J. (1967). *Death in life: Survivors of Hiroshima.* New York: Simon & Schuster.

Lifton, R. J. (1973). *Home from the war.* Boston: Beacon.

Lifton, R. J. (1986). *The Nazi doctors.* New York: Basic Books.

Lifton, R. J. (1988). Understanding the traumatized self: Imagery, symbolization, and transformation. In J. P. Wilson, *Human adaptation to extreme stress.* New York: Plenum.

Maddi, S. R. (1967). The existential neurosis. *Journal of Abnormal Psychology, 72,* 311–325.

Williams, C. C. (1983). The mental foxhole: The Vietnam veterans' search for meaning. *American Journal of Orthopsychiatry, 53,* 4–17.

Changing Demographics

The New Old

Gerontological Psychology

The Western Perspective

Timothy A. Salthouse

The material to be discussed in this chapter is necessarily selective because gerontological psychology is far too large a topic to provide comprehensive coverage of the field within a single chapter. I have nevertheless attempted to maximize the breadth of the coverage by relying on articles published in one of the major journals in the field, *Psychology and Aging*, during the last four years to help identify major topics for inclusion. The coverage is still selective because some areas (e.g., death and dying) are not well represented in that journal and also because my lack of familiarity with some areas that are published in the journal may mean that I have not fully appreciated the significance of a given topic.

The chapter is organized into two major sections. The first and largest section consists of a broad survey of contemporary research in gerontological psychology. A discussion of important trends and future directions constitutes the second section.

Survey of Major Topics

Work

The working years typically span the range from about 18 to 65 years of age, although many people clearly work at older ages. Furthermore, the option of working beyond traditional retirement age is now available to most people because of the virtual elimination of mandatory retirement age policies for nearly all occupations in the United States. However, as the average age of workers increases, so also have there been increases in concerns about the productivity of the workforce. In addition, the effects of social, physical, and mental aspects of work on adults of all ages is another topic that is growing in importance as greater numbers of people are working for 40 or more years of their lives.

Some gerontological research directly relevant to work has been conducted, with a few studies focused on job satisfaction (Warr, 1992), on the effects of job-related training (Czaja & Sharit, 1993), and on the influence on attitudes and productivity of discrepancies between the age of the supervisor and the age of the supervisee (Vecchio, 1993). One particularly interesting study concerned with age differences in managerial decision making was conducted by Streufert, Pogash, Piasecki, and Post (1990). In this study, groups of adults within three age ranges were asked to work as a team in a simulated management situation. Relatively few performance differences were found between teams consisting of 28- to 36-year-old and 45- to 55-year-old participants, but teams consisting of 65- to 75-year-old participants made fewer decisions and were less strategic in their decisions than the other groups.

Few studies investigating relations between aging and work have been conducted in actual work situations. This is unfortunate because questions can be raised about the validity of simulations and about the generalizability of short-term laboratory studies to actual occupational environments.

Considerably more research has been conducted on abilities presumed to be relevant to work performance, such as cognitive, sensory, and motor abilities. However, most of that research has focused on the relations between age and abilities, and few investigators working within a gerontological perspective have attempted to link abilities to measures of occupational productivity or success in training. Research of this type has been reported within the fields of industrial-organizational psychology and personnel psychology, but because it is possible that the relations between ability predictors and criterion measures of job performance vary as a function of the age of the individual, additional research is needed to investigate determinants of work performance across the adult years.

Cognition

Cognition is a very active area of research within gerontology, and as much as 50 percent of the recent literature on psychological aging may be concerned with aspects of cognitive functioning. Because of the very large number of studies in this area, several different topics within the general realm of cognition will be discussed.

Much of the gerontological research on intelligence has been based on psychometric procedures, typically consisting of a battery of tests designed to assess distinct reasoning and numerical, spatial, and verbal abilities (Avolio &

Waldman, 1994; Schaie & Willis, 1993). Research of this type has clearly established a pattern of differential aging in which measures of knowledge or acquired information tend to be relatively preserved across the adult years, whereas measures of the efficiency of novel processing are generally found to decline with increased age. Although the pattern of distinct types of spared and impaired functioning seems well accepted, there is still little agreement regarding the reasons for the different types of age relations. Among the possibilities that have been proposed are that stable and declining abilities reflect different amounts of overlearning, different requirements for processing (e.g., access to previously stored information versus generation of new solutions), or functioning of different portions of the brain.

One topic concerned with psychometric intelligence that has been the focus of much research is the role of health status on the relations between age and cognitive functioning. At one time it was postulated that various types of disease-induced deterioration might be responsible for all of the negative relations observed between age and measures of cognitive functioning. That view is no longer widely accepted largely because of results indicating that age-related declines are found in measures of psychometric intelligence in samples of adults judged to be in excellent health (Salthouse, Kausler, & Saults, 1990). However, there is still considerable interest in how various diseases known to increase in prevalence with age affect cognitive functioning. In addition, several studies have investigated whether there is a precipitous decline in cognitive abilities immediately prior to death (i.e., the terminal drop phenomenon).

Another topic related to psychometric intelligence that has received considerable attention is whether certain kinds of activities facilitate the maintenance of cognitive functioning, and if so, what mechanisms are responsible for the preservation of abilities that would otherwise decline with increased age. Activities ranging from physical exercise, to membership in social clubs, to cognitively demanding hobbies such as solving anagrams or crossword puzzles have been investigated (Gold et al., 1995; Hawkins, Kramer, & Capaldi, 1992; Shay & Roth, 1992). Although many researchers probably believe that there is some validity to the "use it or lose it" hypothesis as applied to cognitive aging phenomena, convincing empirical support for this interpretation is still quite sparse (Salthouse, 1990).

Another topic that has been the focus of research within the general area of intelligence has to do with conceptions and perceptions of intelligence. To illustrate, Berg and Sternberg (1992) conducted a study examining what people think intelligence is and what perceptions they have about changes in their own level of intellectual functioning as they age. Baltes and colleagues have focused on wisdom as a prototypical form of cognition that is often believed to increase with age. In addition to trying to establish valid measures of the wisdom construct, these investigators have also attempted to establish that their measures of wisdom are not simply alternative indices of aspects of personality or of intelligence (Baltes, Staudinger, Maercker, & Smith, 1995; Staudinger, Smith, & Baltes, 1992).

Memory is almost certainly the topic within the field of aging and cognition that has been the focus of the greatest amount of empirical research. Recent studies have investigated memory for a wide variety of material, ranging from memory of unrelated words and prose, of various types of spatial information (Arbuckle, Cooney, Milne, & Melchior, 1994; Cherry & Park, 1993; Uttl & Graf, 1993), of eyewitness events (Adams-Price, 1992), of sources of information (Schacter, Osowiecki, Kaszniak, Kihlstrom, & Valdiserri, 1994), of performed activities (Kausler, Wiley, & Lieberwitz, 1992; Norris & West, 1993), and of actions to be performed in the future (Einstein, Holland, McDaniel, & Guynn, 1992; Maylor, 1993). One of the most popular topics at the current time concerns the distinction between traditional assessments of memory (based on explicit or direct tests) and memory revealed without explicit awareness or deliberate recollection (known as implicit or indirect memory). Because several studies have reported that age differences are much smaller when memory is assessed indirectly, it has been suggested that many of the memory problems of older adults may be in accessing or retrieving information and not in encoding or storing it (e.g., Howard & Howard, 1992; Park & Shaw, 1992; Schacter, Cooper, & Valdiserri, 1992; Wiggs, 1993).

A number of research projects have focused on interventions in the form of memory-training programs (e.g., Verhaegen, Marcoen, & Goosens, 1992). Several studies have been successful at increasing performance of adults of all ages in a variety of memory tasks, but it is not yet clear whether those effects persist over time and whether the magnitudes of the training gains vary as a function of age. This latter issue is important because only if the benefits of training are larger in older adults than in young adults would the experiential intervention reduce or eliminate age differences in memory. In other words, the disuse interpretation that age differences originate because of experiential deficits would not be supported unless the additional experience in the form of training had a greater impact on the older adults who are presumably disadvantaged by disuse. Nevertheless, training effects can still be of practical interest if they are effective in improving the memory functioning of older adults because the increased level of performance may allow the individual to function independently when he or she might not otherwise be able to do so.

Another important theoretical issue that remains unresolved is whether the rate of forgetting is faster with increased age (Giambra & Arenberg, 1993). A substantial amount of research seems to suggest that, at least under certain conditions, processes of encoding and retrieval are impaired with increased age. However, there are conflicting results with respect to whether information is lost more rapidly among older adults. Little or no differences seem to be evident with short intervals of up to several hours, but there are several reports of more rapid declines for older adults compared to young adults as the intervals between presentation and test increase to days or weeks.

Working memory is a form of memory that has attracted much interest in recent years because it is hypothesized to be central to many aspects of cognition. Working memory differs from earlier notions of short-term memory primarily because it explicitly incorporates aspects of processing as well as storage. Several reports of age differences in measures of working memory have been published, and working memory has been implicated in the age differences in several other cognitive tasks (Babcock, 1994; Gilinsky & Judd, 1994).

Metacognition refers to knowledge about one's own cognitive processes. Because metacognition involves monitoring the status of one's own cognitive system and selecting effective strategies, it has been postulated to be a potentially important factor in adult age differences in memory and other cognitive functions (Bieman-Copland & Charness, 1994). However, results have been mixed with respect to the existence of age differences in measures of metacognition. There are some reports of older adults performing at lower levels than young adults (e.g., in the selection of efficient strategies), but other reports of equivalent performance of young and old adults (e.g., in the accuracy of predicting one's subsequent level of memory performance). One type of research that has apparently not been conducted and yet should be informative is determination of the extent to which metacognitive factors contribute to adult age differences in cognitive performance. For example, if appropriate measures of metacognition could be obtained, then one could use statistical control procedures to determine if the age-related effects in the cognitive measures are reduced or eliminated when the metacognitive measures are controlled. This kind of research should be an important priority for metacognition investigators because research on the topic of metacognition is often justified by the suggestion that cognitive deficits may be caused by impaired metacognitive functioning, but no direct tests of the hypothesized causal relations have apparently been published.

Research on attention has also flourished in recent years, perhaps in part because of an assumption that fairly basic attentional processes may be fundamental to the age differences in other cognitive abilities. Selective attention refers to the focus on some aspects of the environment rather than others. It is often investigated with visual search tasks in which one has to determine whether a target is present in the visual field (Madden, Connelly, & Pierce, 1994; Rogers, 1992). Even after extensive practice, adults in their 60s and 70s have been found to be substantially less efficient than adults in their 20s at detecting targets in a visual display. Divided attention is most frequently investigated by requiring research participants to perform two or more tasks simultaneously (Crossley & Hiscock, 1992). Although there is some controversy regarding the most appropriate methods of assessing dual-task performance, a fairly consistent finding is that there is a decline with increased age in the ability to divide or share attention among several concurrent activities.

In the last several years there has been increased interest in the topic of inhibition or the suppression of the processing of irrelevant information (Kane, Hasher, Stoltzfus, Zacks, & Connelly, 1994; Kramer, Humphrey, Larish, Logan, & Strayer, 1994; McDowd & Filion, 1992; Sullivan & Faust, 1993). One reason for this interest is that a decrease in inhibitory capabilities has been postulated to contribute to age differences in selective attention and possibly also to differences in measures of higher order cognition.

Much of the research effort in attention has concentrated on identifying good (i.e., reliable and valid) measures of each hypothesized type of attention. What currently seems to be lacking, however, is evidence that common constructs are being assessed with measures derived from different paradigms. Valuable information relevant to the convergent and discriminant validity of attention constructs could be provided from a few large-scale studies in which correlations among the attention measures obtained from different paradigms were examined.

Perhaps inspired by a dissatisfaction with the apparent artificiality of laboratory methods, or possibly from a desire to examine more complex phenomena, a number of researchers have investigated age differences in new domains related to cognition. Some of this research has been classified as involving everyday cognition, but the basis for categorizing some types of cognition as everyday and others as something else has never been clearly articulated. Regardless of the labels, however, interesting research has been reported contrasting adults of different ages in learning and using routes in familiar and unfamiliar environments (Lipman & Caplan, 1992; Simon, Walsh, Regnier, & Krauss, 1992) and in assembling devices from procedural instructions (Morrell & Park, 1993). Even more complex behaviors that have been studied are medication adherence (Park, Morrell, Frieske, & Kincaid, 1992) and problem solving and comprehension in cancer treatment decisions (Meyer, Russo, & Talbot, 1995), although these particular behaviors are likely to be determined by personality and motivational factors at least as much as by cognitive abilities.

A growing amount of research has been concerned with specifying the causes of the age-related differences in cognitive functioning. Two broad types of mediators can be distinguished: distal and proximal. Distal mediators are those originating from a much earlier period in the individual's life, such as educational or early environment experiences. Proximal mediators are factors operating at the time of the assessment that contribute to the observed level of performance. The proximal mediators are obviously caused by more distal factors, but they may nonetheless be a meaningful level of analysis to help bridge the gap between distal determinants and current levels of performance (Salthouse, 1991).

One of the key theoretical issues in cognitive aging research at the current time concerns the nature of both distal and proximal mediators of age differences in cognition. Some researchers have proposed that the proximal mediators can be conceptualized in terms of processing resources, which are hypothetical entities that possess the properties of existing in limited quantitites and serving to enable or enhance cognitive performance. Several types of processing resources have been proposed, and various measures of those resource constructs have been subjected to investigation. To illustrate, metaphors based on space (working memory), energy (attentional capacity), and time (rate of processing) have been used in discussions of processing resource constructs. Although there is still little consensus regarding the precise nature of processing resources, there does appear to be some agreement about how processing resource hypotheses might be investigated. That is, first, valid (and reliable) measures of the processing resource should be identified. Second, evidence of negative relations between the measures and age but positive relations between the measures and other measures of cognitive functioning should be obtained. And third, it should be demonstrated that the relations between age and cognition are reduced when measures of the construct are statistically controlled (or experimentally equated). Some progress in this direction has been achieved with measures based on processing speed and working memory conceptualizations of processing resources (Babcock, 1994; Gilinsky & Judd, 1994; Salthouse, 1994).

Research concerned with linkages between brain functioning and cognitive functioning across the adult life span has also increased in the last decade. Within psychology most of the research has relied on behavioral measures presumed to reflect functioning in particular portions of the brain. For example, the left hemisphere has been hypothesized to be specialized for processing verbal information, and the right hemisphere has been hypothesized to be specialized for processing spatial information. Other regions of the brain are also sometimes thought to be specialized for particular functions, although the nature and extent of specialization are still controversial. To illustrate, the frontal lobes have sometimes been speculated to be involved in various planning, abstraction, attention, and inhibition functions, but questions have been raised about the validity of these speculations (Reitan & Wolfson, 1994).

Several studies have investigated age differences on measures postulated to reflect functioning in different regions of the brain (Cherry, Hellige, & McDowd, 1995; Parkin & Walter, 1992; Salthouse, 1995; Spencer & Raz, 1994). However, the typical finding has been that older adults perform at lower levels than younger adults in most of the measures, and thus it is not clear whether the results are consistent with localization of age-related cognitive impairments.

Relatively little research concerned with sensory abilities has been reported in psychological journals focused on aging. However, a recent article by Lindenberger and Baltes (1994) stimulated considerable interest by reporting that decreased sensory functioning might serve as a possible mediator of the relations between age and measures of cognitive or intellectual functioning. Somewhat similar findings have been reported by Anstey, Stankov, and Lord (1993), and thus the role of sensory factors on the relations between age and cognition needs to be explored more closely.

A number of studies have also appeared on adult age differences in aspects of motor behavior. Most of them have been concerned with learning, or production, of repetitive patterns (Bosman, 1993; Haaland, Harrington, & Grice, 1993; Harrington, & Haaland, 1992; Howard & Howard, 1992; Jagacinski, Greenberg, Liao, & Wang, 1993; Pratt, Chasteen, & Abrams, 1994), although detailed analyses of age differences in grasping and other fine hand movements have also been reported (Bennett & Castiello, 1995). In addition, several articles have been published describing age trends in athletic achievements, either in track and field competitions or in the ages of peak performance of professional baseball players (Schulz, Musa, Staszewski, & Siegler, 1994).

Personality

The overriding theme of much of the research on personality is the dynamic of stability versus change (Helson & Wink, 1992). Many aspects of personality, especially as assessed with self-report questionnaires, seem to remain stable across age. However, some changes have been reported, and they tend to be most evident with projective test and in-depth interview forms of assessment. An important issue in contemporary research in the area of aging and personality is how to explain the aspects that remain stable and the aspects that appear to change with age.

The self is another active area of gerontological research. The primary focus within this topic is on how one's conception of self changes as we age, particularly with respect to the dimensions or aspects of our lives that we emphasize or value (Ryff, Lee, Essex, & Schmutte, 1994). One of the reasons this research is potentially important is that one's self-conception has been hypothesized to be related to the individual's physical or mental health status (Heidrich & Ryff, 1993; Hooker & Kaus, 1994).

A number of concepts introduced by theorists of adult development have also inspired research in gerontology. For example, some research has been conducted on the midlife crisis, the period of turmoil postulated to be associated with the transition into middle adulthood. Among the issues that have been explored are the existence and prevalence of the midlife crisis and the determinants of crises when they occur. Studies have also focused on generativity during middle and late adulthood (McAdams, de St. Aubin, & Logan, 1993; Peterson & Klohnen, 1995), a theme mentioned in the writings of Eric Erikson.

Some personality research has examined possible age differences in attributional style and control beliefs (Brandtstadter & Rothermund, 1994; Nurmi, Pulliainen, & Salmela-Aro, 1992). One of the central questions in this area is how people explain the events that happen to them, and whether they attribute them to forces under their control or to factors over which they have little or no influence. Research on relations between aging and control beliefs is of interest because it has been hypothesized that there is a decrease in sense of personal control with increased age, and other research has revealed that an individual's sense of control is related his or her level of both physical and mental health.

A related topic that has received some research attention is life goals, and whether there are differences in what people want out of life at different periods in their lives (Rapkin & Fischer, 1992). Life satisfaction is another topic that has been investigated by gerontological researchers, with the primary question being whether the amount of enjoyment or satisfaction with life remains constant across the adult years, or whether it varies systematically as a function of the period in one's life.

Emotionality has also been the focus of a moderate amount of gerontological research. Issues that have been investigated within this area are whether emotions are more intensely experienced at different periods in adulthood, whether spouses in long-term relationships share similar patterns of emotional expression, and whether emotions have a greater role in one's personality or cognitive system during older adulthood than during young adulthood (Barefoot, Beckham, Haney, Siegler, & Lipkus, 1993; Blanchard-Fields, Jahnke, & Camp, 1995; Carstensen, 1992; Carstensen, Gottman, & Levenson, 1995; Carstensen & Turk-Charles, 1994; Lawton, Kleban, & Dean, 1993; Lawton, Kleban, Rajagopal, & Dean, 1992; Malatesta-Magai, Jonas, Shepard, & Culver, 1992). Some research has also examined stress and whether there are variations in the amount of stress expressed or in the factors affecting the level of stress at different periods in adulthood (Spiro, Schnurr, & Aldwin, 1994; Thompson, Norris, & Hanacek, 1993).

Social Relations

Social support refers to the network of people who serve as friends, advisers, and confidants (Levitt, Weber, & Guacci, 1993). As with the sense of personal control and with self-conceptions, the quality or extent of one's social support system has been found to be related to physical and mental health outcomes (Finch & Zautra, 1992). Furthermore, social support systems may increase in importance with age as one's spouse and close friends die and weaken the individual's social network.

Intergenerational relations are of interest because they deal with the interactions between adults of different ages, such as those between adult children and elderly parents. An emerging phenomenon that is of growing concern is the existence of older adults (e.g., 70-year-olds) caring for their elderly (e.g., 90-year-old) parents. More traditional roles, such as parenting and grandparenting, have also been investigated in an attempt to gain a better understanding of the social world of adults. One of the goals of research in this area is to determine whether there are different patterns of interpersonal relationships at various periods in adulthood, and if so, to identify the factors responsible for those differences.

Caregiver burden is another topic that has received considerable research attention (Bodnar & Kiecolt-Glaser, 1994; Cicirelli, 1993; Hooker, Monahan, Shifren, & Hutchinson, 1992; Pruchno & Kleban, 1993). Researchers are aware that the primary responsibility of caring for an elderly parent frequently falls heavily on daughters, but little is yet known about the specific coping mechanisms used to deal with this burden. Research has also attempted to identify what aspects of caregiving are most stressful and what kinds of interventions may be most effective in reducing the stress and anxiety of providing care to relatives whose physical and mental functioning is deteriorating.

Retirement

The phenomenon of retirement has increased in importance in recent years because, as people live longer, they are spending a much greater period in retirement than in the past. For example, in recent years in the United States, the age of retirement has been steadily decreasing, with many people retiring by the age of 60 or earlier. If this trend continues, it could mean that in the near future almost 30 years (i.e., from about age 55 to 85, which is the hypothesized average human life span) of one's life will be spent in retirement. To place this number in perspective, it should be noted that it is much longer than the number of years most people devote to education and is nearly as long as the amount of time many people currently spend in gainful employment.

One of the topics related to retirement that has been the focus of several research studies is the identification of predictors of the timing of, and satisfaction in, retirement (Floyd et al., 1992; Higginbottom, Barling, & Kelloway, 1993; Taylor & Shore, 1995)—that is, what factors (such as health, financial status, avocational interests, and job satisfaction) influence the decision of when to retire and what factors (including those mentioned above) determine the level of happiness during retirement.

Mental Health

What are the major mental health problems in later adulthood, and what can be done about them? Depression is almost certainly the most frequent psychopathology in later adulthood, but estimates of the exact prevalence vary greatly (Kessler, Foster, Webster, & House, 1992; La Rue, Swan, & Carmelli, 1995). Research in the area of late-life depression has been concerned with diagnosis of depression and with evaluation of the efficacy of alternative treatments for depression. One issue that has emerged from the research is the need to use different criteria in the diagnosis of depression among the elderly because some physical symptoms (e.g., insomnia and appetite fluctuations) seem to be associated with normal aging (Williamson & Schulz, 1992).

Alzheimer's disease is an extremely important issue to society because there is currently no cure, the disease is extremely debilitating and progressive, and the prevalence increases dramatically with age. In fact, some estimates are that as many as 47 percent of 85-year-olds may have Alzheimer's disease (Evans et al., 1989). Psychological research has focused on diagnosis with different types of measures; on the characterization or classification of subtypes and stages; and on personality, behavioral, and cognitive changes (O'Leary, Haley, & Paul, 1993; Siegler, Dawson, & Welsh, 1994; Strauss, Pasupathi, & Chatterjee, 1993; Teri et al., 1992).

Independent Living

What factors determine whether a person is capable of living independently? The ability to live independently and to make responsible decisions is sometimes referred to as competence, but how can this be assessed? Several scales have been developed to evaluate the degree to which an individual can perform activities of daily living, but there are still questions about the validity of most instruments used to assess competence.

When an individual is no longer capable of living independently, what happens when he or she is placed in an institution? Some research suggests that there is an increase in dependency, and it is important to determine whether this is induced by staff behaviors and environmental contingencies or whether it occurs spontaneously (Baltes, Neumann, & Zank, 1994; Baltes & Wahl, 1992).

Death and Dying

What processes occur in the last stages of life, and are there ways to minimize grief of both the individual and his or her family and friends during this period? Unfortunately, although the topic of bereavement has been the focus of some speculation, relatively little research has appeared in the psychological journals focused on gerontology.

Future Directions

Major Themes in the Field

In this section I will describe what I believe are the major questions confronting researchers in the psychology of aging. These themes are adapted from the framework introduced by Baltes and Willis (1977), who suggested that there were three goals of theories in adult development: description, explanation, and intervention.

The first goal can be characterized by the question of *what*, in the sense that the initial goal of research is to describe the relevant phenomena. That is, research is needed to describe the differences, or lack of differences, associated with increased age.

The second theme can be characterized by the question of *why*, in that the next goal of research should be to explain the patterns that have been observed. Most current efforts at explanation tend to treat age-related phenomena in isolation, but a shift toward broader perspectives may be occurring. That is, instead of attempting to account for age-related differences in single measures, more integrative explanations are beginning to focus on broader or higher level theoretical constructs and on the patterns of interrelations among several constructs.

The third them in research can be characterized by the question of *so what*. That is, at some point in the evolution of a field, the research must be concerned with application and intervention. If there are no ultimate or long-range consequences of the research, then that research may never have value or real meaning. The long-term benefits of the research should, therefore, always be considered if the work is ever to make a genuine contribution to society.

As in other areas of psychology, gerontological research consists of a mixture of descriptive, theoretical, and applied approaches. If one believes that the three research themes outlined above progress in stages, however, it is probably fair to characterize much of the research in gerontological psychology as intermediate between the descriptive (*what*) and the theoretical (*why*) stages. If this interpretation is accurate, important goals for the future should be the development and investigation of theoretical explanations for psychological aging phenomena, followed by attempts to evaluate theoretically based interventions.

Important Issues

As noted earlier, with the demographic shifts in society, the average age of the workforce is increasing. It is therefore desirable to determine if productivity decreases with increased age in certain jobs and, if so, to learn what can be done to minimize those declines. Research is also needed to learn how to capitalize on the skills and abilities that do not decline with age in order to maximize the effectiveness of the workforce of the future. Possible influences of work and the work environment on the individual will also be of growing importance if some people are spending longer periods of their lives working.

Causes of age-related cognitive declines need to be identified, both at the behavioral level—either in terms of distal (e.g., shifting patterns of activity) or proximal (e.g., reductions in processing resources) factors—and at the neurophysiological level. Some of the declines are relatively minor, but others can have major consequences for psychological well-being. For example, declines in memory that prevent a bridge player from playing at his or her former level of competitiveness could lead to a loss of self-esteem even if they do not jeopardize the individual's ability to live independently. Determination of why cognitive functioning declines with increased age in healthy normal people is also important to provide a better understanding of the causes of pathologies associated with aging.

Factors affecting the choice to retire and degree of satisfaction with retirement should also be important topics for future research. As more people spend greater periods in retirement, it is essential that a better understanding be developed of this phase of adulthood.

Early detection of Alzheimer's disease and other pathologies of later life is important because, when interventions are eventually developed, they are almost certainly going to be more effective if applied at the initial stages in the disease. Psychologists therefore have important roles in the development of sensitive diagnostic instruments, as well as in determining what can be done to ease the burden that falls on those responsible for caring for Alzheimer's patients.

Promising Methods, Designs, and Analyses

Longitudinal investigation will probably always be the optimal developmental research method because only by following the same individuals can the researcher investigate changes occurring within individuals. These changes could be caused by endogenous (maturational) or exogenous (experiential) factors, but in either case, they can be investigated most efficiently by means of longitudinal research. More reports of longitudinal research are beginning to appear

(Hultsch, Hertzog, Small, McDonald-Miszczak, & Dixon, 1992; Zelinski, Gilewski, & Schaie, 1993), but most of it is still relatively short term (i.e., two to seven years). Nevertheless, these studies are useful additions to the literature because many of the earlier longitudinal studies had very limited sets of variables and consequently provided a narrow assessment of the relevant constructs. Furthermore, at least some of the new studies will likely be continued to yield longer term longitudinal information.

Statistical analysis techniques should become more powerful in the future, with more use of correlation-based techniques and less exclusive reliance on *t* tests and analyses of variance designed to evaluate differences in mean level of performance. In addition, techniques should be employed that allow the magnitude of the observed effects to be considered and not just whether differences are statistically significant. Future research should also focus on theoretical constructs rather than on single observed variables and on the relations among constructs rather than simply on the constructs in isolation.

Meta-analyses will likely play a larger role in research in the future because they provide an objective means of integrating results across many independent studies. Several meta-analyses have been reported in recent years (Laver & Burke, 1993; La Voie & Light, 1994; Verhaeghen et al., 1992), but even more will likely be appearing in the future.

Finally, in the future more research in gerontological psychology will almost certainly involve a greater amount of multidisciplinary interaction to link constructs across neighboring disciplines, such as sociology and biology. One example of an exciting new boundary area is behavioral genetics, and several articles on genetic influences in late-life behavior have already appeared (Carmelli, Swan, & Cardon, 1995; Finkel & McGue, 1993). Another underinvestigated area that is likely to yield valuable information about social influences on aging is cross-cultural comparison of age-related phenomena.

Suggested Readings

Major journals in the field are *Psychology and Aging, Journal of Gerontology, Psychological Sciences, Experimental Aging Research*, and *Aging and Cognition*. Edited handbooks that provide a broad coverage of many areas are the *Handbook of the Psychology of Aging* (Birren & Schaie, 1990) and the *Handbook of Aging and Cognition* (Craik & Salthouse, 1992). Several excellent textbooks for undergraduate courses on this topic are those by Cavanaugh (1993), Schaie and Willis (1991), and Schulz and Ewen (1993).

References

Adams-Price, C. (1992). Eyewitness memory and aging: Predictors of accuracy in recall and person recognition. *Psychology and Aging, 7*, 602–608.

Anstey, K., Stankov, L., & Lord, S. (1993). Primary aging, secondary aging, and intelligence. *Psychology and Aging, 8,* 562–570.

Arbuckle, T. Y., Cooney, R., Milne, J., & Melchior, A. (1994). Memory for spatial layouts in relation to age and schema typicality. *Psychology and Aging, 9,* 467–480.

Avolio, B. J., & Waldman, D. A. (1994). Variations in cognitive, perceptual, and psychomotor abilities across the working life span: Examining the effects of race, sex, experience, education, and occupational type. *Psychology and Aging, 9,* 430–442.

Babcock, R. L. (1994). Analysis of adult age differences on the Raven's Advanced Progressive Matrices Test. *Psychology and Aging, 9,* 303–314.

Baltes, M. M., Neumann, E. M., & Zank, S. (1994). Maintenance and rehabilitation of independence in old age: An intervention program for staff. *Psychology and Aging, 9,* 179–188.

Baltes, M. M., & Wahl, H. W. (1992). The dependency-support script in institutions: Generalization to community settings. *Psychology and Aging, 7,* 409–418.

Baltes, P. B., Staudinger, U. M., Maercker, A., & Smith, J. (1995). People nominated as wise: A comparative study of wisdom-related knowledge. *Psychology and Aging, 10,* 155–166.

Baltes, P. B., & Willis, S. L. (1977). Toward psychological theories of aging and development. In J. E. Birren & K. W. Schaie (eds.), *Handbook of the psychology of aging* (2d ed.). New York: Van Nostrand Reinhold.

Barefoot, J. C., Beckham, J. C., Haney, T. L., Siegler, I. C., & Lipkus, I. M. (1993). Age differences in hostility among middle-aged and older adults. *Psychology and Aging, 8,* 3–9.

Bennett, K. M. B., & Castiello, U. (1995). Reorganization and prehension of components following perturbation of object size. *Psychology and Aging, 10,* 204–214.

Berg, C. A., & Sternberg, R. J. (1992). Adults' conceptions of intelligence across the adult life span. *Psychology and Aging, 7,* 221–231.

Bieman-Copland, S., & Charness, N. (1994). Memory knowledge and memory monitoring in adulthood. *Psychology and Aging, 9,* 287–302.

Birren, J. E., & Schaie, K. W. (1990). *The handbook of the psychology of aging* (3d ed.), San Diego: Academic Press.

Blanchard-Fields, F., Jahnke, H. C., & Camp, C. (1995). Age differences in problem solving style: The role of emotional salience. *Psychology and Aging, 10,* 173–180.

Bodnar, J. C., & Kiecolt-Glaser, J. K. (1994). Caregiver depression after bereavement: Chronic stress isn't over when it's over. *Psychology and Aging, 9,* 372–380.

Bosman, E. A. (1993). Age-related differences in the motoric aspects of transcription typing skill. *Psychology and Aging, 8,* 87–102.

Brandtstadter, J., & Rothermund, K. (1994). Self-percepts of control in middle and later adulthood: Buffering losses by rescaling goals. *Psychology and Aging, 9,* 265–273.

Carmelli, D., Swan, G. E., & Cardon, L. R. (1995). Genetic mediation in the relationship of education to cognitive function in older people. *Psychology and Aging, 10,* 48–53.

Carstensen, L. L. (1992). Social and emotional patterns in adulthood: Support for socioemotional selectivity theory. *Psychology and Aging, 7,* 331–338.

Carstensen, L. L., Gottman, J. M., & Levenson, R. W. (1995). Emotional behavior in long-term marriage. *Psychology and Aging, 10,* 140–149.

Carstensen, L. L., & Turk-Charles, S. (1994). The salience of emotion across the adult life span. *Psychology and Aging, 9,* 259–264.

Cavanaugh, J. (1993). *Adult development and aging.* Pacific Grove, Calif.: Brooks-Cole.

Cherry, B. J., Hellige, J. B., & McDowd, J. M. (1995). Age differences and similarities in patterns of cerebral hemispheric asymmetry. *Psychology and Aging, 10,* 191–203.

Cherry, K. E., & Park, D. C. (1993). Individual difference and contextual variables influence spatial memory in younger and older adults. *Psychology and Aging, 8,* 517–526.

Cicirelli, V. G. (1993). Attachment and obligation as daughter's motives for caregiving behavior and subsequent effect on subjective burden. *Psychology and Aging, 8,* 144–155.

Craik, F. I. M., & Salthouse, T. A. (1992). *Handbook of aging and cognition.* Hillsdale, N.J.: Lawrence Erlbaum.

Crossley, M., & Hiscock, M. (1992). Age-related differences in concurrent-task performance of normal adults: Evidence for a decline in processing resources. *Psychology and Aging, 7,* 499–506.

Czaja, S. J., & Sharit, J. (1993). Age differences in the performance of computer-based work. *Psychology and Aging, 8,* 59–67.

Einstein, G. O., Holland, L. J., McDaniel, M. A., & Guynn, M. J. (1992). Age-related deficits in prospective memory: The influence of task complexity. *Psychology and Aging, 7,* 471–478.

Evans, D. A., Funkenstein, H. H., Albert, M. S., Scherr, P. Q., Cook, N. R., Chown, M. J., Hebert, L. E., Hennekens, C. H., & Taylor, J. O. (1989). Prevalence of Alzheimer's disease in a community population of older persons: Higher than previously reported. *Journal of the American Medical Association, 262,* 2551–2556.

Finch, J. F., & Zautra, A. J. (1992). Testing latent longitudinal models of social ties and depression among the elderly: A comparison of distribution-free and maximum likelihood estimates with nonnormal data. *Psychology and Aging, 7,* 107–118.

Finkel, D., & McGue, M. (1993). The origins of individual differences in memory among the elderly: A behavior genetic analysis. *Psychology and Aging, 8,* 527–537.

Floyd, F. J., Haynes, S. N., Doll, E. R., Winemiller, D., Lemsky, C., Burgy, T. M., Werle, M., & Heilman, N. (1992). Assessing retirement satisfaction and perceptions of retirement experiences. *Psychology and Aging, 7,* 609–621.

Giambra, L. M., & Arenberg, D. (1993). Adult age differences in forgetting sentences. *Psychology and Aging, 8,* 451–462.

Gilinsky, A. S., & Judd, B. B. (1994). Working memory and bias in reasoning across the life span. *Psychology and Aging, 9,* 356–371.

Gold, D. P., Andres, D., Etezadi, J., Arbuckle, T., Schwartzman, A., & Chaikelson, J. (1995). Structural equation model of intellectual change and continuity and predictors of intelligence in older men. *Psychology and Aging, 10,* 294–303.

Haaland, K. Y., Harrington, D. L., & Grice, J. W. (1993). Effects of aging on planning and implementing arm movements. *Psychology and Aging, 8,* 617–632.

Harrington, D. L., & Haaland, K. Y. (1992). Skill learning in the elderly: Diminished implicit and explicit memory for a motor sequence. *Psychology and Aging, 7,* 425–434.

Hawkins, H. L., Kramer, A. F., & Capaldi, D. (1992). Aging, exercise, and attention. *Psychology and Aging, 7,* 643–653.

Heidrich, S. M., & Ryff, C. D. (1993). Physical and mental health in later life: The self-system as mediator. *Psychology and Aging, 8,* 327–338.

Helson, R., & Wink, P. (1992). Personality change in women from the early 40s to the early 50s. *Psychology and Aging, 7,* 46–55.

Higginbottom, S. F., Barling, J., & Kelloway, E. K. (1993). Linking retirement experiences and marital satisfaction: A mediational model. *Psychology and Aging, 8,* 508–516.

Hooker, K., & Kaus, C. R. (1994). Health-related possible selves in young and middle adulthood. *Psychology and Aging, 9,* 126–133.

Hooker, K., Monahan, D., Shifren, K., & Hutchinson, C. (1992). Mental and physical health of spouse caregivers: The role of personality. *Psychology and Aging, 7,* 367–375.

Howard, D. V., & Howard, J. H. (1992). Adult age differences in the rate of learning serial patterns: Evidence from direct and indirect tests. *Psychology and Aging, 7,* 232–241.

Hultsch, D. F., Hertzog, C., Small, B. J., McDonald-Miszczak, L., & Dixon, R. A. (1992). Short-term longitudinal change in cognitive performance in later life. *Psychology and Aging, 7,* 571–584.

Jagacinski, R. J., Greenberg, N., Liao, M. J., & Wang, J. (1993). Manual performance of a repeated pattern by older and younger adults with supplementary auditory cues. *Psychology and Aging, 8,* 429–439.

Kane, M. J., Hasher, L., Stoltzfus, E. R., Zacks, R. T., & Connelly, S. L. (1994). Inhibitory attentional mechanisms and aging. *Psychology and Aging, 9,* 103–112.

Kausler, D. H., Wiley, J. G., & Lieberwitz, K. J. (1992). Adult age differences in short-term memory and subsequent long-term memory for actions. *Psychology and Aging, 7,* 309–316.

Kessler, R. C., Foster, C., Webster, P. S., & House, J. S. (1992). The relationship between age and depressive symptoms in two national surveys. *Psychology and Aging, 7,* 119–126.

Kramer, A. F., Humphrey, D. G., Larish, J. F., Logan, G. D., & Strayer, D. L. (1994). Aging and inhibition: Beyond a unitary view of inhibitory processing in attention. *Psychology and Aging, 9,* 491–512.

La Rue, A., Swan, G. E., & Carmelli, D. (1995). Cognition and depression in a cohort of aging men: Results from the Western Collaborative Group Study. *Psychology and Aging, 10,* 30–33.

Laver, G. D., & Burke, D. M. (1993). Why do semantic priming effects increase in old age?: A meta-analysis. *Psychology and Aging, 8,* 34–43.

La Voie, D., & Light, L. L. (1994). Adult age differences in repetition priming: A meta-analysis. *Psychology and Aging, 9,* 539–553.

Lawton, M. P., Kleban, M. H., & Dean, J. (1993). Affect and age: Cross-sectional comparisons of structure and prevalence. *Psychology and Aging, 8,* 165–175.

Lawton, M. P., Kleban, M. H., Rajagopal, D., & Dean, J. (1992). Dimensions of affective experience in three age groups. *Psychology and Aging, 7,* 171–184.

Levitt, M. J., Weber, R. A., & Guacci, N. (1993). Convoys of social support: An intergenerational analysis. *Psychology and Aging, 8,* 323–326.

Lindenberger, U., & Baltes, P. B. (1994). Sensory functioning and intelligence in old age: A strong connection. *Psychology and Aging, 9,* 339–355.

Lipman, P. D., & Caplan, L. J. (1992). Adult age differences in memory for routes: Effects of instruction and spatial diagram. *Psychology and Aging, 7,* 435–442.

Madden, D. J., Connelly, S. L., & Pierce, T. W. (1994). Adult age differences in shifting focused attention. *Psychology and Aging, 9,* 528–538.

Malatesta-Magai, C., Jonas, R., Shepard, B., & Culver, L. C. (1992). Type A behavior pattern and emotion expression in younger and older adults. *Psychology and Aging, 7,* 551–561.

Maylor, E. A. (1993). Aging and forgetting in prospective and retrospective memory tasks. *Psychology and Aging, 8*, 420–428.

McAdams, D. P., de St. Aubin, E., & Logan, R. L. (1993). Generativity among young, midlife, and older adults. *Psychology and Aging, 8*, 221–230.

McDowd, J. M., & Filion, D. L. (1992). Aging, selective attention, and inhibitory processes: A psychophysiological approach. *Psychology and Aging, 7*, 65–71.

Meyer, B. J. F., Russo, C., & Talbot, A. (1995). Discourse comprehension and problem solving: Decisions about the treatment of breast cancer by women across the life span. *Psychology and Aging, 10*, 84–103.

Morrell, R. W., & Park, D. C. (1993). The effects of age, illustrations, and task variables on the performance of procedural assembly tasks. *Psychology and Aging, 8*, 389–399.

Norris, M. P., & West, R. L. (1993). Activity memory and aging: The role of motor retrieval and strategic processing. *Psychology and Aging, 8*, 81–86.

Nurmi, J. E., Pulliainen, H., & Salmela-Aro, K. (1992). Age differences in adults' control beliefs related to life goals and concerns. *Psychology and Aging, 7*, 194–196.

O'Leary, P. A., Haley, W. E., & Paul, P. B. (1993). Behavioral assessment in Alzheimer's disease: Use of a 24-hr. log. *Psychology and Aging, 8*, 139–143.

Park, D. C., Morrell, R. W., Frieske, D., & Kincaid, D. (1992). Medication adherence behaviors in older adults: Effects of external cognitive supports. *Psychology and Aging, 7*, 252–256.

Park, D. C., & Shaw, R. J. (1992). Effects of environmental support on implicit and explicit memory in younger and older adults. *Psychology and Aging, 7*, 632–642.

Parkin, A. J., & Walter, B. M. (1992). Recollective experience, normal aging, and frontal dysfunction. *Psychology and Aging, 7*, 290–298.

Peterson, B. E., & Klohnen, E. C. (1995). Realization of generativity in two samples of women at midlife. *Psychology and Aging, 10*, 20–29.

Pratt, J., Chasteen, A. L., & Abrams, R. A. (1994). Rapid aimed limb movements: Age differences and practice effects in component submovements. *Psychology and Aging, 9*, 325–334.

Pruchno, R., & Kleban, M. H. (1993). Caring for an institutionalized parent: The role of coping strategies. *Psychology and Aging, 8*, 18–25.

Rapkin, B. D., & Fischer, K. (1992). Personal goals of older adults: Issues in assessment and prediction. *Psychology and Aging, 7*, 127–137.

Reitan, R. M., & Wolfson, D. (1994). A selective and critical review of neuropsychological deficits and the frontal lobe. *Neuropsychology Review, 4*, 161–198.

Rogers, W. A. (1992). Age differences in visual search: Target and distractor learning. *Psychology and Aging, 7*, 526–535.

Ryff, C. D., Lee, Y. H., Essex, M. J., & Schmutte, P. S. (1994). My children and me: Midlife evaluations of grown children and of self. *Psychology and Aging, 9*, 195–205.

Salthouse, T. A. (1990). Influence of experience on age differences in cognitive functioning. *Human Factors, 32*, 551–569.

Salthouse, T. A. (1991). *Theoretical Perspectives on Cognitive Aging*. Hillsdale, N.J.: Lawrence Erlbaum.

Salthouse, T. A. (1994). The nature of the influence of speed on adult age differences in cognition. *Developmental Psychology, 30*, 240–259.

Salthouse, T. A. (1995). Differential age-related influences on memory for verbal-symbolic information and visual-spatial information. *Journal of Gerontology: Psychological Sciences, 50B*, P193–P201.

Salthouse, T. A., Kausler, D. H., & Saults, J. S. (1990). Age, self-assessed health status, and cognition. *Journal of Gerontology: Psychological Sciences, 45,* 156–160.

Schacter, D. L., Cooper, L. A., & Valdiserri, M. (1992). Implicit and explicit memory for novel visual objects in older and younger adults. *Psychology and Aging, 7,* 299–308.

Schacter, D. L., Osowiecki, D., Kaszniak, A. W., Kihlstrom, J. F., & Valdiserri, M. (1994). Source memory: Extending the boundaries of age-related deficits. *Psychology and Aging, 9,* 81–89.

Schaie, K. W., & Willis, S. L. (1991). *Adult development and aging.* New York: HarperCollins.

Schaie, K. W., & Willis, S. L. (1993). Age difference patterns of psychometric intelligence in adulthood: Generalizability within and across ability domains. *Psychology and Aging, 8,* 44–55.

Schulz, R., & Ewen, R. B. (1993). *Adult development and aging.* New York: Macmillan.

Schulz, R., Musa, D., Staszewski, J., & Siegler, R. S. (1994). The relationship between age and major league baseball performance: Implications for development. *Psychology and Aging, 9,* 274–286.

Shay, K. A., & Roth, D. L. (1992). Association between aerobic fitness and visuospatial performance in healthy older adults. *Psychology and Aging, 7,* 15–24.

Siegler, I. C., Dawson, D. V., & Welsh, K. A. (1994). Caregiver ratings of personality change in Alzheimer's disease patients: A replication. *Psychology and Aging, 9,* 464–466.

Simon, S. L., Walsh, D. A., Regnier, V. A., & Krauss, I. K. (1992). Spatial cognition and neighborhood use: The relationship in older adults. *Psychology and Aging, 7,* 389–394.

Spencer, W. D., & Raz, N. (1994). Memory for facts, source, and context: Can frontal lobe dysfunction explain age-related differences? *Psychology and Aging, 9,* 149–159.

Spiro, A., Schnurr, P. P., & Aldwin, C. M. (1994). Combat-related posttraumatic stress disorder symptoms in older men. *Psychology and Aging, 9,* 17–26.

Staudinger, U. M., Smith, J., & Baltes, P. B. (1992). Wisdom-related knowledge in a life review task: Age differences and the role of professional specialization. *Psychology and Aging, 7,* 271–281.

Strauss, M. E., Pasupathi, M., & Chatterjee, A. (1993). Concordance between observers in descriptions of personality change in Alzheimer's disease. *Psychology and Aging, 9,* 475–480.

Streufert, S., Pogash, R., Piasecki, M., & Post, G. M. (1990). Age and management team performance. *Psychology and Aging, 5,* 551–559.

Sullivan, M. P., & Faust, M. E. (1993). Evidence for identity inhibition during selective attention in old adults. *Psychology and Aging, 8,* 589–598.

Taylor, M. A., & Shore, L. M. (1995). Predictors of planned retirement age: An application of Beehr's model. *Psychology and Aging, 10,* 76–85.

Teri, L., Truax, P., Logsdon, R., Uomoto, J., Zarit, S., & Vitaliano, P. P. (1992). Assessment of behavioral problems in dementia: The revised memory and behavior problems checklist. *Psychology and Aging, 7,* 622–631.

Thompson, M. G., Heller, K., & Rody, C. A. (1994). Recruitment challenges in studying late-life depression: Do community samples adequately represent depressed older adults? *Psychology and Aging, 9,* 121–125.

Thompson, M. G., Norris, F. H., & Hanacek, B. (1993). Age differences in the psychological consequences of Hurricane Hugo. *Psychology and Aging, 8,* 606–616.

Uttl, B., & Graf, P. (1993). Episodic spatial memory in adulthood. *Psychology and Aging*, 8, 257–273.

Vecchio, R. P. (1993). The impact of differences in subordinate and supervisor age on attitudes and performance. *Psychology and Aging*, 8, 112–119.

Verhaeghen, P., Marcoen, A., & Goosens, L. (1992). Improving memory performance in the aged through mnemonic training: A meta-analytic study. *Psychology and Aging*, 7, 242–251.

Warr, P. (1992). Age and occupational well-being. *Psychology and Aging*, 7, 37–45.

Wiggs, C. L. (1993). Aging and memory for frequency of occurrence of novel, visual stimuli: Direct and indirect measures. *Psychology and Aging*, 8, 400–410.

Williamson, G. M., & Schulz, R. (1992). Physical illness and symptoms of depression among elderly outpatients. *Psychology and Aging*, 7, 343–351.

Zelinski, E. M., Gilewski, M. J., & Schaie, K. W. (1993). Individual differences in cross-sectional and 3-year longitudinal memory performance across the adult life span. *Psychology and Aging*, 8, 176–186.

12

A Life-Span Approach to the Study of Psychogerontology in Russia

Vera A. Kol'tsova, Natasha B. Meshalkina,
& Yury N. Olegnik

A common theme in psychogerontology is that it is necessary to review salient events in the life history of an older person as a means of understanding that individual in his or her old age. So, too, we begin our analysis of the field of psychogerontology in contemporary Russia by taking a longitudinal look at its past. The use of a life-span approach to psychogerontology, as a field of study, illustrates both the philosophy and the methods used by developmental psychologists who specialize in aging.

Russian scientific literature on old age shows that 19th-century interest in the psychological aspects of aging was widely dispersed among several disciplines, with numerous publications in the fields of philosophy, biology, and medicine all appearing within this 100-year span. Psychogerontology developed from the interdisciplinary intersection of these traditional areas of study. Modern psychogerontology, which is now an independent branch of knowledge, still shows the influence of its multidisciplinary origins.

One of the earliest Russian texts on psychogerontology was written by Kalinichenko (1839). It was a published set of lectures on the influence of old age on mental abilities and morals that Kalinichenko delivered in Kharkov, a major city in Ukraine. In these lectures, he discussed age-related changes in physical and psychological functioning, including the loss of physical strength, the "fading" or reduction in the intensity of feelings (and emotions), the gradual decay of memory, and a reduction in the richness of imagination. Kalinichenko concluded that the negative effects of aging are primarily physical, and it is those psychological functions that are most reliant on physical functioning that show the greatest effects of aging. By contrast, he believed that the higher psychic functions become increasingly strong and more energetic with age. The author insisted that the aging "psyche" gained greater independence from the passions and emotional attachments that consume younger adults. As libido diminishes, older adults are released from the "problems" of everyday vanities. With the approach of eternity, older adults become more phlegmatic and indifferent to many of the less significant issues in life. Changes of this sort give the appearance of wisdom because younger adults interpret the independence from everyday vanities as an indication that their elders have become wiser. In other words, the attribution of wisdom to older adults is based on their disengagement from life's more trivial matters, an attitude that is perceived by younger adults as the manifestation of wisdom. In old age, "the higher qualities of psyche stand more visibly, more overwhelmingly, and more strongly" (Kalinchenko, 1839, p. 18).

A decade later, Vetrinsky (1848) combined philosophical and psychological perspectives in his treatise on old age. According to Vetrinsky, the psychological changes that occur as individuals approach their own death are related to unhappiness and loss and not to the more neutral "disengagement" from life that Kalinchenko hypothesized. Vetrinsky enumerated the reasons why aging is associated with unhappiness: the elderly can no longer engage in many activities that they had found pleasurable in their younger years; they must adapt to their increasingly weaker bodies; many sensory pleasures are diminished; and finally, the rapid approach of death is often feared. Vetrinsky also pointed out that despite the limitations imposed by an aging body, it is not an entirely negative stage in the life span. The elderly are often capable of providing insightful advice based on their many years of experience. Older adults often seem better able to show patience, a trait that seemed to Vetrinsky to improve with advancing age. Older adults can often achieve a level of respect that was denied to them when they were younger; it is a time when they reflect upon past kindnesses and good deeds that they had exhibited at younger ages, a pastime that can bring much pleasure in one's older years. Thus, old age is a time for reflection and review of one's life.

The work of these Russian pioneers in psychogerontology is notable for several reasons. It is coincident with the birth of psychology from its more traditional parent fields of philosophy and biology, and both traditions can be found in these early works. Both Kalinchenko and Vitrinsky exemplify the most advanced thinking of the second half of the 19th century, when empirical science made its most rapid advance in Russia and other parts of the world.

Another related theme that emerged near the end of the 19th century was reflections on longevity. Tarkhanov (1891) wrote one of the earliest psychological articles on this topic, which he titled "The Longevity of Animals, Plants, and People." He reasoned that death naturally occurred because the cells of the body are limited in their ability to repair and reproduce. His work in the biology of old age emphasized the biology of cell differentiation. In a surprisingly contemporary approach to questions about life span, Tarkhanov analyzed the statistical data on longevity that were available at that time. Specifically, he computed correlations between longevity and selected aspects of the geographical environment, marital status, and other social variables. The author added a self-description of the aging process to his statistical analysis. Here is a translation of his personal account of growing old:

> At the very beginning, the coming of old age treads so slowly that the individual hardly knows it, hardly realizes that it is approaching. He is still brisk and cheerful; he is still energetic enough to go on with his normal lifestyle. Nevertheless, the most observable signs of the weakening process become visible as the changes in organic tissue reveal themselves. Feelings of strength and health do not disappear suddenly, but fade and weaken gradually. As the internal organs change, external signs of aging also begin to appear. (Tarkhanov, 1891, pp. 493–494)

Tarkhanov was specific in the ways in which he chronicled the weakening of his body. His emphasis on perceptual and cognitive changes also mirrors contemporary research. Before the start of the 20th century, Tarkhanov observed that sight and hearing became diminished with increasing age, with the result that all of perception was reduced. Intellectual abilities waned, muscles no longer responded to will, and movement, once initiated, became inaccurate and unsteady. Not surprisingly, the older adult prefers to remain immobile with longer periods during which the body is at rest. The aging of the central nervous system assumes primary importance. Tarkhanov reflected that deficits are first found in the "nervous nodes" of the brain, beginning in the frontal gyrus, then moving to the base of the brain. He believed that the first portions of the brain to atrophy were the most recently developed structures—first the frontal lobes, then structures within each hemisphere, and finally in the spinal cord. Brain changes were responsible for the numerous problems in body functioning that develop in old age, such as the losses in voluntary movements, thinking, and emotions.

Thus, Tarkhanov was among the first scientists to investigate the relationship between mind and body and the interaction of heredity and environment. He introduced a set of principles that provided the theoretical underpinnings for longevity and early death.

1. Any organ or entire organism that functions in an exaggerated manner (i.e., a notion that is close to the idea of working overtime) degenerates most quickly and loses its ability to continue normal functioning.
2. Organs and organisms can also degenerate quickly if they are seldom used for their intended functions. Thus, both overuse and underuse are associated with early loss of function.
3. Change in the extent to which an organ or organism is used is an important component of "normal" life. Periods of work and rest are needed to maintain healthy functioning. In order to maintain a physically healthy body, it is important to change the degree to which any organ is used.

4. Because the physical body weakens in old age, mental aspects of one's health need to be maintained to compensate for physical losses. Physical and mental health are equally important.

5. It is important to avoid aggravation in old age.

From these five points, he elaborated a program for human longevity that contained prescriptions for physiological, hygienic, and psychological factors. It is easy to see how these factors would be applied to a plan for long life.

Into the 20th Century

Psychophysiological laboratories were established in Russia at the end of the 19th century. The earliest experiments were conducted in clinics that served the older population and in laboratories in theoretical biology. Alelekov (1892) experimentally analyzed a variety of physiological processes, including the electrical excitability of nerves and muscles; muscle strength; reflexive responsivity; visual, auditory, olfactory, and haptic acuity; and peculiarities of old people in the areas of memory, articulation, walking, handwriting, and speech defects. Again we find a surprisingly contemporary analysis in that he differentiated visual and auditory memory from memory for names, figures, and behavioral incidents. Alelekov concluded that the most differentiated and complex aspects of psychological functioning were the ones that weakened first as individuals age, a conclusion that suggests that he was familiar with the work of his predecessors in this area.

Sergei Botkin (1832–1889) was the founder of the Russian School of Clinical Medicine. He has been honored for his outstanding contributions by having a well-respected hospital in Moscow named for him. Also, a type of viral hepatitis is named for him. Thus, his name and reputation are well known in modern Russia, almost 100 years later. Botkin took advantage of his unique and prestigious position to conduct an intensive investigation of older adults. As the trustee of the St. Petersburg Almshouse, he had a ready supply of needy subjects. After his death, a special commission was established to present his findings on the elderly to the scientific community. Of particular note was his work in the area of hearing loss in the elderly, which was the subject of a dissertation that was completed by a student who continued with Botkin's work after Botkin died (Bogdanov-Berezovsky, 1894).

A somewhat more philosophical and inner-directed approach was taken by Ivan Sikorsky (1842–1919), a professor of psychology at Kiev University and the founder of pedogogical psychology in Russia . Sikorsky (1901) provided a psychological description of old age: "The old man's psyche is different from the psyche of those younger" (p. 15). Readers may be surprised to learn that in this case, "different" was used to indicate an improvement. According to Sikorsky, the psyche is at its zenith in old age; no other age can compare to old age in terms of benefits from life experience and having the highest moral standards. The old man finds his psyche freed and cleansed of personal interests and expectations. In the course of living, experiences with loss, misery, and disappointment provide a type of liberation from the mundane: "Old age stays just in itself; it is outside our usual interests" (Sikorsky, 1901, p. 18).

Russian Psychogerontology Comes of Age

The genesis of the field of psychogerontology can be traced to the period of rapid growth in the knowledge base of related fields—general biology, physiology, and hygiene. At the start of the 20th century, both the theories of dying and aging and the practice of rejuvenation (engaging in activities that supposedly would reverse the aging process) emerged as strong areas of interest. Most of the theories of aging began in the natural sciences. The Russian biologist Ilya I. Mechnikov (1908, 1913) was a prominent figure in this area. The first Russian to be awarded a Nobel Prize (1908), Mechnikov is known for his work in the fields of microbiology, virusology, comparative pathology, and embryology. He proposed a theory of immune system functioning, a topic of great interest to contemporary psychogerontologists. His work was known throughout Europe through his connections with the Pasteur Institute in Paris.

He proposed a theory of aging known as *orthobiosis*, which pertained to the entire life cycle. Normal human development is taken as the ideal life pattern, one that results in a long and active life into old age, until one feels satiated with life. A dominant theme in Mechnikov's work is the struggle against premature aging. He believed that premature aging could by prevented by returning to "natural harmonies." One way of achieving natural harmony was to remain free of diseases that caused early signs of aging. The other goal was to make old age a productive, creative, and active time of life. According to orthobiosis, it was possible to double one's life span by selecting the correct life experiences, which consisted of a carefully prescribed system of social, hygienic, food-taking, and financial rules (Mechnikov, 1913; Shmidt, 1920).

Mechnikov (1908) proposed the phagocytic theory to explain the reasons for aging. The body and mind atrophy in old age because of the fight between phagocytes (these are produced in connective tissues and emerge after auto-intoxication) and the "noble" kinds of tissue—nerves and muscle tissues. To conquer the aging process, Mechnikov wrote, is to heighten the abilities of noble tissues to defend themselves against the aggressive phagocytes. Mechnikov proposed a special counterphagocytic serum to assist in the defense of the noble tissues.

Modern readers may scoff at these theories, but Mechnikov was among the first Russians to use the most advanced principles of science available at the time to understand the process of aging. His conceptions of old age were based on evolutionary theory. The cellular-level conceptualization of aging proposed by Mechnikov remained popular long after his death, and it was further developed and refined for many years by his disciples. For example, Shmidt (1915, 1923) described the psychological attributes of old age using the framework proposed by Mechnikov. He considered it a great pity that the human psychic development was so slow that the height of human intellect is not achieved until the beginning of old age. Psychic and nervous disorders, memory loss, and other detrimental attributes of old age are caused by phagocytes in the brain. In complete agreement with Mechnikov, Shmidt, a student of Mechnikov's, wrote that "when tissues become defective and the cells are destroyed, the instinct for death begins—that is, instinctive weariness of life and the desire for calm and rest" (Shmidt, 1920, p. 141).

The work of Sechenov and Pavlov, two Russian psychologists who are well known in the Western scientific literature, served as the basis for another carefully developed theory of aging. Vvedensky, a student of Sechenov's, applied basic notions of nervous activity to the field of aging. These applications served as the basis for the distinctly Russian activity theory, a highly influential theory in Soviet psychology. Vvedensky differentiated two determinants of behavior: one was self-determined, the other was determined by the external environment. In order to work productively, one needs to maintain an effective balance between work and rest so that work can be productive and the individual can conserve the ability to engage in high-level intellectual activities through very old age.

A common theme in the psychology of aging is the notion that the body wears out over time. Disease, loss, stress, starvation, pain, and similar experiences cause premature aging (Belousov, 1923). Of particular concern were the psychological consequences of diseases. According to Soviet psychologists in the 1920s and 1930s, every disease leads to the inhibition of the nervous system, which results in nervousness, poor spirits, moodiness, irritation, and grumbling—in short, the personality characteristics of old men. Over time, the moods of aging men change from grumpiness to sadness and grief. The cognitive deficits of old age are caused by a slowed metabolism, which results in insufficient nutrition of the nervous cells in the cerebral cortex. The elderly show reduced fluency in their ability to think and have poorer imaginations than when they were younger. The internal and external environments seem to change in old age. Nature seems to lose its "blossoming" and is perceived to be as senile and decrepit as the old man himself. The more attention the elderly pay to their internal universe, the harsher and sadder their moods become (Belousov, 1923).

Another theme from the 1920s that has a surprisingly modern appeal is the centrality of hormones as a purported cause of aging (Zavadovsky, 1923, 1924). In the morphogenetic approach to investigations of old age, Zavadovsky combined Mechnikov's phagocyte theory of aging with a hormone theory of aging. He considered aging as a natural development directed by the glands and the hormones they secreted, the battles between the noble tissues of the body and the phagocytes, and the interaction of these two dynamic processes within the body.

The practice of rejuvenation emerged and flourished in the short period of the New Economic Policy (NEP) (see chapter 5, "Russian Advertising in Search of Psychology," for a brief description of this policy that took place shortly after the Communist revolution of 1917). A variety of different conceptualizations served as a basis of this practice. The rejuvenation practice is satirized in the short novel *Dog's Heart*, written by the famous Russian writer Mikhail Bulgakov. Bulgakov began his career as a physician, and this training provided him with the competence to write about medical issues. The author was highly talented in many different areas, as seen in his immensely popular masterpiece *The Master and Margarita*, a story in which the main characters include Pontius Pilate and the Savior. In *Dog's Heart*, the writer creates a scenario involving the hypothetical practice of surgery rejuvenation via organ transplantations. In typical Bulgakov fashion, he goes beyond the merely fantastical and writes about reviving the dead via transplantations and the social problems that arise after that sort of surgery. As is frequently the case, the popular literature of the period provides insights into the most advanced thinking of the time. The novel is satirical and mimicking. It mocks the theories and practices aimed at regaining youth in old age and life after death.

Bogomoletz (1927, 1938) criticized both the eugenic conceptions in science and the rejuvenation practices that were popular earlier in the 20th century. He saw little support for the idea that old organisms could be rejuvenated in their old age. He believed that the aging process should be regulated throughout the entire life span. "The main principle of the rational regulation of one's life is the regulation of work. The entire organism must work. The rest periods should forestall fatigue; rest periods should be the prophylaxis and not cure" (Bogomoletz, 1938, p. 91). Based on his research in the area known as mental hygiene, Bogomoletz criticized the idea of regaining youth in old age. A poor balance in the way one schedules work and rest periods and the psychic cost of never-ending "tiny aggravations" of day-to-day living cause a nervous breakdown, a process that results when nervous cells lose their ability for chemical regeneration and the organism prematurely wastes away (Bogomoletz, 1938). Three systems regulate the speed at which individuals age: physical aspects of the body, social environmental stimuli, and the individual's psychological makeup. It should be noted that the social environment was the main cause in virtually all theories of human behavior that were proposed during the Soviet period. Explanations of behavior that were grounded in the theory of evolution were permissible before the Revolution of 1917 but fell into disfavor after 1917. Social-environmental theories were the basis of almost all of the work in gerontology in the Communist period after the revolution.

In 1929, Rybnikov proposed that old age research should be organized as a special branch of science with the unified research objective of understanding age-related functioning. Based on his background as a psychologist, Rybnikov (1929) advocated that old age research should take into account the accumulated knowledge about all the influences on the elderly that had occurred during their younger years. As a model of this new field of human development, Rybnikov introduced pedology as its own scientific area concerned with the health, growth, education, and psychological well-being of children. Pedology became a popular area of research that attracted the most gifted experts in education, defectology, and psychology in the 1920s and 1930s. Unfortunately, the model of developmental inquiry Rybnikov proposed (i.e., pedology) had a short and unhappy life as a scientific field: a dozen years after his proposal, Communist Party officials declared that pedology was hostile to proletarian needs, incorrect, and harmful. As might have been expected, official sanctions against the field of pedology foretold the fate of its sister field, gerontology. Rybnikov had planned to give initial priority to pedology, with the work in old age based on the knowledge obtained by pedologists. He had hoped that the field of human development would develop in the same sequence as individuals, with studies of childhood preceding studies of old age. When pedology met with an early death, plans to study old age were abandoned.

In the 1930s, the Institute for Medical Labor Examination, which was responsible for establishing norms for working capacity and working ability, disability, aptitude for special professions, and early retirement (owing to especially hard or harmful kinds of work, etc.), conducted research on the working abilities of the elderly. The director of the institute, Grigoriev, stated the problem this way: the characteristics of older individuals who maintain their ability to work was to be investigated. The experimental group included workers (metal craftsmen and turners) over 60 years of age. The control group included workers of the same professions who were 30 to 40 years old. Various dependent measures were collected via interviews, observations at workplaces and at home, clinical examinations, studies of their working habits, and personal knowledge of the subjects. The results of this research program were published in a collected volume *Starost' i trudosposobnost* (1937). Working capabilities turned out to be a complex multidimensional construct with social, physiological, and psychological factors and with compensatory mechanisms that allowed the workers to overcome the debilitating effects of age. For example, memory impairments might be compensated by the automaticity gained by professionals and by effective ways to reduce the need for physical strength on their job.

The First Conference on Psychogerontology

Pre–World War II development of gerontology was summarized at the conference on human longevity held in the Soviet Union in 1938 (the first scientific conference on gerontology ever held in the world) and in the review monograph by Nagorny (1940), which was published at Kharkov, Ukraine. Nagorny analyzed the leading theories of aging: loss of life energy, chemical and colloid chemistry theories, theories based on the idea that organs wear out over time, insufficient somatic cells theories, autointoxication theories, disharmony theories, differentiation and specialization theories, irregulation theories, internal contradictions theories, and others. It presents an overview of the theory and research in gerontology popular just prior to World War II.

After the war, the gerontologists organized in an attempt to create a united field of scientific and applied inquiry. In 1957, a professional section on gerontology was registered at the Moscow Naturalistic Society (a noninstitutionalized society that allowed some nonstandard research areas to gain a semiofficial status). Finally, in 1960, gerontology obtained official status: the Institute of Gerontology and Experimental Pathology was organized at Kiev, Ukraine. Two years later, the Moscow office subdivision of this institute was organized. Because of this official recognition, problems of old age gained greater visibility and importance at medical institutes, centers for the disabled, and psychological institutions (Kiev, Moscow, Leningrad, Kharkov, and others). The period of the 1950s through the 1960s saw the institutionalization of old age as an official research field.

Gerontology quickly became differentiated into numerous subfields. Gerontologists created the social sciences branch of gerontological research (Alexandrova, 1965, 1974), and the specialized psychogerontological field was installed "as a special branch of old age and longevity research" (Alexandrova, 1965, p. 11). The aims of this branch were the study of the influences of psychological factors on the general aging processes. Thus, the 1960s was a decade of active psychogerontology research. The acceptance of psychogerontology and its rapid growth was due to the general demographic trend in the USSR: a substantial portion of the population was growing older. In addition, the historical periods during the rule of Nikita Khrushchev and the early years of Leonid Brezhnev were notable for governmental support of programs for the elderly and, at the same time, for extending the age limit for retirement. These are likely reasons for providing financial support to the researchers in psychogerontology.

Experimental research with the elderly covered a broad range of interests. Specifically, studies of visual perception were conducted by Alexandrova (1961, 1963) and Makarov (1952); Grekov (1964) investigated the verbal associations of older people (70 to 90 years old); conditioned reflexes in old age were investigated by Bzhalava (1963) and Molotkova (1960). It is interesting to note that they concluded that old age leads mainly to defects in inhibition, a topic that is currently being debated in Western research with the elderly. Psychoneurological syndromes of old age were characterized by Rudzit (1963). As can be seen from this list, a wide variety of interests in gerontology were addressed.

An influential and popular theory of aging was proposed by Boris G. Ananiev (1957, 1965), the leader of the Leningrad School of Psychology. He believed that the human ontogenesis included all of the known phases and periods of development. According to Ananiev, these phases and periods are interconnected and determine the individual aging process. He also supported a genetic approach to gerontological problems. Ananiev used his (and his co-workers') research results to formulate the idea of ontogenetic geterochronity, a theory that allowed him to create a typology of aging. The typology differed as a function of gender, nervous system activity, and neuroregulation processes (Ananiev, 1965). Aging was divided into two types: divergent and convergent. This differentiation was supported by Alexandrova's (1974) analysis of age and creativity that used for their data the biographies of prominent European painters, sculptors, writers, musicians, lawyers, and other accomplished people. For all of the creative individuals, the divergent type of aging was characteristic of the way they achieved their accomplishments. It was concluded that divergent aging, in which the hemispheres of the brain were highly interconnected, provides energetic resources to the entire organism. This sort of brain organization was believed to be a beneficial arrangement for the preservation of the intellect.

A Reversal of Government Support

In the 1960s, the field of psychogerontology was rapidly expanding. It was a time of financial support from the government and high demand from society, in general. Theoretical platforms were formulated; original research ideas were experimentally tested; and effective and creative leaders emerged. The institutions and research groups were hard working. But by the end of the 1970s, this favorable situation changed. The main reason for the change was the sociopolitical situation unfolding in the Soviet Union. At the end of 1970s, the top political leaders were all rather old. The graying of the politburo was caused by the permanent occupation of the leading positions by a few elite members and the rules used for the selection of the top leaders. The selection process demanded that the candidate for a top position be moved from one level of managerial position to the next, so that he would have time to gain solid life experience and the opportunity to develop excellent bureaucratic work habits. As a result, the top positions in the USSR were occupied by elderly leaders. This period of state leadership acquired the nickname "gerocraty" because the bureaucrats were all geriatric. It is not difficult to guess the attitudes of gerocrats toward research results that documented serious decrements in old people's cognitive, emotional, intellectual, and volitional abilities: irritation, at least; open hostility, more likely.

Unlike pedology, psychogerontology was not officially blamed for society's ills or officially censored. Nevertheless, research with older population groups was continuously reduced. Without official support of research concerning the elderly, the entire branch of gerontological science lost its identity by gradual reductions. We hypothesize that the real reasons for the reductions in psychogerontological research lie in a governmental tactic that was well known and characteristic of that period. When an area of inquiry waned dramatically and quickly without official sanctions, it was almost always caused by the combination of dispersed responsibility for the decisions regarding resources and secret bureaucratic regulations that escaped the documentation requirements of official government decisions. The point is that the negative "opinions" regarding this field of study from those responsible for overseeing research were transmitted from the higher levels of bureaucratic administration to the lower levels. As a result, the field of psychogerontology was so drastically reduced that the most official task assigned to the society was to keep records about longevity. In real terms, this meant keeping a tally of the oldest citizen, who always seemed to be someone living in a remote region of the Caucasuses.

Studies of Aging in the New Russia

Although every society undergoes changes, the rapid and massive transformations in the social and political life that occurred during the last decade in Russia are probably unprecedented. Still, the results of decades of both formal and informal ideological sanctions against the study of psychogerontology are long-lasting. Currently, there are no pressures to avoid research in the psychology of aging, but new laboratories and studies in this area are slow to return. The relative paucity of contemporary work is documented in a monograph by Duplenko (1985), in which he reports that for the 1970s and early 1980s, "the number of publications on the psychology of aging is the range of .9–1.1 percent of all the publications on aging processes" (p. 137). Most current aging work in former Soviet countries concerns the medical and social aspects of longevity, with little interest paid to the psychology of old age. In the two decades prior to the 1990s, no psychological reports were published by the Institute of Gerontology in Kiev, an institute whose sole purpose was to serve as a center for aging research.

The most recent psychological research in aging is primarily applied. Data are largely gathered during visits to boarding homes for the elderly, and publications in gerontology journals tend to emphasize topics like adjustment to life in these boarding facilities. This trend can be seen in a recently published book by Dement'eva and Oustinova (1991) that focused on applied work on topics like how to welcome and support new residents in boarding facilities for the elderly.

There are many difficulties in reestablishing laboratories for the scientific study of aging after decades without work in this area. For example, scientific researchers lack the contemporary age-normative data that they need for representative sampling. Despite these difficulties, work is progressing, especially in the areas of cognitive aging. Changes are most profound in the areas of problem solving, imagination, and creativity. We now know that older adults have particular difficulties in finding and understanding analogies and in synthesizing information from multiple sources. Researchers report an increase in agnosia (difficulties interpreting sensory information), detriments in space and time orientation, aphasia (severe difficulties in language production), and the ability to remember new information. New work has also emphasized the unevenness of cognitive aging, which can be marked with long periods of little change or rapid change followed by uneven plateaus. Certainly, some of the changes that appear to be purely cognitive are, in part, caused by decreased sensitivity to auditory and visual stimuli.

Personality changes that are most common in old age are frequent crying spells, which signal deep depression, and increased irritability. Dominant personality traits include grumpiness, egocentricism, greediness, suspiciousness, and hypochondriasis. Old people tend to have conservative views; they are negative in their assessment of the present and future, and they recall the past as being better than it objectively was. Despite this negative list of characteristics, all is not negative for the elderly. Many adapt quite successfully to new conditions and situations.

Despite all of the difficulties that the field of psychogerontology in the Soviet Union has faced, research in this area is growing, albeit slowly. Experimental work is being conducted, publications on the topic are welcome in psychological journals, psychogerontology courses are being taught, and professional meetings are gaining in popularity (for example, a colloquium was held in Moscow in 1994, and an international teleconference in 1994–1995). The process of renewal in psychogerontology is still needed to overcome the void that resulted from government actions in the 1970s and early 1980s. The entire infrastructure for the field was destroyed and now needs to be re-created. An efficient infrastructure must be in place in order for high-quality psychogerontological work to flourish. We also need to increase the rate of information exchange with our colleagues from other countries and arrange for rapid translations into Russian of the newest basic publications, to update teaching materials for courses in psychogerontology, to recruit perspective researchers, to establish joint projects at the leading foreign research centers, to publish specialized journals on psychogerontology, and to organize meetings, including international conferences, devoted to contemporary topics in psychogerontology. The authors hope that the Russian psychological community will find ways to achieve all of these goals, and the history of psychology in the new Russia will never again tell of periods when research in a selected area is either officially forbidden or unofficially discouraged. We can only guess at the types of knowledge that we might now have if the psychology of aging had been allowed to follow its natural trajectory. Like the most valued psychological attributes of the elderly themselves, we hope that the field has gained wisdom from these negative experiences.

References

Alelekov, A. N. (1892). Starost': Klinicheskoje issledovanije v oblasti nervnoj sistemy i psikhofiziologii. (Old age: clinical research of the nervous system and psychophysiology.) Ph.D. in medicine thesis. University of St. Petersburg. (In Russian.)

Alexandrova, M. D. (1961). Zritel'no-prostranstevennoje razlichie kak komponent trudosposobnosti. (Visual-spatial difference as a component of work capability.) In *Problemy vosprijatija prostranstva i prostranstvennykh predstavlenij* (Problems of spatial perception and spatial presentations). Leningrad: Russian Federative Republic Academy of Pedagogical Sciences. (In Russian.)

Alexandrova, M. D. (1963). Ob individual'no-vozrastnykh osobennostiakh granitz tzvetovogo polja zrenija. (On individual and age specifics of the limits of color vision field.) In *Problemy obshchej i industrial'noj psikhologii* (Problems of general and industrial psychology). Leningrad: Leningrad State University Press. (In Russian.)

Alexandrova, M. D. (1965). *Ocherki psikhofiziologii starenija.* (Essays on the psychophysiology of aging.) Leningrad: Leningrad State University Press. (In Russian.)

Alexandrova, M. D. (1974). Problemy sotzial'noj i psikhologicheskoj gerontologii. (Problems of social and psychological gerontology.) Leningrad: Leningrad State University Press. (In Russian.)

Ananiev, B. G. (1957). O sisteme vozrastnoj psikhologii. (On the system of aging psychology.) *Voprosy Psikhologii, 5.* (In Russian.)

Ananiev, B. G. (1965). Introduction to M. D. Alexandrova, *Ocherki psikhofiziologii starenija.* (Essays on the psychophysiology of aging.) Leningrad: Leningrad State University Press. (In Russian.)

Belousov, N. F. (1923). *Starost' i smert'.* (Old age and death.) Kharkov: Glavpolitprosvet. (In Russian.)

Bogdanov, A. A. (1927). *Bor'ba za zhiznesposobnost'.* (The struggle for vital capacity.) Moscow: Novaya Moskva. (In Russian.)

Bogdanov-Berezovsky, M. F. (1894). Funktzija slukhovogo apparata v starosti. (The function of acoustic mechanism in old age.) Ph.D. in medicine thesis. University of St. Petersburg. (In Russian.)

Bogomoletz, A. A. (1927). *Zagadka smerti.* (The riddle of death.) Moscow: Narkomzdrav. (In Russian.)

Bogomoletz, A. A. (1938). *Prodlenie zhizni.* (Life prolongation.) Kiev: Ukrainian Republic Academy of Sciences. (In Russian.)

Bzhalava, I. Sh. (1963). K psikhologii involiutzionnoj melankholii. (On the psychology of involutional melancholy.) In *Eksperimental'nyje issledovanija po psikhologii ustanovki* (Experimental research on the psychology of attitudes) (vol. 2). Tbilisi: Georgian Republic Academy of Sciences. (In Russian.)

Dement'eva, N. F., & Oustinova, Z. V. (1991). *Formy i metody mediko-sotsial'noi reabilitatsii netrudosposobnykh Grazhdan.* (Forms and methods of medical and social rehabilitation of the disabled.) Moscow: Tsentral'nyi Nauchno-Issledovatel'skii Institut Ekspertizy Trudosposobnosti I Organizatsii Truda Invalidov. (In Russian.)

Dogel', A. S. (1922). *Razlichnye formy proyavleniya ahirzni.* (Different forms of life.) Petrograd: Mysl. (In Russian.)

Duplenko, Yu. K. (1985). *Starenie: Ocherki razvitiya problemy.* (Aging: Essays on the problem of development.) Leningrad: Nauka. (In Russian.)

Grekov, B. A. (1964). Rezul'taty slovesnogo eksperimenta u litz starshe 70 let. (Results of verbal experimentation with people over 70.) In *Trudy Leningradskogo Instituta Ekspertizy Trudosposobnosti Invalidov* (Proceedings of the Institute for Expertise on the Working Capacity of the Disabled). Leningrad. (In Russian.)

Kalinichenko, I. O. (1839). *O vlijanii vozrastov chelovecheskoj zhizni na umstvennye i nravstvennye sposobnosti.* (On the influence of age on human intellect and morals.) Kharkov: University Print. (In Russian.)

Makarov, P. O. (1952). *Nejrodinamika zritel'noj sistemy cheloveka.* (Neurodynamics of the human visual system.) Leningrad: Leningrad State University Press. (In Russian.)

Mechnikov, I. I. (1908). *Etjudy optimizma: Etjudy o prirode cheloveka.* (Essays of optimism: Essays on human nature.) Moscow: Nauchnoe Slovo. (In Russian.)

Mechnikov, I. I. (1913). *40 let iskanija ratzional'nogo mirovozzrenija.* (Forty years in search of a rational beliefs system.) St. Petersburg: Nauchnoe Slovo. (In Russian.)

Mil'man, M. S. (1923). Uchenie o roste, starosti, i smerti. (A theory of growth, old age, and death.) *Zhurnal Teoreticheskoi I Prakticheskoi Meditsiny* (Journal of Theoretical and Practical Medicine), *1,* 3–4. (In Russian.)

Molotkova, I. A. (1960). Sravnitel'noje izuchenie v vozrastnom aspekte uslovnykh refleksov u cheloveka pri razlichnykh bezuslovnykh podkreplenijakh. (Comparative investigation of aging aspects in human conditioned reflexes with unconditioned reinforcements.) In *Fiziologija i patologija starosti* (Physiology and pathology of old age), in *Trudy Leningradskogo Instituta Ekspertizy Trudosposobnosti*

Invalidov (Proceedings of the Institute for Expertise on the Working Capacity of the Disabled). Leningrad. (In Russian.)

Nagorny, A. V. (1940). *Problema starenija i dolgoletija.* (A problem of aging and longevity.) Kharkov: Kharkov State University Press. (In Russian.)

Rudzit, A. A. (1963). Kharakteristika osnovnykh psikhonevrologicheskikh sindromov starosti. (Characteristics of the main psychoneurological syndromes of old age.) Ph.D. thesis. University of Leningrad. (In Russian.)

Rybnikov, I. A. (1929). K voprosu o psikhologii starosti. (On the psychology of old age.) *Voprosy Psikhologii,* 2(1), 16–32. (In Russian.)

Shmidt, P. Ju. (1915). *Bor'ba so starost'ju.* (Fight against aging.) Petrograd: P. P. Soikin Print. (In Russian.)

Shmidt, P. Ju. (1920). Starost' i smert' po ucheniju I. I. Mechnikova. (Old age and death according to I. I. Mechnikov's conception.) In *Zagadka Zhizni* (The riddle of life). Gosizdat. (In Russian.)

Shmidt, P. Ju. (1923). *Teorija i praktika omolozhenija.* (A theory and practice of rejuvenation.) Petrograd: Prakticheskaya Medizina. (In Russian.)

Sikorsky, I. A. (1901). Tri vozrasta. (Three ages.) In I. A. Sikorsky (ed.), *Psikhologicheskij ocherk, posvjaschennyj junosham i startzam* (A psychological essay dedicated to young and old men). Kiev: I. K. Kushnerev & Co.. (In Russian.)

Starost' i trudosposobnost'. (Old age and work capability.) (1937.) Leningrad: Lenoblispolkom & Lensovet. (In Russian.)

Tarkhanov, I. R. (1891). Dolgoletie zhivotnykh, rastenij i ljudej. (Longevity of animals, plants, and human beings.) *Vestnik Evropy,* 5–10. (In Russian.)

Vetrinsky, I. Ja. (1848). *Russkie pis'ma o schastlivoj zhizni po jeje vozrastam.* (Russian letters on happy life according to age.) St. Petersburg: I. & S. Loskoutovy. (In Russian.)

Voronov, S. A. (1923). *O prodlenii zhizni.* (On life prolongation.) Moscow: M. & S. Sabashnikovy. (In Russian.)

Voronov, S. A. (1927). *Starost' i omolozhenie.* (Old age and rejuvenation.) Moscow-Leningrad: Gosizdat. (In Russian.)

Zavadovsky, B. M. (1923). *Problema starosti i omolozhenija v svete uchenija o vnutrennej sekretzii.* (A problem of old age and rejuvenation in the light of internal secretion theory.) Moscow: Krasnaya Nov'. (In Russian.)

Zavadovsky, B. M. (1924). *Vozmozhna li bor'ba so starostju?* (Is the fight with old age possible?) Moscow: Gosizdat. (In Russian.)

PART THREE

PREJUDICE AND

INTERETHNIC

HOSTILITIES

It is a common worldwide theme: people who belong to an identifiable group that is different from one's own group are perceived to be inferior in multiple ways. As seen in the chapters in this section, membership in a nondominant group usually results in the perception that the "other" is less intelligent, less moral, and different in many negative ways from the dominant group. In many Western societies, the main dimensions of group membership that serve as the basis for prejudice are race, religion, sex, and immigrant status; in the countries that were once part of the Soviet Union, it is almost always ethnicity, although prejudice against Jews also has a long and brutal legacy in Russian history. In a recent article on life in the post-Soviet countries, Hockstader (1995) made this observation: "Racism abounds here. Racism, especially anti-Semitism, is commonplace; many are unaware that it may give offense. The myth of multiculturalism died along with Soviet power" (p. 1).

In the American chapters that discuss prejudice and discrimination, Pamela Trotman Reid and Nicole E. Holland differentiate among related concepts and explain several models that have been proposed as a way of understanding the dynamics and dimensions of the in-group–out-group phenomenon. Jonathan S. Kaplan and Stanley Sue explain how a psychological model of human diversity permits differences but creates an atmosphere for acknowledging and accepting them rather than adhering to the idea that people are similar across and within groups. They provide evidence that prejudice is less overt but still prevalent in contemporary American life.

The three related chapters by post-Soviets show similarities and differences with the American perspective and each other. The chapter contributed by Estonians

Aksel Kirch, Marika Kirch, Vello Pettai, and Tarmo Tuisk provides a uniquely post-Soviet view in which ethnic Russians are facing legally sanctioned discrimination and prejudice based on whether they can trace their ancestry to Estonian soil before or after World War II. The historical events in the countries of the Baltic Sea, other newly independent states, and some countries in Eastern Europe provide a look at a type of prejudice and discrimination that is unknown to many Westerners. It is based on the involuntary takeover of their homeland by the Soviet authorities 50 years ago, and it is the children and grandchildren of these unwelcome "guests" who are now finding themselves as noncitizens in the only country they have ever known. The bloodless secession from the Soviet Union has created a new class of "stateless" people who are losing their jobs and their status in the newly independent countries that had been Soviet republics.

Ukraine, like Estonia, is a newly independent republic in which issues of language are also salient reasons for anti-Russian prejudice. Using one's own native language is more than a mere convenience; it is a source of great national pride and highly symbolic of national freedom. This theme was seen in a recent news story in which the author's guide through the Ukraine was particularly helpful because, according to the author, the guide understood bereavement and exile. The guide told of his father's death in the Gulag. The crime for which he had been jailed was "repeatedly teaching the Ukrainian language" (Weisman, 1996, p. 18). For many Ukrainians, their language is worth dying for because it symbolically stands for their culture and identity.

However, many important differences between Ukraine and Estonia have affected the extent and expression of prejudice. The economic health of Ukraine is closely tied to the Russian economy, a fact that seems to be responsible for the recent improvement in Ukrainian attitudes toward ethnic Russians. The Ukrainian data are based on a social distance scale in which respondents indicated how "closely" they were willing to interact with members of different ethnic groups. Evgueny Golovakha and Natalya Panina report in their chapter that Ukrainians admitted to wide differences in the degree to which they believe members of other ethnic groups are acceptable.

Another new phenomenon in the new Russia is the recent influx of refugees. The bloody war in Chechnya and other Caucus areas has created a new class of people who have lost everything, including their homeland. Escaping the brutalities of war, these displaced persons have had to adjust to life in a strange land, where they are often not wanted, where customs are different from those they know, and where new ethnic clashes are encountered. The immigrants fled from wars that were based on ethnicity and now find themselves as a minority group in a strange place, often with little or no money and few, if any, living relatives. The massive and multiple problems of these bereaved people have created a new set of psychological adjustment issues, of which ethnic prejudice is only one of many. For the first time in many decades, substantial numbers of immigrants are entering Russia, a reversal of the usual direction Russians have known. Studies of the perceptions and problems of these people are described in Galina U. Soldatova's chapter, "Strangers in the Homeland: Ethnopsychological Problems of Forced Immigrants in Russia."

References

Hockstader, L. (1995). For Russian women, new era means more sexism. *International Herald Tribune*, 23 September, pp. 1, 8.

Weisman, A. (1996). Unraveling the mystery of my father. *Los Angeles Times Magazine*, 21 January, 18–21, pp. 30–32.

13

Strangers in the Homeland

Ethnopsychological Problems of
Forced Immigrants in Russia

Galina U. Soldatova

They came to the Soviet Union/Russia because they had no choice—refugees from war-torn areas who fled to save their lives, criminals of conscience who came seeking political asylum, and forced deportees who had decided they must leave the place they had known as home. Unwilling immigrants have flooded into the Soviet Union/Russia in the last several years. First, they faced the traumatic events that caused them to leave their homelands, and now they face a new set of serious adjustment problems that include the need to adapt to an unfamiliar culture, uncertainty about their future, poverty and financial dependence, and the humiliation of having to ask for aid from relatives, strangers, and the government bureaucracy.

Few immigrants entered the Soviet Union for several decades following the Second World War (called the Great Patriotic War in Russia), but the demographics have changed dramatically in the last five to ten years. An accurate account of the number of immigrants who have entered the Soviet Union/Russia is difficult to ascertain because official statistics vary greatly between a low estimate of 1 million and a high estimate of 4 million individuals (Kozlov, 1995). Some cities and regions have strict limitations on the number of individuals who can live there, so the number of immigrants in these regions is surely underestimated. In order to be an official resident of Moscow, for example, one needs a legal document called a *propiska*, and a *propiska* can be obtained legally only by those who have an official place of employment in Moscow or a similar legitimate reason for residing there.

In 1990, Russian academics and government officials were unprepared for the special problems that these immigrants faced because they had not experienced immigration in their lifetime. When the new wave of immigration began, no institutional mechanisms were in place to deal with the problems of large numbers of displaced persons. Psychologists were unprepared for the psychological problems that these people brought with them or developed after they arrived, and they were suddenly confronted with the need to develop a new field of study to service a population with specific issues of adjustment, fears, and psychological sequelae stemming from their displacement.

As might be expected, immigrants in Russia represent distinct ethnic groups that have fled interethnic conflicts in neighboring and nearby countries. During the last ten years, Russian research on interethnic relations has focused almost exclusively on between-group hostilities and armed conflicts because prejudice and war have been much more prominent themes in ethnic relations than cooperation and peace. As regions of the Soviet Union began to break away and form independent states, ethnic confrontations in these regions intensified as various groups jockeyed for positions of political power. The weaker groups were often persecuted as century-old hatreds flared. The bloodless coup in the former Soviet Union turned bloody in the outlying regions. This chain of events created the flood of immigrants into Russia beginning around 1990. For these reasons, studies of and services to immigrants in Russia are intimately linked to the psychology of ethnic relations. In order to provide meaningful psychological assistance to refugees, service providers and academics must have an understanding of the refugees' experiences with their own and other ethnic groups.

A Short Chronology of Interethnic Conflicts in North Caucasus

In this chapter, I present the results of social psychological research on forced immigrants from and into the North Caucasus region. The research described was conducted in 1991–1992 and 1994–1995. I began work with a team of psychologists from Moscow University. We worked first with refugees from the city of Baku who had been granted temporary shelter in Moscow. In order to understand these displaced persons, it is important to examine the reasons for their forced exodus. In January 1990, a bloody massacre occurred in Baku, the capital of Azerbaijan (now an independent state, but part of the Soviet Union in 1990). The first victims were the Armenians living in Baku. Following the first round of slaughter that targeted Armenians, the Soviet army entered the city, shooting indiscriminantly. People from many ethnic groups were killed in this second round of slaughter, but the Azerbaijanians, who are Muslim, were particularly hard-hit. After this double massacre, the Russians living in Azerbaijan and those of other non-Muslim ethnic groups left Baku in fear for their lives and began their journey as refugees. Thus, non-Muslim groups from Baku were the first wave of immigrants into the Soviet Union since the end of World War

II. They were the first subjects in a series of studies of new immigrants groups (Soldatova, Shaigerova, & Shlyagina, 1995).

In October and November 1991, a team of researchers assembled in Vladikavkaz, the capital of the North Caucasus republic of North Ossetia. The Ossetian nation is an ethnic group made up of people with mixed Iranian and Caucasian origins. In Vladikavkaz, the refugee group consisted of 350 subjects who identified themselves as Ossetians who had recently fled from hostilities in Georgia (now an independent state). The Ossetians who had lived in southern Georgia claimed their own independence and attempted to secede from the larger state of Georgia. A fierce civil war resulted from their declaration of independence, and the Ossetians in Georgia fled into North Ossetia, which is part of Russia. At the time of our initial visit in 1991, approximately 100,000 Ossetians from Georgia were in exile in North Ossetia. When we visited again in April 1995, the number of Ossetian immigrants was estimated at 34,000. (Data were provided by the Migration Bureau of North Ossetia.) When considered in the context of the percentage of the population, these figures translate to 16 percent of the population of North Ossetia who were immigrants in the peak period 1991–1992.

Vladikavkaz was overrun with ethnic Ossetians, and many of the new immigrants participated in the bloody battles between the Ossetians and the Ingush, another ethnic group. The Ingush nation separated from the Chechens in 1992 (for details, see Soldatova, 1995). For decades, the Ingush and the Chechens were united in a single autonomous republic in the Russian Federation. These two ethnic groups were very close throughout much of modern history. They were similar linguistically and in their cultures, but the Ingush were more loyal to the Moscow officials than the Chechens. In the early 1990s, some territories neighboring both Ingushetia and Ossetia were experiencing multiple ethnic battles, as both ethnic groups were fighting for their monoethnic claims to these territories. As a result, new immigrant groups emerged. Many of the ethnic Russians who had settled in these states also became refugees because they were no longer welcome in the new nations formed from native ethnic groups. Thus, the unique situation had emerged in which ethnic Russians are immigrants to Russia as they flee from new republics that were part of the Soviet Union only a short time ago.

This situation, in which multiple ethnic groups fight for the sole right to claim an area as their own, is common as the former Soviet republics strive for independence. Almost all of the newly independent republics, and many of those that wish to become independent, engage in systematic and cruel actions designed to frighten ethnic Russians and other Russian-speaking peoples so that they will leave the regions and reduce the number of nonnative inhabitants. In this way, political activity is combined with ethnic conflict. This is why Russians from Chechnya also immigrated to Vladikavkaz. Many of the Russian immigrants had relatives in the Moscow area and were examined in Moscow when they came to stay with their relatives.

It is important to differentiate among these various groups of displaced persons because they represent different peoples with different sorts of problems. The Ossetian immigrants from Georgia were fluent in the Georgian language and had adopted the cultural norms and daily behavior patterns characteristic of the Georgian nation. They were easily identifiable as displaced persons in their new home in North Ossetia because of their distinct dialect. Many of their daily habits were disapproved of by the North Ossetian residents of Vladikavkaz. By contrast, the Russian immigrants had a very different background. They (or their parents or grandparents) had moved into Chechnya in the period between 1944 and 1957. This is the same time that large numbers of Chechens and Ingush were deported to Kazakhstan, in Middle Asia. The forced move of the Chechens and Ingush was one of Stalin's most brutal acts against ethnic groups in the North Caucasus. Many of those deported by Stalin died during his reign of terror. With the native ethnic groups removed to forced labor camps, Grozny, the capital of Chechen, was inhabited by ethnic Russians and other Russian-speaking groups (e.g., Ukrainians). After 1957, the deported Chechens and Ingush who survived the harsh period of forced labor were granted permission to return to their homeland. When they returned, the deportees tried to exclude the Russian inhabitants from the most privileged and powerful positions, which included employment in government and in commerce (Soldatova & Dement'eva, 1994). In general, the Russian and native (or titular) ethnic groups lived together in "strained harmony" for several decades.

The political situation changed greatly in the 1990s. Djohar Dudaev, the aggressive new leader of Chechnya, demanded complete independence from Russia. The hostilities between the Chechens and Russia were soon felt by the Russians living in the area. The Chechens took over in all aspects of Chechen life. The Russians lost many civil rights and soon became victims of numerous criminal acts. The death and suffering of so many Chechen and Ingush during the Stalin years were now avenged on the children and grandchildren of the Russian victors.

Forced deportees from Chechnya told of Russian-speaking people who were killed, robbed, and deprived of their employment or who had suffered in innumerable other ways. It is difficult to determine the exact numbers attacked because of their use of the Russian language or ethnic background. Attacks on prominent Russians became frequent. The rector of Grozny University, who was a professor of psychology, was shot dead without reason or warning. It is as though the decades between the bloody deeds of the Stalinist years and the present only made the desire for revenge grow more intense.

Not surprisingly, many Russians left these hostilities and became refugees in North Ossetia, even before the bloodiest battles began in 1994. Many chose to go to North Ossetia because they had a history of contacts with the people in this region and felt that they would adapt more readily if they remained together as a group in North Ossetia than they would if they were to scatter to the northern regions of Russia. These Russians had lived in the North Caucasus and differed in many obvious ways from relatives who may have remained in Moscow or other cities and villages in more distant regions of Russia.

The anti-Dudaev (Chechen) wars grew more intense beginning in December 1994 and continuing into 1995 and 1996. Finally, the bloody battles were reported in world news, and many people in English-speaking countries became aware of the large numbers of people being maimed or massacred in the conflict. As in any war, the number of refugees mushroomed as hostilities intensified. In the first quarter of 1995, the Russian Federal Migration Bureau registered 320,000 refugees from Chechnya. In August 1995, the Committee for Civil Coaction placed the number of refugees from the capital city of Grozny alone at 400,000. Although the earlier refugees were primarily Russian and Ossetian, the latest group included every ethnicity, even native Chechens who left their war-torn homes in search of safety. Some of the Chechens planned to return to their homes when the war waned, but others knew they could never return and must build a new life in a new place.

Problems of Refugees

Imagine what life was like for those who were fortunate enough to escape these ethnic wars. Close friends, neighbors, and relatives were lost. Many were dead. Others were simply lost; they could be dead, safe in another refugee camp, or in hiding—no one knows. The refugees must share crowded living space with strangers; they have no money for living expenses; they face bureaucratic entities whom they must ask for help; the future is uncertain at best, and the present is bleak. As described in the chapters on post-traumatic stress syndrome, all of the symptoms that emerge following extreme stress can be found in large numbers of refugees. These immigrants have no country. The Soviet Union is gone, and the republic that had been their home during the period of the Soviet Union has rejected them. For these displaced persons, the identity crisis is now doubled because of the dissolution of the Soviet Union and ethnic wars at home. This unique combination of losses enforces the national-ethnic core of their identity. Masses of people have migrated from their homeland because of their ethnic status. Interethnic interactions acquire the status of immense personal significance, which led us to predict that one of the psychological consequences of ethnic conflict would be heightened ethnic identity among the unwilling immigrants.

Experimental Investigations

In order to obtain a meaningful psychological picture of immigrant groups, we compared them on a variety of measures with similar ethnic groups who had not been subject to the traumas of forced immigration.

The comparison groups differed somewhat in each study, with the following groups being used overall: native (titular) Tartars and native Russians in Tatarstan, an autonomous republic on the Volga River; native Russians and Ossetians in North Ossetia; and Muslim Tartars, Russians, and native (titular) Tuvians (Buddhists) living in Tuva, an autonomous republic in South Siberia. Samples consisted of 700 subjects from each of these regions—350 ethnic Russians and 350 non-Russians. All subjects were from urban areas. The data are described more fully in "Nationalism, Ethnic Identity, and Conflict Management in the Russian Federation," a project in which the author participated.

The immigrants were divided into two groups based on the reason they emigrated. Forced deportees are those who left their homelands before they had reason to believe that they would soon be killed or harmed. The deportees, although they may not have wanted to leave, nevertheless made the deliberate and conscious decision to emigrate. They recognized that it was a necessary action and managed to take the economically and psychologically difficult steps to leave. By contrast, refugees left war-torn areas only after it became clear that they would soon be killed or harmed if they stayed. The refugees had endured more direct suffering than the deportees because the refugees delayed their exodus and emigrated under direct and immediate threats. Both groups had been subject to personally difficult life events and were faced with the problems of adjusting in a new culture, but the deportees acted sooner than the refugees and were more personally responsible for their immigrant status.

The refugees from South Ossetia were interviewed in Vladikavkaz, and the refugees from Grozny (Chechnya) were interviewed during their visits to Moscow because the war zone moved very close to Vladikavkaz, which made it too dangerous to conduct research there. Data collection was extremely difficult, even when it was conducted in Moscow. In order to obtain the information we needed, the refugees had to recall their most heartbreaking and traumatic experiences. Data collection was frequently accompanied by crying spells, and the researchers had the difficult task of determining whether the subjects were able to handle the harsh memories and reflections. Subjects in Vladikavkaz had to recall their painful experiences while, at the same time, they were nervously expecting another attack from the Ingush.

Research Instruments

A variety of measures of psychological functioning were obtained, with different measures from different subgroups. In addition, subjects were interviewed about their feelings, beliefs, and personal histories. We used several different normed instruments to assess the psychological functioning of the forced immigrants. The first was a modified (shortened) version of the Kuhn "Who Am I?" Test (Burns, 1979). In the shortened version of the "Who Am I" Test, subjects provide five terms that are central to the way they respond to this question about their self-identity.

The second was the Ethnic Identity Scale (Soldatova, 1994, 1995), which consists of three measures: the degree to which other ethnic groups are perceived as negative; the threshold for negative feelings toward other ethnic groups; and the level of aggression toward other ethnic groups. It presents 30 statements that the subject must respond to by selecting a number along a 5-point scale that indicates the extent to which the subject agrees or disagrees with each statement. These measures are used to identify the type of ethnic identity of a respondent and the degree of ethnic tolerance.

The third instrument was the Diagnostic Attitude Test (Ktsoeva, 1987), which is a variation of the semantic differential method. In this version of the semantic differential, subjects are given 40 scales with one end point labeled with a negative adjective (e.g., "greedy") and the other end point labeled with a neutral adjective that varies along the same dimension (e.g., "thrifty"). The subject indicates where she or he falls along this continuum.

The fourth instrument, the Rozentsveig Frustration Test (Test Rosentsveiga, 1990), assesses stable individual reactions to frustration. It provides measures of the dominant direction of a reaction to frustration—that is, whether the individual tends to blame himself or herself (reproach) or to blame an external factor as the cause of frustration. It also indicates the extent to which the individual seeks to reduce conflict. Also provided are measures of the type of reaction to frustration that is most typical—that is, whether the individual emphasizes the outside factors that cause the frustration or engages in self-defense because the subject perceives himself or herself as the main cause. Finally, it provides an index of the level of social interaction and the extent to which an individual will comply with group norms. This test has excellent test-retest reliability and is valid for all ethnic groups.

The fifth instrument, the Buss-Durkee Aggression Questionnaire (Buss & Durkee, 1957; Oprosnik Bassa-Darki, 1990), is often used along with a test of frustration because frustration often results in aggression. Ethnic conflicts seem to frequently involve aggressive actions and reactions. Measurements include irritation, negativism, grudges, guilt, suspicion, and type of aggressiveness—indirect, physical, or verbal.

Results

As expected, 90 percent of the Russian refugees responded in strong negative terms to questions posed by the interviewers about the status of Russians in Grozny, Chechnya. When asked about their decision to leave Chechnya, they told about their fears and exclusions from the major activities in the society. Here are some typical answers: "If I stayed in Grozny, my children would have no future"; "We had financial problems because I could not work." The most frequently given first reason for leaving was the escape from the ongoing war, to save their lives, and to get away from the constant fear under which they were living.

When asked what would allow them to return to Chechnya, they noted that they needed a guarantee for their safety, they would have to be able to return to their previous way of living, and they would need to be confident that there would be respect among the various ethnic groups. Half of the group could not imagine any condition that would allow their return. Many of the refugees from Chechnya who went to North Ossetia did so because they expected help from relatives and friends who were living there. Many also expected that the residents of North Ossetia would have favorable attitudes toward them. They noted the historically good relations between the two regions: "Ossetians and Cossacks were always on good terms." Eighty percent of the respondents believed that they were very safe or fairly safe in North Ossetia. These ethnic Russians who had lived for decades in the North Caucasus felt that they were closer to the people of North Ossetia than to the ethnic Russians from other "Russian" parts of Russia. Even though they were fluent in the Russian language, they were culturally distinct from the rest of the ethnic Russians because of their different experiences in life.

Transformations in Ethnic Identity

Using the popular Kuhn "Who Am I?" Test, we compared the descriptive terms provided by the two groups of immigrants—forced deportees and refugees—with those provided by two nonimmigrant control groups—Ossetians and Russians living in North Ossetia, in the city of Vladikavkaz. Some striking differences emerged with this technique. The refugees used specific terms like "homeless," "pauper," "jobless," and "refugee" 43 percent of the time. The forced deportees and the two control groups gave answers that are more general in nature, with 80 to 90 percent of the terms coming from categories such as being a human being, a professional identification, a family role such as spouse or father, and a "citizen of Russia." In adddition, ethnicity was a dominant characteristic for all of the nonimmigrant (comparison) groups. The immigrants usually failed to mention this characteristic. The refugees are much less likely to perceive themselves as members of a country or family unit. Instead they defined themselves by the tragic elements in their lives. The loss of identity was discussed in the chapter on post-traumatic stress syndrome, and readers who have already read that chapter will not be surprised to find that the refugees used phrases and terms like "no one needs me" and "unprotected," "dependent," and "having no rights." Other used extremely negative terms like "shadow," "wretched," "good-for-nothing," "dregs," and "scum of society." The key elements of their self-identity are altered by their refugee status.

Transformations in Interethnic Interactions

There are many possible long-term reactions of immigrants who faced persecution because of their ethnicity. One possibility is that their affiliation with their own ethnic group could fade. Immigrants could abandon ethnic identifications and seek stable support from groups that are not formed on the basis of ethnicity. Alternatively, ethnic identity could become "hyperbolized," with the result that the individual becomes increasingly hostile to other ethnic groups. Anecdotal evidence suggests that interethnic hostilities intensify in these situations, a hypothesis that we tested with the Ethnic Identity Scale. Subjects responded with the degree to which they agreed or disagreed with statements that were grouped into six categories (1) ethnic tolerance/intolerance (norms show a positive identification with one's own ethnic group and no evidence of discrimination toward other groups): "I am able to deal with a representative of any ethnic group, in spite of racial and national differences"; (2) ethnonihilism: "I have problems getting along with the people of my own ethnicity"; (3) ethnic indifference: "I never took the problems of ethnicity seriously"; (4) ethnocentrism or ethnoegoism: "I get irritated when I have close contacts with other ethnic groups"; (5) ethnoisolation: "I believe that marriages between people in different ethnic groups lead to erosion of ethnicities"; (6) ethnic fanaticism: "I believe that to uphold the well-being of one's group, nothing is forbidden."

Normally, good ethnic identity means that the individual has positive attitudes toward her or his own group and those of other groups, with a slight preference for one's own group. This sort of pattern is correlated with high levels of tolerance for others and openness to interethnic contacts. By contrast, feelings of ethnic inferiority and denials of the ethnocultural values of one's own group are symptomatic of feelings of shame about the members of one's own ethnic group.

The last three scales on this instrument, ethnoegoism (ethnocentrism), ethnoisolation, and ethnofanaticism, combine to form a seventh scale, hyperidentity. Hyperidentity is marked by a transition from the normal slight preference for one's own ethnic group to absolute assurance in its superiority to all others. Hyperidentity leads to intolerance and the tendency to react to interethnic conflicts in an aggressive and violent manner. The transition to hyperidentity begins with ethnoegoism (or ethnocentrism), which is the belief in the superiority of one's own ethnic group and the belief that another ethnic group is the cause of one's misfortunes. Even casual contact with members of the "other" ethnic group creates feelings of discomfort and irritation for individuals who are ethnocentric. The second stage of hyperidentity has all of the attributes of the first stage plus the notion that it is necessary to remove the influences of the "other" ethnic group from the larger culture. The "other" group is perceived as unnatural or alien to the natural order. Such individuals may, for example, espouse extremely negative attitudes regarding interethnic marriages. There is a high degree of overt xenophobia and the belief that it is morally right to resolve the problems of one's own ethnic group at the expense of the "other" ethnic group. The most extreme form of hyperidentity is the belief that it is a necessity to purge one's country (or village or other place of residence) of the "other" ethnicities. In order to improve one's own superior ethnic group, it is justified to deprive other groups of their human rights, material property, and life. The well-being of one's own group justifies these sacrifices by other groups.

Scaled scores for forced deportees, refugees, and the control subjects are shown in table 13.1. In interpreting the numbers in table 13.1, keep in mind that the higher the tabled value, the more often the attitudes described by the scale were endorsed by a group. As seen in table 13.1, the refugee group shows a higher tendency than the forced deportees for ethnonihilism and hyperidentity. Contrasted to the forced deportees, the refugees have more negative attitudes toward their own ethnic group, are more likely to blame the Russian Federation for their present plight, and are indifferent toward other ethnic groups. I believe that these results could be due to the post-traumatic stress that left them passive and apathetic, a greater indifference to ethnic matters in prewar Grozny, or some combination of the two. Forced deportees seemed to be especially sensitive to matters of ethnicity, a tendency that was seen in prewar interviews with members of this group.

In general, I have found that for the subjects tested in this study and numerous other studies that I have conducted in which forced deportees were compared to refugees, the deportees were more optimistic. They described their current situation as "not so bad," "I can stand it." By contrast, the refugees used descriptions like "impossible to endure" and "disastrous." The control subjects showed more optimism than the forced deportees, both in this study and in several others that my colleagues and I have conducted. The combination of an increase in intolerance for other ethnic groups and decreased optimism seems to covary. Other researchers have found that the refugees are impatient for relief from the stressful conflict (Vasilyuk, 1995).

Stereotypes

Because generalized beliefs about the members of different groups seemed important in understanding the adaptation of immigrants, we investigated autostereotypes (generalized beliefs about one's own ethnic group) and heterostereotypes (generalized beliefs about other ethnic groups). In this study, we

Table 13.1. Scaled Scores on 7 Dimensions of Ethnic Identity

Type of Identity	Forced Deportees	Refugees	Control
Ethnic intolerance	17.4	16.9	18.2
Ethnonihilism	5.1	7.2	4.1
Ethnic indifference	9.7	13.2	11.4
Ethnoegoism (ethnocentrism)	6.4	6.9	5.8
Ethnoisolation	5.7	7.1	5.2
Ethnic fanaticism	6.4	7.1	4.8
Hyperidentity (composite of last 3 scales)	18.5	21.1	15.8

were concerned with the forced immigrants' stereotypic beliefs about the dominant ethnic group in their former homeland and in their new place of residence. Stereotyping is cognitive and emotional categorization based on expectations about groups of people.

Three different groups of subjects were tested using the Diagnostic Attitude Test: Ossetian-forced deportees from Georgia, Russian-forced deportees from Grozny, and Russian refugees from Grozny. In addition to assessing autostereotypes and heterostereotypes, subjects also provided responses about themselves as individuals. This scale was called "beliefs about self." The data from the Diagnostic Attitude Test are presented in table 13.2. In interpreting these values, keep in mind that the higher the value, the more positive the stereotype.

"Beliefs about self" from the two groups of deportees are virtually the same as their autostereotypes (beliefs about their own ethnic group) and significantly ($p < .05$) more positive than their heterostereotypes. The dominant ethnic group at their new residence is the Ossetians in North Ossetia. The Ossetians in North Ossetia are described by the two groups of immigrants as "communicative," "quick-witted," and "diplomatic."

The heterostereotypes about the dominant ethnic group from their former homes are negative, with the highest negative value assigned to the Chechens by the Russian deportees. Both the Georgians and the Chechens were described as "aggressive," which is not surprising given that these ethnic groups are at war with the ethnic groups that are immigrants. Other common descriptors were "hypocrites," "stubborn," and "arrogant." Although these data are not presented in the table because they were not a major focus of these studies, the Russian refugees also maintained negative stereotypes of Russians in Moscow. Many of the same terms used to describe Chechens in their former homelands were used for Russian Muscovites. We believe that is because the refugees found the Rus-

Table 13.2. Stereotypes of Forced Deportees and Refugees

	Beliefs about Self	Autostereotypes	Heterostereotypes of Dominant Ethnic Group	
			At New Residence	At Former Residence
Ossetian forced deportees from Georgia	.34	.31	.21	−.06
Russian forced deportees from Grozny	.28	.30	.24	−.12
Russian refugees from Grozny	.35	.17	−.02	−.01

sian Muscovites to be cold and indifferent to their plight. The stereotypes about Muscovites were even more negative than those for Chechens. The ethnically Russian refugees were extremely negative about both groups.

The data on stereotypes support the earlier findings on ethnonihilism. The refugees show more negative feelings toward their own ethnic group than the deportees and controls, a result that is also confirmed with these data. For the deportees, their ethnic negativism is selectively targeted toward their aggressors and those from whom they expected assistance but who were indifferent to their plight. The refugees, who suffered to greater extent than the deportees because of their ethnic group membership, are more negative to their own group than the deportees. It is possible that the stress following their traumatic experiences has caused them to be more negative overall.

Responsiveness to Frustration

Long-term residence in areas with high levels of interethnic conflict affects all of the inhabitants of the war zone and those in neighboring areas. Psychological reactions include low tolerance for frustration, mass neuroticism, anxiety, irritation, and despair. The reduced tolerance for frustration is the potentially most debilitating of these reactions because it increases the likelihood of aggression and is manifested by higher levels of internal agitation. The Rozentsveig Frustration Test was used to assess the way in which deportees and refugees responded to frustrating circumstances.

As a group, the deportees are characterized by high levels of extrapunitive reactions—that is, they blame external forces for their present condition. They openly blamed the hostile Chechens for their forced immigrant status. Their responses suggested that they had been expecting the war in Chechnya and believed that the conflict was inevitable. Their scores show that the forced deportees were eager to resolve their difficult situation by themselves and did not want to accept external aid. The refugees did not tend to blame any group or individual for their current status. They show many signs of psychological distress, including isolationism, vulnerability, and the interpretation of many events as threatening. But their response is more passive than that of the deportees; they are less likely to ascribe blame and less likely to seek actively for solutions to their problems. Their responses show that they are more helpless and hopeless than the deportees.

Aggressiveness as a Means of Adaptation

Putting aside individual differences in levels of aggressiveness, one likely group-level response to the extreme conditions the immigrants are facing is to increase their overall level of aggression. At the time of the data collection, the subjects were immigrants facing the daunting task of finding living accommodations for their families, earning or otherwise acquiring sufficient funds for their daily living, and learning how to survive in a new culture. Level and type of aggression was measured with the Buss-Durkee Aggressiveness Questionnaire. This instrument yields several subscores of aggressiveness, which are listed in table 13.3. As in previous sections, comparisons are made among forced deportees, refugees, and control subjects. In this experiment, the control group was 52 Russian Muscovites. The higher the value in the table, the stronger the type of aggressiveness appears in the sample.

The results from the Buss-Durkee Aggressiveness Questionnaire show that the deportees were more aggressive than both the refugees and the control subjects. Aggression for this group shows that they are not passive and helpless people. My colleagues and I believe that the higher level of aggression among the deportees shows that they are energized to participate in their own adaptation. By contrast, the refugees appeared more depressed and apathetic. In interpreting these data, it is important to keep in mind the fact that many of the refugees had escaped from Grozny only three months prior to their participation in this research. Although they were less aggressive than the deportees, they were more hostile and seemed ready to respond negatively to even the slightest new misfortune. Again, data from other experiments tend to support these conclusions. Refugees from Georgia tended to be highly suspicious and to respond with hostility. One-third of the Georgia refugees reported that the dominant ethnic group in their new place of residence was "mocking them every time they turned their backs" and were "contemptuous and scornful," but they could not cite any concrete examples of these behaviors.

A large percentage of the deportees (40%) and refugees (30%) approved of violence as a means of taking control of a difficult situation. We provided normative comparison data in a study entitled *Nationalism, Ethnic Identity, and Conflict Management in Russia Today* (Soldatova, 1995). Data on aggressiveness were collected from residents in Tatarstan, North Ossetia; in Tuva (an autono-

Table 13.3. Type and Degree of Aggressiveness

Type	Forced Deportees	Refugees	Control
Physical aggression	6.2	4.3	5.1
Indirect aggression	3.9	3.0	3.5
Verbal aggression	7.8	7.3	6.3
Irritation	5.8	5.9	4.9
Negativism	2.9	4.0	2.7
Grudges	5.8	5.6	4.4
Suspicion	6.0	4.1	3.8
Guilt	6.4	6.4	6.0
Aggression index	17.9	14.6	12.7
Hostility index	9.6	11.3	8.6

mous republic in the Altai mountains in the southern portion of Russian Siberia); and in Jakutia (an autonomous republic in northern Siberia with extremely cold winters that is renowned for its production of diamonds). All of these regions are sites of ethnic tensions, but they do not have the ethnic wars that are raging in Chechnya and Georgia. Overall, only 13 percent of the inhabitants of these regions approved of aggression as a means of handling interethnic disputes. These data show that the immigrants were several times more likely to endorse aggression that the peoples from these comparison regions.

In order to provide a meaningful framework for interpreting these studies, I borrowed from the typology offered by Bochner (1982). I modified his classifications in several ways so that their usage in this manuscript is unique to this study. The term *intermediate* is used according to Bochner's definition. I have substituted the term *national* for Bochner's term *chauvinist* because *chauvinist* elicited negative reactions from Russians. The third style that I delineated—neurotic ethnophobe—is original in this study and has no counterpart in Bochner's original classifications: (1) *Intermediates* are able to engage in nonhostile interactions with members of other ethnic groups. They have a normal ethnic identity (positive for their own group and other groups but somewhat more positive for their own group). Intermediates are best able to adapt to changes in ethnosocial realities and other changes in cultural environment. They are able to resolve conflicts with negotiations and their identity structure is stable. (2) *Nationals* are those with hyperidentity, which underlies their belief that their own ethnic group is superior to others. They are not eager to engage in any contact with other ethnic groups and are more ready than intermediates to use aggressive means to resolve interethnic group conflicts. (3) *Neurotic ethnophobes* are intolerant of other ethnic groups and are hostile to their own ethnic group. Those who show this behavioral style are most likely to show depressive reactions or even serve as the leaders in ethnic wars who justify their violations of the human rights of other ethnic groups because better circumstances for their own superior ethnic group will result.

All three of these behavioral styles can be further divided into the categories "active" and "passive," which describes an individual's likelihood to act on these underlying feelings and beliefs. Data presented here and in other referenced sources show that the post-traumatic stress and crisis in identity formation that immigrants suffer cause a reduction in the proportion of immigrants who exhibit the adaptive behavioral style of intermediates. The same circumstances show an increase in the percentage of nationals and neurotic ethnophobes.

The massive numbers of recent immigrants in Russia have many needs. Financial support is essential, as are rehabilitation programs and psychological counseling. In addition, the research reported here suggests that they need assistance in changing their behavioral styles so that they conform to the more adaptive intermediate style. They also need assistance in changing their status from immigrants who are unwilling residents in a strange land to former immigrants who have normal ethnic identities and who have become participants in a society that accepts them as full citizens.

Acknowledgments   Research was supported by the John D. and Catherine T. MacArthur Foundation.

References

Bochner, S. (1982). The social psychology of cross-cultural relations. In *Cultures in contact*. New York: Oxford University Press.

Burns, R. (1979). *The self-concept: Theory, measurement, and behavior.* New York.

Buss, A. N., & Durkee, A. (1957). An inventory for assessing different kinds of hostility. *Journal of Consulting Psychology*, 21.

Kozlov, V. (1995). Nashi bezhentsy i pereselentsy. (Our refugees and forced deportees.) *Segodnya*, 13 October. (In Russian.)

Ktsoeva, G. U. (Soldatova) (1987). Ethnic stereotyping: An empirical study. *Soviet Journal of Psychology*, 7(2), 224–235.

Oprosnik, Buss-Darki (1990). The Buss-Darki questionnaire. In *Praktikum po psikhodiagnostike: Psikhodiagnostika motivatsii i samoregulyatsi* (pp. 6–12). Moscow: Moscow University Press. (In Russian.)

Soldatova, G. U. (1994). Psikhollogicheskoe issledovanie etnicheskoj identichnosti v usloviyakh mezhetnicheskoj napryazhennosti. (Psychological research of ethnic identity in the conditions of interethnic tenseness.) *Natsional'noje soznanie i natsionalizm.* (In Russian.)

Soldatova, G. U. (1995). Inter-ethnic tension in the Republics of the Russian Federation: Tolerance versus aggression. In G. V. Lapidus & Renee de Nevers (eds.), *Nationalism, ethnic identity, and conflict management in Russia today* (pp. 55–65). Stanford, Calif.: Stanford University Press.

Soldatova, G. U., & Dement'eva, I. (1994). Russians in the North Caucasian Republics. In V. Shlepentokh, M. Sendich, & E. Pain (eds.), *The new Russian diaspora: Russian minorities in the former Soviet Republics* (pp. 122–141). New York: M. E. Sharpe.

Soldatova, G. U., Shaigerova, L. A., & Shlyagina, E. I. (1995). Narusheniya etnicheskoj indentifikatsii u russkikh migrantov. (Russian migrants' ethnic identification defects.) *Sotsiologicheskii Zhurnal*, 3, 144–150. (In Russian.)

Vasilyuk, F. E. (1995). Tipologiya perezhivznii razlichnykh kriticheskikh situatsii. (Typology of suffering of different critical situations.) *Psikhologicheskii Zhurnal*, 16(5), 104–115. (In Russian.)

14

Changing Ethnic and National Identities in Estonia

Aksel Kirch, Marika Kirch, Vello Pettai,
& Tarmo Tuisk

When Western readers think about the former Soviet Union, they tend to think of Moscow, St. Petersburg, and the Russian majority. Except for experts or those with special interests, Westerners tend to forget or underestimate the critical differences among the peoples and republics that constituted the Soviet Union—differences that are so fundamental that they invalidate generalizations from the Russian portions of the Soviet Union to the other republics. The former Soviet republics that are now independent countries and those that are still struggling for their independence are made up of ethnically distinct groups with their own languages and cultural heritages. Estonia, like its Baltic neighbors, Lithuania and Latvia, was an independent country for several decades in the 20th century. It was under czarist rule at the turn of the century, enjoyed independent statehood during the period between World War I and World War II, then was forcibly annexed onto the Soviet Union. Most recently, Estonia declared its independence for the second time in this century in 1991. Older Estonians can still recall the takeover of their country by the Soviet Union at the end of World War II and, with it, the change to Russian as their official language and the loss of prestigious jobs and amenities to Russians who were sent to oversee the new Soviet Estonia. For many Estonians, the Russians who settled there at the end of the war were intruders who assumed privilege and status among the native Estonians. The stage was set for an uneasy alliance between the Russian families who settled in Estonia in the 1940s and the native Estonians and ethnic Russians who had been living there prior to World War

II. The ethnic tensions that exist in modern Estonia have their origins in the postwar migration.

Prejudice and discrimination among ethnic groups in post-Soviet Estonia are closely linked to the process of ethnic identity. The native Estonian population is now in charge of its own destiny as Estonians decide who is entitled to the status of citizen in the newly independent country. To the native Estonians, Russians who had lived in Estonia prior to World War II are legitimate "immigrants" who should automatically qualify for citizenship, but those who came after World War II were unwelcome conquerors and should not be automatically entitled to Estonian citizenship, even if they and their families have lived there as model citizens for the last 50 years. Thus, at least four groups currently coexist in modern Estonia: native Estonias, pre–World War II Russians, post–World War II Russians, and small numbers of other assorted ethnicities and foreigners.

Prejudice and discrimination are based on salient aspects of group membership. An "us–them" group identification must evolve for prejudice to flourish because it is cognitively impossible to act differently toward members of one's own group and those in another group if the actor cannot identify the basis for group membership. The frequent shifts in national status and group hierarchies that have occurred in Estonia and other non-Russian republics have created an ideal breeding ground for prejudice and discrimination among ethnic groups. Native Estonians were forced to change their national language and were accorded a kind of second-class citizenship in their own country when the Soviets annexed Estonia. Now the native Estonians are creating the same conditions for Estonian Russians. The way in which ethnic Estonians and Russians living in Estonia perceive each other and the changes in the identities of these groups (especially among the Russian population in Estonia) will have a major influence on the future social, political, and economic interactions between Estonians and Russians in their state. To date, interethnic relations have been relatively peaceful and stable; however, nationalist Estonians who are eager to rectify the wrongs of decades spent under (Russian) Soviet rule are passing new laws that are detrimental to neighbors of Russian descent.

Estonia, like the other two Baltic states, took advantage of the collapse of the Soviet Union in 1991 to reclaim its independence. The secession from the Soviet Union was accomplished peacefully, although the specter of a bloody ethnic conflict had been predicted by the local populace and the political pundits prior to the secession. In this chapter, the authors, who are ethnically Estonian, analyze relations between Estonians and Russians and recent shifts in ethnic and national identity, both critical factors in the postsocialist transition in this newly independent state.

We use Estonia as a model for describing and generalizing the situation in the other ethnically distinct former Soviet republics, especially the three Baltic states (Kirch & Kirch, 1992). We believe that general lessons can be learned from the Estonian experience that can be applied to other situations around the world where ethnic communities desire their independence from a larger country in which they have minority status. In support of this conclusion, we examine two recently completed studies. The first is published in the book *The Baltic States: The National Self-Determination of Estonia, Latvia and Lithuania*, edited by Graham Smith (1994). The second is a research report by Harri Melin (1995), "Ethnicity and Social Class in the Baltic Countries." Interested readers are also referred to Geistlinger and Kirch (1995) and Kirch and Kirch (1992).

The restoration and consolidation of Estonian independence began in 1988 and was made official in 1991. The independence of Estonia created numerous fundamental changes in society that had a crucial impact on the ethnic and national consciousness of everyone living in Estonia. Perhaps the most salient change caused by the declaration of Estonian independence was a reversal of interethnic relations, with the Estonians becoming the ethnic majority in terms of status and privilege and the other groups of non-Estonians transformed into ethnic minorities, who were now subject to new laws that accorded lesser status to them. In addition to the reversal of status hierarchies among ethnic groups, changes in territorial, political, social, regional, and religious identities for all the inhabitants of Estonia were created along with national independence. Estonians were now free to take a religious identity and a new national identity, resume the official use of the Estonian language, and determine their own laws. All Estonians had been communists and Soviets (at least officially), but in reality few Estonians embraced the communist doctrine. There were only 55,000 Communist Party members among Estonia's 600,000 adults. Thus, less than 10 percent of all Estonians chose to join the Communist Party.

We began our studies of the processes and consequences of the shifts among Estonia's ethnic groups with the assumption that changes in the way groups perceive themselves and others are quite different in scope, magnitude, and intensity for Estonians and Russians. For the Estonians, the creation of an independent Estonia has meant a strengthening of their ethnic identity and a restoration of their European heritage. For Russians living in Estonia, it has required an acceptance of a new political identity (adaptation to the Estonian state) and a slow restoration of the Russian ethnic identity of their ancestors in place of Soviet identity. New groups with hyphenated identities (multiple identities) have been formed as all of Estonia's residents search for ways of resolving what has been a sociological and psychological identity crisis (Hutnik, 1991).

Ethnic Russians and Russophones

Estonia has long had ethnic minorities. Between the two world wars, when it was an independent country, Estonia was approximately 88 percent Estonian, with Russians, Germans, Swedes, and Jews making up most of the remaining non-Estonian population. (Although Jews are a religious group, they are considered a separate ethnic group in Russia. This "ethnic" identity is marked on passports to distinguish them from "ethnic" Russians.) The contemporary non-Estonian minority (now numbering around 35% of the population), however, is largely the product of Soviet-sponsored migration policies during the post-war era. As a result, the minority population of Estonia was transformed, now representing mostly Russians (29%), Ukrainians (3%), and Byelorussians (1.5%).

This Soviet legacy is obvious in Estonia's statistics. In 1989, Estonia's share of foreign-born residents (i.e., born outside Estonia) was one of the highest in Europe: among the urban population it was 32 percent; in rural areas, 11 percent; and in the total population, 26 percent (Tepp, 1994). Among ethnic Russians living in Estonia today, approximately 50 percent are Soviet-era immigrants who came from various regions of Russia (from Leningrad to Vladivostok), Ukraine, Byelorussia, and other regions of the former Soviet Union. Only a small percentage (5 to 7%) were born in prewar Estonia or are descendants of prewar residents. The remaining non-Estonians are Russians who were born during the Soviet period in Estonia (43%).

Among Byelorussians and Ukrainians living in Estonia, most have lost their original ethnic identity and have adopted Russian as their main language. In the late 1980s and early 1990s, some of those from other non-Russian regions of the Soviet Union sought to rediscover their ethnic roots by forming cultural associations, but others classified themselves as simply the "Russian-speaking population," indicating a significant post-Soviet identity vacuum for these people. Thus, the Russian and Russian-speaking population in Estonia is formed from people of many different generations and backgrounds whose everyday language is Russian. In reality, this is a heterogenous group linked only by a common language. They do not form a special Russian community, nor do they have much in common with other immigrants or descendants of immigrants from the varied republics of the former Soviet Union. They are not an internally integrated minority group and do not share the cohesiveness of other ethnic groups. To borrow a phrase from Marx, one might say they are a minority in themselves but not a minority for themselves. Although they all live mainly in the big cities of northern Estonia (Tallinn, Kohtla-Ja rve, Narva), they have different educational levels and professional skills and widely divergent lifestyles and attitudes. Some members of this heterogenous group favored the Estonian independence movement; some have learned Estonian; and some do not want to become Estonian citizens. Thus, sociologically it is extremely important to characterize Russians and Russophones in Estonia as different groups with different wants and different options available to them.

Most Russians and Russian-speaking people were denied automatic citizenship under Estonia's citizenship laws that were passed in 1991–1992. The Estonian argument for these citizenship laws was based on the contention that under Soviet rule, Estonia was an illegally occupied state and therefore those people who settled in Estonia during that period entered the country illegally and could now only be granted citizenship based on Estonia's own terms. In this sense, the argument is purely legal. However, its consequences were strongly ethnopolitical because the vast majority of Soviet-era immigrants are Russian, and they make up most of the Russian-speaking minority in the country. Many high-level professions now or soon will require a near-native fluency in the

Estonian language (e.g., professors, school teachers, government services). Very few adults can expect to obtain this level of language proficiency, which means that they already have or soon will lose their jobs. They find themselves in a country where they and their families have lived since the 1940s, now unemployed, unemployable, and without citizenship. Estonian Russians had been the privileged class in the Soviet era; now they are the underclass. Thus, this overlap of citizenship and ethnic cleavages has de facto deepened the Russian-Estonian divide, although it has still not led to any direct conflict. Rather, faced with the requirements of naturalization, many Russians seem even more atomized, and the purely political link among them has not prompted a clear unification of forces or identities.

Identity Cleavages

If we compare Estonians and Russians as groups, we find that the main dimensions of national identity for each group during the Soviet period were constructed differently. For the Estonians, ethnicity meant an ethnocultural identity; for the Russians, ethnicity meant a state (or Soviet) identity. This has been the main reason why the Estonians and Russians experienced the period of disintegration of the Soviet empire from different perspectives and with different emotions. Estonians, as the citizens of a subjected nation, aspired to national-political self-determination, to the restoration of a link between nation and state. Russians either sought to defend the status quo, which was favorable to them, or were unable to react. With the dawning of perestroika in the Soviet Union, the Estonians recognized a great opportunity for separation and for the strengthening of their ethnic identification. Many Russians, however, felt a sense of disappointment at the lost of their accepted (Soviet) identity. Without the Soviet Union, who were these strangers in a familiar land? As the historic events surrounding perestroika and glasnost were unfolding, they were given different interpretations. The Estonians saw a chance for restoring their former identity; the Russians saw an identity vacuum that brought with it a need to redefine the components of their personal and collective identity.

The central dilemma facing Estonia's Russians was the perception that they belonged to the Soviet state; for them, being Russian was categorically identical to being Soviet. Prior to 1991, the Russians living in Estonia were not eager to believe that their motherland could actually collapse, leaving them without an identity and at the mercy of their native Estonian neighbors. A survey that was administered in 1990 in four Estonian cities showed that only 15 percent of the Russians believed, at that time, that there was no future for the socialist system (Lepane, 1991). The end of this former world power was literally unbelievable to the Estonian Russians, who had much to lose if the Soviet Union disintegrated. The breakup of the socialist system was obviously one of the factors that would frame the identity crisis faced by many Russian people, especially those living in newly independent republics.

At the same time that Russians living in Estonia lost their main identification as Soviets, they had to confront additional identity crises. The restoration of Estonian independence created major changes in their lives that were more tangible and immediate than psychological questions of group identification. The Russians also became an ethnic minority in an independent Estonian state. Had Estonia stayed in the Soviet Union or the Commonwealth of Independent States, Russians in Estonia would not have experienced the profound drop in the social and political hierarchies. Instead of representing one of the most powerful states in the world, they became a minority group in a small but fiercely independent republic. Their rapid loss of status was a second area of crisis in self-identification for the Russian population in Estonia (A. Kirch, 1994). Minority status (in its political sense of loss of power) and the corresponding identity crisis were previously unknown to Estonia's Russians (approximately 480,000) because only 5 to 7 percent (or 35,000) of these Russians were descendants of Estonia's historical (prewar) Russian minority, who had lived at least three generations in Estonia. The descendants of the prewar Russians were given citizenship under the citizenship laws passed in 1993, a status that few had attained in prewar Estonia.

Third, the shift in majority-minority paradigms between Estonians and Russians has also changed important aspects of the culture and type of civilization in Estonia and should profoundly alter many aspects of everyday life well into the next century. Estonia is situated on the edge of Europe. The political events of history have, at times, linked Estonia to the Western sphere of Europe and at other times to the Eastern civilizations. Our research shows that there are significant differences between the attitudes of Estonian and Russian respondents, who see Estonian culture in quite different civilizational contexts. For the Estonians, their cultural orientation focuses on the Nordic countries and on Germany; for Russian respondents, their perception is of a broad Russian-Baltic cultural sphere more isolated from the West. As Estonia becomes increasingly Westernized, Russians in Estonia will also find that their general cultural orientation will be at odds with those of the country in which they live, or they will have to become Westernized as well.

Samuel P. Huntington (1993) has captured the multiple difficulties that Estonian Russians face with these words: "Cultural characteristics and differences are less mutable and hence less easily compromised and resolved than political and economic ones. In the former Soviet Union, communists can become democrats, the rich can become poor and the poor rich, but Russians cannot become Estonians." Although it is questionable whether all communists can really become democrats, it is clear that significant cultural differences complicate the minority integration process and Estonian Russians may not be able to change their ethnic identity. Estonians who had suffered from prejudice and discrimination by Russians are now reversing the status hierarchy, and the Russians cannot legally declare themselves to be Estonians or easily assume an Estonian ethnic identity.

Given the fact that Estonia is now a multiethnic country with laws that confer rights and privileges based on ethnicity, it is important to find ways that

people living in a multiethnic state amid unstable political and economic circumstances can avoid conflict and achieve cooperation and integration. For
Estonia and all other republics of the former Soviet Union, this is a period of
profound change. We believe that a smooth transition from Soviet Estonia to
independent Estonia is most likely if all people maintain their ethnic identities
while they are integrating into Estonian society under a common national identity. Thus, we advocate an acceptance of multiple ethnic identities within a
unified political system.

A New Diaspora Identity?

Surveys in Estonia have shown that ethnic identification among Estonians and
Russians has intensified: both groups of respondents strongly identify themselves
with their own ethnic culture (M. Kirch, 1994). It is important to point out, however, that for Russians, feelings concerning their cultural identity became increasingly important since 1993, while we believe that ethnicity has been of major importance for native Estonians for many years. In 1986, fewer than 20 percent of
Russian respondents said that they consider themselves definitely, or for the most
part, to be people of Russian culture; by 1993, this group had increased dramatically to 96 percent. Still, in the same year, the results also appeared to indicate
that the idea of Soviet identity (as defined through identification with "Soviet
culture") continued to be quite significant. More than half of the Russian respondents (59%) defended the idea of Soviet culture and saw themselves as representatives of it (M. Kirch, 1994). For Estonians, data from the same survey showed
that ethnic identification has always been of primary importance.

More interesting aspects of the change in identity can be seen using a methodology called identity structure analysis (ISA). This technique was developed
by Peter Weinreich (1989). Based on a set of questions in which respondents
compare their value orientations to those of other reference groups, we were
able to measure respondents' sense of closeness (or distance) from those other
groups. These measures of "psychological distance" provide a quantification of
the respondent's identity structure. Surveys that used these techniques were
conducted in March 1993 and April 1995 with 200 Estonians and 200 Russians
in four different Estonian cities. The reference groups included members of the
respondent's own ethnic group, members of the opposite ethnic group, the
Estonian government, and the European Union. With this method, we were able
to chart a relational map of where respondents perceive themselves and their
group to be in society.

The index of contraidentification (negative attitudes or greater distance between oneself and the group one is compared to) that was derived using the 1993
and 1995 data sets shows a low level of distancing in Estonians' attitudes toward
Estonians as a whole, the Estonian government, and the European Union. The
contraidentification indexes for the native Estonians were extremely high toward Russia's Russians and less high toward Estonian Russians. Among local

Russians, the results were mixed. Empathetic (positive) identification with local Russians, as well as with local Estonians, is greater in small cities and in the countryside than among Russians living in Estonia's large cities. Positive attitudes toward the Estonian government was at a medium level, and attitudes toward the opposite ethnic group (i.e., the Estonians) was at a high level.

The critical measure that indicates a change in identity by the Estonian Russians is seen in their attitudes toward Russia's Russians. Here, we see that the Estonian Russians' identification is ambiguous. On the one hand, their contra-identification with Russia's Russians is at a moderate level; on the other hand, there exists quite a high empathetic identification with Russia's Russians. Moderate scores on both positive and negative attitudes toward Russians living in Russia show that the Russians living in Estonia are experiencing a high degree of identity conflict. This means that Russians feel some ethnocultural resonance with Russia's Russians, but they also sense a relatively high identity conflict with Russia's Russians. Based on these findings, we believe that there exists an embryo of local Russian identity, where Estonian Russian people consider themselves quite different from Russia's Russians. These perceptions are supported by the data in table 14.1. As seen in table 14.1, both the native Estonians and Estonian Russians identify more emphatically (in a positive way) with the Estonian Russians (those who settled in Estonia prior to World War II) than with the Russian Russians.

Prospects for the Future

The process of integration is multidimensional. It depends on the Russian's readiness to integrate into the new Estonia, as well as on the Estonian's willingness to cooperate with the non-Estonian population. In this chapter, we have stressed some of the identity changes taking place in Estonia, which feed the process of

Table 14.1. Contra-Identification and Empathic Identification with Others

	Estonian Government	Estonians	Estonian Russians	Russia's Russians	European Union
Empathic identification of Estonians	0.82	0.77	0.53	0.38	0.58
Empathic identification of Estonian Russians	0.49	0.57	0.72	0.54	0.50
Contra-identification of Estonians	0.26	0.22	0.41	0.55	0.24
Contra-identification of Estonian Russians	0.39	0.36	0.28	0.37	0.19

Note: Data collected in May 1995. A higher number indicates a higher level of identification.

interethnic relations. Prejudice and interethnic difference, it has been argued, have been mostly factors of these identities and the perceived gaps between them.

The ethnic identity of Estonians has intensified since the early 1990s. The identity of Russians in Estonia, meanwhile, has largely been influenced by the Soviet era and has slowly been moving away from this state or regime identity. As the time since the collapse of the Soviet Union increases, we are seeing the formulation of a localized ethnic identity among Estonian Russians, a trend that should contribute to their adaptation to a minority status in Estonia. This adaptation is going to be a long-term process that will culminate only when Estonian Russians adapt to the Estonian culture and become fluent in the language of Estonia. Both of these changes are necessary for full participation in the newly created Estonian state. The change in legal status may be likely to follow if Estonian Russians become more like native Estonians and assume the mores of Estonian culture.

References

Geistlinger, M., & Kirch, A. (1995). *Estonia: A new framework for the Estonian majority and the Russian minority*. Vienna: Braumueller.

Huntington, S. P. (1993). The clash of civilizations? *Foreign Affairs, 72*, 101–105.

Hutnik, N. (1991). *Ethnic minority identity: A social psychological perspective*. Oxford: Clarendon.

Kirch, A. (1994). From a change of evaluation to a change of paradigms: Estonia, 1940–1993. In M. Kirch and D. D. Laitin (eds.). *Changing identities in Estonia: Sociological facts and commentaries* (pp. 6–10). Tallinn: Akadeemia Trükk.

Kirch, A., & Kirch, M. (1992). *National minorities in Estonia: Ethnicity and conflict in the post-Communist world, the Soviet Union, Eastern Europe, and China*. K. Rupesinghe, P. King, & O. Vorkunova (eds.) (pp. 89–105) New York: St. Martin's.

Kirch, M. (1994). Identificational diversity in Estonia: Grounds for integration or grounds for disintegration? In M. Kirch & D. D. Laitin (eds.), *Changing identities in Estonia: sociological facts and commentaries* (pp. 31–41). Tallinn: Akadeemia Trükk.

Kirch, M., & Kirch, A. (1995). Search for security in Estonia: New identity architecture. *Security Dialogue, 26*, 439–449.

Lepane, L. (1991). Russians and the social conditions in Estonia: Psychological issues in the political transformation of Central and Eastern Europe. University of Helsinki, *Research Reports, 3*.

Melin, H. (1995). Ethnicity and social class in the Baltic countries. Paper presented at the 2nd European Conference for Sociology, Budapest, 30 August–2 September.

Smith, G. (ed.). (1994). *The Baltic states: The national self-determination of Estonia, Latvia, and Lithuania*. London: Macmillan.

Tepp, L. (1994). In- and out-migration of Estonia: Estonian statistics. *Monthly of Statistical Office of Estonia, 9*, 25–36.

Weinreich, P. (1989). Variations in ethnic identity: Identity structure analysis. In K. Liebkind (ed.), *New identities in Europe: Immigrant ancestry and the ethnic identity of youth* (pp. 41–74). Gower: Hants.

15

Interethnic Intolerance in Post-Soviet Ukraine

Evgueny Golovakha & Natalya Panina

The population of modern Ukraine is an uneven mix of various ethnicities. According to the last general census (1989), the 51.5 million Ukrainians are composed of 72.7 percent Ukrainian nationals, 22.1 percent Russians, .9 percent Jews, and 4.3 percent "other." Although Ukrainian history contains less of the sort of interethnic conflict that resulted in armed rebellions than occurred in other parts of the former Soviet Union, recent events have caused increased tensions among the ethnic groups in modern Ukraine. Several ethnic groups have been forced to move to Ukraine because of conditions caused by the breakup of the Soviet Union. For example, the Crimean Tartars have been re-settling in Ukraine, which has caused problems as they adapt to life in a new country. The bigger problem, however, is the unknown consequences of the "Ukrainization" policy that makes Ukrainian the official language of this newly independent country. Of course, ethnic Russians who have been living in Ukraine are worried about the change in language because only those who are fluent in Ukrainian will be able to hold high-level positions in government, academia, and political life. There are also large numbers of ethnic Ukrainians, especially in East Ukraine, whose mother tongue is Russian. They fear that they will be outcasts in their own country because of the new language requirements. Members of this large group have an ambivalent identification with modern Ukraine because their parents or grandparents decided to make the dominant language of their time Russian, which was taught and learned at home, in the belief that this choice was in the best interest of their offspring.

The intensity of interethnic conflicts varies by region. The eastern and southern regions belonged to Russia during the last three centuries and are deeply ingrained in Russian culture and identity. Similarly, the western regions have strong cultural ties to Poland and Austria-Hungary and strong identification with these European countries. The area now known as Ukraine was united when it became part of the Soviet Union; the unification was accomplished when Ukraine was ruled by the Soviet government in Moscow. Its disjointed history and unification by Russia (perceived by some Ukrainians as a foreign power) are the reasons that the crucial ethnosocial problems concern Ukrainian-Russian relations specifically and national-ethnic intolerance in general.

The New Ukrainian Minority—Russians

Russians have assumed many roles in the past. They have been, at various times, aggressors and saviors, the blessed and the damned, depending on the time in history and the perspective from which their actions were viewed. But Russians have always been the indisputable masters in their own land. They were always the landlords, even when the land they claimed as their own was populated with other ethnic groups and cultures. For the first time, the situation has changed, and it is now the time of the Russian diaspora, when Russians scattered in distant countries have minority status. The new Russian minority is suffering from the intolerance shown by other ethnic groups, while at the same time Russians need to reorient to their role as the "national minority," a role that is deeply resented because it represents their fall from dominance.

The Russians living in Ukraine always believed that the Russian culture was indigenous to the region. Rifts between these two new countries have arisen from their different approaches to the economy, politics, and the military. Furthermore, Russians primarily live in the most industrialized regions of Ukraine. They are one-third of the population in Ukraine's five eastern regions and a majority of the population in the Crimea. In fact, some political factions in Russia consider these regions to be part of Russia and not part of the new Ukraine. By contrast, the western part of Ukraine, where Russians are 3 to 8 percent of the population, especially the area known as Galychyna, is strongly opposed to the Moscow influence in Ukrainian life. Thus, it is difficult to draw a single picture of ethnic relations in Ukraine.

An Old Minority Group—Ukrainian Jews

Relations among the various ethnic groups in Ukraine become even more complicated when viewed from the perspective of Ukrainian Jews. According to national polls, Jews in Ukraine were as supportive of the formation of an independent state as the native Ukrainians were, but there was also some vocal opposition in the Jewish community. The destruction of the Soviet totalitarian system had many benefits for the Jews because it allowed opportunities for social, cultural, and political activities that were supportive of Jewish life—activities that were strictly forbidden under communism. Many independent Jewish organizations have been formed in the last few years, and Jewish cultural centers, newspapers, and magazines have quickly been established.

On the other hand, the size of the Jewish population has been shrinking throughout the entire former Soviet Union and in Ukraine. One of the most painful problems for Ukrainian Jews is the same as that faced by many Ukrainians in eastern regions: loss of their own language. Over 90 percent of Ukrainian Jews consider Russian to be their native language. Most Jews maintained their identity as an ethnic group because of the "cultural genocide" that was conducted against them by the Communist Party. They remained firmly identified as Jews because they were targeted for discrimination and thus could not assimilate either by will or by gradual shifts toward the dominant culture. Of course, this sort of "negative identification" (i.e., identification with the group that is most discriminated against) has led to mass emigration and deportation of Jews.

The Last Jew in Ukraine?

We do not believe that this situation will lead to the eventual exit of all Jews from Ukraine. Some members of the Jewish intelligentsia feel strong spiritual links to Ukraine and recognize the vast contributions that Jews have made to Ukrainian culture. We also believe that the transition to a market economy will attract the most active and experienced businessmen from the Jewish community. Some of these businessmen are returning to Ukraine from Israel and the West, countries to which they fled during Soviet rule. Finally, there is now no official policy of state-sanctioned anti-Semitism, as there had been in the past, so many Jewish families believe that it may now be possible to solve the problems of national identification in ways that will be beneficial to the Jews.

Interethnic Tolerance amid Economic Decline

Social tensions are rising at a rate that is proportional to the decline in the standard of living in Ukraine. These are the worst possible conditions for interethnic tolerance and cooperation. When similar events occurred in other former Soviet republics—for example, Chechnya and Georgia—the outcomes were bloody clashes and civil wars that pitted different ethnic groups against each other in a battle for scarce resources. In a study conducted between 1989 and 1991 by the Central Ukrainian Department of All-Union Center of Public Opinion Research and the Institute of Sociology of the National Academy of Sciences, it was found that, in Ukraine, the greatest concern of all citizens was fear of interethnic conflict. The fear remained high even though there had been no serious conflicts in Ukraine. Fear peaked in 1992, when almost half of the adult population in Ukraine (49%) considered the possibility of interethnic conflict to be a major threat. Although half of all adults believed that these conflicts were highly likely, only 3 percent of the respondents said that they had been personally involved in a conflict involving ethnicity. We believe that the disparity in these numbers shows that the beliefs of many adults were influenced by events in other republics where vicious wars between ethnic groups were raging. In order to understand the factors that contribute to interethnic conflict and the perception that such conflicts are likely, we studied the feelings of various groups of Ukrainians toward other ethnic groups.

An Empirical Investigation

We administered a series of questionnaires to a random sample of 1,752 adults in April 1992 and 1,807 adults in May 1994 who were selected to be representative of Ukrainian population with respect to region of residence, type of settlement (city or town), nationality, sex, age, and educational level.

Bogardus Scale of Social Distance

We needed a scale that would measure the level of tolerance toward different ethnic groups. An ideal measure for this is the Bogardus Scale of Social Distance (Bogardus, 1925; Park, 1924), which allows us to assess the social attitudes of an individual toward members of other ethnic groups. The "distance" is an index of one's readiness to become close to members of other ethnic groups or refusal to accept them without considering the personal attributes of the target individual. The Bogardus Scale has been widely used in Eastern Europe (Kol'tsov, 1989; Ktsoeva, 1985; Pantic, 1991). For example, in response to questions about members of an ethnic group (e.g., Jews), the respondent would select one of the following options:

1. I agree to accept them like . . . members of my own family (1 point), close friends (2 points), neighbors (3 points), colleagues (4 points), inhabitants or residents of my country (5 points), tourists (6 points).
2. I do not accept them (7 points). Thus, a score of 1 indicates maximum tolerance and a score of 7 indicates maximum intolerance.

We applied the Bogardus Scale of Social Distance to a list of 23 nationalities in two studies (Kyiv, August 1990 and July 1991). The results were highly reliable (Golovakha & Panina, 1991; Golovakha, Panina, & Churilov, 1992). Additional studies using this scale were carried out in April 1992 and May 1994.

The April 1992 study was conducted approximately half a year after Ukraine acquired the status of an independent state. The second study was conducted in May 1994, two years after the establishment of the separate country of Ukraine. Mean social distance for each administration regarding 18 ethnic groups is presented in table 15.1. These data show an orientation on the part of a national sample of Ukrainians toward "national separation."

Table 15.1. Mean Scores on Bogardus Social Distance Scale for 16 Ethnic Groups, April 1992 and May 1994

	April 1992	May 1994	Change
Ukrainians	1.55	1.83	+0.28**
Russians	2.46	2.25	−.0.20**
Byelorussians	2.85	2.70	−0.15*
Poles	3.77	4.45	+0.68**
Jews	4.18	3.83	−0.36**
Hungarians	4.24	4.59	+0.35**
Americans	4.31	4.42	+0.11
Germans	4.43	4.48	+0.05
Romanians	4.56	4.69	+0.13*
Crimean Tartars	5.09	4.55	−0.54**
Georgians	5.26	4.86	−0.40**
Gypsies	5.55	5.09	−0.46**
Slovaks		4.55	
Moldavians		4.59	
Serbs		4.77	
Turks		4.91	

Note: Higher numbers indicate greater social distance.
*$p < .05$.   **$p < .01$.

As seen in table 15.1, many ethnicities have a mean score greater than 5, which indicates that members of these groups have not acquired the status of permanent residents among the Ukrainian population. These groups are also at greatest risk for serious interethnic conflicts because of the way they are perceived by a representative sample of adults living in Ukraine. Although full-scale war has not erupted in Ukraine, as in some other republics, a type of soft xenophobia has been created, in which some ethnic groups are isolated from the others and ethnicities that are mostly associated with foreign countries are least tolerable.

It is particularly instructive to consider the relative position of Jews in the social distance scale. Historically, anti-Semitism in Ukraine has been a major concern both within Ukraine and in the international arena where Ukraine's treatment of its Jewish population has attracted a great deal of negative attention. The treatment of the Jews by the Ukrainians during World War II was particularly atrocious, even when viewed against the backdrop of the mass killings, genocide, degradation, and torture of World War II. The data in table 15.1 show that Jews are not considered just another example of outsiders because Jews do not belong to those groups that are perceived as "most different from us." They are more accurately perceived as a group from which most Ukrainians want to maintain their distance but are among those who inhabit the country. Results regarding Jews showed wide differences when the geographic area in which the data were collected was considered. Tolerance was greatest in large cities (the Kyiv sample had a mean of 3.44; other large cities, 3.67); intolerance grew as population density decreased (small towns, 4.25; villages, 4.56; all $p < .05$).

The Social Reality of Xenophobia

Communist ideology served as a pressure cap on interethnic relations that was blown off when the totalitarian system deteriorated. This conclusion is supported by the results of a factor analysis on the data obtained with the social distance scale. Three separate factors emerged, accounting for a total of 82 percent of the variability. By far the largest factor, accounting for 66 percent of the variance, was xenophobia. Essentially what this factor showed was that if you discount answers about Ukrainians, Russians, and Byelorussians, there is a high probability that anyone who expresses nontolerance of any of the remaining ethnic groups will also express nontolerance toward all of the other remaining ethnic groups. Those who provided answers that showed they were willing to have close relations with members of one of these groups responded in the same way for all other groups. This finding suggests that among Ukrainians there is a general trait of nontolerance or tolerance toward members of ethnic groups other than those of "Eastern Slavonic origin."

The remaining two factors are relatively weak, accounting for 12.3 and 4.4 percent of the variance, respectively. The second factor was labeled "general national tolerance." In our optimistic view, we believe that it represents a tendency toward tolerance. The third factor, although weak, suggests a "pro-Western" orientation. These two factors offer some hope for the future development of positive attitudes toward members of ethnic and national groups other than one's own.

A comparison of the social distance data in 1992 with the data collected two years later show some interpretable changes. In the first two years of modern Ukraine, intolerance of Western countries, specifically the United States and Germany, remained unchanged for Ukrainians. Nontolerance toward ethnic groups living in Ukraine (Crimean Tartars, Gypsies, and Jews) decreased, perhaps reflecting a tendency to see members of these groups as part of one's country, but nontolerance toward its Eastern European neighbors (Poland and Hungary) increased.

Regional Differences

A comparison of the social distance data by region in which it was collected also shows definite trends, reflecting the social and political processes that have transpired in the earliest years of the newly independent Ukraine. Social opinion and national tolerance are important determinants and reflections of political actions regarding politically sensitive issues, such as the problems in the Crimea and conflict between the Russian Black Sea fleet and Ukraine's desire to use its own naval power in this strategically critical sea. Regional distributions of the social distance data in 1992 and 1994 surveys are presented in table 15.2.

When the data are arrayed by region, it is easy to see that there has been a small but definite improvement in tolerance toward various ethnic groups in

Table 15.2. Mean Scores on Bogardus Social Distance Scale Distributed by Region, April 1992 and May 1994

	April 1992	May 1994
Kyiv	4.01	4.49
Western	4.31	4.33
Central	4.87	4.25*
Eastern	4.71	4.64
Southern	4.71	4.68
Crimea	4.63	4.44
Ukraine (average)	4.63	4.44*

Note: Higher numbers indicate greater social distance. The large difference for Kyiv failed to achieve statistical significance because it was based on only 90 respondents and there was much variability in their responses.
*$p < .01$.

most regions of Ukraine. Despite the general improvement in attitudes, overall scores remain above the midpoint of 4.0, thus reflecting more nontolerance than tolerance. The central portion of Ukraine has a traditional-archaic orientation, which means that local interests supersede global ones for most of the inhabitants, and this orientation influences the development of political events and philosophy. The shift in preferred social distance from members of various ethnic groups was also seen in the 1994 presidential election, with the population of this area splitting its vote into two blocs—one with a western Ukrainian orientation and the other with an eastern Ukrainian orientation. The differentiation of voting blocs in an area that was formerly homogeneous in its political actions shows that the independence of Ukraine is having an effect in even the more remote geographical areas.

Regional data were also analyzed separately for indicators of tolerance toward Ukrainians and Russians. These are the two largest ethnic groups and the two groups most likely to engage in heated conflict because of contentious issues that reflect historical events (e.g., the annexation of Ukraine by the Soviet/Russians) and linguistic issues that threaten employability and cultural traditions (i.e., the change to Ukrainian as the official language). These data are presented in table 15.3. There has been a considerable improvement in attitudes toward Russians in the central and southern regions of Ukraine and a worsening of attitudes toward Russians in Crimea in the first two years of modern Ukraine's independence. These regional differences reflect variations in the status of the language problem for inhabitants of these regions. The survey that was conducted in May 1994 also asked a question about everyday language use. Language-use data by region is shown in table 15.4.

Overall, in Ukraine the percentage of adults who speak only Ukrainian, only Russian, or either depending on circumstances is approximately equal. However, there are large regional differences in everyday language use. In Kyiv, for example, almost half of the population speak both languages in their homes,

Table 15.3. Social Distance Scores toward Ukrainians and Russians by Region in 1992 and 1994

Region	Preferred Social Distance toward Ukrainians		Preferred Social Distance toward Russians	
	1992	1994	1992	1994
Kyiv	1.67	1.55	2.17	2.08
Western	1.37	1.75**	3.14	2.97
Central	1.33	1.41	2.58	1.79**
Eastern	1.58	2.03	2.05	2.24
Southern	1.86	2.02	2.84	2.22**
Crimea	2.27	2.76**	1.83	2.34*
Ukraine (mean)	1.55	1.83	2.45	2.25**

Note: Higher numbers indicate greater social distance.
*$p < .05$. **$p < .01$.

but in western Ukraine, there is a strong tendency to speak only Ukrainian. The newly independent Ukraine enacted a state policy that all official documents were to be in Ukrainian, a fact that was greeted with much hostility in those regions where most people are most fluent in Russian. The election of L. Kuchma as president of Ukraine in 1994 was strongly determined by those regions in which Russian is the dominant language because he ran on a platform that included making Russian the official language of Ukraine and strengthening economic ties with Russia. There are two important reasons why Ukrainians might want to maintain economic ties with Russia: salaries are much higher in Russia, and the purchasing power of the Russian ruble is higher in Ukraine than the Ukrainian currency.

The economic situation in Ukraine is so difficult that three-fourths of the population manage to survive only by growing produce on their own small plots (according to the Sociological Service of the Democratic Initiatives Center survey conducted in February 1994, in which the authors participated). Especially

Table 15.4. Responses by Region to the Question: What Language do You Speak in Your Family?

Region	Ukrainian Only	Russian Only	Depends on Circumstances
Kyiv	16%	39%	46%
Western	79	5	16
Central	60	8	32
Eastern	13	53	35
Southern	22	47	31
Crimea	4	86	11
Ukraine (mean)	37	33	30

for those in the western regions, there is a strong preference to sell their produce in Russia, where they will make more money, than in Ukraine. For these reasons, we believe that the improvement in attitudes toward Russians is caused by these economic factors.

Economic Beliefs and Interethnic Tolerance

As shown in the previous section, there is a strong link between attitudes toward various ethnic groups and the perceived effect members of an ethnic groups will have on one's economic status. These are hard times for Ukrainians because the transition to a market economy has created a new and more desperate poverty than previously existed. We believe that the greater one endorses the change to a market economy, the better the attitudes toward members of other ethnic groups. For example, we have found that ethnic tolerance is lowest among those who prefer "low prices with a lack of consumer goods" and highest among those who prefer "high prices but with abundant goods and services." In general, negative attitudes toward entrepreneurial activity, private property, and other manifestations of a market economy are correlated with negative attitudes toward members of various ethnic groups. Support for this conclusion is found in the social distance data when they are separated on the basis of how respondents answered questions about the transition in the economy. Among those who responded in the affirmative to the question "Is it necessary to go through with the transition to the market economy?," the mean social distance score was 4.15. In comparison, those who agreed with the statement "We should return to the economic system that existed before the transition began" had a mean social distance score of 4.61.

These data, along with the others already presented, suggest that as the economic conditions in Ukraine improve, increased tolerance for ethnic groups should also result.

Summary

Several conclusions can be drawn from the social distance measures collected in Ukraine in 1992 and 1994. First, the period immediately following the establishment of modern Ukraine was marked with national separatism. Those ethnic groups that were not present in large numbers in Ukraine were perceived as most distant. Second, a general type of xenophobia explained much, but not all, of the variability in the responses. By knowing a respondent's attitude toward any group (other than Ukrainian, Russian, and Byelorussian), you could assume with high probability that the individual has the same attitude toward members of the other groups. Third, there has been a general increase in tolerance, showing some slow but real changes in a positive direction. Fourth, attitudes toward Ukrainians and Russians vary widely by region probably because of the different language traditions and economic influences caused by the move to independence.

The economy is an important determinant of interethnic attitudes. The higher salaries and greater purchasing power gained by close associations with Russia have helped to improve attitudes toward ethnic Russians. Similarly, a positive free-market orientation is correlated with increased interethnic tolerance, and a negative free-market orientation is correlated with an increase in interethnic nontolerance. It seems that what is good for the economy is also good for interethnic relations, a point that cannot be ignored in a time of great sociopolitical change.

References

Bogardus, E. S. (1925). Measuring social distance. *Journal of Applied Sociology*, 9, 299–308.
Golovakha, E., & Panina, N. (1991). Inter-ethnic relations and ethnic tolerance in Ukraine. In *Jews and Jewish topics in the Soviet Union and Eastern Europe* (vol. 14, pp. 27–30). Jerusalem.
Golovakha, E. I., Panina, N. V., & Churilov, N. N. (1992). *Kiev, 1990–1991: Sotsiologicheskie reportazhi*. (Kiev, 1990–1991: Sociological reports.) Kiev: Naukova Dumka. (In Russian.)
Kol'tsov, V. B. (1989). Sotsial'naya distantsiya v mezhnatsional'nom obschenii: Opyt postroeniya integral'nogo pokazatelya. (Social distance in interethnic communication: An attempt to construct an integral coefficient.) *Sotsiologicheskie Issledovaniya* (Sociological investigations), 2, 26–29. (In Russian.)
Ktsoeva, G. U. (Soldatova) (1985). Metody izucheniya etnicheskikh stereotipov. (Methods of investigation of ethnic stereotypes.) In *Sotsial'naya psikhologiya i obschestvennaya praktika* (Social psychology and social practice) (pp. 225–231). Moscow: Nauka. (In Russian.)
Pantic, D. (1991). *Nacionalna distanca gradana jugoslavije: Jugoslavija na kriznoj prekpetnici*. Beograd: IDNCPIJM.
Park, R. E. (1924). The concept of social distance. *Journal of Applied Sociology*, 8, 339–344.

16

Prejudice and Discrimination

Old Paradigms in New Models
for Psychology

Pamela Trotman Reid & Nicole E. Holland

In a southwestern county in Georgia, African American students were routinely assigned to low-achieving classes, even when they had high test scores; white students were assigned to classes for high achievers even with low scores (Associated Press, 1995).

"Today, gay men and lesbians continue to be the targets of violence. Over 90 percent have been subjected to antigay verbal abuse or threats. Almost one-quarter reported they had been physically attacked" (Strong & DeVault, 1994, p. 723).

Ann Hopkins was denied a partnership in her firm because the male members did not feel comfortable with the image she conveyed (*Price Waterhouse v. Hopkins*, 1989).

These real-life vignettes demonstrate prejudice and discrimination in a variety of social settings. They are exemplars of both blatant and subtle bias and may be considered representative of what occurs in a variety of social settings and circumstances. Nevertheless, we should not take the proclivity of humans to discriminate as justification for such behavior. Instead, we can try to understand what leads us to strive for homogeneity in our designation of group membership and to resist strongly perceived threats to status and the status quo.

Definitions of Terms

Our discussion of prejudice must begin with the identification of the basic terms used: prejudice, racism, sexism, stereotypes, and discrimination. To discuss how individuals operate in a social setting, perhaps we might first agree that most people naturally group themselves and others into categories or groups. Groups to which individuals believe they belong are called "in-groups." In-group members are believed to share beliefs, attitudes, or some other characteristic. "Out-group" members are those others who are seen as different.

Prejudice

The word *prejudice* is derived from the Latin *praejudicium*, meaning "previous judgment" (Webster's Ninth New Collegiate Dictionary, 1984). Psychological definitions of prejudice typically accept this notion of preconceived conclusions and move to further explicate the concept. For example, Klineberg (1968) explained the concept as "an unsubstantiated prejudgment of an individual or group, favorable or unfavorable in character, tending to action in a consonant direction" (p. 439). Simpson and Yinger (1985) described prejudice as "an emotional, rigid attitude (a predisposition to respond to a certain stimulus in a certain way) toward a group of people" (p. 21). Finally, Allport (1954) included the negative dimension in his definition, "thinking ill of others without sufficient warrant" (p. 7).

As these definitions reflect, social scientists have identified three domains on which definitions of prejudice typically focus: attitudinal, cognitive, and emotional (Allport, 1954; Duckitt, 1994; Ehrlich, 1973). Strictly speaking, one may consider prejudice to occur in both positive and negative directions. Over time, however, the meaning of prejudice has come to convey only the negative and to be considered in a relatively pejorative sense.

Racism

One form of prejudice, directed toward individuals based on the biological definition of the group to which they belong, is called racism. Racism includes the beliefs that race (1) determines the traits, characteristics, and abilities of individuals; (2) provides the basis for comparative judgments; and (3) justifies the subordination of members of a particular group (Duckitt, 1994; Rothenberg, 1992).

Racism is deeply embedded in U.S. culture, and a variety of definitions have been developed to describe it. Thus, racism has been defined in political terms "as the principle of social domination, by which a group that is seen as biologically inferior is exploited economically and oppressed socially and psychically" (Duran, Guillory, & Villaneueva, 1990, p. 215, citing Blauner, 1969). In psychology it has also been frequently defined from an intrapersonal perspective (Reid, 1988)—that is, in terms of individual pathology or disturbed personal characteristics (Biassey, 1972; Comer, 1980; Delany, 1980).

In the United States, issues related to race have been historically and inextricably intertwined with economics, politics, and other aspects of social life. In addition to the pervasive influence of race through all social systems, racism has been found to be intentional and unintentional, conscious and unconscious, individual and institutional (Brewer, 1994; Duckitt, 1994; Jones, 1981; Rothenberg, 1992). Thus, to the average citizen, "prejudice" most often means "racism." Even psychologists have linked the constructs and have often used them interchangeably (Ponterotto & Pederson, 1993).

Sexism

Sexism, the belief that women are inferior, has been simply defined as "prejudice or discrimination against women." Like racism, sexism implies a mode of negative expression and affect. It involves the generalization of behavior to both individuals and groups, and it engenders a sense of inferiority and powerlessness in the designated individuals, girls and women (Reid, 1988).

Although racism occurs in various patterns worldwide, its manifestation is often exclusive to particular settings and circumstances. Sexism, on the other hand, appears to be virtually universal in scope (Reid, 1988). We find evidence of this universality in many diverse cultures. For example, Orthodox Hindus claim that women can never achieve salvation, unless they are reborn as men. Mormons maintain that women have inferior religious status. In their daily prayers, Orthodox Jewish men thank God that they were not born female. And the majority of Christian religions restrict the priesthood and highest levels of ministry to men.

There is evidence that both sexism and racism evolve from childhood socialization and societal expectations and are informed by culturally defined values. However, it is interesting to note that psychologists have focused on different explanations for sexism. Ashmore and DelBoca (1981) distinguished between explanations of prejudice that focused on intrapersonal factors and those that emphasized interpersonal relations. Sexism has been frequently described as societally induced and politically encouraged (Hyde, 1985).

Feminist scholars, as well as others, have insisted that social forces lie at the root of women's role limitations. While some researchers have discussed the anxiety men feel about changing female roles, feminist theorists have not labeled individuals with sexist attitudes as pathological (Reid, 1988). Indeed, the popular view is to accept or excuse individual acts against women because they constitute socially accepted practice.

Stereotypes

Prejudice in all of its forms depends upon the use of stereotypes—that is, cognitive structures used to store beliefs. Stereotypes are exaggerated belief systems through which we are able to create categories. As noted by Allport (1954) and Fiske (1993), stereotypes function to justify or rationalize our conduct in relation to the categories we create. Bethelehem (1985) also described the utility of stereotypes as enabling a person to respond to a particular individual in the same way one would respond to any other in that social category. Stereotypes may lead to both positive and negative generalizations; however, as with prejudice, contemporary interpretations are weighted on the negative side of the continuum.

Gardner (1994) proposed that stereotypes maintain information shared by one's own group, shown to be excessive and unjustified, and assumed to distinguish one group from another. Ashmore and DelBoca (1981) also suggested that stereotypes function in several ways to orient us to the social environment. First, stereotypes offer a cognitive orientation that reduces and simplifies the vast amount of information we face on a daily basis. Second, they provide a psychodynamic orientation that helps to protect and defend our ego or sense of self-worth. And third, they help individuals to relate to the in-group and identify out-group members. The utility of the above functions appears to yield sufficient motivation for the continued existence of stereotypes even when evidence refuting their validity is presented (Snyder & Miene, 1994).

Discrimination

While prejudice, racism, and sexism refer to belief systems, discrimination addresses the behavioral component of these beliefs and "refers to one's actions toward a person as a function of group membership" (Schroeder, Johnson, & Jensen, 1985, p. 83). It is important to note that prejudiced attitudes and biased beliefs do not necessarily lead to discriminatory behavior (LaPiere, 1934). However, historically, members of the powerful majority have routinely denied access to economic, educational, political, and social opportunities to members of powerless or minority groups (Brewer, 1994; Lalonde & Cameron, 1994; United States Commission on Civil Rights, 1992). Recent examples of discrimination may be found in federal policies (e.g., exclusion of gay men and lesbians in the military), local mandates (e.g., lower funding of schools with predominantly African American or Latino students), and individual actions (e.g., personal attacks against ethnic minorities on college campuses).

A Brief History of Research on Prejudice

"American psychology up to 1920 was lily-white, consisting essentially of native or imported Anglo-Saxons (if we do not take the definition of this term too literally), with an occasional Jew or half-Jew thrown in. . . . From the twenties on, however, ethnics began to move into the profession in ever-increasing numbers. . . . It was not until the sixties that Italian, Greek, and all other 'ethnic' names showed up in large numbers among our journal authors. Blacks were, of course, even further behind. . . . Between 1920 and 1966 the ten leading departments produced over 3700 Ph.D.s in psychology, a survey found only eight of them to have been blacks" (Samelson, 1978, pp. 271–272).

Prejudice and discrimination have existed in many nations and for many centuries; still, these functions may be claimed as the foundation of society in the United States. Religious, ethnic, and racial prejudices were evidenced in the United States from days of the earliest settlements, and while progress may be claimed in many arenas, there can be no pronouncement of a resolution to the difficult issues (Tobach & Rosoff, 1994). The presence of psychologists as participants in trying to explain or prevent prejudice is a relatively recent phenomenon. We can see how their research helped to shape the public discourse and contributed to the general world understanding.

Examining Anti-Semitism and Racism

For more than six decades, psychologists have struggled to analyze and evaluate a variety of sociopolitical issues involving prejudice and discrimination, most typically framed in terms of intergroup relations. Dominating the social research agenda throughout the 1940s, 1950s, and 1960s were the problems of anti-Semitism and other anti-ethnic or racist views (e.g., LaPiere, 1934; Hartley, 1946). The philosophy and strategies of Hitler, who transformed religious and racial discrimination from personal actions into governmental policies, mobilized the efforts of a number of psychologists who focused their efforts on addressing such social injustice.

Researchers such as Allport (1954) and Adorno and others (1950) articulated psychological explanations that were both personal (i.e., characterizations of personality such as authoritarian) and structural (i.e., representations of group needs and goals such as cohesion). In preparing the defense against the egregious injustices of the war, they were also well positioned to offer assistance to the cause of African Americans. Indeed, the legal challenges prepared by civil rights organizations benefited from the definitions of racism, explications of authoritarian personality, and descriptions of how racist behavior may be manifest.

We would present an unrealistic view of the research of that era, however, if we only cite the useful and antiprejudice literature. For every set of investigations that outlined the damage and the pathology of prejudice, there were others offering justifications and apologies for racial, religious, and gender-based discrimination. While the proponents of equity have demonstrated the impact of social forces on both victims and perpetrators of discrimination, the researchers promoting discrimination have typically relied on genetic explanations.

Indeed, as Duran, Guillory, and Villanueva (1990) wrote, "Psychology has been a very useful tool in the effort to control oppressed people. The profession openly assists oppressive systems to continue to perpetuate supremacy. This is particularly evident in professional practices such as testing, research, diagnosis, treatment, and training" (p. 212). Recently, psychologists have renewed the debate instigated by proponents of the notion that social inequities can be best explained by genetic differences. In spite of seriously flawed analyses and distorted assumptions, these notions justified in the name of psychological research have reached vast audiences (Kamin, 1995).

Moving toward Diversity

During the years after World War II, the focus on white-black relations and on anti-Jewish sentiment so dominated the attention of psychologists and the public that other forms of discrimination received scant, if any, attention. As the sexual revolution of the 1960s overpowered the drive for the civil rights of black Americans, white women took over the social arena. Owing in large part to the successes of affirmative-action policies, developed initially to remedy racial discrimination in education and employment settings, the number of white women researchers grew and they began to examine the inequities owing to sex or gender (Deaux, 1995). (The number of African American and other American ethnic minorities also grew, although much more slowly; thus, the numbers and the research focused on these ethnic populations remain small. See Bernal & Castro, 1994; Reid, 1994b).

The explosion of interest in research on women and gender equity was followed by attention to other groups who found themselves left out of the mainstream of society and psychology: gays and lesbians, the aged, the disabled, and victims of abuse and violence. The movement to recognize the diversity of American populations became important for both political and scientific reasons. Yet psychological research remained hampered by the dominance of the white male perspective throughout the research process—that is, this perspective permeated assumptions, terminology, measures, and analyses (Tobach & Rosoff, 1994; Wallston, 1981).

Paradigms for Prejudice

"Every Jew by now has to realize that he is merely tolerated as a guest in Germany and has to submit absolutely to the laws of the host country" (*Sturmer*, 1939, cited by Kaplan, 1995).

"After World War I the Negro (Black) boys strutted around proud of their service and their uniforms. But White people became angry and said, 'Who do they think they are?' My brother asked, 'What more do I have to do to prove I'm an American, too?'" (Delany, Delany, & Hearth, 1993, p. 103).

Nancy Wang (1995), a Chinese American, is frequently asked where she comes from, because only white Americans are seen as real Americans. She writes, "I'm fifth-generation American. . . . Am I not American by now?"

Psychology's attempts to understand prejudice have focused on the development of explanatory paradigms. These models have covered a variety of circumstances and agendas, from biological to political to personal. None successfully explains all conditions under which we find manifestations of prejudice. Duckitt (1992) concurs with this analysis and claims that the paradigms that have evolved are in response to specific social and historical circumstances. Nevertheless, it is interesting to review the various determinants used in the analysis of prejudice. These determining factors include power, personality, identity, and social relationships.

Models of Power

Power has been used as a factor in analyzing the experience of prejudice for certain groups over certain periods of time and across macro systems, such as economic, educational, or political institutions. The use of historical and sociocultural perspectives has led theorists to propose a relationship between prejudice and power that is recurring and sustained. According to Winter (1973), power refers to the intentional influence of one party over another. The party may be an individual or a group. Majority groups, according to Moscovici's (1985) analysis of social influence, exert their power primarily through coerciveness. The dominant group (typically the majority) exacts conformity to the group norms from the minority. For example, racism and sexism are often seen as related to power, in that each process demands the relative inequality of status. Indeed, the implication of social power was included in Chesler's (1976) definition of racism as "acts or institutional procedures which help create or perpetuate sets of advantages or privileges for whites and exclusions or deprivations for minority groups" (p. 22).

When Meyers (1984) traced the history of the term "minority group" to its usage in Europe, he found that as early as 1913 social scientists drew parallels between the situation of blacks in the United States and European national minorities—for example, Slavs and Ukrainians. He concluded that the essential issue in problems involving prejudice is that of power. The connection between prejudice and political power was also embraced by Samelson (1978). In his research on the shifting focus of studies from race psychology to prejudice, he documented the decline in the comparisons of African Americans to European minorities and linked it to the lessening of national interest in immigration restrictions. Samelson (1978) also analyzed psychology's attention to so-called Nordic superiority and pointed to its connection with opinions widely held in the United States during the early 1920s. He noted that testing for differences in intelligence between European races was prevalent until about the 1930s, when the public shifted its perspective from "racial homogeneity to interracial harmony" (p. 271).

Models Based on Personality

Models for explaining prejudice have also been based on intrapersonal factors, such as personality. For example, Thompson (1982), who conducted a psychopolitical analysis of discrimination, suggested that resistance to new or different groups was best explained by the projections of inner angers and fears stemming from insecurities of the in-group members. To accept personality as a factor in prejudice, we must assume that certain people are more likely to lend themselves to biased beliefs (e.g., the authoritarian personality). Indeed, one form of this model suggests that angry and defensive people will often be prejudiced (Peterson, Doty, & Winter, 1993).

The motivating factor for aggressive discrimination against particular outgroups was the focus for much of the research that followed World War I. Hovland and Sears (1940) suggested that discrimination was the result of ingroup frustration. Katz and Braly (1933) used Princeton University students, in what became a historic study, to define prejudice as irrational and based on personality type. Later, Allport's (1954) classic, *Prejudice*, laid the foundation for a theory still accepted by most social psychologists today. He posed that prejudice emanates from negative emotions and attitudes.

Following Allport's analysis and thesis connecting hostile attitudes to discriminatory behavior, psychologists paid considerable notice to defining the authoritarian personality and connecting it to prejudice. Lack of substantiation and limited usefulness caused attention to this personality type to subside during the 1980s. Stone (1995) recently traced the rise and fall of interest in the authoritarian personality and suggested that the decline was based on methodological flaws, not conceptual ones. He suggested that there is still a need to understand the syndrome that links aggressiveness, prejudice, and submission to authority. He also pointed to the resurgence of research focused on this personality construct as coincident with the reappearance of fascism in the United States and in Europe, as noted in the popular press.

Models Based on Identity

Social identity theorists (Hogg & Abrams, 1988) contend that selection procedures used by people for social functioning are rarely carried out in an objective or dispassionate manner. The lack of objectivity appears to be due to self-involvement. That is, we typically categorize people in relationship to ourselves—like me or not like me. (This theme also appears in the Russian chapter on political psychology.) Because the identity of the individual is so closely associated with the group's identity and group membership, Hogg and Abrams believe that it is clear why in-group stereotypes tend to be favorable and outgroup ones are derogatory and unfavorable.

The use of out-groups as scapegoats for in-group problems is easier for ingroup members when they establish markers to denote the differences between themselves and the out-groups. Some out-group characteristics are easily recognized, such as ethnic membership or gender. When the distinguishing characteristics are less obvious, the in-group may attempt to heighten them; hence, Nazis made Jews wear yellow stars. Or the in-group may otherwise distort the out-group characteristics: Nazi researchers paid significant attention to Jewish facial features (Kaplan, 1995). Frequently out-group members are dehumanized and depersonalized in some way to make differential treatment more acceptable. (Disenfranchised people, for example, are viewed as living by lower standards—

i.e., less ethical, less moral, less human.) What psychology has described through numerous investigations into group behavior is the tendency of individuals to treat out-group members not as individuals but as depersonalized "others."

Social Relationship Model

The social relationship model focuses on the way the prejudiced person responds to a situation. It is argued that social lives, rather than the nature of minds, are responsible for prejudice (Lewis, 1992). Indeed, many researchers have attempted to explicate the relevant dimensions of in-group versus out-group behavior. Studies by Billig and others (Billig, 1973; Billig & Tajfel, 1973; Rabbie & Horwitz, 1988) demonstrate that the mere division of people into groups with little justification (e.g., based on a coin toss) resulted in biased evaluations. Ferguson and Kelley (1964) found that discrimination that favors in-group members and discriminates against out-group members occurred even without explicit competition.

Tajfel (1972) indicated that competition for resources was a real factor in intergroup discrimination and that such discrimination was perceived as benefiting both the in-group and the individual as a member of that group. Thus, in times of financial exigency or resource scarcity, it becomes of paramount importance to decide who is "in" and to influence "in" members to conform to group expectancies and attitudes. We must remember that group rules dictate that members who deviate from the majority position may find themselves forced to leave the group. The competitiveness between in-groups and out-groups has become particularly intense in current times owing to financial difficulties.

What psychologists found as far back as 1955 was that "in the long run group uniformity is secured at the expense of group success and group adaptation to the environment" (Muscovici, 1988, p. 350). This finding refers to experimental work that demonstrated that the social pressure of a group to conform is stronger than reality, stronger than knowledge of appropriate behavior, even stronger than group achievement. Such pressure has been found to effectively operate in opposition to the group's interests. Discrimination can also be increased or decreased by varying factors, such as the salience and magnitude of group differences, levels of in-group cohesiveness, and cooperation or competition between groups. The paradox for social psychology, according to Muscovici, is to explain how a group can change if the social power of the group typically forces compliance to the norms from its members. He claims that the only possible solution is to recognize that minority groups can influence the majority. Thus, innovation, creativity, growth, and development in new directions are possible only if there is "deviance."

Outcomes of Prejudice and Discrimination

Prejudice and discrimination are not merely hypothetical constructs; they represent real-world phenomena. Thus, attention must be directed to their outcomes. Not surprisingly, most research has focused on the effects on the groups toward whom discrimination has been directed. For example, oppressed people (such as African Americans) have been found to be plagued with self-hatred and identity problems because of negation of their humanity (Fannon, 1963; Memmi, 1965). Similarly, women typically have lower levels of self-esteem or expectancies for their own success than men (Laws, 1975; Murrell, Olson, & Frieze, 1995).

In addition to such intropunitive or self-directed reactions to prejudice, Allport (1954) also identified extropunitive reactions. He indicated that these might be positive, such as increased efforts to succeed or strengthening of in-group ties. However, more often prejudice leads victims to develop feelings of blame and to target outside forces by acting with hostility or suspicious prejudice toward other groups, aggression, and revolt.

Increasingly, however, researchers have documented the impact not only on the recipients of discrimination but also on proponents of biased attitudes and actions. Dennis (1981) is one of the few who examined white reactions to being immersed in a tradition of racism. From his study of white people's autobiographies, he extracted the deleterious effects: ignorance of blacks, duality of consciousness developed from the double ethical standards, and conformity to norms. Terry (1981) and Karp (1981) also discuss how racism "undermines and distorts" white people's view of themselves and serves to isolate them from potential friends and allies. Additionally, emotional consequences were found to include guilt and shame, and some found that extreme prejudice may constitute a mental illness (Skillings & Dobbins, 1991).

We do not discount findings that demonstrate that majority groups members may suffer ill effects from the prejudicial views of the society; however, we must agree with Ridley (1989) that benefits also accrue to those in the majority. Thus, it is found that whites experience a number of positive outcomes from societal prejudice directed against others. These benefits include social privilege, economic status, political power, and even gains in psychological status (e.g., feeling special). To these benefits, Simpson and Yinger (1985) add sexual advantages, prestige, and maintenance of the status quo (change is often frightening, sameness is comforting). With so many advantages for the in-group, the difficulty in combating prejudice becomes readily apparent.

New Directions in Research on Prejudice

Attention to research on prejudice has waxed and waned, as we have noted earlier. It appears that we may be approaching a period of increased interest coinciding with (1) current attacks on ethnic minority opportunities in the public sector, (2) social and political gains by women, (3) greater acceptance for gays and lesbians, and (4) policies to recognize the needs of disabled and disadvantaged. It should be recognized, however, that even with the many and varied groups of individuals seeking power and societal status, the prototype

of all negative attitudes and discriminatory behavior for Americans continues to be racism—that is, attitudes against blacks (Ponterotto & Pederson,
1993). Ironically, while Myrdal (1970), in remarks to the Nobel Prize committee, was announcing the diminution of the inferiority doctrine and the
resolution of racial tensions, Jensen (1969) and others were resurrecting the
notions of genetic differences. Klineberg (1986) noted that the pronouncement almost 30 years ago of the end of racial tensions proved to be remarkably premature.

Increasing Complexity

As we approach the end of this millennium, racial and ethnic tensions are still
with us. Gender discrimination and other forms of bias also remain. Hatred
based on faulty generalizations and unfounded assumptions continues to impact our society. As in the past, psychologists are found on all sides of the question. On the side of reducing tension, some models have been proposed and
research efforts have been directed at uncovering and understanding the processes involved. Many of these current discussions involve a reformulation of
past theories. The new proposals, however, have been responsive to criticisms
of psychology's failure to adequately account for the complexity in identity
development and personality caused by diversity and domination by the majority (Gaines & Reed, 1995; Reid, 1993, 1994a).

Ponterotto (1991), for example, developed a reformulation in which he linked
his conceptualization of prejudice with Allport's discussion of definition, origins, and manifestation. However, he also extended the analysis to explain
racial tensions of the late 1980s and 1990s by presenting a developmentally se-
quenced approach to multicultural awareness as a mechanism for prejudice
prevention. As he reformulated strategies to combat racism, others have been
focused on sexism. Until recently, these processes have been treated as discrete,
if parallel. When the effects of racism have been studied, it has been assumed
by most examiners to affect men and women equally. Similarly, sexism has been
presumed to pose an identical problem for white women and for women of color
(Burnham, 1994).

As white women have ignored issues of ethnicity, men of color have ignored
sexism. Women of color, then, have fallen into the interstices of research and
theory on racism and sexism. They are lumped together with men of color
when racial comparisons are made and with white women when gender comparisons are made (Reid, 1988). Researchers appear to believe that racism
is experienced in some settings and sexism in other settings, so the experiences may be compared. In fact, racism and sexism, rather than serving as alternative sources of a similar prejudice, may actually have an interactive effect.
Smith and Stewart (1983) suggested that racism and sexism should be examined in relationship to each other. A model that incorporates a contextual
and interactive framework is recommended for a more complex and accurate
representation.

Appreciating Diversity

While researchers in the past also sought ways to prevent prejudice and discrimination, considerable bias was found in the research conducted in ethnic minority communities. Many white researchers found the pathology they expected while ignoring strengths and adaptive capacities. An additional problem in research on race and ethnicity has been the assumption that greater homogeneity exists among ethnic populations than among the majority community. Thus, very little attention has been given to differences in socioeconomic status, differences in cultural background, or even sex and age differences (Jackson, Chatters, & Neighbors, 1986; Reid, 1994a; Reid & Kelly, 1995).

The steady increase in research on positive attributes of ethnic minority communities may be seen to correspond to the slowly increasing numbers of ethnic minority researchers (Reid, 1994b). A modern-day case may also be made to relate changes in current attitudes toward women with the existing social, political, and economic climates. White women, for example, have experienced significant increases of participation in politics as economic status has changed (Deaux, 1995). The higher cost of living made it necessary for families to have two incomes; status in the economic arena led to strength in the political arena. Similarly, political and economic power promoted freedom in social settings. Social opportunities have led to economic successes, but they have also caused male ambivalence and resentment (Fiske & Glick, 1995).

Understanding the Majority

Almost 20 years ago, Samelson (1978) remarked that "social psychologists have made valuable contributions to our understanding of 'race relations.' But could even greater contributions have been vitiated by an unreflected attitude toward their own role?" (p. 274). Now, more so than before, the impact of racism on perpetrators has been examined and meaningful behavior revealed.

In discussing the relationship between the dominant in-group and the out-group, Reid (1988) strongly suggested an impact on the perception of the discrimination. That is, for white men or women, racism and discriminatory practices can be perceived as affecting only members of the out-group, a segment of the population that can be ignored and dismissed. Therefore, it was deemed difficult for these in-group members to see themselves as participants or collaborators in racist practices. As Pence, Pendleton, Dobbins, and Sgro (1982) suggested, white people do not believe that the elimination of racism will actually provide any personal gain for them. Instead, the contrary belief exists— namely, that it is only the out-group who will gain from it.

Fiske (1993) appeared to concur. Her research led her to contend that the powerful majority does not need to pay attention to the powerless. Her hypothesis is that a mutually reinforcing interaction between power and stereotyping exists, leading those in control to use stereotypes more often as a shorthand way to deal with the masses of out-groups. Major (1995) pursued this issue further as "the psychology of entitlement." She asserted that social-comparison biases may prevent an awareness of disadvantage. In addition, she declared that attribution biases actually legitimate disadvantage. In an attempt to examine antecedents and consequences of these beliefs, she has taken a relatively new track and focused not on the existence of prejudice and discrimination but on how members of groups evaluate their circumstances.

Others have also tried to revise existing paradigms by examining, for example, satisfied female workers (Crosby, 1982) and satisfied working wives (Biernat & Wortman, 1991). Such studies are rare, however, and research comparing the satisfaction of African Americans to whites are even more rare and typically use inadequate samples (Jackson, Chatters, & Neighbors, 1986).

Summary

Overt prejudice appears to be increasing nationally and worldwide. Discrimination, both subtle and blatant, is more in evidence. Accordingly, we see more psychologists attending to this phenomenon and its apparent concomitant factors (e.g., Bernal & Castro, 1994; Fiske, 1993; Weiner, 1993). While some researchers prepare to address this situation as an emerging problem, anecdotal evidence of today seems disconcertingly similar to examples of racism from decades past.

While new twists to definitions and approaches are being developed, the old explanatory models still seem to hold. Thus, it holds true that negative attitudes are related to power, personality, and social conditions. Justifications for demeaning stereotypes now, as in the past, seem to depend on assumptions of biological inferiority or superiority of one group over another (Tobach & Rosoff, 1994). Researchers who seek strategies for the prevention of hostilities continue to recommend "humanizing" the powerless through attention to individual difference rather than accepting the dehumanizing influences of overgeneralizations.

Indeed, our review of the psychology of prejudice and discrimination appears to reveal that we are putting old paradigms in new models, a process that does not enhance or improve the product. We are, therefore, concerned that our society and our discipline appear to be repeating some of the distasteful aspects of the past. Are the projects and products to combat the harmful impact of prejudice, thus far, offering more than repackaged strategies? Probably the most encouraging development is the slowly emerging view that new, more sophisticated and complex perspectives, tactics, and applications will be needed for the future. These will necessarily account for the multiple identities of both the stereotyped and those who are stereotyping and the varied contexts in which they find themselves.

References

Adorno, T. W., Frenkel-Brunswik, E., Levinson, D. J., & Sanford, R. N. (1950). *The authoritarian personality*. New York: Harper.
Allport, G. W. (1954/1979). *The nature of prejudice*. Reading, Mass.: Addison-Wesley.
Ashmore, R. D., & DelBoca, F. K. (1981). Conceptual approaches to stereotypes and

stereotyping. In D. L. Hamilton (ed.), *Cognitive processes in stereotyping and intergroup behavior* (pp. 1–35). Hillsdale, N.J.: Lawrence Erlbaum.

Associated Press (1995). Ga. race tracking in schools exposed. *The Press of Atlantic City, New Jersey*, 13 June, p. A8.

Bernal, M. A., & Castro, F. G. (1994). Are clinical psychologists prepared for service and research with ethnic minorities?: Report of a decade of progress. *American Psychologist, 49,* 797–805.

Bethelehem, D. W. (1985). *A social psychology of prejudice.* New York: St. Martin's.

Biasey, E. L. (1972). Paranoia and racism in the United States. *Journal of the National Medical Association, 64,* 353–358.

Biernat, M., & Wortman, C. B. (1991). Sharing of home responsibilities between professionally employed women and their husbands. *Journal of Personality and Social Psychology, 60,* 844–860.

Billig, M. (1973). Normative communication in a minimal intergroup situation. *European Journal of Social Psychology, 3,* 339–343.

Billig, M., & Tajfel, H. (1973). Social categorization and similarity in intergroup behavior. *European Journal of Social Psychology, 3,* 27–52.

Blauner, R. (1969). Internal colonialism and ghetto revolt. *Social Problems, 16,* 393–408.

Brewer, M. B. (1994). The social psychology of prejudice: Getting it all together. In M. P. Zanna & J. M. Olson (eds.), *The psychology of prejudice: The Ontario symposium* (vol. 7, pp. 315–329). Hillsdale, N.J.: Lawrence Erlbaum.

Burnham, L. (1994). Race and gender: The limits of analogy. In E. Tobach & B. Rosoff (eds.), *Challenging racism and sexism: Alternatives to genetic explanations* (pp. 143–162). New York: Feminist Press.

Chesler, M. A. (1976). Contemporary sociological theories of racism. In P. A. Katz (ed.), *Towards the elimination of racism.* New York: Pergamon.

Comer, J. P. (1980). White racism: Its root, form, and function. In R. L. Jones (ed.), *Black psychology* (2d ed.). New York: Harper and Row.

Crosby, F. (1982). *Relative deprivation and working women.* New York: Oxford University Press.

Deaux, K. (1995). How basic can you be?: The evolution of research on gender stereotypes. *Journal of Social Issues, 51,* 11–20.

Delany, L. T. (1980). The other bodies in the river. In R. L. Jones (ed.), *Black psychology* (2d ed.). New York: Harper and Row.

Delany, S., Delany, A. E., & Hearth, A. H. (1993). *Having our say: The Delany sisters' first 100 years.* New York: Kodansha.

Dennis, R. M. (1981). Socialization and racism: The white experience. In B. P. Bowser & R. G. Hunt (eds.), *Impacts of racism on white Americans* (pp. 71–85). Beverly Hills: Sage.

Duckitt, J. H. (1992). Psychology and prejudice: A historical analysis and integrative framework. *American Psychologist, 47,* 1182–1193.

Duckitt, J. H. (1994). *The social psychology of prejudice.* Westport, Conn.: Praeger.

Duran, E., Guillory, B., & Villaneuva, M. (1990). Third and fourth world concerns: Toward a liberation psychology. In G. Stricker, E. Davis-Russell, R. W. Hammond, J. McHolland, K. Polite, & B. E. Vaughn (eds.), *Toward ethnic diversification in psychology education and training* (pp. 211–217). Washington, D.C.: American Psychological Association.

Ehrlich, H. J. (1973). *The social psychology of prejudice.* New York: Wiley.

Fannon, F. (1963). *The wretched of the earth.* New York: Grove.

Ferguson, C. L., & Kelley, H. H. (1964). Significant factors in overevaluation of own group's product. *Journal of Abnormal and Social Psychology, 69,* 223–228.

Fiske, S. T. (1993). Controlling other people: The impact of power on stereotyping. *American Psychologist, 48,* 621–628.

Fiske, S. T., & Glick, P. (1995). Ambivalence and stereotypes cause sexual harassment: A theory with implications for organizational change. *Journal of Social Issues, 51,* 97–115.

Gaines, S. O., Jr., & Reed, E. S. (1995). Prejudice: From Allport to DuBois. *American Psychologist, 50,* 96–103.

Gardner, R. C. (1994). Stereotypes as consensual beliefs. In M. P. Zanna & J. M. Olson (eds.), *The psychology of prejudice: The Ontario symposium* (vol 7, pp. 1–31). Hillsdale, N.J.: Lawrence Erlbaum.

Hartley, E. L. (1946). *Problems in prejudice.* New York: King's Crown.

Hogg, M. A., & Abrams, D. (1988). *Social identifications: A social psychology of intergroup relations and group processes.* London: Routledge.

Hovland, C. I., & Sears, R. R. ((1940). Minor studies of aggression: VI, Correlation of lynching with economic studies. *Journal of Psychology, 9,* 301–310.

Hyde, J. S. (1985). *Half the human experience: The psychology of women* (3d ed.). Lexington, Mass.: Heath.

Jackson, J. S., Chatters, L. M., & Neighbors, H. W. (1986). The subjective life quality of black Americans. In F. M. Andrews (ed.), *Research on the quality of life* (pp. 193–213). Ann Arbor: Institute for Social Research.

Jensen, A. R. (1969). How much can we boost I.Q. and scholastic achievement? *Harvard Educational Review, 39,* 1–123.

Jones, J. M. (1981). The concept of racism and its changing reality. In B. J. Bowser & R. G. Hunt (eds.), *Impacts of racism on white Americans* (pp. 17–49). Beverly Hills: Sage.

Kamin, L. J. (1995). Book review: Behind the curve. *Scientific American,* February, 99–103.

Kaplan, G. (1995). Irreducible "human nature": Nazi views on Jews and women. In E. Tobach & B. Rosoff (eds.), *Challenging racism and sexism: Alternatives to genetic explanations* (pp. 188–210). New York: Feminist Press.

Karp, J. B. (1981). The emotional impact and a model for changing racist attitudes. In B. P. Bowser & R. G. Hunt (eds.), *Impacts of racism on white Americans* (pp. 279–314). Beverly Hills: Sage.

Katz, D., & Braly, K. (1933). Racial stereotypes of one hundred college students. *Journal of Abnormal and Social Psychology, 28,* 280–290.

Klineberg, O. (1968). Prejudice: The concept. In D. Sills (ed.), *Encyclopedia of the social sciences* (vol. 12, pp. 439–448). New York: Macmillan.

Klineberg, O. (1986). SPSSI and race relations, in the 1950s and after. *Journal of Social Issues, 42,* 53–59.

Lalonde, R. N., & Cameron, J. E. (1994). Behavioral responses to discrimination: A focus on action. In M. P. Zanna & J. M. Olson (eds.), *The psychology of prejudice: The Ontario symposium* (vol. 7, pp. 33–54). Hillsdale, N.J.: Lawrence Erlbaum.

LaPiere, R. T. (1934). Attitudes versus actions. *Social Forces, 13,* 230–237.

Laws, J. L. (1975). Psychology of tokenism: An analysis. *Sex Roles, 1,* 51–68.

Lewis, M. (1992). Many minds make madness: Judgment under uncertainty and certainty. *Psychological Inquiry, 3,* 170–172.

Major, B. (1995). From social inequality to personal entitlement: The role of social comparisons, legitimacy appraisals, and group membership. In M. Zanna (ed.), *Advances in experimental social psychology* (vol. 26). New York: Academic Press.

Memmi, A. (1965). *The colonizer and the colonized*. Boston: Beacon.

Meyers, B. (1984). Minority group: An ideological formulation. *Social Problems*, 32(1), 1–15.

Moscovici, S. (1985). Notes toward a description of social representation. *European Journal of Social Psychology*, 18, 211–250.

Murrell, A. J., Olson, J. E., & Frieze, I. H. (1995). Sexual harassment and gender discrimination: A longitudinal study of women managers. *Journal of Social Issues*, 51, 151–167.

Myrdal, G. (1970). Biases in social research. In A. Tiselius & S. Nilsson (eds.), *The place of values in a world of facts: Nobel symposium* (vol. 14, pp. 155–164). New York: Harper & Row.

Pence, E., Pendleton, W. C., Dobbins, G. H., & Sgro, J. (1982). Effects of causal explanations and sex variables on recommendations for corrective actions following employee failure. *Organizational Behavior and Human Performance*, 29, 227–240.

Peterson, B. W., Doty, R. M., & Winter, D. G. (1993). Authoritarianism and attitudes toward contemporary social issues. *Personality and Social Psychology Bulletin*, 19, 174–184.

Ponterotto, J. G. (1991). The nature of prejudice revisited: Implications for counseling intervention. *Journal of Counseling and Development*, 70, 216–224.

Ponterotto, J. G., & Pedersen, J. G. (1993). *Preventing prejudice: A guide for counselors and educators*. Newbury Park, Calif.: Sage.

Price Waterhouse v. Hopkins (1989). 490 U.S. 228.

Rabbie, J. M., & Horwitz, M. (1988). Categories versus groups as explanator concepts in intergroup relations. *European Journal of Social Psychology*, 18, 117–123.

Reid, P. T. (1988). Racism and sexism: Comparisons and conflicts. In P. A. Katz & D. Taylor (eds.), *Eliminating racism* (pp. 203–221). New York: Plenum.

Reid, P. T. (1993). Poor women in psychological research: Shut up and shut out. *Psychology of Women Quarterly*, 17, 133–152.

Reid, P. T. (1994a). Development of gender and class identities for African Americans. Paper presented at the Annual Conference of the American Psychological Association, Los Angeles, Calif.

Reid, P. T. (1994b). The real problem in the study of culture. *American Psychologist*, 49, 524–525.

Reid, P. T., & Kelly, E. (1995). Research on women of color: From ignorance to awareness. *Psychology of Women Quarterly*, 18, 477–486.

Ridley, C. R. (1989). Racism in counseling as an adverse behavioral process. In P. B. Pedersen, J. G. Draguns, W. J. Lonner, & J. E. Trimble (eds.), *Counseling across cultures* (3d ed., pp. 55–77). Honolulu: University of Hawaii Press.

Rothenberg, P. S. (1992). Defining racism and sexism. In P. S. Rothenberg (ed.), *Race, class, and gender in the United States: An integrated study* (pp. 5–8). New York: St. Martin's.

Samelson, F. (1978). From "race psychology" to "studies in prejudice": Some observations in the thematic reversal in social psychology. *Journal of the History of the Behavioral Sciences*, 14, 265–278.

Schroeder, D. A., Johnson, D. E., & Jensen, T. D. (1985). *Contemporary readings in social psychology*. Chicago: Nelson-Hall.

Simpson, G. E., & Yinger, J. M. (1985). *Racial and cultural minorities: An analysis of prejudice and discrimination* (5th ed.). New York: Plenum.

Skillings, J. H., & Dobbins, J. E. (1991). Racism as a disease: Etiology and treatment implications. *Journal of Counseling and Development, 70,* 206–212.

Smith, A., & Stewart, A. J. (1983). Approaches to studying racism and sexism in black women's lives. *Journal of Social Issues, 39,* 1–15.

Snyder, M., & Miene, P. (1994). On the functions of stereotypes and prejudice. In M. P. Zanna & J. M. Olson (eds.), *The psychology of prejudice: The Ontario symposium* (vol. 7). Hillsdale, N.J.: Lawrence Erlbaum.

Stone, W. F. (1995). The rise, fall, and resurgence of authoritarianism research. *SPSSI Newsletter* (Society for the Psychological Study of Social Issues), April, p. 14.

Strong, B., & DeVault, C. (1994). *Human sexuality.* Mountain View, Calif.: Mayfield.

Tajfel, H. (1972). The devaluation by children of their own national and ethnic groups: Two case studies. *British Journal of Social and Clinical Psychology, 11*(3), 235–243.

Terry, R. W. (1981). The negative impact on white values. In B. P. Bowser & R. G. Hunt (eds.), *Impacts of racism on white Americans* (pp. 119–151). Beverly Hills: Sage.

Thompson, H. O. (1982). A case study in social psychology. *Political Psychology, 3,* 221–248.

Tobach, E., & Rosoff, B. (1994). *Challenging racism and sexism: Alternatives to genetic explanations.* New York: Feminist Press.

United States Commission on Civil Rights (1992). The problem: Discrimination. In P. S. Rothenberg (ed.), *Race, class, and gender in the United States: An integrated study* (pp. 9–19). New York: St. Martin's.

Wallston, B. (1981). What are questions in psychology of women?: A feminist approach to research. *Psychology of Women Quarterly, 5,* 597–617.

Wang, N. (1995). Born Chinese and a woman in America. In J. Adleman & G. Enguidanos (eds.), *Racism in the lives of women: Testimony, theory, and guides to antiracist practice* (pp. 97–110). New York: Harrington.

Webster's (1984). *New World Dictionary* (2d ed.). New York: Warner.

Weiner, B. (1993). On sin versus sickness: A theory of perceived responsibility and social motivation. *American Psychologist, 48,* 957–965.

Winter, David (1973). *The power motive.* New York: Free Press.

17

Ethnic Psychology in the United States

Jonathan S. Kaplan & Stanley Sue

Throughout history, human beings have had to deal with individual and group differences on many dimensions. Two of the most important dimensions are ethnicity and race. Ethnic and racial groups often mirror the fears, prejudices, and hostilities, as well as the curiosity, benevolence, and understanding, of one group of people toward another. The history of the United States is strongly embedded in ethnicity and ethnic relations. When the founding fathers sought freedom and democracy and the establishment of a new country in the Americas, the seeds were laid for conflict with the indigenous people—the Native Americans—and for the introduction of African slavery. Years of ethnic and racial strife, including a civil war, the civil rights movement, and the controversies over affirmative action, immigration, and racial genetic differences in intelligence have bedeviled the history of the United States. Yet, in many ways, tremendous progress over time has been made in race and ethnic relations.

In this chapter, our goal is to describe developments in ethnic psychology—namely, the study of ethnicity and ethnic relations in the United States. We shall see how the field of psychology has attempted to study and explain ethnic differences and relationships. We conclude by indicating the implications of the research on ethnicity.

Ethnic psychology has been defined as the examination of psychological variables within an ethnic group in order to discover the relationships between characteristics of that ethnic group, other groups with which it is in contact, and the corresponding intergroup interactions (Berry, 1994). Put another way, ethnic psychology strives to explain psychological differences and similarities between ethnic groups based on the qualities of each ethnic group. Thus, the field is concerned with diverse issues, such as ethnic differences in academic achievement, intelligence, psychopathology, prejudice, communication, and personal relationships.

For purposes of this chapter, we discuss ethnic groups at a broad, macrolevel, limited to the nonwhite ethnic groups of African Americans, Hispanic Americans, Asian Americans, and Native Americans. (In the earlier part of this century, however, ethnic psychology often focused on white ethnic groups, such as the Irish, Italians, and Jews—e.g., Giordano & Levine, 1975.) In the United States, the recent growth rate of these minority ethnic groups is considerably higher than white European Americans. From 1980 to 1990, whites underwent a 6 percent growth in population. In contrast, African Americans grew by 13.2 percent, Hispanics by 53 percent, and Asian Americans by 95 percent (LEAP Asian Pacific American Public Policy Institute, 1993). Together with Native Americans, these ethnic groups constituted approximately 25 percent of the total U.S. population in 1990 (U.S. Bureau of Census, 1990). Within the next century, ethnic minorities will outnumber the white population in some states (Cross, Bazron, Dennis, & Isaacs, 1989). Therefore, the United States has become increasingly multiethnic—indeed, it is one of the most multiethnic countries in the world— and it is instructive to examine the issues and problems that arise from the interaction of different ethnic Americans.

In this chapter, our specific goal is to present a broad overview of the past, present, and future of ethnic psychology. Our discussion covers the following four areas:

1. We define *ethnicity* and outline related issues in order to provide an appropriate framework for discussion.
2. We present a very brief overview of the historical experiences of different ethnic groups in the United States as a background to facilitate understanding of ethnic relations in this country. Both racism (negative attitudes and beliefs about nonwhite groups) and discrimination (the corresponding poor treatment of nonwhite ethnic groups) characterize the historical relationships between white Americans and nonwhite ethnic groups.
3. We describe the past and present psychological models that attempt to explain ethnic differences. The evolution of these different perspectives demonstrates advances in scientific thinking, along with progress in the public consideration of ethnic issues.
4. Our final section outlines the challenges that face ethnic researchers in psychology.

Definition and Discussion of Ethnicity

The term "ethnicity" was originally derived from the Greek word for nation, *ethnos*. Herein, an ethnic group is defined as "a group socially distinguished or set apart, by others or by itself, primarily on the basis of cultural or nationality characteristics" (Feagin, 1989, p. 9). It is important to note that this is a social definition, not a biological one. However, outward physical similarities may also exist within certain ethnic groups.

Berry (1994) noted that ethnic groups have both objective and subjective components. They are united with a common lineage and culture that can be observed objectively from outside the group. In addition, an ethnic group subjectively defines its own sense of identity and group membership. When conducting research on different ethnic groups, it is therefore essential to determine beforehand what component(s) of ethnicity may explain the results.

In addition to the subjective and objective components, there are many different "levels" of ethnicity based on the specificity of the group under examination. Within each broad ethnic category (e.g., Asian American), there is a considerable amount of heterogeneity in terms of cultural values and historical experiences in the United States (Sue, Zane, & Young, 1994; Uehara, Takeuchi, & Smukler, 1994). As one provides more detail about the specific ethnic subgroup under study, one moves to a different level of analysis. For example, among Asian Americans, individuals may have originally descended from China, Korea, Japan, India, Taiwan, the Philippines, Southeast Asia, or even countries in South America. At the level of these more specific subgroups, systematic ethnic differences may appear (e.g., between Chinese Americans and Japanese Americans). Further subdivisions may also be possible: Chinese Americans who originally emigrated from mainland China may differ from immigrants who came from Taiwan or Hong Kong. Thus, research on Asian Americans may not be truly representative of Chinese Americans; research on Chinese immigrants from Taiwan may differ from findings with Chinese Americans born in the United States.

To create a visual example of ethnicity as a categorical variable, picture it as a pyramid: the broad, macrolevel descriptions (e.g., Asian American or Hispanic American), which include many different subgroups, appear at the bottom. More detailed group designations cause one to move up to higher levels of the pyramid until the apex of a highly specified group (e.g., third-generation, middle-class Chinese American college students) is reached. If one is comparing different levels within a pyramid, one is doing intraethnic research. Comparisons of different pyramids can be likened to interethnic research.

This ethnicity pyramid will help one determine whether or not cross-ethnic studies are conducting comparisons at the same level of ethnicity. For example, in a study of Mexican Americans, are they being compared—on a similar level of specificity—to Chinese Americans? Or are they being contrasted to Asian Americans in general, who represent a broader ethnic level? Naturally, either comparison may be empirically or theoretically justified depending on the nature of the experiment. In summary, when studying different ethnic groups, one should delineate the appropriate level of discourse, or ethnic (sub)group, to be clear about exactly who is being compared. Naturally, when conducting an experiment and interpreting its results, it is important to stay within those boundaries unless one is testing the generalizability of findings across different levels of ethnicity.

In psychological research, as well as everyday society, ethnicity is often confused with race and culture (Betancourt & Lopez, 1993). Essentially, culture is a collection of subjective norms that could apply to any kind of group, not only different ethnicities. So a common culture exists in the United States, in the workplace, in opera audiences, and so on. Race, on the other hand, is typically defined in terms of shared physical characteristics, such as skin color, hair type, and facial structure, that evolved from geographically isolated in-group breeding (Zuckerman, 1990). The traditional anthropological distinctions consist of Mongoloid, Negroid, and Caucasoid. However, as we discuss later, these categories have not withstood criticisms from modern-day research in genetics.

The Major Ethnic Minority Groups

African Americans

In 1619, the first Africans arrived in the United States as indentured servants. During the 17th and 18th centuries, the period of their servitude gradually extended to a life of slavery as a result of state laws, court precedents, and systematic maltreatment at the hands of the white slave owners (Burkey, 1978). Typically, African slaves were forced to work on plantations and small farms as field workers. As the interests of the white farm owners expanded in tobacco and cotton, their need for African labor also increased.

The ubiquitous oppression of the African slaves was often justified by both biblical and "scientific" sources (Guthrie, 1976; Thomas & Sillen, 1972). Some white Americans believed that, owing to their dark skin, the Africans were the cursed descendants of Noah's son Ham, as described in the Book of Genesis (Guthrie, 1976). Others argued that Africans were created before man and, accordingly, were not even human (Smith, 1993). Physicians of the time also described the Africans as having smaller, primitive brains and psychologies well suited for servitude (Thomas & Sillen, 1972). As a result, the slaves were denied basic human rights and subjected to beatings, psychological traumas, and squalid living conditions. Family members were often separated from each other. Laws concerning slavery were designed to safeguard the property rights of the slave owner and protect the safety of the white public (Hornsby, 1991).

The egalitarian principles embodied in the American Revolution started a series of manumissions in which black slaves were set free by their owners. The invention of the seed-separating cotton gin effectively reversed this trend, however. Cotton became a highly profitable crop, but it required large amounts of manual labor for cultivation and harvesting. As a result, the U.S demand for slave labor increased from 500,000 in 1776 to 4 million in 1861 (Burkey, 1978; Hornsby, 1991).

In 1865, following a bloody civil war, the Thirteenth Amendment to the U.S. Constitution officially abolished slavery. In the following years, African Americans technically were granted the same rights as other citizens, including the right to vote. However, racism, discrimination, and hatred directed against African Americans became more firmly entrenched in American life, thus preventing African Americans from attaining a better standard of living. In 1896, the U.S. Supreme Court case of *Plessy v. Ferguson* stated that "separate but equal" facilities could be established for blacks and whites. Consequently, African Americans were segregated within society and given inferior treatment, owing to the omnipresence of white racism. Public areas such as water fountains, bathrooms, and buses were divided into "colored" and "white" sections. In the South, Jim Crow laws essentially denied African Americans the right to vote through the imposition of barriers at the polls, such as literacy tests and poll taxes.

In 1954, the Supreme Court decision in *Brown v. Board of Education of Topeka, Kansas* declared that segregated school facilities were unequal and therefore unconstitutional. In the following decade, five civil rights acts were passed that established inviolable voting rights for African Americans and prohibited discriminatory practices in public areas and government programs.

In the 1960s, the civil rights movement demanded equal rights for African Americans and other minority groups. African Americans began to establish a positive self-consciousness on a national level. Black leaders such as Martin Luther King, Jr., Malcolm X, and Stokeley Carmichael provided energy and determination for the movement toward equal rights for African Americans. During this time, the government-sponsored program of affirmative action was designed to facilitate minority access to better employment positions and educational programs.

In recent years, African Americans have reached a higher level of prominence in American society. They occupy more prestigious political, social, and economic positions than ever before. However, there are still many threats to African Americans in this country. Poor socioeconomic conditions, high rates of drug use and criminality, and the persistence of American racism represent just a few of the serious obstacles facing African Americans today.

Hispanic Americans

Hispanic Americans are a very diverse group, composed of people from Mexico, Cuba, Puerto Rico, and Central and South America. Because Mexican Americans represent the vast majority of Hispanics in the United States (Martinez, 1986), their history will be documented here.

The original people of Mexico were conquered by Spain around 1522. Merging with the native population, the Spanish settlement grew northward from 1530 to 1800 into the present-day states of Texas, California, and New Mexico (Novas, 1994). While some people were direct descendants of the Spanish colonists, most inhabitants were of mixed ancestry between the Spanish and the indigenous people of Mexico.

White American traders had their first contact with Mexicans along the Santa Fe Trail in the late 1700s and 1800s. In addition to business relationships, some traders formed matrimonial ties with the local population and settled down in the Mexican territories. As the fledgling nation of the United States expanded westward in the 18th and 19th centuries, Mexicans fell into areas that were controlled by the American government. The increase of white settlers in the Southwest relegated the Mexican inhabitants to a minority, second-class status.

Fearing overcrowding on the East Coast, the country soon embarked on a popular journey of aggressive nationalism in the 19th century. Coined in 1845, the phrase "Manifest Destiny" proclaimed that Americans had the God-given right to rule the continent from coast to coast (Samora & Simon, 1993). As more settlers moved westward, conflicts slowly emerged between whites and Mexicans and between both groups against the Mexican government (Moore & Pachon, 1970; Samora & Simon, 1993).

The United States was at war with Mexico from 1846 to 1847. After early Mexican victories, the U.S. government prioritized the war effort, which produced a quick American victory. Through the Treaty of Guadalupe Hidalgo, the United States gained control of vast areas of Mexican territory, including Texas, California, New Mexico, and Arizona. Eighty thousand Mexicans thus became de facto citizens of the United States (Meier & Ribera, 1993).

The development of large farming interests, together with the railroad and mining industries, forced many Mexican ranchers and farmers out of business. Mexican Americans reluctantly assumed the subservient role of laborers or tenants in these businesses in order to support themselves and their families (Meier & Ribera, 1993; Moore & Pachon, 1970). Living in poor health and housing conditions, these workers characteristically earned low wages and moved often to follow the seasonal demands of different industries (Moore & Pachon, 1970).

Owing to the anti-Asian immigration acts of the 1880s and 1900s, Mexico provided a large number of laborers to work in American business ventures. The 1924 Immigration Act did not place any restrictions on immigration within the Western Hemisphere, so Mexican workers flocked across the border to fill the high demand for cheap labor (Novas, 1994).

When the Great Depression of 1930–1933 devastated American business, many Mexican workers were left jobless and dependent on government-sponsored programs. A movement within the United States called for the deportation of Mexican workers; 500,000 were sent back to Mexico during the 1930s (Novas, 1994). Later, in the 1940s, Mexican laborers were again welcomed into the country in the face of an agricultural crisis and the wartime demand for manufactured goods.

In the 1960s and 1970s, an increased ethnic consciousness developed among Mexican Americans. During this time, Cesar Chavez formed the first successful farm workers' union, which achieved better rights and a higher minimum wage from Californian grape growers. In addition, more militant, separatist movements led by Reis Tijerina and Rodolfo Gonzalez called for the return of federal properties unlawfully seized from Mexican property owners to their original heirs (Novas, 1994).

Today, Mexican Americans and other Hispanics report high levels of physical problems and psychological distress relative to the white population (Fabrega,

1995; Roberts, 1980). The discrimination against this minority group continues as well. Most recently, the state of California passed a resolution (Proposition 187) to deny social services to illegal immigrants. This law is targeted at undocumented Mexicans living in the country, but it undoubtably affects Mexican Americans whose rightful citizenship will be questioned.

Asian Americans

Often considered as a single ethnic group, Asian Americans actually include over 25 distinct ethnic groups, each with its own unique history in the United States (Uba, 1994). Owing to space limitations, we present a very brief description of the experiences of Japanese Americans, Chinese Americans, and Southeast Asians in this country.

Japanese Americans   Seeking work as farm laborers, Japanese immigrants started coming to the United States during the 1880s. In 1906, Executive Order 589 and, in 1907, the Gentlemen's Agreement restricted Japanese immigration. In response, many male Japanese who had settled here quickly arranged marriages with Japanese women overseas (known as "picture brides") in order to start families in the United States. So, by the passage of the Immigration Act of 1924, which totally restricted Japanese immigration, about 130,000 to 150,000 Japanese were living in this country (Uba, 1994).

   The most significant event affecting Japanese Americans was Executive Order 9066, issued by President Franklin Roosevelt during World War II. Because the United States was at war with Japan, people of Japanese ancestry were considered to be possible conspirators against the American war effort (Hatamiya, 1993). Consequently, in a wave of severe persecution and paranoia, the federal government removed Japanese Americans from their homes and incarcerated them in poorly accommodated internment camps, where they remained for the duration of the war. This presidential order deprived Japanese Americans of their rights to due process and equal protection under the law in flagrant violation of the U.S. Constitution: two-thirds of the 120,000 internees were American citizens by birth, and thus their civil liberties should have been protected and inviolable (Daniels, 1971, Irons, 1983, as cited in Takaki, 1989). As a result of the internment, many Japanese Americans lost their jobs, homes, and possessions. This victimization psychologically traumatized the internees and their children (Nagata, 1991).

Chinese Americans   The history of Chinese immigration in the United States has significantly affected the size and characteristics of Chinese American families over time (Glenn, 1983; Wong, 1985). Chinese Americans first started coming to the United States during the mid-19th century in order to find employment as farmhands, miners, or railroad workers (Chan, 1991). Emigration from China was severely curtailed by the 1882 Exclusion Act and totally cut off by the 1924 Immigration Act (Hing, 1993). During this time period, many laws were directed against the Chinese, including special taxes and restrictions in housing and employment (Daniels, 1988; Glenn, 1983). A Supreme Court decision classified Chinese women as laborers, thus subjecting them to immigration law restrictions. The Chinese American population was correspondingly limited, as Chinese men were unable to meet potential wives and start families in the United States (Hing, 1993).

During World War II, the United States began accepting a small quota of Chinese immigrants. Later, after the Communist victory in China, the United States encouraged Nationalist scientists and professionals to settle here (Uba, 1994). Today, Chinese arrive under the auspices of the 1965 Immigration Act (and its 1990 extension), which allows the immigration of individuals with special skills or people whose families reside in the United States (Hing, 1993). Because immigration quotas are no longer based on race, the number of Chinese immigrants has risen as individuals arrive from China, Taiwan, and Hong Kong (Uba, 1994). At present, only 37 percent of Chinese Americans are born in the United States; the rest are foreign-born immigrants (Sue, Zane, & Young, 1994).

Southeast Asians   The various groups of Southeast Asians suffered many different traumas associated with their migration to the United States. The Vietnamese, for example, first started coming after the victory of North Vietnam in 1975 (Uba, 1994). Most of these immigrants paid great sums of money in order to escape on overcrowded, dilapidated boats. Once at sea, they suffered from starvation, disease, and attacks by pirates who robbed, raped, and killed many of the refugees (Niem, 1989). Similar atrocities befell the citizens of Laos and Cambodia (Uba, 1994). In 1975, the Pathet Lao seized power in Laos. This regime soon embarked on a campaign of extermination directed at its opponents, including the hill tribes of Hmong and Mien, who helped the CIA during the Vietnam War. Also in that year, Pol Pot, leader of the Khmer Rouge, took over in Cambodia. He forced millions of people into harsh labor camps, splitting up families in the process. Deemed a threat to society, intellectuals were targeted for annihilation.

The traumatic experiences of Southeast Asian refugees do not end once they arrive in the United States. Many problems arise here as well, including unemployment (Belser, Johnson, & Turner, 1993), language difficulties (Niem, 1989), and disruptions in family life and traditions (Abe, Zane, & Chun, 1994).

Today, there is a popular belief that Asian Americans constitute a well-adjusted, "model minority" based on their high rates of academic achievement and presumably low rates of psychopathology and social deviance (Sue & Morishima, 1982; Sue, 1994; Sue, Nakamura, Chung, & Yee-Bradbury, 1994). Consequently, some people use Asian Americans as a yardstick to measure other ethnic groups, in effect saying, "Asians Americans have done well in this country, so if you find yourself in a disadvantaged position, the fault lies in you, not American society."

The arguments against this position are fourfold. First, as we have outlined earlier, the discriminatory experiences of each ethnic group are unique and widely varied (Fairchild, 1991); thus, their relative positions in present-day society are not indicative of progress along similar paths. Second, while some Asian Americans are doing well, many (e.g., recent immigrants) still experience significant hardships (Sue, 1994). A third contention is that Asian Americans still have to work harder than whites in order to reach similar levels of success. Finally, Asian Americans have been able to better themselves through the use of education to overcome restrictions in upward mobility (Sue & Okazaki, 1990). Even so, an environment persists that allows Asian Americans only to go so far. For example, a prevailing stereotype is that Asian Americans make good workers, not good leaders. Thus, the "model minority" myth is replete with criticisms.

Native Americans

Estimates of the number of Native American tribes that existed prior to the arrival of English colonists range between 200 (Burkey, 1978) and 400 (Churchill, 1993). These tribes centered on kin groups involved in a symbiotic relationship with their natural surroundings. Initially, Native Americans had good relations with the European traders, who depended upon them for furs and pelts. The situation soon soured, however. Economic opportunities spawned greed in some native tribes, which promoted the abandonment of traditional means of subsistence. Whole animal species were wiped out as a result of excessive hunting. The introduction of alcohol as a way to take advantage of Native Americans during trade negotiations promoted alcoholism. All of these factors, combined with the westward movement of the fur trade, sunk the eastern tribes into a state of poverty and misery (Josephy, 1994).

In addition to the disruptions caused by trading, the native population declined drastically owing to disease and warfare following the arrival of the Europeans (Thornton, 1987). Epidemic diseases, such as smallpox, cholera, and whooping cough, almost devastated whole tribes of Native Americans (Oswalt, 1978). Severe hardship ensued as a result of the loss of tribal leaders, the lack of faith in native shamen, and holes in the cooperative fabric of tribal living (Walker & LaDue, 1986). The native population fell from over 5 million people in 1492 to only 600,000 in 1800 (Thornton, 1987).

The present-day Bureau of Indian Affairs traces its roots to 1824, when management of Native Americans was assigned to the secretary of war (Trimble, 1988). Evidently, the colonists did not foresee peaceful coexistence with the native population. Soon thereafter, in 1830, the Indian Removal Act forced eastern tribes, including the Creeks, Cherokee, and Choctaw, to relocate to isolated areas in the Midwest. The expulsion of the Cherokee from Georgia, known as the Trail of Tears, typified a pattern in which Native Americans were relocated to less desirable pieces of land until the United States, succumbing to its economic or expansionistic needs, violated existing treaties and forced them to move again (Burkey, 1978). The federal government repeatedly ignored the boundary restrictions contained in its treaties with different tribes (Jackson, 1881), often resorting to coercive purchases or outright annexation (Foreman, 1932).

In 1854, the Kansas-Nebraska Act confined Native Americans to remote reservations in order to remove them as a barrier to westward migration. The lands set aside for reservations dwindled in size as the number of settlers and land speculators increased in those areas. In addition, the 1887 Dawes Act broke up reservations into small plots assigned to individuals; the 48 million remaining unassigned acres were gradually sold to white settlers and businesses (Josephy, 1994).

The U.S. oppression of Native Americans was not a peaceful process. Many armed battles arose between whites and various native tribes whenever settlers infringed on tribal lands. For example, approximately 70,000 Native Americans perished from war or disease in the decade following the 1849 discovery of gold in California (Burkey, 1978).

In the 20th century, the federal government began efforts to assimilate Native Americans into mainstream society. Full citizenship was granted to Native Americans in 1924. The establishment of voting rights varied from state to state, with some states (New Mexico and Arizona) withholding such privileges until 1948 (Trimble, 1988). The 1934 Indian Reorganization Bill gave them the right to self-government on the reservations through governmentally appointed tribal councils (Churchill, 1992). However, during the Great Depression, the life of Native Americans was again disrupted as government-sponsored public works projects infringed on tribal land and destroyed the local ecosystems upon which many tribes depended for subsistence (Walker & LaDue, 1986).

In the 1950s, the government tried to relocate Native Americans to urban centers in order to provide them with job training and employment opportunities. This effort helped some Native Americans achieve a higher socioeconomic status, but many were unable to make the transition. Thornton (1987) predicts that the urbanization movement will produce three notable changes in the Native American population: a decline in the growth rate, an increased number of interethnic marriages, and a loss of tribal affiliations.

In 1975, the Indian Self Determination Act and the Indian Health Care Improvement Act finally allowed tribal input in the planning of social service programs on reservations. Today, Native American communities are plagued with problems of alcoholism, violence, suicide, and depression (Mail & Johnson, 1993; May & Dizmang, 1974; Walker & LaDue, 1986).

Explanatory Models in Ethnic Psychology

Psychological research has uncovered ethnic differences in many different areas, including the following: academic achievement (Whang & Hancock, 1994); emotional expressions (Matsumoto, 1993); child rearing (Kelley & Tseng, 1992; Levine & Bartz, 1979; Reis, 1993); cognitive styles (Huang & Sisco, 1994; Shade, 1986); marital interactions and attitudes (Cromwell & Cromwell, 1978; Farber, 1990; Oggins, Veroff, & Leber, 1993; Oggins, Leber, & Veroff, 1993; Uzzell, 1986); and rates of psychopathology (Robins & Regier, 1991). In the United States, these research findings have been viewed from a variety of perspectives. Many psychological models have been proposed to explain both categorical (e.g., psychiatric symptomatology) and dimensional (e.g., intelligence test scores) differences between ethnic groups. These models represent not only advances in scientific thinking about ethnic differences but also reflections of public opinions characteristic of the time period in which the model was proposed. For example, the focus on innate biological characteristics as the fundamental source of differences between people was originally derived from the writings of Charles Darwin and Gregor Mendel. However, the popularized version of this perspective—which touted the genetic inferiority of ethnic minorities—aptly demonstrated the blatant racism endemic in the United States during the 19th and early 20th centuries.

At the time of writing, there have been five major explanatory models in ethnic psychology. Sue, Ito, and Bradshaw (1982) and Sue (1983) described the first three models as focusing on genetic inferiority, environmentally caused deficits, and cultural pluralism. In the past decade, the two competing theories of symbolic racism and social dominance have emerged as a fourth model to explain white racism in political matters. In vogue today, the final model has ethnic psychology subsumed within the larger arena of human diversity. In the following section, the models are presented in roughly chronological order in terms of their emergence and popularity. For illustrative purposes, an empirical example is also interpreted within the context of each model.

Inferiority Model

Because of centuries of religious, racial, and colonial persecution, it is not surprising that the first paradigm used to explain ethnic differences was based on racist thinking. Innate biological characteristics, as described by Charles Darwin and Gregor Mendel, were considered to be responsible for a minority ethnic group's failure to thrive. This "natural inferiority" of different ethnic groups provided justification for the continuation of discrimination and oppression. The argument proceeds as follows: if a group is inherently incapable of attaining a better position in society, then there is no point in adjusting the existing environment to provide preferential or equal opportunities. Nonwhite ethnic group members were considered to be misfits in a "civilized" world and thus suitable only for menial jobs and disdainful treatment. The notion of genetic inferiority characterized the discriminatory and persecutory practices inflicted against African Americans in the United States (Klineberg, 1935). This doctrine also provided the scientific justification for slavery, which originated from the religious and ethnocentric prejudices of Western Europe. The disadvantaged position of African Americans, and other minorities, in this country was seen to result from inherent biological factors, not years of oppression and exclusion (Thomas & Sillen, 1972; Kovel, 1970).

Biological explanations for racial and ethnic differences are not supported by research in human genetics, however. Although racial categories are based on similar phenotypes, the underlying genetics within each racial group are remarkably dissimilar. Indeed, research has discovered more genetic differences intraracially than interracially (Jackson, 1992; Zuckerman, 1990; Nei & Roychoudhury, 1974). Recent findings in the Human Genome Project at Stanford University also show that true genetic differences between people have almost no relationship to traditional racial distinctions (Begley, 1995). Thus, some researchers (Fairchild, Yee, Wyatt, & Weizmann, 1995; Sun, 1995; Yee, Fairchild, Weizmann, & Wyatt, 1993) have concluded that the concept of race includes a notable social component.

The inferiority model is perhaps most associated with the controversy surrounding racial differences in intelligence and intelligence test scores. Guthrie (1976) noted that the first intelligence testing of African Americans was done by Josiah Morse and Alice Strong in 1912. Not surprisingly, they concluded that African American children were mentally younger than white children. Based on his study in 1915, W. H. Pyle later declared that African Americans had only two-thirds of the mental capacity of whites (Guthrie, 1976). Intelligence testing of army recruits in World War I also testified to the intellectual inferiority of African Americans.

Since that time, a number of additional authors have reported lower I.Q. scores among African Americans than among white European Americans (Montie & Fagan, 1988; Reynolds, Chastain, Kaufman, & McLean, 1987; Seligman, 1992; Jensen, 1969; Jensen & Reynolds, 1982; Rushton, 1994). Some researchers proclaim these lower results to be caused by genetic deficiencies (Jensen, 1969; Jensen, 1976; Rushton, 1994; Rushton, 1995). Support for this argument is gathered from studies that show intelligence to be a highly heritable trait (e.g., Boomsma, 1993; Chipuer, Rovine, & Plomin, 1990; Jensen, 1976; Plomin, 1989).

The position that genetically mediated racial differences exist in intelligence has been criticized from many angles, however. For example, Crane (1994) argues that the environmental factors—not genetics—play a significant role in racial I.Q. differences. As a direct refutation of J. P. Rushton's work, which finds racial differences in cranial capacity (Rushton, 1994), Cernovsky (1993) states that head size is not related to intelligence or race. Furthermore, Grubb (1987) reasoned that if African Americans are truly genetically inferior in intelligence, then the occurrence rate for severe mental retardation among blacks would be higher than among whites; he found no such differences, however. Numerous researchers have also challenged the heritability estimates of intelligence (e.g., Erdle, 1990; Mackenzie, 1984; Schonemann, 1989; Wahlsten, 1994).

In addition, there are many criticisms of the intelligence tests themselves and their application to nonwhite populations. For example, in his book *The Mismeasure of Man* (1981), Gould criticizes the very notion of having a single numerical measure of intelligence, as well as its corresponding ranking system. After all, Frenchman Alfred Binet developed the first intelligence test to distinguish between normal and mentally retarded schoolchildren, not as a continuous scale of intelligence (Kamin, 1974). Other authors have argued against the use of intelligence tests for ethnic minorities in particular. For example, Lopez and Taussig (1991) showed that a difference in language introduces a test bias when assessing Hispanic Americans. Furthermore, variables that systematically covary with ethnicity, such as educational achievement and socioeconomic status, may cause ethnic and racial differences to appear in test results (Ehrlich & Feldman, 1977). A Western cultural bias may also exist in the test items and components used to define intelligence (Ehrlich & Feldman, 1977; Guy, 1977). Despite the overwhelming and varied evidence against the application of the inferiority model to ethnic differences in intelligence, the controversy continues, as evidenced by the recent publication of *The Bell Curve* (Herrnstein & Murray, 1994), which argues for the genetic-intellectual inferiority of African Americans.

Deficit Model

As a reaction to the proposition that genetics—or "nature"—explains ethnic differences in psychological research, the deficit hypothesis developed. Based on Gordon Allport's landmark book *The Nature of Prejudice* (1954) and fueled by the civil rights movement in the 1960s, this model proposed the opposite extreme: the locus of ethnic differences lies in the environment—or "nurture"—not in the individual.

In his book, Allport (1954) stated that prejudice is composed of erroneous generalizations and hostility. Both of these ingredients are "natural and common capacities of the human mind" (p. 17). Prejudice is subsequently applied in the rejection of out-groups who do not share the same well-regarded characteristics of one's in-group; the formal distinctions between in-groups and out-groups are derived from normal psychological processes.

The deficit model built upon these premises by stating that the consequences of prejudice (i.e., verbal rejection, discrimination, and physical attack [Allport, 1954]) create stress for minority groups that greatly hinders their ability to thrive (Sue, 1983). Kramer, Rosen, and Willis (1973) took the position that "racist practices undoubtedly are key factors—perhaps the most important ones—in producing mental disorders in Blacks and other underprivileged groups" (p. 355). Racial discrimination and segregation in housing, education, and employment restrict the opportunities available to ethnic minorities. Furthermore, severe persecution can lead to self-hatred and a loss of self-respect in oppressed ethnic groups (Baldwin, 1979; Saenger, 1953).

The deficit model has been applied to ethnic differences in mental health. For example, several studies have reported higher rates of schizophrenia (Steinberg, Pardes, Bjork, & Sporty, 1977) and some anxiety disorders (Blazer, Hughes, George, Swartz, & Boyer, 1991; Eaton, Dryman, & Weissman, 1991; Neal & Turner, 1991) in African Americans, accompanied by more severe symptomatology (Adebimpe, Chu, Klein, & Lange, 1982; Kleiner, Tuckman, & Lovell, 1960). The deficit model, therefore, proposes that white racism produces these higher rates of mental distress in African Americans (Carter, 1994). Gary (1981) suggested that the oppression characteristic of institutionalized racism produces self-destructive psychological coping mechanisms, such as substance use and suicide, in African American men. The fear of racism may also cause African Americans to act paranoid or secretive in therapy situations (Ridley, 1984) and thus prevent the establishment of a trusting therapeutic relationship (Hankins-McNary, 1979). Perhaps institutionalized racism affects the admission rates or quality of care in psychiatric facilities (Flaherty & Meagher, 1980; Wade, 1993). Evidence also suggests that racism is responsible for the poor physical health of some nonwhite ethnic groups (Krieger, Rowley, Herman, Avery, & Phillips, 1993).

The deficit model has both advantages and disadvantages in terms of explaining ethnic differences (Sue, 1983; Sue et al., 1982). On the one hand, its focused attention on the environment provides a closer examination of racial discrimination and the poor social and living conditions of some minorities, which may hinder their ability to thrive. In 1954, psychological research into the harmful effects of segregation formed the basis of the U.S. Supreme Court decision in *Brown v. Board of Education* to end the separation of black and white schoolchildren (Sue, 1983; Yee et al., 1993). On the other hand, the deficit model still cast minorities as inferior (Thomas & Sillen, 1972). By only looking at the weaknesses of a specific ethnic group relative to white Americans, it neglected areas of good or superior functioning in the nonwhite group. Klineberg (1981) described this problem as the replacement of nature by nurture in explaining the inferiority of African Americans.

Cultural Pluralism

Originally proposed by Horace Kallen in 1915, cultural pluralism arose as an idealized description of ethnic group relations to counteract the coercive efforts of assimilation and Americanization directed against ethnic minorities. Kallen (1924) rejected the popular idea of the melting pot, which proffered that American ethnic groups were combining with the dominant Anglo-Saxon culture to produce a new, universal American identity. Instead, he proposed that ethnic groups should remain distinct cultural entities while promoting universal American values. For example, groups would promote democratic principles through voting and political participation. Kallen used the phrase "unity in diversity" to represent the ethnic groups' acceptance of common American values and traditions, combined with the groups' preservation of their own unique culture (Krug, 1976).

Gordon (1964) identified three themes that punctuated Kallen's writings on cultural pluralism. First, Kallen believed that, in contrast to all other groups to which an individual may belong (e.g., political party or religious group), ethnic group membership is an involuntary process that fosters personality development. Because an individual is not able to change his ethnicity, he must come to terms with it. Second, cultural pluralism embodies the ideals of democracy because it does not force minorities to conform to the dominant American culture. Thus, one is free to embrace the values of his ethnic group and/or American society to any degree he desires. And finally, the United States benefits from the interactions of diverse ethnic groups within its boundaries. Individual ethnic groups are able to contribute parts of their cultural heritage to the national culture directly, as well as indirectly, thereby promoting positive relationships with other ethnic groups.

Cultural pluralism may operate at several different levels in society (Gordon, 1978). At the most basic level, each ethnic group maintains all intimate and family relationships within itself. Contact with other ethnic groups is formal, impersonal, and characterized by tolerance. The more advanced stage of "good group relations" includes primary personal relationships that cross ethnic boundaries. At this level, public institutions are well integrated with different ethnic groups. The point at which ethnicity is no longer a salient feature in personal relationships is dubbed the "community integration" level. People of diverse ethnic backgrounds interact within a common, intimate social structure. In keeping with the central tenets of cultural pluralism, the cultural and ethnic identities of individuals are well respected and valued but are also combined with an appreciation of the commonalities of all people. Because cultural pluralism places a high emphasis on allowing ethnic groups to decide their own levels of identification and integration in American society, a mixed level also exists. Herein, individuals could live primarily within their own ethnic group (i.e., at the tolerance or "good group relations" level) or participate in a larger communal brotherhood (i.e., at the community integration level). These latter individuals would likely have only a marginal affiliation with their own ethnic group.

Unlike the premises of the inferiority and deficit models, cultural pluralism is not a theory or a description of real-life circumstances (Sue, Moore, Iscoe, & Nagata, 1984). Rather, it is an ideology that sets the stage for social interventions. Sue et al. (1984) outlined the following three values contained in a culturally pluralistic perspective: (1) a mutual respect for the presence of cultural differences; (2) an awareness of the strengths inherent in those differences; and (3) active support of the rights of different ethnic groups to retain their cultural heritage. The application of these principles to interethnic relations would presumably lead to a better understanding and camaraderie between ethnic groups.

The influence of cultural pluralism in psychology can be seen in research on ethnic identity. Like cultural pluralism, the concept of ethnic identity received increased attention during the ethnic-consciousness movements of the 1960s (Phinney, 1990). Essentially, ethnic identity seeks to discern an individual's relationship to his own ethnic group and to the larger, dominant white society. In most ethnic identity paradigms, the individual progresses from a state of unawareness of his own ethnic identity, through an ethnocentric fixation upon it, to a stage in which he has integrated his ethnic self together with his relationship to the white culture. These latter two levels are similar to the first and second stages of cultural pluralism as posited by Gordon (1978).

Symbolic Racism

Following the *Brown v. Board of Education* decision and the civil rights movement, politics tried to provide equal opportunities in education and employment for nonwhite ethnic groups, together with the desegregation of public facilities. While white Americans were supportive of egalitarianism (Taylor, Sheatsley, & Greeley, 1978), they also opposed specific policies designed to facilitate equality and desegregation, such as affirmative action and the busing of schoolchildren to provide diversified learning environments (Pettigrew, 1979). Schuman, Steeh, and Bobo (1985) found that whites were more positive to egalitarian attitudes than to egalitarian policies. Bobo (1988) described this discrepancy as "a gap between 'principles and implementation.'"

In order to explain the voting behavior of white Americans who opposed desegregation and affirmative action, the theories of symbolic racism and social dominance have been recently proposed. Whites were voting against black political candidates and policies of desegregation and affirmative action (e.g., busing), even when such issues did not significantly affect their self-interests. Flagrant, "traditional" racism was unable to explain the observed voting behavior, so a more subtle form of prejudice was conjectured.

The theory of symbolic racism states that white opposition to certain racial policies is caused by an adherence to traditional American values of individualism and meritocracy combined with antiblack affect (Kinder & Sears, 1981). In 1988, Sears outlined the three central propositions of the model. First, symbolic racism significantly affects racial policy preferences and voting decisions in elections in which race is an issue. Second, symbolic racism has a greater impact on political issues than "traditional" racism. And third, symbolic racism is a more salient feature of whites' political responses than personally relevant racial threats. This final tenet highlights the fact that symbolic racism deals with abstract concepts and symbols rather than concrete interests of the self or group. Research on symbolic racism has shown it to be a better predictor of white opposition to busing (Sears & Kinder, 1985) and African American candidates (Kinder & Sears, 1981) than simply self-interest or traditional racism.

In contrast to symbolic racism, social dominance theory proposes that antiegalitarian attitudes fuel racist voting decisions. As a hegemonic in-group, whites adopt a social dominance orientation by favorably comparing themselves to African Americans, who represent a negative reference out-group. This social dominance orientation not only fuels discrimination against African Americans but also supports socially accepted attitudes that justify an unequal distribution of societal resources. These attitudes and beliefs are known as legitimizing myths. Social dominance theory also assumes that most conflicts between groups occur as a result of the unequal social hierarchy, which provides an evolutionarily adaptive function in reconciling intragroup conflict and better organizing groups to compete for scarce resources (Sidanius, 1993)

A recent study of symbolic racism and social dominance theory (Sidanius, Devereux, & Pratto, 1991) found more support for the latter theory than the former one. While symbolic racism was related to white resistance to racial policies of equal opportunity and preferential treatment for minorities, it was not significantly related to feelings of meritocracy, one of the theory's central tenets. In contrast, the test of social dominance theory showed that anti-egalitarianism was related to legitimizing myths (including symbolic racism) and resistance to equal opportunities for minorities. Thus, there is some evidence that social dominance may better explain the rationale behind white racist voting behavior than symbolic racism.

Human Diversity

The newly emerging model in ethnic psychology is simply known as human diversity (e.g., Trickett, Watts, & Birman, 1993, 1994; Chin, De La Cancela, & Jenkins, 1993). Basically, this new area seeks to broaden the scope of research beyond racial, ethnic, or cultural issues to include other groups that have unique differences, strengths, needs, histories, and discriminatory experiences. This research will include ethnic groups and other populations that historically have been victims of discrimination, such as women, gays and lesbians, and individuals with disabilities. Members of the dominant culture (i.e., white male heterosexuals) are included as well. Thus, one of the central premises is that everyone in society has a unique culture, both independently and in relationship to a larger society.

Watts (1994) outlined the following four paradigms to conducting research within the framework of human diversity: population-specific psychology, cross-cultural psychology, sociopolitical psychology, and intergroup theory. Population-specific psychology posits that by understanding an oppressed population's worldview and its environmental circumstances, one is able to identify patterns distinctly applicable to that population. These patterns become the basis for theories that then can be applied to research or interventions within that specific population. Cross-cultural psychology looks for both universal and unique cultural attributes between two or more cultural groups. Instead of examining one group exclusively, cross-cultural psychologists gain understanding of populations through explicit comparisons to each other. This perspective allows for the influence of culture into our psychological theories of affect, behavior, and cognition. Sociopolitical psychology examines the oppression against nondominant groups by an elite group, both as a process and as an outcome. By focusing on the present ideology of oppression and injustice, one strives to ultimately change or replace the current sociopolitical system. Finally, intergroup theory examines group processes at the most general level by incorporating cultural, societal, and other factors that impinge upon the formation, structure, identity, and dynamics of all groups.

As an example of population-specific psychology, research has recently started to examine the concept of "loss of face" in Asians and Asian Americans (e.g., Ja & Aoki, 1993; Kuo & Kavanaugh, 1994; Leong, Wagner, & Kim, 1995). Based on cultural phenomena, this construct posits that Asians are concerned with the maintenance of harmony in interpersonal relationships; behavior will be circumscribed in order to prevent oneself and others from losing respect in the eyes of the group. Loss of face may be examined in many different contexts, including school environments, business meetings, and psychotherapy sessions. For example, the tendency of Asian Americans to underutilize mental health services relative to the white population may reflect concerns about saving face. Applications such as this one will provide better understanding of Asians and Asian Americans.

Future Challenges in Ethnic Psychology

The future of ethnic psychology will likely encounter the following five major challenges: (1) the limitations of ethnicity as an explanatory variable; (2) the difficulty of investigating individuals who have a mixed ethnic background; (3) the refinement of handling ethnicity in research; (4) the development of culturally valid assessment measures; and (5) the cyclical nature of beliefs.

First, we, as researchers, need to move beyond ethnicity as a way of explaining differences (Betancourt & Lopez, 1993). As traditionally employed, ethnicity is essentially a categorical variable, not an explanatory one. It is also entangled with differences in social class (Adler et al., 1994; Ehrlich & Feldman, 1977). Rather than providing an additive stress, differences in socioeconomic status interact with ethnicity, so it is not possible simply to remove the effects of income and education (Adler et al., 1994; Kessler & Neighbors, 1986; Ulbrich, Warheit, & Zimmerman, 1989). In other words, being poor and African American is fundamentally different from being poor and white. As a result, we need to ask more specific questions, like "What is it about being Asian American or African American or Hispanic American that makes one different?" In order to uncover the causal mechanisms that lie beneath ethnic differences, we must find constructs that are capable of providing better explanations than simply ethnicity.

These new variables may be explicitly related to notions of race, ethnicity, or culture. Racial identity, ethnic identity, acculturation, and cultural competence are all promising examples used to explain differences both between and within ethnic groups. In addition, variables may be applied that cut across ethnic lines. These variables may possess better predictive validity than simple ethnic group membership. For example, the theory of interdependent and independent self-construals (Markus & Kitayama, 1991) may provide better indicators of behavior and cognitions than ethnicity. That is, two independently oriented individuals from disparate ethnic backgrounds may act more similarly than two people who share the same ethnicity but different self-construals. Individualism/collectivism (see Triandis, McCusker, & Hui, 1990) is an example of a construct that has been previously applied to explain the similarities between seemingly disparate societies, as well as the differences between presumably similar societies. It is also possible that variables that have traditionally examined individual and group differences in personality psychology and social psychology (e.g., introversion and extraversion) may be adapted for use with cultural and ethnic groups.

A second issue confronting ethnic researchers is how to conceptualize individuals with a diverse ethnic background. For example, how should a child whose parents are African American and Asian American be treated in research? Would the child be considered as belonging specifically to either ethnic group? Both? Neither? As the number of different ethnic groups increases in our society, so will the number of mixed ethnic pairings and their offspring. These individuals may represent a new challenge to existing research strategies, but they also provide interesting insights into many research areas, such as prejudice and self-identity.

A third problem confronting researchers is how to appropriately treat ethnicity in research. If we agree that ethnicity is socially defined and has both objective and subjective components as defined by Berry (1994), then how do we define our research subjects? Do we rely on the subject's self-report as belonging to a specific ethnic group? Do we assign subjects to multiethnic conditions based on their outward physical appearance? Our answers to these questions necessarily limit our investigations and conclusions. Zuckerman (1990), for example, points out that conclusions of genetic differences in intelligence between racial groups are invalid if the racial group of the subjects is simply based on self-report. Because little is known about the cultural and genetic makeup of the subjects, any conclusions about the origin of group differences are premature.

In recent years, psychological studies have been forced to include a diverse sample across ethnic and gender lines. This movement provides a welcome opportunity to expand the applicability of research findings beyond white male undergraduates who major in psychology. Unfortunately, an unintended result is that many researchers simply toss in a few minority subjects with little consideration of how they contribute to the overall research design beyond a simple categorical designation. This neglect of the possible effects of ethnicity is simply bad science. Even if the dependent variables under investigation do not seem amenable to ethnic effects, there is the possibility that ethnicity may confound results owing to the very nature of how and where research is conducted. Given the complexity of cross-racial and cross-ethnic interactions, the ethnicity of the experimenter(s) may influence the behaviors or reports of the subjects (Sue et al., 1982).

The fourth challenge to ethnic psychology is the development of culturally valid assessment measures. Many psychological tests have been designed by white male researchers and standardized on white subjects. Should test items selected by whites, coupled with profiles based on white subjects, be used with nonwhite ethnic groups? Maybe so, maybe not. Some tests may indeed be valid and reliable for use with different ethnic groups. However, because research has found biases in the application of some tests to nonwhite ethnic groups, one should be careful in the interpretation of a subject's performance by considering the bases of the test results. For example, if a subject or patient is not a native English speaker, the psychologist may give less weight in his overall assessment of tests conducted in English. In the future, psychological research should strive to cross-validate assessment tests and widen standardization samples.

The final challenge revolves around the cyclical nature of racial and ethnic beliefs. It seems that some arguments never die. For example, the notion that African Americans are genetically inferior in intelligence was popularly held until the civil rights movement. It is now being revived by publications such as the book *The Bell Curve*. The cyclic nature of sentiments can also be seen in political attitudes toward immigrants and multiculturalism. The United States has experienced periods when immigrants have been unwelcome and have been victims of great hostility. At other times, immigrants have been viewed as adding to the strength and vitality of the country. Currently, there is an unfortunate rise in anti-immigrant sentiments and a tendency toward ethnocentricism. To progress as a discipline and society, we need to recognize our common future and work toward better relations between ethnic groups. A rehash of moot findings in the absence of new evidence is both fruitless and counterproductive. As a society, we need to recognize the benefits of improved interethnic relations and build upon the unique strengths of each ethnic group. In doing so, we must try to reduce ethnic conflicts, not provoke them.

Summary

Incorporating American history and empirical research, we have outlined the field of ethnic psychology in the United States. Our presentation of the historical experiences of nonwhite ethnic groups demonstrated how ethnic relations in this country have been tainted with racism and discrimination. We also discussed the theoretical models that have been applied to explain findings of ethnic differences. The development of these models and their application to particular research findings shows the progression of thinking about ethnic differences in both psychology and public opinion. In other words, the unfolding history of ethnic relations in the United States has been mirrored by changes in popular and scientific thinking about ethnic differences. In the 19th and first half of the 20th century, the early model of inferiority highlighted the low functioning of nonwhite ethnic groups and tried to explain their failure to thrive in terms of genetic differences between ethnic groups. In the 1950s, the deficit model emerged as an effort to explain ethnic differences in terms of environmental pressures; research began to study the effects of discrimination and prejudice. However, the underlying message was that nonwhite ethnic groups still performed more poorly than whites. In the hope of promoting mutual respect and harmony, cultural pluralism gained popularity in the 1980s and has tried to emphasize the interconnectedness of different ethnic groups. Unfortunately, as the theories of symbolic racism and social dominance demonstrate, racism and discrimination still exist, though in a more camouflaged form. Finally, the human diversity model seeks to acknowledge discrimination as a common factor that applies to all disadvantaged groups in society. In summary, the effects of discrimination and racism have been progressively more recognized in American society. As a result, their influence on the explanatory models of differences between ethnic groups has also increased.

Now and in the future it will be useful to compare and contrast ethnic psychologies from different societies. Are the processes underlying ethnic prejudice and discrimination similar in different countries? Why do ethnic conflicts in some countries result in violence? To what extent can the solutions for ethnic strife found in one country be used in another? These are the important and interesting questions that need to be addressed. By comparing the approaches to ethnic psychology in different societies, as is being done in this book, we may be able to put an end to ethnically motivated conflicts and work toward improving the status of different ethnic groups and the quality of interethnic relationships.

References

Abe, J., Zane, N., & Chun, K. (1994). Differential responses to trauma: Migration-related discriminants of posttraumatic stress disorder among Southeast Asian refugees. *Journal of Community Psychology*, 22, 121–135.

Adebimpe, V. R. (1981). Overview: White norms and the psychiatric diagnosis of black patients. *American Journal of Psychiatry*, 138(3), 279–285.

Adebimpe, V. R., Chu, C. -C., Klein, H. E., & Lange, M. H. (1982). Racial and geographic differences in the psychopathology of schizophrenia. *American Journal of Psychiatry*, 139(7), 888–891.

Adler, N. E., Boyce, T., Chesney, M. A., Cohen, S., Folkman, S., Kahn, R. L., & Syme, S. L. (1994). Socioeconomic status and health: The challenge of the gradient. *American Psychologist*, 49(1), 15–24.

Allport, G. W. (1954). *The nature of prejudice*. Reading, Mass.: Addison-Wesley.

Baldwin, J. A. (1979). Theory and research concerning the notion of black self-hatred: A review and reinterpretation. *Journal of Black Psychology*, 5(2), 51–77.

Begley, S. (1995). Three is not enough: Surprising new lessons from the controversial science of race. *Newsweek*, 13 February, pp. 67–69.

Belser, M., Johnson, P., & Turner, R. (1993). Unemployment, underemployment, and depressive affect among Southeast Asian refugees. *Psychological Medicine*, 23, 731–743.

Berry, J. W. (1994). An ecological perspective on cultural and ethnic psychology. In E. Trickett, R. J. Watts, & D. Birman (eds.), *Human diversity: Perspectives on people in context* (pp. 115–141). San Francisco: Jossey-Bass.

Betancourt, H., & Lopez, S. R. (1993). The study of culture, ethnicity, and race in American psychology. *American Psychologist*, 48(6), 629–637.

Blazer, D. G., Hughes, D., George, L. K., Swartz, M., & Boyer, R. (1991). Generalized anxiety disorder. In L. N. Robins & D. A. Regier (eds.), *Psychiatric disorders in America: The epidemiologic catchment area* (pp. 180–203). New York: Free Press.

Bobo, L. (1988). Group conflict, prejudice, and the paradox of contemporary racial attitudes. In P. Katz & D. Taylor (eds.), *Eliminating racism: Profiles in controversy* (pp. 53–84). New York: Plenum.

Boomsma, D. I. (1993). Current status and future prospects of twin studies in the development of cognitive abilities: Infancy to old age. In T. J. Bouchard Jr. & P. Propping (eds.), *Twins as a tool of behavioral genetics* (pp. 67–82). Chichester, England: Wiley.

Burkey, R. M. (1978). Ethnic and racial groups: The dynamics of dominance. Menlo Park, Calif.: Cummings.

Carter, J. H. (1994). Racism's impact on mental health. *Journal of the National Medical Association, 86*(7), 543–547.

Cernovsky, Z. Z. (1993). J. P. Rushton's aggregational errors in racial psychology. *Journal of Black Psychology, 19*(3), 282–289.

Chan, S. (1991). *Asian Americans: An interpretive history*. New York: Twayne.

Chin, J., De La Cancela, V., & Jenkins, Y. (1993). *Diversity in psychotherapy: The politics of race, ethnicity, and gender*. Westport, Conn.: Praeger.

Chipuer, H. M., Rovine, M. J., & Plomin, R. (1990). LISREL modeling: Genetic and environmental influences on IQ revisited. *Intelligence, 14*(1), 11–29.

Churchill, W. (1992). Preface: The open veins of native North America. In M. A. Jaimes (ed.), *Fantasies of the master race: Literature, cinema, and the colonization of American Indians*. Monroe, Maine: Common Courage Press.

Churchill, W. (1993). *Struggle for the land: Indigenous resistance to genocide, exocide, and expropriation in contemporary North America*. Monroe, Maine: Common Courage Press.

Crane, J. (1994). Exploding the myth of scientific support for the theory of black intellectual inferiority. *Journal of Black Psychology, 20*(2), 189–209.

Cromwell, V. L., & Cromwell, R. E. (1978). Perceived dominance in decision-making and conflict resolution among Anglo, black, and Chicano couples. *Journal of Marriage and the Family, 40*(4), 749–759.

Cross, T., Bazron, B., Dennis, K., & Isaacs, M. (1989). *Towards a culturally competent system of care: A monograph on effective services for minority children who are severely emotionally disturbed*. Washington, D.C.: National Institute of Mental Health, Child and Adolescent Service System Program.

Daniels, R. (1971). *Concentration camps USA: Japanese Americans and World War II*. New York: Rinehart & Winston.

Daniels, R. (1988). *Asian America: Chinese and Japanese in the United States since 1850*. Seattle: University of Washington Press.

Eaton, W. M., Dryman, A., & Weissman, M. M. (1991). Panic and phobia. In L. N. Robins & D. A. Regier (eds.), *Psychiatric disorders in America: The epidemiologic catchment area* (pp. 155–179). New York: Free Press.

Ehrlich, P. R., & Feldman, S. S. (1977). *The race bomb: Skin color, prejudice, and intelligence*. New York: Quadrangle.

Erdle, S. (1990). Limitations of the heritability coefficient as an index of genetic and environmental influences on human behavior. *American Psychologist, 45*(4), 553–554.

Fabrega, H., Jr. (1995). Hispanic mental health research: A case for cultural psychiatry. In A. M. Padilla (ed.), *Hispanic psychology: Critical issues in theory and research* (pp. 107–130). Thousand Oaks, Calif: Sage.

Fairchild, H. (1991). Scientific racism: The cloak of objectivity. *Journal of Social Issues, 47*(3), 101–115.

Fairchild, H. H., Yee, A. H., Wyatt, G. E., & Weizmann, F. M. (1995). Readdressing psychology's problems with race. *American Psychologist, 50*(1), 46–47.

Farber, N. (1990). The significance of race and class in marital decisions among unmarried adolescent mothers. *Social Problems, 37*(1), 51–63.

Feagin, J. R. (1989). *Racial and ethnic relations* (3d ed.). Englewood Cliffs, N.J.: Prentice-Hall.

Flaherty, J. A., & Meagher, R. (1980). Measuring racial bias in inpatient treatment. *American Journal of Psychiatry, 137*(6), 679–682.

Foreman, G. (1932). *Indian removal: The emigration of the five civilized tribes.* Norman: University of Oklahoma Press.

Gary, L. E. (ed.) (1981). *Black men.* Beverly Hills: Sage.

Giordano, J., & Levine, M. (1975). Mental health and middle America. *Mental Health, 59*(4), 26–31.

Glenn, E. N. (1983). Split household, small producer, and dual wage earner: An analysis of Chinese-American family strategies. *Journal of Marriage and the Family, 45*(1), 35–46.

Gordon, M. M. (1964). *Assimilation in American life: The role of race, religion, and national origins.* New York: Oxford University Press.

Gordon, M. M. (1978). *Human nature, class, and ethnicity.* New York: Oxford University Press.

Gould, S. J. (1981). *The mismeasure of man.* New York: W. W. Norton.

Grubb, H. J. (1987). Intelligence at the low end of the curve: Where are the racial differences? *Journal of Black Psychology, 14*(1), 25–34.

Guthrie, R. V. (1976). *Even the rat was white: A historical view of psychology.* New York: Harper & Row.

Guy, D. P. (1977). Issues in the unbiased assessment of intelligence. *School Psychology Review, 6*(3), 14–23.

Haller, J. S., Jr. (1971). *Outcasts from evolution: Scientific attitudes of racial inferiority, 1859–1900.* Urbana: University of Illinois Press.

Hankins-McNary, L. D. (1979). The effect of institutional racism on the therapeutic relationship. *Perspectives in Psychiatric Care, 17*(1), 25–30.

Hatamiya, L. T. (1993). *Righting a wrong: Japanese Americans and the passage of the Civil Liberties Act of 1988.* Stanford, Calif.: Stanford University Press.

Herrnstein, R. J., & Murray, C. (1994). *The bell curve: Intelligence and class structure in American life.* New York: Free Press.

Hing, B. O. (1993). *Making and remaking Asian America through immigration policy, 1850–1990.* Stanford, Calif.: Stanford University Press.

Hornsby, A., Jr. (1991). *Chronology of African-American history: Significant events and people from 1619 to the present.* Detroit: Gale Research.

Huang, J., & Sisco, B. R. (1994). Thinking styles of Chinese and American adult students in higher education: A comparative study. *Psychological Reports, 74*(2), 475–480.

Irons, P. H. (1983). *Justice at war: The story of Japanese American internment cases.* New York: Oxford University Press.

Ja, D. Y., & Aoki, B. (1993). Substance abuse and treatment: Cultural barriers in the Asian-American community. *Journal of Psychoactive Drugs, 25*(1), 61–71.

Jackson, F. L. C. (1992). Race and ethnicity as biological constructs. *Race and Ethnicity, 2*, 120–125.

Jackson, H. (1881). *A century of dishonor: A sketch of the United States government's dealings with some of the Indian tribes.* Norman: University of Oklahoma Press.

Jensen, A. R. (1969). How much can we boost I.Q. and scholastic achievement? *Harvard Educational Review, 39*(1), 1–123.

Jensen, A. R. (1976). Race and the genetics of intelligence: A reply to Lewontin. In N. J. Block & G. Dworkin (eds.), *The I.Q. controversy: Critical readings* (pp. 93–106). New York: Pantheon.

Jensen, A. R., & Reynolds, C. R. (1982). Race, social class, and ability patterns on the WISC-R. *Personality and Individual Differences, 3*(4), 423–438.

Josephy, A. M., Jr. (1994). *500 nations: An illustrated history of North American Indians.* New York: Knopf.

Kallen, H. M. (1924). *Culture and democracy in the United States.* New York: Boni & Liveright.

Kamin, L. J. (1974). *The science and politics of I.Q.* Potomac, Md.: Lawrence Erlbaum.

Kelley, M. L., & Tseng, H. -M. (1992). Cultural differences in child rearing: A comparison of immigrant Chinese and Caucasian American mothers. *Journal of Cross-Cultural Psychology, 23*(4), 444–455.

Kessler, R. C., & Neighbors, H. W. (1986). A new perspective on the relationships among race, social class, and psychological distress. *Journal of Health and Social Behavior, 27*(6), 107–115.

Kinder, D. R., & Sears, D. O. (1981). Prejudice and politics: Symbolic racism versus racial threats to the good life. *Journal of Personality and Social Psychology, 40*(3), 414–431.

Kleiner, R., Tuckman, J., & Lovell, M. (1960). Mental disorder and status based on race. *Psychiatry, 23,* 271–274.

Klineberg, O. (1935). *Race differences.* New York: Harper & Brothers.

Klineberg, O. (1981). International educational exchange: The problem of evaluation. *American Psychologist, 36,* 192–199.

Kovel, J. (1970). *White racism.* New York: Pantheon.

Kramer, M., Rosen, B. M., & Willis, E. M. (1973). Definitions and distributions of mental disorders in a racist society. In C. V. Willie, B. M. Kramer, & B. S. Brown (eds.), *Racism and mental health.* Pittsburgh: University of Pittsburgh Press.

Krieger, N., Rowley, D. L., Herman, A. A., Avery, B., & Phillips, M. T. (1993). Racism, sexism, and social class: Implications for studies of health, disease, and well-being. *American Journal of Preventive Medicine,* Supplement, *9*(6), 82–122.

Krug, M. (1976). *The melting of the ethnics: Education of the immigrants, 1880–1914.* Bloomington, Ind.: Phi Delta Kappa Educational Foundation.

Kuo, C. -L., & Kavanaugh, K. H. (1994). Chinese perspectives on culture and mental health. *Issues in Mental Health Nursing, 15*(6), 551–567.

LEAP Asian Pacific American Public Policy Institute (1993). *The state of Asian Pacific America: Policy issues to the year 2020, a public policy report, executive summary.* Los Angeles: LEAP and UCLA Asian American Studies Center.

Leong, F. T. L., Wagner, N. S., & Kim, H. H. (1995). Group counseling expectations among Asian American students: The role of culture-specific factors. *Journal of Counseling Psychology, 42*(2), 217–222.

Levine, E. S., & Bartz, K. W. (1979). Comparative child-rearing attitudes among Chicano, Anglo, and black parents. *Hispanic Journal of Behavioral Sciences, 1*(2), 165–178.

Lopez, S. R., & Taussig, I. M. (1991). Cognitive-intellectual functioning of Spanish-speaking impaired and nonimpaired elderly: Implications for culturally sensitive assessment. *Psychological Assessment, 3*(3), 448–454.

Loring, M., & Powell, B. (1988). Gender, race, and *DSM-III*: A study of the objectivity of psychiatric diagnostic behavior. *Journal of Health and Social Behavior, 29*, 1–22.

Mackenzie, B. (1984). Explaining race differences in IQ: The logic, the methodology, and the evidence. *American Psychologist, 39*(11), 1214–1233.

Mail, P. D., & Johnson, S. (1993). Boozing, sniffing, and toking: An overview of the past, present, and future of substance use by American Indians. *American Indian and Alaska Native Mental Health Research, 5*(2), 1–33.

Markus, H. R., & Kitayama, S. (1991). Culture and the self: Implications for cognition, emotion, and motivation. *Psychological Review, 98*(2), 224–253.

Martinez, C., Jr. (1986). Hispanics: Psychiatric issues. In Charles B. Wilkinson (ed.) *Ethnic psychiatry.* New York: Plenum.

Matsumoto, D. (1993). Ethnic differences in affect intensity, emotion judgments, display rule attitudes, and self-reported emotional expression in an American sample. *Motivation and Emotion, 17*(2), 107–123.

May, P. A., & Dizmang, L. H. (1974). Suicide and the American Indian. *Psychiatric Annals, 4*(11), 22–28.

Meier, M. S., & Ribera, F. (1993). *Mexican Americans/American Mexicans: From conquistadors to Chicanos.* New York: Hill and Wang.

Montie, J. E., & Fagan, J. F. (1988). Racial differences in IQ: Item analysis of the Stanford-Binet at 3 years. *Intelligence, 12*(3), 315–332.

Moore, J. W., & Pachon, H. (1970). *Mexican Americans* (2d ed.). Englewood Cliffs, N.J.: Prentice-Hall.

Nagata, D. K. (1991). Transgenerational impact of the Japanese-American internment: Critical issues in working with the children of former internees. *Psychotherapy, 28*(1), 121–128.

Neal, A. M., & Turner, S. M. (1991). Anxiety disorders research with African Americans: Current status. *Psychological Bulletin, 109*(3), 400–410.

Nei, M., & Roychoudhury, A. (1974). Genetic variation within and between the three major races of man, Caucasoids, Negroids, and Mongoloids. *American Journal of Human Genetics, 26*, 421–443.

Niem, T. T. (1989). Treating Oriental patients with Western psychiatry: A 12-year experience with Vietnamese refugee psychiatric patients. *Psychiatric Annals, 19*(12), 648–652.

Novas, H. (1994). *Everything you need to know about Latino history.* New York: Plume Books.

Oggins, J., Leber, D., & Veroff, J. (1993). Race and gender differences in black and white newlyweds' perceptions of sexual and marital relations. *Journal of Sex Research, 30*(2), 152–160.

Oggins, J., Veroff, J., & Leber, D. (1993). Perceptions of marital interaction among black and white newlyweds. *Journal of Personality and Social Psychology, 65*(3), 494–511.

Oswalt, W. H. (1978). *This land was theirs: A study of North American Indians* (3d ed.). New York: Wiley.

Pettigrew, T. F. (1979). Racial change and social policy. *Annals of the American Academy of Political and Social Science, 441*, 114–131.

Phinney, J. S. (1990). Ethnic identity in adolescents and adults: Review of research. *Psychological Bulletin, 108*(3), 499–514.

Plomin, R. (1989). Environment and genes: Determinants of behavior. *American Psychologist, 44*(2), 105–111.

Reis, J. (1993). Black and white adolescent mothers' child-rearing beliefs and behaviors. *Infant Mental Health Journal, 14*(3), 221–233.

Reynolds, C. R., Chastain, R. L., Kaufman, A. S., & McLean, J. E. (1987). Demographic characteristics and IQ among adults: Analysis of the WAIS-R standardization sample as a function of stratification variables. *Journal of School Psychology, 25*(4), 323–342.

Ridley, C. R. (1984). Clinical treatment of the nondisclosing black client: A therapeutic paradox. *American Psychologist, 39*(11), 1234–1244.

Roberts, R. E. (1980). Prevalence of psychological distress among Mexican Americans. *Journal of Health and Social Behavior, 21*(2), 134–145.

Roberts, R. E. (1990). Prevalence and psychological distress among Mexican Americans. *Journal of Health and Social Behavior, 21*(2), 134–145.

Robins, L. N., & Regier, D. A. (eds.) (1991). *Psychiatric disorders in America: The epidemiologic catchment area study.* New York: Free Press.

Rushton, J. P. (1994). The equalitarian dogma revisited. *Intelligence, 19*(3), 263–280.

Rushton, J. P. (1995). *Race, evolution, and behavior: A life history perspective.* New Brunswick, N.J.: Transaction Publishers.

Saenger, G. (1953). *The social psychology of prejudice: Achieving intercultural understanding and cooperation in a democracy.* New York: Harper & Brothers.

Samora, J., & Simon, P. V. (1993). *A history of the Mexican American people.* Notre Dame, Ind.: University of Notre Dame Press.

Schonemann, P. H. (1989). New questions about old heritability estimates. *Bulletin of the Psychonomic Society, 27*(2), 175–178.

Schuman, H., Steeh, C., & Bobo, L. (1985). *Racial attitudes in America: Trends and interpretations.* Cambridge, Mass.: Harvard University Press.

Sears, D. (1988). Symbolic racism. In P. Katz & D. Taylor (eds.), *Eliminating racism: Profiles in controversy* (pp. 53–84). New York: Plenum.

Sears, D. O., & Kinder, D. R. (1985). Whites' opposition to busing: On conceptualizing and operationalizing group conflict. *Journal of Personality and Social Psychology, 48*(5), 1148–1161.

Seligman, D. (1992). *A question of intelligence: The I.Q. debate in America.* New York: Birch Lane Press.

Shade, B. J. (1986). Is there an Afro-American cognitive style? An exploratory study. *Journal of Black Psychology, 13*(1), 13–16.

Sidanius, J. (1993). The psychology of group conflict and the dynamics of oppression: A social dominance perspective. In S. Iyengar & W. J. McGuire (eds.), *Explorations in political psychology* (pp. 183–224). Durham, N.C.: Duke University Press.

Sidanius, J., Devereux, E., & Pratto, F. (1991). A comparison of symbolic racism theory and social dominance theory as explanations for racial policy attitudes. *Journal of Social Psychology, 132*(3), 377–395.

Smith, J. D. (1993). Introduction. In J. D. Smith (ed.), *Anti-black thought, 1863–1925,* vol. 6, *The Biblical and "scientific" defense of slavery: Religion and "the Negro problem"* (part 2, pp. xxv–xxix). New York: Garland.

Steinberg, M. D., Pardes, H., Bjork, D., & Sporty, L. (1977). Demographic and clinical characteristics of black psychiatric patients in a private general hospital. *Hospital and Community Psychiatry, 28*(2), 128–132.

Sue, S. (1983). Ethnic minority issues in psychology: A reexamination. *American Psychologist, 38*(5), 583–592.

Sue, S. (1994). Mental health. In N. Zane, D. T. Takeuchi, & K. Young (eds.), *Confronting critical health issues of Asian and Pacific Islander Americans* (pp. 266–288). Newbury Park, Calif.: Sage.

Sue, S., Ito, J., & Bradshaw, C. (1982). Ethnic minority research: Trends and directions. In E. E. Jones & S. J. Korchin (wds.), *Minority mental health*. New York: Praeger.

Sue, S., Moore, T., Iscoe, I., & Nagata, D. (1984). Ethnic minority groups in community psychology. In S. Sue and T. Moore (eds.), *The pluralistic society: A community mental health perspective*. New York: Human Sciences Press.

Sue, S., & Morishima, J. (1982). *The mental health of Asian Americans*. San Francisco: Jossey-Bass.

Sue, S., Nakamura, C. Y., Chung, R., & Yee-Bradbury, C. (1994). Mental health research on Asian Americans. *Journal of Community Psychology, 22*(2), 61–67.

Sue, S., & Okazaki, S. (1990). Asian-American educational achievements: A phenomenon in search of an explanation. *American Psychologist, 45*(8), 913–920.

Sue, S., Zane, N., & Young, K. (1994). Research on psychotherapy with culturally diverse populations. In A. E. Bergin & S. L. Garfield (eds.), *Handbook of psychotherapy and behavior change* (4th ed., pp. 783–817). New York: Wiley.

Sun, K. (1995). The definition of race. *American Psychologist, 50* (1), 43–44.

Takaki, R. (1989). *Strangers from a different shore: A history of Asian Americans*. Boston: Little Brown.

Taylor, D. G., Sheatsley, P. B., & Greeley, A. M. (1978). Attitudes towards racial integration. *Scientific American, 238*, 42–49.

Thomas, A., & Sillen, S. (1972). *Racism and psychiatry*. Secaucus, N.J.: Citadel.

Thornton, R. (1987). *American Indian holocaust and survival: A population history since 1492*. Norman: University of Oklahoma Press.

Triandis, H. C., McCusker, C., & Hui, C. H. (1990). Multimethod probes of individualism and collectivism. *Journal of Personality and Social Psychology, 59*(5), 1006–1020.

Trickett, E. J., Watts, R. J., & Birman, D. (1993). Human diversity and community psychology: Still hazy after all these years. *Journal of Community Psychology, 21*(4), 264–279.

Trickett, E. J., Watts, R. J., & Birman, D. (1994). Towards an overarching framework for diversity. In E. J. Trickett, R. J. Watts, & D. Birman (eds.), *Human diversity: Perspectives on people in context* (pp. 7–26). San Francisco: Jossey-Bass.

Trimble, J. E. (1988). Stereotypical images, American Indians, and prejudice. In P. Katz & D. Taylor (eds.), *Eliminating racism: Profiles in controversy* (pp. 181–202). New York: Plenum.

Uba, L. (1994). *Asian Americans: Personality patterns, identity, and mental health*. New York: Guilford.

Uehara, E., Takeuchi, D., & Smukler, M. (1994). Effects of combining disparate groups in the analysis of ethnic differences: Variations among Asian American mental health service consumers in level of community functioning. *American Journal of Community Psychology, 22*(1), 83–99.

Ulbrich, P. M., Warheit, G. J., & Zimmerman, R. S. (1989). Race, socioeconomic status, and psychological distress: An examination of differential vulnerability. *Journal of Health and Social Behavior, 30*, 131–146.

United States Bureau of Census (1990). *Census of population and housing: Summary of social, economic, and housing characteristics*. Washington, D.C.: U.S. Department of Commerce, Economics, and Statistics Administration, Bureau of the Census.

Uzzell, O. (1986). Racial and gender perceptions of marriage roles at a predominantly black university. *Western Journal of Black Studies, 10*(4), 167–171.

Wade, J. C. (1993). Institutional racism: An analysis of the mental health system. *American Journal of Orthopsychiatry, 63*(4), 536–544.

Wahlsten, D. (1994). The intelligence of heritability. *Canadian Psychology, 35*(3), 244–260.

Walker, R. D., & LaDue, R. (1986). An integrative approach to American Indian mental health. In C. B. Wilkinson (ed.), *Ethnic psychiatry* (pp. 143–194). New York: Plenum.

Watts, R. J. (1994). Paradigms of diversity. In E. J. Trickett, R. J. Watts, & D. Birman (eds.), *Human diversity: Perspectives on people in context* (pp. 49–80). San Francisco: Josey-Bass.

Whang, P. A., & Hancock, G. R. (1994). Motivation and mathematics achievement: Comparisons between Asian-American and non-Asian students. *Contemporary Educational Psychology, 19*(3), 302–322.

Wong, B. (1985). Family, kinship, and ethnic identity of the Chinese in New York City, with comparative remarks on the Chinese in Lima, Peru, and Manila, Philippines. *Journal of Comparative Family Studies, 16*(2), 231–254.

Yee, A. H., Fairchild, H. H., Weizmann, F., & Wyatt, G. E. (1993). Addressing psychology's problems with race. *American Psychologist, 48*(11), 1132–1140.

Zuckerman, M. (1990). Some dubious premises in research and theory on racial differences: Scientific, social, and ethical issues. *American Psychologist, 45*(12), 1297–1303.

PART FOUR

ECOLOGICAL AND ENVIRONMENTAL PSYCHOLOGY

Regardless of national boundaries, we all breathe the same air, drink the same water, fish from the same oceans, and farm in common soil. Pollution does not obey national boundaries or need a visa to waft over or leak into foreign lands and waters. But concerns about the environment extend beyond the problems of pollution. Poachers are decimating the flora and fauna of the Russian Far East as they search for ingredients for "traditional" folk medications that bring temptingly high prices—bear gallbladders, sea cucumbers, tiger skins, and other natural products with no demonstrable health effects. Large portions of the Siberian forest have been clear-cut, and the waters of Lake Baikal, the largest freshwater lake on earth, are seriously contaminated. Environmental epidemiologists have noted that two generations of Russians have produced industrial, conventional, and radioactive waste that is exacting a toll on the environment of former Soviet countries (Specter, 1995).

Westerners are facing similar pillage of their natural resources; some native wolves and buffalo have neared extinction, for example, only surviving after the problem reached critical levels. The development of environmental responsibility must become a national and international priority, a task that is especially difficult when the local population is very poor and at the mercy of those who are willing to pay huge sums of money to dump chemicals into their streams, hunt their native animals, or strip their rich forests.

The emerging field of environmental and ecological psychology is concerned with the psychological variables that affect person-environment interactions.

Environmental and ecological psychology extend into human-built settings as well as natural ones. The ways in which cities are designed and living arrangements are engineered have an effect on the way people live their lives. A city that is easy to navigate means that more people will travel through it; a neighborhood with safe play areas will result in more children and adults gathering together; and a home that is spacious and private will create a different pattern of family interactions than an overcrowded and shared living space.

The post-Soviet perspective on ecological and environmental psychology was written by Latvian psychologists Sergei Deryabo and Vitold Yasvin. In their chapter, they discuss the importance of developing a pro-green attitude and describe their research findings on how children develop a pro-environmental belief system. The American chapter in this part is written by Paul A. Bell and Eric D. Sundstrom. These authors focus mainly on the way city and neighborhood design influences how people use those spaces. Both pairs of authors recognize the interaction of people with the physical world around them as an important variable in modern life. This is a growing area, and we expect much more research and interest in how people can protect the environment and how the environment influences our lives.

Reference

Specter, M. (1995). Russia's declining health: Rising illness, shorter lives. *New York Times*, 19 February, pp. 1, 12.

18

Environmental Psychology

Evolution and Current Status

Paul A. Bell & Eric D. Sundstrom

Environmental psychology has existed as a branch of psychology for approximately 30 years. It focuses on the ways in which features of the physical environment affect, and are molded by, individuals, groups, communities, and social entities as large as entire cultures. One definition depicts environmental psychology as the study of transactions between individuals and their physical settings (Gifford, 1994), reflecting the premise that the relationship of people to their physical environment is one of mutual influence and exchange (Stokols & Altman, 1987).

In this chapter we provide an overview of the evolution and current status of environmental psychology in the United States, and we describe research examples to illustrate the field's main methods and assumptions. We begin by outlining the background and characteristics of the field. We briefly describe prominent theoretical perspectives and areas of research, then give illustrative research examples, including studies of noise as an environmental stressor, reactions of employees after their work environments were renovated to incorporate open-plan offices, and residential preferences and design features related to crime prevention. We conclude with a brief discussion of future directions of environmental psychology.

Environmental Psychology: In the Beginning

The first documented use of the term "environmental psychology" was in a paper delivered by William H. Ittelson at a meeting on hospital planning (Ittelson,

1964). The premise of the paper—which had also been addressed by others (e.g., Sommer & Osmond, 1961)—was that aspects of hospital design, such as wall color, furniture arrangements, or amount of private space, can have therapeutic impact. The term *environmental psychology* gained currency in the context of research on the design of institutional, residential, and work environments—including neighborhoods and entire communities—to maximize human functioning (Proshansky & Altman, 1979; Proshansky, Ittelson, & Rivlin, 1970; Sommer, 1969).

An early example of thinking by environmental psychologists was Osmond's (1957) hypothesis that seating arrangements influence social interaction. So-called sociopetal space was supposed to encourage conversation through seating that places people within comfortable distance, facing toward each other directly enough for convenient eye contact. Sommer and Ross (1958) tested Osmond's idea in a newly refurnished geriatrics ward for women at a Saskatchewan hospital, where patients appeared depressed and withdrawn; the hospital administrators had invited the consultants to address the problem. Sommer and Ross noticed that the chairs on the ward were lined up along the walls, side by side, all facing the center of the large room. They persuaded the staff to rearrange the chairs into circles around tables, the "sociopetal" arrangement. Counts of conversations before and after the environmental intervention revealed that after a few weeks the frequency of conversations had nearly doubled.

Sommer and Ross's informal experiment on the design of a hospital ward room illustrates a common tool of environmental psychologists: environmental design research. A typical project begins with analysis of the setting's goals and existing environment-behavior relationships, followed by development of a design intended to meet the goals of the setting. The new design is introduced into part or all of the setting, and measurements are collected before and after renovation for postoccupancy evaluation (Preiser, Rabinowitz, & White, 1988) of the effects of the design intervention and for tests of scientific hypotheses. Several such projects evaluated designs for hospitals and residential treatment centers and identified specific features associated with increased social interaction among patients (Cherulnik, 1993; Preiser, Vischer, & White, 1991).

Environmental psychology has evolved a focus on designing and changing built environments to meet human needs and on research to identify links between behavior and environment. Simultaneously an applied and a scientific subfield of psychology, environmental psychology draws on other branches, such as social and human factors psychology, as well as other disciplines (Bell, Greene, Fisher, & Baum, 1996; Sundstrom, Bell, Busby, & Asmus, 1996). In studying and implementing design changes, environmental psychologists seek habitability or congruence between the design and human needs.

Characteristics of Environmental Psychology

The origin of environmental psychology as an applied branch of psychology has had implications for its evolution. Emphasis on planning and design prompted an interdisciplinary orientation and encouraged multimethod research in intact settings and existing environments. Theory underlying both research and application has been eclectic and diverse, but it is used in service of a holistic perspective.

Interdisciplinary Orientation

Projects, books, and conferences involving environmental psychologists often include professionals from other disciplines: architects, urban planners, interior designers, facility managers, and others.

Multimethod Research in Field Settings

Although many environmental psychologists conduct controlled laboratory experiments, the orientation toward application has tended to encourage studies of existing, built environments and natural settings. Accordingly, most research reported in environmental psychology journals occurs in field settings and is quite applied. A related implication is that research methods tend to be diverse and eclectic: field experiments, surveys, correlational field studies, quasi-experimental designs, obtrusive and unobtrusive observation, and case study methods are all common tools in the research repertoire of environmental psychology.

Eclectic Theory

In studying intact settings, environmental psychology has drawn on other subfields of psychology. For example, principles of perception play a major role, particularly Gestalt principles and related concepts in architectural design, as well as perceptual implications for aesthetics and preference in built and natural environments. Perception is also important for understanding noise, heat, and detection of pollution. Studying attitudes toward and satisfaction with particular settings calls on the attitude formation and change literature of social psychology. Many environment-behavior relationships involve social behavior, such as attraction, aggression, and helping, so environmental psychologists draw on the social psychology literature concerning these behaviors as well. Since much human use of space involves personal space, crowding, and territory, environmental psychologists draw on social psychological and ethological expertise for these topics. Clinical and community psychology also provide rich material for environmental psychologists' study of environmental stress (e.g., commuting stress or crowding stress) and human response to disasters, including technological catastrophes and natural disasters. There is also a growing emphasis on environmental cognition, such as way finding and mental maps of built and natural environments, and the contributions of cognitive psychology are prominent in environmental psychologists' study of these topics. Efforts to encourage people to conserve resources typically employ reinforcement strategies derived from the psychology of learning.

Holistic View

Although environmental psychologists may dissect a given setting into various components for detailed study, there is an assumption that behavior and environment interact in ways that cannot be fully appreciated unless the setting is studied as a whole. We do gain knowledge by examining individual components, but we gain the best perspective by studying intact units. Thus, environmental psychology assumes we have the most to gain by studying environment-behavior relationships in applied settings. Moreover, environmental psychologists assume that environment-behavior relationships run both ways; over time, the environment influences human behavior and human behavior influences the environment, so the least bias in our research occurs when we study the interrelationship between behavior and environment over extended periods of time (Altman & Rogoff, 1987).

Theoretical Perspectives

Research has used several theoretical perspectives, many of which are borrowed from other branches of psychology. Dominant models or approaches include adaptation, stress, overload, understimulation, privacy regulation, and behavior constraint.

Adaptation

A dominant perspective in studying environment-behavior relationships relies on the concept of adaptation, which refers to adjustments of behavior or perception, or alteration of the environment itself, to enable continued habitation of a particular setting. For example, people adapt to restricted space in a prison or a submarine by withdrawing from social interaction or by erecting artificial barriers to limit interaction (such as by hanging bedsheets across the room). People adapt to noise by shouting to be heard, screening out intrusive sounds, or adding noise-attenuating barriers.

Stress

According to the environmental stress model, components of the environment such as noise, extreme temperature, or environmental disaster challenge individual and group mechanisms for adaptation. Cognitive appraisal of stressors as threatening sets in motion these coping responses, which may be problem focused (e.g., attempts to stop the stressor) or palliative (e.g., use of psychological defense mechanisms such as denial). If coping is unsuccessful, physiological and psychological exhaustion can result. If coping is successful, there can also be negative aftereffects, such as reduced frustration tolerance, or positive aftereffects, such as increased self-confidence.

Overload

Another common model in environmental psychology derives from cognitive processing and information overload. This load or overload model assumes that we have a limited capacity to process information about the environment. When too much information is present—as is often the case in commercial sections of large cities—we attend to the most central or relevant information and ignore less important cues. Milgram (1970), for example, used this model to explain why incivilities can develop in large cities: to cope with overload, we screen out cues that signal us that other people need help.

Understimulation

In contrast, the understimulation perspective examines behavioral consequences of too little stimulation, such as in sensory deprivation studies (e.g., Zubek, 1969). Although negative consequences of deprivation are often discussed (e.g., heightened anxiety), research also shows that REST (Restricted Environmental Stimulation Therapy) can be therapeutic for hypertension, addictions, and other disorders (e.g., Barabasz & Barabasz, 1993).

Adaptation Level

Yet another theoretical perspective examines optimal stimulation. Borrowing from Helson (1964), Wohlwill (e.g., 1974) proposed that people have an ideal level for different types of environmental stimulation. An environment that falls outside this optimal level will be distressing, while one that meets the adaptation level will be most habitable.

Behavior Constraint

The behavior constraint approach to environment-behavior relationships is one of several control models. When components of a setting lead to loss of perceived control, psychological reactance or attempts to restore control occur. If these attempts are unsuccessful, learned helplessness can occur. Institutional environments such as prisons or nursing homes may be especially vulnerable to such control issues.

Other Models, Ecological Psychology, and Staffing Theory

Numerous other theoretical perspectives can be found in environmental psychology, such as arousal models, privacy regulation models, and environmental press. We might make special mention of Barker's ecological psychology approach, which examines the behavior setting, the cultural purpose and operation of the setting, and the consequences of overstaffing or understaffing the setting (e.g., Barker, 1968). This perspective has proved especially useful in studying large versus small schools and overcrowding in national parks, for example.

A model combining many of the elements of these theoretical perspectives has been proposed by Bell et al. (e.g., 1996). This eclectic model posits that objective physical conditions and individual factors influence perception of an environment. If components of the setting are outside the optimal range of stimulation, arousal, stress, overload, or reactance may occur. Coping follows, which if successful leads to adaptation and potential aftereffects and if unsuccessful leads to continued and intensified reactions, as well as aftereffects.

Areas of Research

As the field of environmental psychology has evolved over the past 30 years, its research has fallen into several identifiable clusters. Clearly, the design of built environments remains a major emphasis. Research in this area focuses on a range of settings, including residences (single-family homes, apartments, dormitories), work environments (offices, factories), institutional environments (hospitals, nursing homes, prisons), learning environments (classrooms for students of all ages, museums, zoos, college campuses), recreation environments (playgrounds, community parks, national parks), neighborhoods (residential, commercial), and entire communities (e.g., rural versus urban comparisons). Although not restricted to built environments per se, much of the study of built environments includes how people use space, including personal space, privacy, crowding, and territoriality. Other research examines physical environmental stressors, such as noise, weather (especially temperature), and pollution. Such stressors can be studied as part of a specific setting (e.g., a city) or in a laboratory, with the assumption of generalization across settings. Other stressors such as natural disasters or toxic spills must be studied as they occur. One research area that relies heavily on laboratory experiments is environmental perception; examples include preferences for architectural styles and aesthetic quality of natural scenes. Preference is also examined in attitude surveys about a specific environment or about environmental issues. A final area of research is resource preservation, such as energy and water conservation, antilitter campaigns, and recycling programs. Research on these topics tends to be extended over time and is typically conducted as a field experiment with one or more interventions. Any given research project in environmental psychology is likely to involve more than one of the above areas. For example, one might study the effects of a design change in a work setting and measure noise levels, territorial behavior, preferences for views of natural scenery, and judgments of the aesthetic quality of the modified rooms.

Owing to the nature of research in environmental psychology, with a focus on improving design in a specific setting, it is often difficult to generate principles that apply across a range of settings. Rather, the careful procedures followed in the design and implementation stages of the research should yield a design that improves the habitability of the setting. We refer to these as the substantive and procedural contributions, respectively, of environmental psychology. We turn now to three examples of research in environmental psychology that illustrate the richness of these procedural and substantive contributions. Our specific research examples include noise as an environmental stressor, changing office designs to an open-plan arrangement, and designing homes and neighborhoods for crime prevention.

Noise as an Example of Environmental Stress

Since much of what environmental psychologists study is specific environmental stressors, regardless of the setting, it is worth summarizing some of the research on at least one stressor across a variety of settings. Since environmental psychologists probably study noise more than any other physical environmental stressor, we have chosen it as our example for cross-setting investigation. Moreover, noise research collectively is an excellent example of the multiple perspectives environmental psychologists employ in addressing issues. Noise studies have included basic theory-building laboratory research, applied research on noise in the classroom, and basic and applied studies on noise and social behavior. As we will see in the next two sections, noise is also an important factor in open-plan office designs and in housing considerations.

Noise and Urban Stress

Glass and Singer (1972) undertook a series of laboratory studies on noise and behavior as a means of investigating urban stress. In their view, the information gained was a respectable analog of the consequences of everyday urban living. Theoretically, noise and other environmental stressors certainly impact arousal. Noise, for example, increases blood pressure and other measures of arousal. Eggertsen, Svensson, Magnusson, and Andren (1987) selected subjects with moderately high blood pressure and exposed them to 105 decibels of noise for 30 minutes. Compared to quieter periods, the noisy periods were associated with elevated systolic and diastolic blood pressure. Glass and Singer showed that noise also impacts autonomic arousal as measured by skin conductance, vasoconstriction, and muscle action potentials.

Given such results, one might expect that noise would impact task performance. However, Glass and Singer found that noise had essentially no impact on simple mental tasks, including same-different comparisons between multidigit numbers, adding three numbers of up to two digits each, and finding a specific letter in a list of words. On the other hand, noise had significant impact on a more complex task. In this dual-task study, subjects had to track a line with a steering wheel simulator, designated as the primary task. A simultaneous secondary task required subjects to listen to a list of numbers and repeat the previous number whenever a new number appeared, which happened every two seconds. Noise had minimal impact on the primary task but substantial delete-rious impact on the secondary task. Such findings suggest that rather than arousal being the major mediator of noise effects, cognitive overload could be more important. That is, noise did not particularly impact performance until it placed an excessive burden on the information-processing demands of the dual-task methodology.

Further support for this interpretation comes from what is perhaps the most significant outcome of the Glass and Singer research: the type of noise can be more important than the mere presence of noise. Specifically, Glass and Singer varied the predictability and controllability of the noise stimulus. In the pre-dictable condition, a 9-second noise burst (usually 108 dB) was presented at 1-minute intervals. In the unpredictable condition, the length of noise bursts (also 108 dB) varied from 3 to 21 seconds in duration between intervals of 15 to 90 seconds. In addition, a perceived control condition was implemented by sometimes telling subjects they could stop the noise any time they wished (analy-ses in the controllability condition were based on subjects who did not stop the noise). For physiological reactivity and for task performance, the results indi-cated greater deleterious impact of the noise if it was uncontrollable and if it was unpredictable.

In addition, these researchers found reliable aftereffects of noise. Once the noise had stopped, subjects were asked to complete paper-and-pencil drawing puzzles, some of which were impossible to solve. By counting the number of times subjects attempted to solve the unsolvable puzzles, the experimenters derived an index of frustration tolerance. Also, subjects were given a proofread-ing task to complete after the noise stopped. For both of these measures, un-predictable and uncontrollable noise had the greatest deleterious impact.

Taken together, these results are usually interpreted in terms of overload and adaptive capacity. Unpredictable and uncontrollable noise is difficult to adapt to and overloads information-processing capacity. Recovery from such stress requires time, which is reflected in reduced frustration tolerance and poorer performance on tasks requiring concentration. As previously indicated, Glass and Singer intended their studies to be an analog of urban stress. Milgram (1970) also invoked an overload model to explain adaptation to the experience of liv-ing in cities: Adaptation to city life was characterized by attending to important cues and ignoring peripheral cues, a circumstance that leads to an impersonal and even asocial atmosphere.

Noise in the Classroom

The results of these carefully controlled laboratory studies have been corrobo-rated in several field settings that have studied the impact of noise on children's classroom performance. For example, Cohen, Glass, and Singer (1973) studied children in a high-rise apartment complex that spanned a freeway in New York City. Children on the lower floors, who were exposed to much more noise, were compared with those on the upper floors, while variables such as socioeconomic status and air pollution levels were statistically controlled. Results indicated that children on the lower floors had poorer hearing discrimination and poorer reading ability—substantial costs for their noise exposure. Similarly, Bronzaft and McCarthy (1975) compared the reading skills of children in a school that was adjacent to elevated railroad tracks. Those on the side of the building facing the tracks had poorer reading skills than those on the quieter side of the building away from the tracks. Amelioration of the situation by installing sound-absorbing insulation in the classroom ceiling and pads on the tracks reduced the noise levels and equalized the reading scores on the two sides of the building (Bronzaft, 1985–1986).

In other studies, Cohen and colleagues (1980, 1981) compared four elementary schools in the flight paths of traffic at Los Angeles International Airport to three quieter schools in similar neighborhoods away from the flight paths. Overflights subjected children in the noisy schools to 95 decibels of noise approximately every 2.5 minutes. Testing for this research was conducted in a quiet research trailer at the schools. Children in the noisy schools had higher blood pressure and poorer cognitive performance, and they also showed signs of helplessness—giving up on a classroom assignment before it was complete. After noise abatement strategies were implemented in some of the noisy classrooms, there was some improvement in cognitive performance and school achievement. However, the abatement classrooms were still more noisy than the quiet control classrooms, and students in the quiet classrooms still had superior performance after the abatement procedures. Moreover, a one-year follow-up of children in the noisy classrooms showed no evidence of adaptation: the effects of the noise did not dissipate over time.

Noise and Social Interaction

Other researchers have examined the impact of noise on social behavior. For example, Mathews, Canon, and Alexander (1974) found that even a noise of 80 decibels increased the distance at which individuals felt comfortable with each other. Also, in a correlational study, Appleyard and Lintell (1972) found less informal interaction among neighbors when traffic noise was greater. Kenrick and Johnson (1979), on the other hand, found that among females, exposure to aversive noise increased attraction toward one who shared the aversive experience with the subject but decreased attraction toward someone not actually experiencing the noise. Siegel and Steele (1980) found that noise led to more extreme and premature judgments about other people but did not cause these judgments to be more negative. All of these results are consistent with an overload interpretation: if noise causes people to narrow their attention and focus on a smaller part of their environment, it may also cause people to pay attention to fewer characteristics of other people. Thus, noise could lead to a distortion in perceptions of other people.

Noise and Aggression

Research on the effects of noise on aggression has shown several interesting results. In a traditional laboratory experiment, Geen and O'Neal (1969) provided subjects with an opportunity to aggress against a confederate "victim" by ostensibly delivering electric shocks to that person. Subjects exposed to a two-minute burst of continuous 60-decibel white noise delivered more shocks, as did subjects exposed to a violent film. In other laboratory research, Donnerstein and Wilson (1976) found that a 95-decibel unpredictable noise increased aggression relative to a 55-decibel unpredictable noise only for angered subjects. Apparently, noise made no difference in the intensity of shocks delivered by nonangry subjects. Konecni (1975) also found this to be the case—noise increased aggressiveness only when subjects had been provoked and made angry. In a second experiment, Donnerstein and Wilson (1976) found that more intense shocks were delivered by angry than nonangry subjects and that unpredictable and uncontrollable noise increased aggression for angry subjects. A 95-decibel noise had no effect on aggression, however, when subjects perceived they had control over it. These experiments suggest, then, that under circumstances in which noise would be expected to increase arousal or a predisposition to aggress (i.e., when subjects were already angry), aggression is increased. However, when the noise does not appreciably increase arousal (as when an individual has control over it) or when the individual is not already predisposed to aggress, noise appears to have little, if any, effect on aggression.

Noise and Helping

Cohen and Lezak (1977) demonstrated that the content of photographic slides depicting social situations was less well remembered under noisy than under quiet conditions when subjects were asked to concentrate initially on material other than the slides. Findings suggest that noise may also interfere with the perception of cues that indicate an individual needs help apparently because it prevents people from perceiving or processing such cues.

In a laboratory experiment, Matthews and Canon (1975) examined the effects of noise on willingness to help a confederate pick up a pile of dropped papers and books. Some 72 percent of the subjects helped in a "normal" noise condition, 67 percent in a 65-decibel condition, and only 37 percent in an 85-decibel condition. In the same article, Matthews and Canon reported a field experiment in which a confederate dropped a box of books while getting out of a car. To emphasize his apparent need for aid, he wore a cast on his arm in half of the experimental situations. Noise had little effect on helping when the confederate was not wearing a cast. But when the confederate wore a cast (high-need condition), a loud noise (87 dB) reduced the frequency of helping from 80 percent to 15 percent compared to a 50-decibel control condition.

A series of studies by Page (1977) also provided evidence that noise can reduce the likelihood that people will help each other. In one study, subjects encountered a confederate who, with an armful of books, had dropped a pack of index cards. They were exposed to one of three levels of noise (100 dB, 80 dB, or 50 dB) at the time they saw the confederate drop the cards. Results of this study suggested that people helped most under low levels of noise. In a second study, subjects saw a confederate drop a package while walking past a construction site. When the jackhammers were being used on the site, noise levels were 92 decibels; when they were not being used, levels were 72 decibels. Thus, depending on the jackhammers, subjects saw a confederate drop a package during one or another level of noise. People were less likely to help the confederate when noise levels reached 92 decibels than they were when it was a relatively quiet 72 decibels. In a third study, people were approached and directly asked whether or not they could provide change for a quarter. Noise once again decreased the likelihood that people would respond favorably to the request. At least two more studies, however (Bell & Doyle, 1983; Yinon & Bizman, 1980) failed to find that noise decreased helping.

On the other hand, Sherrod and Downs (1974) demonstrated that one aftereffect of noise can be decreased helping and that perceived control can reduce this negative influence. In that study, subjects participated in a proofreading task while simultaneously monitoring a series of random numbers presented on audio tape. Three conditions were established: (1) a control condition in which the numbers were superimposed on the pleasing sounds of a seashore (e.g., waves striking the beach); (2) a complex noise condition in which the numbers were superimposed on a round of Dixieland jazz and another voice reading prose; and (3) a perceived control condition using the same tape as the complex noise condition but with the subjects told they could terminate the distracting noise if they so desired. After 20 minutes in one of these situations, subjects left the laboratory and were approached by an individual asking their assistance in filling out forms for another study. The most help was volunteered by subjects in the seashore sound condition, for whom noise was least noxious. Subjects in the perceived control condition offered more help than subjects in the uncontrollable complex noise condition. Thus, the effects of noise on helping behavior depend on several factors, among which are perceived control of the noise, volume of the noise, and stimulus characteristics of the person needing assistance.

Summary of Noise Effects

Altogether, research on noise indicates that it increases autonomic arousal, places demands on information-processing capacity, and can impair cognitive performance and increase aggression while decreasing helping behavior. Moreover, these effects are more severe with unpredictable and uncontrollable noise, which is more difficult to adapt to than predictable and controllable noise. These effects are noticeable under a variety of controlled laboratory conditions and in numerous field settings.

Residential Design

Preferences

Despite the range of residential alternatives available, research on design preferences shows that residents of the United States and Canada overwhelmingly prefer single-family homes over apartments, condominiums, or other alternatives. Environmental psychologists and others have concluded that this preference is largely due to privacy issues. Single-family homes permit more restrictions on access by those who are not occupants. They tend to reduce interior noise levels and visual intrusion, as well. On the other hand, considerable satisfaction can be attained by those who reside in other forms of housing. For example, Paulus, Nagar, and Camacho (1991) compared satisfaction among U.S. army families who resided in apartments versus mobile homes. Satisfaction was high for both types of housing because of perceived choice, expectation of improved conditions in the future, and comparison with past housing. Those satisfied with mobile homes especially emphasized low noise levels, low perceived crime risk, more distance between units, more privacy, and compatibility of housing with raising children. Those satisfied with apartments cited attractiveness, convenience of services, adequacy of recreation facilities, fire and weather safety (e.g., feeling safer in case of a tornado), and other people in the complex. This last correlate suggests a phenomenon that seems to hold across a variety of settings and cultures: residential satisfaction is closely associated with social ties to family and neighbors. For example, in a classic study of the consequences of large-scale dislocation of a run-down neighborhood in order to renovate it during the U.S. urban renewal movement, Fried (1963) observed that resulting disruption of social ties with former neighbors was a major source of dissatisfaction among those who were supposed to benefit from the intervention effort. In another example of the importance of social ties, Ebbesen, Kjos, and Konecni (1976) appealed to the "environmental spoiling hypothesis" to explain how neighbors who disturb the neighborhood (e.g., through loud noise, failure to keep up property, or disrespect for the preferences of others) can lead to intense neighborhood dissatisfaction. These findings make it clear that design features are but one component of satisfaction.

   One way that single-family homes give more control over privacy is how they structure space. By segmenting space into individual rooms for specific functions (sleeping, eating, bathing, and so on), home designs give control over interactions that will occur among occupants. To the extent that physical barriers are not designed into the home, occupants adapt by using dominance hierarchies to determine who gets to use specific spaces. Cultures can even be classified along a continuum according to the degree to which their usual housing designs segment space.

Designing for Crime Prevention

A growing concern in many parts of the world is an actual or perceived increase in crime, especially crime against people and property. Environmental psychologists have been particularly interested in studying whether specific designs can decrease the incidence of such crimes. Fear of crime seems related to designs that provide refuge for perpetrators and lack of perceived escape routes for victims (Day, 1994; Fisher & Nasar, 1992; Loewen, Steel, & Suedfeld, 1993; Nasar & Fisher, 1992). Although many design factors have been studied for their potential to prevent crime, three that are of notable interest are defensible space, exterior appearance, and restricted access to entire neighborhoods. The concept of defensible space has been promoted by Newman (e.g., 1972). The idea is to design buildings so that space appears to belong to an individual or group. Defensible spaces could lead to lower crime for several reasons (Taylor, Gottfredson, & Brower, 1984). First, they could have a direct effect. It may be that spaces that look "defensible" lead potential offenders to assume that residents will actively respond to intruders, a notion that has been supported in work by Brower, Dockett, and Taylor (1983). In multifamily housing, for example, public hallways or other areas accessible to anyone should be eliminated because they are less likely to be defended against intruders. Adding porches and windows promotes surveillance of the area. Second, as suggested by Newman, defensible space may cause the formation of local ties among residents. This may occur because it makes people feel safer, which causes them to use the space more, to come into increased contact with neighbors, and, ultimately, to develop more common ties. Individuals with more ties are more apt to intervene to "defend" their neighborhood, are better able to discriminate neighbors from strangers, and, because shared norms develop, are more likely to know what types of activities should go on and what types should not (Taylor & Brower, 1985). The latter analysis was supported in research by Taylor et al. (1984). Smaller entries shared by 3 or 4 families rather than 10 or 20 families will encourage immediate neighbors to get to know each other and to recognize who belongs and who does not belong in the immediate area. Of course, defensible space can deter crime only if the social fabric (e.g., trust among neighbors) is present to carry out the defense (e.g., Merry, 1981). Finally, defensible space could lessen crime since it may strengthen people's territorial functioning (i.e., because areas characterized by defensible space are well bounded and more defensible, they may elicit more proprietary attitudes). For example, Taylor, Gottfredson, and Brower (1980) suggest that some critical environmental features for controlling crime are signs of defense, signs of appropriation, and signs of incivility. Signs of defense are symbolic and real barriers directed toward strangers that keep unwanted outsiders away. Signs of appropriation are territorial markers suggesting that a space is used and cared for. Signs of incivility are physical and social cues (e.g., environmental deterioration) that indicate a decay in the social order. These territorial signs give information to other residents and to strangers, which affects whether or not crime occurs. Taylor et al. believe that territorial signs that deter crime are more common in homogeneous neighborhoods and where there are strong local social ties. As opposed to Newman's model, then, these authors suggest that sociocultural variables and social conditions, in addition to design, determine territorial cognitions and behaviors and ultimately the level of crime in a neighborhood (e.g., Newman & Franck, 1982; Taylor et al., 1980, 1984).

Several studies have examined the effects of exterior appearance of homes on their susceptibility to crime. Brown and Bentley (1993) found that burglars were especially wary of signs that residents would show territorial concern. Specifically, burglarized homes differed in that the symbolic barriers they possessed were public, as opposed to private. For example, burglarized homes had fewer assertions of the owner's private identity (e.g., name and address signs), more signs of public use (e.g., public street signs in front of them), and fewer attempts at property demarcation from the street (e.g., hedges, rock borders). They also had fewer actual barriers (e.g., fewer locks or fences to communicate a desire for privacy and deter public access). Also, on streets where burglaries occurred, there were fewer traces (e.g., signs of occupancy) that showed the presence of local residents. Burglarized houses had fewer parked cars and fewer sprinklers operating, and residents were less apt to be seen in their yards by the researchers. In this regard, a garage was significant, since it often made it ambiguous whether or not people were home (e.g., a garage without windows can disguise the absence of the car). More burglaries occurred in homes without garages, perhaps because the absence of cars made it likely that these homes were empty. In houses where burglaries occurred, detectability (the potential for exercising surveillance) was also lower, and neighboring houses were less visually accessible (see also Perkins, Meeks, & Taylor, 1992; Perkins, Wandersman, Rich, & Taylor, 1993). Interestingly, MacDonald and Gifford (1989) found that signs of territorial defense could indicate to burglars that valued goods were inside a residence.

A fairly recent means of promoting territorial defense in cities is to barricade streets to keep nonresidents out (Crowe, 1991). A cul-de-sac design in a residential area serves a similar function: traffic access is reduced so that residents may be more vigilant and criminals more conspicuous if they cruise through the area to scout out a target. In areas with a gridlike street pattern, it is more difficult for neighbors to know who "belongs" in the area and who does not. By barricading strategic points in the neighborhood, residents hope to make cruising through the neighborhood by criminals more difficult. Barriers can be barrels filled with sand and linked by long boards, concrete construction barriers, or attractively designed brick walls with landscaping. Barricades are not without controversy; often, lower income residents or those in mostly minority neighborhoods contend that barricades are designed to keep them out of well-to-do majority residential areas. Do barricades work? Atlas and LeBlanc (1994) report on a study of Miami Shores, a community in Florida that erected barriers over a period of years. Compared to crime rates in other communities, some crime rates in Miami shores were lower after installation of the barricades. Part of the reduction, however, may have been due not to the barriers themselves but to the need for neighbors to work together to implement the plan.

Summary of Crime Prevention Design

The research on residential designs intended to prevent crimes is not without societal and academic controversy. Although implementing certain features such as defensible space and blocking off neighborhoods seem to reduce crime at least somewhat, it is impossible in field studies to determine whether the results are due to physical design changes, social changes, or both. Moreover, societies must be willing to deal with the fallout of some interventions, such as blockading streets against "outsiders."

Summary

Environmental psychology has been an exciting field in North America for three decades. The richness of the field stems from its emphasis on using basic and applied research and a multidisciplinary perspective to address real-world problems that arise when humans encounter their built and natural environments. The research topics so addressed seem limitless. Even though the focus of environmental psychology seems largely applied, numerous theoretical perspectives have been employed that cross the research domains. By drawing on a knowledge base that includes social psychology, cognitive psychology, psychology of learning, perception, and community psychology, among others, environmental psychology has helped to show the joint relevance of these different content areas to specific real-world problems. Given the accomplishments of environmental psychology since its inception, the future of the field seems bright as long as humans show concern about their interactions with their environment.

References

Altman, I., & Rogoff, B. (1987). World views in psychology: Trait, interactional, organismic, and transactional perspectives. In D. Stokols & I. Altman (eds.), *Handbook of environmental psychology* (vol. 1, pp. 7–40). New York: Wiley Interscience.

Appleyard, D., & Lintell, M. (1972). The environmental quality of city streets: The residents' viewpoint. *Journal of the American Institute of Planners, 38*, 84–101.

Atlas, R., & LeBlanc, W. G. (1994). Environmental barriers to crime. *Ergonomics in Design*, October, pp. 9–16.

Barabasz, A. F., & Barabasz, M. (1993). *Clinical and experimental restricted environmental stimulation: New developments and perspectives.* New York: Springer.

Barker, R. G. (1968). *Ecological psychology.* Palo Alto, Calif.: Stanford University Press.

Becker, F., & Steele, F. (1995). *Workplace by design.* San Francisco: Jossey-Bass.

Bell, P. A., & Doyle, D. P. (1983). Effects of heat and noise on helping behavior. *Psychological Reports, 53,* 955–959.

Bell, P. A., Greene, T. C., Fisher, J. D., & Baum, A. (1996). *Environmental psychology* (4th ed.). Fort Worth: Harcourt Brace.

Bronzaft, A. L. (1985–1986). Combating the unsilent enemy—Noise. *Prevention in Human Services, 4(1–2),* 179–192.

Bronzaft, A. L., & McCarthy, D. P. (1975). The effects of elevated train noise on reading ability. *Environment and Behavior, 7,* 517–527.

Brower, S., Dockett, K., & Taylor, R. (1983). Residents' perceptions of territorial features and perceived local threat. *Environment and Behavior, 15,* 419–437.

Brown, B. B., & Bentley, D. L. (1993). Residential burglars judge risk: The role of territoriality. *Journal of Environmental Psychology, 13,* 51–61.

Cherulnik, P. D. (1993). *Applications of environment-behavior research: Case studies and analysis.* New York: Cambridge University Press.

Cohen, S., Evans, G. W., Krantz, D. S., & Stokols, D. (1980). Physiological, motivational, and cognitive effects of aircraft noise on children: Moving from the laboratory to the field. *American Psychologist, 35,* 231–243.

Cohen, S., Evans, G. W., Krantz, D. S., Stokols, D., & Kelly, S. (1981). Aircraft noise and children: Longitudinal and cross-sectional evidence on adaptation to noise and the effectiveness of noise abatement. *Journal of Personality and Social Psychology, 40,* 331–345.

Cohen, S., Glass, D. C., & Singer, J. E. (1973). Apartment noise, auditory discrimination, and reading ability in children. *Journal of Experimental Social Psychology, 9,* 407–422.

Cohen, S., & Lezak, A. (1977). Noise and inattentiveness to social cues. *Environment and Behavior, 9,* 559–572.

Crowe, T. (1991). *Crime prevention through environmental design: Applications of architectural design and space management concepts.* Boston: National Crime Prevention Institute/Butterworth-Heinemann.

Day, K. (1994). Conceptualizing women's fear of sexual assault on campus: A review of causes and recommendations for change. *Environment and Behavior, 26,* 742–765.

Donnerstein, E., & Wilson, D. W. (1976). Effects of noise and perceived control on ongoing and subsequent aggressive behavior. *Journal of Personality and Social Psychology, 34,* 774–781.

Ebbesen, E. B., Kjos, G. L., & Konecni, V. J. (1976). Spatial ecology: Its effects on the choice of friends and enemies. *Journal of Experimental Social Psychology, 12,* 505–518.

Eggertsen, R., Svensson, A., Magnusson, M., & Andren, L. (1987). Hemodynamic effects of loud noise before and after central sympathetic nervous stimulation. *Acta Medica Scandinavica, 221,* 159–164.

Fisher, B., & Nasar, J. L. (1992). Fear of crime in relation to three exterior site features: Prospect, refuge, and escape. *Environment and Behavior, 24,* 35–56.

Fried, M. (1963). Grieving for a lost home. In L. J. Duhl (ed.), *The urban condition* (pp. 151–171). New York: Basic Books.

Geen, R. G., & O'Neal, E. C. (1969). Activation of cue-elicited aggression by general arousal. *Journal of Personality and Social Psychology, 11,* 289–292.

Gifford, R. (1994). Environmental psychology. *Encyclopedia of Human Behavior, 2,* 265–277.

Glass, D. C., & Singer, J. E. (1972). *Urban stress.* New York: Academic Press.

Helson, H. (1964). *Adaptation level theory.* New York: Harper & Row.

Ittelson, W. H. (1964). Environmental psychology and architectural planning. Paper presented at the American Hospital Planning Association Conference on Hospital Planning, New York.

Kenrick, D. T., & Johnson, G. A. (1979). Interpersonal attraction in aversive environments: A problem for the classical conditioning paradigm. *Journal of Personality and Social Psychology, 87,* 572–579.

Konecni, V. J. (1975). The mediation of aggressive behavior: Arousal level versus anger and cognitive labeling. *Journal of Personality and Social Psychology, 32,* 706–712.

Loewen, L. J., Steel, G. D., & Suedfeld, P. (1993). Perceived safety from crime in the urban neighborhood. *Journal of Environmental Psychology, 13,* 321–331.

MacDonald, J. F., & Gifford, R. (1989). Territorial cues and defensible space theory: The burglar's point of view. *Journal of Environmental Psychology, 9,* 193–205.

Mathews, K. E., & Canon, L. K. (1975). Environmental noise level as a determinant of helping behavior. *Journal of Personality and Social Psychology, 32,* 571–577.

Mathews, K. E., Canon, L. K., & Alexander, K. (1974). The influence of level of empathy and ambient noise on the body buffer zone. *Proceedings of the American Psychological Association Division of Personality and Social Psychology, 1,* 367–370.

Merry, S. E. (1981). Defensible space undefended: Social factors in crime control through environmental design. *Urban Affairs Quarterly, 16,* 397–422.

Milgram, S. (1970). The experience of living in cities. *Science, 167,* 1461–1468.

Nasar, J. L., & Fisher, B. (1992). Design for vulnerability: Cues and reactions to fear of crime. *Sociology and Social Research, 76,* 48–58.

Newman, O. (1972). *Defensible space.* New York: Macmillan.

Newman, O., & Franck, K. (1982). The effects of building size on personal crime and fear of crime. *Population and Environment, 5,* 203–220.

Osmond, H. (1957). Function as the basis of psychiatric ward design. *Mental Hospitals, 8,* 23–30.

Page, R. A. (1977). Noise and helping behavior. *Environment and Behavior, 9,* 559–572.

Paulus, P. B., Nagar, D., & Camacho, L. M. (1991). Environmental and psychological factors in reactions to apartments and mobile homes. *Journal of Environmental Psychology, 11,* 143–161.

Perkins, D. D., Meeks, J. W., & Taylor, R. B. (1992). The physical environment of street blocks and resident perceptions of crime and disorder: Implications for theory and measurement. *Journal of Environmental Psychology, 12,* 21–34.

Perkins, D. D., Wandersman, A., Rich, R. C., & Taylor, R. B. (1993). The physical environment of street crime: Defensible space, territoriality, and incivilities. *Journal of Environmental Psychology, 13,* 29–49.

Preiser, W. F. E., Rabinowitz, H. Z., & White, E. T. (1988). *Post occupancy evaluation.* New York: Van Nostrand Reinhold.

Preiser, W. F. E., Vischer, J. C., & White, E. T. (eds.) (1991). *Design intervention: Toward a more humane architecture.* New York: Van Nostrand Reinhold

Proshansky, H., & Altman, I. (1979). Overview of the field. In W. P. White (ed.), *Resources in environment and behavior* (pp. 3–36). Washington, D.C.: American Psychological Association.

Proshansky, H. M., Ittelson, W. H., & Rivlin, L. G. (eds.) (1970). *Environmental psychology: Man and his physical setting.* New York: Holt, Rinehart and Winston.

Scheflen, A. E. (1971). Living space in an urban ghetto. *Family Process, 10,* 429–450.

Sherrod, D. R., & Downs, R. (1974). Environmental determinants of altruism: The effects of stimulus overload and perceived control on helping. *Journal of Experimental Social Psychology*, *10*, 468–479.

Siegel, J. M., & Steele, C. M. (1980). Environmental distraction and interpersonal judgements. *British Journal of Social and Clinical Psychology*, *19*, 23–32.

Sommer, R. (1969). *Personal space: The behavioral basis of design*. Englewood Cliffs, N.J.: Prentice-Hall.

Sommer, R., & Osmond, H. (1961). Symptoms of institutional care. *Social Problems*, *8*, 254–263.

Sommer, R., & Ross, H. (1958). Social interaction on a geriatrics ward. *International Journal of Social Psychiatry*, *4*, 128–133.

Stokols, D., & Altman, I. (eds) (1987). *Handbook of environmental psychology*. New York: Wiley.

Sundstrom, E., Bell, P. A., Busby, P. F., & Asmus, C. (1996). Environmental psychology, 1989–1994. *Annual Review of Psychology*, *47*, 485–512.

Taylor, R. B., & Brower, S. (1985). Home and near-home territories. In I. Altman & C. Werner (eds.), *Human behavior and environment: Current theory and research*, vol. 8, *Home environments* (pp. 183–212). New York: Plenum.

Taylor, R. B., Gottfredson, S. D., & Brower, S. (1980). The defensibility of defensible space: A critical review and a synthetic framework for future research. In T. Hirshi & M. Gottfredson (eds.), *Understanding crime*. Beverly Hills: Sage.

Taylor, R. B., Gottfredson, S., & Brower, S. (1984). Understanding block crime and fear. *Journal of Research in Crime and Delinquency*, *21*, 303–331.

Wohlwill, J. F. (1974). Human response to levels of environmental stimulation. *Human Ecology*, *2*, 127–147.

Yinon, Y., & Bizman, A. (1980). Noise, success, and failure as determinants of helping behavior. *Personality and Social Psychology Bulletin*, *6*, 125–130.

Zubek, J. P. (ed.) (1969). *Sensory deprivation: Fifteen years of research*. New York: Appleton-Century-Crofts.

19

Environmental and "Green" Psychology in the Former Soviet Union

Sergei Deryabo & Vitold Yasvin

There are more people alive today than ever before in history, yet the size of the planet that we inhabit remains unchanged and the earth's nonrenewable natural resources are declining. At the same time, we have developed the potential to destroy or render uninhabitable huge portions of our planet. The possibility of a worldwide environmental crisis is real. How do people think and feel about the world in which they live, and how can psychologists understand how some people come to value their environment and others treat it with total disregard?

Like any rapidly expanding area of interest, one of the barriers to communication and development in the field is the problem of defining new words and using labels for new concepts in a consistent manner so that people can communicate about developments in the field. The word *ecology*, for example, has taken on multiple meanings, and although the proliferation of meanings shows that an increasing number of academic disciplines are concerned with this field, it has also resulted in a peculiar version of the Tower of Babel, in which everyone is uttering the same word but meaning a different concept.

When the word *ecology* was introduced in 1866 by Earnest Gekhel, it was used as a label for the scientific study of the interrelationships of organisms with their environment. We doubt he could imagine that this obscure field of study would assume such prominence that his new term would be used by young schoolchildren or that scientists from a variety of backgrounds would devote their life's work to this newly named field. In an attempt to reduce the ambiguity conveyed by the word *ecological* in the psychological literature, the following four distinctions are proposed.

1. Psychological ecology: a field of ecology. When used in this way, the word *psychological* is used to modify or describe an area of ecology. Psychological ecology refers to the way in which physical aspects of the environment, such as variations in temperature, light, air pollution, ambient levels of radiation, sound intensity or frequency, gravitational pull, and water quality, affect human psychical functioning. For example, in the aftermath of the Chernobyl disaster, there has been much concern in the former Soviet Union and Scandinavian countries about the effect of high levels of radiation on biological systems. Areas of investigation that would fall under the heading psychological ecology include studies of the way variations in radiation levels affect memory, attention, and personality traits like feelings of lethargy or depression. Studies of the way people develop specific phobias about exposure to high radiation levels or the way they interpret governmental assurances or warnings about radiation levels would be excluded from this rubric.

2. Gibson's ecological approach in psychology: a specific school of thought within psychology. When used in this context, the word *ecological* has a specific and somewhat idiosyncratic meaning. It is associated with a particular view of perception that was espoused by James Gibson (1979), in which he used the framework of ecology as a way of studying visual perception. In his view, the study of psychology must include the notion that humans develop in an environment, and perception of the environment is inherent in the optic array that "allows" visual perception. More specifically, it is a particular view of perception that emphasizes the meaning that is in the stimulus array, instead of the opposite view that emphasizes the role of the observer in creating meaning from sensations. This particular approach to the study of perception is not relevant in this chapter and is mentioned only for the benefit of those readers who are familiar with Gibson's theory and who find Gibson's specific use of the word *ecological* confusing.

3. Environmental psychology: an area of psychology. Environmental psychology is the study of human behavior as it is influenced by and occurs within an environment. This is an area of psychology that has grown considerably since the 1980s. A dominant view among environmental psychologists is that humans and their environment are a single system, so attempts to study them as separate entities will not yield meaningful results. The increasing popularity of this paradigmatic shift is one reason that so many psychologists left their laboratories and now prefer to conduct their studies in natural settings. A central concept in environmental psychology is that humans influence their environment and the environment, in turn, influences humans. An example of research that would be included under this heading is a study of the effects of crowding. As the density of a population increases within a limited area, many features of the environment change (e.g., air, water, and soil quality, noise levels) and many aspects of human behavior change (e.g., aggression most likely will increase,

people speak louder, odors are more perceptible). How do these changes affect both human and environmental responses? Popular topics of study that fall under this category are the relationship between environmental variables and human stress responses and the way people form representations of their surrounding areas, a topic known as environmental cognition.

4. Ecological psychology: the study of pro-environmental attitudes and behaviors ("greenmindedness" or "green psychology"). The psychological study of how people develop the ethic of caring for and preserving the environment or, at the opposite extreme, destroying and disliking it is an increasingly popular area of specialization within psychology that needs to be differentiated from environmental psychology. Ecological psychology is fundamentally different from environmental psychology in terms of the underlying issues that it is investigating. In this text, we use the terms *green psychology* or *greenmindedness* to denote this area of study and to differentiate it from similar-sounding specialties. It refers to human interactions with and attitudes toward flora and fauna. (We thank Dmitry Leontiev of Moscow State University for suggesting the term *greenmindedness*.)

Perhaps the most compelling reason for the study of green psychology is the belief that an ecological crisis cannot be avoided without radical changes in human knowledge of ecological principles and an appreciation of nature. The perspective of green psychologists, relative to that of psychologists in other areas of specialization, is comparable to that of the well-known perceptual shift that accompanies a figure-ground reversal. Psychologists who are acquainted with the literature in perception know that the term *figure-ground* refers to the perception that a "figure" or central object is perceived as standing out from its background. If we showed most people a picture of a woman standing in front of a row of trees, almost universally, they would describe the photo in this way. When a figure-ground reversal occurs, what was formerly seen as background becomes the central figure and the former figure is seen as background. In this example, a figure-ground reversal means that the photo might be perceived as a row of trees with a person obscuring the view of some of them. The trees and not the person assume the primary importance of the figure. This is exactly the sort of reversal that characterizes the study of green psychology (Deryabo & Yasvin, 1994a, 1994b).

Environmental Psychology

Active study of environmental psychology in the Soviet Union and the former Soviet republics has been possible only in the last 10 to 15 years. The absence of psychological investigations in these areas during the most stringent years of communism was consistent with the official ideological stance of that time. According to official political theory, the environment is a major determinant of human behavior. The use of the word *environment* is misleading in this manifesto because it is taken to mean only certain aspects of the environment. It was declared that social class structure is the aspect of the environment that leads to undesirable actions, and only when class structure is destroyed can desirable actions and the greatest happiness be achieved. When used in this context, the environment does not include air and water quality or the other sorts of attributes of the environment that concern environmental psychology.

Although the official communist ideology and concern for the natural environment could have coexisted, it was clear to those in charge that natural aspects of the environment were not as critical as the problem of eliminating class structure. Every other endeavor was of lesser importance. In other words, communism was defined by its opposition to the pollution of the social environment by class structure; pollution of the natural environment was not of interest. Again, we see how use of the same terms to convey multiple meanings makes communication difficult.

The whole scope of the environment in psychology was perceived as a biologically based approach to the study of behavior in the Soviet Union. The *biologization* of a phenomenon—that is, the use of biology as the primary means of understanding it—was a pejorative term. It was used as a criticism of work that did not acknowledge the supreme importance of social and class factors, the most important factors according to the dominant ideology.

Another strike against psychology that prevented its early development in the field of environmental studies (as well as many others) was the perception that psychology focuses on the individual. Under a belief system in which social and class variables were declared to be of primary importance, the emphasis on individual differences and individual behavior was incompatible with the way research should be conducted and the way scientists should think. This meant that psychological research groups that dealt with problems of the environment could not be formed prior to the political period defined by glasnost (openness) and perestroika (restructuring). Thus, before the era that permitted an openness to new ideas, the field of environmental and ecological studies was dominated by geographers, architects, and sociologists—scientists who did not threaten the prevailing view of the appropriate framework for understanding how people interact with their environment. Psychology played only a minor role in the early development of the field.

Most important, the essential premise of the psychological approach—that people and the environment interact—was negated under communism because people had little choice about how they interacted with or selected environments. Such transactions between humans and nature were more often mandated by official policies and actions than by choice (Heidmets & Kruusvall, 1988; Rappoport, 1989). Again, many examples can clarify this point. Consider the development of large industrial centers, which were completely planned by the party. Such industrial centers were frequently built on large rivers so that transport of materials could be accomplished easily. The most frequent plan for development was to build huge plants on one side of the river and massive housing structures on the other. For reasons that defy understanding, the plants always seemed to be situated so that the pollution emanating from them would be blown toward the massive housing units. There was no possibility of moving downwind from the plants because that was not where the housing units were built. So it was not possible to achieve even something as simple as selecting a site for living that was subject to less direct pollution.

A severe housing shortage is a continuing problem in the countries that once constituted the Soviet Union. A disproportionate share of the income and labor was pumped into the "industrial-military" complex and was spent for "defense" purposes, space exploration, and ideologically useful purposes such as the support of communist oganizations abroad. One result of these state-mandated priorities was the scarcity of consumer goods and a lower standard of living than that experienced in the industrialized countries of the West.

For the most part, people were assigned to a factory and a town where they were to work. After arriving at the assigned site, they were often required to wait long periods before housing became available. Until then, they lived in dormitories that were crowded and that did not permit much privacy. As housing became available, often after a wait of several years, it was assigned according to a formula. A family of one or two people was entitled to a one-room flat (small apartment); three people were entitled to two rooms; and four people were entitled to three rooms. Housing assignments were usually made only once in a lifetime (unless an individual was required to move out of the area for some reason), so if you were given a one-room flat, you and any future family that you might have would all live in the same one room, quite probably for the rest of your life. Because of this policy, couples would plan pregnancies around the date when flat assignments were expected to be made in order to qualify for an additional room. This is another example of the way official policies indirectly dictated such personal choices as family planning.

Several key aspects in the fundamental tenets of communism created the uniquely Soviet way of comprehending nature. The communist view of the world was monological, as opposed to dialogical. In other words, the prevailing idea was that the person dominated the environment—the influence was in one direction. This is opposed to the integration of person and environment, a more interactive and dialogical approach to the world. As long as the worldview was unidirectional, psychologists could not work in this field because it was a fundamentally different worldview from one that would be advocated by most psychologists.

In addition, psychology was thought to be incompatible with the study of ecology and environment because one of the basic communist emphases was uniformity, a principle that placed an additional physical limitation on psychology's ability to study interactive processes with nature. The principle of uniformity did not allow much leeway in the adaptation of space to fit the unique needs and predilections of the users. Among the many actions that are attributed to Stalin is the construction of incredibly large and imposing buildings known as "Stalin skyscrapers." Seven of these huge buildings are scattered throughout Moscow, and the eighth was given to the Soviet Union's "younger brother," Poland. Thus, a visitor to Warsaw from Moscow would have the immediate impression that he had not gone very far because it would look the same as many neighborhoods in Moscow.

There is an apocryphal story that some students have lived all of their college years in the large Stalin skyscraper on the campus of Moscow State University without ever leaving the building. Although it would hardly be an enviable life, it certainly would be possible because the building contains classrooms, living accommodations (for faculty and students), buffets, laundry facilities, movie theaters, a few museums, barbers, clothing and food stores, and any other service that can be imagined. Of course, such stories are exaggerations that few Western readers can appreciate without spending some time in these massively imposing structures.

There is a comedic Russian movie called *The Irony of Fate* that parodies the principle of uniformity. In this movie, the protagonist becomes drunk one evening and is mistakenly put on a plane instead of his friend. When he arrives at the destination, he doesn't notice that he is not in his home city because everything looks the same. He hails a taxi and gives the driver his home address. The driver takes him to the same address in the new city. The protagonist then uses his key to open the door to an apartment that has the same number and the same lock as the one he has at home. The furniture is the same as that in his own apartment, a fact that Soviet viewers could easily believe because there were only a few choices for furniture. As might be imagined, the plot thickens when we learn that he has unknowingly entered the apartment of a beautiful woman. But such is the irony of fate. Comedy has always been a good strategy for dealing with oppressive situations, such as cramped, uniform, massive, and communal living environments.

Studies in Environmental Psychology: Urban Images

Much of the Soviet work in environmental psychology concerned the way people know and use their knowledge of cities. A series of studies clearly showed that the physical characteristics of an area are less important in how mental representations of space are created than the experiences that one has traveling through and living within a space (Belyaeva, 1977; Berezin, 1975; Kolejchuk, 1983; Lapin, 1991). A series of studies showed systematic distortions in personal images of urban areas. For example, the relative size of different portions of a city shrinks or expands depending on the social significance and cultural traditions and rituals of the section of the city being investigated (Akhtzezer & Ilyin, 1975; Vishnevsky, 1983).

Nickolskyaya (1980) and Glazychev (1984) investigated the drawings of town sites made by professional artists and schoolchildren. They linked the drawn images with verbal descriptions of the areas depicted. For example, drawings of the skyline of a town with which subjects were familiar were matched with descriptive terms. All of the words used in the matching task connoted particular emotions designed to reveal the way the subjects felt about the town. This unique method of responding provided information about both the degree of factual correspondence to the real skyline and subjective feelings about the personal significance that the town held for the respondent.

Soviet investigators also found that the image people have of an area is dependent on the way they travel within it. Discrete areas of town are connected by the way people travel through them (Dobritzina, 1984). Using these findings, we would expect that someone who travels long distances from home to a few places within Moscow via the metro (underground subway) would think of Moscow as a few centers of activity connected by relatively short distances that are devoid of activity. As might be expected, those who live within the center of town perceive the town very differently from those who live in suburban areas (Kogan, 1982; Veshinsky, 1983).

One's own location is the center of one's personal universe. When villagers in the areas surrounding Moscow were asked to estimate the populations of nearby villages, they most often underestimated the size of the population in the other villages and overestimated the size of their own village (Fedulov, 1988). It is clear that personal images of urban areas are formed by the way each person uses the area and moves through it. Personal images are more dependent on actual experience than on map knowledge, at least for those with extensive experience in an urban setting.

Seemingly minor aspects of the physical environment often determine the way it is used and perceived. For example, people tend to stroll (i.e., walk slowly) when wide pavements are available and to hurry when pavement width narrows (Pijir, 1971). If the use of wide paved areas for walking was intended to allow the rapid movement of people, the design failed to produce this outcome because it seems better suited for leisurely walking since people can stop to speak to each other and slower, less steady walkers (young children, the elderly, the physically disabled) find the wide pavements safer and more conducive to outings.

Desirable Qualities of Urban Living Areas

Soviets have had little or no choice about the characteristics of their physical living space, such as where (within a very large area) it is located, its size, and its type. Although they had no choice, under some conditions, it was possible to exchange or swap living accommodations with a willing party. Often people would advertise information about their own flat and the one that they would like to swap it for. For example, an advertisement might have read that an individual had an eighth floor two-room flat in a particular location that he would like to swap for a flat in another location. Of course, he would prefer a larger apartment, but this was true of almost everyone. Medvedkov (1974) conducted an analysis of "apartment change certificates," the registration records of exchanges in apartments, in order to understand what sort of housing people tended to prefer. The study of housing certificates showed how people made choices within the realities of Soviet society.

Other researchers used questionnaire and survey data to compile a list of factors that are important indices of the quality of an environment. Barbash (1986), Backlanova (1977), and others found that the most important variables were the number of trees and shrubs in the area; availability of services such as laundry, shopping, and movies; and the absence of uncompleted construction (with the seemingly interminable problems of noise, mud, and large equipment because large construction projects seem to go on forever).

When people made choices among cities, the primary factors were a comfortable climate and the administrative status of the town (Vasilyev, Sydorov, & Khanin, 1988). This is a concept that most Western readers will not understand without some background information. Under the Soviet system, all population areas were assigned a type of classification. Moscow, the capital of the country, was unique and had the highest classification. The capitals of each of the Soviet Union's 15 republics received the second highest classification, followed by regional centers or cities of moderately large size, smaller towns, and finally the collective farms known as *kolhoz*. The higher a living area was in this hierarchy, the more goods and services it received. For example, Moscow had the greatest quantity and variety of food and other consumer items. Thus, it is not hard to understand why the most desirable living areas were those with high administrative status.

A second hierarchy was also important. Some factories, mines, and other large complexes and their surrounding towns obtained a privileged status for the receipt of food and consumer goods. These strategic sites would sometimes receive a better assortment of products than a neighboring site of higher status, so the hierarchy of a work site was also a determinant in the type of living that was desirable.

The disparity between the large cities and small towns was quite large, with the result that Moscow was a highly desirable place to live. After Brezhnev declared that Moscow was to be a "model city," this further increased the status differences between Moscow and the rest of the huge Soviet Union. When Moscow was filled with foreign tourists for the 1980 Olympic Games, a large variety of consumer goods became available for the first time. Such delicacies as salami, Coca-Cola, Fanta orange soda, imported cheese that came presliced, and, of course, blue jeans could be found in Moscow stores. These goods were so desirable and rare that no Soviet citizens who lived outside of Moscow were allowed into the city during that period. (Soviets had their official address stamped inside their passport so that proof of their home address was readily available.)

Based on a review of the research literature and studies of their own, Estonian psychologists Heidmets and Kruusvall (1988; Kruusvall & Heidmets, 1986) suggested the following principles for the design of living spaces more compatible with the preferences of the people who live in them. They suggested a change from the huge multistoried rectangles that were most commonly used as housing to buildings that have between two and four stories. They also recommended that the number of units in each building be reduced and that the buildings be detached from each other (wall-to-wall housing is the current norm). They also advocated a planned community in which entire neighborhoods are designed according to sections, with one section reserved for services, another for inter-actions among inhabitants, and another for children. They coined the term *ter-ritorial deprivation* to describe situations in which children grow up without sufficient space for the usual activities of childhood. They suggested that chil-dren who are "space deprived" behave in ways that show "lack of initiative, hesitation, and fear" (Heidmets, 1989; Niit, 1983).

The Estonian psychologists showed their belief in the interaction of people and the environment in their suggestion that real social units (families, neigh-bors) have the opportunity to alter the environment in ways that make sense for their particular needs and wants—an important idea in the Soviet Union, which was founded on the principle of alienating citizens from their environ-ments. The origins of the principles of alienating environments are seen in early work on creating utopian environments (Panchenko, 1982, 1986). In the so-called utopian societies that served as models for totalitarian societies, the environ-ment was planned in ways that served the administrative needs of the govern-ment first and the needs of the citizens who were to live there second. While we know nothing about the thoughts of the inhabitants of these utopian worlds, Heidmeits and Kruusvall (1988) found that two-thirds of the inhabitants of the suburbs would prefer not to be living there.

The Soviet Cult as Reflected in Architecture

Every totalitarian regime is based on a set of beliefs that are carried to an ex-treme. These "cults" provide the guiding principles for much of the activity under the regime and have widespread influence beyond their original intent. Eight extreme beliefs of communism were applied to the architecture and envi-ronmental design that typified the Soviet Union (Rappoport, 1989).

1. Uniformity. The uniformity of the Soviet buildings, both inside and out, has already been described. It lends a strange sense of déjà vu when citizens travel to distant locations and, except in historical areas, see the same facades, enter familiar hallways, and live with furniture that is identical to what they left at home.

2. Quantity. The cult of quantity is easily summarized with the familiar say-ings, "The more the better, and the bigger the better." Housing built in Soviet times consisted of mammoth rectangles, arrayed as far as the eye could see. Of course, they all looked alike. Quality was always secondary to quantity, a belief that was justified under the ethic of economy. The walls were paper-thin as a cost-savings measure, a fact that also made it convenient for neighbors to spy on each other. The telltale sounds of *Voice of America* coming over a radio could be heard by one's neighbors, a fact that is amplified in the chapters in this book on the psychology of lies. Environments that were conducive to spying assumed

particular political significance during the most repressive periods in history, when participation in certain activities resulted in midnight raids and deportation to Stalin's infamous labor camps.

3. Respect for science. Science was the highest good (after communism), and respect for science was very high. If Soviet scientists said that the water quality was "within norms," who were ordinary citizens to voice their suspicions or question the deliberately vague description? Any such complaints would be answered with, "Don't you trust Soviet scientists?" There was only one correct answer to this question.

4. Living for the future. Soviet society was future oriented. Interestingly, this did not include any concern for conserving natural resources for future generations. Citizens became used to the constant disorder and hassle of construction sites because they were justified by the explanation that they were building a better Soviet society for tomorrow. The cult of the future was parodied in a short novel by Andrei Platonov, a Russian writer with a highly peculiar and difficult-to-translate style. In one of his allegorical stories, "Kotlovan" (A pit), the main characters live inside giant pumpkins. They are motivated by tales of the great society they are building. Every day they toil at a large construction site, where they prepare the foundation for a great building to be used in an even greater society. Every day they hear stories about the massive and monumental building they are constructing and their devotion and fervor grow stronger. As the plans for the building grow, so does the need for a strong foundation. A large building of such importance needs a deep basement, so every day they dig deeper and deeper to prepare a basement that will be worthy of such a grand building. They are probably still digging this great basement for this great building for an even greater future society.

5. Secrecy. The theme of secrecy appears in several places in the chapters in this book written by psychologists from the former Soviet Union. Secrecy was apparent in the design of the environment. Enclosed regions were erected behind tall walls, fences were a common part of the architecture, and narrow entrances that could be traversed only by the few persons with appropriate clearance became a standard design.

Secrecy also meant that some large and rather obvious land masses seemed to disappear. For example, a small, beautiful island in St. Petersburg figures prominently in Russian history because it was a favorite spot of Peter the Great's. In Soviet times, it became the Marine Military Research Center, obviously designated a secret place. Tour guides were instructed not to mention the island as their tour groups passed it. All references to the island disappeared from Soviet tour books. For all civil purposes, the island ceased to exist.

6. Anonymity. Old cities were given new Soviet names instead of their former historical ones, which linked them with the past. Numerous smaller towns and countless streets underwent changes in their names. Names were easily altered and identities were easily lost. Each time a prominent leader, usually a party "higher up" but sometimes others who had made genuine contributions such as writers (e.g., Maxim Gorky) or cosmonauts (e.g., Yuri Gagarin), died, a wave

of renaming of towns, streets, mines, colleges, channels, public libraries, and industries followed.

7. Hypocrisy. Western readers may wonder how the environment reflected the cult of hypocrisy. This aspect of communism could be seen in the declarations and signs proclaiming that various changes were made "in the name of the people." For example, if a large group needed a bus stop at a particular location, this bus stop was added with great fanfare "in the name of the people." However, "the people" seemed to inspire only small and meaningless changes. An industrial town was renamed for Brezhnev after his death, and a statute of him appeared in his birthplace "in the name of the people," but no one seems to recall any cry from the people to change their environment to honor this less-than-popular Soviet leader.

8. Estrangement. Thin walls and communal living meant that people constructed their own private walls by hiding their emotions and not talking freely except among their most trusted friends because they might be overheard. The results of these living conditions were greater separateness and isolation among the crowds than might have resulted from more private living arrangements.

Of course, these environmentally mediated influences on the psychology of the Soviet people could not be spoken of or investigated under Soviet systems. They represent new areas of study that are now possible and are likely to attract new investigators as topics in environmental psychology grow in worldwide importance.

Anthropocentric and Ecocentric Views

Modern society is essentially anthropocentric in its attitudes toward the natural environment. A human-dominated way of thinking about the environment has led to ecological catastrophes and promises even worse disasters for the future. By contrast, the philosophy of green psychology is rooted in the idea that people and other living things are mutually dependent and interactive. It is drawn from Russian religious philosophy, theoretical conceptions of noosphere, American environmentalism, and universal ethics. We propose eight dimensions for the differences between these two philosophies (Deryabo & Yasvin, 1994a), shown in table 19.1.

The Development of Green Psychology

We describe here a study (Deryabo, 1995; Deryabo & Yasvin, 1994b) conducted with children aged 10 to 17 years. We have not collected data from younger children, but the Swiss psychologist Jean Piaget offered a developmental account of how children think about the world at younger ages. According to Piaget, children younger than 7 years old perceive natural phenomena, like the sun and

Table 19.1. Eight Dimensions that Characterize Differences between Anthropocentric and Ecocentric Views of Nature

Anthropocentric	Ecocentric
1. Value and Harmony	
Nature has no value of its own. Harmony has no meaning in this context.	Nature has inherent value. People need to live in harmony with nature.
2. Hierarchy	
Because people have consciousness, they have higher worth than other living things.	Because people have consciousness, they are responsible for the care of other living things.
3. Interaction	
The purpose of nature is to provide humans with maximum satisfaction of their needs.	The needs of all living things are equally important. People and nature are important to each other.
4. Ecological Imperative	
Anything that is good for human existence is permitted.	Anything that destroys ecological balance is forbidden.
5. Rights of Nature	
Only humans have rights.	All living things have equal rights.
6. Ethics	
The concept of ethics only applies to human-human interactions.	The concept of ethics applies to human-human interactions and human interactions with other living things.
7. Co-evolution	
People evolve and use nature for their own purposes.	Both humans and nature are mutually dependent for their continued evolution.
8. Conservation	
Save natural resources for future use by humans.	Save nature for its own sake.

wind, as made by people for their use. Between ages 7 and 10, children perceive nature less as something to be used (i.e., pragmatic) and more as animistic. Children in this age range begin to think more scientifically than at younger ages, and the developmental markers for the growth of scientific thought in this age range have been studied by the Russian developmental psychologist Lev Vygotsky (1962).

We were particularly concerned with the way children come to develop ideas about the conservation of natural resources and the ways in which they understand nature. To examine these questions, we sampled 1,007 children (approximately equal numbers of boys and girls) selected from each of the ten schools in Daugavpils, the second largest city in Latvia, which was a Soviet republic earlier in this decade. A series of specially constructed questionnaires (Deryabo & Yasvin, 1995) was used to assess the way children and adolescents comprehended four different concepts in green psychology: nature as aesthetic (nature is beautiful), conservation (it is important to save and protect nature), a pragmatic view (nature is a commodity we should use), and a cognitive/educational view (desire to learn more about nature). Because there are important differences in the way nature is perceived, we sorted the data into three groups representing different feelings about nature: (1) children who seemed to have little liking for nature and were not eager to conserve it but perceived it as aesthetic; (2) children who scored midway on the liking of nature scale, were willing to interact with nature, and wanted to learn more about it but were not particularly interested in conservation; and (3) children who liked nature the most, were likely to participate in nature-conserving activities, and wanted to learn more about it. The nature-loving children and teens also had the most favorable attitudes toward conservation in the future and viewed nature nonpragmatically—that is, they did not think it should be used exclusively for human purposes.

Questions about the pragmatic use of nature did not follow an obvious developmental pattern, but concern for conservation was more likely among the older children. We are using the information that we gained from this study to design a program that will teach them about the natural world. The program will encourage them to see the beauty in nature and to understand that it cannot survive unless someone cares enough to protect it (Yasvin & Pupin', 1993; Yasvin, 1994; Yasvin, 1995). Perhaps if this education is provided, we can grow a nation that will value and take care of its environment. We invite our Western counterparts to join us in this activity.

References

Akhtzezer, A. T., & Ilyin, P. M. (1975). *Zadachi razrabotki spetzialnykh otzenok territorii v usloviyakh nauchno- tekhnicheskoi revolyutzii.* (On the problems of working out special criteria of territorial assessment under scientific-technical revolution.) Izvestiya AN SSSR. Ser.: Geography. (In Russian.)

Backlanova, T. A. (1977). Territorialnaya podvizhnost naseleniya kak osnova otzenok sredy v usloviyakh krupnogo goroda. (Migration processes as the basis for environment assessment in a city.) In *Urban environment and the way to its optimization*. Moscow. (In Russian.)

Barbash, N. B. (1986). *Metodika izucheniya territorialnoi differentziatzii gorodskoi sredy*. (Methods to study territorial differentiation of the urban environment.) Moscow. (In Russian.)

Belyaeva, E. L. (1977). *Arkhitekturno-prostranstvennaya sreda goroda kak objekt zritelnogo vospriyatiya*. (Architectural-spatial urban environment as the object of visual perception.) Moscow. (In Russian.)

Berezin, M. P. (1975). *Prostranstvo, vospriyatiye, povedeniye: Stroitelstvo i arkhitektura*. (Space, perception, behavior.) Leningrad. (In Russian.)

Deryabo, S. D. (1995). *Prirodnyi objekt kak "znachimyi drugoi."* (Natural object as "significant other.") Daugavpils, Latvia). (In Russian.)

Deryabo, S. D., & Yasvin, V. A. (1994a). *Ekologicheskaya psikhodiagnostika*. (Ecological psychodiagnostics.) Daugavpils, Latvia. (In Russian.)

Deryabo, S. D., & Yasvin, V. A. (1994b). Kul'turno-istoricheskaya obuslovlennost' krizisa evropeiskogo ekologicheskogo soznaniya. (The cultural and historical cause of the European ecological awareness crisis.) *Culture and Word*, November. (In Russian.)

Deryabo, S. D., & Yasvin, V. A. (1995a). *Metodiki diagnostiki i korrektzii v ekologicheskom vospitanii*. (Diagnosis and correction methods in ecological education.) (In Russian.)

Deryabo, S. D., & Yasvin, V. A. (1995b). Priroda: Objekt ili subjekt otnosheniya lichnosti. (Nature: Object or subject of personality's attitude.) *Shkola zdorovya, 1*. (In Russian.)

Dobritzina, I. A. (1984). K postanovke v dizaine problemy obespecheniya orientatzii v srede sovremennogo goroda. (On the problem of the formation of contemporary urban environment orientation in designing.) *Proceedings of VNIITE* (Research Institute of Design), *44*. (In Russian.)

Fedulov, S. V. (1988). *Geograficheskoye izucheniye obraza zhizni: Metodologicheskiye i metodicheskiye aspekty*. (Geographical investigation of lifestyle: Methodological and methodical aspects.) Ph.D. thesis, Moscow State University. (In Russian.)

Glazychev, V. L. (1984). *Sotzialno-esteticheskaya interpretatziya gorodskoi sredy*. (Social-ethical interpretatrion of the urban environment.) (In Russian).

Heidmets, M. (1989). Gorodskaya sreda kak sotzialnaya problema. (Urban environment as a social problem.) In *Urban environment* (part 1). Moscow. (In Russian.)

Heidmets, M., & Kruusvall, Y. (1988). Dva puti optimizatzii sredy zhiznedeyatelnosti v gorode. (Two ways of the environment optimization in the city.) In *Anthropoecological assessment and optimal urban environment formation*. Leningrad. (In Russian).

Kogan, L. B. (ed.) (1982). *Sozialno-kulturniye funkzii goroda i prostranstvennaya sreda* (Sociocultural functions of the city and spacial environment.) Moscow. (In Russian.)

Koleichuk, V. F. (1983). Zritelnii obrasy prostranstva: Opyt experimentalnogo analiza. (Visual images of space: An experience of experimental analysis.) *Proceedings of VNIITE* (Research Institute of Design), *40*. (In Russian.)

Kruusvall, Y., & Heidmets, M. (1986). O putyakh povysheniya sotzialnoi effektivnosti zhiloi sredy. (On the ways to increase social effectiveness of living environment.) In *Reproductive processes in a city*. Tallinn. (In Russian.)

Lapin, E. A. (1991). Sovremennaya psikhologiya okruzhayushchei sredy: Sostoyaniye i perspectivy. (Contemporary psychology of the environment: Present state and perspectives.) In *The problems of ecological psychoacoustics*. Moscow. (In Russian.)

Medvedkov, Y. V. (1974). Modeli ekologii cheloveka v geografii: Teoriya i metodika geograficheskikh issledovanii ekologii cheloveka. (Models of human ecology in geography: Theory and methods of geographical investigations of human ecology.) Moscow. (In Russian.)

Nickolskaya, L. V. (1980). Liniya i slovo. (Line and word.) *Stroitelstvo i arkhitektura Leningrada, 10*. (In Russian).

Niit, G. (1983). Plotnost lyudei i chuvstvo stesnionnosti: Teorii i gipotesy-Chelovek v sotzialnoi i fizicheskoi srede. (Density of the population and the feeling of constraint: Theories and hypotheses.) In *Man in social and physical environment*. Tallinn. (In Russian.)

Panchenko, D. V. (1982). Yambul i Kampanella [o nekotorykh mekhanismakh utopicheskogo tvorchestva]. (Yambul and Campanella [on some mechanisms of utopean creativity].) In *Antique heritage in the Renaissance culture*. Moscow. (In Russian.)

Panchenko, D. V. (1986). Utopicheskii gorod na iskhode Renessansa (Doni and Kampanella). (Utopian city on the edge of the Renaissance [Doni and Campanella].) In *Urban culture: Middle age and the beginning of the new times*. Leningrad. (In Russian.)

Pijir, P. M. (1971). Issledovaniye peshekhodnogo dvizheniya na ulitzakh zentralnikh raionov krupneishikh gorodov. (Investigation of the pedestrian movement in the streets in the downtown of the largest cities.) Ph.D. thesis, Moscow. (In Russian.)

Rappoport, A. G. (1989). K estetike totalitarnikh sred. (On the aesthetics of totalitarian environments.) In *Urban environments* (part 1). Moscow. (In Russian.)

Vasilyev, G. L., Sidorov, D. A., & Khanin, S. E. (1988). Vyyavleniye potrebitelskikh predpochtenii v sfere rasseleniya. (Investigations of consumers' residential preferences.) *Vestnik Moskovskogo Universiteta, 2*. (In Russian.)

Veshinsky, Y. G. (1983). Planirovka, svet, orientatziya. (Planning, light, orientation.) *Gorodskoye khozyaistvo Moskvy, 4*. (In Russian.)

Vishnevsky, E. H. (1983). O "krivizne" gorodskogo sotzialnogo prostranstva (na primere Moskvy). (On "distortion" of the urban social space in Moscow.) In *Psychology and architecture* (part 2). Tallinn. (In Russian.)

Vygotsky, L.S. (1962). *Thought and speech*. Cambridge.

Yasvin, V. A. (1994). Pedagogical management of forming a personal attitude to nature: Culture, ecology, pedagogical process. Daugavpils, Latvia.

Yasvin, V. A. (1995). The fundamentals of ecological psychopedagogics for pre-school pupils: A teacher at the pre-school—What does it mean? Unpublished manuscript.

Yasvin, V. A., & Pupin', M. F. (1993). Organizatzionniye osnovy sotzialno-pedagogicheskogo dvizheniya "EKO-DO." (Organizational basis of the social-educational movement "ECO-DO," or "ecological way.") (In Russian.)

Conclusion

Two Faces of Psychology

Diane F. Halpern *&* Alexander E. Voiskounsky

The contemporary issues examined throughout this book reflect how psychological concepts have been defined and investigated in the United States and the countries that once constituted the Soviet Union. During the past 100 years, when psychology was developing as a scientific discipline, few academic exchanges took place between these two major world powers. The past century can be described as a time of mistrust, misunderstanding, and fear, beginning with Western-Russian/Soviet hostilities early in the century, uneasy alliances during the Second World War, the frigid chill of the Cold War, and now a great thaw with much uncertainty about the future relationship between the countries of the West and the former Communist countries.

Several themes emerge from the paired perspectives on contemporary psychological issues. Although no psychologists or team of psychologists can "speak" for all of their colleagues, each chapter in this comparative text was written by outstanding psychologists who are recognized and respected in their own countries for their expertise in the topic on which they have written. Thus, we can consider these chapters representative of the best thinking and writing by psychologists in the former Soviet Union and the United States. We list here some of the conclusions that we have gleaned from the chapters.

1. Sociopolitical context is a strong determinant of the way in which psychology has developed in the United States and former Soviet Union. Evidence for the strong influence of place, historical period, political system, and social

system on the way psychology has been defined and investigated can be found in every set of chapters. Consider, for example, the way the field of psychogerontology developed in the United States and in the Soviet Union. The free-market economy in the United States emphasized the importance of work because an individual's standard of living most often depended on how well and how hard the individual worked. Americans often view their work as more than a source of income; for many, work is so central to their lives that it is also key to their identity. At the same time, the nature of modern work has become increasingly complex and cognitive in nature. One of the dominant goals in the psychology of aging in the United States is to find ways to slow or reverse intellectual decline so that older adults can continue to work.

By contrast, the Soviet government overtly and covertly discouraged research into the psychology of aging, especially into those psychological topics that pertained to an age-related intellectual decline. With few exceptions, the heads of the Communist Party were very old men. The system required many long years of devoted service before an individual could rise to a high-level government post, so it was only in old age that most officials could attain the highest offices. These elderly bureaucrats did not want to fund research that might show a cognitive decline in old age. There were other reasons, as well, for the paucity of psychological research on aging in the Soviet Union. Every aged individual was guaranteed a retirement in exchange for a lifetime of work. These old people were no longer the producers in society, so the bureaucrats insisted that the limited research money would not be wisely spent if the subjects and beneficiaries of the research were the nonproductive elderly.

We also see the strong influence of sociopolitical context on the way people think about lying and the times and occasions they are willing to lie. The U.S. Constitution's Bill of Rights ensures that all citizens can speak the truth without fear of retaliation and that the press is free to print the truth. Thus, there is a guaranteed legal right to speak and write the truth (or, anything else one might want to speak or write, with very few exceptions). The United States also has a strong religious tradition that prohibits lying. In the Soviet Union, the religious doctrines that defined lying as a sin were revoked, lies in the service of communism were elevated to the "highest good," and truth tellers were often punished. If a plant manager failed to announce that the plant had met and exceeded its production quotas, the manager might soon be among the workers. The truth as to whether the production quotas really were met was not as important as saying that they were because such a statement instilled confidence in the communist system. In addition, the human rights notion that free speech is a protected and inalienable right never developed in the Soviet Union. Thus, very different attitudes toward lying existed, depending on the political belief system.

Alcoholism in Russia is also attributed, in part, to the suppression of free speech. Among the many reasons why Russians drink so heavily is the fact that alcohol lowers inhibitions and liberates the tongue, so that normally timid men are able to speak the truth, an act they dare not do when they are sober. Alcoholism is a multifaceted problem, and its prevalence in the United States and other countries that protect free speech clearly shows that restrictions on speech are only a contributing factor to high rates of alcoholism.

Among many other examples of the importance of sociopolitical context on psychological variables, it seems that prejudice is inherent in the human condition. We tend to group people on the basis of some characteristic, and then we perceive other groups as relatively homogeneous, inferior to our own, and a threat to the limited resources that our own group so rightfully deserves (e.g., employment, land, housing). Despite this sad conclusion, prejudice is rooted in very different circumstances in countries of the former Soviet Union and the United States. In the former Soviet countries, prejudice exists among ethnic groups, especially when ethnic groups are vying for land they believe is historically theirs and for the right to use their native language in everyday transactions. Prejudice in the United States is not based on the possibility that one ethnic group might leave the union and claim a portion of the land as its own. American-style prejudice is based on some salient group characteristic, which is most likely race, sex, sexual orientation, or age. Discrimination against minority groups was overt and bloody earlier in this century, especially prejudice against African Americans (omitting the earlier periods of slavery and the Civil War). Modern prejudice and discrimination are now less overt. They can be found among biases in deciding who should get a home mortgage and other credit decisions and in hiring and firing, where criteria tend to be subjective.

Although sociopolitical context is important, it is only one influence on human thoughts and behaviors and the way the field of psychology evolves. There are both similarities and differences between prejudice in the former Soviet countries and the United States variety. In the Soviet Union, Jews were perceived as a distinct ethnic group, even if they came from different regions and had different customs from each other. In the independent countries, this situation is much the same. Jews have been the scapegoat for all of Russia's ills for many centuries, and they have endured countless pogroms and bloody acts of violence (including the active participation of some Soviet republics in the extermination of Jews during World War II). As modern Russia reembraces religion, religious intolerance has increased. The virulent rhetoric of some fascist political candidates in Russia shows that anti-Semitism is still widespread and acceptable to many people. These candidates have proposed that only blue-eyed blonds should be allowed to appear on television and that all Jews should be deported. By contrast, no political candidate in America could blatantly endorse prejudice or discrimination. If a political candidate in the United States were to state publicly that all members of a minority group would be deported if he were elected, this candidate would not obtain much public support, and all of the major political parties would rush to denounce him. Despite these differences, the underlying psychological processes for prejudice and discrimination seem similar. A minority group is identified and then blamed for a wide variety of societal ills. Thus, although distinctive features of prejudice can be attributed to time and place, commonalities transcend sociopolitical norms.

2. There are major differences in the dominant research paradigms, with former Soviets preferring to use self-report data and Americans preferring to use dependent measures that do not require self-report. The Western tradition is, in general, empirical, whereas the post-Soviet paradigm seems amenable to descriptive methods and to the use of existential explanations, although we recognize that there is a continuum of methods and the differences are more a matter of degree than of kind. Again, we cite a few examples to support this conclusion. Consider the Russian chapter on political psychology. The experimental paradigm that was used was the semantic differential technique. As explained in this chapter, subjects rated various political statements along a series of bipolar scales. That is, they reported their feelings and thoughts about the political statements. The data were analyzed with several highly sophisticated multivariate techniques. The authors used the most advanced computerized programs for data analysis, so the preferences for self-report are not due to the lack of complex computer programs. Semantic differential techniques were also used in the advertising chapter written by a former Soviet. The contemporary use of semantic differentials in the United States and other Western countries is rare. Self-report measures were also the basis for the studies by former Soviets on lying, alcoholism, post-traumatic stress disorder, and ethnicity and prejudice. The relative absence of self-report in the American psychological literature and its prevalence in studies by former Soviets show an important difference in the way psychologists in these two countries think about the study of psychological processes.

Self-report measures are based on the underlying assumption that much can learned from listening to the way subjects respond to questions about their thoughts, emotions, and behaviors. In fact, the nearly universal use of these measures in the chapters written by former Soviets suggests that many view it as the primary way of investigating mental life. On the other hand, Americans have been influenced by ideas and data that show that people often think and act in ways they themselves cannot understand. For example, the concept of implicit memory (Roediger, 1990) is based on empirical findings that show that people have knowledge they cannot describe in words and they do not consciously know they have. These implicit or tacit memories affect thinking and acting in ways that are unknown to the subject. Unconscious and preconscious processes influence all of us, so that no one can provide an adequate description of her or his own thoughts and feelings.

We note here that this volume contains chapters about areas of research that are relatively new in the former Soviet countries. For this reason, the studies reported here represent a starting point for investigations of these new areas. Self-report methods are well suited for pioneer studies in areas that are still being defined. Additional paradigms will undoubtedly emerge as these new topics of investigation are developed further.

Much can be learned from both approaches. Both sorts of data can be used to study human psychology in ways that enrich our understanding. We are like the blind men who feel different parts of the elephant; our perceptions are shaped by the methods we use and what we "see" from our limited perspectives. Additional methods will provide other views of this elephant we call psychology.

3. Despite the differences created by sociopolitical context and the use of different research paradigms, the behavior and feelings of former Soviets and Americans are remarkably similar. It is clear that people act and think in ways that are shaped by their life circumstances. It is also clear that there are many differences in the way Americans and former Soviets define the field of psychology and the methods they use to collect the data that informs their theories. Despite these differences, the responses of people to similar situations seem remarkably similar. In other words, we believe that if Americans had been born in Russia, they would act and think in ways that are similar to the ways Russians act and think, and vice versa. We think that the many differences between former Soviets and Americans are only "culture deep" and that they could be substantially reduced in one generation if the culture underwent a radical change. Modern Russia has undergone a sudden and radical change. If our beliefs are correct, we will find that the psychology of former Soviets and Americans will become increasingly similar and merge into a psychology of people, or at least of people with similar cultures in industrialized societies.

Consider, for example, the pair of chapters on post-traumatic stress disorder. Veterans from the wars in Chechnya, Afghanistan, Vietnam, and the Persian Gulf demonstrated huge differences in the nature of their war experiences, including their feelings about whether the fighting was just or unjust, the challenges presented by climate, the type of warfare and killing involved, the extent to which they witnessed or participated in torture, and the closeness of their contacts with death and dying. Despite these differences and the cultural differences in the way men are supposed to express their anguish, the symptoms of post-traumatic stress are essentially the same. That is, the human reaction to unspeakable horrors does not depend on one's political belief system, country of origin, or other psychosocial variables.

The similarity between Americans and former Soviets in their reactions to everyday environmental design and to nature can be seen in the pair of chapters that address environmental/ecological psychology. When sidewalks are wide, people walk slowly and linger to greet neighbors; when safe, open areas are available, children play in them; and when natural areas can be found, people flock to them to enjoy the beauty and serenity of nature. There is a universality to human nature.

4. For post-Soviet psychologists, the great wealth of Russian literature contains prototypical examples of psychological phenomena; American psychologists rarely reference literary works when discussing their field. Few countries have produced as much great literature as the Soviet Union and Russia. And there are probably few other places on earth where serious fiction and poetry are loved more. Not only do these great literary masterpieces amuse and inform, like books in other countries, but also they are believed to contain the "Russian soul." In this book, the chapters written by former Soviets refer to books by their much-loved Russian authors. The characters in these books and their dilem-

mas breathe life into dull psychological concepts. They are known to all, and like a dear relative, provide a bond among all former Soviets.

It is difficult to know why love of the written word is so strong in the former Soviet countries. Perhaps the rich beauty of the Russian language expresses slight nuances with great accuracy, or perhaps fiction was one of the few areas that was open to personal expression (although literature and other art forms were carefully controlled under communism and long before it). In the West, the link between literature and psychology is weak. A work of literature is very rarely referenced in an American psychology book.

One of the authors in this book, Olga Mitina, remarked that the frequent reference to literature in Russian scientific papers is a deliberate strategy that shows that the author is well read and highly educated. To understand these literary examples, the reader needs to know the great Russian novels. On the other hand, the literary references are a deliberate sign of status and may not reflect a love of great literature, as we had hypothesized. Whatever the reason, it is a striking difference between the American and post-Soviet chapters.

As we mentioned earlier, we believe that the massive changes in Russia will result in greater similarity between former Soviets and Americans. Unfortunately, it seems that the former Soviets are reading less now that television and video games are more widely available. It is little wonder why so many former Soviets do not welcome these aspects of American culture into their society.

5. The nature of psychology is rapidly changing in post-Soviet countries; the rate of change is much slower in the West. This conclusion could have been anticipated before reading the chapters in this volume because many of the areas we identified as contemporary were officially off-limits to psychologists during the Soviet regime. For the former Soviets, there is no historical tradition for many of the topics studied. For example, political psychology was under the sole purview of the propaganda office. Very few studies on this critical topic were published in open-access journals before the recent reforms were enacted. Research in gerontology was officially discouraged; there was no need for studies on advertising or prejudice because there were few consumer choices and the ideal communist had no prejudices. Similarly, ecological psychology is a wholly new field for former Soviets that demanded urgent attention after the disaster at Chernobyl.

6. We have much to learn from each other. How can psychologists from the former Soviet Union catch up in areas that have little or no history in their countries? It is possible for modern Russians and citizens of other former communist countries to learn from Western history in psychology. Although not all of the research findings will be valid for former Soviets, they can serve as a starting point for a field that is new and therefore without its own learning curve. For example, Russia now has a large influx of refugees, the first large immigrant movement in decades. America has a long history of accepting immigrants from other countries with customs and language very different from those of majority groups in America. The American immigration experience can be used to

help Russians plan and deliver services to this new class of Russians, some of whom are ethnic Russians, returning to a "homeland" they barely know.

Former Soviets do not have to rediscover the knowledge in psychology that was developed over the last hundred years, although much of it will have to be adapted to account for the many differences between American and Soviet life. Americans, on the other hand, can immediately benefit from the flurry of activity and research taking place in the former Soviet countries. Methods and topics that Americans have overlooked or rejected in their earlier research can be examined in a new light now that data are emerging from the former Soviet countries.

This short list of conclusions does not do justice to the rich array of theories and research that are described by the authors in this volume. Recent political events created a unique opportunity to compare the way political and social contexts influenced psychologists in their thinking about contemporary issues in two societies built upon diametrically opposed principles. We hope that readers have accepted our invitation to view the world from a vantage point 180 degrees removed from their own and to partake of vistas that can be seen only from the other side of the world. It is our hope that this new perspective allows all of us to see ourselves and the rest of the world more clearly and completely than our usual monocular point of view allows.

Reference

Roediger, H. L., III (1990). Implicit memory: Retention without remembering. *American Psychologist, 45*, 1043–1056.

Index